D1539011

THE AGE OF REAGAN

Also by STEVEN F. HAYWARD

THE AGE
OF REAGAN

THE CONSERVATIVE
COUNTERREVOLUTION
1980–1989

STEVEN F. HAYWARD

CROWN
FORUM
NEW YORK

Copyright © 2009 by Steven F. Hayward

All rights reserved.

Published in the United States by Crown Forum,

an imprint of the Crown Publishing Group,

a division of Random House, Inc., New York.

www.crownpublishing.com

CROWN FORUM with colophon is a registered trademark of

Random House, Inc.

Library of Congress Cataloging-in-Publication Data is available upon request.

ISBN: 978-1-4000-5357-5

Printed in the United States of America

10 9 8 7 6 5 4 3 2 1

First Edition

To Phil Ryan, who taught me the endurance for such a project; and James Holton and Harry V. Jaffa, my first teachers in politics

CONTENTS

———◆———

AUTHOR'S NOTE

I BEGAN THIS two-volume project more than ten years ago in the belief that Edmund Morris's then-forthcoming official biography would be too narrow in scope, and more broadly that Reagan would fare poorly at the hands of what John Patrick Diggins calls the "media-academic complex." The full catalogue of dismissive judgments of Reagan during his political career could fill a large encyclopedia. Michael Kinsley, an astute observer of politics, is typical of established liberal opinion with this judgment of Reagan from 1986: "It seemed to us, the carping critics, that this man was not terribly bright, not terribly thoughtful or well informed, not terribly honest, and in most other ways not up to the most important job in the world." Or this, from the *Nation:* "Those without a sense of irony about American politics may find it hard to believe that a man of such limited vision, mediocre intellect, and narrow comprehension can cut a figure of world-historical importance."

Although Reagan left office in 1989 with his popularity with the American people intact, it was the near-universal opinion of the commentariat that the eventual verdict of history on his governance would be negative, perhaps harshly so. Calvin Coolidge left office with high popularity too but, after two generations of rough handling by academic historians, became a president of low regard. Reagan was surely going to be "Coolidgized." An *American Heritage* magazine survey of journalists and historians taken around the time Reagan left office ranked him as the second most overrated president, behind, surprisingly, John F. Kennedy.

But over the past decade, starting well before Reagan's passing in 2004, the most unexpected thing occurred: liberals started to like him. Not all of him, to be sure, and therein lies a tale and the necessity for a broad-gauge book such as this. There are two main reasons for the upward revision in Reagan's stock. The first was the dramatic and unexpected end of the Cold War and the demise of the Soviet Union. Causation is complicated and disputed, but even Reagan's critics allow him a substantial role in the outcome. The second reason for the positive reappraisal was the revelation, starting about ten years ago, of Reagan's extensive writings—radio addresses, letters, speeches, and finally his personal diary—which displayed a lively and informed mind and a greater depth of character than hitherto imagined. At long last we had found the rest of him, to answer his most famous movie line.

The Cold War is the most dramatic aspect of Reagan's story, but this left a gap in the Reagan literature, and a frequent interpretive disjunction, as too many observers, especially the liberals, draw a distinction between Reagan's foreign policy and his domestic policy. Too often his domestic policy is either ignored or treated roughly. As this narrative argues, they need to be seen as a unity. Too many of the treatments of Reagan try to abstract from his ideology, which is like, to borrow G. K. Chesterton's phrase, trying "to tell the story of a saint without God."

What follows is an integrated, analytical narrative, covering the whole of the Reagan presidency. Even at this length, I have had to be selective and often too concise, leaving out not only valuable detail but also entire episodes. (The long agony of the savings and loan disaster is omitted, for example, in part because it was a diffuse and bipartisan fiasco.) Above all, this is intended to be a study in statesmanship—reflecting in narrative form on some permanent questions that we are still working out in our current political scene. Although I have—and have always had—strong pro-Reagan sympathies, this narrative does not shrink from noting his weaknesses or from strongly criticizing his mistakes and errors, both large and small. Unlike the criticisms of media know-it-alls or ideological opponents, however, the criticisms here are intended to illuminate the deeper, permanent problems of politics and policy. The first volume of *The Age of Reagan* attempted to explain the deeper sources of the inevitability of Reagan's election in 1980. The present chronicle of the ups and downs of his presidency attempts to explain Reagan's durability and his legacy for politics today.

A word about the pace of the book: it is slightly lopsided. The early chapters linger in great detail on the first year of the Reagan presidency, which was its most important year not only because it was the most eventful but also because it laid down the baseline for more than two decades of subsequent political argument between left and right. That year was a genuine turning point, and as such, it deserves treatment in depth. It is also necessary to tell this part of the Reagan story in its fullness, as it is a case study in the difficulty of plotting a genuine change in the course of the nation's affairs.

Steven F. Hayward
Cambria, California

THE AGE OF REAGAN

PROLOGUE

THE LION AT THE GATE

———✦———

Mr. Gorbachev, tear down this wall!
—PRESIDENT REAGAN AT THE BRANDENBURG
GATE, WEST BERLIN, JUNE 12, 1987

M OST OF HIS senior aides didn't want him to say it. Indeed, they
tried repeatedly to talk him out of it. *You'll embarrass your host,
West German chancellor Helmut Kohl. You'll anger and provoke Mikhail
Gorbachev, with whom you've just started making progress on arms control.
You'll whip up false hope among East Germans—for surely the Berlin Wall
isn't coming down anytime soon. Besides, Germans have grown used to the
wall.* The ultimate reason: *You'll look naive and foolish, Mr. President.*

"Virtually the entire foreign policy apparatus of the U.S. government," Reagan speechwriter Peter Robinson recalled, tried to stop Ronald
Reagan from saying "Tear down this wall," including Reagan's secretary of
state, George Shultz, and the new national security adviser, General Colin
Powell.[1] "Some Reagan advisers," the *New York Times* reported without
naming names, "wanted an address with less polemics."[2] The State Department and the National Security Council (NSC) persisted up to the last
minute trying to derail it; one meeting between Powell and White House
communications director Tom Griscom was, participants say, "tense and
forceful."

Reagan had to intervene against his own advisers. Ken Duberstein, serving then as Reagan's deputy chief of staff, has offered different accounts of
how the conversation went, but the gist of it was like this:

REAGAN: I'm the president, right?

DUBERSTEIN: Yes, sir, Mr. President. We're clear about that.

REAGAN: So I get to decide whether the line about tearing down the wall stays in?

DUBERSTEIN: That's right, sir. It's your decision.

REAGAN: Then it stays *in*.[3]

But even this wasn't the end of the effort to deflect the president from his purposes. While Air Force One was in flight to West Berlin, State and the NSC sent by fax one more speech draft to the plane without the Berlin Wall line. It went into the trash.

Today Reagan's personalized call to "tear down this wall" is recognized as the most memorable line of his presidency, and Reagan's role in the surprising and swift end of the Cold War the most celebrated aspect of his statecraft. Some of the people who opposed the line and tried to stop it now claim to have written it and been for it all along.

The Berlin Wall speech is a perfect microcosm of Ronald Reagan's entire political career. Reagan, the *New York Times* said in its news story about the Berlin Wall speech, "revived a *long-dormant* debate over the Berlin Wall" (emphasis added).[4] "Long dormant" for whom? Perhaps for the *Times* and American liberals, but certainly not the people of East Germany. That's precisely the point: Reagan revived lots of long-dormant debates great and small about our political life. Indeed, the dominant theme and focus of this narrative is to survey and tie together the massive number of arguments Reagan opened up on nearly every front of American political life.

The ruckus over the Berlin Wall speech highlights two important things about Reagan, one now more widely recognized, and one still obscure. The first is Reagan's insight, which is now acclaimed even among liberals who disagree with his philosophy. The second key aspect of Reagan's statecraft that emerges from his staff's opposition to the Berlin Wall line, and many similar episodes throughout his presidency, is the extent to which Reagan battled not only with the Democratic opposition but also against the conventional reflexes of much of his own party and staff. Often, in fact, Reagan's fights with members of his own party were fiercer than his fights with Democrats. And there was still a third faction he had to battle—the news media. It was not so much the media's liberalism as its *adversarialism*, grown to gargantuan dimensions in the decade after Watergate. The conformist mentality of the media on stories large and small meant that objectively, as the Marxists used to say, the media served the interests of Reagan's opposition.

These aspects of Reagan's political story are directly related on multiple levels, but we should take stock of his insight and imagination first. Reagan's insight always seemed to be married to an uncanny sense of timing. Throughout his presidency, and especially in his face-to-face meetings with Gorbachev, Reagan seemed to know when to press hard with provocative positions and when to strike a more irenic pose. Friends and critics alike have drained tankers of ink trying to decipher Reagan's unusual habits of mind.[5] His imagination and his penchant for analysis by anecdote are usually deployed for the purpose of denigrating his intelligence, which conveniently overlooks the fact that analysis by anecdote is the method of Plato's dialogues. Modern social science tries to reduce thinking either to an orderly, replicable process of formal logic and quantitative models or to the context of a person's life.

But insight doesn't work this way. Insight, the philosopher Bernard Lonergan notes in his magisterial study of the subject, is reached "not by learning rules, not by following precepts, not by studying any methodology . . . [Insight] is a function not of outer circumstances but of inner condition, pivots between the concrete and the abstract, and passes into the habitual texture of one's mind." Insight is discovery, not deduction; it shares the same element of genius that creates great new art. "Were there rules for discovery," Lonergan adds, "then discoveries would be mere conclusions. Were there precepts for genius, then men of genius would be hacks."[6]

Certainly there is insight at work in Reagan that was missing from other leading anti-Communist figures of modern times, with the significant exception of Winston Churchill, who also thought the Cold War need not be a permanent condition.[7] Lincoln wrote that all nations have a central idea, from which all their minor thoughts radiate. The same can be said of great statesmen. Churchill's central insight was that the distinction between liberty and tyranny is real and substantial—a distinction too often obscured in modern social science or willfully avoided by pusillanimous politicians. Reagan's central idea was a variation of Churchill's—that unlimited government is inimical to liberty, certainly in its vicious forms such as Communism or socialism, but also in its supposedly benign forms, such as bureaucracy.

Thus there was a seamless quality to Reagan's domestic policy outlook and his Cold War grand strategy. Many of the histories and biographies now appearing, however, obscure the fact that Reagan's foreign policy and domestic policy were of a piece. As Reagan's role in the ending of the Cold War has come into much sharper relief over the past few years, the epic nature of that struggle is causing us gradually to lose focus on most other aspects of Reagan's presidency, in part because the philosophy behind Reagan's domestic ideas remains as controversial today as it was then. Apart from the Cold War, the conventional wisdom is that Reagan's presidency ranged from fiasco (such as his economic policy) to disaster (the Iran-Contra scandal), just as many historians judge Churchill's pre–World War II career as largely a failure or disaster.[8]

This represents a willed narrowness of historical imagination. Reagan cannot be understood in such a compartmentalized way, and his acknowledged success in one arena—the Cold War—cannot be disconnected from his larger political genius, which extended to domestic affairs as well. That Reagan regarded statism as a continuum rather than as a dichotomous problem of East and West was made clear in his 1982 speech in Westminster, where he said: "[T]here is a threat posed to human freedom by the enormous power of the modern state. History teaches the dangers of government that over-reaches—political control taking precedence over free economic growth, secret police, mindless bureaucracy all combining to stifle individual excellence and personal freedom." Reagan's conflation of "secret police" and "mindless bureaucracy" was no coincidence, as his next sentence made plain: "Now, I'm aware that among us here and throughout Europe there is legitimate disagreement over the extent to which the public sector should play a role in a nation's economy and life"—in other words, *I know you're not all as freedom-loving as me and Margaret Thatcher*—"but on one point all of us are united: our abhorrence of dictatorship in all its forms."

The point is, the same principles that animated Reagan's Cold War statecraft also directed his domestic policy vision. The domestic policy story is more diffuse and complex. Much of it turns on arcane aspects of legal and regulatory philosophy, cost-benefit analysis, and eye-glazing fiscal numerology. It lacks the personal drama of foreign policy and the Cold War against the Evil Empire. Reagan never stood in front of the Federal Trade Commission or the Environmental Protection Agency and said, "Mr. Regulator—tear down this rule!" But he figuratively had this attitude. One revealing diary entry from 1986 reads: "The villain in the case is the Fed. Drug Administration [he meant the Food and Drug Administration], and they are a villain."

The fundamental unity of Reagan's statesmanship asserted here necessarily opens up for debate the question of whether Reagan's domestic record is commensurate with his foreign policy achievements. This question involves issues that historians have typically neglected but which lie at the fault line of partisan division today.

It became fashionable during the contentious presidency of George W.

Bush for some liberals to wax nostalgic about Reagan, but during Reagan's time in office the Left hated Reagan just as lustily as they hated Bush, and with some of the same venomous affectations, such as the *reductio ad Hitlerum*. The key difference is that there was no Internet during Reagan's years with which to magnify these derangements, and the twenty-four-hour cable TV news cycle was in its infancy. But the signs were certainly abundant. In 1982 Madame Tussauds Wax Museum in London held a vote for the most hated people of all time, with the result being Hitler, Margaret Thatcher, Ronald Reagan, and Dracula.[9] A Democratic congressman, William Clay of Missouri, would charge that Reagan was "trying to replace the Bill of Rights with fascist precepts lifted verbatim from *Mein Kampf*."[10] The argument Reagan propelled to the fore in 1980 has not yet been resolved a generation later. In one sense, Reagan's story is unfinished.

*   *   *

OF COURSE, POLITICAL argument is seldom finally resolved in America, as the persistence of die-hard sympathizers of Southern secession 140 years after Appomattox demonstrates. What can be discerned are clear turning points—*realignments* is the term political scientists and historians use—in political thought and party dominance. The political story of the 1980s, and the central focus of this narrative, is how the previously regnant liberalism and the Democratic Party reacted and adapted (or failed to adapt) to Reagan's challenge, and second, how Reagan transformed the Republican Party in his own image.

The question of political realignment is nowadays controversial within academic opinion. Historians and journalists accept the idea wholeheartedly; political scientists are split.[11] Even those who embrace the concept agree that realignments have happened only a few times in American history: in 1800, when Thomas Jefferson's Democratic-Republican Party obliterated the Federalist Party of John Adams; in 1860, when Abraham Lincoln's new Republican Party displaced the Democratic Party and controlled the presidency for fifty-six of the next seventy-two years; and again in 1932, when FDR's New Deal ended decades of Republican rule in Washington and established the Democrats as the dominant party for the next forty-eight years.

It was not at all clear in 1980 whether Reagan's landslide victory marked the beginning of another such realignment. To be sure, many conservatives who had been talking of the "silent majority" for years thought Reagan's election represented the breakthrough they had been predicting at least since

Kevin Phillips's 1969 book *The Emerging Republican Majority*. Polls taken in the aftermath of the 1980 Reagan landslide showed Republicans pulling nearly even with Democrats on party identification among voters—a dramatic change from the period immediately following Richard Nixon's resignation, when the proportion of voters who identified themselves as Republican fell to 18 percent in one poll. Republicans had temporarily occupied the executive citadel before (see Dwight Eisenhower, Richard Nixon), but liberals understood these administrations to have been temporary aberrations. Besides, Eisenhower and Nixon governed domestically from slightly left of center.

Yet for all of Reagan's dominance, Republicans failed to make much ground in the House of Representatives after 1980, confounding the realignment thesis and lending reassurance to Democrats that they were, after all, still the natural governing majority. As the half-life of the 1980 election wore off, voting preference polls began to show a comfortable Democratic advantage once again. This circumstance made it less obviously compelling to Democrats that they had to change in order to prosper with the voters—allowing the party to proceed in the condition the psychobabblists call denial. Meanwhile, the ambiguous situation unnerved many conservatives, who, even before Reagan's presidency concluded, began to despair that Reagan and their cause had come up short.

The extent to which conservatives were frustrated with Reagan much of the time, particularly during his second term, is another aspect of the Reagan years that has receded from view. The categorical imperatives of ideological fervency are the lifeblood of party politics, but often distract from perceiving real changes and achievements. It is striking to compare Reagan, now the unchallenged conservative icon, with Franklin Roosevelt, the liberal icon, for both suffered from the contemporaneous disappointment of their ideological supporters.

An extended comparison between Reagan and FDR reveals a deeper aspect of political realignment that is usually not captured in the simple model of one party replacing another as the majority. Each man took on his own party and by degrees successfully transformed it, while at the same time frustrating and deflecting the course of the rival party.

This process occurred slowly and against much resistance. Like conservatives in the Reagan era, liberals during FDR's time were often frustrated with him and thought the New Deal fell far short of what it should accomplish. The *New Republic* lamented in 1940 "the slackening of pace in the New Deal," and also that "the New Deal has been disappointing in its second phase." The philosopher John Dewey and Minnesota's Democratic governor, Floyd Olson, among others, complained that the New Deal hadn't gone far enough to abolish the profit motive as the fundamental organizing principle of the economy, and Socialist Party standard-bearer Norman Thomas scorned FDR's "pale pink pills." Historian Walter Millis wrote in 1938 that the New Deal "has been reduced to a movement with no program, with no effective political organization, with no vast popular party strength behind it, and with no candidate."[12] Much the same kind of thing was said about Reagan at the end of his second term. Midge Decter wrote in *Commentary*: "There was no Reagan Revolution, not even a skeleton of one to hang in George Bush's closet." "In the end," concurred William Niskanen, chairman of Reagan's Council of Economic Advisers, "there was no Reagan Revolution."[13]

Liberal ideologues who despaired over the limits of the New Deal overlooked that FDR had to carry along a large number of Democrats who opposed the New Deal. Reagan similarly had to carry along a number of Republicans who were opposed to or lukewarm about his conservative philosophy. This problem would dog Reagan for his entire presidency. Influential conservative columnist Robert Novak would observe in late 1987: "True believers in Reagan's efforts to radically transform how America is governed were outnumbered by orthodox Republicans who would have been more at home serving Jerry Ford."[14] Harvard government professor Harvey Mansfield understood the challenge Reagan faced as early as 1980, observing, "The debate in American politics today, one can say with little exaggeration, is within the Republican party between those with ideas and the prudent distrusters of ideas."[15]

Had it been within the power of the "prudent distrusters" of the GOP establishment in 1980, the party's presidential nomination would surely have gone to Gerald Ford, George H. W. Bush, Howard Baker, Bob Dole, or John Connally before Reagan. By 1980 many Republicans in Washington could be considered victims of the political equivalent of the Stockholm syndrome, in which hostages come to sympathize with their captors. Having been in the minority for so long, many Washington Republicans had come to absorb the premises of establishment liberalism, preferring to offer a low-budget version of the Democratic platform.

Reagan's dramatic landslide election in 1980, and the mandate it conferred, might be said to pose two problems: Democrats had to figure out how to oppose Reagan; Republicans, how to contain him. Even though GOP senators owed their newfound and much coveted committee chairmanships to

Reagan's coattails, old establishment bulls were distinctly unenthusiastic about the new president. Bob Dole and Pete Domenici, key senators on the Finance Committee, laid repeated roadblocks in the path of Reagan's economic policy. Mark Hatfield, the new chairman of the Appropriations Committee, opposed Reagan's proposals to cut social spending, eliminate cabinet departments, and privatize the Bonneville Power Administration ("over my dead body," the senator roared). His fellow Oregonian Robert Packwood, chairman of the Republican Senatorial Campaign Committee, attacked Reagan as an obstacle to a Republican realignment. Charles Percy, chairman of the Foreign Relations Committee, openly criticized Reagan's arms control diplomacy and often put holds on Reagan's diplomatic appointees. Percy found ample Republican support from Larry Pressler and Charles Mathias. Several of these senators had contested Reagan for the GOP nomination in 1980 and were unchastened by their rout, chiefly because they thought themselves better qualified to sit in the Oval Office. Reagan once remonstrated Howard Baker: "Remember, Howard, I'm president and you're not."[16]

Much of the time these and other GOP senators acted as though they were in opposition; they shared little or none of Reagan's partisan spiritedness, giving proof to Eugene McCarthy's quip that the principal function of liberal Republicans "is to shoot the wounded after the battle is over." Reagan noted this problem from time to time and expressed privately a high degree of contempt for Capitol Hill Republicans. In a diary entry in 1984, complaining about Hatfield's opposition to an administration position on the budget, the president ruefully comments: "With some of our friends we don't need enemies." In another diary entry, Reagan refers to Lowell Weicker as "a pompous, no good fathead" and on a separate occasion complains that "Weicker had the gall to question me—I think I did him in." More than once after a disappointing show of support from congressional Republicans, Reagan writes in his diary, "We had rabbits when we needed tigers."

The party split in the Senate existed also in the House, where Reagan's own political staff knew they couldn't count on as many as twenty northeastern Republicans, though the more populist and freewheeling nature of the House enabled the insurgent conservatives greater latitude to assert themselves. On the other hand, Reagan received staunch support for his defense and foreign policy from Democratic senator Henry "Scoop" Jackson, and populated his administration with important Democrats such as Max Kampelman, Eugene Rostow, and Jeane Kirkpatrick.

The lesson of FDR and Reagan is that remaking one's own party can be more difficult than beating the opposition party in elections. Woodrow Wilson wrote that "if the president leads the way, his party can hardly resist him." Perhaps, but the longer tenure in Washington of most House and Senate members, combined with the prerogatives of the separation of powers, feeds their intransigence. FDR grew impatient as his own party blocked his legislative agenda during his second term, and thus he attempted to purge the Democratic Party of anti–New Dealers in the 1938 election cycle. This gambit failed worse than his court-packing scheme and resulted in a Republican rout at the polls. (Democrats lost seventy-one House seats and five Senate seats in 1938.)

Reagan, whether by temperament or conviction or both, rejected any notion of leading a Republican purge. To the contrary, he replicated his two-front struggle against liberalism and establishment Republicanism within his own senior staff at the White House, resulting in the well-advertised split between the so-called ideologues and pragmatists. Lawrence Eagleburger, who served in Reagan's State Department and later briefly served as secretary of state under President George H. W. Bush, observed early in Reagan's first term that the administration resembled "a coalition government" more akin to what might be seen in a multiparty parliamentary government in Europe. Movement conservatives bristled at seeing the GOP establishment so well represented in Reagan's inner circle, and, to be sure, the "pragmatists" were more adroit at infighting and using press leaks in attempts to alter Reagan's course.

At the same time, movement conservatives and the media alike did not perceive how well this arrangement served Reagan, or indeed how it matched his California experience, where Reagan blended moderate Republicans from the campaign of his vanquished primary foe, George Christopher, alongside movement conservatives. Reagan tried to explain it, as in this exchange from a 1981 press conference:

QUESTION: There have been specific reports that your Secretary of State and Secretary of Defense are not getting along and that they argue in front of you. Can you comment on those reports?
PRESIDENT REAGAN: The whole Cabinet argues in front of me. That was the system that I wanted installed.[17]

In a manner that eludes many historians, political scientists, and reporters, the most successful presidencies tend to be those that have factional disagreement within their inner councils, whereas sycophantic administrations tend to get in the most trouble. Fractiousness in an administration is a sign of health:

the Jefferson-Hamilton feud in Washington's administration, the rivalry within Lincoln's cabinet, and the odd combination of fervent New Dealers and conventional Democrats in FDR's White House provided a dynamic tension that contributed to successful governance. Though the partisans of the distinct camps in the Reagan White House would be loath to admit it, their feuding probably contributed to better policy in many cases. An attempted Reaganite purge, of either the party or his own staff, might well have backfired and snuffed out the spontaneous slow-motion revolution within the party that was already under way, and which gained new momentum in the 1990s under the spur of figures such as Newt Gingrich.

Gingrich himself frequently expressed frustration with Reagan. "Ronald Reagan is the only coherent revolutionary in an administration of accommodationist advisers," he complained in 1984. "The problem was that Reagan's people were so excited by victory, they forgot they didn't control the country. They didn't control the House and they didn't really control the Senate. They didn't in fact have real power, but psychologically they acted as if they did."[18] At one White House meeting late in the second term, after Gingrich laid out complaints about important things the administration had left undone, Reagan put his arm around the young Georgia congressman and said in his typically gentle fashion, "Well, some things you're just going to have to do after I'm gone."

To be sure, the so-called pragmatist-ideologue split in the White House was reflected in the widely varying character of different agencies and cabinet departments. Where there was a concentration of movement conservatives, such as at the Justice Department, the Federal Trade Commission, and the Office of Management and Budget, there were substantial efforts to make fundamental policy changes and to tame the permanent bureaucracy. In departments or agencies that lacked a critical mass of ideologues, such as the Department of Education during Reagan's first term, or the Department of Labor, there was little or no conservative reform.

Twenty years later, nearly every Republican claims to be a Reagan Republican, as Reagan has become the standard against which to measure Republicanism, just as FDR became the standard for two generations of Democrats. Many of the so-called pragmatists of the Reagan years are now in the political wilderness, and admit to having been had by the wily Reagan.

*   *   *

REAGAN'S ORGANIZATIONAL DISREGARD of the biblical injunction "be ye not unevenly yoked" (in the King James version) was only one aspect of his character, imagination, and political practice that observers found difficult to understand. Taking their cue in part from Reagan's befuddled official biographer, Edmund Morris, historians and political scientists are increasingly drawing a veil over inquiries into Reagan's innermost character, acknowledging that there was more to Reagan than they knew, but still conveying (if only tacitly) that he was something of a fluke. Despite the growing acclaim for Reagan, the standard line remains that he was personally "remote," that the "real Reagan" somehow remained hidden and mysterious. "At his core," the *Washington Post*'s Haynes Johnson wrote, "[T]here was something unknown or unknowable about Ronald Reagan."[19] This extends beyond his personal characteristics to his political thought process as well. Even some of Reagan's ideological sympathizers follow this track. Midge Decter wrote in 1991, "It will, one day, take a truly gifted writer, perhaps a novelist, to solve the puzzle of such a man."

Numerous observers have put forward compelling insights into this or that aspect of Reagan, but no one seems to feel capable of capturing the whole. Even Mrs. Reagan has validated this view, telling Lou Cannon in 1989, "You can get just so far to Ronnie, and then something happens."[20] Much has been made of the withdrawal of children of an alcoholic parent, but it is also true that Reagan's kind of reserve would be entirely unremarkable in a private citizen. We have become so accustomed to public figures and celebrities baring their souls to Barbara Walters that we find it odd when a prominent person disdains to do so, and unable to reconcile the spectacle of geniality and privacy. Although many of Reagan's Depression-era generation embraced the baby boomer practice of emotional public introspection, there is reason to regard Reagan as a more authentic figure.[21]

The incredulity that a man with such extraordinary views and such an unconventional background could sweep to the pinnacle of power is testimony to the isolation of Washington, D.C., and the parochialism of the media and political class. The political class regards only official appointments and long tenure in elected office as genuine "experience," and deprecates the way in which private participation in public affairs can prepare someone for high office.[22] President Carter told an interviewer the day after the 1980 election that he had spent the first two years of his presidency as "a student," and that Reagan "will have the same things to learn that I had to learn." "No previous president of the United States," Rowland Evans and Robert Novak wrote, "had so bizarre a preparation for political office."[23]

This is quite wrong, for the heterodox notion should be considered that Reagan was one of the best-prepared men ever to become president. By the time he was elected president, he had spent more than thirty years thinking about politics and participating in public life in a meaningful way, starting with his tenure as head of the Screen Actors Guild in the late 1940s during an especially politicized time. His travels in the 1950s on behalf of General Electric represent his period of serious self-education in politics—an underappreciated factor in Reagan's saga that I have written about in detail elsewhere.[24]

The important point to grasp is that Reagan approached politics from the standpoint of a *citizen* rather than as an aspiring politician or intellectual. In the abstract the American idea of self-government militates against a professional political class, even though it was understood at the time of the Founding that political leadership would be mostly an elite preoccupation. For every Adams, Lodge, Taft, Roosevelt, Kennedy, or Bush who rose to prominence on the basis of family background, there was a Truman, Eisenhower, Nixon, Carter, Reagan, or Clinton who rose from obscurity, reminding us of the essential egalitarianism of American political opportunity, and most importantly that Americans should never come to believe there is a fundamental distinction between *citizens* and *rulers*.

For the better part of the last century, however, advanced political opinion gradually formalized the view that contemporary government was an expert affair, increasingly remote from the comprehension of ordinary citizens. The enthusiasm for administrative government by expert elites was the root of our problems, Reagan thought. His stance as a citizen-politician in his first race for governor of California in 1966 was undoubtedly an effective posture, but it was just as undoubtedly sincere. Well into his presidency Reagan still self-consciously referred to the federal government as "they" rather than "we."

Reagan understood instinctively that modern liberalism represented a rejection of the constitutional premises of self-government. Many liberals, following in the footsteps of Woodrow Wilson, explicitly attacked the American Founding and the Founders' understanding of the Constitution as defective. Most contemporary liberals have little use for the Declaration of Independence, the *Federalist Papers,* James Madison, or even Thomas Jefferson, the father of the Democratic Party. When liberals are not actively hostile to the Founders and their way of thinking, they are uninterested. The usable political tradition for most liberals begins with Franklin Roosevelt and the New Deal.

Hence the core of Reagan's political purpose was recovering an appreciation for the Founders' understanding of the principles and practice of American government. This was central to his rhetoric to a much greater extent than it was to that of any other modern president of either party. Political scientist Andrew Busch conducted a content analysis of major presidential speeches from Lyndon Johnson through Reagan and found that Reagan cited the Founders three to four times as often as his four predecessors. Reagan mentions the Constitution ten times in his memoirs, often in a substantive way; Carter, Ford, Nixon, and Johnson mention the Constitution a grand total of zero times.[25] "We're for limited government," he said in his 1988 State of the Union speech, "because we understand, as the Founding Fathers did, that it is the best way of ensuring personal liberty and empowering the individual so that every American of every race and region shares fully in the flowering of American prosperity and freedom."

Although the American Founding was central to Reagan, his conservatism was idiosyncratic and unorthodox, which may say as much about the condition of American conservatism in 1980 as it does about Reagan. The main line of modern conservatism, emanating chiefly from William F. Buckley Jr.'s *National Review,* defined itself as "[s]tanding athwart history, yelling Stop!" This kind of conservatism, though intellectually rigorous, is too backward-looking and aristocratic for America, the land of immigrants, upward mobility, and constant transformation. The patriotism of traditional conservatism, though fervent, was often refracted through an old European lens. Though Reagan was a devoted *National Review* reader and friend of Buckley, he was not that kind of conservative. And while Reagan was the annual headliner for the Conservative Political Action Conference—the Woodstock for movement conservatives—he typically described conservatism in populist rather than ideological terms. George Will noted that "[Reagan] is painfully fond of the least conservative sentiment conceivable, a statement from an anti-conservative, Thomas Paine: 'We have it in our power to begin the world over again.' Any time, any place," Will complained, "that is nonsense."[26] That is the voice of traditional, Edmund Burke–style conservatism. It was not the idiom of Reagan; his belief in America's dynamism was at the core of his optimism about the future, and that dynamism has profoundly unconservative effects at times.

Reagan's constitutional statesmanship arrived at a necessary moment. Reagan came to office at a time when the nation's self-doubt and pessimism about the future were at an all-time high, and this doubt extended to the very form of the nation's government itself. The presidency, it was said, was an office inadequate for modern times. By implication, the Constitution was obsolete. The self-doubt about America's prospects and her institutions essentially raised the question of whether constitutional self-government was still possible at all.

This represented a startling turnaround in the space of less than a decade. At the time of Richard Nixon's resignation at the flood tide of Watergate, the prevailing sentiment, exemplified in Arthur Schlesinger's best-selling book, was that we had most to fear from an imperial presidency. Four years of Jimmy Carter's flailing led political elites to the opposite view, that the presidency, or the federal government in general, wasn't nearly imperial enough.

The popular historian Barbara Tuchman expressed the thinking of the intellectual elite: "The job of President is too difficult for any single person because of the complexity of the problems and the size of government. Maybe some form of plural executive is needed, such as they have in Switzerland."[27] *U.S. News and World Report* wondered: "Perhaps the burdens have become so great that, over time, no President will be judged adequate in the eyes of most voters."[28] Columnist Joseph Kraft wrote on the eve of the election: "As the country goes to the polls in the 47th national election, the Presidency as an institution is in trouble. It has become, as Vice President Mondale said in a recent interview, the 'fire hydrant of the nation.' " *Newsweek* echoed this sentiment: "The Presidency has in some measure defeated the last five men who have held it—and has persuaded some of the people who served them that it is in danger of becoming a game nobody can win. . . . [T]he job as now constituted is or is becoming impossible, no matter who holds it."[29] Political scientists Robert Wright and Fred Greenstein wrote: "Recent history offers little cause for optimism about Ronald Reagan's chances of governing the American people to their satisfaction."[30] British journalist Godfrey Hodgson observed that Reagan "has aroused expectations that he cannot fulfill. Disappointment will turn into disillusionment, and excessive expectations will curdle into unreasonable resentment. That has happened, in one way or another, to each of the last half dozen presidents. Why should Ronald Reagan be an exception?"[31]

Many others concurred. Political scientist Theodore Lowi stated: "The presidency has become an impossible job . . . because the presidency has become too big, even for the likes of FDR."[32] Elsewhere Lowi wrote, "The probability of [presidential] failure is always tending toward 100 percent." James MacGregor Burns, author of *The Deadlock of Democracy,* concluded: "The greatest problem of America in modern times is the despair and disillusion of thoughtful people with the apparent incapacity to solve our problems under an antiquated governmental system, booby-trapped with vetoes, and a purposely designed self-limiting division of power."[33] Everett Carll Ladd wrote in *Fortune* magazine, "The experience of recent years strongly suggests that personal ability and character, while vitally important, are insufficient to assure success to a contemporary presidency. For the institutional setting quite simply has become adverse. A kind of 'vicious circle' of declining performance has been initiated." The big question, for Ladd, was: "Can *anybody* do it?" Surveying the field of candidates who wanted to succeed Jimmy Carter, Ladd thought not, and worried about the implications: "The consequences of yet one more failure in this unique office would impose appalling stress on the whole political system."[34] Like Tuchman, Ladd thought the office was no longer equal to the times. "The institutional resources available to the President, relative to what he is expected to do, remain seriously deficient."

This was more than idle parlor talk. Congress considered a resolution to form a Commission on More Effective Government that would be charged with making "a comprehensive review of our system of government." President Carter's White House counsel, Lloyd Cutler, caused a stir with a widely noted article in the fall 1980 issue of *Foreign Affairs* calling for extensive constitutional reforms to make the presidency more powerful, including giving the president the power to dissolve Congress and call for new elections, as prime ministers can do in most parliamentary governments.[35] "We're going to be having this same conversation about Ronald Reagan in two years' time, or maybe one," Cutler said after Carter's rejection at the polls.[36] President Carter embraced the view of the feebleness of the presidency in his farewell address to the nation a week before leaving office in 1981, noting that the presidency is "at once the most powerful office in the world and the most severely constrained by law and custom. . . . Today we are asking our political system to do things of which the Founding Fathers never dreamed. The government they designed for a few hundred thousand people now serves a nation of almost 230 million." Translation: *Don't blame me—I was hamstrung by this impotent office.*

For the chorus of intellectuals and political elites who thought wholesale reform of the presidency and the Constitution was necessary, Reagan seemed the least likely person to reverse the perceived decay of the presidency, for the simple reason that most reform ideas required making the federal government more powerful, while Reagan called for making the federal government smaller and less powerful. Reagan's electoral success supposedly confirmed the theme that our entire political system had slipped off the rails. Tuchman huffed that "[t]he methods we use today in presidential elections—image making, paid political advertisements and the like—*lead to the wrong people winning office.* . . . [P]eople of any quality and self-respect cannot take it" (emphasis added).

The highest measure of Reagan's achievement is that after eight years of his presidency, the Iran-Contra disaster notwithstanding, all talk of the presidency as an inadequate institution had vanished into the mists, and has not returned. The *National Journal* polled presidential scholars in 1985, finding that a large majority thought Reagan had succeeded in "reviving trust and confidence in an institution that in the post-Vietnam era had been perceived as being unworkable."[37] Charles McDowell, national political reporter for the *Richmond Times-Dispatch* and a regular TV presence on *Washington Week in Review* during Reagan's presidency, said in 1986: "If somebody had told me in 1979 that Ronald Reagan by common consent would be ranked with Franklin Roosevelt as one of the two most important presidents of the century I've lived in, I would have walked away from such a trivial person, shaking my head and saying there's no hope for any of us if anyone thinks that. And now I think that."[38] The *Washington Post*'s Haynes Johnson offered a similar mea culpa: "I thought Ronald Reagan was the most ignorant major candidate I'd ever seen running for president. I misjudged him. I was wrong."[39] Johnson, whose politics tilt to the left, added, "I think it was a healthy thing that Ronald Reagan was elected president."

*   *   *

EVEN IF THE depth of Reagan's insight, personal virtues, and political achievement are gradually becoming recognized, he is still likely to remain the Rodney Dangerfield of modern American presidents—he gets little respect from the intellectual class and much of his political peer group. There is a large superficial reason for this: the gravity of the office has tugged noticeably at the facial features of all of our other recent presidents, but not Reagan. Dwight Eisenhower had a heart attack and a stroke during his time in office; Lyndon Johnson's basset hound face drooped as Vietnam casualty figures soared; Richard Nixon's jowls got jowlier; Jimmy Carter's Cheshire cat grin disappeared beneath the furrows of worry and strain.

As Reagan became the oldest person ever to be president a few months into his first term, it was assumed that the physical exactions would be even more evident. Shortly after the 1980 election a Metropolitan Life Insurance Company study found that being president shortens a person's life expectancy nearly as much as cigarette smoking—on average, by 3.9 years (or 5.2 years among twentieth-century presidents). Twenty-two of the (at that time) thirty-five deceased presidents had failed to live to their normal life expectancy. Reagan, Met Life projected, could expect to live another eleven years, to 1992.

Yet Reagan, seventy-seven years old at the end of two terms in office, seemed to show little physical wear and tear. His facial appearance was nearly as fresh and unruffled as the day he first arrived in 1981, despite having suffered a serious gunshot wound and two cancer surgeries. Reagan's age-defying performance seemed to be evidence that it was all an act, just another Hollywood production. Surely if he had been fully "engaged" in his own presidency, the strain of the office would have shown up in his appearance. It is only as Reagan became the oldest living ex-president and new testimonials from his doctors came to light about his extraordinary fitness that we have begun to perceive that Reagan was as physically unique as he was mentally unique.

Reagan can be said to be like Edgar Allan Poe's case of the purloined letter: the real Reagan was hidden in plain sight. This is certainly true from a purely historical and political point of view. Reagan's ascent on the world stage is one of the most remarkable in history, and he will baffle and fascinate historians for decades to come. What Reagan said and did is more significant than whatever tangled subconscious aspects of his character may or may not exist at some obscure level. This narrative pays special attention to Reagan's words—speech being the most basic political act, but one that too many modern political thinkers wrongly deprecate. Reagan did not mind being called the Great Communicator, so long as it was understood that, for him, *what* he was communicating outweighed how well or badly he did it. Lincoln too could have been known as the Great Communicator but for the fact that the aim of his words became the deed of the nation, thereby bestowing on him the higher title of the Great Emancipator. Reagan was too modest to have claimed for himself the title that the substance of his words and deeds point to: the Great Liberator. Yet that is the legacy he ultimately deserves—and not simply for winning the Cold War.[40]

This is the story of how Ronald Reagan forged that legacy.

PART I

———⟫●⟪———

THE IMPRISONED
LIGHTNING

CHAPTER I

"THE TOWN TREMBLED":

From Election Day to Inauguration Day

*No strongly centralized political organization feels altogether
happy with individuals who combine independence, a free
imagination, and a formidable strength of character with
stubborn faith and a single-minded, unchanging view
of the public and private good.*
—Isaiah Berlin on Winston Churchill

Washington, D.C., awoke on Wednesday, November 5—the
day after Ronald Reagan's election—to an unimaginable scene. Reagan's victory had been anticipated, but the depth and sweep of it had not. His ten-point margin in the popular vote translated into a 489–49 landslide in the electoral college; Reagan won forty-four states, Jimmy Carter just six. Unlike Nixon's forty-nine-state landslide in 1972, Reagan had long coattails: a twelve-seat GOP pickup—and a majority for the first time in twenty-four years—in the Senate, and a thirty-three-seat pickup in the House, enough for a working majority.[1] The political landscape was littered with the carcasses of slaughtered Democratic bulls. By Thursday the magnitude of the election was starting to course through the news cycle. "The election was a shocker," *Washington Post* columnist David Broder wrote in a front-page article with the banner headline "A Sharp Right Turn." "The conservative victory could hardly be more complete." For establishment Washington it was as if a barbarian horde had sacked the city. "The Town Trembled," read another *Post* news headline.

The *Post* editorial page was less restrained than the stately Broder. The *Post* house editorial, "Tidal Wave," admitted that "[s]omething of gigantic proportions happened—must have been happening for a long while—and the capital and the political wise men were taken by surprise. . . . [A]n 'anti-Washington,' 'anti-establishment' political storm warning was missed by Washington and the establishment."[2] Reagan had predicted since the early 1960s that a "prairie fire" of conservative populism would someday sweep the nation; on November 4 it appeared that Reagan had finally struck the match. The *Post* blamed "the used-up, unrenewed and reflexive quality of so much Democratic Party thought and dogma these days." Democratic Senator Paul Tsongas of Massachusetts summed up the election's meaning in one sentence: "Basically, the New Deal died yesterday."

The Style section of the *Post* may have been a better barometer than the staid news pages at capturing how truly aghast was the social sentiment of elite Washington. Columnist Henry Allen wrote: "It's like one of those old horror movies where the atom bomb rouses the dinosaurs from the ice they've slumbered in all those eons . . . and all of a sudden you can hear the cry going up in liberal strongholds: The Reagan People are coming."

John P. Roche, a former head of the liberal Americans for Democratic Action, wrote in 1984 that Reagan's election was "an 8-plus earthquake on the political Richter scale, and it sent a number of eminent statesmen—Republican and Democratic—into shock."[3] It was a welcome shock in at least one important establishment neighborhood: the stock market rallied sharply the day after the election, with the Dow Jones Industrial Average soaring fifteen points to 953.16 on record volume of eighty-five million shares. The dollar rallied sharply on overseas currency markets. (The "Reagan rally" proved short-lived; the following day the market slumped again after banks raised their prime lending rate by a full point, to 15.5 percent.)

If American elites and intellectuals were wary of Reagan, among opposition leaders in Eastern Europe Reagan's victory was a glimmer of hope. Lech Walesa, the leader of the Polish resistance, remarked to American reporters after the election that "Reagan was the only good candidate in your presidential campaign, and I knew he would win."[4] Soviet leader Leonid Brezhnev sent Reagan a telegram of congratulations that the *Washington Post* described as "noticeably cooler" than the message sent to Jimmy Carter four years earlier. According to the *New York Times,* "Soviet officials, whose job it is to study the United States, said they were depressed by the defeat of such Democratic advocates of détente as Senators George McGovern, John Culver, and Frank Church."

Back in the United States, the far Left twitched with predictable paroxysms of paranoia. In Berkeley, more than two thousand people turned out to protest Reagan's election for three nights in a row, forgetting the irony that it was the Berkeley Free Speech Movement in 1964 that had helped propel his entry into politics. To borrow Yogi Berra's solecism, it was déjà vu all over again: police arrested fifty-four people for occupying the chancellor's office.[5]

To the agitated Left, Reagan's election meant only one thing: the dark night of American fascism was about to descend. Eddie Williams, head of what the *Washington Post* described as "the respected black think tank, the Joint Center for Political Studies," reacted to Reagan's landslide thus: "When you consider that in the climate we're in—rising violence, the Ku Klux Klan—it is exceedingly frightening."[6] This was not far removed from Fidel Castro's opinion about Reagan offered right before the election: "We sometimes have the feeling that we are living in the time preceding the election of Adolf Hitler as Chancellor of Germany." Libya's Kaddafi was not to be left out of the parade, saying, "Reagan is Hitler number 2!" (This is admittedly confusing, since most radical Arab leaders like Hitler.)

Kaddafi's and Castro's *reductio ad Hitlerum* could also be found in the American press. *Los Angeles Times* cartoonist Paul Conrad drew a panel depicting Reagan plotting a fascist putsch in a darkened Munich beer hall. Claremont College professor John Roth wrote: "I could not help remembering how forty years ago economic turmoil had conspired with Nazi nationalism and militarism—all intensified by Germany's defeat in World War I—to send the world reeling into catastrophe. . . . It is not entirely mistaken to contemplate our post-election state with fear and trembling." Harry Stein wrote in *Esquire* that the voters who supported Reagan were like the "good Germans" in "Hitler's Germany."[7] Sociologist Alan Wolfe wrote in the *New Left Review:* "The worst nightmares of the American left appear to have come true."[8] In the pages of the *Nation*, Wolfe's nightmare took a familiar shape: "[T]he United States has embarked on a course so deeply reactionary, so negative and mean-spirited, so chauvinistic and self-deceptive that our times may soon rival the McCarthy era."[9] The *Bulletin of Atomic Scientists,* keeper of the "Doomsday Clock," which purported to judge the risk of nuclear annihilation, moved the hands on the clock from seven to four minutes before midnight.[10]

Triumphant conservatives were more than willing to stoke the Left's paranoia. The election seemed to be more than merely the turning out of the bums; it was, as Harvard's Harvey Mansfield Jr. put it, "a general repudiation of the values of the 1960s."[11] The *Washington Post*'s Haynes Johnson quoted an unnamed conservative political activist saying, "This country's going so far to the right you won't recognize it."[12] In Oklahoma and Wyoming, Republican enthusiasts placed roadside billboards proclaiming: WELCOME TO THE REAGAN REVOLUTION.

*   *   *

ALTHOUGH THE FROTHIER expectations of partisans at both ends of the political spectrum would turn out to be overwrought, the shock of the 1980 election would have a long half-life. For movement conservatives, Reagan's election was a golden moment whose like shall never come again. There was a clear sense of destiny, the overwhelming feeling that Our Time Was Coming. Reagan's decisive victory in 1980 produced an upwelling of sentiment leagues ahead of the usual thrill of electoral victory.

Democrats would take nearly a year to recover their bearings and go on the political offensive again. The media and the Washington establishment had set themselves up for a shock with their pre-election predictions of a close vote. Pollster Burns Roper admitted, "The Press, political analysts and political strategists all missed the magnitude and breadth of the sweep."[13] A week before the election, the *New Republic*'s Morton Kondracke wrote that "it seems more likely by the day that Ronald Reagan is not going to execute a massive electoral sweep. In fact, the movement of the presidential campaign suggests a Carter victory."[14] David Broder had written: "There is no evidence of a dramatic upsurge in Republican strength or a massive turnover in Congress." Though polls in the days leading up to the election showed Reagan ahead of Carter, most were near or within the margin of error, and everyone was predicting a late-night nail-biter. The *New York Times* poll three days out had Reagan ahead by a single point; veteran California pollster Mervin Field said, "At the moment there is a slight movement toward Carter." George Gallup said, "This election could very well be a cliffhanger just like 1948."[15]

During the last forty-eight hours, after most major media and polling organizations had completed their final polls, voters broke sharply to Reagan. The combination of public disgust with Carter and Reagan's reassuring performance in the debate the previous Tuesday provided the catalyst for the Republican surge. Only the two campaigns, each conducting relentless tracking polls, knew what was happening. Both Reagan's pollster, Richard Wirthlin, and Carter's, Pat Caddell, saw the same results from their final polls over the last two days before the election. Caddell's polls showed that Reagan's margin moved up to five points on Sunday and grew on Monday to ten points.

The pollster's alarm deepened when he saw that the "generic" vote for Democratic House and Senate candidates was plummeting along with Carter. "The disaffection was spreading across the board," Caddell told *Public Opinion* magazine after the election.

While Caddell, a brilliant if idiosyncratic analyst of public opinion, had always been wary of Carter's chances for reelection, most of Carter's inner circle was incredulous at their fate. For months White House chief of staff Hamilton Jordan had been so confident of victory over Reagan that he openly predicted, "It's not even going to be close." Wirthlin couldn't believe what he was seeing either and, knowing Reagan to be guarded until the votes were counted ("I remember President Dewey," Reagan often said), put his final poll results in the bottom drawer of his desk and didn't tell the candidate.[16]

Reagan passed Election Day calmly, voting early in the same Pacific Palisades precinct as Lawrence Welk, Sylvester Stallone, and Los Angeles Dodgers broadcaster Vin Scully. Asked by reporters how he felt about his prospects, Reagan said, "You know me, I'm too superstitious to answer anything like that." His horoscope—Reagan was an Aquarius—for that day read: "Ideal day to spend more time on home affairs so that everything there is more harmonious." And so he did. After voting Reagan went to get a haircut at his usual Beverly Hills barber (Druckers) and then lunched on tuna salad at home. Ed Meese and Mike Deaver, top advisers since the California years, dropped by his house after lunch to talk over transition planning. In Washington, the phone company activated phone lines at the office space the Reagan campaign had secured for the transition. Over at the campaign command post at the Century Plaza Hotel, the early exit poll results were confirming what Wirthlin called "those numbers no one could believe." The TV networks were seeing the same thing with their exit polls of more than twenty-three thousand voters. ABC News political director Hal Bruno said afterward, "Our exit polls told us by 1 p.m. that it was going to be a landslide."[17]

Despite the confidence of his pollsters, Reagan still expected it to be a long night. He was stepping into the shower when NBC News "officially" declared Reagan the winner at 5:15 p.m. Pacific time, even though only 4 percent of the vote had been counted. (A few days before the election, NBC anchorman John Chancellor had said, "I think we'll be here until way after midnight before we can predict the winner.") Nancy Reagan had to roust the president-elect from the shower to take President Carter's concession phone call.[18] While Reagan's campaign aides were erupting in giddiness at the Century Plaza, Reagan appeared serene and relaxed during dinner with fifty of his closest longtime supporters at the Bel Air home of steel magnate Earle Jorgensen, causing *Newsweek* to speculate that "perhaps jubilation, like depression, is not in his emotional repertoire."[19]

Reagan clearly relished the moment when he appeared before supporters at the Century Plaza Hotel after the polls closed on the West Coast. "There's never been a more humbling moment in my life," he told the rapturous crowd. Then he invoked the memory of his two most distinguished predecessors:

> Do you know, Abe Lincoln, the day after his election to the Presidency, gathered in his office the newsmen who had been covering his campaign, and he said to them: "Well boys, your troubles are over now; mine have just begun."
>
> I think I know what he meant. Lincoln may have been concerned in the troubled times in which he became President, but I don't think he was afraid. He was ready to confront the problems and the troubles of a still-youthful country, determined to seize the historic opportunity to change things.
>
> I am not frightened by what lies ahead. And I don't believe the American people are frightened by what lies ahead. Together, together we're going to do what has to be done. I aim to try and tap that great American spirit that opened up this completely undeveloped continent from coast to coast and made it a great nation, survived several wars, survived a great Depression, and we'll survive the problems that we face right now.

                              *   *   *

IT WAS NOT clear in November 1980 whether Reagan's election would entail a decisive break with the enervated 1970s, as John F. Kennedy's election signaled a sharp turn from the staid 1950s. On the surface it was supposed that Reagan was Eisenhower redux, that the political cycle had run full circle: Reagan would try to take us back to the 1950s. It was an easy mistake to make about the nation's soon-to-be oldest president, who often spoke in nostalgic terms about the good old days of his Hollywood career. The paradox of Reagan was what might be called his old-fashioned futurism. As Lou Cannon put it, "Reagan spoke to the future with the accents of the past"; George Will's equally serviceable formula was "He does not want to return to the past; he wants to return to the past's way of facing the future." Reagan's variety of future-oriented optimism rooted in historical attachment has become almost unrecognizable in the age of a postmodernism that is openly contemptuous of history and historical experience.

The sense of national crisis in 1980 was palpable, more so than at any other time since 1932. Persistent high inflation and unemployment had shattered the nation's confidence that it could fine-tune the economy. This was more than just a crisis in economic doctrine; it seemed to herald the end of the American Century. Starting in 1979, for the first time since public opinion surveys had begun to be taken, the majority of Americans doubted that the future would be better than the past, or even equal to the present. The number of Americans who told the Gallup poll that the country was on the wrong track hit a new peak of 84 percent in August 1979; 67 percent agreed with the statement that the United States was in "deep and serious trouble." A popular bumper sticker of the time read: GOD BLESS AMERICA—AND PLEASE HURRY.

In its year-end wrap-up edition in 1979, *Newsweek* observed that "[t]he whole country seems slightly traumatized on the brink of the '80s" and that there was "a growing sense that the country's institutions and leaders were no longer up to managing problems that were simply too complex to grasp." *Time* magazine essayist Lance Morrow thought the same thing: "From the Arab oil boycott in 1973 onward, the decade was bathed in a cold Spenglerian apprehension that the lights were about to go out, that history's astonishing material indulgence of the U.S. was about to end." Columbia University's Amitai Etzioni said of the 1970s that "[t]he trauma and scars had the same psychological impact on America that the loss of the empire had on Britain." Former secretary of defense James Schlesinger told *Newsweek* that he worried that the ebbing of American power and influence in the world might become a rout and that "the '80s look to me like a period of bleakness and confrontation." This powerful undertow of pessimism, it was assumed, would drag Reagan under as well.

The seeming decrepitude of America extended beyond the intellectual class to popular culture. The highest-rated television program of the moment was the prime-time soap opera *Dallas,* whose central character was a grasping, amoral oil man, J. R. Ewing. Ewing was the archetypal antihero for antiheroic times, portraying what prosperity still existed to be wholly decadent. When an unknown assailant shot Ewing in the last show of the 1980 season, "Who shot J.R.?" became an international obsession. London bookmakers gave odds on the suspected killer and took in several hundred thousand dollars in wagers. The episode that revealed the answer, broadcast two weeks after Reagan's election in November, received the highest TV viewership in history up to that point. That the show centered around oil, the commodity thought to be at the heart of America's economic difficulties, undoubtedly added to the show's fascination. *Dallas* was hardly unique among Hollywood products; studies of TV shows and movies from the time found that a disproportionate number of films depicted businessmen and commerce as corrupt.[20] The message to viewers, in other words, was that private sector institutions were as dysfunctional as our political institutions.

The faltering economy was not the only source of gloom about America's future. The nation's continuing agony over the fate of fifty-two hostages held in Iran underscored the perception of ebbing American power. The shadow over all of these disparate strands was the growing power and assertiveness of the Soviet Union. "The Soviet drive for empire," Eugene Rostow said during his Senate confirmation hearings to be head of the Arms Control and Disarmament Agency, "is accelerating in momentum and is becoming more and more difficult to contain."[21] In the weeks immediately after the election, the West feared a Soviet invasion of Poland to put down the burgeoning Solidarity trade union movement. Both the outgoing Carter administration and the incoming Reaganites made several high-profile public statements warning the Soviets against such a move, but the United States, tied down with Iran, could do little but complain.

There was not much encouragement to be found from other democracies, few of which could be said to be thriving. Freedom House's annual survey of freedom in the world found that "not free" and "partly free" nations outnumbered free nations by a two-to-one margin.[22] (Among the "not free" and "partly free" categories was most of Latin America.) The French author Jean-François Revel would soon climb the best-seller lists in Europe and the United States with the prediction that democracy was about to be revealed as a historical accident, "a brief parenthesis that is closing before our eyes."[23]

Over in Britain, Prime Minister Margaret Thatcher, Reagan's closest ideological match, was faltering badly. The economy had not improved, and her public opinion ratings had fallen to 31 percent, an all-time low for a modern British prime minister in the second year in office. Polls showed that the Labour Party would beat the Conservative Party by ten points if an election were held then, a prospect that alarmed Reagan's incoming foreign policy team. Richard Allen, who would become Reagan's first national security adviser, sent Reagan a memo worrying that Thatcher had "lost her grip on the political rudder" and that a return to power of the Labour Party "could prove harmful to our security interests." The Labour Party adopted a charming and classy slogan at their 1980 party conference: "Ditch the Bitch." The *Times* of London published a petition signed by 364 British economists saying there was "no basis in economic theory or supporting evidence" for Thatcher's economic policy, which borrowed too heavily from American free marketeers. Large-scale urban rioting in England in the summer of 1980 and 1981 was thought to be a harbinger of what might occur in the United States under Reagan—especially if he cut federal social spending.

In fact, the United States was on the cusp of a period of renewal, some of which would have occurred even if Reagan had not been elected. The 1980s would be the most creative and productive decade since the 1920s, though not without surprises and setbacks along the way. Sharp cultural turns rarely have obvious or definite points of departure, yet the election of Reagan can be seen in retrospect to be about as bright a line between epochs as is possible. The 1980s would quickly take on a distinctive style, as the last cohort of the erratic baby boom generation came to maturity while the nation's oldest president came to power. To that point the main current of youth was thought to be countercultural, but the annual survey of the American Council on Education showed that students entering college in the fall of 1980 were more interested in power, money, and status than at any other time in the past fifteen years; business management was the most popular major. The generation gap that had opened in the 1960s now reversed itself: the yippies (short for members of the Youth International Party) became yuppies—young urban professionals.[24] In one of those coincidences that is hard to dismiss entirely, Marshall McLuhan, the "prophet of grooviness," died on December 31, 1980, symbolically closing the books on the 1960s and 1970s.

This turn of the wheel was ratified on TV in 1982 when *Family Ties'* Alex Keaton replaced *All in the Family*'s Mike Stivic ("Meathead") as the pop culture representation of the next generation. Alex's ex-hippie parents wondered where they had gone wrong as their precocious, tie-wearing, über-capitalist teenage son placed a photo of William F. Buckley Jr. in his bedroom. Later in the series, young Alex swooned for a young lady because she shared his enthusiasm for Milton Friedman. Alex Keaton was the ideal Youth for Reagan yuppie icon. *Family Ties*, not surprisingly, became Ronald Reagan's favorite TV show, and Alex his favorite character. Reagan is reported to have offered to do a cameo appearance on the show; the producers disregarded it.

Median household income in 1981 was $24,000; an income of $50,000 was in the top 5 percent of the income distribution—a figure to keep in mind when reviewing the debate on the Reagan tax cuts. The median price of a house was $64,600, while the average price of a new car from Detroit was about $8,000. During the 1970s the crime rate increased 50 percent, on top of a 111 percent increase in the 1960s. It was another Democratic vulnerability. New York Democrat Charles Schumer, first elected to the House in 1980, remarked later: "I didn't understand why Reagan won until I got to Washington. Crime was ripping apart my district. And who is writing the crime legislation? The ACLU. They weren't just at the table; they were *writing* it."[25] Possibly related to the crime rate was the divorce rate, also up nearly 50 percent in the 1970s, and 136 percent higher than 1960. In 1960, one-quarter of all marriages ended in divorce; in 1980, half of all marriages were ending in divorce.

The nation had been said to be on the brink of the computer age for at least the past twenty years, but by 1980 the promise of the computer era was beginning to manifest itself more widely in everyday life. Computers would be to the 1980s what radios and automobiles had been to the 1920s—the device that would transform both work and home life in profound ways. IBM introduced its first desktop PC in 1980; at the moment, the leading desktop computer, costing $999 and capturing 40 percent of the market, was the Tandy TRS-80. The most common consumer interaction with computers came in the form of video games such as Space Invaders, Asteroids, and—above all—Pac-Man. When asked if he knew about Pac-Man, Reagan quipped: "Someone told me it was a round thing that gobbles up money. I thought it was Tip O'Neill." By 1983, *Time* magazine would for the first time eschew a human being for its "Man of the Year," naming instead the personal computer "Machine of the Year." (An indicator of how immature the sector still was at this point is the fact that Microsoft got only one brief mention in the long *Time* feature, and Bill Gates was not mentioned at all.) There were only about a million desktop PCs in the United States at the beginning of 1981, half of which were being used just to play games such as Pac-Man, but it was predicted that the number could rise to eighty million by the year 2000. (A woeful underestimate: the Census Bureau today reports that fifty-four million households had computers in 2000, but the number in business locations was surely a large multiple of that.) Word-processing software was on the market, but spreadsheets, graphic design programs, and e-mail software for consumers were still in development.

A look at the American scrapbook for the early 1980s finds the genesis of other now-taken-for-granted totems of contemporary life. The Federal Communications Commission was preparing to grant the necessary authority to begin cellular telephone service, even though the technology had been around for more than twenty years. The first popular handheld cell phone, the Motorola DynaTAC 8000X, would appear in 1983; the size of a brick, the DynaTAC cost $3,995, and its battery charge lasted only thirty minutes. United Airlines announced plans in early 1981 to put pay phones on its DC-10 planes—an air travel first. "If it works out," *Advertising Age* huffed, "make room for the cigarette and slot machines." Little did they know. Polartec fabric was introduced in 1981, though it didn't catch on big in garments until the 1990s. Rollerblades made their first appearance in 1980 and have proven more durable than the Hula-hoop. The Sony Walkman cassette player flew off the shelves, becoming the unplanned but essential accessory to Rollerblades. A little lower on the technological food chain was the 3M company's introduction of Post-it notes, dealing a setback to the dream of a paperless office. NutraSweet made its debut, as did the 20¢ first-class postage rate. The *New England Journal of Medicine* reported new research that cholesterol caused heart disease, another blow to good-tasting rich food. MTV made its debut on August 1, 1981; its first music video was "Video Killed the Radio Star" by the Buggles. For the first several months, MTV was reluctant to run Michael Jackson videos because the network feared a white audience wouldn't want to watch black performers. Bad-boy tennis pro John McEnroe popularized a new slogan with his high-decibel rants at Wimbledon line judges: "You cannot be serious!" A "weekend warrior" pastime caught on: paintball. Liberal cultural critics, in a foreshadowing of the deepening culture war, immediately criticized paintball as "fascist behavior in the woods." Think of what might have been said if it had been cowboys and Indians.

*   *   *

THE MAGNITUDE OF Reagan's victory did little to remove the widespread doubts about his views and ability to be leader of the free world. As Richard Wirthlin put it, Ronald Reagan was by now very well known, but still not known *very well*.[26] For all of Reagan's well-advertised views on the federal government, PBS television's Paul Duke could still say, "No one quite knew what to expect when the new Republican Administration took possession of the government in 1981."[27] This was media-speak for *Surely Reagan can't seriously propose to govern the way he has talked for the last twenty years.* Robert J. Samuelson wrote in the *National Journal:* "It must be slowly occurring to the folks at Ronald Reagan's transition headquarters that the ideas that won the election won't suffice to run the government."[28]

The *New York Times* made this theme into a journalistic art form in the days after the election. *Times* political reporter Howell Raines took comfort in the fact that "the real message of his governorship was that, despite his conservative talk, and despite the expectations of right-wing supporters who wanted him to roll back the clock to a laissez-faire society, Mr. Reagan's was a stable and scandal-free administration that provided the same basic services as the liberal regimes that had preceded it."[29] Another news story quoted an unnamed foreign source saying, "A politician is not expected to put his campaign speeches into practice when he becomes President of the United States."[30] The *Times*'s business page reported that "for the most part, those interviewed believe that, as President, Mr. Reagan will be more moderate and balanced than his campaign rhetoric might suggest."[31]

Two days after the election Reagan held his first press conference as president-elect in Los Angeles, and many of the questions had this theme as their premise. Reagan didn't take the bait. One reporter asked the president-elect, in light of the fact that he had received millions of votes from independents and Democrats, "[D]o you still feel wedded to the Republican Party platform?" Reagan: "I think it would be very cynical and callous of me now to suggest that I'm going to turn away from it." Another reporter asked "how much consideration" he would give to the advice of "these new conservative organizations and the Moral Majority and people like the Rev. Jerry Falwell." Reagan answered tartly: "I'm not going to separate myself from the people who elected us and sent us there." (This showed remarkable loyalty on Reagan's part, for leaders of the religious Right were constantly putting their foot into their mouth with statements that cried out for repudiation. Falwell, for example, remarked in 1980: "America has less than 1,000 days as a free nation unless there is divine intervention.") Reagan also reiterated his support for a constitutional amendment to ban abortion. Then he departed for a few days' rest at his Santa Barbara ranch.

Reagan's smooth steadfastness at this press conference brought to mind the famous comment prompted by Barry Goldwater's statement at the 1964 Republican convention: "Extremism in defense of liberty is no vice." "My God," Theodore White recalled hearing someone say, "he's going to run as Barry Goldwater." Now Reagan provoked the same apprehension, except now it wasn't a thought experiment. *Ronald Reagan is really going to be president.*

To a surprisingly large extent the public shared the establishment's doubts and apprehensions about Reagan. Despite his thumping electoral victory he recorded the lowest public approval rating—51 percent—of any incoming president in the history of the Gallup poll. Reagan's heterodox views, endlessly assailed by the media, were surely one reason for this high quotient of public doubt. Anyone who pledged such a decisive break with the past was bound to cause a polarization of public opinion.[32]

*   *   *

MEANWHILE, DEMOCRATS HAD to figure out how they were going to adapt and react to Reagan. Republicans had elected presidents before in the New Deal era. This time was different. Two things about the 1980 election raised a new alarm: the way in which Reagan's conservatism represented a departure from other modern Republican presidential contenders such as Nixon and Eisenhower, and the GOP breakthrough in Congress. Having lost the White House and the Senate, liberals were down to a precarious toehold in the House of Representatives. Although Democrats had a numerical majority of 243 to 192, conservative southern Democrats would give Republicans effective command of the House. Democrats were panicked that Republicans might go on to win a majority in the House in the 1982 election. House Speaker Tip O'Neill's biographer John A. Farrell summarized the mood: "Lose the House in 1982 and there would, indeed, be a revolution. Lose the House and lose most of the Great Society, and much of the New Deal. Lose the House and there could, in fact, be realignment."[33] Worse, it appeared that the Democrats were becoming less and less competitive on the presidential level. With the population shifts to the Republican-leaning Sunbelt states, there was starting to emerge talk of a Republican "lock" on the electoral college and, therefore, the presidency.

In addition to the instinct for denial, Democrats could take some comfort in a few facts. Below Reagan, the 1980 election was closer than it seemed. In fact, Democratic Senate candidates outpolled Republican Senate candidates on a nationwide basis by a large margin.[34] Republicans had captured the Senate by winning the tight races in small states—if not a fluke, then at least the political equivalent of an inside straight. Many Democrats and political analysts said that Reagan's massive win reflected less support for his ideas than a rejection of Jimmy Carter. Tip O'Neill told his Democratic House colleagues, "I think there was a small minority, ten or fifteen percent, who voted for Reagan, who really wanted to deliver a mandate. We know why we lost the election. We had an unpopular presidential candidate, inflation was high and so was unemployment."[35]

But could not the same thing have been said of Franklin Roosevelt's victory over Herbert Hoover in 1932, especially since FDR campaigned on an orthodox platform of balancing the budget that gave no hint of the shape of the New Deal to come? Realignments are determined by whether the winning party coming out of an election produces a new governing philosophy that enables it to win an enduring majority in successive elections. One confirmation of a realignment is whether the former majority party changes its character to accommodate the successful formula of the new majority party. Several subsequent elections are required to ratify that a realignment has indeed taken place.

Thus the question of how Reagan would govern was bound up indissolubly with the question of how liberals would respond to him. The political story line of the 1980s, and indeed of the entire epoch since Reagan's first national victory, consists mainly of the dynamics of liberalism's attempt to reconstitute itself in the face of a mature conservative challenge. The problem for liberal Democrats was that, as the progressive party, they were without new progressive ideas to put forward and were in the position of having to defend older progressive programs, especially entitlements, which were now, Harvard's Harvey Mansfield noted, "progressive only in their uncontrolled cost." It was not an advantageous position. The general rule of sports applies equally to politics: if you are on defense, it is difficult to score.

The immediate question facing liberal Democrats was who would lead the opposition to Reagan. The presidential front-runners for 1984, Ted Kennedy and Walter Mondale, would obviously be important figures, but institutional dynamics dictated that Tip O'Neill, as the highest-ranking Democrat in Congress, would be the de facto leader of the Democratic opposition. Was this a good idea? Nearly every media profile of O'Neill described him as "rumpled." The gray-haired, bulbous-nosed, heavyset (coat size: 52 stout) O'Neill was a career pol of the old school.[36] He had served as Speaker of the Massachusetts House of Representatives in the late 1940s. He won his seat in Congress in a tough election in 1952 (not without some Chicago-style voting "irregularities," it is alleged), replacing another Irish politician named John F. Kennedy, who was moving up to the Senate. He rose slowly through the ranks of the House, becoming Speaker in 1977 at the same time Jimmy Carter came to town.

O'Neill seemed an unlikely matchup for the telegenic Reagan. He described himself as an "old-hat FDR-liberal Democrat" and boasted that "I've been one of the big spenders of all time; it's true, I am a big spender." There was no good cause for which he wouldn't support new spending. O'Neill was so much on the side of "the little guy" that he even boasted of getting federal funding for research to enable dwarfs to grow six inches taller. *Newsweek* called O'Neill "a cartoonist's caricature of urban liberalism on its last legs."[37] He was a favorite target of Republicans. A brash freshman Republican congressman from Long Island, John LeBoutillier, called O'Neill "big, fat, and out of control—just like the federal government." O'Neill would make sure that LeBoutillier became a one-term congressman at the next election. During the 1980 campaign, a Republican TV commercial had suggested the decrepitude of the Democratic Congress with an image of a cigar-smoking O'Neill look-alike riding along in an aging limousine that ran out of gas. O'Neill had lustily reciprocated, dismissing Reagan as a "matinee idol" and deliberately mispronouncing Reagan's name throughout the fall campaign, calling him "REE-gan." O'Neill seldom appeared on the Sunday TV news shows, where Washington conducts its semi-official political conversation. His forte was backroom wheeling and dealing, but this moment demanded someone who could argue the liberal case publicly as well as plot strategy against Reagan.

In the short run, O'Neill figured, a tactical retreat would be necessary. Liberals and the Democratic Party would live to fight another day, in large part because the headwaters of left-liberal sentiment run deep into the wellsprings of modernity and cannot be turned back by a single election rout, no matter how dramatic. More immediately, O'Neill knew that if the Democrats obstructed Reagan completely, they would be blamed if the economy failed to turn around. Besides, the House Speaker shrewdly calculated, if they gave Reagan enough rope, he might hang himself. O'Neill understood, as he put it to a colleague, that when you win a big election, "you've got to deliver."

*   *   *

ONE OF JIMMY Carter's many mistakes as president was his deliberate aloofness from the Washington social elite, and Reagan, representing an ideology inimical to Washington's status, stirred even greater apprehension among this class. Reagan knew this, and launched a charm offensive even before he took office.

The president-elect made the first of three pre-inauguration trips to Washington on November 17. The very next night, at the exclusive F Street Club, he hosted an intimate dinner whose guest list included the leading

Democrats in Washington's social scene. "Some people couldn't even believe they'd been invited," the *Washington Post* reported. "The first couple of calls I got," said Nancy Reynolds, the aide who arranged the dinner, "were people who said, 'Are you sure this is serious? It's not a practical joke? I'm a Democrat.' "[38] "There's only one letter's difference between 'president' and 'resident,' " Reagan said to his assembled guests. Two nights later Reagan renewed his charm offensive at a dinner columnist George Will hosted at his home. Reagan was seated between AFL-CIO president Lane Kirkland and Jeane Kirkpatrick, and he swapped stories with Kirkland, a fervent anti-Communist, about resisting Communist influence in organized labor.

On the first full day of his visit, Reagan called on congressional leaders at the Capitol (Congress was holding a lame-duck session), where he had his first of many encounters with House Speaker Tip O'Neill. Reagan and O'Neill would make a great show over the next few years of getting along with each other publicly, an edifying demonstration of civility in politics. Privately both men quickly developed a large fund of contempt for the other, bordering on personal animosity, despite calling each other by their first names and swapping endless Irish jokes. The friction began at this first meeting. O'Neill was not initially impressed with Reagan and said to him, "You've been a governor of a state, but a governor plays in the minor leagues. You're in the big leagues now." (O'Neill had said the same thing to Jimmy Carter four years before.) Reagan replied, "Oh, you know, no problem there." Despite the genial response, O'Neill's comment represented the very kind of Washington haughtiness that set Reagan's teeth on edge. Aides to the president-elect were incensed.

Reagan also acceded to a request for a meeting from a potential challenger to his reelection in 1984: Massachusetts senator Ted Kennedy. They had never met before. Kennedy's aides told reporters that the senator had urged Reagan to consider human needs in deciding where to cut the budget.[39] (Kennedy would soon have to lay off fifty-six members of his staff as a consequence of the Republican takeover of the Senate.)

The most important feature of this first visit to Washington was Reagan's one-on-one meeting with President Carter on November 20, after which Carter told reporters that he and Reagan had established a "good working relationship." But he was privately appalled that Reagan took no notes and asked few questions as Carter talked for more than an hour and reviewed more than a dozen issues that the incoming president would face. (Carter, ever the thorough engineer, had met with individual members of President

Ford's cabinet during the transition in 1976.) Carter thought Reagan had no interest in anything he had to say—which is, perhaps, exactly the impression Reagan wanted to give. Carter's campaign innuendo that Reagan was a racist had especially angered the Republican, and it would be unsurprising for him to have been more reserved than usual toward someone for whom he had built up a healthy supply of contempt. Still, Reagan paid closer attention than Carter thought. At the end of the meeting, Reagan asked to have a copy of Carter's three-by-five card listing the issues covered. He then walked across the street to his transition office and gave a twenty-minute recapitulation of Carter's briefing to his senior aides, prompted only by the note card.[40]

*   *   *

MUCH OF REAGAN'S first visit to Washington was for show (during a courtesy call on the Supreme Court, Reagan watched George H. W. Bush sign the guest book and noticed for the first time that his vice president–elect was left-handed). But behind the scenes he had already set to work on the serious business of assembling a government. Reagan showed his practical side in how he managed the eleven-week transition period between Election Day and his inauguration on January 20. Both incoming and outgoing administrations always say publicly that the transition to a new administration is going "smoothly" and "orderly." In fact transitions are always chaotic. Reagan's transition, despite its squabbles and contentiousness, was arguably the least chaotic in modern times. This is chiefly because Reagan woke up the day after the election with the best prepared government-in-waiting in American history already well in motion.

Uppermost in the minds of Reagan and his closest aides were the memories of Nixon's frenzied and ineffective transition in 1968, and the broader problem of how to get meaningful control of the executive branch in a way that enables a new president to move quickly. Nixon and Carter had failed badly at this, as would Bill Clinton in 1993. In a phrase that became an overused cliché, Reagan and his team wanted to "hit the ground running."

Two things are required to master this problem: personnel and program. The two factors are inextricably linked; Reagan and his inner circle hewed to the adage "Personnel is policy." With more than three thousand jobs to fill in the executive branch, a president-elect has the daunting task of identifying suitable appointees and getting them through the cumbersome background check and clearance process. This process is always frantic, inefficient, and nearly unmanageable. There are only about one thousand working hours between the election and Inauguration Day. To fill all the executive branch appointments by January 20 would require naming three people per hour. The Reagan administration would not fill up most of the lower positions until months after the inauguration.[41] The central personnel problem, however, is not speed but finding qualified appointees who will be loyal to the new president and his program. Between personal ambition and the blandishments of the Washington bureaucracy, this is difficult to ensure. The conservative sage M. Stanton Evans quipped that too many conservatives come to Washington intending to drain the swamp, only to find out after they arrive that Washington is less a swamp than a hot tub.[42] Reagan, to his credit, was never much impressed with Establishment credentials. When told that his prospective secretary of transportation, Drew Lewis, was a Harvard Business School graduate, Reagan quipped, "So much for his liabilities."

Ed Meese reflected on the personnel problem the day after the election: "Too often Cabinet members become activists for their departments. Constitutionally, Cabinet members are supposed to be extensions of the President to carry out his policies." Equally important are the subcabinet appointees. Nixon decided to let his cabinet secretaries make their own selections for subcabinet and staff positions, a decision he immediately regretted.[43] Reagan and Meese decided, months before the election, that personnel selections would be closely controlled through the White House, and even went so far as to recruit a veteran executive headhunter, Pendleton James, to be the point man for staffing the administration. James quietly set up shop in Alexandria, Virginia, several weeks before the election. By Election Day James already had hundreds of résumés on file and an organizational scheme in place for matching people with jobs.

In selecting his cabinet, Reagan directed his transition team to develop a list of three names for each post, from which he would make his choice. That a certain portion of Reagan's longtime California entourage—known as the "Kitchen Cabinet"—would receive senior positions was a given, just as Georgians had dominated Jimmy Carter's administration. Kitchen Cabinet members such as Justin Dart, Holmes Tuttle, William Wilson, and Henry Salvatori were closely involved in the vetting process for senior appointments (they had a formal name: the Executive Advisory Committee) and naturally promoted people well known to them or who seemed to have the right Reaganite convictions. The Kitchen Cabinet even had its own office space during the transition and interviewed numerous prospective appointees. This attracted media criticism like bees to flowers; the *Washington Post*'s Haynes Johnson described the Kitchen Cabinet as "a perfect expression of Social Darwinism"—the only kind of Darwinism liberals oppose—that "bespoke something more than insensitivity toward others less fortunate and a renouncing of public responsibility to ameliorate social distress." The "something more" Johnson was not shy in labeling: "reaction."[44]

Reagan, however, was given neither to cronyism nor to ideological litmus tests, despite declaring with typical pith a few days after the election, "There's an awful lot of talent in people who haven't learned all the things you can't do." This could be seen most emphatically in Reagan's prompt choice for White House chief of staff. Everyone assumed it would be Ed Meese, who had risen to that post under Governor Reagan in Sacramento. Reagan surprised everyone by selecting James A. Baker III, whose previous loyalties had been to Gerald Ford and George Bush *against* Reagan. It was Reagan's first personnel announcement, made two days before his initial visit to Washington.

There are conflicting accounts of the factors behind Reagan's decision to pick the supremely able Baker, ranging from Meese's reputation for being too unorganized to manage the White House paper flow to Reagan's intuition about the utility of having someone with prior Washington experience as chief of staff.[45] Other accounts say that Reagan's other longtime close aide, Michael Deaver, refused to work under Meese and plotted with others to convince Reagan to pick Baker.[46] To these insider explanations must be added the political calculation that selecting Baker would provide a strong bond to Vice President Bush. Machiavelli would have approved: best to keep your potential enemies close, binding their interest to your success. Reagan had done much the same thing in his first race for California governor in 1966, incorporating into his campaign the staff of the opponent he had defeated in the Republican primary, George Christopher. Baker would acquire the reputation as a champion leaker to the media, and his glowing press notices offer the most compelling evidence of the charge. *New York Times* White House reporter Steven Weisman, for example, wrote that Baker was "shrewd and affable," a sure sign that Baker promptly returned Weisman's phone calls.

Baker would prove to be a superb chief of staff in the ordinary sense, largely because he operated according to a simple rule: on every issue, it was crucial that "the President wins." This is not to say that he subordinated his own political preferences or never engaged in subterfuges to influence Reagan. He was mostly unsuccessful in these attempts, because Reagan's surface geniality concealed an iron will, and also because Reagan had sufficient counterweights to Baker's tergiversations.

By degrees Reagan arrived at a scheme that combined Baker, Meese, and Deaver as virtual co-equals in what became known as "the troika." Baker would manage political affairs and organize the White House (meaning he controlled the all-important flow of paper to the president). Meese would oversee policy development as counselor to the president with cabinet rank— essentially minister without portfolio, or, as it would turn out in practice, minister with every portfolio.[47] Deaver became deputy chief of staff in charge of scheduling, public relations, and the all-important job that never showed up on any formal organizational chart or job description: handling the cares of first lady Nancy Reagan. "I always imagined," Deaver later remarked, "that when I died there would be a phone in my coffin, and at the other end of it would be Nancy Reagan."

The troika's combination of Baker's managerial skills, Meese's policy sense, and Deaver's public relations instincts served Reagan well in many re- spects. But it would also be the source of conflict and intrigue during Rea- gan's first term—the locus classicus of a perceived split between conservative "ideologues" and moderate "pragmatists." Although the three men enjoyed mostly cordial relations, their staffs were often at daggers drawn, sometimes going as far as to sit separately or across the table from one another in White House meetings. Deaver once joked that he owed the success of his weight loss to observing a diet during which he ate only on days when the senior staff members were speaking to one another. These divisions meant that the White House was often negotiating with itself.

Although the conservative/pragmatist split would come to be exagger- ated to some extent (especially by a news media always looking to stir up mischief and conflict for the good copy it provided), the kernel of truth be- hind the perception of a split could be summed up in a single appointment: Richard Darman. James Baker brought Darman into the White House as head of the Legislative Strategy Group, the political unit responsible for pushing Reagan's policy proposals through Congress. Darman was a Har- vard graduate—reason enough for conservative suspicion—and a protégé of Elliot Richardson, the bête noir of the Right during the Nixon years. Darman was smart, talented, and hardworking but, by his own admission, a fish out of water. To his many critics, he was the Rasputin of the Reagan administra- tion. Darman's conservative critics joked: "Why do people take an instant dislike to Darman?" Answer: "It saves time." Darman's memoir, *Who's in Control?* offers unintentionally comic confirmation of his lack of sympathy with Reagan's views and purposes. "[W]hat was I doing among the would-be-bronc-busters? . . . I was still very much imbued with the spirit of the Kennedy era." Not a good sign.

"This much is true," Darman wrote by way of introducing his deviations from Reaganism: "America is naturally progressive"—a code phrase for saying America is naturally liberal. "And more simply," he added, "it was unclear whether 'big government' had really grown so big. It depended on how one measured . . . [I]t was new to me to find ideology to be the driving force for so many Reaganauts."[48] To his credit, Darman never joined the Reagan-is-dumb-and-out-of-touch parade, and he fulsomely described Reagan in positive terms.[49] But he deprecated the talk of a "Reagan revolution," adding that "I had some doubts whether the incoming Reaganauts would even be able to get effective hold of government," a statement that by itself should have opened Darman's eyes about whether government had grown too big and the need for some kind of political revolution. "Such a man, so faint, so spiritless / So dull, so dead in look, so woebegone" (*Henry IV,* Part 2).

The selection of Baker to be chief of staff, along with the prominent inclusion on the transition team of a number of establishment Republicans from the Nixon and Ford administrations including Darman, alarmed conservative movement leaders. *Congressional Quarterly* observed barely a week after the election that "Reagan and his closest associates quickly moved to put a centrist stamp on the incoming Republican administration."[50] There could hardly be worse news for the conservative press. The newspaper *Human Events*—one of Reagan's favorite periodicals—wrote that "less than three weeks after the election, the euphoria in the conservative community is already dissipating somewhat . . . [C]onservatives have a right to feel somewhat distraught."[51] Direct-mail wizard Richard Viguerie complained to the *Washington Post* that "the names we're seeing now do make us nervous. It looks like it might be old home week for the Nixon-Ford administration."[52] Columnist Kevin Phillips echoed Viguerie: "The President-elect seems to be leaning to a cabinet full of the same proven don't-rock-the-boat experts who bored the nation to death during the Gerald Ford Administration." James Reston noted in the *New York Times:* "It is a paradox that those who were most determined to elect Mr. Reagan now seem more worried about what he will do as President than those who opposed him."

Conservatives were especially on guard against the return of Henry Kissinger or any of his acolytes. *Human Events* ran a lengthy editorial attacking the front-runner to be secretary of state, Nixon administration veteran George Shultz, saying that the prospect of his appointment "sent shivers down the spine of some hard-liners in the Reagan foreign policy camp."[53] The newspaper kept score on lesser appointments as well, criticizing the inclusion of "such liberal women" as Elizabeth Dole and worrying especially about the potential appointment of a Ford administration budget aide named Paul O'Neill—the same Paul O'Neill whom President George W. Bush would sack from Treasury in 2002. ("O'Neill is considered a menace by those who want to trim federal spending," *Human Events* reported.)[54] Conservative columnist John Lofton succinctly expressed the New Right's personnel philosophy: "There will be no Reaganism without Reaganites." He added, "There are even moments when I wonder how much of a hard-core Reaganite Reagan is."

The practical problem for Reagan's transition was that there were only a limited number of movement conservatives with sufficient expertise or experience for appointment to senior positions in the administration. Reagan aide Lyn Nofziger said, "As far as I am concerned, anyone who supported Reagan is competent." But the transition team, following Reagan's well-established inclinations from his years as California governor, preferred competence and experience over ideological purity in most cases, which meant relying on what were labeled Nixon-Ford retreads. It should also be kept in mind that many leaders of the so-called New Right had not been Reagan backers in the first place, having preferred other candidates in the Republican primaries in 1980, so their complaints did not receive much sympathy in Reagan's inner councils.

And so as the New Right grumbled, Reagan assembled his cabinet. Lou Cannon later offered the judgment that "[o]verall, bombthrowers were conspicuous by their absence in the Reagan cabinet."[55] The notable exception to the seeming moderation of the cabinet was Interior Secretary James Watt, whose appointment generated howls of indignation from liberals and the media. He liked to say things such as that Indian reservations were "a failed experiment in socialism," a statement that is substantively correct but politically indiscreet. For statements such as this Watt received bad press from the moment he was appointed. His owlish glasses, bald head, and thin jaw made him a favorite subject for caricature by editorial cartoonists. He was a land use lawyer from Colorado and an utterly sincere and ingenuous evangelical Christian, fitting in perfectly with a key segment of the Reagan constituency but making him a Martian to the Washington press corps. Watt was in close harmony with Reagan, so much so that he sometimes is falsely credited with originating the slogan "Let Reagan be Reagan." (In fact, William Clark originated that famous rallying cry in Sacramento during Reagan's governorship.)

Yet for the supposed moderation of the cabinet, it should be observed that Reagan exuded a magnetic field that tended to turn moderate Republicans by degrees into Reaganite conservatives. The example of Caspar Weinberger is the preeminent case in point. Weinberger had been a liberal Republican in California in the 1960s; he backed Rockefeller against Goldwater in 1964, and George Christopher against Reagan in the Republican primary for governor in 1966. But in his subsequent service for both Reagan and President Nixon he became a thoroughgoing Reagan loyalist. (This wasn't enough for some conservatives; North Carolina senator Jesse Helms voted against Weinberger's confirmation, arguing that he wasn't conservative enough to head the Pentagon.) Reagan had this effect on people, and would again with a number of his appointees, such as Senator Richard Schweiker, his erstwhile running mate in 1976, who raised hackles among conservatives for his big-spending ways in the Senate. But as Reagan's secretary of health and human services, he moved noticeably to the right and pleased conservatives.

This process was manifest in Reagan's eventual selection for treasury secretary. Reagan's first two picks for Treasury turned him down, deterred chiefly by the new public financial disclosure rules.[56] Reagan's surprise pick for Treasury was Donald Regan, the chairman of Merrill Lynch. The Right erupted in incredulity and disappointment. In a 1972 book Regan had endorsed Nixon's wage and price controls and said sympathetic things about higher taxes. Worse, under Regan's direction Merrill Lynch's political action committee had made campaign contributions to several liberal Democrats in the most recent election cycle. More recent statements from Regan suggested a closer harmony with Reagan's economic views, and indeed Regan would end up being one of the president's most loyal and effective servants on economic policy. One step he took to acquaint himself with Reagan's purposes was to read the Republican Party's 1980 platform and many of Reagan's old speeches on economic issues. He readily aligned himself with supply-side economics; "I saw that there was remarkable consistency in the President's public utterances."[57]

The surprise of the Regan appointment was not atypical. Few of the cabinet selections went according to the initial speculation. One member of Reagan's inner circle, Caspar Weinberger, had run the Office of Management and Budget (OMB) under President Nixon, where he had earned the nickname "Cap the Knife" for his frugal inclinations, and was thought likely to reprise his role at OMB. But Weinberger didn't want to return to OMB. He wanted to be secretary of state. He wound up as secretary of defense, where he could exert a strong pull on foreign policy.[58] William Casey too wanted to be secretary of state, but he was made director of the Central Intelligence Agency, where he arguably would play a larger role in achieving Reagan's purposes than he would have at State. Meanwhile, George Shultz was widely expected to be secretary of state, but Reagan did not appoint him (at least initially).

Along with the surprise of some of Reagan's cabinet selections was the nontraditional way they were unveiled to the public. Typically the president-elect makes a great show of appearing with and announcing cabinet selections himself. Presidents-elect going back to John F. Kennedy had followed this practice. Reagan felt no need to step into the spotlight, and allowed Ed Meese or a transition team spokesman to announce most of his cabinet selections while he remained in seclusion at home or up at the ranch. This gave rise to the first news stories that Reagan was "out of touch" with his own government, establishing a theme about Reagan that continues to this day. "Reagan on the Sidelines: Reagan Often Seems Remote from Administration-Shaping Process" read the *Washington Post* headline in mid-December. The *Post* thought it odd that Reagan would be chopping wood at his ranch the same day his secretary of state was announced. This led naturally to a flurry of official denials and explanations from Reagan's senior staff that kept the story alive for another news cycle, even though the original story was not news at all but a "media analysis," that is, journalistic opinion disguised as news coverage. "Reagan 'Is Really Running Things,' Meese Tells Press," read a *Post* headline the next day. A week later, the theme ran again. "Meese Insists Reagan Isn't Hiding Out," said the *Post* headline on December 29.

Thus began the persistent theme that Reagan was lazy, uninformed, uninterested, and a creature of his staff—a reputation that has only slowly receded. It is true that Reagan didn't have much interest in who was selected to run the lesser cabinet positions. Reagan's failure to recognize his own secretary of housing and urban development at the White House months later (he greeted Secretary Sam Pierce as "Mr. Mayor") is unfailingly cited as proof of Reagan's remoteness from his own government, which overlooks the fact that Reagan once failed to recognize his own son at the boy's prep school graduation ceremony. (Reagan's inability to recall names and faces is one notable recurring failure of his otherwise superb memory. Martin Anderson quipped that if Nancy Reagan should be away for more than two weeks, Reagan would need to be reintroduced to her.) Yet the conclusion that Reagan's key cabinet selections were done by automatic pilot without his active direction is mistaken. This is most clearly shown by Reagan's handling of the selection of secretary of state.

William Casey did not get the State appointment, because, it was said, he mumbled. Instead, the post went to Alexander Haig, who merely dissembled—a more familiar skill in modern diplomacy. Haig's appointment followed a circuitous route. The Kitchen Cabinet had been fully behind George Shultz, who had served as secretary of labor and treasury under Richard Nixon. Just one person was not on board with the pick: Ronald Reagan. His stated reason for his reluctance about Shultz was that both Caspar Weinberger and Shultz were then senior executives with the Bechtel Corporation, and Reagan thought it inappropriate to have two executives from the same company at the apex of his cabinet.[59] There were two unstated deeper reasons. Reagan had met Alexander Haig in 1979 and seen eye to eye with him about foreign policy, remarking to Deaver after that meeting that he'd like to have Haig in his cabinet. He originally thought Haig, a former general and NATO commander, would be ideal for the Pentagon, but law required the secretary of defense to be a civilian. So Reagan thought to put him at State instead. Then too, there was intrigue against Shultz and in favor of Haig from an important but unacknowledged source—Richard Nixon.

Nixon sent Reagan an eleven-page memo of general advice ten days after the election. The former president was blunt in his assessment of Shultz as a potential secretary of state: "I do not believe that he has the depth of understanding of world issues generally and the Soviet Union in particular that is needed for this job." Nixon suggested separately in phone conversations with Reagan insiders that Shultz's loyalty was doubtful. Knowing that his favorite choice—Kissinger—had no chance at returning to State, Nixon made the case for Haig. "He would reassure the Europeans, give pause to the Russians . . . He is intelligent, strong, and generally shares your views on foreign policy. Those who oppose him because they think he is 'soft' are either ignorant or stupid."[60] That last line was an oblique reference to the fact that Haig had been a Kissinger deputy in the Nixon White House and therefore bore the taint of Kissinger's hated détente.

Reagan seldom went directly against the clear consensus of his advisers. But in this case the transition team had ranked Shultz as the top candidate for the State post, ahead of Haig. In fact, Meese and Deaver were said to have major doubts about Haig and pressed Reagan to offer the appointment to Shultz. Reagan, Lou Cannon was the first to observe, did something so clever that no one noticed. As Deaver remembers the phone call, Reagan said to Shultz, "Well, George, I'm here with some of the fellows, and I'm calling to see if you'd like to come back to Washington with me."[61] Reagan usually told prospective appointees the specific office he was offering them, and could be very forceful in persuading reluctant people to make the sacrifice of joining the administration. But he didn't mention the State Department to Shultz, who didn't know what office Reagan might have in mind (he thought it might be Treasury) and did not want to be put in the awkward position of asking and then having to turn down an undesired post. As Shultz recalls, he replied: "Well, I'd like to help you in any way I can, but I like what I'm doing, so proceed in your own way." Reagan offered State to Haig the next day.

Was Reagan's neglecting to mention the State Department a careless oversight or deliberate? Although Deaver later told Lou Cannon that the conversation was a "misunderstanding" (Deaver thought Shultz knew he was going to be offered the State Department; Shultz didn't), Cannon is more convincing that Reagan's anodyne approach to Shultz was an intentional manipulation, allowing Reagan to get the person he really wanted while mollifying his closest advisers.[62]

Haig, meanwhile, wanted the job but had reservations about joining the Reagan administration. Remembering the way Nixon and Kissinger had defenestrated the State Department, Haig "wanted to know if Mr. Reagan, in fact, wanted a secretary of state." Reagan understood this problem and had planned to downgrade the status of the national security adviser in his administration. Reagan readily agreed to Haig's vision of being Reagan's "vicar" of foreign policy. Just to be sure, however, Reagan sent one of his most trusted friends, California Supreme Court justice William Clark, to be the number two man at the State Department to look over Haig's shoulder, and to be the de facto "American desk" at Eurocentric Foggy Bottom.

Cannon concluded that "the overall record of the transition contradicts the conventional wisdom that the president-elect was largely a bystander during the selection of his cabinet. . . . Overall, the transition was a stylistic and political triumph for Reagan."[63] Presidential scholars agree. One study concluded that "the Reagan transition was the most carefully planned and effective in American political history."[64]

*   *   *

STAFFING A NEW administration is the tip of the iceberg visible above the waterline. The larger unseen task is planning in detail what policies the new administration wants to pursue. The Reagan transition had a policy-planning process that was actually further along than its personnel operation.

In the modern administrative state, it typically takes new appointees months to figure out an agency's policies and how they work in practice. By then it is too late. The combination of bureaucratic inertia along with the axis of special interest groups and congressional backstopping (known in the political science literature as the "iron triangle") makes it difficult or impossible for presidential appointees to get command of an agency and make fundamental changes in its course. This is partly by design; a central purpose of modern liberalism is to institutionalize liberal governance in order to make it permanent or beyond the reach of elections. The incoming Reaganites, whose publicly professed goal was to shrink the size and scope of the federal government, had taken steps to deal with this problem.

Modern presidential campaigns all have issue task forces that morph into transition planning task forces after an election, and it is these task forces that attempt to generate action plans for appointees to follow. Reagan's forty-eight task forces, with more than 450 participants, had been in place longer than most, dating back to early 1979 in some cases. (Reagan had seventy-four advisers on economic policy alone.) Transition task forces can be chaotic and are not necessarily central to an incoming president; in many cases they are used for show, as a means of involving campaign supporters and seeing whether potential appointees are serious in their knowledge and commitment to government. Reagan's were serious and were the most elaborate and extensive such effort to date.

But to find out what the Reagan administration wanted to do in detail, it was necessary to buy just one book: *Mandate for Leadership. Mandate* was a project of an independent effort of the Heritage Foundation, which in the late 1970s was not the high-profile Washington powerhouse it is today; the *Mandate* project was the breakthrough that established the think tank's prominence. More than a year before the election Heritage surmised that a conservative—probably Reagan—was likely to win the presidency, and decided to set up an independent, parallel set of issue task forces with an eye toward generating a detailed agenda for each major federal agency and policy area. A typical chapter about a cabinet department or federal regulatory agency itemized specific programs to be cut or eliminated, grants to be cancelled, regulations to be changed, executive orders to be repealed or amended, and statutes to be reformed. Heritage had twenty task forces with more than three hundred participants (some of whom were also on Reagan's official transition task forces). The effort culminated in a compendious 1,093-page book that conveniently was ready in galley form days after the election. Reagan passed out prepublication copies of *Mandate* to his incoming cabinet secretaries and senior staff in December. *Mandate for Leadership* became a rare think tank product on the bestseller list in the Washington, D.C., area. Conservatives and the media snapped it up to see what they could expect; bureaucrats bought it to see what they should fear.

If there was to be a Reagan Revolution, however, it would not be carried off through policy wonkery alone. It would require a sustained political offensive—air cover, so to speak—from the White House. Reagan's inner circle developed a detailed plan, complete with a time line for presidential action during the first year in office, that came to be known as the Initial Actions Project. The final report of the Initial Actions Project is a remarkable assessment of how Reagan's political strategists thought about Reagan's political standing and the strategy he would need to follow if he was to succeed. The report conceived the moment in broad and ambitious terms: "The election was not a bestowal of political power, but a stewardship opportunity for us to reconsider and restructure the political agenda for the next two decades. The public has sanctioned the search for a new public philosophy to govern America."65

David Gergen (who became White House communications director in Reagan's first term) and Richard Wirthlin were the principal authors of the Initial Actions Project, and their final forty-nine-page report had a simple premise: President Reagan needed to get off to a strong start in his first days and weeks in office, and the best way to do this was to stay focused overwhelmingly on his economic program. "How we begin will significantly determine how we govern." This may seem so obvious as to go without saying, except that Jimmy Carter had botched his opening months in office and never recovered. Learning from and avoiding Carter's mistakes was uppermost in the minds of Reagan's strategists. "When Jimmy Carter assumed the Presidency," Gergen and Wirthlin observed, "he tried to move on many fronts simultaneously—energy, welfare reform, government reorganization, a tax stimulus package, tax reform. It left the Congress and the country unsure about what he really cared about. *He had so many priorities that he had no priorities*" (emphasis in original).66

There was a real risk that Reagan's presidency could be similarly diffuse. Reagan's longtime domestic policy adviser Martin Anderson noted Reagan's capacious conservatism: "We didn't need to develop any new ideas for Ronald Reagan. He had been examining public policy issues for most of his adult life. He had a long, long list of specific policy changes that he thought were very important and that he wanted to make right now."67 In addition to Reagan's own manifold policy inclinations, the fervent constituency—the movement—

that had helped to propel him into office had its own demands that would need to be accommodated; many conservatives were eager to seize the moment and right fifty years' worth of big-government wrongs; while social conservatives were especially concerned about abortion, school prayer, and other moral issues.

The priority for Reagan was easy to figure out. Reagan's team didn't say, "It's the economy, stupid," as Bill Clinton did twelve years later, but they might have. There were important aspects of foreign and defense policy that needed immediate attention, but Reagan and his team understood that restoring the economy was the prerequisite for a successful foreign and defense policy. They also knew that the first few months of 1981 would be their only window of opportunity, since that is when any new president carries the most clout with Congress and the public, and since in this particular circumstance the Democrats, having suffered large losses in the election, would be temporarily disoriented and dispirited.

The main task facing Reagan's strategists, therefore, was how to craft a political offensive to overcome the dizzy opposition. This would provide the central drama for Reagan's first year in the White House.

*   *   *

RONALD REAGAN WAS poised for a strong start, and circumstances transformed his inauguration on January 20 into a triumphant bookend that matched the force of his Election Day victory. For one thing, two weeks of bitterly cold weather gave way to spring-like temperatures on Inauguration Day, which seemed fitting for a new president from California. But the main factor in magnifying Reagan's inauguration was the imminent release of the American hostages in Iran, which occurred almost simultaneously with Reagan's assuming the reins of power. The hostages' release had been finally agreed after weeks of tortuous negotiations and several last-minute legal and financial snags that had kept Carter up overnight before Inauguration Day. The wear on Carter was evident when Reagan and his entourage arrived at the White House later in the morning to ride over to the Capitol. Some of Reagan's aides were shocked at Carter's "ashen" appearance.

Carter had hoped to be able to announce the hostages' release on TV before noon, in the last few minutes of his presidency. But the Iranians, in a deliberate final humiliation of Carter, kept delaying the hostages' departure from the Teheran airport. They were still sitting on the runway in their Algerian airplane as Reagan began his inaugural address. Even the Algerians, who had served as intermediaries in the negotiations, didn't trust Iran; they had sent fifty commandoes to guard their plane at the Teheran airport. In a magnanimous gesture, Reagan had instructed Michael Deaver to interrupt him in the middle of his inaugural address if news came of the hostages' departure, so that he could call Carter up to the podium to make the announcement. But the Iranians waited until five minutes after Reagan finished speaking to give clearance for the plane to leave, so it fell to Reagan, speaking to a congressional luncheon in the Capitol after his swearing in, to announce the happy news.

The fear of Reagan likely played a role in the Iranians' inclination to settle with Carter. Following Reagan's election, a joke came into currency: "What's flat as a pancake and glows in the dark? Iran after Reagan becomes president." Reagan played to type during the transition, making several tart statements about Iran, such as calling the Iranian captors "criminals" and saying, "I don't think you pay ransom for people that have been kidnapped by barbarians." The *Washington Post* speculated: "Who doubts that among Iran's reasons for coming to terms now was a desire to beat [Reagan] to town."[68]

The tension of the hostage release added genuine drama to America's preeminent democratic ritual. Most Americans watching on television saw a split-screen scene, with Reagan juxtaposed next to the darkened night sky of Teheran. The *Washington Post*'s TV critic Tom Shales wrote, "Perhaps not since the funeral of John F. Kennedy have Americans kept so diligent a vigil before their television sets." The media found irresistible the dramatic parallel between this moment and something that might have come from Reagan's previous career. The *Washington Post* editorial page wrote, "It was a scene as theatrical as any in which Mr. Reagan played in Hollywood," while *New York Times* columnist James Reston (who was not an admirer of Reagan) called the moment a "theatrical triumph . . . In his long years as an actor and a politician, Ronald Reagan never had such a perfect setting on the American stage, let alone the world stage." Separately in the *Times,* Howell Raines wrote that Reagan played the scene as if straight out of a Frank Capra movie.

The high drama of the hostages' release distracted somewhat from Reagan's inaugural address, in which Reagan signaled that he indeed intended to govern according to his conservative principles. The speech is worth a close reading for its structure as well as its argument—the more so as Reagan wrote most of it himself, with the assistance of Ken Khachigian.

One remarkable aspect of the address is how little of it was devoted to foreign policy, given the prominence with which Reagan had crusaded against American weakness toward the Soviet Union. Reagan devoted only four short paragraphs—just 224 words out of a total of 2,425—to foreign policy toward the end of the speech, almost a perfunctory mention. Unlike John F. Kennedy's almost wholly foreign-oriented inaugural address, Reagan's focused on the domestic health of the nation. (Also unlike Kennedy, who changed the word *enemies* to *adversaries* in the final draft of his inaugural address, Reagan deliberately used the phrase *enemies of freedom*.)

The most obvious messages of the address concerned the connection among big government, the poor economy, and Reagan's rejection of the pessimism of the moment. It was the first inaugural address in fifty years that appealed to the idea of limited government. He began with a review of the condition of the economy:

These United States are confronted with an economic affliction of great proportions. We suffer from the longest and one of the worst sustained inflations in our national history. It distorts our economic decisions, penalizes thrift, and crushes the struggling young and the fixed-income elderly alike. It threatens to shatter the lives of millions of our people. Idle industries have cast workers into unemployment, causing human misery and personal indignity. Those who do work are denied a fair return for their labor by a tax system which penalizes successful achievement and keeps us from maintaining full productivity.

While pledging to reverse this state of affairs, Reagan fired his first broadside against the established order, declaring: "In this present crisis, government is not the solution to our problem. Government *is* the problem. . . . It is no coincidence that our present troubles parallel and are proportionate to the intervention and intrusion in our lives that result from unnecessary and excessive growth of government." Liberals could scarcely imagine hearing such heresy from the presidential podium. Although many liberals had been shaken by the disasters of the last fifteen years, from Vietnam and the Great Society through Carter's ineffectual rule, there was never a point at which the fundamental premises of modern liberalism were attacked from the pinnacle of American power. The moment seemed very far removed from when a liberal intellectual such as Robert Maynard Hutchins could declare: "The notion that the sole concern of a free society is the limitation of governmental authority and that that government is best which governs least is certainly archaic. Our object today should not be to weaken government in competition with other centers of power, but rather to strengthen it as the agency charged with the responsibility for the common good."

Reagan represented his aim not in the context of mere economic policy but as a restoration of free government as the Founders intended it to work. He rejected the reformist theme that the presidency, or our democracy in general, was inadequate to the times.

> From time to time, we have been tempted to believe that society has become too complex to be managed by self-rule, that government by an elite group is superior to government for, by, and of the people. But if no one among us is capable of governing himself, then who among us has the capacity to govern someone else?

Reagan had so fully internalized the thought of so many of his political forebears such as Jefferson, Lincoln, and Roosevelt that it is not clear whether he knew he was paraphrasing them. Reagan had said much the same thing about self-government in his first inaugural address as California governor in 1967. Where he got it is no mystery. In his first inaugural address in 1801, President Thomas Jefferson said: "Sometimes it is said that man can not be trusted with the government of himself. Can he, then, be trusted with the government of others? Or have we found angels in the forms of kings to govern him? Let history answer this question." Unlike Hutchins and other liberals, Reagan didn't think Jefferson's philosophy was "archaic."

Reagan said, "It is time to check and reverse the growth of government, which shows signs of *having grown beyond the consent of the governed*" (emphasis added). Note here that he rested his argument against the growth of government not on the ground of efficiency or effectiveness but on the constitutional ground of *consent*. This had been a constant theme of Reagan's political teaching for more than twenty years, but one that was rarely heard from America's political class—even from conservatives. He was careful, though, to qualify his critique of government:

> It is my intention to curb the size and influence of the Federal establishment and to demand recognition of the distinction between the powers granted to the Federal Government and those reserved to the States or to the people. . . . Now, so there will be no misunderstanding, it is not my intention to do away with government. It is rather to make it work—work with us, not over us; to stand by our side, not

ride on our back. Government can and must provide opportunity, not smother it; foster productivity, not stifle it.

"On these principles," Reagan concluded with emphasis, "*there will be no compromise.*"

Throughout his entire discussion of the political and economic principles he would follow, Reagan weaved several arguments against the pessimistic declinism that had overtaken the nation. "It is time for us to realize that we're too great a nation to limit ourselves to small dreams. We're not, as some would have us believe, doomed to an inevitable decline." *As some would have us believe* was a not-so-oblique reference to his predecessor, Jimmy Carter, sitting a few feet away. Four years before, Carter had used his inaugural address to endorse the idea of "limits to growth" and counsel Americans to begin diminishing their expectations for the future. "We have learned that 'more' is not necessarily 'better,' " Carter said, "that even our great Nation has its recognized limits."

But Reagan went beyond merely refuting the small-is-beautiful juice that liberals had attempted to make out of limits-to-growth lemons. He connected his rejection of the nation's pessimism, his political teaching about limited government, and his confidence in economic revival to the idea of heroism. One of the corollaries of the idea of limits to growth and diminished expectations was that heroism is anachronistic. "We have every right to dream heroic dreams," Reagan said.

> Those who say that we are in a time when there are no heroes just don't know where to look. You can see heroes every day going in and out of factory gates. Others, a handful in number, produce enough food to feed all of us and then the world beyond. You meet heroes across a counter, and they're on both sides of that counter. There are entrepreneurs with faith in themselves and faith in an idea who create new jobs, new wealth and opportunity. They're individuals and families whose taxes support the government and whose voluntary gifts support church, charity, culture, art, and education. Their patriotism is quiet, but deep. Their values sustain our national life. Now, I have used the words "they" and "their" in speaking of these heroes. I could say "you" and "your," because I'm addressing the heroes of whom I speak—you, the citizens of this blessed land.

So far this is no more than a garden-variety salute to the American every-man, a staple of American political rhetoric. But Reagan integrated this shop-worn theme into the heart of his teaching about the principles of American democracy. He did it in a way that went beyond mere words.

Reagan's 1981 inaugural was the first in the nation's history to be held on the west front of the Capitol building. From the west front, facing the Mall and looking out across the broad expanse of the nation, Reagan took note of the famous national monuments to "the giants upon whose shoulders we stand"—Washington, Jefferson, and above all Lincoln. About Lincoln, Reagan said: "Whoever in his heart would understand the meaning of Amer-ica, will find it in the life of Abraham Lincoln." He also took note of the heroism of the Founders in establishing our constitutional order.

Then Reagan drew the nation's attention to another set of monuments visible in the far distance—the headstones of Arlington National Cemetery. Here Reagan made out the argument that self-government requires all Amer-ican citizens to be heroes in a sense. "Each one of those markers is a monu-ment to the kind of hero I spoke of earlier." He then selected the example of one ordinary American who did an extraordinary deed comparable in merit to the giants such as Washington and Lincoln.

> Under one such marker lies a young man, Martin Treptow, who left his job in a small town barbershop in 1917 to go to France with the famed Rainbow Division. There, on the western front, he was killed trying to carry a message between battalions under heavy artillery fire. We're told that on his body was found a diary. On the flyleaf under the heading, "My Pledge," he had written these words: "Amer-ica must win this war. Therefore I will work, I will save, I will sacri-fice, I will endure, I will fight cheerfully and do my utmost, as if the issue of the whole struggle depended on me alone."

Reagan noted that current circumstances didn't require Americans to make the ultimate sacrifice, as had Treptow; he drew an equivalence between the virtue of Treptow and ordinary citizens as a way of summoning Ameri-cans to think themselves worthy of their liberty. Reagan closed: "We can and will resolve the problems which now confront us. And, after all, why shouldn't we believe that? We are Americans."

The news media faithfully reported the content of the speech but missed its deeper theme. They jumped all over a factual problem in the speech: Martin Treptow is buried not in Arlington National Cemetery, as Reagan had implied, but in Wisconsin. Lou Cannon later discovered that Reagan's staff had learned this in advance, but Reagan didn't want to drop the story, or confuse the flow of his narrative by saying Treptow is buried in Wisconsin while alluding to Arlington Cemetery and the other national monuments visible in the distance.[69] For the media, this was yet another example of Reagan playing fast and loose with facts. "It would prove a portent of his presidency," Cannon wrote. Reagan's substantive message connecting the virtue of ordinary citizens such as Treptow—does it really matter where he is buried?—to the virtue of the nation as the common source of the nation's greatness was lost to the media mind.[70]

A few commentators grasped Reagan's theme and didn't like it. In a foreshadowing of a skirmish line to come in the 1980s, *Washington Post* columnist Richard Cohen displayed liberalism's increasing reflex for victimology by writing that "Ronald Reagan says [Treptow] is a hero. He might just call himself a victim. . . . Heroes can be victims." Cohen thought a welfare mother struggling to keep her family together was equally or more worthy of heroic praise.[71] *New York Times* columnist Tom Wicker thought Reagan effective in employing the "hackneyed theme of the nation's greatness" but tut-tutted about "the danger in too much exceptionalist fervor."[72] This discomfort with ritualistic expressions of American greatness and the natural patriotism they elicit is one of the odd tics of modern liberalism that has contributed to the public's diminished esteem for liberals.[73]

But these discordant notes amounted to idle back chatter on a day of otherwise euphonious commentary for Reagan's formal arrival. The release of the hostages not only removed a major problem for the incoming president but also added significantly to the tailwind that all incoming presidents enjoy during their so-called honeymoon period. Reagan's campaign theme had been "a new beginning," and there was almost a palpable sense of a break with the past midday on January 20. In *The Age of Roosevelt*, Arthur Schlesinger Jr. wrote that "[t]he fog of despair hung over the land" as Franklin Roosevelt assumed office in 1933, but that with FDR's inaugural address, "[a]cross the land the fog began to lift." Many commentators had drawn a comparison between Roosevelt's moment in 1933 and Reagan's moment in 1981. Wilbur Mills, the legendary former chairman of the House Ways and Means Committee, told a reporter: "[T]he situation today is as dangerous as the one Roosevelt faced. I really believe it."[74] Henry Fairlie, a writer of moderate liberal sensibilities, was almost giddy at the spectacle: "It is almost a heresy for someone of my beliefs to say that this transition takes my mind back to 1933. Yet how can one deny it? This is not Truman to Eisenhower, or Eisenhower to Kennedy, or Johnson to Nixon, or Ford to Carter. This is a feeling of a nation with its own mandate."[75]

The conjunction of the end of America's hostage agony with Reagan's ascension caused people to think that maybe, just maybe, the country had turned a corner. The day after Reagan's inaugural the *Washington Post* wrote: "[B]y the time he left the Capitol, America seemed a different place."

CHAPTER 2

DUNKIRK

—»◦«—

*There are no doubt some who would prefer to put off a tax cut in
the hope that ultimately an end to the Cold War would make possible an
equivalent cut in expenditures—but that end is not in view and to
wait for it would be costly and self-defeating.*
—PRESIDENT JOHN F. KENNEDY,
1963 STATE OF THE UNION MESSAGE

T HE NATION'S ECONOMIC conditions began slipping toward near
panic in the two weeks after the 1980 election as Representative Jack
Kemp (R-N.Y.) prepared to fly west to California to meet with President-elect
Reagan and his other economic advisers on November 16.[1] The ebullient
Kemp, the former NFL quarterback who above all others was responsible for
elevating the idea of a 30 percent income tax cut to the top of the national
agenda, had reason to be anxious. Although the economy had started growing again—slowly—over the summer, economic sentiment was unsettled. Interest rates surged sharply following the election, with the prime rate rising 4
percentage points, to about 19 percent, in early December, and the Federal
Reserve hiking its main discount rate to 16 percent, up from 9 percent over
the summer. Auto sales were down 10 percent from the year before; nonetheless, inflation had become so deeply ingrained that Detroit's big three announced price hikes. Housing starts were in free fall. Several large money
center banks, including Wells Fargo, stopped offering fixed-rate thirty-year
mortgages, the bread and butter of home purchasing. Chase Manhattan Bank
floated the ridiculous rumor that the incoming Reagan administration had
plans to impose wage and price controls. Unemployment stood at 7.4 percent,

but many economists were publicly predicting that the nation was headed back into a recession. One of them, Reagan adviser Alan Greenspan, told the *New York Times* that "we are going to stall out in a matter of weeks." On top of all this bad news, the federal budget deficit was soaring beyond previous estimates. Two weeks before Inauguration Day, a worried Reagan said: "What was a setback was to find that the economic problem, bad as it was when I was campaigning, is a lot worse since the campaign has ended."[2]

Fear of continued out-of-control inflation was at the root of the high anxiety. Inflation showed little sign of abating from double-digit annual rates, and the President's Council on Wage and Price Stability—a White House unit that Reagan would abolish within days of taking office—issued a gloomy year-end forecast that food prices would rise by more than 10 percent in the coming year, and energy prices by 20 to 40 percent. "No American President since Franklin Roosevelt," Reagan's Initial Actions Project noted, "has inherited a more difficult economic situation. . . . 1980 may well have been the most critical year for the American economy in half a century." "For all his optimism," *Newsweek* magazine thought, "Ronald Reagan may spend his first year in the White House presiding over precisely the same economic mess with which he tarred Jimmy Carter: high inflation, higher interest rates and an unavoidable recession."[3]

Congressman Kemp carried with him to Los Angeles a twenty-three-page memorandum to the president-elect suggesting a bold course of action. Kemp was listed as an author of the memo, but its principal author was another Republican congressman, thirty-four-year-old David Stockman of Michigan—a person destined soon for greater things. There was little of substance in the memo that wasn't in previous Martin Anderson campaign policy papers going back to 1979, but the flamboyance of the Kemp-Stockman memo caused it to become front-page news when it was later leaked (most likely by iconoclast Jude Wanniski).[4] As an ex-quarterback who won several championships, Kemp knew when it was time to throw the long bomb. The very title of the memo conveyed the portent of the moment: "Avoiding a GOP Economic Dunkirk." Kemp had originally suggested that what Reagan needed to do was the economic equivalent of the Inchon landing in the Korean War, but Stockman substituted the World War II battle of Dunkirk for Inchon when composing their memo. Inchon was an act of boldness that routed a superior force; Dunkirk, for all its heroism, was an act of retreat before a superior force. As Churchill reminded Britons, "Wars are not won by evacuations." It is revealing that Stockman preferred Dunkirk to Inchon for his metaphor. It is also ironic that he conceived of the Dunkirk analogy, given that when trouble did come in the Reagan years, he sought the first lifeboat.

Sprinkled with colorful language about "reckless" government social programs amounting to "an automatic 'coast-to-coast soup line' " and "McGovernite no-growth activists" at regulatory agencies, the memo was at heart a political proposal: "President Reagan should declare a national economic emergency soon after inauguration." The symmetry with Franklin Roosevelt in 1933 was obvious; Kemp and Stockman even suggested that Reagan frame his economic policy on a one-hundred-day timetable. Anything less, they argued, risked political ruin for President Reagan and the Republican Party.[5]

Thus began the central domestic policy saga that would dominate the entire two terms of the Reagan presidency, and that continues to this day.

*   *   *

RONALD REAGAN CAMPAIGNED on a clear economic plan consisting of tax cuts, budget cuts, sound monetary policy, and regulatory reform, but within days of his election the plan was in political trouble.[6]

Three of the four parts of Reagan's economic program were uncontroversial; in fact, a matter of degree was the only difference between Reagan and Carter on budget cutting, regulatory relief, and monetary restraint. The Stockman-Kemp "Economic Dunkirk" memo created a stir because of the fourth part of Reagan's economic program, the factor that caused his policy to become known as Reaganomics—the proposal to cut income tax rates by 30 percent over the next three years. Reagan wanted the first 10 percent cut to be retroactive to January 1, 1981; less noticed than the income tax cut was a companion proposal to relax depreciation rules to spur business investment.

Cutting income tax rates is today Republican orthodoxy, but in 1980 and 1981, it was anything but. The phrase on most lips at the time was that economic theory was "in crisis." "By any economic standard," economist Michael Boskin wrote, "the decade of the 1970s was the worst relative performance since the Great Depression."[7] Keynesian policy was thought to be the principal cause of, rather than a plausible remedy for, this deterioration. But if Keynesianism was discredited, it was far from clear to the mainstream of economic thought that the new doctrine known as supply-side economics was a worthy successor.

Supply-side economics is a yeasty confection. It is no less controversial today than it was then, even though its proponents represent it as no more than a restatement of neoclassical economics.[8] A variety of succinct definitions were offered; several economists described supply-side economics as merely microeconomics applied to macroeconomic aggregates.[9] This formula will mean little to noneconomists. In its simplest formulation, supply-side economics can be summed up in two words: *taxes matter.* Taxes matter to each individual decision to save, invest, produce, or consume. And the sum of individual decisions adds up to whether the economy is robust or stagnating.

By whatever definition supply-side economics is understood, it represented an audacious break with existing economic thought, and its advocates, who quickly became known as supply-siders, were nothing if not audacious in their representation of its promised effects. "Nothing like them had appeared on the national scene since the early New Dealers," the *Washington Post*'s Haynes Johnson wrote of the brash tax-cutting insurgents. Lawrence Lindsey, who would later serve as President George W. Bush's chief economic adviser, wrote, "The supply-side challenge of [1981] was the greatest challenge to a reigning economic dogma since the overthrow of classical economics in the 1930s."[10] Herbert Stein, senior economic adviser to Presidents Nixon and Ford and a critic of supply-side economics (it was Stein who first came up with the label, in fact, back in the mid-1970s), wrote that Reagan "has chosen a rather eccentric school of economics and economists and has eschewed the opportunity of reducing responsibility for error by staying close to the mainstream."[11]

Stein's use of *eccentric* to describe the supply-siders may conceal a certain amount of personal pique on the part of other schools of conservative economic thought. For decades conservative dissenters from Keynesian statism endured the smug certitude of more prominent liberal economists. Milton Friedman, an adviser to Barry Goldwater's 1964 campaign, had been dismissed as belonging to an "ingenious sect" and "a minority position among economists."[12] By 1980 Friedman had a Nobel Prize on his mantle, as did another free market champion, Friedrich Hayek; the heterodox views of the Chicago School on everything from monetary policy to regulation and antitrust had won wider respect. Now along came the young, uppity supply-siders threatening with their unproven ideas to usurp the hard-won position of eminences such as Friedman, Hayek, Stein, Greenspan, George Stigler, Murray Weidenbaum, and others.

The breathtaking audacity of supply-side economics can be best appreciated by reference to the simple theoretical construct explaining *how* taxes matter that became almost a household phrase: the Laffer curve. Economist Arthur Laffer, the legend goes, drew an inverted U-shaped curve on a restaurant napkin over lunch in 1975 to depict how lowering income tax rates might produce *higher* tax revenues. The drawing on a restaurant napkin, supposedly made for then White House chief of staff Dick Cheney, may not have actually happened (neither Laffer nor Cheney recalls this taking place), but it made for a great image of an "aha" moment. So durable was the Laffer curve that it entered the popular culture and made an appearance in the 1986 feature film *Ferris Bueller's Day Off,* where a sonorous Ben Stein (Herbert Stein's son) attempts to explain it to a sleepy high school class.

The Laffer curve also led to a major misconception about the core idea of supply-side economics. High income tax rates had two main distorting effects. First, high tax rates—the top tax rate on unearned income (which meant investment income) in 1980 was 70 percent—discouraged productive investment and caused wealthier taxpayers to invest in unproductive tax shelters. This represented a massive misapplication of capital. High tax rates along with inflation also raised the cost of capital significantly, and in the latter half of the 1970s both productivity growth and the rate of new business start-ups fell sharply. Second, with inflation pushing more and more middle-income taxpayers into higher tax brackets (the phenomenon known as bracket creep), tax rates were causing people to reduce their supply of labor. Cutting income tax rates across the board, as the Kemp proposal would do, surely would induce changes in investment behavior by wealthy taxpayers that would cause those brackets to report higher income. This had already occurred among higher brackets in Britain following Margaret Thatcher's reductions of the even higher income tax rates there. Cutting rates would also provide incentive for people to supply more labor. But in the short run income tax revenue would fall from taxpayers in the lower brackets whose tax liability was not determined by investment choices and other discretionary factors. The question was whether increased overall economic growth and changes in investment behavior by upper-income taxpayers would *immediately* result in higher revenues at lower rates.

In their exuberance for their idea, Laffer, Kemp, and a few other supply-siders suggested that cutting tax rates would indeed produce higher tax revenues through faster economic growth. In other words, *tax cuts would pay for themselves.* At one point Laffer wrote that "each of the 10 percent reductions in tax rates would, in terms of overall tax revenues, be self-financing in less than two years. Thereafter, each installment would provide a positive contribution to overall tax receipts."[13]

In fact, few if any of the economists advising Reagan found Laffer's scenario to be plausible. Milton Friedman sensibly pointed out that if tax revenues increased after a tax cut, then tax rates had not been cut far enough. Alan Greenspan estimated that only about 20 percent of the lost revenue would be made up by higher economic growth. Other estimates were higher, though still nowhere near Laffer territory. The Chase Econometrics model projected that 41 percent of the tax cut would be recovered the first year, rising to 72 percent by the seventh year.[14]

Even if Laffer was not precisely right about tax cuts immediately paying for themselves, he was right about a broader point: government revenue estimates of changes in tax policy were wholly static and made no allowance for changes in economic behavior in response to different tax rates. In other words, the government's revenue models assume that taxes don't matter. This had been proven wrong in the late 1970s, when the capital gains tax cut in 1978—the first supply-side breakthrough—had generated increased revenue. The government models all assumed that the cut would lose revenue.

There was much more to supply-side theory than simply stimulating higher economic growth. Contrary to the conventional wisdom that saw a large tax cut as a powerful inflationary force leading to still-higher interest rates, supply-siders thought that lower tax rates would be *deflationary* and help *reduce* interest rates. The logic of this bold insight goes to the core of supply-side theory. Following the classic definition of *inflation* as "too much money chasing too few goods," supply-siders thought that increasing the output of economic goods would lower inflationary pressures. Also, the high inflation and high taxes of the 1970s had caused a disproportionate investment in tangible assets (such as real estate and precious metals) as an inflation hedge whose tax liability could be postponed indefinitely. Therefore, the supply-siders argued, lower income tax rates would make financial assets, such as stocks and bonds, more attractive investments, and this process would bid down the yields on stocks and bonds. The expansion of productive capital investment and the total capital stock, and the shift to financial assets, would make it possible to support a larger budget deficit and still have falling interest rates. The supply-siders also correctly anticipated that the American economy would become a more attractive destination for foreign capital. One supply-sider told the *Wall Street Journal*'s Robert Bartley that the Saudis would finance America's higher budget deficit; this prediction turned out to be exactly correct.

Over the long run the supply-side argument that lower tax rates lead to higher economic growth and a broadened tax base was also correct, as we shall see. But this does not happen instantly, and the large deficit Jimmy Carter was leaving behind was seen as the most important short-run problem along with inflation. The Laffer-style supply-side exuberance that tax cuts would pay for themselves and be deflationary became the basis for the charge that supply-side amounted to the economics of the free lunch. Brookings Institution economist Henry Aaron, for example, called the Laffer curve "the Laetrile of economics"—Laeterile then being a popular but bogus cancer treatment.[15] This became a favorite talking point. Walter Heller, the Keynesian éminence grise of the Kennedy administration, also said, "[S]upply-side economics is a kind of Laetrile for the cancer of inflation." (Heller's other attempted antitax-cut witticism was nearly as flat: "Waiting for supply-side economics to work is like leaving landing lights on for Amelia Earhart.") Otto Eckstein, another old-school Keynesian veteran of the Kennedy administration, resorted to *reductio ad Harvard Yard:* "I wouldn't let a freshman in my beginning economics course at Harvard leave class with that idea. The conclusion that a tax cut will stimulate the economy is as unsubstantiated as ever. Completely off the wall."[16]

This view was not limited to Democrats, who nowadays instinctively oppose cutting taxes. Many leading Republican economists, who could be thought of as the old guard, scorned the idea. Herbert Stein derisively called it "the economics of joy." Alan Greenspan remarked, "I'm for cutting taxes, but not for Laffer's reasons. I don't know anyone who seriously believes his argument." George Stigler, another Chicago School economist headed for a rendezvous with the Nobel Prize, dismissed supply-side economics out of hand. "Laffer is no longer a very serious scholar," Stigler said in 1978. "He is playing the role of a propagandist, and as such he is performing some service. But I would not base a $125 billion tax cut on his work." "From the very beginning of his academic career," Reagan's domestic policy adviser Martin Anderson noted, "Laffer was treated almost as an outcast."[17] Former Federal Reserve chairman Arthur Burns said: "One listens with a sense of dismay to those candidates who promise to cure inflation by massive cuts in taxes."[18] The most vivid and memorable attack came from Reagan's principal opponent in the Republican nomination contest in 1980, George Bush; Bush said that supply-side tax cutting amounted to "voodoo economics." (For their part, the supply-siders referred to the old guard as "the deep root-canal" school of economics.)

The news media were only too happy to amplify the doubts of establishment Republicans. The election results had hardly been tabulated before a media echo chamber generated a high-decibel din about how Reagan would surely have to give up on his tax cut plan. The *New York Times* gleefully reported, "In the Senate, where the Republicans will hold sway, Bob Dole of Kansas, the Republican who will head the Finance Committee, has said that in his opinion one year's tax relief would suffice and a three-year bill would 'fuel inflation.' "[19] Dole's view was identical to Jimmy Carter's criticism of Reagan's plan during the campaign. The senator told another reporter that the Kemp proposal "hasn't been tested. It may be the greatest idea since sliced bread, but there are still reservations."

The *Washington Post* reported ten days after the election (on the very day Kemp presented the "Economic Dunkirk" memo to Reagan in Los Angeles) that supply-siders hoping Reagan would go ahead with their program "are going to be disappointed. . . . There is little sentiment on [Reagan's] economic policy coordinating committee, however, for getting the tax-cut cart too far in front of the spending-cut horse."[20] An anonymous member of Reagan's economic advisory committee told the *Post* that sometime in 1981 there would be a showdown with the supply-side purists, and implied that the supply-siders would have to give in. Two days later the *Post* fired another broadside with a headline suggesting that Reagan's prescription had already proven to be a failure in England: "Thatcher's Conservative Policies Fail to Revive Economy." The *Post*'s economics writer, Hobart Rowen, who never saw a tax cut he didn't hate, wrote: "By the end of the [congressional] session, supply-side tax theory may be back on the shelf." Surely, Rowen speculated, new Treasury Secretary Donald Regan's "more traditional instincts" would rein in these radicals. (In fact, Regan became an early convert and rugged supporter of the supply-siders.)

The newsweeklies were not to be left out of the act. "If Reagan gets his way, inflation may well worsen," *Newsweek* echoed in late November. "In fact, some Reagan advisers would not be unhappy if a House still controlled by Democrats scaled back their tax-cut proposals, relieving the pressure for big budget cuts."[21] A week later *Newsweek* returned to the theme: "The prospects for any more than the first leg of Reagan's 10-10-10 tax cut seem to be fading." The story quoted a "well-wired Congressional tax expert" as saying that the Kemp tax bill "will be dialed back in the Republican-controlled Senate as well as in the House."[22]

The campaign to separate Reagan from his central economic idea was relentless. Indeed, the central story of the entire Reagan presidency might be said to be how he managed to keep to his purposes and principles in the face of an unremitting onslaught from every side—often including from his own political party, White House staff, and his family. (The same pattern repeated itself in foreign affairs.)

It is in this context that the Kemp-Stockman "Economic Dunkirk" memo and the November 16 meeting should be understood. This was the first meeting of Reagan's economic advisers after the election, and therefore the first time that Reagan confronted the responsibility of forming policy, as opposed merely to proposing campaign themes. The supply-siders feared that the old guard would urge Reagan to back away from the full 30 percent tax cut in the face of rising deficit projections, or at the very least to postpone tax cuts until spending cuts could be achieved. Given Washington's bias against spending cuts, the supply-siders thought, a move to make tax cuts a "reward" for spending restraint would effectively cause Reagan's tax cut proposal to evaporate.

Armed with the "Economic Dunkirk" memo, Kemp came to the November 16 meeting ready to do battle against the predicted backsliding—an audacious role considering that he was the only noneconomist in Reagan's economic advisory group. He needn't have fretted; the chairman of the economic advisory group, George Shultz, was among the voices on the committee who emphatically argued that Reagan should stick with the full 30 percent income tax cut. The committee did begin to backtrack in other key areas. For example, it dropped the proposal to lower the top rate on unearned income from 70 percent to 50 percent, chiefly for political reasons. It was thought that the idea would be attacked as a "giveaway to the rich." (Democrats would revive this idea within a few months.) The committee also suggested that the Reagan administration drop the idea of indexing the income tax for inflation to eliminate bracket creep. In addition, the advisory group rejected the idea of declaring an economic emergency in the style of Roosevelt in 1933, although the media mentioned the idea repeatedly for the next two months.

While this meeting went well for the supply-siders, its slight trims were a harbinger of what would unfold as the major internal policy skirmish line of the Reagan presidency. Members of the old guard thought the supply-siders were being "paranoid" (a quote given anonymously to a reporter by a member of the advisory group), yet it was quite reasonable for the insurgent supply-side movement to think that it would be outmaneuvered. One of the things that made the supply-side phenomenon so extraordinary is that there were so few supply-siders. William Niskanen, a member of Reagan's Council of Economic Advisers, observed: "As of 1981 there were no distinctive supply-side texts, no [college] courses, no distinguished scholar, and no school of supply-side economists."[23] In fact, there weren't even enough supply-siders to staff all of the important economic positions in the new administration. In the White House itself there were no supply-siders. The White House staff, supply-sider Paul Craig Roberts ruefully observed, "were unwilling to assume the risks of change for the sake of someone else's issue."[24] The unsung supply-side heroes of the Reagan administration staff wars turned out to be those who ended up together in a critical mass at the Treasury Department— Roberts, Bruce Bartlett, Norman Ture, and Steve Entin, who would conduct a determined campaign to keep the original tax cut proposal intact in the face of opposition from every corner of Washington. Had these officials been scattered to different government bureaus instead of Treasury, the tax cut story might have taken a very different course.

The eventual policy divisions among Reagan's advisers arose, oddly enough, from their fundamental *agreement;* as with medieval theological disputations, sometimes the bitterest arguments over particulars arise from a general agreement about universals. Reagan's advisers all agreed that government was too big, that taxes and spending were too high, and that inflation had to be tamed through sensible monetary policy. But there were profound disagreements over how different aspects of Reagan's policy mix should fit together, which aspect deserved more emphasis than the others, and what the economic effects would be in both the short and long terms. "Reaganomics was a compromise from the beginning," Roberts wrote; "a conglomerate, if you will, of three points of view: supply-sider economics, monetarism, and traditional Republican budget balancing."[25] Murray Weidenbaum, William Niskanen, and William Poole, members of Reagan's Council of Economic Advisers, put the matter delicately in a retrospective account of this trying period. Working out the details and the rationale of Reagan's economic plan "proved to be a difficult undertaking because the Reagan economic program, like the Reagan constituency, reflected a range of views on economic policy . . . There was broader agreement on the substance of the program than on the reasons for the major proposed changes in economic policy."[26]

Most fortunate for the supply-siders, they would have one very important ally in the White House—the president himself.[27] Reagan had always been for cutting taxes, chiefly because reducing revenue constrains the growth of government. He was following the attitude of his favorite contemporary economist, Milton Friedman, who liked to say that he was for any tax cut at any time for any reason. But before 1980 Reagan had said on numerous occasions that a severe recession would be required to cure the nation's inflation. ".Frankly," he told Robert Novak in 1978, "I'm afraid this country is just going to have to suffer two, three years of hard times to pay for the binge we've been on."[28] But then Reagan came to embrace the supply-side view that the economy could be revived and inflation brought down through tax cuts. In his speeches, radio addresses, and newspaper columns starting in the fall of 1978, he began singing the praises of Kemp and his tax-cutting philosophy.

By the time he reached the White House, Reagan had fully absorbed the logic of the purest strain of supply-side—including, it must be said, its chief misconception. The story has been widely recalled that Reagan's instinctive enthusiasm for supply-side economics stemmed from his experience in the movie business, where highly paid actors frequently found that after making one or two movies they were in the 91 percent tax bracket. Why make another picture that year if you kept only 9¢ on the dollar? So, Reagan would say, they quit working every year by June and sat around the Brown Derby restaurant talking about oil deals (almost certainly for their tax shelter potential).[29]

Yet here it must be suggested that Reagan's economic literacy was far more profound than the anecdotal accounts would indicate. (This didn't stop him, however, from needling his economic advisers as practitioners of the dismal science.) Reagan, remember, was an economics major at Eureka College, graduating *before* the Keynesian revolution in economics in the 1930s. To the conventional wisdom, this was a handicap; for the supply-siders, it was a great benefit. To the extent that supply-side economics represented a revival of certain pre-Keynesian precepts, it was not necessary to convert Reagan from a deeply ingrained conventional view. As Herbert Stein noted, "Ronald Reagan's views of economic policy were probably more precisely defined than those of any other recent [presidential] candidate."[30]

Reagan's intuitive economic literacy was often best on display in the give-and-take of press questions or debate. In his campaign debate with Jimmy Carter, he responded to Carter's attack that tax cuts would be inflationary with a sharp rhetorical question: "I would like to ask the president why it is inflationary to let the people keep more of their money and spend it the way they like, and it isn't inflationary to let him take that money and spend it the way he wants?" When unprecedented deficits mounted and pressure grew to raise taxes because high deficits crowd out private market access to capital, Reagan retorted with a variation of this insight. Why is it, he would say, that a deficit crowds out investment but taxes don't? No convincing rejoinder was ever offered. Reagan knew that there was an important difference to economic incentives and capital formation whether he borrowed money or taxed it.

Reagan's natural facility with economics can be seen in his discussion of a question about inflation at an early press conference. The response clearly reads as an original thought and not as a canned, staff-prepared answer to an anticipated question. A reporter asked, "Mr. President, in your list of inflationary forces last night, why did you not mention the increase in gasoline prices and home heating fuels?" The premise of this question, common to economic reporting at the time, is that price increases cause inflation, which is akin to the logic that wet sidewalks cause rain. Reagan's reply makes clear he understood that inflation was primarily a monetary phenomenon and not the result of commodity shortages or other mysterious animal spirits:

> Why in the list of inflationary forces did I not mention gasoline prices and home heating fuel prices? Well, I have to believe that to a certain extent, I know that that's an unusual situation, prices are not so much the *cause* of inflation—price rises—they're the *result*.

Reagan could have quit here, resting on the monetarist understanding of inflation. But he then addressed what was thought to be different about the oil market—the quasi-monopolistic behavior of the OPEC cartel.

> And when I say there is something different in that one, yes. When the OPEC nations with the near monopoly power now take advantage of that position and just simply raise the price to suit themselves, that is a price over and above the normal response to inflation.
>
> One economist pointed out a couple of years ago—he didn't state this as a theory, but he just said it's something to look at—when we started buying the oil over there, the OPEC nations, 10 barrels of oil were sold for the price of an ounce of gold. And the price was pegged to the American dollar. And we were about the only country left that still were on a gold standard. And then a few years went by, and we left the gold standard. And as this man suggested, if you looked at the recurrent price rises, were the OPEC nations raising the price of oil or were they simply following the same pattern of an

ounce of gold, that as gold in this inflationary age kept going up, they weren't going to follow our paper money downhill? They stayed with the gold price. Of course, now, if we followed that, why, they should be coming down, because the price of gold's coming down. But I think that that's like the inflation-contributing factor that you'll have sometimes simply because of a poor crop. That is not based on the economy, that's simply supply and demand. And if there's a crop failure and you've got a bigger demand than you have supply, the price goes up.[31]

Although the answer has the typical fractured syntax and rambling quality of many of Reagan's off-the-cuff remarks, it is nevertheless extraordinary. Reagan here shows that he knows that oil prices, even with OPEC's market concentration, are destined to come down if there is monetary restraint and a decontrolled market for oil. One of his first actions after taking office was immediately removing the final price controls on oil, a step Jimmy Carter had resolutely resisted. Carter had begun a slowly phased price decontrol that might have taken longer than waiting for Godot to arrive.

The conventional wisdom was that oil prices would surely head higher as a result of Reagan's move. Democrats and liberal interest groups seemed to compete with each other for the most fulsome expression of economic illiteracy. In the annals of public policy prognostication it is difficult to find such a wide assembly of wrongheadedness. Senator Howard Metzenbaum of Ohio took to the Senate floor the next day to predict, at a time when gasoline prices had reached an average high of $1.41, that "we will see $1.50 gas this spring, and maybe before. And it is just a matter of time until the oil companies and their associates, the OPEC nations, will be driving gasoline pump prices up to $2 a gallon." Senator Don Riegle of Michigan said, "It will hurt our people within a matter of days." Senator Dale Bumpers of Arkansas had previously predicted that "without rationing, gasoline will soon go to $3 a gallon," and now added that "[d]econtrol is designed to see how much we can squeeze out of the American people before they take to the streets." Maine's Senator George Mitchell said, "Every citizen and every family will find their living standards reduced by this decision."[32]

Instead oil prices started falling almost immediately and dropped steadily, with pump prices reaching a national average of 89¢ a gallon in the spring of 1986. Oil imports from OPEC fell by two million barrels a day by the end of 1982. Reagan's integrated view of oil prices, inflation, and the value of the dollar is especially remarkable in comparison with the Carter administration, which never seemed to understand inflation, ascribing it to animal spirits or, at one point, even to the moral failings of Americans.

But Reagan's enthusiasm for the supply-side insurgency led him to contribute to the view that tax cuts would pay for themselves. Leading supply-siders have gone to great lengths in the intervening years to deny or qualify the idea that tax cuts would pay for themselves right out of the starting gate. "The prediction [of immediately higher revenues]," Robert Bartley wrote in 1992, "is not one any of us really ever made."[33] Martin Anderson said the same thing in his 1988 memoir, *Revolution*. Anderson says it was a "myth that Reagan and his key economic advisers believed that large tax cuts would produce more revenue. And even when dozens of the finest economists in the land examined and blessed Reagan's comprehensive economic program, and even though neither they, nor Reagan, nor any of Reagan's senior aides ever made any such outlandish claim, the myth continued, year after year."[34]

It is narrowly true that none of Reagan's advisers made the claim that tax cuts would immediately pay for themselves, chiefly because neither Jack Kemp nor Jude Wanniski held an administration appointment. And *none* of the official economic and budget forecasts the Reagan administration produced predicted that growth would pay for the entirety of the tax cut. But Reagan *did* make such claims himself. In an early press conference after his formal economic plan was finally unveiled, Reagan replied to a question as follows:

> Every major tax cut that has been made in this century in our country has resulted in even the government getting more revenue than it did before, because the base of the economy is so broadened by doing it. We only have to look at the last few experiences with cuts in the capital gains tax, and you find that the very next year after the rate was lowered, the government got more revenue from capital gains tax than it's been getting at the higher rate. What happens? People up there who are now worried about and busying themselves with tax shelters, if it becomes profitable to move out into risk-taking adventure and investments, they then are encouraged to move out and into that.
>
> Back when Calvin Coolidge cut the taxes across the board, and more than once, the government's revenues increased. When Jack Kennedy did it in the 2-year program and his economic advisers, they were all telling him—I can remember the figures—they told him

that the government would lose $83 billion in revenue, and the government gained $54 billion in revenue, I think is the figure, that it actually went up. So, they had made quite a sizeable financial error in their estimates. Jack Kennedy's line about it was, "a rising tide lifts all boats." And this is what we believe that the tax proposals that we've made, what they're aimed at. . . . And we're just convinced that what has happened before, every time, is going to happen again.

This was not a one-off comment casually made. Reagan said virtually the same thing at a press conference eight months later, when the first installment of his tax cut plan went into effect.

QUESTION: Mr. President, some of your critics are saying that by cutting taxes and at the same time spending more for the military you are, like Lyndon Johnson, saying it was possible to have guns and butter at the same time, and that it won't work for you any more than it did with Johnson and that it will, indeed, damage the economy. What do you say to that?
REAGAN: Well, the great difference is the tax portion of our program, because when we say cutting taxes, we're really leaving a word off. There is a difference between reducing rates and reducing tax revenues. And we only have to look back just shortly before Lyndon Johnson's term to when John F. Kennedy was President and when he followed the policy across the board, against the same kind of economic advice that we've been getting, that he couldn't do that. But he cut those tax rates, and the government ended up getting more revenues, because of the almost instant stimulant to the economy. Now, that's what's being called today—they didn't use the term then— "supply-side economics."
And you don't even have to stop at that one. If you look at our reductions in capital gains tax, if you go back to the twenties when Mellon was the Secretary of the Treasury under Coolidge and was doing this, every time, that kind of a tax cut brings us back—I've told, I think, some of you before—to a principle that goes back at least, I know, as far as the fourteenth century, when a Moslem philosopher named Ibn Khaldun said, "In the beginning of the dynasty, great tax revenues were gained from small assessments. At the end of the dynasty, small tax revenues were gained from large assessments." And we're trying to get down to the small assessments and the great revenues.

Reagan's fulsome belief that tax cuts would increase revenues served as the basis for much of the criticism and ridicule that would be directed at

Reaganomics. This was unfortunate, for the central insight of supply-side economics would be largely vindicated over the course of the 1980s. But that was not the only source of liberal scorn for Reagan's political economy, nor the only aspect of his independent turn of mind on the subject.

*   *   *

MINUTES AFTER REAGAN took the oath of office at noon on January 20, Clement E. Conger, the White House curator, took down Thomas Jefferson's portrait in the cabinet room and replaced it with the portrait of . . . Calvin Coolidge. Coolidge! Was there a Republican from a previous era that enlightened opinion held in lower regard? Surely this was proof, as if further evidence were needed, that the government had been taken over by hopeless reactionaries. As historian Thomas B. Silver summarized the Coolidge predicament: "Coolidge has been subjected to more ridicule perhaps than any other president in American history. His policies are regarded by most historians as beneath contempt."[35]

Reagan's admiration for Coolidge was a matter of record. He told *Newsweek* in mid-January: "But if you go back, I don't know if the country has ever had a higher level of prosperity than it did under Coolidge. And he actually reduced the national debt, he cut taxes several times across the board. And maybe the criticism was in both cases that they weren't activist enough. Well, maybe there's a lesson in that. Maybe we've had instances of government being too active, intervening, interfering. You have here a couple of cases of men who were abiding by the rule that says if it ain't broke don't fix it."[36] He returned to this theme in July in an interview with the *Washington Post*'s Haynes Johnson: "Now you hear a lot of jokes about Silent Cal Coolidge, but I think the joke is on the people that make jokes because if you look at his record, he cut the taxes four times. We had probably the greatest growth and prosperity that we've ever known. And I have taken heed of that because if he did nothing, maybe that's the answer [for] the federal government."

Expressing fondness for a neglected Republican tax cutter was one thing. Putting his portrait in the White House cabinet room was another. The media were incredulous when Reagan did just that as soon as he took office— particularly because the Coolidge portrait displaced one of *Thomas Jefferson*. For example, columnist (and former Democratic speechwriter) Mark Shields wrote, "[D]on't try and tell me that Calvin Coolidge could ever substitute for Thomas Jefferson. That's almost a national sacrilege."[37]

Coolidge thus became a lever by which the media and the Democratic opposition could suggest that Reagan and his economic ideas were simple-minded, outdated, dangerous, and contemptible, all within the veneer of "objective" reporting. *Newsweek:* "But it is quite by design that he has chosen, in Cal Coolidge, a role model who slept eleven hours a day, took two-month vacations and did not splinter his lance on every problem in town."[38] Haynes Johnson, who called Coolidge "the patron saint of business," wrote, "At times Reagan sounds as if he were advocating a return to laissez-faire and the laid-back policies (meaning none) of a president he admires, Calvin Coolidge." Senator Ted Kennedy complained that Reagan "saddled us with the tattered old philosophy of Calvin Coolidge that will work no better in the 1980s than in the 1920s."

Coolidge's policies, especially his tax cuts, are said to have been at the root of the "false prosperity" of the 1920s that contributed to the crash of 1929 and the subsequent Great Depression. ("Business leadership led straight to the Panic of 1929," wrote historian John Hicks in *Republican Ascendancy*.) Activist, enlightened government, it is implied, would have prevented the Great Depression. As the 1980s wore on and gave way to the 1990s and the ascension of Bill Clinton, Reagan's economic policies would be stigmatized as "false prosperity" just as the 1920s had been described.

There was never any serious effort to develop this argument substantively. None of the extensive media commentary on Reagan's interest in Coolidge examined the tax cuts or economic record of the Coolidge era, a remarkable lapse given the centrality of tax cuts to Reagan's agenda. In place of analysis, journalists liked to practice ventriloquist journalism, whereby an ostensibly objective news reporter quotes the dismissive judgment of some authority to make the journalist's argument for him.

Haynes Johnson offered a textbook example of ventriloquist journalism, combined with sleight of hand, in his treatment of the Coolidge-Reagan connection. Johnson was especially fond of Frederick Lewis Allen (whom Johnson still considered "the premier historian of the '20s"), who thought that "the most original thing about Coolidge was his uncompromising unoriginality."[39] In his 1991 book on the Reagan years, *Sleepwalking Through History,* Johnson reprised Allen's thesis, only this time with a different target: "The most original thing about Reagan, like Coolidge, was his uncompromising unoriginality." Johnson quotes Allen at length: "Calvin Coolidge honestly believed that by asserting himself as little as possible and by lifting the tax burdens of the rich he was benefiting the whole country—as perhaps he was. And it was perfectly in keeping with the uninspired and unheroic political temper of the times."

Johnson writes, "The point is not some invidious analogy linking the failures of Coolidge prosperity with the promise of the Reagan economic program," but in the same sentence he notes that Reagan's program contains "similar governmental approaches to those employed by Coolidge—the tax cuts, the get-government-off-our-backs attitudes, the prime-the-pump, *help-the-rich-first, and let-the-rest-trickle-down philosophies now in place*" (emphasis added). A few paragraphs later Johnson drops all artifice and makes the "invidious analogy" directly: "The danger today, as it was in the '20s, comes from putting too much faith in simple solutions." Enter now the ventriloquist dummy to lend authority to Johnson's point of view. In this case, Johnson had to go all the way to an obscure management symposium in Saint-Gall, Switzerland, to find a little-known Wall Street figure to assail Reagan's economic views. Albert M. Wognilower, a managing director of First Boston Corporation, "warns against a tendency to seek 'simplistic but self-defeating "solutions" to the various internal conflicts' facing the country." (Liberals missed the irony that Reagan was unmoved by the financial sector's anxieties, answering a reporter's question about Wall Street's misgivings about tax cuts with "I have never found Wall Street a source of good economic advice.")

Johnson's treatment is typical of the media malpractice when it came to Coolidge and the tax cuts of the 1920s. From the media, readers learned almost nothing substantive about Coolidge or his economic program. All of the leading histories of the Coolidge era (written chiefly by liberal authors) on which contemporary journalists such as Johnson relied convey the simple-minded view that Coolidge and his Treasury secretary, Andrew Mellon, merely wanted to cut taxes for the rich. Arthur Schlesinger Jr.'s account has it that Coolidge "concentrated on cutting taxes for millionaires." (The one notable exception to this came from, of all people, John Kenneth Galbraith. In his book *The Great Crash,* Galbraith wrote: "A whole generation of historians has assailed Coolidge for the superficial optimism which kept him from seeing that a great storm was brewing at home and also more distantly abroad. This is grossly unfair.")

In fact, Coolidge cut income taxes three times (not four, as Reagan told Haynes Johnson), and those cuts did not by any means benefit millionaires only. Coolidge's chief target each time was the emergency income surtax rates that had been enacted during World War I but which had not been lowered after the war ended, as is typical of many "temporary" or "emergency" government measures. The surtax kicked in at an income of $6,000, and the top rate was 73 percent. A household earning a $1 million income in 1924 paid a net tax of $550,000. Coolidge lowered the top surtax rate from 73 percent to 25 percent, and later to 20 percent. He also cut the lowest tax bracket from 4 percent to 1.5 percent. He raised the income threshold at which the surtax took effect from $6,000 to $10,000, which removed thousands of households from the income tax rolls entirely. While Coolidge's tax cut was pejoratively described as a giveaway to the rich, 70 percent of the tax reduction went to households with income under $10,000 (about $120,000 in today's dollars). This is one reason the Coolidge tax cuts were broadly popular with Americans. The most ironic aspect of the Coolidge tax cuts was their *progressivity*: the proportion of the total income tax burden paid by those earning $100,000 and above increased from 28 percent in 1921 to 61 percent in 1928.

Coolidge understood the supply-side logic of his tax cuts in exactly the manner predicted by the Laffer curve. In his 1924 State of the Union message to Congress, Coolidge argued that "the larger incomes of the country would actually yield more revenue to the Government if the basis of taxation were scientifically revised downward. . . . There is no escaping the fact that when the taxation of large incomes is excessive they tend to disappear." He had said the same thing earlier in the year at a Lincoln Day dinner:

> I agree perfectly with those who wish to relieve the small taxpayer by getting the largest possible contribution from the people with large incomes. But if the rates on large incomes are so high that they disappear, the small taxpayer will be left to bear the entire burden. If, on the other hand, the rates are placed where they will produce the most revenue from large incomes, then the small taxpayer will be relieved.

Coolidge—and the Laffer curve—turned out to be right during the 1920s. In 1922, the surtax yielded only $77 million from taxpayers with incomes above $300,000, down from $243 million in 1919 and $220 million in 1918. By 1927, by which time the top surtax rate had been reduced to 20 percent, the Treasury netted $230 million from taxpayers with incomes over $300,000. The first year after Coolidge's 1924 tax cut saw a decline of $127 million in total income tax revenues, though, as economist Lawrence Lindsey discovered upon sifting the data, tax receipts from taxpayers with incomes over $100,000 *increased*. In other words, *all* of the lost revenue came from lower and middle incomes.[40] This had the effect of shifting the relative tax burden onto upper-income taxpayers—exactly the opposite of the claims of tax cuts critics then and now. By 1928 income tax revenues had risen $310 million above where they had been before the first tax cut, and 61 percent of total tax revenues came from taxpayers with incomes over $100,000. Only 4 percent of income tax receipts came from taxpayers with incomes under $10,000.

Reagan might have cited an unlikely precedent earlier than Coolidge for his supply-side views—Woodrow Wilson. In a message to Congress in 1919, Wilson said: "The Congress might well consider whether the higher rates of income and profits tax can in peacetimes be effectively productive of revenue, and whether they may not, on the contrary, be destructive of business activity and productive of waste and inefficiency. There is a point at which in peace times high rates of income and profits taxes destroy energy, remove the incentive to new enterprise, encourage extravagant expenditures and produce industrial stagnation with consequent unemployment and other attendant evils."

Rather than cite this Democrat, Reagan did something infinitely more infuriating: he invoked the authority and experience of John F. Kennedy.

*   *   *

IN 1963, PRESIDENT Kennedy proposed income tax rate cuts of almost the same scale as Reagan's nearly two decades later. The shorthand JFK slogan the supply-siders adopted was "A rising tide lifts all boats." But Kennedy's fulsome public rhetoric in support of his tax cut proposal was nearly identical to Reagan's in 1981. The current income tax system, Kennedy told the Economic Club of New York in the fall of 1962, "siphons out of the private economy too large a share of personal and business purchasing power. . . . [I]t reduces the financial incentives for personal effort, investment, and risk-taking." It would also *raise revenues*.

> Our true choice is not between tax reduction, on the one hand, and the avoidance of large Federal deficits on the other. It is increasingly clear that no matter what party is in power, so long as our national security needs keep rising, an economy hampered by restrictive tax rates will never produce enough revenue to balance our budget just

as it will never produce enough jobs or enough profits. Surely the lesson of the last decade is that budget deficits are not caused by wild-eyed spenders but by slow economic growth and periodic recessions, and any new recession would break all deficit records.

In short, it is a paradoxical truth that tax rates are too high today and tax revenues are too low and *the soundest way to raise the revenues in the long run is to cut the rates now*. The experience of a number of European countries and Japan have borne this out. This country's own experience with tax reduction in 1954 has borne this out. And the reason is that only full employment can balance the budget, and tax reduction can pave the way to that employment. The purpose of cutting taxes now is not to incur a budget deficit, but to achieve the more prosperous, expanding economy which can bring a budget surplus. (Emphasis added)

In his subsequent *Economic Report to Congress*, JFK made the point more directly: "The ultimate increases in the continuing flow of incomes, production, and consumption will greatly exceed the initial amount of tax reduction." And in a special message to Congress that accompanied the transmittal of his formal tax cut proposal, he said, "Total output and economic growth will be stepped up by an amount several times as great as the tax cut itself. . . . Within a few years of the enactment of this program, Federal revenues will be larger than if present tax rates continue to prevail. . . . It would be a grave mistake to require that any tax reduction today be offset by a corresponding cut in expenditures." Kennedy returned to this theme often throughout 1963, and even had a line promoting the tax cut in the speech he was on his way to deliver in Dallas on November 22. (Kennedy's tax cut was not enacted until after his death, in 1964.)

It was bad enough that Reagan was hijacking the image of the boy prince of modern liberalism; worse than this larceny was the way the supply-side barbarians turned the Kennedy era's Keynesian understanding of tax cuts on its head. *Wait a minute!* protested the Keynesian veterans of the Kennedy era; *our tax cut was a classic example of stimulating aggregate demand* (the economic term for spending more money). *JFK's revenue predictions were based on the Keynesian multiplier effect, wherein a dollar sent to the private economy through a tax cut would stimulate several dollars' worth of consumption.*[41] *Investment incentives were the last thing on our mind. Moreover, inflation in the early 1960s was very low, so there was little risk that a tax cut would fan inflation. These uncredentialed, upstart supply-siders,* the liberals fumed, *are accusing us of not understanding our own policy. A tax cut in 1981,* the old-timers screamed, *will send inflation through the roof.* "What they do not tell you," an incredulous Ted Kennedy complained, "is that inflation was then 2 percent and today it is 12 percent."

The supply-siders marshaled impressive evidence that the JFK tax cuts had significant effects on supply-side capital formation and investment. Growth in the gross domestic product (GDP) accelerated to over 5 percent the year following the tax—more than a full percentage point above the long-term postwar growth rate of 3.4 percent. Capital spending jumped by a third in the first two years after rates were cut; the personal savings rate increased 50 percent—the amount saved was greater than the cash delivered by the tax cut itself, suggesting that people were indeed reacting quickly to the increased relative reward for savings and investment over consumption. As supply-side theory would have predicted, productivity growth jumped by nearly a full percentage point. Even though the top marginal income tax rate was cut from 91 to 70 percent, taxes paid by those earning more than $50,000 (equivalent to about $135,000 in 1981) increased nearly 40 percent between 1963 and 1965—a vindication of one of the key tenets of supply-side thinking and a rebuttal to the main attack against tax cuts.[42] Consumption rose less than the Keynesian models predicted. Lawrence Lindsey estimates that the tax cut generated three-quarters of the increase in the growth rate in the 1960s, while increased demand, Keynesian-style, accounted for only one-quarter of the higher growth. Lindsey concluded: "The tax cuts of 1964 were a major cause of the longest economic expansion then on record, which continued until 1970."[43] Moreover, Lindsey argues, "high-income taxpayers reported so much more taxable income that more revenue was collected under the lower tax rates than would have been collected under the higher tax rates prevailing before the tax cut."

The Keynesian old guard was caught flat-footed by the supply-side fervor. Except for the argument about inflation, the old Keynesians often seemed incoherent in their protests against Reagan's proposed tax cuts.[44] Walter Heller argued that "there is no scientific evidence that [the Kennedy tax cut] paid for itself." But Bruce Bartlett dug up a statement Heller made in the 1960s that the tax cut "was the major factor that led to our running a $3 billion surplus by the middle of 1965 before escalation in Vietnam struck us." Heller had to repudiate the statement, saying it had been "an unguarded response to a leading question by an exuberant Hubert Humphrey during a

Congressional hearing years ago." The Brookings Institution, the Democratic-leaning think tank whose leading economists were opposed to Reagan's tax plan, published a book in the spring of 1981 that confused the argument further, at least for the media. *How Taxes Affect Economic Behavior* agreed with the central supply-side premise that high tax rates discouraged investment and the supply of labor, but disagreed that tax cuts would pay for themselves. Still other liberal economists, such as 1981 Nobel Prize winner James Tobin, said on NBC's *Meet the Press* that "there were some supply-side tax cuts, it's true, in the Kennedy Administration."

Beyond the spectral argument about economic theory lay a profound divide over political principle on two levels. The most significant aspect of the challenge to liberal orthodoxy was not so much whether tax cuts were more effective on the supply side or the demand side but its premise that the decisions and actions of the private market were more powerful than government intervention. By implication, supply-side economics represented a rebuke to the premises of activist government, and therefore of liberalism. In other words, supply-side economics was more important as an ideological challenge to liberalism than as a technical challenge to Keynesianism.[45] The Reagan administration's first *Economic Report of the President* noted this fact: "This plan for national recovery represents a substantial break with past policy. The new policy is based on the premise that the people who make up the economy—workers, managers, savers, investors, buyers, and sellers—do not need the government to make reasoned and intelligent decisions about how best to organize and run their own lives." This helps explain the fury of the liberal reaction to Reagan's invocation of Kennedy's tax cuts. (The Kennedy comparison continues to drive liberal Democrats out of their mind today. In 2003 Senator Ted Kennedy objected to TV ads recalling President John F. Kennedy's praise of tax cuts.)

This dimension of the supply-side challenge went largely unstated because of its abstract character, but the second aspect of the argument loomed large, and still does today. Because across-the-board tax cuts would deliver their largest nominal dollar reductions to the people who pay the most income tax, it was argued that tax cuts were tilted unfairly to the rich. This became the chief liberal talking point against the Reagan plan. John Kenneth Galbraith, renowned for his supposed wit, told a reporter, "We used to say the theme of the New Deal was 'the forgotten man.' I think, about the Reagan administration, you'd say it is 'the forgotten rich man.' "[46] "There is something else they do not say," Ted Kennedy complained; "President Kennedy's tax cut concentrated relief on middle income families. [Reagan's] tax cut would give the most to the wealthiest segment of our society."[47]

Senator Kennedy was wrong: JFK's tax cut had its largest effects at the top rates, a fact that was not lost on a few liberals in 1964. The *New Republic*'s TRB (Richard Strout) complained that the tax cuts would chiefly benefit the rich. But in the Kennedy years the imperative of growth trumped liberalism's redistributionist impulse, in large part because liberals of that earlier era were confident that growth itself would enable the government to finance ambitious social spending programs; in other words, growth was seen as indirect redistribution.

By the end of the 1970s, however, liberalism had come to embrace the polar opposite—the limits to growth. The supposed scarcity of oil and natural resources of the 1970s was merely symptomatic of a new era of low or no growth that constricted the hitherto broad horizons of liberalism. Indeed, it might be said that within the space of a single decade, the central governing challenge of liberalism changed from allocating abundance to rationing scarcity. Jimmy Carter had ratified this thinking in his infamous Camp David retreat in the summer of 1979, where he told one group of visitors, "I think it's inevitable that there will be a lower standard of living than what everybody had always anticipated, constant growth. . . . I think there's going to have to be a reorientation of what people value in their own lives. *I believe that there has to be a more equitable sharing of what we have. . . .* The only trend is downward" (emphasis added).

In other words, liberalism's redistributionist impulse metastasized into a zero-sum mentality holding that anyone's gain must entail someone else's loss. (A favorite and influential liberal title in the early 1980s was economist Lester Theroux's *The Zero-Sum Society*.) If our economy is a zero-sum game, then it is *not fair* that wealthier Americans would get larger tax relief than middle- and lower-income Americans. Even if wealthier Americans saved and invested more, liberals had so little of their previous confidence in growth that it was inconceivable the economy could spread its blessings across all income groups. This was the basis of the charge that tax cuts were "trickle-down economics." When Reagan invoked JFK's slogan, "A rising tide lifts all boats," liberals began responding, "What about the boats stuck in the mud?"

Fairness is the great lodestar of American politics. It is derivative of the principle of equality as enshrined in the Declaration of Independence, which is why fairness is usually at the center of American political scrums. The polar extremes of the debate are *fairness as equal opportunity,* which means people should be rewarded for their own efforts, versus *fairness as equality of result,* which requires some measure of redistribution regardless of individual effort. In the 1980s this debate came into sharper relief as the two parties became more explicitly identified with the two poles of the debate, which can be summarized more succinctly as the debate between *opportunity* (the GOP) versus *entitlement* (the Democrats). Indeed, as Harvey Mansfield wrote, the elections of the 1980s can be seen as a continuous referendum on this divide.[48]

In the context of post–New Deal liberalism, fairness would seem to be a Democratic trump card, as people seldom ask how fair it is for the government to tax up to 70 percent of someone's earnings. However, fairness as equality or entitlement gets limited traction for Democrats for a simple reason: there is a sharp limit to class envy in America. Even low-income Americans aspire to be high-income Americans someday, and rightly see high tax rates as an obstacle to achieving their dream. George McGovern was shocked in 1972 when working-class voters reacted strongly against his proposal for confiscatory inheritance tax rates. In other words, more Americans regard fairness as opportunity than as entitlement or egalitarianism.

There is a stark irony in the shape of the debate over tax cuts in the early 1980s. The two political parties had virtually changed places with each other. In 1964, Senator Barry Goldwater voted against the Kennedy tax cut, fearing it would increase the federal budget deficit. (So did a young Kansas congressman, Bob Dole.) In *The Conscience of a Conservative,* Goldwater expressed the orthodox conservative view: "I believe that as a practical matter spending cuts must come before tax cuts. If we reduce taxes before firm, principled decisions are made about expenditures, we will court deficit spending and the inflationary effects that invariably follow." In 1981 this became the argument of Democrats (and not just in 1981; in 2003 Democratic Senate majority leader Tom Daschle used arguments nearly identical to Goldwater's in opposition to President George W. Bush's tax cuts). In 1981, Goldwater would vote for the tax cut.

✻   ✻   ✻

AMIDST THE HAIRSPLITTING arguments over the distinctions between the Kennedy and Reagan tax cuts, Goldwater's comment from 1964—that tax cuts should be the reward for spending cuts—contained the one surviving point of agreement within the narrow confines of the conventional wisdom. But of course there are always excuses for not cutting spending, as Kennedy noted in the epigraph to this chapter. While the spending-cut/tax-cut nexus remained prominent with mainstream Republican economists and among many of Reagan's top advisers, the hardcore supply-siders rejected this linkage because of its association with Hooverite austerity. This divergence in economic premises set the stage for furious internecine controversy within the new administration. There was considerable ambiguity and confusion going forward, because Reagan wanted to slash government spending in any case as a means of reducing the size and scope of government. It set the stage for a two-front political war, one front within the administration itself over balancing tax cuts and spending cuts, and the main front against liberals who opposed both tax and spending cuts. If liberals disliked cutting taxes, they were near apoplexy over cutting federal spending. It was one thing to cut taxes and thereby reduce revenues to the government; cutting spending programs that in many cases fueled Democratic interests constituted a direct attack on the Democratic Party's power.

The difficulty in cutting spending is that Congress, not the president, controls spending—especially so since the Budget Act of 1974 reduced the president's already limited power over the purse strings. Since the Budget Act, spending growth had exploded; during the Carter years, the federal budget grew at *twice* the rate of inflation. Reagan's team knew they had to strike fast in Congress to achieve meaningful results, while the new president enjoyed his "honeymoon" period and the opposition was in disarray. Reagan's Initial Actions Project noted: "For the moment, the spending constituencies are not in the ascendance. With no general elections until November 1982 the leverage of organized spending interests is at its nadir." *Intimidated* was the word the media employed most often to describe the sentiment among congressional Democrats.

Two days after the election Reagan aides announced that they would seek immediate cuts in spending programs under the 1981 fiscal year Carter budget that Congress had already approved, rather than wait for a new budget cycle to begin the following October. The first idea floated was a 2 percent across-the-board reduction in all programs except defense. Even though this amounted to only about $13 billion, the idea proved unworkable for the same reasons Reagan had had to abandon a 10 percent across-the-board spending cut in the California state budget during his first year as governor in 1967.

Success at making serious spending cuts would require a detail-oriented point man who could master the clever schemes of the spendthrift bureaucracy and dissect the arcane codes of the federal budget. A previous executive branch reform had created the Office of Management and Budget (OMB) in the White House to give the president a mechanism to get command of spending, though it remained exceedingly difficult to do in practice. The seemingly perfect person for OMB emerged: third-term Michigan congressman David Stockman, author of the "Economic Dunkirk" memo. Stockman was a wunderkind of the House, where he had distinguished himself in just two terms as a slayer of liberal ideas. Congressman (later Senator) Phil Gramm, no slouch himself in the brains department (Gramm had a Ph.D. in economics), said that "Stockman was the smartest member of Congress." He matched his intelligence with hard work, bordering on nerdy monomania. As a young congressional staffer, Stockman had read ten years' worth of back issues of *Congressional Quarterly* so that he would be familiar with any issue that came up. He also saved more than $15,000 from his modest staff salary, which he used to help fund his first run for office in 1976. It was said that Stockman might be the only human being who actually read the entire federal budget, devouring it with the same thoroughness that most men devote to the *Sports Illustrated* swimsuit issue. He applied his smarts and hard work with devastating effect in the House. Stockman's critiques of Carter's hospital cost containment plan and Carter's energy plan were instrumental in their collapse in Congress. Just thirty-four years old in 1980, Stockman was clearly on the rise. He was included, along with Arkansas governor Bill Clinton, in *Time* magazine's 1979 survey "50 Faces for the Future."

Reagan initially offered Stockman the post of secretary of energy, but Stockman declined. It was a brazen step for Stockman; ordinarily a congressman wouldn't get another chance at a senior-level appointment. But Stockman hungered for OMB; indeed, one biographer says that Stockman's ambition to head OMB began as early as 1970, after he had read a leading textbook on the budget process. It has to be one of the more peculiar political ambitions ever seen inside the Beltway.[49] His close congressional ally Jack Kemp arranged both for Robert Novak to write a newspaper column boosting Stockman for OMB and for Stockman to meet with Senator Paul Laxalt, who was in the thick of assembling Reagan's team. The plotting and scheming worked.

Stockman was already well known to Reagan because he had served as the stand-in for Jimmy Carter in Reagan's debate rehearsals in October 1980. Reagan said later that Stockman had been tougher than Carter himself. Reagan recalled this when he telephoned Stockman in early December 1980 to offer the OMB appointment: "Dave, I've been thinking about how to get even with you for that thrashing you gave me in the debate rehearsals. So I'm going to send you to OMB." Stockman seemed the ideal Reagan revolutionary, and he would become the central figure in the drama over economic policy in 1981. His appointment was met with enthusiasm among conservatives, as his association with Kemp created the impression that he was a full-throated disciple of supply-side economics. But Stockman would turn out to be a disastrous appointment—he became the Robert McNamara of the Reagan administration—from which supply-side economics has never fully recovered.

Stockman himself would later characterize his role as "the Trotsky of the supply-side movement." In retrospect the signs of Stockman's disharmony with Reagan should have been more easily recognized, for the odyssey of David Stockman encapsulates the crosscurrents and confusions of the baby boom generation. Raised in a Republican family on a rural Michigan farm, Stockman got caught up in the radical fervor of the New Left when he arrived at Michigan State University in 1964, where he drew the attention and surveillance of the Michigan state police. He intended to study agriculture and return to the farm; instead, he studied Marxism, joined the radical Students for a Democratic Society, burned his draft card, grew his hair long, bought a guitar so he could croon Bob Dylan songs to coeds, and eventually ended up at Harvard Divinity School, where God is barely a dying memory. Stockman didn't just strike the radical pose; he helped organize anti–Vietnam War protests and participated in the most famous of the antiwar hijinks, the October 1967 March on Washington. Stockman downplays this period to some extent in his 1986 memoir, *The Triumph of Politics*, dismissing it as "my coffee house period."

At Harvard, where he went to avoid the draft, he began to have second thoughts. About this time he encountered the anti-utopian works of Reinhold Niebuhr and Walter Lippmann. "The scales fell from my eyes as I turned those pages," Stockman recalled. Then in one of those strange twists of fate that seem to occur with regularity in American life, Stockman became the live-in babysitter for Daniel Patrick Moynihan, who at that time was commuting back and forth from Cambridge to his post in the Nixon White House. This ended up providing Stockman with his entrée into the real world of politics.

Through Moynihan's connections Stockman went to Washington in 1970 to work for Illinois congressman John Anderson. Anderson was chairman of the House Republican Conference, and he installed Stockman, then just twenty-five, as its executive director. Anderson was a liberal Republican, as became evident when he ran for president as a left-leaning independent in 1980. (It was Stockman's history with Anderson that originally brought

Stockman to the Reagan campaign's attention as they sought a stand-in for Reagan's debate preparations in 1980.) Though Stockman was thought to be an ideological conservative when he arrived on his own in the House, he voted with Anderson 80 percent of the time and supported abortion, opposed school prayer, and joined the last outpost of Rockefeller Republicans, the Ripon Society, which by then was long past its peak influence. He boasted that he had not voted for Richard Nixon in 1972.

Stockman did not hold Reagan in high regard either. "I considered him a cranky obscurantist," Stockman wrote in his bitter memoir, "whose political base was barnacled with every kook and fringe group that inhabited the vasty deep of American politics."[50] He added: "I would never be comfortable with what I viewed as the primitive, right-wing conservatism of my grandfather or Goldwater—or Reagan."[51] Stockman expressed various signs of contempt for Reagan, such as referring to Reagan's old speeches and writings as "The Scrolls" and comparing the president's intellect to "a trench—narrow, but deep." In the 1980 presidential campaign Stockman initially backed John Connally, then switched to George Bush when Connally's candidacy proved stillborn. As Martin Anderson reflected later, "Anyone who could love John Connally, the godfather of wage and price controls under President Nixon, couldn't be all good."[52] Pat Moynihan quipped: "Stockman is peerless. I have never known a man capable of such sustained self-hypnotic ideological fervor. One day he arrives at Harvard preaching the infallibility of Ho Chi Minh. Next thing you know, he turns up in Washington proclaiming the immutability of the Laffer Curve."[53]

Everyone missed the signs of what the *Wall Street Journal*'s Robert Bartley identified as Stockman's "intellectual instability" and "congenital restlessness."[54] He professed to be a supply-side true believer, and he brought to the coming budget battle the energy and intellect that Reagan needed. (Though for all his learning at Michigan State and Harvard, he apparently never took a course in economics.) As Martin Anderson described Stockman's ascension, "He joined the administration with the enthusiasm of a new puppy, eager and urgent, bounding and leaping through the federal budget with wild-eyed passion. . . . Stockman turned out to be a superb leader for OMB." Another enthusiastic endorsement came from Alan Greenspan: "He's the brightest guy around." Whereas the Reagan team initially thought budget cuts in the range of $13 billion to $18 billion would be hard to get, Stockman came along with a plan to cut $41 billion out of the next budget, and more than $100 billion a year by 1986. Reagan and his top aides were dazzled. Stockman would later admit, "I instilled so much confidence by appearing to know all the answers."

The OMB director would have cabinet rank in the Reagan administration, and at thirty-four, Stockman was the youngest cabinet member in 160 years. His youth and brashness made inevitable a clash with Treasury Secretary Don Regan, especially when Stockman received more media attention and came to be regarded as the de facto point man for Reagan's economic program. (Less than a month into the new administration, a tight shot of Stockman landed on the cover of *Newsweek* with the headline "Cut, Slash, Chop.") Regan was old enough to be Stockman's father and, Martin Anderson observed, sometimes treated his OMB director like a child. Regan started making jokes about the difficulty of keeping Stockman under control before inauguration day.

The largest disharmony with President Reagan was not ideological but temperamental. Martin Anderson observed: "Stockman was profoundly pessimistic by nature. If he were ever to write a history of American baseball, he would probably describe Ted Williams this way: even at the height of his career, Williams managed to get base hits only 40 percent of the time and struck out repeatedly."[55]

Yet Stockman was the indispensable person, because Reagan decided he would unveil the full details of his economic program in a State of the Union speech before a joint session of Congress on February 18—less than a month after taking office, and before many appointees to key economic posts had been confirmed and put in place. (Reagan was the first president since Kennedy to give a State of the Union address in his first month in office.) Most incoming administrations make only minor adjustments to the budget plan their predecessors have assembled for the upcoming fiscal year, but the Reagan team knew it had to throw out the Carter budget. The Reagan administration would produce not merely its own plan but a full-scale *Economic Report of the President* to explain it (even though the outgoing Carter administration had already published its own edition of this annual report).

Stockman didn't wait for inauguration day to begin assembling a budget, even though he didn't get much cooperation from the outgoing Carter budget officials in terms of access to OMB data and budget models. Soon he was seen carrying around a thick black notebook under his arm that contained his target list of budget cuts. Senate majority leader Howard Baker called it "the book of cuts and wounds."

Here it must be noted that *budget cuts* is one of those Washington misnomers that defies a commonsense understanding of things. Although Stockman itemized $467 billion in spending reductions spread over the next five years, *federal spending was still projected to rise by $257 billion during that period,* which hardly amounts to shrinking government. Reagan more precisely described what he sought to do as "reducing the rate of growth of federal spending." He would often illustrate this point in conversation with staff by putting his arm at a 45-degree angle while saying, "Spending has been growing like *this,*" and then, lowering his arm to a 30-degree angle, he would complete the thought: "And we need to reduce the growth rate to something like *this.*" The media generally failed to report this dynamic accurately, but there were occasional exceptions. *Time* magazine noted: "For all its radicalism, Reagan's plan calls for something much less than a repeal of Lyndon Johnson's Great Society, let alone Franklin Roosevelt's New Deal. Among the spending programs that Reagan picked as targets, only a few would be axed completely; most of the others would not only continue but would grow, albeit more slowly."[56] This clarity didn't last long; by April *Time* would be describing Reagan's cuts as "draconian." *Newsweek* used the same adjective. This was hardly the stuff of a revolution, and ironically the Reaganauts' boastful talk of the Reagan Revolution lent credence to the liberals' attack that the new president was dismantling the social safety net in fundamental ways.

Stockman's own view was more radical than Reagan's. Stockman didn't just want to trim the rate of spending growth; he really did want to mount an assault on the fundamental pillars of the welfare state. He argued at the time, "The idea that has been established over the past ten years, that almost every service that someone might need in life ought to be provided, financed by the Government as a matter of basic rights, is wrong. We challenge that. We reject that notion." His budget plan called for abolishing dozens of programs entirely (ultimately 144), including a popular $3.7 billion job training program, the Legal Services Corporation, trade adjustment assistance for displaced workers, and the Economic Development Administration, which provided subsidies to business. He also planned for lower spending growth in the school lunch program, unemployment benefits, the food stamp program, and federal aid for mass transit projects. Dozens of other federal grant programs would be shrunk and consolidated into much smaller block grants, where many could be expected to die of fratricide as state and local officials fought over how to allocate the money.

But a fateful decision was reached early in 1981, based on a tactical mistake of Stockman's. Although Reagan's Initial Actions Project understood clearly that the window for serious budget cuts would close quickly, the plan Stockman presented to the cabinet on February 10, about a week before Reagan was scheduled to unveil his budget program, did not propose any cuts in the largest entitlement programs such as Medicare, veterans' benefits, Head Start, Supplemental Security Income, or summer youth jobs programs— programs that account for nearly 40 percent of domestic spending and that tend to grow on automatic pilot. "It wasn't that we intended to spare those programs," Stockman explained later, "it was simply that we hadn't yet got around to cutting them."

If this was Stockman's view, he didn't explain it forcefully enough to Reagan or the cabinet on February 10, for it was decided to make a political virtue of "exempting" these "social safety net" programs from budget cuts as a way of deflecting the criticism that Reagan was assaulting the poor.[57] Sure enough, Stockman's ringing challenge to the premises of the welfare state was repudiated. Treasury Secretary Donald Regan told reporters: "I think Dave went a little too far in that statement. When people are in need or unemployed, they can expect that the Government will help them." And so there appeared in Reagan's speech a week later the following pledge:

> Those who, through no fault of their own, must depend on the rest of us—the poverty stricken, the disabled, the elderly, all those with true need—can rest assured that the social safety net of programs they depend on are exempt from any cuts. The full retirement benefits of the more than 31 million social security recipients will be continued, along with an annual cost-of-living increase. Medicare will not be cut, nor will supplemental income for the blind, the aged, and the disabled. And funding will continue for veterans' pensions. School breakfasts and lunches for the children of low-income families will continue, as will nutrition and other special services for the aging. There will be no cut in Project Head Start or summer youth jobs. All in all, nearly $216 billion worth of programs providing help for tens of millions of Americans will be fully funded.

Democrats and liberal activists still screamed. Senator Howard Metzenbaum declared, "We are wreaking unbelievable havoc on the lives of millions of poor Americans." House Speaker Tip O'Neill said Reagan was "taking a meat ax" to vital social programs. In other words, Reagan got no less partisan heat and criticism for having put several large entitlement programs off-limits, and by doing so increased the budget pressure on the remaining programs that were on the table for cuts.

And then there was an oddity in the plan that would come back to haunt the White House: the specified budget cuts fell $44 billion short of the total amount needed for the budget to reach projected balance by 1984. Stockman included this amount in a line item identified with an asterisk as "future savings to be proposed." This became known as "the magic asterisk"; according to Stockman, it was his private euphemism for going after Social Security, which Reagan had for the time being placed off-limits, even though there was some bipartisan sentiment on Capitol Hill to consider some cuts in Social Security spending.[58]

Stockman started doing something else that would have potent ramifications for himself and Reagan's economic policy several months down the road: he agreed to begin meeting regularly with the *Washington Post*'s national affairs editor, William Greider, who proposed to write an in-depth story about how the supply-side experiment unfolded. Stockman trusted Greider, but more important than trust was the intellectual vanity that led him to think he could make a convert—even as he had been a convert—out of the very left-wing Greider. "My intellectual impulse," Stockman explained later, "was to try to penetrate the citadel of establishment opinion makers," especially in the pages of the *Washington Post*. "They were the modern secularists I was trying to convert."[59] The Stockman-Greider sessions, usually over breakfast at the Hay-Adams Hotel across Lafayette Square from the White House, did indeed turn into a confessional—for Stockman.

Beyond the details of what specific budget cuts could be achieved lay a more fundamental task of economic policy: the Reaganites needed to develop a five-year baseline economic forecast against which tax and spending changes could be scored. This seemingly obscure bureaucratic topic actually proves central to the argument over Reagan's economic legacy.

Determining how much spending needs to be cut to achieve a balanced budget over a period of several years requires estimating how much revenue will come in and how much government spending will increase. This is not dramatically different from what a household does when it sits down at the kitchen table to plan a monthly budget: how much is your income going to be, and what do you think your expenses are going to be? When income and expenses don't match up, most families make adjustments. In the case of the federal budget, making estimates of future revenues and expenses depends on the assumed rate of economic growth. *Accurate* long-range macroeconomic forecasting is almost impossible; forecasts seldom match the reality of what ensues beyond a year or two. At best the forecasting exercise is an educated guess and is useful for clarifying policy choices and the economic premises behind those choices. Yet the federal government persists to this day in issuing annual five-year forecasts.

The standard account of the first month of the Reagan presidency, to which several of Reagan's own aides such as David Stockman would later subscribe, is that the administration made up unrealistic or even phony forecasts to justify the tax cut, deliberately obscuring the large budget deficits that subsequently ensued. It quickly came to be said that someone named Rosy Scenario generated the administration's economic forecast. The phrase first appeared in a *Washington Post* headline on February 7, and like other media-bestowed monikers, "Rosy Scenario" became a hardy perennial commensurate with Lyndon Johnson's "credibility gap," Nixon's "secret plan" to end the Vietnam War, and Jimmy Carter's "malaise" speech.[60] Like these other infamous totems, it is inaccurate and incorrect.

The administration did fall into fractious infighting over which economic forecast it would use and the economic rationale by which it would explain its policy. The nub of the argument was this: the economy's growth rate in the late 1970s had been anemic (3.2 percent in 1979, −0.1 percent in 1980), yet the supply-side theory predicted that tax cuts would produce a strong spurt in growth almost immediately. The outgoing Carter administration had projected 1982 real (that is, inflation-adjusted) GDP growth of 3.5 percent, but supply-siders at the Treasury Department thought a growth rate over 5 percent was justified. The forecast the Reagan economic team finally settled on, after debate among Treasury, the Council of Economic Advisers, and OMB, estimated growth at 4.2 percent for 1982, 5.0 percent in 1983, and 4.5 percent in 1984. It was these allegedly unrealistic numbers that came to be the cornerstone of Rosy Scenario.

But were the estimates that far out of line? By contrast, the Congressional Budget Office projected 2.5 percent growth for 1982, while the Blue Chip forecast (a consensus of Wall Street projections) expected 3.7 percent growth. Though optimistic, the administration's 4.2 percent projection was far from absurd or unprecedented; the annual growth rate in the 1960s, after Kennedy's tax cut, had been as high as 8 percent. The Reagan projections were actually *lower* than the growth rates of the first two years of Carter's presidency—5.5 percent growth in 1977, 4.8 percent in 1978. In 1976 the outgoing Ford administration had projected 6.5 percent growth for 1977 and 1978, which by comparison could have been called the Raging Sunflower Scenario. And the Carter administration's last budget forecast, amazingly enough, projected 3.5 percent growth in 1982, not that far below what Reagan's team expected. William Niskanen of Reagan's Council of Economic Advisers rightly protested in his memoir: "The initial Reagan forecasts did not deserve the later characterization as a 'rosy scenario,' however optimistic they appeared in retrospect."[61]

The non-supply-side economists at the Council of Economic Advisers and at OMB, however, noted what they saw as a contradiction in the Treasury forecast. In order to bring inflation down, it was assumed, the Federal Reserve would reduce the growth of the money supply, which the Fed had let get out of hand in the summer and fall of 1980 (in an attempt, Milton Friedman thought, to assist Carter's reelection chances). But lower monetary growth, according to orthodox economic thinking, would restrain GDP growth.

This dispute turned on some of the technical aspects of monetary theory, especially the velocity of money, which in commonsense terms means how quickly a dollar turns over in the economy. More broadly, the argument was about whether it is possible to restrain high inflation without slower growth or even a recession. The conventional view was that high growth led the economy to overheat, which pushed inflation higher. The supply-siders, however, argued the heterodox view that it was not inherently impossible for a nation to reduce inflation while enjoying higher growth. Paul Craig Roberts pointed to Japan, which had made a steady and gradual transition from 24 percent inflation and negative growth in 1974 to a robust 6 percent growth with 3.6 percent inflation in 1979—this during the same period that oil prices were soaring.[62] (Unlike the United States, Japan imported virtually all of its oil.) The Treasury supply-siders argued that their scenario would work if a gradual reduction in money growth accompanied a steady decline in inflation. The Reagan forecast predicted that inflation would drop according to the following schedule: 1981, 11 percent; 1982, 8.2 percent; 1983, 6.2 percent; 1984, 5.4 percent; 1985, 4.7 percent. *Besides,* some of the supply-siders said, *if you really want to tame inflation, we have another answer for you: return to the gold standard.* This was always the point in the discussion where jaws dropped or neck veins bulged among the more traditional economists; it really did start to seem like voodoo economics, even to so hearty a Reagan stalwart as Milton Friedman.

The argument over the forecast was matched in its intensity by the argument over how the policy was to be understood and explained to the American people. A truncated *Economic Report of the President* would be released along with the policy details on February 18. This report became the focus of as much debate as the economic forecast itself. The Treasury Department contracted with George Gilder to write an introduction to the report. Gilder had just ascended to the top of the best-seller list, and earned himself a glowing profile on *60 Minutes,* with his supply-side treatise *Wealth and Poverty.*[63] A better wordsmith for the Reagan revolution could hardly be conceived. Indeed, the dust jacket for *Wealth and Poverty* contained an effusive endorsement from David Stockman: "It shatters once and for all the Keynesian and welfare state illusions that burden the failed conventional wisdom of our era."

Yet Gilder's introduction was discarded. The supply-side analysis that the Treasury Department suggested for the report was also largely laid aside. The news media duly noted the spectacle of the administration debating itself, as the time-honored practice of fighting policy through media leaks proceeded at fever pitch. Leaks suggested that economists in the White House, who had final say over the *Economic Report of the President,* were not comfortable with endorsing the supply-side view of "the way the world works," to borrow Jude Wanniski's iconoclastic supply-side title.

A certain amount of pettiness and ego may have figured in the infighting. Who were Gilder and Wanniski anyway? They were certainly not economists, and they committed the unpardonable sin of writing about economics in plain English. Moreover, who would benefit politically from a full presidential endorsement of supply-side theory? The main beneficiary would be Jack Kemp rather than the person who had said supply-side thinking amounted to "voodoo economics"—Vice President Bush. It is never too early in Washington to think about the politics of presidential succession. An anonymous White House aide confirmed that such a motivation existed, telling *Time* magazine: "There are worse things than having daylight between this Administration and Jack Kemp."[64] The supply-siders at Treasury were dismayed at this turn of events. Roberts sent a memo to a Treasury colleague: "I think it is extraordinary that the first Reagan economic report (even if a mini-report), the first explicitly supply-side President ever elected to office provides no explanation whatsoever of the new policy that he is the carrier of and for which he had made so many claims."[65]

The source of Roberts's frustration is easily seen in the report that was finally issued on February 18. "The *leading edge* of our program," the report said, "is the comprehensive reduction in the rapid growth of Federal spending" (emphasis added). Not until near the very end of the report was there the slightest nod to the supply-siders: "In contrast to the inflationary demand-led booms of the 1970s, the most significant growth of economic activity will occur in the supply side of the economy." That was it. For the supply-siders, the austere ghost of Herbert Hoover was haunting their waking dreams, especially when the details of the plan were changed to call for delaying the first 10 percent cut in income tax rates to July 1, instead of being retroactive to January 1 as Reagan had originally proposed.

All of this infighting over the theory and the forecast would expose the Reagan economic plan to severe criticism. The administration's economic forecast determined how much the budget would need to be cut to reach a balanced budget. If the theory backing up the forecast wasn't credible, Congress wouldn't go along with the Reagan plan and the market might respond with even higher interest rates. Most of the Council of Economic Advisers in the White House, along with Stockman at OMB, didn't think the supply-side scenario of rapid, noninflationary growth was credible. Safer to go with a conventional theory than to embrace those crazies over at Treasury. But by sticking with a conventional framework that emphasized budget cuts over supply-side stimulus, the budget plan would of necessity require the spending cuts to be very large and stretch over the next several years.

To understand the dilemma that the Reagan team faced, look at the numbers. Carter left behind a deficit of $59 billion for 1981; Reagan's team hoped to cut that back to $54 billion and then cut the deficit to $45 billion in 1982 and $23 billion in 1983. By 1984, the plan projected, there would be a narrow budget surplus of $500 million, increasing quickly to $30 billion by 1986. But at the same time the tax cut would reduce revenues by about $500 billion over the next five years (so much for the idea that the Reagan plan claimed the tax cut would pay for itself) and defense spending would go up.

More important, the numbers reveal that reducing federal spending as a share of GDP was more important to the administration's plan than balancing the budget—a point lost on Reagan critics both then and now. The Reagan team projected federal spending to decline from 23 percent of GDP in 1981 to 19 percent by 1986. This was a significant change, since spending had risen under Jimmy Carter from 18 percent of GDP in 1976 to 22 percent in 1980. In fact, under Carter's old budget plan, government spending as a share of GDP would have risen to 24 or 25 percent by 1986. The only way Carter would have avoided large deficits, had he been reelected, was through large tax hikes.

Despite the uncertainty, haste, and infighting going on within Reagan's councils, the compromise plan unveiled on February 18 offered a credible scenario, *if* all of its assumptions were borne out. As will be seen, neither the growth rates nor the budget cut targets were achieved. Yet it was the tax cut that would get the lion's share of the blame for the deficits that came. Hindsight in such matters is always perfect, but a sound rule of historical interpretation should be invoked here—namely, to seek to understand past moments as they were understood *at the time* by the people on the spot. As this narrative goes forward it should be kept in mind that although the administration's economic forecast turned out to be wrong, *all the rival public and private sector forecasts were wrong too.*

*   *   *

ACCORDING TO ONE 1980s trivia book, Reagan ate 112 jelly beans on February 18 before heading up to Capitol Hill to unveil his plan, though who could have kept count of such a thing? Reagan's speech followed the outline of the economic report, with the bulk of the message summarizing $41 billion in budget cuts, sometimes in exacting detail ("the Export-Import Bank loan authority [should] be reduced by one-third in 1982"). Reagan's defense of the tax cut was noticeably less assertive than it had been on the campaign trail in the fall.

After more than two decades the speech reads flat and boring. The dramatic effect of speaking for the first time before a joint session of Congress, with its bursts of ritualistic applause at every pregnant pause, masked the fact that it was an uninspiring speech. Reagan hadn't liked the draft his speech-writing department sent to him, and he rewrote it himself. For once Reagan's muse deserted him—perhaps a case of jitters over his first address to a joint session of Congress; the speech bore few of his trademark rhetorical flourishes. *Time* magazine noted that the speech, "studded with statistics, lacked Reagan's unique verbal tang."[66] But Reagan could make the telephone directory sound like Pericles's funeral oration, and the speech had its intended effect. A poll the next day showed two-thirds of the public backing Reagan's plan; phone calls to the White House ran eleven to one in Reagan's favor.

Thus was the stage set for one of the most remarkable political battles of modern American history, stretching through the spring and summer of 1981. Although Reagan was in a strong position, the opposition to both his budget cuts and his tax cuts was already rumbling. Speaking to a group of visiting state legislators a few days before his speech, Reagan predicted: "I can assure you, by morning I'll be hung in effigy. The screams will be heard from border to border and coast to coast."

James Baker and others described the three top priorities of the Reagan administration in those early months of 1981 as "the economy, the economy, and the economy." This is only figuratively true. Reversing forty years of economic policy was not Reagan's only top goal; he also sought to reverse twenty years of foreign policy drift. While circumstances required that he move at light speed on the economy, the circumstances of foreign policy in 1981 dictated that he move very slowly. To this part of the story we now turn.

CHAPTER 3

"LIE, CHEAT, STEAL . . ."

We were not to know it at the time, but 1981 was the last year of the West's retreat before the axis of convenience between the Soviet Union and the Third World. . . . "There is new leadership in America, which gives confidence and hope to all in the free world."
—MARGARET THATCHER, *THE DOWNING STREET YEARS*

IN ONE OF the favorite conservative books of the pre-Reagan era, *Suicide of the West,* James Burnham wrote: "A political figure who suggests that Peace may not be unqualifiedly the supreme object of national policy runs the risk of being scalped at sunrise by the leading hatchetmen of liberal journalism." Reagan, who was familiar with Burnham through his regular column in *National Review,* might have had Burnham somewhere in the back of his mind when, in his first press conference as president nine days after inauguration, leading media hatchetman Sam Donaldson asked Reagan what he thought the Soviet Union's long-range intentions were.[1] "Do you think, for instance," Donaldson asked, gilding his question, "the Kremlin is bent on world domination that might lead to a continuation of the Cold War, or do you think that under the circumstances détente is possible?"

In the course of pursuing the presidency, Reagan had moderated several of his saucier positions on domestic issues such as Social Security and the Civil Rights Act of 1964. Donaldson's question was designed to see whether Reagan would now trim his hard-line rhetoric about the Soviet Union, and Donaldson's use of the phrase "world domination" was a specific reference to what liberals long thought a laughable and unserious tic of conservative anti-Communist rhetoric. More broadly, what was on the minds of the foreign policy elite was whether Reagan, like Richard Nixon before him, would embrace at least a modified détente once in office.

Reagan's answer stunned the room:

> Well, so far détente has been a one-way street that the Soviet Union has used to pursue its own aims. . . . I know of no leader of the Soviet Union since the revolution, and *including the present leadership,* that has not more than once repeated in the various Communist congresses they hold their determination that their goal must be the promotion of world revolution and a one-world Socialist or Communist state. . . . Now, as long as they do that and as long as they, at the same time, have openly and publicly declared that the only morality they recognize is what will further their cause, meaning they reserve unto themselves *the right to commit any crime, to lie, to cheat,* in order to attain that, that that is moral, not immoral, and we operate on a different set of standards, I think when you do business with them, even at a détente, you keep that in mind. (Emphasis added)[2]

That was it. Next question.

There was an audible gasp among the press corps in the briefing room. Some of Reagan's own aides, cowering in the corners of the room, blanched. This was not the way world leaders talked about other nations. This was the most blunt presidential language since Harry Truman dressed down Soviet foreign minister Vladimir Molotov two weeks after succeeding Franklin Roosevelt in 1945. "I've never been talked to like that in my life," Molotov complained to Truman, who replied tersely, "Carry out your agreements and you won't get talked to like that."[3]

At least Truman said this in private, not to a public press conference. The Soviets had long since pegged Reagan as, in the words of Anatoly Dobrynin, the Soviet ambassador to the United States, "an extreme right-wing political figure" who was a vehicle for "representatives of the most conservative, chauvinist, and bellicose part of American politics." Of course, Dobrynin's description is not that different from what many career staff in the State Department and the CIA were thinking and saying about Reagan. (Alexander Haig wrote in his memoirs that upon arriving at the State Department he found that "the fear was abroad that a legion of right-wing activists were going to march in and start conducting American diplomacy according to the rules of a political rally.") Likewise, many career staff probably sympathized with Dobrynin's recollection that "[t]hose early Reagan years in Washington were the most difficult and unpleasant I experienced in my long tenure as ambassador. Ronald Reagan's presidency revived the worst days of the Cold War."[4]

*   *   *

TODAY RONALD REAGAN'S association with the surprising end of the Cold War in the late 1980s is his most prominent attribute in the public mind. While this accolade is fully deserved, in fact he did not come to office with a detailed foreign policy commensurate with his economic policy—that is, a specific action plan that would shape decisions on hot spots such as Central America and the Middle East, as well as opening a new avenue of engagement with the Soviet Union. To be sure, however, he had a general strategy and several guiding principles. Reagan's central insight into the problem of superpower relations was that the current mode of interaction, which had attempted to convert political differences into technical differences that could be bargained away through the arms control process, needed to be swept away, just as much as the debilitating income tax rates needed to be swept away to fix the American economy.

Here the domestic and foreign parallel is apt and again shows the unity of Reagan's statecraft. At some level, Reagan understood that just as the economy required a period of painful readjustment to right itself, reorienting superpower relations would require a difficult period of readjustment as well. It would have to start by saying no and increasing Cold War tensions to crystallize the fundamental moral problem at the root of the conflict. Reagan had long yearned to be able to say *nyet* across the table to the Soviets in the face of a bad arms control deal such as the second Strategic Arms Limitation Treaty (SALT II), even as he proceeded to build up America's military power as a deliberate means to bring pressure on the Soviets. He would get this chance several times during his presidency before finally saying *da*, but before that he had to find more than a new framework for negotiations. He needed to be able to get the Soviets to the negotiating table on his own terms.

In contrast to economic policy, where the crisis of the moment demanded rapid action, reversing the inertia of the long years of détente required patience. Hence Reagan got off to a slow start on foreign policy. Partly this was by design: the paramount importance of focusing on the economy in 1981 meant that, as a practical matter, foreign policy would have to wait. Besides, the key aspect of Reagan's policy was a defense buildup, and this would take time. Although the outline of what Reagan would summarize as a strategy of "peace through strength" had long been present, the robust and aggressive strategy that would become known as the Reagan Doctrine was not yet in sight. In the first year of his presidency, the administration's foreign policy statements came in dribs and drabs, usually in response to media questions. Secretary of State Haig made some waves—more than the White House would have preferred—and Reagan's occasional improvisations were not always helpful. Reagan offered no grand vision, in contrast to his four nationally televised speeches about his economic policy in his first six months.

In April a *Washington Post* headline declared, "100 Days and Still Groping for a Foreign Policy." The Reagan foreign policy team, the *Post*'s Robert Kaiser wrote, is "not at all ready to explain a coherent approach to world problems." *New York Times* foreign affairs columnist Anthony Lewis chimed in: "In 100 days the Reagan Administration has set a record for confusion and contradiction in foreign policy." The *Wall Street Journal* ran an editorial entitled "The Foreign Policy Vacuum." *Newsweek,* observing that Reagan's foreign policy had been "marred by a confusion of signals on a series of issues" quoted an anonymous White House aide as saying, "We know where we want to go. We just don't know quite how to get there."[5] William Safire wrote that Reagan was "embarrassingly unprepared on foreign policy." *Pravda* got in on the act, zinging Reagan's "zigzag" foreign policy. Walter Laqueur wrote in *Commentary* at the end of the year: "Reviewing the first year of the Reagan foreign policy one is driven to the conclusion that a strategy is not yet in sight."[6] Even Reagan's friends at *National Review* noted the "disarray" and "untidiness" of Reagan's foreign policy in the spring of 1981 and returned to this theme in the fall, lamenting that "we still lack an overarching strategic design in our foreign policy."[7] While Reagan was naturally less perturbed than the media chin-pullers by this seeming lack of coherence, he did acknowledge the perception in a personal letter he wrote to a friend in July 1981. "I know I'm being criticized for not having made a great speech outlining what would be a Reagan foreign policy. I have a foreign policy; I'm working on it. I just don't happen to think that it's wise to always stand up and put in quotation marks in front of the world what your foreign policy is."[8]

Beneath the implied canniness of Reagan's remark that his purposes might be better served by a degree of Machiavellian concealment, it is necessary to recover the world as Reagan found it in 1981 to understand both his eventual policy and his achievement. While in economic policy the crisis atmosphere and massive public support gave him the upper hand necessary to push through his tax cut plan in the face of bitter opposition, in foreign affairs circumstances were more ambiguous, and the opposition to Reagan's conception of the world was even more bitter and entrenched. A nation's foreign policy is like an oceangoing supertanker: its forward momentum (or what might be called the bias toward continuity) makes it difficult to change direction quickly. Reagan inherited a foreign policy establishment, including many within his own party, that longed for a resumption of the palmy days of détente as it had unfolded under President Nixon (not to mention our European allies, who were deeply wedded to an accommodationist policy toward the Soviet bloc). This guaranteed that there would be a fierce institutional undertow against any bold initiatives Reagan might conceive. Public opinion was afflicted with cognitive dissonance: the public supported a military buildup and "standing up to the Russians" but favored negotiations and remained wary of U.S. intervention.

At the root of both the elite attitude of appeasement and the public nervousness about asserting American power was the lingering crisis of self-doubt that had come to be known as the "Vietnam syndrome." The still-too-fresh memory of Vietnam would provide the backdrop for foreign policy disputes in the 1980s and the template through which especially liberals analyzed nearly every American involvement beyond U.S. borders. (The Left still does today, as the discourse over the Iraq War demonstrated.) The searing memory of Vietnam had roughly the same clouding effect on America's outlook as World War I had on Great Britain during the 1930s: the British averted their gaze from Hitler's rise and sloughed off Churchill's warnings. Reagan had fully absorbed this lesson. Although the election of 1980 was clearly seen as the end of the New Deal era in domestic affairs, it was less clear whether or how it would mark the end of the Vietnam syndrome in foreign affairs.

In a nutshell, the Vietnam syndrome could be said to be the doubtfulness of America's military capacity and resolve along with a presumptive guilt about the role of American power and influence in the world. For a certain cast of mind, Vietnam was not merely a military and foreign policy folly but the paradigmatic expression of modern America's imperial overreach and misperception about the nature of the superpower struggle. Many liberals had invested considerable intellectual capital in the Vietnam syndrome and would not yield easily to a return to Cold War thought. *New York Times* foreign affairs columnist Anthony Lewis, for example, wrote in the 1970s, "The United States is the most dangerous and destructive power in the world." The president of a major university went further in 1971: "In 26 years since waging a world war against the forces of tyranny, fascism, and genocide in Europe we have become a nation more tyrannical, more fascistic, and more capable of genocide than was ever conceived or thought possible two decades ago. We conquered Hitler but we have come to embrace Hitlerism." The British writer Malcolm Muggeridge had called this kind of thinking "the great liberal death wish."

Beyond the liberal intelligentsia was a confused public. Military doctrine could be reformed and tactical prowess could be rebuilt, but the apprehensive mood of the nation could not be fixed merely with a larger defense appropriation. Reagan's remark during the 1980 campaign that the Vietnam War had been a "noble cause" set off a media firestorm.[9] The wounds of Vietnam received a fresh salting right at the outset of his presidency when a controversial design for a Vietnam War memorial on the National Mall was selected from among fourteen thousand competing entries in a contest. A Yale University architecture student named Maya Lin proposed what she called "a rift in the earth" consisting of a black marble V-shaped wall featuring the names, in chronological order, of all 57,692 men killed in Vietnam. Critics noted that most memorials are made of white rather than black marble, and rise above the landscape rather than disappearing below it. The monument seemed calculated to express in less than subtle form the antiwar movement's understanding of Vietnam: the soldiers had sacrificed their lives for nothing. *National Review* spoke for numerous critics in judging that "it will be a perpetual disgrace to the country and an insult to the courage and the memory of the men who died in Vietnam."[10] Clearly the passions over Vietnam had not subsided.

During the ebbing days of Vietnam in the early 1970s the United States was overcome by a sense of strategic exhaustion, for which détente had been the perfect relief. Even though détente had come apart, most foreign policy thinkers felt that it would be better to try to revive détente in some form rather than return to the tense atmosphere of outright confrontation from the 1950s and early 1960s. That approach had nearly blown up the world in 1962. Détente, for all its failings, had held out the promise that such a prospect was unnecessary.

Therein lies the nub of the problem as Reagan saw it in 1981. Between the strategic exhaustion of the post-Vietnam era and the corrosive effect of self-deluding and revisionist liberalism, the fundamental conflict between the West and the East had given way to the view that it was all somehow a "misunderstanding" that would yield to the solvents of "confidence-building measures."[11] Reagan understood that it was not possible to build genuine bilateral confidence when one of the parties had lost its own. Cold War historian Derek Leebaert noted that "Reagan came to office saying nothing about communism's threat that John Kennedy had not declared twenty years before." Yet in the intervening years the disaster of Vietnam and the false dawn of détente had sapped the moral courage of the West such that JFK's language seemed baroque, at least to the chattering classes. It was now permissible to say that the United States and the Soviet Union had "different" values, but it was beyond the pale to suggest that Soviet values were "evil."

Yet Reagan wanted to do much more than simply return to a robust anti-Communist foreign policy; he had spoken openly to his aides of wanting to *win* the Cold War, a hitherto unthinkable notion. Most notably, he told his future national security adviser, Richard Allen, sometime in 1979 that his view of the Cold War was simple: "We win, they lose. What do you think of that?" Reagan rejected coexistence and agreed with the orthodox conservative view that containment was a losing strategy in the face of determined revolutionists. Following Lincoln's policy on slavery, Reagan wanted to place Communism on the course of ultimate extinction. Like Lincoln just after his election in 1860, Reagan probably didn't think it could be done during his presidency (as indeed it wasn't). But as with Lincoln in 1861, events would unfold in a course he did not foresee.

Reagan never fully articulated his view on winning the Cold War during his 1980 campaign or at the outset of his presidency; he probably knew it was so far beyond conventional thinking that it would lose him votes, and in the early weeks of his administration he knew that prudence dictated a nearly exclusive focus on passing his economic plan in Congress, before his precious Capitol Hill clout started to decay. In some ways Reagan's approach turned the Marxist dialectic on its head: to end the Cold War, it was necessary to bring it back to full strength, in order to heighten the contradictions of the Communist system rather than those of the capitalist system. This would require patience as well as steady determination.

Reagan has been described as an "old man in a hurry," but in fact he displayed remarkable patience in allowing his foreign policy to take shape. First he needed to make his own government as well as the Soviet Union realize that he meant what he said. Lots of smart and influential people simply didn't believe Reagan, or at least didn't believe he could craft a serious hard-line policy in the face of massive institutional pressure to yield. Henry Kissinger had reassured Anatoly Dobrynin shortly before the election that if Reagan won, he would not continue with his harsh anti-Soviet rhetoric. Nixon, in a separate communication with Dobrynin two days after the election, offered a similar assurance. But Reagan didn't let up, even after his shocking "lie, cheat, and steal" comment at his first press conference led the media and the foreign policy establishment to push him to moderate his language. In early March Reagan reaffirmed his view in a TV interview with Walter Cronkite: "They have told us that their goal is the Marxian philosophy of world revolution and a single one-world Communist state, and they're dedicated to that." In essence Reagan's view was straightforward: why should we think they don't mean what they say at their annual party congresses and manifestoes? Western sophisticates always wanted to change the subject in the face of such an uncomfortable question.

That Reagan didn't relent on his rhetoric came as a shock to the Soviets— and America's European allies. West German chancellor Helmut Schmidt, Reagan's first foreign visitor after the election, spent ninety minutes trying to persuade Reagan to abandon his anti-Communist rhetoric in the interest of preserving harmony within NATO. Reagan responded by telling Schmidt his favorite joke about Soviet leader Leonid Brezhnev: Brezhnev was showing off his collection of expensive foreign cars to his mother, who said, "That's fine, son, very fine. But what happens if the Commies come and take it all away?" Reagan aide Richard Pipes observed that this joke sent Schmidt to "the verge of apoplexy . . . [W]ith his humorous digression Reagan was conveying: 'Don't tell me what to do about the Soviet Union. My mind is quite made up.' "[12] Reagan's attitude, Dobrynin wrote, led to "angry and emotional" meetings of the Politburo in Moscow in the weeks after Reagan took office. The Politburo realized that "détente could not be recovered as long as Reagan remained in power. . . . [T]he collective mood of the Soviet leadership had never been so suddenly and deeply set against an American president."[13] KGB chief Yuri Andropov frankly warned at a Politburo meeting in May 1981 that Reagan was likely to launch a nuclear attack against the Soviet Union. Andropov ordered the KGB to organize a special surveillance program in the United States—code-named Operation RYAN—to look for signs of preparations for an attack.

Reagan liked to quip about détente: "Détente—isn't that what a farmer has with his turkey—until Thanksgiving Day?" He understood what Dobrynin, but not the U.S. foreign policy elites, admitted: "Soviet leaders after Stalin were content to see détente as a form of class struggle."[14] International relations professor Angelo Codevilla described détente more directly as "a sophisticated attempt to bribe the Soviets not to use their guns."[15] Beyond the flabbiness of détente, though, Reagan's outlook appeared to be sympathetic with a deeper strain of conservative pessimism (liberals called it paranoia) about the long-term prospects for the East-West confrontation. Many conservatives thought the West was going to lose.

Lose the Cold War? Today the very notion is considered ridiculous. The outcome seems obvious with the benefit of hindsight, and it is becoming an act of provocative revisionism merely to recapture the facts and perceptions of the time. The neo-Kantian framework for understanding the world that Reagan sought to overthrow nowadays champions the view that Reagan's confrontational policy *delayed* the end of the Cold War. The ground of this debate has searching implications for policy in the age of terrorism.

A good summary statement of the conservative outlook on the Cold War can be found in the writings of James Burnham. In *Suicide of the West,* Burnham wrote: "If communism continues to advance at the rate it has in fact maintained since it began operating as a distinct organization in 1903, it will achieve its goal of world power before the end of this century: well before that, indeed, because the continuing advance of communism, combined with Western withdrawals from regions not yet communized, would throw the world strategic balance decisively in favor of the communist enterprise some time before the direct extension of its rule over all the world."

All of the trends in the two and a half decades since Burnham penned these words bolstered his judgment. Margaret Thatcher agreed that "the West had been slowly but surely losing" the Cold War.[16] Jimmy Carter's outgoing CIA chief, Stansfield Turner, reported that "since the mid-1970s, an assertive, global Soviet foreign policy has come of age." The first National Intelligence Estimate produced under Reagan concluded, "This more assertive Soviet behavior is likely to persist as long as the USSR perceives that Western strength is declining and as it further explores the utility of its increased military power as a means of realizing its global ambitions."[17]

A look at the global chessboard in 1981 found the Soviets or their proxies on the move in nearly every region of the world. The most notable Soviet presence was in Afghanistan, where by 1981 the Soviets had deployed eighty thousand combat troops. Soviet forces fought with a ferocity that showed they were determined to pacify the country. A fierce resistance (which the United States partially supplied) stymied Soviet efforts, such that they never effectively controlled more than 20 percent of the nation. The CIA judged that the Soviets had their hands full digesting Afghanistan, but no one could be sure that the move wasn't the first step in a plan to achieve Peter the Great's ambition of gaining a warm-water port for the Russian empire on the Indian Ocean. The suspicions deepened when considered alongside Soviet activities of supplying arms and advisers to several African and Middle Eastern governments and to guerilla factions fighting the governments in several more. In addition to arms shipments, the Soviets were playing the foreign aid game to the hilt, dispensing $34 billion in the second half of the 1970s (including $2 billion a year to Cuba). We also knew from human intelligence—a highly placed mole inside the Warsaw Pact military command—that the Soviets had a serious war-fighting plan to sweep quickly through Western Europe, beginning with decapitating nuclear strikes at key NATO installations.

The most ominous trouble spot outside Eurasia was Central America, where revolutionary Nicaragua was serving as a conduit for Soviet and Cuban arms shipments to rebels in troubled El Salvador. (American-made weapons seized from the Salvadoran rebels turned out to be weapons that had been lost to North Vietnam during the Vietnam War.) In early 1981 Salvadoran rebels launched what they called their "final offensive," but it failed to topple the government. Nevertheless, the Nicaraguan-Salvadoran intrigue looked like an effort to destabilize a region on America's doorstep, a step in the strategic encirclement of the United States that anti-Communists had long predicted. When Reagan dispatched two dozen military advisers to El Salvador, the American Left, on hair trigger against American intervention anywhere, warned that Central America might become "another Vietnam." "U.S. out of El Salvador" or the less coherent "No Vietnam War in El Salvador" became popular graffiti slogans in Berkeley, Madison, Ann Arbor, Cambridge, Greenwich Village, and other fashionable neighborhoods. A popular bumper sticker read: EL SALVADOR IS SPANISH FOR VIETNAM.

The question of nuclear arms overshadowed considerations of geopolitics. Liberals had been proven wrong about Soviet strategic intent. In 1965 Defense Secretary Robert McNamara confidently declared, "There is no indication that the Soviets are seeking to develop a strategic nuclear force as large as ours." But that's exactly what they did, during which time the CIA consistently underestimated the extent of the buildup. In 1981 the United States still had the edge in the total number of nuclear warheads—the United States had eight thousand warheads to the Soviets' six thousand—but the Soviets were leaping ahead in the number of accurate land-based missiles and the megatonnage of their warheads; at present rates of production (allowed under the unratified SALT II treaty) the Soviets were expected to have sixteen thousand warheads by 1985.[18] (In 1981 the Soviets had five ICBM assembly plants producing missiles; the United States had none.) The combination of increasing stockpiles of warheads fitted on an arsenal of accurate land-based missiles was the basis for what Reagan called America's "window of vulnerability."

In the mid-1970s Henry Kissinger asked, "What in the name of God do you do with nuclear superiority?" Winning a nuclear war seemed unthinkable, though signs appeared occasionally in Soviet military doctrine that could convey the impression that they thought they might be able to. The most recent edition of the Soviet military encyclopedia contained references to the possibilities of winning a nuclear exchange, and Soviet military doctrine was replete with references to Karl von Clausewitz's classic understanding of war as a continuation of politics.[19] (There was special emphasis on Clausewitz's principles of surprise and concealment.) This could be discounted as military bravado intended for the indoctrination of the troops, but what was to be made of the extensive civil defense preparations in the Soviet Union?

Short of intending to win a nuclear war, an equal or superior nuclear force provided more latitude for Soviet action and would constrict the West's options in any regional crisis. This was already apparent in the Middle Eastern crisis of 1973. In addition to building up its nuclear forces, the Soviets had augmented its conventional forces. As of 1980 the Soviet Union had 4.8 million men under arms, with 180 divisions, backed up by 50,000 tanks and 20,000 artillery pieces. They were building 1,000 fighter aircraft a year, and in Eastern Europe alone the Soviets fielded 3,500 bombers and fighter aircraft. The Pentagon estimated that the Soviets' military production capacity expanded by a third during the 1970s.

The configuration of these forces indicated they had in mind more than just homeland defense.[20] The Soviets were building a high-seas fleet, complete with a new generation of battleships and aircraft carriers that would complicate NATO's command of the North Atlantic in any prospective war. The new Soviet navy had evolved well beyond being a counterforce to U.S. naval dominance. The Soviets were also developing amphibious attack capabilities and were staging elaborate amphibious exercises with non–Eastern European allies such as Syria.[21] In addition to the Syrian exercises, U.S. intelligence noted extensive Soviet military liaison activity with Yugoslavia, South Yemen, Ethiopia, and Kuwait, leading some analysts in the summer of 1981 to speculate that "Moscow may be touching bases in anticipation of a full-scale Middle Eastern war within the next six months."[22]

Even the pro-détente, appeasement-minded Europeans were now alarmed about the Soviet Union. According to one West German poll, the number of Germans who felt threatened by the Soviets nearly doubled—from 35 to 63 percent—between 1979 and 1980. In Canada, 62 percent told pollsters they believed the chance of nuclear war was greater than a decade before; in 1970, the number had been only 10 percent. In the Netherlands, 39 percent—a high number for the Low Countries—believed the Soviets were a "serious danger." In Britain, 64 percent said they believed Warsaw Pact military forces were stronger than NATO forces (53 percent of West Germans also held this view). More ominously, 65 percent of Britons believed that a third world war was coming; almost half guessed that it would come within the next five years.[23] A fictional narrative of what such a war would be like, retired British general Sir John Hackett's *The Third World War: August 1985,* was a runaway best-seller on both sides of the Atlantic in 1979 and 1980. "The warning was as clear as any given by Hitler before the Second World War," Hackett wrote in words that echoed Ronald Reagan. "The steady build-up of offensive military power was not only wholly consistent with a determination to impose Soviet-Russian ends by force of arms if necessary. It was hardly consistent with anything else."

Although the Western alliance triumphed in Hackett's grim narrative, his scenario depended on two notable points. First, it assumed that the Western alliance, following the flaccidity of the 1970s, had engaged a significant rearmament program starting in the early 1980s, providing the West with the means to trump Soviet arms. Second, it envisioned a Soviet Union emboldened by the weakness of a Republican southern governor elected to succeed President Carter in 1984. Obviously Hackett wrote that before the 1980 election of Reagan was in prospect, yet it raised the pertinent question of whether this genial new president would exhibit weakness.

Before Reagan's election the United States and the NATO alliance agreed to increase defense spending to counter the Soviet buildup. But Moscow compelled a much tougher decision than mere dollars. Since the mid-1970s the Soviet Union had deployed hundreds of multiple-warhead intermediate-range nuclear missiles—SS-20s—in Ukraine and other western locations, which brought all of Europe within range. The deployment of SS-20s completely upended the existing deterrent logic of NATO. Western defense doctrine rested the defense of Europe against superior Soviet conventional forces on the American nuclear umbrella; in other words, the threat of an American nuclear strike on the Soviet Union held the Soviets in check. The potential flaw in this deterrent was whether the United States would be willing to put its own cities at risk of retaliation from Soviet intercontinental ballistic missiles (ICBMs).

So in 1979 the NATO allies reached the difficult decision to deploy American intermediate-range, single-warhead nuclear missiles—108 Pershing IIs and 464 cruise missiles—in Europe as a counter to the Soviet missiles. This hardly represented an out-of-control arms race; even a full deployment of this battery would leave the Soviets with a four-to-one advantage in total intermediate range warheads. But deployment wouldn't take place until 1983, during which time it was hoped that there might be an arms control agreement with the Soviet Union to reduce the number of SS-20s and remove the need to deploy the American missiles. In fact, many European leaders didn't want the Pershing and cruise missiles deployed, and agreed to the gambit as a bluff. West Germany was the crucial venue for missile deployment and the weakest link in the alliance. Willy Brandt, the former chancellor of West Germany and the chairman of the ruling Social Democratic Party (SPD), declared, "The SPD has cast its decision [to support deployment] not in order that arms will necessarily be increased, but rather so that there can be negotiations on disarmament."[24] The entire issue was closely bound to the SALT negotiations; other senior voices in West Germany's SPD said that the U.S. failure to ratify SALT II would create "a new situation" with regard to deployment of intermediate range missiles.

The Soviets sensed the obvious opportunity to drive a wedge between the United States and Europe, particularly since Reagan's hard-line rhetoric was so unwelcome in Europe. Through propaganda the Soviets would undoubtedly try to turn Reagan's tough posture to their advantage. As a result, Reagan had to proceed carefully, convincing the Soviets that he meant business while keeping the Europeans calm and steady enough to follow through with deployment if negotiations failed. Although the action around the periphery in Asia, Africa, and Central America dominated headlines, the central venue was still Europe. If the Soviets could decouple Europe from the United States, all kinds of possibilities would open up, both economic and military.

Beyond the European question lay the problem of America's window of vulnerability. The Soviets' buildup of ICBMs in the 1970s had brought them to the point where they could deliver three warheads on every American missile silo and every other strategic target using only about half of their missile force. Such a prospect rendered obsolete American nuclear doctrine of massive retaliation and escalation dominance. Although the United States also had a potent arsenal of missile-firing submarines and heavy (though aging) strategic bombers, only land-based missiles were thought to have the accuracy to destroy key Soviet targets in a counterforce strike. The rise of the Soviets' overpowering arsenal had been totally unexpected; in the early 1970s the CIA's intelligence assessments—and Henry Kissinger—had believed that the Soviets would not risk the benefits of détente by building a missile force designed to win a war.[25] And the Soviets showed no signs of slowing down. Even with the most generous game-theory assumptions about the caution of the men in the Kremlin, it was impossible to explain Soviet motivations with an answer that was not disquieting.

Jimmy Carter had agreed without enthusiasm to the development of a new, mobile ICBM, known as the MX. Two hundred MX missiles, each capable of accurately delivering ten independently targeted warheads, would be deployed by 1989. Carter proposed basing the MX missile on a mobile "racetrack," in which missiles would be shunted along hundreds of miles of underground rails connecting forty-six hundred concrete shelters in Utah and Nevada. The Soviets wouldn't know where the missiles were, and wouldn't be able to target all the possible sites without using a large portion of its ICBMs. Building the underground rail basing system would have been the largest construction project in the history of mankind, requiring more concrete than the entire interstate highway system. It was a preposterous idea, and was dead by the time Reagan took office. So Reagan had to solve the problem of finding a way to deploy a mobile missile that had no means of mobility, and that as a result was just as vulnerable as the existing Minuteman missile.

*   *   *

UNDERNEATH THE OVERT signs of gathering Soviet strength, however, were signals of latent weakness. As U.S. intelligence began generating more accurate estimates of Soviet military preparations in the late 1970s, it also began to detect deepening economic and social trouble. In the early 1960s the Soviet Union had boasted that its economic program would generate "the highest standard of living in the world" by 1980, but in fact, as Soviet scholar Martin Malia described the situation, "by the 1980s much of the country was literally crumbling into ruin." On a table of global living standards, the Soviet Union ranked about sixtieth.[26] Third world students who came to the Soviet Union to study often found a standard of living lower than at home. The CIA had judged that the Soviet economy had grown at an annual rate of

3 percent during the first half of the 1970s, slowing to 2.3 percent annual growth from 1976 to 1980. Official Soviet statistics reported growth about twice these levels. In reality, the Soviet economy was shrinking.[27] One sign of their trouble was a steep decline in agricultural production under the watch of the young new agriculture minister, Mikhail Gorbachev. Although the Soviet Union had more than four times the number of tractors as the United States, it managed to produce only one-third as much food.

The Soviets' downward spiral probably began as far back as the 1960s and would have been more acute but for the generous trade credits, investment, and subsidized agricultural sales that flowed from the first flowering of détente under Nixon, along with the oil boom of the 1970s.[28] The Soviets' oil exports accounted for nearly 80 percent of their hard currency earnings in the late 1970s and early 1980s, and mitigated the increasing decrepitude of their economy. The Soviet system was still grinding out centrally directed five-year plans, and official statistics reported that the production targets were being met. Commercial ministries to manage the machine continued to grow, but central bank subsidies to basic industries would rise to 8 percent of GDP by the mid-1980s. Soviet industry was so inefficient that it required three times as much material and labor as a Western country would need to manufacture a comparable product. By the late 1970s, the deterioration had become so pervasive that 40 percent of the state's construction projects were abandoned before completion, up from an estimated 1.7 percent in the 1960s.[29] British historian Robert Skidelsky observed, "The Soviet state deliberately fostered monopolies and gigantomania in order to coordinate production: 73 percent of enterprises had over 1,000 employees."[30]

Measuring an economy without real prices was always a difficult task, which explains the uncertainty and large margin of error in everyone's estimates—including those of the Soviets themselves. Soviet economic accounting was so fraudulent that the KGB used its own spy satellites to estimate domestic crop harvests.[31] While guesses about growth rates might be wildly inaccurate, there were telltale signs of erosion, such as declining exports of raw materials.

The accumulating anecdotes were arguably more revealing. Shortly after the 1980 election the *Los Angeles Times* and *Washington Post* both ran bemusing stories about three separate freight trains bound for Odessa that simply disappeared, victims apparently of piracy. Suspicious conservatives wondered whether these kinds of stories were deliberate misinformation, intended to reinforce the view that the Soviet Union was little threat to the

West. (After all, Soviet intelligence services operated a Directorate of Deception precisely for this kind of misinformation.) Ronald Reagan was not among them. He would refer often to the Soviets' "Mickey Mouse economy," and he loved hearing stories of economic absurdities such as the missing trains. Reagan instructed the State Department to collect Soviet jokes and send them along to him in weekly memos. Paul Goble, head of the Balkan desk at State, collected more than fifteen thousand Soviet jokes during the 1980s. Reagan would later use them on Soviet leaders.[32]

The declining economy had one overarching implication: the Soviet Union could not go on increasing defense spending 4 to 5 percent a year without exacting further deprivations on Russian consumers. U.S. intelligence picked up signs of growing consumer discontent, predicting that it "will cause the regime of the 1980s serious economic and political problems." The lengthening lines for consumer staples were obvious; accounts of strikes appeared in the Soviet press. The commonplace joke in the Soviet Union became "They pretend to pay us, and we pretend to work." For the first time in 1980, the CIA predicted that the Soviet economy would decline in the next decade. Unknown to Western intelligence, some inside Soviet leadership had reached the same conclusion. The KGB's foreign intelligence directorate ran a computer simulation to project future global economic trends and concluded that the United States was winning—and the USSR now losing—the Cold War.[33]

Some of the best indications that the Soviet Union was breaking down came not from intelligence services but from, of all places, the U.S. Census Bureau. In 1980 two Census researchers, poring over official and unofficial Soviet statistics, realized that the health of the Soviet population was collapsing. In the 1950s, Soviet life expectancy was reported to be greater than that of the United States (68.7 years in the USSR compared to 68.2 in the United States in 1950).[34] The Soviets also boasted an infant mortality rate lower than Austria's and Italy's, and close to Belgium's and West Germany's. Demographer Nick Eberstadt noted: "In the face of these and other equally impressive material accomplishments, Soviet claims about the superiority of their 'socialist' system, its relevance to the poor countries, and the inevitability of its triumph over the capitalist order were not easily refuted."[35] But in the 1970s life expectancy suddenly dropped by six years from its 1950s level. For people in their fifties, death rates jumped 20 percent; for people in their thirties, 30 percent. Infant mortality slumped to the level of semi-developed nations such as the Dominican Republic and Panama, but these nations were moving steadily up while the Soviet Union was falling. Birth defects were rising by 5 to 6 percent a year, while the average Soviet woman of child-bearing age had six to eight abortions. This translated into 10 million to 16 million abortions *per year.* (The comparable figures for the United States were 0.5 abortions per woman and roughly 1.5 million abortions per year.) Eberstadt noted, "The only country in modern times to have suffered a more serious setback in life expectancy was the 'Democratic Republic of Kampuchea,' Pol Pot's Cambodia. Clearly, something in Russia is going very, very wrong."

Alcoholism in the Soviet Union was rising in inverse proportion (and probably in direct relation) to life expectancy. Per capita alcohol consumption was estimated to be twice as high as in the United States or Sweden (a half liter per capita per day), though the actual level was likely higher. Soviet households spent as much of their household budget on booze as American households did on food, and alcohol sales may have accounted for as much as one-third of domestic trade volume, as it was the one consumer product even the Soviets' dysfunctional economic system could provide in abundance.[36] Managers in the workplace reportedly judged whether workers were sober enough for their jobs by whether they were able to stand. Most major factories had alcoholic wards where drunk workers could dry out.

More than a million Soviet hospital beds were in facilities that lacked hot water; one-sixth of hospitals had no running water at all, and 30 percent lacked indoor toilets. Some of the Soviet rot began to approach the level of farce: Eberstadt noted that one of the leading cardiac clinics in Moscow was on the fifth floor of a building that lacked an elevator.[37] Eberstadt concluded: "Measured by the health of its people, the Soviet Union is no longer a developed nation." The CIA, meanwhile, missed this entirely, with a senior CIA figure writing in 1977 that the Soviet record in public health was "outstanding."[38]

The decline in public health, like the decline in the nation's economy, could be easily traced to the nation's disproportionate commitment of resources to its military. The supreme effort to build a global military power of the first rank was taking an appalling toll on the economy. The Soviets later admitted that their military spending was more than twice the highest CIA estimate. The Soviet Union, as Martin Malia put it, wasn't a country with a military-industrial complex; it *was* a military-industrial complex. But the decline in public health along with a declining birthrate meant that the Soviet workforce was starting to shrink, and the country would soon begin to face a severe labor shortage. Within the foreseeable future there would not be enough men available to keep up its current troop strength, a fact not lost on military commanders.[39]

Less clear was whether the Soviet leadership class, isolated from the people over whom it ruled, perceived the necessity of reform, or if it did, whether it could act on the impulse.[40] By the early 1980s it was fashionable to refer to the ruling cadre of the Central Committee of the Communist Party as the "gerontocracy." The elderly leadership class in the Kremlin had been propelled into their Party careers as a result of Stalin's murderous Great Purge of the late 1930s, with who knows what distortion to their souls; Brezhnev had been appointed to his first government post (head of strategic rocket forces) by Stalin himself. Russian scholar Leon Aron notes that the Twenty-sixth Party Congress of 1981—Brezhnev's last—"was a strange affair at which the cymbals of victory reverberated through an atmosphere filled with the faint but distinctive smell of decay."[41] By 1981, the seventy-four-year-old Brezhnev, hobbled by a series of strokes and barely able to function, could be seen drooling on himself on his rare appearances on Soviet television. Rather than removing him, however, the Politburo merely nominated him for still more medals. Lenin—the "incandescent" Lenin, as Churchill called him—would have been appalled.

Brezhnev had argued in a secret speech to party leaders in the mid-1970s that by the mid-1980s the "correlation of forces"—the Soviet term used to describe the East-West balance of power—would favor the Soviets and give them the means to take the initiative against the West. Yet by 1981 it might be said that the correlation of forces was swinging in favor of the West. But did this make the Soviet Union less dangerous, as Western liberals argued, or *more* dangerous? The Soviet Union was underfed and overarmed, a dangerous combination. Cold War historian Derek Leebaert reflected: "The fiercely armed yet sclerotic giant might not be long for this world, but no one knew what convulsions, fatal to far more than itself, might disfigure its last moments. The longer the Soviet Union survived in this condition, the greater the chance that something might go horribly wrong."[42] Senator Pat Moynihan argued the case at the time:

> The Soviet empire is coming under tremendous strain. It could blow up. The world could blow up with it. . . . The problem is that the internal weaknesses of the Soviet Union have begun to appear at the moment when its external strength has never been greater. Edward Luttwak has described the present Soviet situation as one of "operational optimism" and "strategic pessimism." The short run looks good, the long run bad. Therefore move. It was the calculation the Austro-Hungarian empire made in 1914.[43]

Moynihan returned to this theme several times in the early 1980s, worrying that desperate Soviet leaders might try "to reverse the decline at home and preserve national unity" by seizing Middle Eastern oil fields.

The collapsing social health, the sclerotic leadership class, and the West's uncertainty about Soviet intentions underscored the USSR's remarkable isolation from the rest of the world, surely the first global power in all of history to be so isolated. The Soviets' self-imposed isolation was increasing at the outset of the 1980s; foreign travel by the *nomenklatura* was sharply reduced beginning in 1981 (with the exception of KGB agents), bringing to mind Churchill's memorable assessment of the USSR written in 1929: "Russia, self-outcast, sharpens her bayonets in her Arctic night, and proclaims through self-starved lips her philosophy of hatred and death."[44] The French writer Alain Besançon said that understanding the Soviet Union requires us to "remain mentally in a universe whose coordinates bear no relationship to our own."

The West proved very poor at this task. Soviet scholars in the United States had a terrible track record of predicting major political changes in the Soviet Union. Leopold Labedz, the longtime editor of *Survey of Soviet Studies*, noted wryly that the only Western journal to predict the ouster of Nikita Khrushchev in 1964 was *Old Moore's Almanac*, which was an astrological journal.[45] (Maybe Nancy Reagan's interest in astrology wasn't so outlandish after all.) Western intelligence, meanwhile, had badly misjudged Soviet military output, the size of the Soviet economy, and Soviet moves throughout the world.

In other words, we didn't have a clue. Better than our intelligence agencies, however, was Ronald Reagan's intuition. Here the most intriguing aspect of Reagan's Cold War strategy comes to the fore. While he warned of the threat of the Soviet military, his instincts told him that the Soviet Union was potentially a house of cards. Perhaps Reagan had a grasp that the general tide of history was moving in his direction. When Margaret Thatcher came to town in February 1981, Reagan said, "Everywhere we look in the world, the cult of the state is dying." The president gave his first public hint of his intuition about the potential demise of the Soviet Union in his commencement address at Notre Dame in May 1981: "The West won't contain Communism, it will transcend Communism. It won't bother to dismiss or denounce it, it will dismiss it as some bizarre chapter in human history whose last pages are even now being written."[46] Ten days later, in a commencement address at West Point, Reagan previewed another rhetorical theme that would later loom large, referring indirectly to the Soviet Union as an "evil force."

Robert Gates, deputy director of the CIA under Reagan (and later director under George H. W. Bush), remarked that "Reagan, nearly alone, truly believed in 1981 that the Soviet system was vulnerable, not in some vague, long-range historical sense, but right then. . . . So he pushed—hard."[47] Indeed, most of the foreign policy establishment, along with the elite intelligentsia, considered it outlandish to suggest that the Soviet system might be weakening. The CIA, Angelo Codevilla noted, "willfully believed in the Soviet Union as a stable communist superpower."[48] Arthur Schlesinger Jr., fresh from a visit to Moscow in 1982, wrote, "Those in the U.S. who think the Soviet Union is on the verge of economic and social collapse, ready with one small push to go over the brink, are . . . only kidding themselves." One prominent group of Western Sovietologists predicted in 1980 that the Soviet economy would continue to grow at a 3.15 percent annual rate through the year 2000. The projection "does not portray a Soviet economy on the verge of collapse."[49] Another leading Sovietologist, Seweryn Bialer of Columbia University, wrote in *Foreign Affairs,* "The Soviet Union is not now nor will it be during the next decade in the throes of a true systemic crisis, for it boasts enormous unused reserves of political and social stability that suffice to endure the deepest difficulties."

Joseph Berliner of Brandeis University and Harvard's Russian Research Center wrote an assessment that deserves to be cited at length to appreciate its comprehensive wrongheadedness:

> The first conclusion is that the [economic] reforms give no evidence of a disposition to doubt the efficacy of the system of central planning as the basis of the economic mechanism. On the contrary, the 1979 Planning Decree affirms the intention to strengthen the planning system by improving the quality of the national plans. In this respect the efforts of the last several decades have probably been successful. The technical equipment now available to planners, including electronic data processing equipment and mathematical modeling techniques for checking the consistency of plans, have no doubt been helpful. We may expect that the plan-making process will continue to improve in the future, although the growing complexity of the economy increases the size of the task from plan to plan.[50]

This is the quality of analysis that emanated routinely from academic departments of Soviet studies and official intelligence agencies right up until the Soviet regime drew its last breath.

*   *   *

CONSERVATIVES SHOULD NOT be exempted from the gallery of intelligent people who missed the signals of Soviet vulnerability. In a sense they had less excuse to miss the cracks in the Communist edifice, in part because conservatives, at least the tradition-minded among them, emphasize the supremacy of the spiritual over the material. And the most significant vulnerability of the Soviet Union on the eve of the 1980s was not its material decrepitude but its spiritual emptiness. Reagan understood this, writing to a friend in the summer of 1981 that "religion might very well turn out to be the Soviets' Achilles' heel."[51]

The challenge first came to sight in the form of an unlikely gnome of a man named Karol Wojtyla, who came from an unlikely place: Poland. Wojtyla is of course better known as Pope John Paul II, and he would become a crucial strategic partner to Reagan during the 1980s. The first non-Italian Pope in 455 years set off alarm bells in the Kremlin when he was selected in October 1978. Before his ascension to the papacy, Wojtyla is reported to have told a group of German bishops that he believed Communism was doomed and might soon collapse.[52] Wojtyla's headline proclamation upon being selected Pope was "Be not afraid!" Be not afraid of *what*? The indirect meaning was clear.

The uncertainty and worry in ruling Communist circles could be seen in the first moments of John Paul's selection; while the news spread instantly across Poland by word of mouth, the state-controlled Polish TV and radio network delayed announcing the news for several hours while the ruling Communist Party worked out its position. A hastily prepared CIA analysis concluded, with typical understatement of the obvious, that a Polish Pope "will undoubtedly prove extremely worrisome to Moscow." (For this keen analysis American taxpayers must pay?) An Italian journalist with good access to the Soviets remarked that "the Soviets would rather have Aleksandr Solzhenitsyn as Secretary-General of the U.N. than a Pole as Pope." The head of the KGB, Yuri Andropov, called the KGB's Warsaw station chief demanding to know, "How could you possibly allow the election of a citizen of a socialist country as Pope?" The Polish ambassador to the USSR was called in for "consultations" in Kiev the day after Wojtyla's selection; one can only speculate what undiplomatic epithets were exchanged. Surely, some Soviets thought, the United States must be behind this.[53]

Poland, the flash point for the outbreak of World War II, the crucible of the Cold War (at Yalta), and the keystone of the Soviet empire in Eastern Europe, would become the point of slippage. In part the growing resistance to Communism reflected the fact that Russian influence and Marxist ideology were broadly detested in Poland. Historian John Lukacs noted at the time, "There is not one intelligent person in Eastern Europe who believes a word of Marxism or Communism. . . . The dissolution of feudalism required hundreds of years. The dissolution of Marxist socialism has taken less than twenty."[54] But the developing rebellion owed much to Poland's religious profile as well. More than 80 percent of the Polish population was Roman Catholic, and the church had long been the one significant focal point of resistance to the Communist regime. "Going to Mass," *Time* magazine noted, "became not only a religious act but a quiet sign of rebellion against the state."[55] Stalin had famously dismissed the importance of the Catholic Church with a quip: "The Pope—how many divisions does the Pope have?"[56] The Soviet Union was about to find out.

The multilingual and charismatic John Paul was a firm anti-Communist; he used to urge parishioners to read samizdat copies of George Orwell's *1984*. He was much more threatening to the Soviet Union than any liberal Eastern bloc politician; he was an intellectual but had maintained a studied distance from politics for much of his life. As such, he had successfully resisted the blandishments of the Polish Communist Party. His frequent preaching about universal human rights, though always carefully worded so as not to attack the state directly, made the government uncomfortable. For a long time the Polish government had been worried that Wojtyla would succeed Cardinal Wyszynski as primate of the Polish Catholic Church. In 1974 a Polish Communist Party official, Andrzej Werblan, had singled out Wojtyla as "the only real ideological threat in Poland."[57] Now he was Pope. His most authoritative biographer, George Weigel, notes that "John Paul II's refusal to accept the Yalta division of Europe as a fact of life was a frontal challenge to postwar Soviet strategy. . . . A Slavic Pope, capable of addressing the restive people of the external and internal Soviet empires in their own languages, was a nightmare beyond the worst dreams of the masters of the Kremlin."[58]

The nightmare was not long in coming. Just months after moving into the Vatican the new Pope announced his intent to visit his home country the following summer; it would be the first-ever visit by a Pope to Eastern Europe. Brezhnev wanted Poland to disallow the Pope's trip entirely, but the Polish government knew this was impossible. Instead the Polish leadership hoped to limit the impact of his visit, haggling over dates and cities to visit, and censoring media coverage of the trip. John Paul originally proposed a two-day visit to Krakow and Warsaw to celebrate the Feast of St. Stanislaw on the nine hundredth anniversary of his death on May 8, 1979, but the Polish government resisted, since this feast day, as George Weigel observed, had "unmistakable overtones of resistance to state power, [and] was simply too much for the regime to contemplate."[59] The Polish government was relieved when the Pope agreed to come in June instead. But John Paul got the better of them: instead of two days and two cities, he would be coming for nine days and visiting six cities. "The regime may have convinced itself," Weigel reflected, "that, by deflecting the visit from the traditional date of Stanislaw's feast, it had won a considerable victory. In fact, the communists had lost a great deal. John Paul happily traded two days for nine, two cities for six."

Millions turned out to see the Pope celebrate what were probably the largest outdoor masses in the history of the church. In Warsaw's Victory Square, the crowd began chanting, "We want God, we want God, we want God in the family circle, we want God in books, *we want God in government orders,* we want God, we want God." Two million turned out for his final mass in Krakow. The government ham-handedly tried to undermine the Pope's visit by circulating a flyer in the public schools that declared, "The Pope is our enemy. . . . Due to his uncommon skills and great sense of humor he is dangerous, because he charms everyone, especially journalists." (One almost wonders whether such a crude broadside wasn't the work of the CIA or secret Catholic sympathizers within the Polish government.) Polish television was careful to focus its camera tightly on the Pope, deliberately avoiding any views of the massive crowds that turned out to see him. These attempts to contain the Pope were hopeless. "For nine days the state virtually ceased to exist," historian Timothy Garton Ash wrote. "Everyone saw that Poland is not a communist country—just a communist state. . . . It is impossible to place an exact value on the transformation of consciousness wrought by the Polish Pope."[60]

There was little doubt about where the real power now lay. The regime cowered. The Soviet ambassador to Poland left the country for the whole week, and the forty thousand Soviet troops based in Poland were confined to quarters, lest any inadvertent provocation occur. The Pope's carefully worded spiritual messages took direct aim at Poland's Communist government and by implication its patrons in Moscow: "The exclusion of Christ from human history is an act against man. . . . There can be no just Europe without the independence of Poland marked on its map." A Polish bishop told *Time* magazine: "The Polish people broke the barrier of fear. They were hurling a challenge to their Marxist rulers." George Will tersely noted: "No Communist leader in Eastern Europe or the U.S.S.R. will ever hear such cheers." John Lukacs concurred: "In Poland the monopoly of the Communist Party is broken beyond repair."[61]

The Soviet leadership in Moscow didn't want to sit back and passively watch events unfold. In November the Politburo passed a six-point policy statement entitled "Decision to Work Against the Policies of the Vatican in Relation with Socialist States." It directed the Communist Parties of the Soviet states bordering Poland to step up propaganda against the Catholic Church. Outside the Soviet bloc, the KGB was ordered to "improve the quality of the struggle against the new Eastern European policy of the Vatican," and above all "to show that the leadership of the new pope . . . is dangerous to the Catholic Church."[62]

Moscow didn't have to wait long for the other shoe to drop. In the middle of August 1980, workers at a shipyard in Gdansk (better known to the prewar generation as Danzig) went on strike to protest sharp increases in food prices by the government. The strike quickly spread to the coal mines of Silesia and other industrial sites; soon more than 750,000 workers (according to official estimates—the real number was probably higher) were off the job. Polish workers in the past had risen up and even rioted against their Communist slave masters to protest price increases and food shortages, in 1956, 1968, and most notably in 1970, when the police and army opened fire on protesters, killing a never-disclosed number. On all the previous occasions, the combination of lethal force and lesser intimidations made the workers skulk back to their jobs and swallow the government's gross economic mismanagement.

This time it would be different. In another irony that seems worthy of being attributed to Providence, the Gdansk shipyard where the first authentic workers' revolt in the Communist world began was named after Lenin. To succeed where previous worker protests had fizzled would require a leader of Lenin-like talent and drive. Such a man came in the form of Lech Walesa, a thirty-seven-year-old unemployed electrician, jailed previously on several occasions for illegal unionizing activities. What Walesa lacked in gainful employment he made up for with abundant charisma. Walesa had red hair and a handlebar mustache, and like Karol Wojtyla was a slight man; many Western press accounts commented on his Chaplinesque appearance. He was a born organizer, and shortly after he climbed the shipyard fence to join the workers (rather than staying off the job, the workers shrewdly decided to occupy the shipyard), he emerged as their leader.

As rumors of a Soviet invasion or a Polish military crackdown grew, the scene at the Lenin shipyard riveted the world's attention. Thousands brought food and flowers to the workers occupying the shipyard. Most ominous for the regime were the pictures of the Polish Pope (who had sent a message supporting the strikers in the first week of their action) hung on the shipyard fence, and the scene of hundreds of workers going to confession and taking communion on the grounds, not only symbolizing the rival power but also defiling the atheist legacy of the shipyard's namesake, Lenin. Soon this incipient labor movement took a name that itself expressed righteous larceny from the so-called ideology of worker empowerment: Solidarity.

Beyond the symbols, though, were some hardheaded demands from Walesa. Solidarity wanted the right to form as a free and independent union, and the right to strike—freedoms unheard of in any Communist country, where the Communist Party claimed to represent the interests of all workers. Events came to a head in late August as the Polish government sat down for negotiations with the strikers inside the shipyard. Walesa theatrically climbed over the shipyard fence at frequent intervals to brief the Western press and the assembled crowds on the progress of the talks.

Signs pointed to a crackdown, with either a rerun of Hungary in 1956 and Czechoslovakia in 1968 or at the very least the imposition of martial law by the Polish government. The threat to the Communist Party's status was not lost on neighboring rulers. The Communist Party rulers in Czechoslovakia, Romania, and East Germany feared that "the Polish disease" would spread next to their countries. The Soviets had good reason for this concern at home, where a series of local strikes had occurred. East Germany and Czechoslovakia in particular urged Moscow to lead a crackdown, and offered to lend troops and tanks for the purpose. The Soviet Union hurriedly drew up contingency plans to send fifteen divisions with up to a hundred thousand troops and fifteen thousand motorized vehicles into Poland for "assistance."

But at this moment the rulers in Moscow and Warsaw blinked. The Polish government apparently decided to play for time, yielding on virtually all of Solidarity's demands. The Gdansk agreement, as it became known, not only guaranteed Solidarity's right to exist as an autonomous union and to go on strike, but also promised to reduce censorship and even to grant access to state TV. In another less-than-subtle sign of the real nature of the political

struggle now under way, Walesa signed the agreement at an outdoor ceremony with a large pen bearing the image of the Pope. The accord was more
than a mere economic agreement; Poles interpreted the episode in explicitly
social terms, and above all stressed that the chief result of the Solidarity movement was an expression of their dignity. Polish poet Stanislaw Baranczak said
it was like coming up for air after living for years under water.[63] In other
words, Solidarity really did represent a spontaneous expression of a recovery
of civil society behind the Iron Curtain. There were actually some tangible
measures to these grand words: according to official statistics, in the months
after the Gdansk accords, suicides in Poland fell by a third, and alcohol consumption dropped by a quarter.[64]

The Soviet Union had not abandoned plans to intervene to stop Solidarity; it had merely postponed an invasion, hoping that Polish authorities could
get control of Solidarity through the fine arts of infiltration and intimidation. Solidarity as an open organization would be easier to control than a
large-scale underground group. After all, Communist intelligence services had
thoroughly penetrated Eastern European human rights groups such as Charter 77 (though this did not diminish the impact of these groups).

Yet contrary to Soviet hopes, Solidarity's initial victory was a disaster for
Polish Communism. A million Poles quit their membership in the Polish
Communist Party over the next few months, reducing its membership to
about two million. A poll taken in the fall found that only 3 percent of Polish
voters would pull the lever for the Communist Party in a free election. Meanwhile, Poles signed up in droves to join Solidarity; the union quickly enrolled
ten million members in regional chapters throughout the country. Most ominous to the rulers was that the membership was overwhelmingly young,
and one-third of the Polish workforce was under the age of twenty-five. The
Communists had lost the next generation. The leader of the Polish Communist Party, Edward Gierek, was sacked. Stanislaw Kania, head of Poland's
intelligence service, replaced him, though increasingly prominent in public affairs and in the communications with the Kremlin was the commander of the
Polish military, General Wojciech Jaruzelski.

The Polish government had no intention of allowing Solidarity to become a full-fledged independent source of power, but the union's momentum
proved unstoppable. In late September Walesa submitted the formal application to have Solidarity registered as a legal trade union. The regime dragged
its feet, and Walesa responded by calling for a one-hour general strike on October 3. Although the state-controlled media refused to broadcast any news

of the strike, Solidarity's own communications network made the strike a nationwide success. The Polish Communist Party Central Committee met for two days of what was described as "vitriolic argument" about what to do. When a judge finally granted Solidarity legal recognition, he added a provision to the union's charter asserting the Communist Party's supremacy over Poland's economy. Solidarity erupted in fresh fury and threatened a day-long general strike. Two days before the strike date, the Polish government backed down and removed the offending clause.

Realizing that the Polish government would be unable to get control of Solidarity, the Soviet Union resumed preparations to intervene late in the year, this time with plans to execute Solidarity leaders by firing squad after summary trials. This then was the state of play in the weeks after the 1980 election, as the CIA, working from detailed reports from its source in the Polish military, briefed President Carter and President-elect Reagan that a Soviet invasion was imminent. President Carter issued public and private messages to the Soviet Union warning of "very grave consequences" if the Soviets intervened in Poland. Carter also got other Western leaders to issue their own warnings to the Soviets (West Germany's Helmut Schmidt warned that "détente could not survive another Afghanistan"), and President-elect Reagan issued a statement backing Carter's actions. AFL-CIO president Lane Kirkland promised to organize a worldwide labor union boycott of Soviet commerce.

For the second time in six months, the Soviets stood down. The Poles had warned the Soviets that Polish resistance to Soviet force might be ferocious; there were even rumors that some units of the Polish military would oppose the Soviet army. The Soviets realized that they had miscalculated Western reaction to their invasion of Afghanistan a year earlier, and that an invasion of Poland would not be a replay of the Czech intervention of 1968.

How much did Soviet fear and uncertainty about the Pope and the incoming American president play into their calculations? It is impossible to say without access to the still-classified transcripts of Politburo deliberations from that period. But there were rumors at the time (incorrect, as it turned out) that the Pope would come to Poland in the event of an invasion, and as the Soviets were struggling with how to come to grips with Ronald Reagan, it is certain that a provocation over Poland would have worked at cross purposes with the incipient diplomatic and propaganda effort to separate the United States from its European allies.

For the time being Solidarity maintained the upper hand, but the Polish story was far from over. This was but the close of the first of three long acts in what became a central drama of the last decade of the Cold War. Although the Soviet and Polish Communists were stymied for the moment in their attempts to subvert or subdue Solidarity by force, they thought patience would bring them more chances to turn the tide. Indeed, as we shall see, subsequent events in Poland would provide the catalyst that finally helped crystallize Reagan's foreign policy after nearly a year of drift and confusion.

The events in Poland reinforced Reagan's instincts about the vulnerability of the Soviet system. In a June 1981 press conference, the first question, from Dean Reynolds of ABC News, was: "Mr. President, last month you told graduates at Notre Dame that Western civilization will transcend communism and that communism is, in your words, 'A sad, bizarre chapter in human history whose last pages are even now being written.' In that context, sir, do the events of the last 10 months in Poland constitute the beginning of the end of Soviet domination of Eastern Europe?"

To this question Reagan responded: "I think the things we're seeing, not only in Poland but the reports that are beginning to come out of Russia itself about the younger generation and its resistance to longtime government controls, is an indication that communism is an aberration. It's not a normal way of living for human beings, and I think we are seeing the first, beginning cracks, the beginning of the end."

Reagan's answer to this would turn out to be exactly correct.

*   *   *

IN ADDITION TO understanding the world situation as Reagan found it upon taking office, it is necessary also to review the starting lineup of his top appointees in foreign policy. The prevailing view of Reagan in Washington, Lou Cannon reminds us at the outset of *President Reagan: The Role of a Lifetime,* was that the White House staff carried Reagan and was responsible for the decisive aspects of policy that emerged from the Oval Office. The prejudice was strongest in foreign policy. Yet Machiavelli reminds us that "good counsel, from wherever it comes, must arise from the prudence of the prince, and not the prudence of the prince from good counsel." In other words, no amount of good advice (and advice is never unanimous) can make up for a lack of judgment by the man at the top; to the contrary, it is the clarity of view of the man at the top that enables advisers to do their jobs constructively. With a few notable exceptions, Reagan showed remarkably good judgment on foreign affairs. This was not always the case with his foreign policy team, and Reagan sometimes had difficulty discerning this. Even when advisers share the essential principles of the president, they will often differ on the application of those principles to day-to-day decisions. Differences on foreign policy were the cause of the worst infighting throughout Reagan's entire presidency.

The adage "Personnel is policy" is perhaps most applicable in foreign affairs, not merely because of the wide sweep of matters that come before the government but also because the senior foreign policy team filters the information and shapes the agenda that reaches the president's desk. This has never gone smoothly in the modern presidency, and Reagan's presidency was no exception. Reagan's attempts to reform the national security and foreign policy apparatus to reduce the natural friction of this domain failed miserably, in part because the inherent nature of the conflict makes the task impossible, and in part because of the personalities of the people involved.

Reagan's initial foreign policy team was, with a few exceptions, arguably the best of his entire presidency. Alexander Haig seemed well suited for the job of secretary of state. He had been a deputy to Henry Kissinger and then chief of staff to President Nixon during the awful final days of the Watergate agony. He had been commander of NATO forces in Europe after leaving the White House, so he was well known to our European allies and understood the dynamics of the Soviet military buildup. He shared Reagan's tough-mindedness about the Soviet Union. Yet he was an unmitigated disaster.

Haig began alienating Reagan and his inner circle starting on Inauguration Day, when the new secretary tried to push through a plan to put himself at the center of all national security policy making. Haig had watched Henry Kissinger control foreign policy from his White House perch as Nixon's national security adviser through the simple expedient of being head of what are known as the Interagency Groups (IGs)—that is, the consultation process on foreign policy making among the State Department, the Pentagon, the National Security Council, and the intelligence agencies. Haig hoped to emulate Kissinger's power, but he was maladroit about pressing for being put at the center of all the IGs. To the White House inner circle, it looked like a power grab; in the press, it was described as an attempted "palace coup." Strobe Talbott observed that Haig fit Churchill's famous criticism of John Foster Dulles as being "the only case I know of a bull who carries his china closet with him."

The inaccurate story was reported in the media that Reagan was still in his inaugural formal wear when Haig tried to get him to sign a formal National Security Decision Directive (NSDD) ratifying the scheme. In fact Reagan never saw it. Haig gave his draft to Ed Meese, who squashed it. The troika—Meese, Baker, and Deaver—were on their guard over Haig from that moment on. Haig came to believe that the troika was out to get him, even as he dismissed them as "second-rate hambones." He disdained his peers in the cabinet too, writing harshly in his memoirs about Cap Weinberger's "foolish statements," adding, "The arduous duty of construing the meaning of Cap Weinberger's public sayings was a steady drain on time and patience."[65] Haig received a humiliating comeuppance in mid-March when the White House announced that Vice President George Bush would head the official crisis management process. The next day Haig wrote out the first of several letters of resignation he would threaten with over the following sixteen months. Reagan had to talk him out of it and issue a public statement affirming Haig's preeminence.

Part of Haig's problem, one Reagan intimate said on a not-for-attribution basis, is that he brought the competitive style and hard-edged mentality (and probably some of the paranoia) of the Nixon White House into the more comfortable and confident Reagan White House, where it fit like a square peg in a round hole. Lou Cannon remarked, "It is difficult to understand why Haig, either at the time or retrospectively, was so totally devoid of insight into Reagan's style of governance." What Haig thought was a take-charge approach seemed more like a takeover approach. Reagan noted in his memoirs that Haig "didn't even want me as president to be involved in setting foreign policy. . . . [H]e wanted to formulate it and carry it out himself." Haig did little to disabuse Reagan or anyone else of this perception, saying in an interview later that "I wouldn't call Reagan a student of foreign affairs. . . . I think that the president at that stage in his life was, on some occasions, less than in total command of an issue."[66] National Security Council staffer Donald Gregg described Haig at cabinet meetings as looking like "a cobra among garter snakes, looking for somebody to bite." Charles Hill, one of Haig's State Department assistants, attributed Haig's abrasiveness to a service academy mentality (Haig was a graduate of West Point) in which "they regard every encounter as a personal confrontation that you have to win." "There was hostility all the time," Martin Anderson recalls.[67] Reagan soon came to share that hostility. NSC aide Richard Pipes observed that Haig's "superior airs visibly annoyed Reagan." Haig, however, was oblivious.

Haig also drew too much attention to himself, even after being asked by James Baker to curtail his TV appearances. He got into a public spat with the Soviets in the early weeks of the administration, and rattled the nation's sabers against Cuba, threatening publicly at one point that the United States needed to "go to the source" of the trouble in Latin America. Privately he advocated that Reagan consider a naval blockade against Cuba, and said at one early national security meeting, "Give me the word and I'll make that island a fucking parking lot," leaving one to wonder whether Haig thought himself secretary of war rather than secretary of state.[68] Reagan's senior aides were alarmed and appalled—alarmed because Haig seemed to be arguing for an openly warlike policy in Latin America, and appalled because an early public fight over Latin America threatened to derail the effort to get the president's tax cut plan through Congress.

Richard Allen, Reagan's national security adviser, was the counterpoint to Haig in almost every way imaginable—stylistically as well as institutionally. Allen was low-key, laid-back, and scholarly rather than bombastic. He had been briefly on Nixon's National Security Council in 1969, until he left after getting crossways with Kissinger. In the 1970s he became a leading critic of détente and wound up as the chief foreign policy adviser to Reagan. Reagan was keenly aware of the infighting that had gone on between the National Security Council and the State Department under Nixon, Ford, and Carter, and sought to avoid that prospect by downgrading the post of national security adviser. Not only would Allen's office be in the basement of the West Wing, rather than the larger main floor office Kissinger had, but he wouldn't even report directly to the president. Allen would be reporting through Meese. The NSC itself shrank along with Allen's office space; the professional staff of the NSC, which had been as many as seventy-five under Kissinger and Zbigniew Brzezinski, was reduced to thirty-three under Reagan.[69]

The downgrade scheme didn't work. The friction between NSC and State is endemic to the institutional overlap, and Reagan was not well served by having barriers between himself and Allen. Allen had the noble intention of acting as a mere staff coordinator between State, Defense, and the intelligence agencies, but in the real world of Washington, weakness in a national security adviser only encourages intransigence among the other principals. "You never really had a day," James Baker said of Reagan's early NSC arrangement, "when the secretary of state and the secretary of defense weren't at each other's throats."[70]

Reagan especially liked to have people with an instinct for public argument in high-profile positions. Two in particular stand out: Jeane Kirkpatrick, whom Reagan selected to be United Nations ambassador, and Max

Kampelman, the one significant holdover from the Carter foreign policy team, whom Reagan wanted to continue in his position as chairman of the U.S. delegation to the Helsinki Final Act monitoring conference in Madrid. The Helsinki Final Act of 1975 lent formal legitimacy to the post–World War II borders of Eastern Europe, which was the Soviets' chief aim in the agreement. This led to bitter criticism at the time, including from presidential candidate Ronald Reagan, that the agreement surrendered the West's moral authority to use the language of the "Captive Nations" about Eastern Europe, and indeed the Soviets celebrated Helsinki as the greatest event since the defeat of Hitler.

However, the West did get a key concession in Helsinki—the commitment of the Soviets and Eastern bloc nations to respect human rights. The Soviets thought they could exploit divisions among European nations and bluster their way through the obvious hypocrisy of their human rights commitment in the follow-up conferences called for in the pact, and they were successful in doing so—until they ran up against Max Kampelman in 1980. Kampelman kept the Soviets on the defensive with relentless detailed accounts of their persecution of Jews and dissidents, and in one closed session even cited the secret 1973 speech in which Brezhnev offered his cynical account of how détente was a ruse to gain advantage over the West. It was an impressive performance that thoroughly irritated the Soviets—exactly the kind of public argument that delighted Reagan. Kampelman would later become one of Reagan's top arms control negotiators.

The notable aspect of these appointments was that Kampelman and Kirkpatrick were both prominent Democrats. Both had been closely associated with Hubert Humphrey's presidential campaign in 1968; Kampelman, in fact, was widely thought to have been Humphrey's pick to be secretary of state had he won the election. That Reagan could reach out to former mainstream Democrats tells us a lot about him—and the drift of the Democratic Party. Kampelman and Kirkpatrick never would have served in a Reagan administration had Reagan succeeded in being elected president in 1968, the time of his first, halfhearted, but nearly successful run for the GOP nomination.

Jeane Kirkpatrick, a professor of government at Georgetown University, had come to Reagan's attention through her famous 1979 *Commentary* magazine article, "Dictatorship and Double Standards." Kirkpatrick's article was a sensation among political intellectuals, and several people passed the article along to Reagan. According to Kirkpatrick's own account, Richard Allen handed Reagan a copy of the article shortly before the candidate boarded a plane in Washington to return to California. Reagan called Allen two hours later when he was changing planes in Chicago, asking, "Who is he?"

"Who is who?" Allen replied.

"Who is this Jeane Kirkpatrick?"

"Well, first, he's a she."[71]

Reagan wrote to Kirkpatrick in December 1979 to praise the article. Her article, Reagan wrote, "had a great impact on me . . . Your approach is so different from ordinary analyses of policy matters that I found myself reexamining a number of the premises and views which have governed my own thinking in recent years." If possible, Reagan closed, "I should very much like to have the opportunity to meet with you and to discuss some of the points you have raised."[72]

Kirkpatrick's appointment was said to be unpopular with some Reagan insiders such as the Kitchen Cabinet, who held against her that she was a Democrat and therefore not a Reagan loyalist. Reagan's decision to give Ambassador Kirkpatrick cabinet rank (following the precedent of Andrew Young under Jimmy Carter) irritated Haig because it meant that Kirkpatrick would have direct access to Reagan and wouldn't need to operate exclusively through State Department channels. Haig—and later George Shultz—regarded Kirkpatrick as a "diplomatic menace" (according to Lou Cannon), and at various times State Department officials acted to undercut her.

But Kirkpatrick had the enthusiastic confidence of the person who counted most—the president. And she did so because she shared his understanding that, as she put it at her Senate confirmation hearing, "[s]peech is an action"—especially in a speech-oriented forum such as the United Nations. She was the ideal person to reprise Pat Moynihan's robust performance of 1975. Kirkpatrick also shared with Reagan an unapologetic view about the so-called dark days of the Cold War in the Truman-Eisenhower years. To the contrary, Kirkpatrick said, "[T]he years of the Cold War were a relatively happy respite during which free societies and democratic institutions were unusually secure. The West was united, strong, and self-assured." At cabinet meetings Reagan would beam at Kirkpatrick and say: "You've taken off that sign that we used to wear that said 'kick me.' "

Reagan's most controversial senior-level foreign policy appointment was William Casey, whom Reagan sent to sort out the CIA. Casey had become chairman of Reagan's faltering 1980 campaign on the day it turned the corner, the New Hampshire primary in February. He was best known as a Wall

Street lawyer and investment banker who had been chairman of the Securities and Exchange Commission (SEC) under President Nixon (he had wanted to head the CIA under Nixon, but got SEC instead). Critics thought him unqualified to head the CIA, which, with the notable exception of George H. W. Bush, typically had been led by Company men or military figures with long ties to the foreign policy establishment. One of Casey's critics was former president Gerald Ford, who said that he was "absolutely surprised" that Reagan selected Casey for the CIA. "He was not qualified to be the head of the CIA," Ford later said, "and his performance justifies my statement."[73]

In fact Casey brought considerable depth to the job. He had served on the President's Foreign Intelligence Advisory Board and had read widely on foreign affairs and intelligence, surely more widely than the members or staff of the congressional intelligence committees. The deeper background he brought to the CIA was his experience with the Office of Strategic Services (OSS), the forerunner to the CIA, during World War II. The OSS, led by the legendary William "Wild Bill" Donovan, had a reputation as a daring, swashbuckling clandestine organization unfettered by either bureaucracy or political constraint. As a member of the OSS, Casey had organized teams of spies to be dropped behind German lines late in the war. Casey's appointment was thought to herald a return to the old rough-and-ready ways of the OSS. For conventional thinkers Casey's "OSS mentality" was the root of his problems; others would count his "OSS mentality" as his greatest asset.

CIA deputy director Robert Gates described Casey as "aggressive, inventive, inexhaustible, [and] as unbureaucratic as anyone can be . . . Casey was one of the smartest people I have ever known and certainly the most intellectually lively."[74] Another of Casey's top deputies, Herbert Meyer, recalled that it was typical for Casey to tell State Department analysts in interagency meetings, "That's the stupidest goddamn thing I ever heard in my life." Though Casey was sixty-seven at the time he became director of central intelligence (DCI), he was a fount of nervous energy. He couldn't sit still in meetings, often fidgeting with paper clips or chewing on the end of his necktie. Gates remarked that "watching Casey eat was not for the squeamish." Casey was most famous for his supposed lack of diction; his "mumbling" became so legendary in Washington that Reagan quipped that Casey was the only CIA director in history who didn't need to use a scrambler phone. On some minutes of National Security Council meetings, Casey's indecipherable comments were recorded as "??????." This seems to have been partly an artifice, though, as many of Casey's interlocutors recall crystal-clear diction on important occasions. Casey seems to have reserved his mumbling for congressional testimony and reporters' phone calls.

Casey had no strong friends or sponsors on Capitol Hill. Senator Barry Goldwater, the new chairman of the Senate Intelligence Committee, had pushed strongly for someone else (Admiral Bobby Ray Inman) to head the CIA, and did not hide his disappointment that his man did not get the nod from Reagan. Some observers attributed Goldwater's coolness to Casey all the way back to 1966, when Casey had challenged a Goldwater-backed candidate for a House seat in New York. Casey's complicated financial history raised congressional and media eyebrows, and several early mistakes generated a rocky relationship with Congress that never abated and which would prove to be a significant liability for the Reagan administration.

Casey reciprocated the Hill's hostility. One of his senior deputies, Duane Clarridge, said that Casey "had a lot of contempt" for congressional oversight committees. With good reason, Casey thought that Congress had intruded too much on the intelligence community with its post-Watergate reforms. The Church-Pike committee hearings in the mid-1970s had developed in response to the refrain from liberals and their media echo chamber that the CIA was a rogue elephant, but the overreaction to CIA missteps of the 1960s and 1970s had nearly euthanized the beast. The reforms, combined with a wave of retirements and dismissals during the Carter years, led to an incredible 90 percent turnover in the CIA's supergrade employees (those with civil service rank of GS-16 through GS-18) between 1975 and 1980.

On top of these problems, morale at the CIA was low. Casey's predecessor, Admiral Stansfield Turner, had not been popular at Langley. The wariness some CIA employees might have had about Casey's overtly political background was mitigated by the fact that the new DCI was close to Reagan, which would count for a lot. Sure enough, Reagan made the post of CIA director a cabinet-level job, which cemented Casey's status at the CIA and within the administration. (Lou Cannon reports, however, that Casey and Reagan met alone only five or six times.)

What Casey found at the CIA was a stifling bureaucracy; Gates wrote that it had slowly turned into the Department of Agriculture. Casey had been around Washington long enough to know that the CIA bureaucracy would not be susceptible to sweeping reform schemes; he had said as much at his confirmation hearings, telling the Senate Intelligence Committee, "This is not the time for another bureaucratic shake-up of the CIA." He also had the requisite distrust of the CIA's inertia. The Soviet dissident Vladimir Bukovsky recalled visiting Casey with a proposal for nasty deeds against the USSR. "It's just great," Casey told him, "but let me give you some advice: don't tell anyone in the CIA about it; they'll screw it up."[75]

He focused instead on trying to get specific divisions of the CIA to conceive of their mission in radically new ways. Casey and Gates did shake up CIA analysts when they announced that henceforth the accuracy of individual reports would be taken into account when it came time for promotions. (Resentful CIA bureaucrats remembered this humiliation eight years later and quietly opposed Gates's nomination by President George H. W. Bush to become CIA director.) Casey brought in new faces from the outside, leased a building in Rosslyn to separate some of his new initiatives from the routine atmosphere of Langley, and became his own case officer after a fashion, traveling abroad frequently to talk firsthand with station chiefs and agents in foreign countries.

Critics believed that Casey and Reagan wanted a revival of cloak-and-dagger clandestine operations, and the subsequent Iran-Contra scandal is offered as the simple proof of this criticism. While this was one element of the Casey program, he was after something more fundamental: he understood that intelligence was not a value-free, depoliticized social science but rather was served and informed by political purpose. As Robert Gates succinctly put it: "Bill Casey came to CIA primarily to wage war against the Soviet Union."

Casey got along smoothly with Weinberger, Allen, and Kirkpatrick and generally saw foreign policy questions the same way. But of course the Reagan foreign policy team divided into factions, with the prickly Haig, most notably, constantly at odds with everyone. Most accounts of Reagan's early foreign policy suppose that infighting among Reagan's advisers accounts for the lack of clear direction in the first year of Reagan's presidency. But perhaps no policy was the right policy. Reagan understood, as Haig did not, that what was most needed in 1981 was patience. He believed that productive relations with the Soviet Union were possible but that it required the recovery of America's confidence and assertiveness. Speeches alone wouldn't make this a reality. Effective policy would require waiting for some opportunities, or perhaps creating some. And so Reagan understood, intuitively at least, that relations with the Soviet Union might have to get worse before they got better.

This necessity, more than a conflict of personalities, accounts for the slow start on foreign policy. One of Reagan's first directives to his cabinet and senior staff was that there were to be no high-level contacts with the Soviet

Union for the first several months of his administration. Reagan wouldn't have his first meeting with Ambassador Dobrynin until 1983. Cap Weinberger said publicly that it would be "at least six months" before arms talks with the Soviets could resume, a statement that did not endear him to Haig, since arms control talks were a matter for the State Department to determine. A number of small signals were sent to make the Soviets understand that the United States would not do business as usual. Ambassador Dobrynin's access to the underground parking lot and private entrance at the State Department was revoked, and he was not informed until he showed up one morning at his customary entrance and was turned away by a low-level guard. Now he had to go in the front door, past the media gantlet, just like the ambassador from Peru or Botswana. Georgi Arbatov, one of the Soviet Union's smoothest agit-prop spokesmen, had his visa restricted, cutting off his hitherto unlimited ability to travel around the United States.

On the other hand, Reagan confounded his tough rhetoric and blunt gestures with the contradictory step of lifting the embargo on grain sales to the Soviet Union that President Carter had imposed after the Soviet invasion of Afghanistan. Reagan had criticized the embargo during the 1980 campaign in his appearances in the farm states (especially in Iowa, site of the all-important first caucus of the election season) and promised that he would lift the embargo if elected. He made the cogent argument that the grain embargo unfairly asked just a single segment of American business—farmers—to make a sacrifice. At his first presidential press conference in late January, Reagan said, "You only have two choices with an embargo: You either lift it, or you broaden it." He returned to the theme in early March in a televised interview with Walter Cronkite: "[I]f we were going to go that route, then it should have been a general embargo." Reagan also noted that the embargo had had little effect on the Soviet Union because none of our allies had gone along with it; other grain-exporting nations, such as Argentina, filled the gap, taking away market share from American farmers.

While Reagan had those arguments on his side, the decision to lift the embargo was not easy to reach, nor did it pass without arousing controversy. When the cabinet first discussed the issue, on February 4, Ed Meese and Agriculture Secretary John Block called for lifting the embargo immediately, while Haig and others argued against the move, saying it would look like a unilateral concession to the Soviets. Reagan agreed to defer the decision but could not delay for long after the Senate, in mid-March, voted 58–36 in favor of lifting the embargo, a tribute to the strength of farm state senators. The president lifted the embargo on April 24, at the very time when tensions over Poland were heating up, and with only short notice to our allies. Notable conservatives pounced on the decision. George Will, for example, wrote that the Reagan administration loved commerce more than it loathed Communism. The front page of *Human Events,* meanwhile, ran the headline "Reagan's First Major Foreign Policy Mistake?"

Lifting the grain embargo was not helpful in achieving the near-term objective of Reagan's foreign policy, which was to smash up the last remaining filigree of détente without openly saying so. Reagan was seeking to strike a tougher attitude toward the Soviet Union without foreclosing the possibility of genuine negotiations. It was necessary to be artful and indirect about this purpose because of diplomatic requirements involving the skittish European alliance. Occasional lapses into candor, including from Reagan himself, always set off a furious reaction in the media and among the diplomatic corps. In mid-March, an unnamed high administration official made some incautious remarks (the official thought he had been speaking off the record) to a Reuters reporter that caused a full-scale ruckus:

> A high U.S. official said today the Reagan administration believes détente is dead and broad negotiations are pointless until Moscow abandons what he called "The most brazen imperial drive in modern history." The official, who asked not to be identified, said the administration planned to confront the Soviet Union on its own terms despite what it realized would be heavy pressure from the allies, especially West Germany, for a more conciliatory line. . . . The official said, "Nothing is left of détente," and "Détente is dead . . ." He said Soviet leaders would have to choose between peacefully changing their Communist system in the direction followed by the West "or going to war. There is no other alternative, and it could go either way."[76]

The anonymous high official was Richard Pipes of the National Security Council, the Polish-born Harvard scholar who had published several articles on the inherently expansionist tendencies of the Soviet Union and why the Soviets thought they could prevail in war against the West, including nuclear war. (The Soviets had, unsurprisingly, protested Pipe's appointment to the NSC.) The predictable furor erupted, with one European newspaper blaring the headline, "Reagan War Threat Horrifies West." Haig, while privately agreeing with Pipes, publicly professed to be "outraged," and apologized to the West German foreign minister for the critical comments that appeared in the article. The White House issued a statement saying the official quoted in the article was not authorized to speak for the administration.

But aside from the sensational war talk, there was a glimpse at the source of the uncertainty about policy: Pipes said that the administration's replacement for détente could be either "warmed over containment" or perhaps something *as radical as the President's economic program*" (emphasis added). What might that look like? No one could—or would—say at this point.

A clear direction in the details of foreign policy might have been reached sooner but for the most harrowing moment of the 1980s—the moment that almost derailed the entire Reagan revolution both in domestic and foreign policy.

CHAPTER 4

THE SHOT HEARD
ROUND THE WORLD

—⟫●⟪—

Whatever happens now I owe my life to God and
will try to serve him in every way I can.
—RONALD REAGAN, PERSONAL DIARY ENTRY, APRIL 1981

O N MONDAY, MARCH 30, 1981, President Reagan's schedule for the day appeared on page A-4 of the *Washington Post*. It was the last time the *Post* published any president's daily schedule.

The fourth item for the day was Reagan's 2:00 p.m. address to the AFL-CIO's Building and Construction Trades Conference at the Washington Hilton on Connecticut Avenue. This might seem an unlikely audience for a Republican president (though Reagan noted with pride that "I'm the first President of the United States to hold a lifetime membership in an AFL-CIO union"), but the appearance reflected the fact that both halves of Reagan's economic plan—budget cuts and tax cuts—were now in trouble. The talk in the media and on Capitol Hill was that Reagan's "honeymoon" was about over. A Gallup poll in mid-March found that Reagan's approval rating was the lowest in the second month of any elected president in polling history (though it was still a robust 59 percent). Democrats were starting to emerge from their post-election shell shock. House majority leader Jim Wright had written in his diary the day before: "The Democratic spirit, so long subdued by the obvious Reagan popularity, is showing signs of life."[1]

Reagan gave the labor audience his standard critique of big government, leavened with his typical jokes, anecdotes, statistics, and letters from citizens, along with a paean to the Polish Solidarity trade union movement. His speech was received politely but coolly, according to most accounts, though this was instantly forgotten because of the immediate sequel. The scene outside the hotel is now etched in the American memory.

The shooting and near death of President Reagan on that March afternoon provides another occasion for reflection on the radical contingency of human affairs and for counterfactual what-if speculation. What if Winston Churchill had been killed when he was struck by a taxi on New York's Fifth Avenue in 1932? What if Lee Harvey Oswald had missed his target in Dallas? Most such speculations are ultimately fatuous, but in the case of Ronald Reagan one can speculate with confidence that the Reagan Revolution, as it came to be known, would not have been consummated under the presidency of George H. W. Bush.

The proximate counterfactual of March 30, 1981, is: what if Secret Service agent Jerry Parr had not ordered the driver to divert the presidential limousine to George Washington University Hospital instead of the White House? The verdict is unanimous: Reagan would have died of his wound. Reagan didn't know he had been shot; he first thought Parr had broken a rib and punctured a lung when Parr shoved the president into the limousine. When the limousine arrived at the hospital, Reagan got out of the car under his own power, even though he was having difficulty breathing and had started coughing up blood en route. He hitched up his pants as he always did and walked to the hospital door, which reassured onlookers that his injuries were minor. But he collapsed just inside the hospital door. The paramedics who first saw Reagan thought he was having a heart attack.

Paramedics had trouble getting a pulse and a blood pressure reading. He was close to going into shock. The first doctor to examine Reagan saw a small hole below Reagan's armpit, and realized that he had been shot. But there was no exit wound; the bullet was still inside. Nancy Reagan arrived at the hospital, frantic. (A small person to begin with, she lost ten pounds over the next month.) It was at this moment that Reagan made the first gesture demonstrating his authentic ruggedness and good nature. Lifting his oxygen mask, he tried to reassure Nancy by quipping, "Honey, I forgot to duck"—the line Jack Dempsey had used after he lost a title fight to Gene Tunney. He also joked to a nurse holding his hand, "Does Nancy know about us?" Reagan's steadiness might have been called the actor's greatest performance, but as there was no script and no director, it gave evidence that he was not just someone who read other people's lines.

The doctors quickly decided that Reagan's high rate of blood loss—he ended up losing almost 50 percent of his total blood volume before the ordeal was over—meant that they would have to perform surgery to find the bullet and close the wound. When he was wheeled into the operating room, Reagan did it again, asking the medical team, "Please tell me you're all Republicans." The lead physician, Dr. Joseph Giordano, was a liberal Democrat, but was equal to the moment, telling Reagan, "Mr. President, we're all Republicans today."

The surgery took more than two hours. The surgeons had to remove several blood clots from Reagan's chest, and had trouble finding the bullet, which had come to rest less than an inch from his heart. Placed on a respirator to help reinflate his collapsed left lung, Reagan awoke at 7:30 p.m. Unable to speak, he continued making jokes in writing: "I'd like to do this scene again—starting at the hotel." The next morning, when the troika turned up to have Reagan sign legislation curtailing milk price supports, he was reassured that the government was running smoothly. Reagan immediately scribbled out a response: "What makes you think I'd be happy to hear that?"

Reagan wasn't all self-deprecation and quips. While he was being prepped for surgery, he pulled his oxygen mask away again to ask, "Who's minding the store?" In the bedlam of the moment, it is not recorded what answer he received, if any. Whatever answer he might have gotten would have been wrong, because the White House was initially a scene of confusion. What followed at the White House had a *Rashomon*-like quality: recollections from the principals about who said what are fragmented and contradictory.

In case of an attack on the president there are carefully worked out contingency plans for a continuity of military command authority (there was no reason, for example, to be particularly concerned with the location of the "football"—the briefcase containing the president's nuclear launch codes and communications gear). But Reagan's circumstances were ambiguous. Vice President Bush was on an Air Force plane over Texas, and although he turned the plane around to return to Washington, his aircraft, amazingly, lacked secure communications ability. Bush, the official head of crisis management, was effectively out of action for the next four hours until he reached Washington. His absence left a command vacuum.

While the troika of Baker, Meese, and Deaver had gone to the hospital to be near Reagan, back at the White House several members of Reagan's cabinet and senior staff assembled in the situation room in the basement, including Defense Secretary Caspar Weinberger, Treasury Secretary Don Regan, Communications Director David Gergen, White House Counsel Fred Fielding, CIA Director Bill Casey, Attorney General William French Smith,

Secretary of State Al Haig, and several others. Communication with the hospital proved to be surprisingly difficult; phone connections kept getting cut off.

With Reagan's condition unclear, the troika decided that the Twenty-fifth Amendment, which stipulates that in cases of incapacity the vice president shall assume the office of the president, should not be invoked. This decision was constitutionally dubious, as the cabinet is supposed to make this decision, not White House staff. Back in the situation room there was confusion about who was in charge of the government. The national security adviser, Richard Allen, ran a tape recorder, providing the only authoritative record of what occurred at the White House. Allen's tape captured the following exchanges:

GERGEN: Al, a quick question. We need some sense, more better sense of where the President is. Is he under sedation now?
HAIG: He's not on the operating table.
GERGEN: He *is* on the operating table!
HAIG: So the . . . the helm is right here. And that means right in this chair [where Haig was sitting] for now, constitutionally, until the Vice President gets here.

Here one can see the origin of the great tempest of the afternoon. In fact, in the national command authority chain, Haig was third in line, behind the secretary of defense and the chairman of the Joint Chiefs of Staff. But that chain of command is operative chiefly in wartime. Command authority in peacetime is more ambiguous. By seniority of cabinet rank, the secretary of state is second in line after the vice president. By order of *succession* in case of a president's death or disability, however, the secretary of state is fourth in line, behind the vice president, Speaker of the House, and president pro tempore of the Senate. Haig was simply mistaken about what the Constitution says.

This distinction would have been largely moot except that at roughly the same time deputy press secretary Larry Speakes was in the press briefing room, on national television before a tumultuous press corps. What was Reagan's condition? Speakes had no new information. Was Reagan in surgery? Speakes could not say. The clincher was: "Who's running the government right now?" Speakes did not know that the bulk of the cabinet was assembled in the situation room, and fumbled badly: "I cannot answer that question at this time." The press corps erupted with incredulity. Ironically, Speakes had been previously scheduled to participate in a briefing on crisis management procedures at four o'clock that afternoon.

The cabinet members in the situation room, where a TV was on, were appalled by Speakes's answers. Haig took it upon himself to rush up to the press briefing room to repair the damage. He bounded up two flights of stairs and, as a recent triple-bypass patient and still a two-pack-a-day cigarette smoker, arrived at the podium sweaty and short of breath. A reporter called out a question: "Who is making the decisions for the government right now? Who is making the decisions?"

Haig answered: "Constitutionally, gentlemen, you have the president, the vice president, and the secretary of state, in that order, and should the president decide he wants to transfer the helm to the vice president, he will do so. As of now, I am in control here, in the White House, pending the return of the vice president and in close touch with him. If something came up, I would check with him, of course." Haig's voice cracked in the middle of his remarks. It was hardly a reassuring performance. To the contrary, reporter Judy Woodruff said, "I had never seen Haig look so shaken or sound so unsteady. It made me wonder just how serious the president's condition was."

Worse interpretations came to mind. Martin Anderson, also present in the situation room, wrote that Haig's demeanor and words "sounded ominously like a veiled grasp for power." The media—and later legions of comedians— came down hard on Haig.[2] Pat Buchanan summarized the media spin as having portrayed Haig as "something of a cross between General Jack D. Ripper in *Dr. Strangelove* and Burt Lancaster in *Seven Days in May*." "It will be in the third paragraph of his obituary," Reagan aide Lyn Nofziger remarked. Former secretary of state Dean Rusk defended Haig, saying that his only problem was that he had not yet learned the special ability of secretaries of state, "how to say nothing at great length." This was manifestly untrue, as Haig already had a well-earned reputation for being a verbose obscurantist when it served his purposes.

Haig's performance led to sharp words when he returned to the situation room. Among other blunders, the secretary of state had told the press that there had been no change in the nation's alert status. It was true that the Def-Con (Defense Condition) status had not been formally changed, because such a move could alarm the Soviet Union. But Defense Secretary Weinberger had ordered the armed forces to elevate their alert status, since Soviet forces were active near the Polish border and two Soviet missile submarines were "out of

the box"—that is, closer to U.S. territory than usual. The possibility of a conspiracy behind Reagan's shooting couldn't be immediately ruled out. Back in
the situation room, Haig now felt chagrined that he didn't know what Weinberger had done. In the discussion that followed Haig barked at Weinberger,
"I am not a liar" (no one had said he was) and "You'd better read the
Constitution."

Despite all the seeming chaos in the White House, Al Haig himself was
the only person in the situation room confused about the chain of authority.
More important, for all the media fury behind the question of who was in
charge, the only essential matter at that moment was the continuity of national command authority, which, because of the multiple contingencies of a
prospective nuclear war, was well worked out and functioning smoothly. The
details of these contingencies are classified and would not be shared with the
media in any event.

The cabinet could have headed off the Speakes and Haig misstatements
had it decided at the outset to invoke the Twenty-fifth Amendment, which
makes the vice president the acting president in the event of the president's
disability. But that amendment had been enacted only in 1967, in the aftermath of the Kennedy assassination. In the uncertain circumstances of March
30, the cabinet was understandably reluctant to invoke this rarely used
amendment.

The issue deepens as more complete details of Reagan's condition emerged
over the years. One of the quips Reagan scribbled on a notepad after waking
up after surgery was Winston Churchill's famous line from his autobiography
My Early Life that "there is no more exhilarating feeling than being shot at
without result." But the bullets missed Churchill. While Reagan survived his
bullet, it was not without "result." In addition to the severe pain of his wounds
(whose treatment required strong medication including morphine), Reagan
contracted a staph infection in the hospital that was as life-threatening as the
bullet wound. He had to be placed back on oxygen and given powerful
antibiotics. Three days after the shooting House Speaker Tip O'Neill was the
first outsider to visit Reagan in the hospital. "He was in terrific pain, much
more serious than anybody thought," O'Neill later said.[3] In an extraordinary
moment, O'Neill, in tears, knelt next to Reagan's bedside, held the president's hand, and recited the Twenty-third Psalm with Reagan.

Although Reagan returned to the White House after thirteen days in the
hospital, his working hours were severely curtailed for weeks. Al Haig, one
of Reagan's first visitors back at the White House, said, "I was shocked when

I saw him. He was a shell of his old self."[4] It would be two months before the president worked a full day. His personal physician said that he didn't think Reagan fully recovered until October, seven months later. Reagan never mentioned his discomfort. His only complaint was that he wouldn't be able to ride a horse for a while.

The White House staff never made any conscious decision to downplay or mislead the public about Reagan's condition, as was the case after Woodrow Wilson's stroke in 1919. It was understood that the uncertainty over a diminished president would be intolerable. Reagan's own jauntiness—his "courage under pressure," as the pundits were quick to pronounce—bestowed on him a heroic quality that would have been foolish to traduce by officially deeming him disabled from his job. Senator Pat Moynihan, who was present in the White House on November 22, 1963, wrote a few days after Reagan's shooting: "In the history of the office has any man ever so triumphed over danger and pain and near death? We are surely proud of him." Even the *Nation* magazine, not ordinarily friendly to Reagan, wrote that his "resilience provided a brief celebration of the tenacity of life and a reassuring glimpse at an appealing aspect of Ronald Reagan's character. . . . One half-expected to read upon awakening from the anesthesia he had quipped, 'Where's the rest of me?' "[5] Certainly the nation was better served by the hope of his recovery rather than the worry of the continuity of his administration.

Somewhere in the back of everyone's mind was the memory of the national tragedy of 1963, and the day after Reagan's shooting the nation breathed a sigh of relief that it had averted a JFK-style nightmare. In fact Reagan's shooting would turn out in the fullness of time to be the inverse of the JFK tragedy. JFK looms large in our mind because he was, as our second-youngest president, the youthful tragic hero, cut down before he could achieve his potential. Reagan, our oldest president, having survived the assassin's bullet, would go on to achieve his full potential and become the conquering hero of the Cold War.

American life quickly began to return to normal. The Academy Awards, postponed while Reagan's life hung in the balance, went forward a night later complete with a good-humored jab at Reagan from master of ceremonies Johnny Carson: "The president has asked for severe cuts in aid to the arts and the humanities. It's Reagan's strongest attack on the arts since he signed with Warner Brothers." A taped message from Reagan to the Academy was played, prompting a laugh of relief over the new meaning to Reagan's comment "Film is forever—I've been trapped in some film forever myself."

The assassination attempt did prompt predictable hand-wringing from the commentariat about what kind of nation we are. Senator Bill Bradley (D-N.J.) took to the Senate floor to proclaim that America was a "sick society," and Ted Kennedy called for more gun control; Pat Moynihan noted the irony that Reagan would instantly veto any new gun control law that Congress might pass.[6] The *Nation* noted that "the only public figure who did not perform the ritual hand-wringing was the President himself."

While Reagan did not indulge any pop sociology over the character of the nation, he was deeply introspective about the intersection between his physical salvation and his spiritual salvation and purpose. Much has been made of Reagan's supposed belief (and his wife's certain belief) in astrology, but it is obvious that the idea of providential destiny was much more important to Reagan's soul. The providential religious overtones of Reagan's view of America were always widely noted, especially his frequent borrowing from John Winthrop's famous sermon about the "shining city on a hill." He also liked to quote from Pope Pius XII: "Into the hands of America God has placed the destinies of an afflicted mankind." Reagan talked much less about his belief in individual providence, though it ran equally strong. Throughout his life Reagan affirmed the view he got from his mother, Nellie: God has a plan for each of us.[7]

This view appears numerous times in his personal letters. After losing the 1976 nomination campaign, Reagan wrote in a letter to a supporter: "Whether it is this job or whether it is early training from long ago just now coming clear, I find myself believing very deeply that God has a plan for each of us. Some with little faith and even less testing seem to miss it in their mission, or perhaps we fail to see the imprint on the lives of others. But bearing what we cannot change, going on with what God has given us, confident there is a destiny, somehow seems to bring a reward we wouldn't exchange for any other. *It takes a lot of fire and heat to make a piece of steel*" (emphasis added).[8]

Did Reagan ponder how being shot was part of God's plan for him? Unsurprisingly, he did not share whatever private thoughts he may have had, but on Good Friday, less than three weeks after the shooting, out of the blue Reagan told Mike Deaver that he wanted to talk to a clergyman. Deaver, an ex-seminarian, arranged for Terence Cardinal Cooke to come down from New York on short notice to visit with Reagan in the family residence at the White House. Reagan told the cardinal: "I have decided that whatever time I have left is for Him." Separately Mother Teresa told Reagan that God had spared him for a purpose. The providential character of Reagan's survival was perhaps confirmed two months later when, in a coincidence that seems hard to dismiss out of hand, Pope John Paul II survived an assassin's bullet in Vatican Square. Providence or not, the Pope's shooting was a sign that the Cold War had entered a dangerous new phase, as many Western intelligence analysts believed the Pope's shooting was a conspiracy involving Soviet-bloc intelligence agencies.

* * *

ONE PRACTICAL RESULT of Reagan's newfound dedication to his providential purpose was a personal letter to Soviet party chairman Brezhnev. In early March, Brezhnev had sent Reagan a long, wide-ranging letter asking for a resumption of arms talks "without delay" along with negotiations on other matters of dispute, and a suggestion for a summit. Brezhnev also floated the idea that would soon become the rallying cry of the Left in the United States and Europe—a freeze on deployment of nuclear weapons in Europe, which would have the effect of ratifying the existing Soviet advantage. The letter pointedly rejected the cornerstone of Reagan's nascent Soviet policy of "peace through strength": "The Soviet Union has not sought and does not seek military superiority, but neither will we permit the building up [of] such superiority over us; intention of that kind and talking to us from positions of strength are absolutely futile."

Reagan replied during his convalescence in the White House, and clearly relished his first official opportunity to argue his favorite themes directly to the world's top Communist. He included his paraphrase of Jefferson's argument about consent of the governed—"If [the people] are incapable, as some would have us believe, of self-government, then where among them do we find people who are capable of governing others?"—a point that was surely oblique to someone marinated in the Marxist doctrine of the dictatorship of the proletariat, according to which bourgeois democratic consent is a chimera of false consciousness. Reagan also repeated his familiar litany about how America did not abuse its one-time nuclear monopoly, but was instead a non-imperialistic force for good in the postwar world: "May I say that there is absolutely no substance to charges that the United States is guilty of imperialism or attempts to impose its will on other countries by use of force." He contrasted this with Soviet aggression in Afghanistan and its use of Cuban proxies in Africa.

The more dominant line of argument in the letter, though, was deeply personal and sentimental. Reagan began by reminding Brezhnev that they had met at Richard Nixon's San Clemente home a decade before: "When we met I asked you if you were aware that the hopes and aspirations of millions and millions of people throughout the world were dependent on the decisions that would be reached in your meetings. You took my hand in both of yours and assured me that you were aware of that and that you were dedicated with all your heart and mind to fulfilling those hopes and dreams." This wasn't just a prelude to establish a personal rapport; it suffused the letter.

"Is it possible," Reagan went on,

> that we have permitted ideology, political and economic philosophies, and governmental policies to keep us from considering the very real, everyday problems of our peoples? . . . Mr. President, should we not be concerned with eliminating the obstacles which prevent our people from achieving their most cherished goals? And isn't it possible some of these obstacles are born of government objectives which have little to do with the real need and desires of our people?[9]

Despite its Reaganesque sincerity, this is curious language, coming close to validating the view that the Cold War was an irrational misunderstanding, perhaps even implying a moral equivalence at some level. Here we see one of Reagan's paradoxes at work: his clear-eyed view of Soviet totalitarianism along with his belief in the power of personal diplomacy. Reagan would often say, in a comment that struck listeners as naive, that if only he could get a Soviet leader to travel through America with him, the Communist scales would fall from the Soviet's eyes. He wrote later that he "aimed at reaching [Brezhnev] as a human being." Yet in other instances he showed that he knew better. In a 1983 personal letter Reagan wrote: "I have never believed in any negotiations with the Soviets that we could appeal to them as we would to people like ourselves."[10]

The State Department had been working on a formal reply for Reagan to sign at the time of his shooting, and was dismayed when they saw the president's handwritten draft. Haig and several members of the NSC thought Reagan's letter would confuse the Soviets, as it seemed to vitiate much of Reagan's own direct public criticisms of the Soviet Union. ("It was so maudlin and so at odds with Reagan's public stance," Richard Pipes wrote.) In one of the rare moments in his presidency, the State Department took a harder anti-Soviet line than Reagan. State rewrote Reagan's letter with very tough language, leaving out the president's personal touches. The State Department letter threw cold water on any prospect for a summit, declaring, "I must be frank in stating my view that a great deal of tension in the world today is due to Soviet actions." It also objected to the Soviets' "unremitting and comprehensive military buildup over the last 15 years, which in our view far exceeds purely defensive requirements and carries disturbing implications of a search for military superiority."

Reagan wasn't happy with the "impersonal" tone of the State Department version but reportedly was prepared to defer to the "experts" at State until several of his White House staff encouraged him to stick to his guns. He ultimately decided to send both the State Department version and his handwritten version as a sort of cover letter. The messages were dispatched on April 24, the same day the ending of the grain embargo was announced.

The conciliatory gesture did no good. Brezhnev replied promptly with a message Reagan accurately described as "icy." *Petulant* and *sarcastic* are adjectives that also could be applied. "All assertions concerning a Soviet military threat," Brezhnev wrote, "or our alleged search for military superiority do not become any more convincing through having them repeated. . . . [E]very new spiral in the arms race has been initiated by the United States." Poland and Afghanistan, Brezhnev argued, were none of the United States' business. And forget about any summit.

Brezhnev's letter was clearly a Foreign Ministry product designed to rebut the State Department letter, for he enclosed a second letter, dated two days earlier, where he addressed Reagan's handwritten letter. While the tone was more personal ("I too recall our brief conversation . . . in June 1973") and less vituperative, Brezhnev contested every claim Reagan made. An "objective" look, the Soviet leader wrote, would show that the United States was to blame for worsening superpower relations and world tensions. He closed the letter with an appeal for "private conversations," which he thought would be more productive than continued letters.

Despite its attempt to match Reagan's personal style, this letter too bore the hallmarks of a foreign ministry draft. Reagan was disappointed that Brezhnev's letter was typed rather than handwritten, as Reagan's had been. He wondered whether Brezhnev had actually seen his letter. "So much for my first attempt at personal diplomacy," Reagan reflected.

But he may have accomplished more than he thought. The Soviets were being forced to argue in broad terms about their basic legitimacy. They had not done this for a long time, and they didn't like it.

*   *   *

WHILE REAGAN'S SHOOTING plainly extended his honeymoon period of suppressed partisan rancor (his approval rating soared to the high 70s), it was not clear whether this would revive his flagging economic plan. Some package of budget cuts was certain to pass, but the more important tax cut was under determined attack. The news media, especially the *New York Times* and *Washington Post,* ran almost daily articles attacking the tax cut and offering every opposition voice an outlet to undermine the idea. Dan Rostenkowski, the powerful chairman of the House Ways and Means Committee, declared in mid-March that Reagan's tax cut was dead, and that he would develop a Democratic alternative. Tip O'Neill declared on March 26: "All factions of the [Democratic] party agree they are against Kemp-Roth" (Congressman Jack Kemp and Bill Roth co-sponsored the tax cut bill). House Democrats started talking of a compromise plan with smaller budget cuts and a modest, one-year tax cut. Reagan called the Rostenkowski proposal "less than half a loaf" and threatened to veto a one-year tax cut. But the White House figured that it was a hundred votes short in the House of being able to pass either its budget or tax cuts. *Newsweek* magazine ran a story headlined "Is the Big Tax Cut Dead?"

But some of the hardest blows came from *Republicans.* White House congressional liaison Max Friedersdorf sent a worried memo to the troika in late March with the understatement that "our staff continues to pick up disturbing intelligence with regard to the tax reduction side. . . . [O]ur problem [is] on the House side and among the Republicans in Ways & Means."[11]

There was a revolt brewing in the Senate too. On April 10, the day before Reagan came home from the hospital, four conservative Republicans joined all the Democrats on the Senate Budget Committee in rejecting Reagan's budget plan. Committee chairman Pete Domenici and the other dissenting Republicans were uncomfortable with the "magic asterisk" of unspecified future cuts, worried about the potential deficits of Reagan's plan, and didn't accept the economic forecasts.[12] But Domenici's real target was not the budget cuts but the tax cut they helped to justify. Rowland Evans and Robert Novak reported in their column, "Domenici's staff proclaimed, with unconcealed delight, that Kemp-Roth was dead." The *Wall Street Journal* editorial page let out a blast headlined "John Maynard Domenici." Domenici wasn't the only significant holdout in the Senate. Meanwhile, Finance Committee chairman Bob Dole was telling reporters that he did not have the votes to pass Reagan's tax cut in his committee.

Complicating the case for deep tax cuts were signs that the economy was beginning to perk up. Domestic auto sales in March jumped 30 percent. The stock market rallied sharply, with the Dow reaching an eight-year high of 1,015.22. In April the first quarter's economic growth figure came in at a strong 6.5 percent (later revised upward to a more robust 7.9 percent). Inflation had dropped from 14 percent in November to 7.5 percent in March, and the prime rate had fallen by half, from 20 percent in December to 10.75 percent. As the near-panic atmosphere of December and January began to ebb, the refrain began that the improving economy meant that deep tax cuts weren't necessary.

Suddenly it was Reagan's economic advisers who started talking down the economy. They pointed to the Index of Leading Economic Indicators, which fell for the third month in a row in February, often a sign of impending recession. "We're losing momentum," a White House source was quoted in the press. With Reagan sidelined by his bullet wound, the Washington spring air was thick with talk of "compromise," which meant Reagan's surrender. Anonymous White House sources indicated to reporters that they were interested. To David Stockman, it appeared that Washington was about to lapse back into business as usual, although, according to Stockman's later account, he was beginning to have misgivings about the size of the tax cut at this point.

There now commenced a round of legislative maneuvering that provided Washington with one of its episodes of high drama and intrigue. In April the Democratic-controlled House Budget Committee passed an alternative budget resolution and tax plan that on paper actually showed a lower deficit for the next fiscal year than Reagan's plan. But Stockman noted that this was done with accounting gimmicks and spending increase deferrals to future years, which meant that the plan featured few real cuts. Meanwhile, the tax cut in the plan would be eaten up by inflation-driven bracket creep within two years. House Republicans shrewdly repackaged Reagan's plan with the help of a renegade Democratic budget committee member, Phil Gramm of Texas, and offered it as a bipartisan substitute to the House Democrats' budget. It became known as Gramm-Latta, after Gramm and Republican Budget Committee member Delbert Latta of Ohio.

The key to victory for either side rested with the group of about forty conservative southern Democratic House members known as the Boll Weevils. The conservatism of the Boll Weevils must be properly qualified: while culturally conservative and hawkish on foreign affairs, most of these Democratic members were not fiscally conservative in the least, and in many cases, owing to their seniority on key fiscal committees, they were champions of pork barrel spending. Most of the Boll Weevils were initially inclined to back their own party's budget plan. Besides, the House Democratic leadership could threaten reprisals against any member who broke ranks—lost committee assignments, no more pork barrel for their districts, and so forth. On the other hand, the White House could credibly threaten to end their political careers entirely. Reagan had run very strongly in the South, and southern House members were wary of having to run against Reagan's enormous popularity back home. The White House knew this and decided to exploit Reagan's popularity by framing the budget vote as a sign of whether "you are for or against the President."

How soon, and in what way, would Reagan rejoin the fight for his economic program? The answer was right away. From his hospital bed Reagan put out the word that he would not retreat from either budget cuts or tax cuts, and he banned any further White House talk of compromise, though leaks and back-channel talk of compromise naturally continued. Even as he was recuperating from his shooting and working limited hours, he began working the phones to a long list of House members thought amenable to a direct appeal from the commander in chief.

With the forces of the White House and the House Democratic leadership finely balanced in a classic Washington battle, Tip O'Neill blundered. He and fourteen other Democratic congressmen went off to Hawaii, Australia, and New Zealand on a junket over Easter break. O'Neill realized the Reagan blitz was on when White House operators tracked down Democratic congressman Tom Bevill, who was along with O'Neill in New Zealand. (When Reagan woke Bevill and found out that it was 4:00 a.m. in New Zealand, the president later recounted, he was tempted to say, "This is Jimmy Carter calling." But "it was too late; he knew who it was.") Reagan reached another Democrat, Eugene Atkinson of Pennsylvania, while the congressman was on a radio talk show. Reagan joined the show live, asked Atkinson for his vote, and got it. Democrats back home grumbled about O'Neill's absence in the midst of Reagan's blitz. O'Neill later admitted that his overseas trip was his biggest political mistake of 1981.

Still figuring to be on the short end of the House vote, the White House wanted Reagan to give a televised address from the Oval Office to generate public support. But the president decided he wanted to try another formal speech before a joint session of Congress. Reagan's April 28 address, coming just thirty days after his shooting, was his first major public appearance, and he was greeted in the packed House chamber with a prolonged hero's welcome. For the first time ever the Secret Service had an agent accompany him down the aisle in the House. Reagan, noticeably thinner—he lost seventeen pounds in the weeks after the shooting—and still looking wan from what only very few knew was a difficult recovery, basked in the moment. Ever the showman, Reagan, with his best twinkle of the eye and trademark grin, responded to the tumultuous welcome with: "You wouldn't want to talk me into an encore, would you?" which led to another long round of cheering and applause.

It would have been odd had Reagan not offered some personal reflection on his shooting, and so he began with a digression to express his thanks for the nation's support and prayers. But the moment also offered him the occasion to reprise an old theme. Back in the 1960s few things had angered Reagan more than the charge that America was a "sick society." He had spoken often against this theme in the past, including a 1970 speech entitled "Ours Is Not a Sick Society."[13] Now was the moment to close the book on that theme once and for all.

> You've provided an answer to those few voices that were raised saying that what happened was evidence that ours is a sick society. . . . Well, sick societies don't produce men like the two who recently returned from outer space. Sick societies don't produce young men like Secret Service agent Tim McCarthy, who placed his body between mine and the man with the gun simply because he felt that's what his duty called for him to do. Sick societies don't produce dedicated police officers like Tom Delahanty or able and devoted public servants like Jim Brady. Sick societies don't make people like us so proud to be Americans and so very proud of our fellow citizens.

Then, in a typical Reagan touch, he pulled a letter from his coat pocket. No one knew for some years that Reagan not only read a large number of the letters sent to the White House, but also replied personally to hundreds of them. "The letter came from Peter Sweeney," Reagan said. "He's in the second grade in the Riverside School in Rockville Centre, and he said, 'I hope you get well quick or you might have to make a speech in your pajamas.' He added a postscript. 'P.S. If you have to make a speech in your pajamas, I warned you.' " As the laughter was dying down, Reagan carefully folded the letter and put it back in his coat pocket to be answered personally later, a sign of its—and his—authenticity.

With this prologue, Reagan got down to business, and didn't mince words.

> It is time to try something new. . . . Six months is long enough. . . . [W]e know that the cure will not come quickly and that even with our package, progress will come in inches and feet, not in miles. . . .
> Our choice is not between a balanced budget and a tax cut.

Properly asked, the question is, "Do you want a great big raise in your taxes this coming year or, at the worst, a very little increase with the prospect of tax reduction and a balanced budget down the road a ways?" With the common sense that the people have already shown, I'm sure we all know what the answer to that question would be.

A gigantic tax increase has been built into the system. We propose nothing more than a reduction of that increase. The people have a right to know that even with our plan they will be paying more in taxes, but not as much more as they will without it.

The option, I believe, offered by the House Budget Committee, will leave spending too high and tax rates too high. . . . In short, that measure reflects an echo of the past rather than a benchmark for the future.

Reagan's arguments were met with thunderous standing ovations several times, including from a large number of Democrats. Speaker O'Neill, sitting behind Reagan, could feel the sentiment of the House surging in Reagan's favor, and during one ovation leaned over to Vice President Bush and said, "There's your forty votes." Afterward House majority leader Jim Wright wrote in his diary: "We've just been outflanked and outgunned." Wright complained that Reagan's speech was "extremely partisan" but "probably very effective." This was an understatement. Capitol Hill was flooded with telegrams and phone calls in support of Reagan.

Reagan ended up getting 63 House Democrats to join all 190 House Republicans in passing the Gramm-Latta substitute budget resolution a week later. The Senate adopted the Reagan budget plan by a similarly lopsided 72–20 vote a week later. O'Neill lamented: "We can't argue with a man as popular as he [Reagan] is."

But argue he and his party did, and as May faded into June, the level of rancor over Reagan's economic plan deepened. The budget resolution provided only the general outline, or spending ceilings, for each broad category of federal spending. A second round of votes would have to be cast to reconcile the resolution with individual appropriation bills from the various congressional committees. Would spending-addicted congressmen stay within the ceilings of Gramm-Latta, which ordered the spending committees to cut total spending for the next fiscal year by $36.6 billion?

With an eye toward the 1982 elections, Speaker O'Neill thought he saw an opening to derail some of Reagan's momentum. O'Neill planned to have the House vote for each budget cut individually, hoping to pile up a record of votes against spending for popular-sounding programs such as school lunches, mass transit aid, job training, black lung disease payments, and so forth. Already the committees that oversaw spending bills—whose powerful chairmen Stockman referred to as "the Politburo of the welfare state"—were chafing under the caps of the budget resolution and employed accounting tricks to meet the budget ceiling without actually having to cut spending. O'Neill's gambit threatened to make the entire budget cutting strategy unravel, one thread at a time.

The White House countered by having Gramm and Latta sponsor their own substitute budget reconciliation bill, known as Gramm-Latta II, which bundled all the budget cuts together in one package that would require only a single up-or-down vote by the House. This set up another test of strength between the White House and the House Democratic leadership, and led to one of the first direct clashes between Reagan and O'Neill. Reagan telephoned O'Neill to ask that Gramm-Latta II be given an up-or-down vote in the House and not blocked by parliamentary maneuvering or a closed rule from the House Rules Committee. O'Neill bristled, telling Reagan: "Didn't you ever hear about the separation of powers? The Congress of the United States will be responsible for spending. You're not supposed to be writing legislation."

Reagan replied, "I know the Constitution."

He also knew his political strength, for the same coalition that passed the first Gramm-Latta budget resolution in early May embraced the Gramm-Latta II reconciliation bill in late June. The White House had handed O'Neill another stinging defeat, albeit by the close vote of 217 to 211. So many southern Democrats had defected to Reagan that O'Neill couldn't credibly threaten to strip them of committee assignments or seniority for fear they would switch parties or vote with Republicans to install a Republican speaker. (The one exception to this calculation was Phil Gramm. O'Neill eventually did bounce Gramm from the House Budget Committee, whereupon Gramm became a Republican.) A battered O'Neill told a reporter back in Boston, "I'm getting the shit whaled out of me."

While O'Neill felt he was getting pummeled, over at the White House some of the sharp-pencil budgeters and economists began to realize dimly that Congress had passed a crappy budget deal. In order to gain the support of the Boll Weevils, the White House had had to make numerous spending concessions. Louisiana congressman John Breaux, for example, received an extension of sugar import quotas, giving rise to his now famous remark "I can't be bought—but I can be rented." Republicans got in on the act too, including Jack Kemp, who fought to preserve mass transit funding for Buffalo. One measure of the haste and frenzy of the backroom dealing was that a staff person's name and telephone number (Rita Seymour, 255-4844), scribbled on the margins of a list of budget items, ended up being mistakenly printed in the final legislation that went on the books.

"The resulting 1,000-page document," Stockman wrote later of the budget deal, "was replete with every loophole, every cut corner, every perversion of fine print in the considerable repertoire of the professional staff."[14] He estimated that the real budget savings was only $16 billion for 1982. Instead of being $44 billion short of a balanced budget by 1984, the budget would now be more than $100 billion in the red. This modest savings would prove to be the high-water mark for serious budget restraint; as Stockman put it, "It was the day on which the United States Congress reached the limit of its ability—and willingness—to reduce spending." Both parties went along with the charade of having made "deep" budget cuts: Republicans wanted to claim a large victory, while Democrats wanted to bemoan "cruel" budget cuts to weaken sentiment for further budget restraint and to be able to boast of the spending they had preserved.[15] None of the programs Stockman targeted for elimination was eliminated, and spending reductions in many other programs never materialized or were far less than claimed.

Five years later in his memoir, Stockman, the former congressman, would profess to be shocked—*shocked!*—that politics would intrude, let alone triumph, in the budget process. Stockman's good friend George Will had predicted this outcome. Writing two weeks before Reagan's inauguration, Will said: "When—if—Reagan does what some aides say he must, when he asks Congress to prune some of the biggest programs of 'big government,' he may find that the number of 'liberals' in the new 'conservative' Congress approaches 535."

Bear in mind that most of the budget cuts that the White House managed to achieve were not really cuts at all. Rather, as noted in Chapter 2, Reagan merely set out to reduce the *growth* of federal spending, which was set according to baseline budgeting, a phenomenon whereby most social spending programs grow on automatic pilot every year according to formulas for caseload. Reagan loved to complain about baseline budgeting all the way back to his time as governor of California. School lunches, student loans, basic welfare (the AFDC program), and Medicaid—in these and many other cases, total year-over-year spending grew after the 1982 budget cuts, but at a lower rate than the baseline formula.[16] Overall spending for all social programs in 1982 was still $53 billion *higher* than in 1980.

But such basic facts went missing from the major news media coverage of the budget debate, which with very few exceptions became a de facto adjunct to the Democratic Party's attacks on Reagan's budget. The method was simple, especially for TV network news: find a person whose benefits were being eliminated or reduced, and dramatize that person's story. *Baltimore Sun* reporter Fred Barnes called it "aggressive victimology."[17] CBS News began using this story line *before* Reagan had even proposed any cuts, broadcasting a story on February 13, 1981 (five days ahead of Reagan's first budget speech), about the plight of Irene O'Brien, who was supposedly going to lose her food stamps. (The CBS story was wrong; O'Brien didn't lose her eligibility.) The drumbeat grew as the budget fight heated up over the spring and summer. CBS was the worst, with its correspondents seemingly in a hyperbole competition. "Hunger in America is back," Bill Moyers said on CBS in the spring, months before Reagan's budget even took effect. Food stamp cuts "are putting people into a 1981 version of the bread line," Charles Kuralt said on the *CBS Morning News.* Commentator Charles Osgood said that the budget-cutting wind has been "blowing strong enough to uproot some government programs—CETA is gone—and tear the roof off some other ones— food stamps for example." Reporter Lesley Stahl asked Reagan at a press conference: "What do you say to the single working mother whose eligibility for Medicaid and for food stamps has been cut? What would you like to say to her today about how she cannot provide medical care for her children or feed them with food stamps?" The other networks marched in lockstep, creating the impression of very large budget cuts.

It made for great television, and would have been less objectionable had the stories of individual hardship been balanced with stories explaining exactly what the Reagan budget cuts entailed. In the case of food stamps, for example, the Reagan budget was said to have cut $1 billion from the 1982 program, from $12.3 billion to $11.3 billion. But the $12.3 billion was the 1982 baseline estimate; the actual spending reduction was only $100 million, from the 1981 spending level of $11.4 billion. The mechanism for restraining spending on food stamps was to tighten eligibility requirements, but the news media failed to explain this point, or got the details badly wrong when they tried. In reality, the Reagan budget lowered the eligibility threshold for food stamps from a gross income below 150 percent of the poverty line ($9,300 for a family of four in 1982) to 130 percent. The change in eligibility (from which the elderly and disabled were exempted) affected less than 4 percent of the total caseload; *twenty-two million* people were still receiving food stamps after the Reagan budget was adopted. But with very few exceptions (ABC being notable), news organizations didn't provide this other side of the story.

In the midst of the budget battle, in fact, there occurred the kind of media scandal that validates conservative resentment of media bias: the *Washington Post* got caught publishing a wholly fabricated story that won a Pulitzer Prize. A young African American *Post* reporter, Janet Cooke, had written a sensational story about an eight-year-old heroin addict she had found on the streets of Washington. But after the story won the Pulitzer, cooler heads began to inquire about the implausibility of the story. What eight-year-old can afford to support a heroin habit? As the story quickly unraveled, conservatives made the point that such a shoddy story got through the editorial process only because it conformed to liberal stereotypes of victimology and minority misery. Cooke was fired and the *Post* embarrassed, but there was little change in elite media editorial outlook.

The media's formidable onslaught on the Reagan budget plan helped Democrats achieve the long-term victory for control of future budgets, even after losing this initial battle. Social spending over the next few years would grow in real terms and as a proportion of the federal budget.[18]

Yet neither side was able to perceive this clearly at the time. All that seemed obvious was that Reagan had won two big legislative victories in a row, which gave him the political capital to revive the centerpiece of his program: the tax cut. Democratic congressman Robert Kastenmeier summed it up in a comment to the *Washington Post*: "The majority party has lost control and this changes the balance of power on everything that is consequential."

The Democratic leadership in the House began to lash out in frustration, complaining that Reagan was dominating Congress. Representative Richard Bolling, the chairman of the House Rules Committee, said, "This is incipient tyranny, a popular president is attempting to tyrannize a whole Congress, a whole people." Majority leader Jim Wright complained, "I don't know what it will take to satisfy them [the White House], I guess for Congress to resign and give them our voting proxy cards." After a decade of Nixon, Ford, and Carter, the imperial Congress was unaccustomed to facing a vigorous and effective chief executive.

*   *   *

IN BETWEEN THE first and second Gramm-Latta budget victories in early May and late June, the White House committed its first major blunder when it decided to touch the third rail of American politics: Social Security. This was always a vulnerable subject for Reagan (and Republicans generally), since over the years he had embraced the idea of making Social Security voluntary, or of privatizing the program much in the manner that is now fashionable.[19] Recognizing the political difficulties, most of Reagan's advisers opposed any meddling with Social Security. Stockman, however, hoped to include deep cuts in later rounds of budgeting. Social Security was badly out of balance—people retiring in 1981 could expect to get back as much as five times the amount they had paid into the system—and it was projected to go broke within the next two to three years, despite having been "fixed" with another payroll tax increase in 1977.

On the morning of May 11 Stockman sprang a reform plan on Reagan, the centerpiece of which was a sharp reduction in monthly benefits for people who took early retirement at age sixty-two. The plan would save $50 billion over the next five years but would mean that hundreds of thousands of people planning to take early retirement would have to change their plans or live on less than they expected. Reagan liked Stockman's plan and approved it on the spot. It is hard to fathom why Reagan embraced this plan; only two months earlier he had rejected a milder proposal to freeze for one year the Social Security cost-of-living increase and to slowly raise the retirement age from sixty-five to sixty-seven, in large part because he had made a campaign promise not to reduce benefits. Although it is not clear whether Stockman fully explained to Reagan the practical effects his technical changes entailed, others present for Stockman's proposal say the president grasped these details readily. Most observers think Reagan's big win on the first round of the budget four days earlier made him overconfident in his political mastery.

Chief of Staff James Baker, realizing that there had been no advance work to gain support for the idea on Capitol Hill, worked quickly to try to get Reagan's fingerprints off it. By the afternoon he had maneuvered to have the plan announced by Health and Human Services Secretary Richard Schweiker rather than the White House. This didn't fool anyone; the *Washington Post* headline the next day read: "*Reagan* Proposes 10% Cuts in Social Security Costs" (emphasis added). The reaction was volcanic. Tip O'Neill called the plan "despicable." Behind the Democrats' outrage was barely concealed glee. Pat Moynihan told *Newsweek:* "We had them on something. This was a genuine entitlement being taken away." He speculated what he imagined smart Republicans must be thinking about this misstep: "My God, the Democrats have an issue here that will confirm every doubt anybody has ever had about us for the last 50 years—that we are going to tear up that social-security card." (It was doubly embarrassing that the Republican National Committee was in the process of sending out a mailing with the boastful headline "President Reagan Keeps Promise, Retirement Benefits Go Untouched.") Not surprisingly, smart as well as dumb Republicans rushed unanimously to join the denunciation. The White House attempted an orderly retreat from the idea, but the retreat became a rout when the Senate voted 96–0 in favor of a resolution condemning any attempt to "unfairly penalize early retirees."

Although the White House quickly put the matter behind them, the stumble lent the Democrats new vigor in their public arguments against the tax cut and Reagan generally. While Democrats may have lacked the confidence to defend themselves as the party of government and higher social spending, they had lost none of their old New Deal–inspired egalitarianism and the concomitant rhetoric of class warfare.

The legislative battle over the tax cut that followed is a classic case study in interest group deal making, ego soothing, and power politics. Most accounts of the 1981 tax cut battle portray it as a "grudge match" (in Stockman's words) just to see who could win. But there was a deeper and more serious reason for the intensity of the fight: a real difference of principle was at stake, a difference that in this case made impossible what otherwise could have been an easy and straightforward compromise. Democrats conceded that Reagan had won the battle for a tax cut. The only question was what kind of tax cut it would be. Democrats opposed across-the-board income tax cuts because people with higher incomes would receive a larger amount of relief than the average taxpayer.

Liberal rhetoric on the issue is revealing. Allowing people to keep more of their own money was called "showering money on the rich," as though all wealth belonged to the government rather than the people. This Democratic attitude is rooted in a fallacy—the idea that wealth is *distributed,* mostly by government, rather than earned by individuals and apportioned by markets. Even if liberalism appealed not to distributionism but to a theory of the social contract under which the wealthy have an obligation to the state, there has never been much of a concrete explication of what the practical limits are.[20]

(George McGovern called for something like a 90 percent tax on all estates above $500,000 in 1972, which he admitted was "confiscatory.")

It was inevitable that the tax cut debate would arouse the fiercest partisan passions because it cut once more to that fundamental issue of American politics, fairness. Political thinkers such as James Madison understood that a regime of equal rights must recognize unequal outcomes, but modern liberals rejected this older understanding, considering such outcomes to be unfair. Conservatives, meanwhile, pointed out that the top 5 percent of incomes in the United States paid about half of all income taxes. Was this fair?

The ultimate epithet against tax cuts was that it amounted to trickle-down economics. James Tobin, a Nobel laureate in economics and a veteran of JFK's New Frontier, argued that Reaganomics meant that "inequality of opportunity is no longer a concern of the federal government." This is a perfect example of ideology and class envy trumping empirical evidence. As Lawrence Lindsey points out, "[T]he evidence suggests that high tax rates help ossify class structure rather than break it down."[21]

The major news media were overwhelmingly sympathetic to the liberal viewpoint about fairness and acted as a megaphone for the Democratic attacks on Reagan's tax cut plan.[22] The *Washington Post*'s Haynes Johnson offered a typical formula: "Stripped of slogans and magic economic curves, supply-side theorems were nothing more than the old selfishness dressed up in new garb for the 1980s. . . . [A]cquisition of wealth had been given a moral rationale."[23] Read the last sentence again: the clear implication is that acquiring wealth is morally dubious. Editors in newsrooms repeatedly let this kind of phrase pass as reporting or news analysis without so much as a hiccup. More often the leading refrain, even in news stories, was that Reagan's budget plans were unfair to the poor and minorities. "The impact of the Reagan cuts on minority groups is likely to be severe," the *Washington Post* reported in a front-page *news* story.[24] Even the Soviet Union joined the attack on Reagan's economic policy. Georgi Arbatov told the *New York Times* that Reagan's policies were an attempt "to cure the entrenched economic ills of the late 20th century simply by returning to the 'good old practices' of 19th-century capitalism."[25] Few noticed the irony that the major American news outlets took the same editorial line about Reaganomics as the Soviet Union.

Then there were the dire predictions of a "long hot summer," that cuts in social programs would spark a revival of 1960s-style urban rioting and racial unrest. Richard Hatcher, the Democratic mayor of Gary, Indiana, emerged from a White House meeting with Reagan to declare, "There are hundreds of

Mount St. Helenses in the streets and alleys of this country. If drastic cuts are made in the programs that go to the heart of the little assistance the disadvantaged receive, I fear for what will result."[26] New York's Democratic governor, Hugh Carey, echoed this prediction, saying that "there will be social upheaval in this country by October because of the Reagan Administration's budget cuts."

Many columnists cited recent riots in Britain that had spread to seventeen cities in what was widely seen as a reaction to Prime Minister Margaret Thatcher's economic and social policies—policies Reagan was about to emulate. Columnist Tom Wicker warned, "[T]he Reagan Administration would be prudent to weigh such parallels as there are, with the idea that what's happening in Britain could presage a recurrence in this country." Similar columns from David Broder, William Raspberry, Henry Fairlie, Russell Baker, Flora Lewis, and Leonard Silk served as the media echo chamber.[27] There never were any riots, then or a year later when unemployment soared.

The bitter rhetoric became sharply personal on June 16, when Reagan gave his first full-scale press conference since the assassination attempt. In the judgment of many White House staffers and media figures, it did not go well; Lou Cannon called Reagan's performance "deplorable." The White House communications office, in what became a routine practice, issued several corrections of facts Reagan had misstated, especially on foreign policy. Reagan's comparatively poor performance in this press conference had more to do with his still-reduced work schedule in the aftermath of his shooting; what time he was working was devoted primarily to his economic plan, and he spent little time on foreign policy.

His focus on economics showed in the most memorable moment of the day. Reagan had closed off the questioning, apologizing for not being able to stay all night to answer every reporter with a question, and was walking away from the podium when the human bullhorn Sam Donaldson called out: "Tip O'Neill says you don't know anything about the working people, that you have just a bunch of wealthy and selfish advisers." Reagan abruptly stopped, turned on his heel, and walked back to the podium with an angry, petulant expression on his face. It was almost as if he were answering a director's cue in a movie.

"One more, just one," Reagan said. "Wouldn't you know that Sam Donaldson would be the one? Sam says that Tip O'Neill has said that I don't know anything about the working man." O'Neill's complete statement, made on ABC's *Good Morning America,* was actually much more pointed than

Donaldson's summary. His full statement to ABC's Charles Gibson was: "He has no concern, no regard, no care for the little man in America. And I understand that. Because of his lifestyle, he never meets those people. And so consequently, he doesn't understand their problems. He's only been able to meet the wealthy." Gibson prodded O'Neill further: "You're saying he's callous?" O'Neill rose to the bait: "I think that he has very, very selfish people around him, people only of the upper echelon of the wealth of this nation, and they are his advisers. I think he'd do much better if he had brought in some people close to him who are from the working force of America, who have suffered along the line, not those who have made it along the line and forgotten from where they've come." O'Neill added the revealing coda: "We are the party of the people. *And we're their guardians*" (emphasis added).

The charge that Reagan had no regard for low-income or working people angered him almost as much as the charge that he was a racist, and he had seethed over O'Neill's comments, which he thought were out of bounds. His answer showed that while he might not be on top of the details of foreign policy, he had the economic arguments down cold:

> I'm trying to find out something about his boyhood, because we didn't live on the wrong side of the railroad tracks, but we lived so close to them we could hear the whistle real loud. And I know very much about the working group. I grew up in poverty and got what education I got all by myself and so forth, and I think it is *sheer demagoguery* to pretend that this economic program which we've submitted is not aimed at helping the great cross section of people in this country that have been burdened for too long by big government and high taxes. From 10 to 50 to 60 thousand dollars covers, certainly, all the middle class, and they pay 72 percent of the tax. And 73 percent of our tax relief or more is going to that bracket of workers. And we're going to do our utmost to keep that bottom rung of the ladder clear for those people that haven't yet started to climb. (Emphasis added)

O'Neill didn't back down. To a union convention in July, he declared: "Let's face it. This is a callous, right-wing administration committed to repealing the Great Society, the New Frontier, the Fair Deal, and the New Deal. It has made a target of the politically weak, the poor, the working people."[28]

And he made it personal again, calling Reagan "a tightwad, a real Ebenezer Scrooge."

The emphasis on the fairness of the tax cut obscured the more serious argument about the potential effect of tax cuts. O'Neill and a number of leading Republicans such as Senator Bob Dole argued that cutting tax rates would lead to huge budget deficits, higher inflation, and higher interest rates. Both Dole and Congressman Barber Conable, the ranking Republican on the House Ways and Means Committee, publicly expressed doubts about the size and duration of Reagan's tax cut and indicated their willingness to broker a compromise with the Democrats on the Democrats' terms. Reagan had to call both Dole and Conable to the White House to impress upon them his insistence on a three-year tax cut. For all of Reagan's persuasive power, the tax cut still looked like a long shot.

*   *   *

FOR ALL OF his indignation, O'Neill was wary of being labeled as an obstructionist and of giving Reagan the easy opportunity to blame Democrats at the next election if the economy failed to improve. Therefore, he promised Reagan an up-or-down vote on the White House tax cut plan, and set out to defeat the president in a straight-up fight. Democrats thought there might be room to craft an alternative tax cut that would be more to their liking, with smaller rate cuts targeted more toward the lower-middle-income brackets that had the added benefit of allowing them to share the political credit for its enactment. The key, once more, would be the southern Boll Weevil Democrats, who had gone with Reagan twice now.

The votes of the Boll Weevils again came with specific price tags. House Ways and Means Committee chairman Dan Rostenkowski quickly acceded to the southerners' demands for tax breaks for the oil and gas industries. The White House, equally determined to win the tax, made concessions of its own, agreeing to reduce the size and delay the implementation of the cut. The Boll Weevils, concerned chiefly about the near-term budget deficit, thought a 30 percent tax cut was too large, so Reagan reluctantly assented to a 25 percent plan. The southern congressmen also wouldn't go along with making the cut retroactive to January 1, as Reagan had originally wanted, or July 1, the date he had already compromised on. Instead they favored a backloaded 5-10-10 formula, with the start date of the first 5 percent tax cut being pushed back to October 1.

Rostenkowski, the point man for the Democrats on taxes, proposed a two-year, 15 percent tax cut skewed toward middle- and lower-income groups. Tip O'Neill played the class warfare card: "If you make over $50,000 a year, ours is better." This was not true: the Democrats' targeted plan did not offer lower tax rates for low and middle incomes than Reagan's 25 percent across-the-board tax cut plan did. It was an appeal to pure envy and resentment.

In the effort to prevent Reagan's full across-the-board tax cut, Democrats reversed fifteen years of tax policy principles. Rostenkowski had bowed to the Boll Weevils' request for relief from the windfall profits tax, which had been a cherished Democratic Party accomplishment just the year before. Soon he was offering more generous business write-offs than Reagan had proposed, which Democrats ordinarily would have blasted as corporate give-aways. The Democrats also offered to ease up on the estate tax. One Reagan aide observed in a memo: "The Democrats have now abandoned any pretense of philosophy and are now engaged in a raw, opportunistic contest . . . a bidding contest to win a game." The chairman of the House Budget Committee, Oklahoma Democrat Jim Jones, admitted as much, telling the *New York Times:* "We're in a bidding war. Any economic foundation for the tax bill has been abandoned." Pat Moynihan called it "an auction of the Treasury."

It was a foolish strategy for Democrats; even if they won the legislative battle, maintaining the principle of higher tax rates for upper incomes would require a much larger reduction in revenue from other tax cuts than if the Democrats had simply acceded to Reagan's original plan. Lower revenue would mean less money to spend for social programs, pork barrel projects, and so forth. How likely was it that they could win a tax cut bidding war? Just as Republicans can seldom promise to outspend Democrats (except on defense), how could Democrats think they could cut taxes better than Republicans?[29]

Only a few Democrats realized that they were playing into Reagan's hands. Freshman Democratic congressman Barney Frank showed the acuity for which he became better known in the 1990s when he told the *Wall Street Journal:* "I think the purpose of [tax cuts] is to reduce the revenue of the federal government so that it simply isn't possible to have very many constructive, directed programs." Pat Moynihan also suspected a Machiavellian intent: if the supply-side theory of tax cuts paying for themselves didn't work and the country had huge deficits, so much the better. Huge deficits would crimp big government for a very long time. Even if huge deficits weren't the deliberate creation of Reaganomics, the budget deficit would dominate Washington politics for the rest of the decade, Moynihan (accurately) predicted.

Two final moves determined the outcome of the tax cut fight. Michigan Democrat William Brodhead proposed something the White House had been too afraid to propose itself—immediately cutting the top rate on unearned income from 70 percent to 50 percent. This looked to tilt the outcome in favor of the Democrats' tax bill until Republican senator Bill Armstrong countered by proposing indexing income tax rates for inflation—a step Democrats could not take. Indexing the income tax for inflation promised to end the automatic-pilot, stealth income tax hikes that the government had enjoyed for the previous decade. The Senate Finance Committee endorsed the idea by a vote of 9–5. Stockman had opposed indexing in the White House proposal, fearing that it would open the budget deficit wider. But now the White House decided to embrace the idea, and this feature proved to be decisive as the House vote neared.[30]

Democrats also floated the idea of a trigger for the second and third years of the tax cut, under which the cut would not take effect unless spending reduction targets were met. (Stockman was sympathetic to this view, writing that he thought tax cuts should be a "reward" for spending restraint.) This has come to be a perennial theme whenever tax cuts have been proposed since the Reagan era; triggers were a popular proposal to attempt to slow up President George W. Bush's tax cuts in 2001 and 2003, for instance. As Reagan immediately pointed out, the trigger was "designed by people who don't really believe in cutting taxes." It provides the best of both worlds for politicians, who can tell their voters that they supported a tax cut, and yet don't have to anger any of the spending constituencies with real spending constraints.

The White House had a handy answer: it was again able to invoke John F. Kennedy, who had opposed a trigger for his tax cuts in 1963. President Kennedy had written to House Ways and Means Committee chairman Wilbur Mills with distinctive supply-side reasoning: "I see no reason for placing any conditions or contingencies on the effectiveness of the second phase of the tax reduction program. . . . Any delay or contingent feature would substantially reduce the effectiveness of the legislation in stimulating the economy, reducing unemployment, and increasing incentives. *This in turn could lead to decreases in revenues below expectations and greater deficits than now projected*" (emphasis added). The trigger idea died aborning.

The outcome was still in doubt when Congress returned from its July 4 holiday break. Reagan's personal lobbying effort was in full swing as he welcomed fifteen of the Boll Weevils up to Camp David for a barbecue. He got commitments to support his tax bill from twelve of them. Another fifty-eight House members, mostly Democrats, came to the White House individually or in small groups to see Reagan in the Oval Office; he got pledges of support from thirty-nine of them. He telephoned another twenty-six House members and got pledges of support from seventeen. The key promise to the Boll Weevils and other renegade Democrats, however, had nothing to do with any specific tax break; more significant was Reagan's pledge not to campaign against any Democrat who backed his tax cut. "I could not in good conscience campaign against any of you Democrats who have helped me," Reagan told them. "I couldn't look myself in the mirror."

Even with Reagan's effective lobbying blitz, the White House still found its vote tally falling short of certain victory in the House. For one thing, a number of liberal Republicans balked at the tax breaks for the oil industry, opposed the third year of the tax cut, and had various other excuses. Representative Marjorie Holt of Maryland told the White House that she would vote against Reagan's bill because she was angry that Mrs. Reagan had visited a drug rehab facility in her district without telling her. Representative Bud Shuster of Pennsylvania, one of the great Republican pork-barrel spenders, was "nervous" about income tax indexing. Several members of both parties cited fears of the budget deficit as reason to oppose one or both tax cut proposals. A number of conservative oil patch Democrats whose votes Reagan needed told the White House that they had to stick with the Democratic leadership because it had bent to their demands. Texas Democrat Charlie Wilson said repeatedly that he had been bought and would stay bought: "You're not worth a damn around this place if you don't keep commitments like that."

In the face of this resistance, the White House decided that Reagan should make another nationwide TV speech. He went on the air on July 27, two days before the tax vote was scheduled in the House. The power of Reagan as the Great Communicator was never more fully displayed than in this speech. More notable than Reagan's persuasiveness, though, was the ideological ferocity of the speech. He scorned "the cries of protest by those whose way of life depends on maintaining government's wasteful ways," and then went on to attack the sincerity of Democrats:

Now, when I first proposed this—incidentally, it has now become a bipartisan measure coauthored by Republican Barber Conable and

Democrat Kent Hance—the Democratic leadership said a tax cut was out of the question. It would be wildly inflationary. And that was before my inauguration. And then your voices began to be heard and suddenly, in February, the leadership discovered that, well, a 1-year tax cut was feasible. Well, we kept on pushing our 3-year tax cut and by June, the opposition found that a 2-year tax cut might work. Now it's July, and they find they could even go for a third year cut provided there was a trigger arrangement that would only allow it to go into effect if certain economic goals had been met by 1983. . . . So what is the purpose behind their change of heart? They've put a tax program together for one reason only: to provide themselves with a political victory.

If I could paraphrase a well-known statement by Will Rogers that he had never met a man he didn't like, I'm afraid we have some people around here who never met a tax they didn't hike.

Reagan then turned to the comparative merits of his tax bill, noting that without his tax indexing feature, inflation and previously enacted payroll tax increases (for Social Security and Medicare) would swallow up any tax cut in just two or three years. To illustrate the effect of indexing, Reagan did something almost no president has ever done in an Oval Office speech: he used a visual aid—a large chart, prepared by Treasury aide Steve Entin—as though he were a classroom teacher:

The majority leadership claims theirs gives a greater break to the worker than ours, and it does—that is, if you're only planning to live two more years. The plain truth is, our choice is not between two plans to reduce taxes; it's between a tax cut or a tax increase. There is now built into our present system, including payroll Social Security taxes and the bracket creep I've mentioned, a 22-percent tax increase over the next 3 years. The committee bill offers a 15-percent cut over 2 years; our bipartisan bill gives a 25-percent reduction over 3 years. Now, as you can see by this chart, there is the 22-percent tax increase. Their cut is below that line. But ours wipes out that increase and with a little to spare. And there it is, as you can see. The red column—that is the 15-percent tax cut, and it still leaves you with an increase. The green column is our bipartisan bill which wipes out the tax increase and gives you an ongoing cut.

From here Reagan turned up the pressure on the Democrats by making the issue a matter of personal honor, telling the story of a Democratic congressman who had a constituent ask him, "What I want to know is are you for 'im or agin 'im?" Reagan closed with an appeal for the public to lobby Capitol Hill: "I urge you again to contact your Senators and Congressmen. Tell them of your support for this bipartisan proposal. Tell them you believe this is an unequalled opportunity to help return America to prosperity and make government again the servant of the people."

Reagan's speech produced the desired response. Phone calls and telegrams poured into Capitol Hill at ten times the normal rate, running twelve to one in Reagan's favor. Tip O'Neill admitted, "We are experiencing a telephone blitz like this nation has never seen. It's had a devastating effect." Washington Democrat Norm Dicks told both sides he was undecided; four hundred pro-Reagan phone calls to his district office helped him make up his mind to go with the president. An unnamed congressman told *Newsweek*, "I sure hope Reagan doesn't go on the tube again and say no more sex." One by one, most of the supposedly rock-solid votes that had been dearly bought with concessions from Rostenkowski were peeling off to Reagan's bill. Missouri Democrat Richard Gephardt said, "[T]he dam broke. . . . It just fell apart."

The final House vote on July 29 was 238–195; forty-eight Democrats defied the party leadership to back Reagan. (Among them was South Dakota's lone representative, Tom Daschle.) Only one Republican voted against Reagan's tax cut—Vermont's Jim Jeffords, a name that would become celebrated for a more brazen betrayal of a Republican president nearly twenty years to the day later, also on the eve of a tax cut vote. In the Senate, Democratic opposition to the tax cut had collapsed a few days before. The Democrats could rally only eleven no votes. Nineteen of the twenty Democratic senators up for reelection in 1982 voted with Reagan. (The sole exception was Ted Kennedy.) The effectiveness of Reagan's television appeals was nearly unprecedented. Although it is common to think every president enjoys the built-in advantage of the bully pulpit, academic studies have found, surprisingly, that nationwide presidential appeals usually have no effect or even a slight negative effect.[31]

Banner headlines about the tax cut had to share the front pages with another spectacular event that occurred the same day: the marriage of Prince Charles and Lady Diana Spencer in England. This prompted a slap from O'Neill: "This has been quite a day for aristocracy: a royal wedding and a royal tax cut." The House Speaker was more gracious in his congratulatory phone call to Reagan, telling the president that he was "stunned" at the rout; Reagan, who had told his staff not to gloat, replied that he was stunned too. Oddly enough, the most memorable misgiving about the tax cut after its passage came not from O'Neill or a liberal icon but from Republican Senate leader Howard Baker, who called the tax cut "a riverboat gamble"—less than a ringing vote of confidence.

The full story requires telling some of the numbers. There were still fifteen income tax brackets—or fifteen different rates—under the Reagan plan. The top rate, starting with income on a joint return of $162,400, fell from 70 percent to 50 percent. For a couple with $30,000 income, the rate fell from 37 percent to 28 percent; at $50,000, the rate fell from 49 percent to 38 percent. A household earning the median income of $22,000 in 1984 saved about $500 in taxes.

Another set of numbers is also important to know: because of all the sweeteners added to the bill to win votes, the revenue loss in the early years from the final tax package was about twice the amount of Reagan's original 30 percent tax cut proposal.

The economic results of the tax cut shall be surveyed in due course, but one important point is that the Reagan tax cut was heard around the world just as loudly and dramatically as the bullets fired at him in March. In the ensuing years, nearly all industrialized nations would emulate the Reagan plan and reduce their marginal income tax rates. Even the Scandinavian social welfare states of Sweden, Norway, and Finland got in on the act. Norway cut its top tax rate from 75 percent to 54 percent, Finland cut rates from 71 percent to 54 percent, and Sweden from 83 percent to 75 percent.[32] (Supply-siders suggest that Sweden's relatively poor economic performance relative to its neighbors is explained by the fact that it didn't cut its tax rates enough.)[33]

*   *   *

ALTHOUGH REAGAN'S THREE big congressional wins weren't achieved in a breathless one hundred days, it was the most impressive presidential start since FDR, and it left Washington equally breathless. Reagan's Initial Actions Project had laid out a two-hundred-day timetable for his domestic agenda, and events had unfolded almost exactly according to script. On top of his recovery from the shooting and his legislative victories came his first Supreme Court appointment in July. Reagan had promised late in the 1980 campaign that he would make a woman "one of his first" appointments to the Supreme

Court. Reagan had left some wiggle room—he hadn't said he'd make a woman his *very* first appointment. In 1981 there were precious few Republican women with the judicial qualifications for such a high appointment, so it was no surprise that the Justice Department sent over to the White House a list of white males recommended for consideration. (Women accounted for fewer than 5 percent of all law school graduates ages forty-five to sixty in 1981.) Reagan sent the list back with the message that he wanted a woman for his very first appointment after all.

Sandra Day O'Connor of Arizona's state supreme court was about the only Republican woman available, and Reagan was satisfied that the Justice Department had found a suitably conservative candidate.[34] (The Justice Department lawyer who vetted O'Connor was Kenneth Starr.) But many conservatives voiced concerns. Terry Eastland, writing in the *American Spectator,* observed that "O'Connor's views on the Constitution and her understanding of judicial review are largely unknown," because she had been on the Arizona Supreme Court for only two years and had written just twenty-nine opinions.[35] George Will wrote: "Some persons will call it courageous, others will call it reckless to pick a nominee who has a thin record of rulings and published reflections on the crucial questions that have divided the Court and the country."[36] Conservative religious leaders feared that O'Connor wasn't sufficiently robust in her opposition to abortion (as an Arizona state senator, she had cast some murky procedural votes that worried pro-life activists). Jerry Falwell said that all good Christians should oppose O'Connor, prompting Barry Goldwater to say that all good Christians should kick Falwell in the ass.

Reagan responded to O'Connor's critics in less colorful language. He addressed the concerns of evangelical writer Harold O. J. Brown in a personal letter: "She has assured me that she finds abortion personally abhorrent. She has also told me she believes the subject is one that is a proper subject for legislation . . . I have full confidence in Mrs. O'Connor, in her qualifications, and in her philosophy."[37]

Reagan's confidence in O'Connor was initially justified. She sailed through an easy Senate confirmation and during her first years on the Supreme Court she was a solid conservative, voting with her Stanford Law School classmate and fellow Arizonan Justice William Rehnquist in as many as 92 percent of the Court's decisions. O'Connor's defection from conservative jurisprudence lay in the future. At the moment, the appointment was hailed as a Reagan triumph.

There commenced a chorus of media reflections on Reagan's strong start. *Philadelphia Inquirer* columnist Tom Fox wrote: "It has been years since America has had the kind of political leadership that Ronald Reagan is providing in the Oval Office. Reagan is a cross between John F. Kennedy (for style, grace, charm, looks, and dash) and Franklin D. Roosevelt (for political insights and an uncanny reading of contemporary moods)." *Time* magazine's Walter Isaacson observed: "Not since the first six months of Franklin Roosevelt's Administration has a new President done so much of such magnitude so quickly to change the economic direction of the nation."[38] Academic opinion would come to ratify these contemporaneous journalistic assessments. Political scientist James Ceaser would write in 1984: "[T]he transformation in American politics that took place in 1981 was probably greater than any that has occurred since the inauguration of Franklin Roosevelt in 1933."[39]

The media and most of the academic commentators missed the deepest parallel between Reagan and Roosevelt, however. To a much greater degree than most presidents, Reagan and Roosevelt employed a sharply partisan approach toward their policy goals. Although on the surface all of Reagan's TV appeals incorporated a bipartisan substitute to the Democratic alternative, his general rhetoric about the Democratic policies that "got us into this mess" had a partisan ideological edge. Reagan was doing to Democrats exactly what Roosevelt did to Republicans in the 1930s: he was gradually delegitimizing them as a plausible governing party, which is exactly what a realigning political leader must do.[40] *New York Times* columnist Russell Baker commented, "In the end the Democrats were agreeable to the death of the New Deal, which took place this week at the Capitol."

Representative Stephen Solarz (D-N.Y.) summarized the glum mood of Democrats when he told a reporter, "Now I know how the Japanese felt when they signed the instrument of surrender on the battleship *Missouri*." Democrats had reason to be frightened. Reagan's pollster, Richard Wirthlin, reported that the Republican Party had drawn nearly even with Democrats in party identification among voters (39 percent GOP to 40 percent Democrat), closing a twenty-point gap that had existed for the past three decades. Another survey showed that if an election were held then, Republican House candidates would outpoll Democrats by eleven points. Pundits across the political spectrum were speculating about how many House seats Republicans were likely to pick up in the 1982 election, with the median guess being about twenty. (Republicans needed twenty-five House seats to gain outright control.) Seventeen House seats were being moved from the Democratic-leaning Frost Belt to the GOP-leaning Sunbelt because of the 1980 Census. The *Washington Post*'s David Broder speculated in his column whether a period of Republican political dominance had arrived, leaving Democrats "consigned to a minority of quarreling factions."

There were signs of an improving national mood to go along with the Republican surge: a *New York Times*/CBS poll found that 46 percent of Americans felt the nation would be better off by 1986, versus 29 percent who thought things would be worse. This was a sharp reversal from the poll taken in 1979, when only 24 percent were optimistic, while 43 percent were pessimistic.

* * *

FOR A WASHINGTON establishment and a world audience still getting to know Reagan, there had been curiosity about whether he had a tougher side, which every president needs when, as inevitably happens, things do not go well. The *Washington Post*'s Haynes Johnson summarized the conventional wisdom on Reagan in a roundup of his first eight months in office: "One word springs forward to describe him. Nice. If that impression has any validity, then the question arises: is being nice what America needs for the 1980s?" Johnson and most of his media brethren did not perceive that, as Martin Anderson described it, beneath Reagan's genial appearance of being a "soft pillow" there was a two-inch rod of chrome steel.[41]

America and the world were about to see Reagan's tough side in action. In a remarkable asymmetry, in the next scene in Reagan's early presidency he took what he thought was purely a domestic action that nonetheless reverberated in the halls of the Kremlin. On August 3, Reagan fired the nation's air traffic controllers.

This chapter of the Reagan story requires some background. Following long tradition, most of organized labor had sided with the Democratic Party and Jimmy Carter in the 1980 election, with the notable exception of the Teamsters, which had strayed from the Democratic reservation before.[42] Another exception that received little notice during the campaign was the small union representing the nation's 16,412 air traffic controllers, the Professional Air Traffic Controllers Organization (PATCO). Reagan had learned that the union's endorsement might be in play, and just three weeks before the election he wrote to PATCO president Robert Poli to express his sympathy with the union's perception of air traffic controllers' situation, such as "too few people working unreasonable hours with obsolete equipment," which "placed the nation's air travelers in unwarranted danger." If elected, Reagan promised, "I will take whatever steps are necessary to provide our air traffic controllers with the most modern equipment available and to adjust staff levels and work days." Above all, he pledged "a spirit of cooperation" with PATCO. The union reciprocated by endorsing Reagan.

Armed with what it considered an IOU from Reagan, in the winter and spring of 1981 PATCO presented the government with ninety-six demands, including a reduction in the workweek to thirty-two hours, an immediate $10,000 raise for every controller, and a 100 percent salary increase over the next three years, which would have put the average controller's salary higher than a cabinet member's and offered fringe benefits much larger than were available to other federal employees.[43] The total cost of PATCO's wish list was estimated at $1.1 billion in the first year alone. "Most Americans regarded the union's demands as ridiculous," *Time* magazine writer William A. Henry observed. Nevertheless, Poli threatened darkly that controllers would strike if their demands were not met, and originally set a strike date of June 22.

The Federal Aviation Administration (FAA), a division of the Department of Transportation, countered with a $40 million offer that included an immediate raise of $4,000 across the board, a higher pay scale for night work, and overtime pay for the last four hours of a forty-hour workweek. It was a larger pay raise than any other category of federal employees would receive in 1981. After some back-and-forth and concessions by each side, Poli and PATCO's executive board signed off on the FAA's offer on the eve of the strike deadline in late June and sent it along to the membership for a vote. "I feel good about it," Poli told reporters.

But for some reason, Poli did an about-face just days later, calling the contract "an insult" and "garbage." Apparently he came under pressure from hard-line factions in the union; "Poli is being beaten around the head by his own people," David Gergen wrote in his notes of a White House meeting over the issue. In late July PATCO's rank-and-file membership rejected the FAA's offer by a margin of 95.3 percent to 4.7 percent. Talk of a strike intensified.

Air traffic controllers were federal employees and were forbidden by law from striking.[44] But PATCO had a history of this kind of tactic. Since its formation in 1968, the union had threatened to strike or initiated a work slowdown six times and had mostly gotten away with it, receiving only a minor slap on the wrist for an organized sick-out in 1970. Similarly, Nixon had responded weakly in 1970 when a wildcat strike by postal workers closed six hundred post offices, and the Carter administration had granted postal employees a large wage increase in response to a threatened strike. PATCO thought Reagan would fold as easily as Carter, especially given the vulnerability of air travel to a controllers' work stoppage.

Reagan, however, warned that a strike would be illegal and that striking workers could be fired. PATCO thought the president was bluffing; the union had not done its homework. Had PATCO not pondered that notorious portrait of Reagan's hero Calvin Coolidge, the man who had rocketed to national fame with his declaration against the Boston police strike of 1919: "There is no right to strike against the public safety by anybody, anywhere, at any time"? (Reagan could also cite his hero FDR, "who proclaimed," Reagan wrote in a private letter to the mother of a striking controller, "that public employment was different and that strikes against the people could not be tolerated.") PATCO also did not note that as governor of California, Reagan had twice stomped on strikes by public sector employees, in one case threatening State Water Resources Department employees that they would be fired if they did not return to work within five days (the minimum period under California law that Reagan had to allow). On the fifth day, the striking workers returned to their jobs—without a raise.

Very early in the process the Reagan administration said that any strike would be illegal and would be dealt with severely, but the emphasis at the White House, as notes on various meetings attest, was on working it out. Transportation Secretary Drew Lewis became directly involved in the negotiations and told the White House that it was important not to back Poli into a corner. But Reagan ordered the Justice Department as early as June 20 to be ready to move quickly to get an injunction against a strike. U.S. attorneys across the country were mobilized to seize strike funds and arrest PATCO officials.

In an act of stunning political tone deafness, Poli chose July 29, the same day that Reagan's tax cut triumphed in the House, to announce a strike deadline of 7:00 a.m. on August 3. Over the next five days negotiations intensified, with the Reagan administration upping its salary package slightly to $50 million. Poli demanded a package costing $681 million and brushed off all government requests for more time. Drew Lewis judged that Poli was trying to set himself up as a martyr. Finally, at 2:30 a.m. on August 3, four and a half hours before the strike deadline, PATCO walked out of the negotiations.

At 10:55 that morning, Reagan and Attorney General William French

Smith came out to meet the press in the White House rose garden and made good on Reagan's threat. Reminding them once again that he was the only president to have belonged to a labor union and to have once led a strike, a grim-faced and plainly perturbed Reagan reiterated that public sector strikes were intolerable: "I must tell those who fail to report for duty this morning they are in violation of the law, and if they do not report for work within 48 hours, they have forfeited their jobs and will be terminated."

There was more. The Justice Department's criminal division readied to arrest PATCO leaders and hit them with $1,000 fines. The administration went to court to get a judge to issue a restraining order against the union, but U.S. marshals found that PATCO's officers had gone into hiding. Across the country the Justice Department attorneys fanned out to court to ask for fines against PATCO. A federal judge in Brooklyn slapped the union with a $100,000-per-hour fine. PATCO's modest strike fund went up in smoke; the fines levied on the union eventually reached $150 million. The Reagan administration also began legal proceedings with the Federal Labor Relations Authority to have PATCO decertified, a process that was accomplished in two months.

The union had discounted administration threats to fire strikers and hire replacements because it takes up to three years to train a controller. Knowing that August was the busiest month for air travel, the union thought it held the high cards. A controller was quoted in *Time*: "The reality is, we are it. They have to deal with us." But Reagan announced plans to have military air traffic controllers fill in for striking controllers, while a quarter of PATCO's membership defied the union's strike order. As a result, air travel disruptions and delays were minimal. While commercial flights were down about 50 percent in the first days of the strike, within ten days replacement commercial flight traffic was up to 70 percent of its prestrike volume. Moreover, sixty thousand applications poured into the FAA to replace the thirteen thousand strikers.

Reagan never looked back, though a few of his advisers worried that an airline accident would be blamed on the White House, with disastrous political consequences. Reagan banned fired controllers from reapplying for their old jobs, an injunction that lasted until 1993, when President Bill Clinton pointedly lifted it as a gesture that the Reagan years were gone for good. By that time, few ex-controllers wanted to go back to the tower. Three years after the strike, 20 percent fewer controllers were handling 6 percent more flights. Poli resigned as president of the moribund union in January 1982, signaling his capitulation. Backtracking furiously, the previously defiant Poli hoped his resignation would restart negotiations and lead to the rehiring of the fired controllers. Reagan offered the small concession that ex-controllers could apply for other federal jobs, but not in aviation. Poli ended up selling real estate in Florida. The union never re-formed.

Reagan rolled up PATCO just as quickly in the court of public opinion. Although the AFL-CIO's Lane Kirkland voiced support for PATCO, no American labor union observed PATCO's picket lines or offered any other tangible help. The public was overwhelmingly on Reagan's side as well. More than six thousand telegrams and phone calls came into the White House over the next week, favoring Reagan's stand by more than a ten-to-one margin. Opinion polls showed strong majority support for Reagan (64 percent in an NBC/AP poll; 52 percent of *union members,* according to another poll).

Smashing the air traffic controllers union has loomed large in populist lore ever since as a "signal" to private sector management that it was now okay to squeeze unions, but this is too simple.[45] (If Reagan had really wanted to send an anti-union message, he would have proposed privatizing air traffic control.) Generally polls showed that public esteem for organized labor was at an all-time low by the time of PATCO's ill-considered gambit.[46] Labor was getting the message. A *Wall Street Journal* headline a month later told the story: "Economic Gloom Cuts Labor Union Demands for Big 1982 Contracts." Fed chairman Paul Volcker later said that Reagan's firing of the PATCO strikers was the single most important anti-inflationary step Reagan took.[47]

There was one unanticipated audience that paid close attention to Reagan's manhandling of the strike: the Soviet Politburo. Since taking office the administration had been looking for an opportunity to demonstrate in some concrete ways its toughness toward the Soviet Union. As is often the case, the most effective opportunity came in an unexpected way and from an unlooked-for place. The White House realized it had gotten Moscow's attention when the Soviet news agency TASS decried Reagan's "brutal repression" of the air traffic controllers.

For the American news media, Reagan's handling of the strike became the opening for a new line of criticism. During the budget fight, the dominant line of criticism was that while Reagan's *policies* might be cruel and uncaring, he himself was a kindly man. Having wondered whether Reagan was too "nice," Haynes Johnson now wrote: "A glimmer of a harsher Reagan emerges. . . . For the first time as president, he has displayed another, less attractive side. Firmness is fine in a president; indeed, it is desirable. But something else came through last week—a harsh, unyielding, almost vengeful and mean-spirited air of crushing opponents. It makes you wonder how he will respond if faced with a direct, and dangerous, foreign challenge, one requiring the most delicate and skillful combination of strength and diplomacy."

*   *   *

A "DIRECT AND dangerous" challenge came hard on the heels of the air traffic controllers strike, and in a place where Reagan deliberately sought it: Libya. Reagan decided to engage in the kind of old-fashioned diplomacy that was far from what modern sensibility regards as "delicate and skillful." He sent his diplomatic message in the form of an aircraft carrier task force.

U.S. relations with Libya had deteriorated since Mohammar Kaddafi took power in a violent coup in 1969 and immediately aligned himself against the West. To call Kaddafi's Libya a rogue state is a disservice to genuine rogues everywhere. Soviet diplomats always soothed Western governments with the line that they found Kaddafi unpredictable and erratic, which of course made him the ideal tool for Soviet proxy ventures. (At the same time, the Soviets sent indications that they would permit the United States considerable latitude to deal with Kaddafi.) Kaddafi expelled the United States from an air force base in Libya, and went so far as to fire on a U.S. C-130 transport plane flying over the Mediterranean during the 1973 Arab-Israeli Yom Kippur war. That same year he wanted to use an Egyptian submarine on temporary loan to torpedo the ocean liner *Queen Elizabeth 2,* en route to Israel's twenty-fifth-anniversary celebration. Egyptian president Anwar Sadat—still on speaking terms with Kaddafi at that point—had to talk him out of it. Kaddafi routinely sent assassination squads to murder Libyan exiles overseas. "It is the duty of the Libyan people constantly to liquidate their opponents . . . at home and abroad, everywhere," he declared. In 1977 he ordered the assassination of the American ambassador to Egypt, Hermann Eilts. Only a blunt warning from President Carter, who had got wind of the plot, forced Kaddafi to abandon the plan.

Kaddafi's murderous ways were reciprocated. In the spring of 1981 the Soviets tipped him off to a plot hatched among a handful of Libyan military officers to shoot down Kaddafi's airplane on his return from a trip to Moscow. Kaddafi foiled the plot by sending a decoy plane, which was indeed shot down. More coup attempts would follow, each unsuccessful.

Kaddafi had revolutionary ambitions. Following the model of Mao, he had his political views, including the abolition of private property and private enterprise, published in what became known as *The Green Book.* "I have created Utopia here in Libya," Kaddafi declared, "not an imaginary one that people write about in books, but a concrete Utopia."[48] Libya had a population of just three million, but its oil riches enabled Kaddafi to make good on his promise to deliver utopia to Libyans, as well as purchasing a formidable arsenal and bankrolling revolutionary mischief on a wide scale (including $300 million to the Sandinistas in Nicaragua). He had tried to assassinate Sadat after Egypt made peace with Israel; Sadat wanted to invade Libya and depose Kaddafi by force, but Jimmy Carter dissuaded him.

Kaddafi made trouble throughout much of Africa and the Middle East. By 1980 the CIA had identified Kaddafi as the chief sponsor behind the increase in terrorism. He shipped weapons on a large scale to the Palestine Liberation Organization (PLO) and to the Irish Republican Army, and by 1981 he was linked to guerilla insurgencies and terrorism in forty-five countries, including all of his immediate neighbors (with the exception of Algeria). His arms purchases from the Soviet bloc were so enormous that much of the equipment sat in the desert uncrated. Kaddafi's desire to acquire nuclear weapons was an open secret.

U.S. forbearance with Kaddafi reached the breaking point after Libya invaded Chad in December 1980. Reagan took up the subject of getting tougher on Libya in his very first National Security Council meeting the day after his inauguration, and made evident in public statements in subsequent days that he intended to oppose Libya's statecraft. The Reagan administration closed the Libyan embassy in Washington and broke off relations in May 1981 after Libya was caught red-handed in an attempt to assassinate a Libyan exile living in the United States. (Twelve African nations had suspended relations with Libya by this point.) Reagan did not end oil purchases from Libya, which at the time was the third-largest foreign oil supplier to the United States. Looking for a way to push back against Kaddafi, Reagan authorized covert aid to the faction in Chad opposed to Libya, and aid to other African nations to counter Libya's aid to guerillas and terrorists. While Reagan's advisers wanted a plan to topple Kaddafi, the usual bureaucratic compromises stopped the covert plan from going that far. Nonetheless, the Reagan administration got its first experience with the fierce partisan undertow against its foreign policy when Democratic congressman Clement Zablocki, a member of the House Intelligence Committee who had been secretly briefed about the CIA effort, leaked the covert operation to the media. (Zablocki received no reprimand for leaking.)

The Pentagon, meanwhile, noted the perfect opportunity to challenge Libya through Libya's territorial claim over the entire Gulf of Sidra, nearly two hundred miles beyond the twelve-mile limit recognized in international law. It was an absurd claim—even the Soviet Union didn't recognize it—but in 1980 President Carter had pointedly ordered the U.S. Navy to stay clear of the Gulf of Sidra. (In addition, the Carter administration concealed from the public several episodes of Libyans harassing American airplanes in international airspace over the Mediterranean.) Now Reagan decided deliberately to hold naval exercises in the gulf, inside Kaddafi's territorial claim, and even chose to announce the exercises ahead of time. *Newsweek,* reporting that the exercises were intended as the "first direct challenge to the Libyan strongman," laid out the ground rules: "U.S. pilots and sailors have orders not to fire at anything but practice targets—*unless fired upon*" (emphasis added).[49] To up the ante, Egypt announced plans to conduct army exercises in the desert near the Libyan border at the same time. (Egypt later cancelled its exercise, fearing it might provoke Kaddafi.)

The episode that followed offered an example of how Reagan's governing style would result in real change. Under previous peacetime rules of engagement (ROE), if an American airplane was fired upon, a pilot would have to request permission from his commander on ship or back at a land base before firing back. Moreover, if an enemy plane turned and fled after firing, American pilots were ordered to withhold fire, which gave tinpots like Kaddafi essentially one free shot at Americans. Unhappy with this state of affairs, the navy had promulgated new rules of engagement allowing pilots to fire back without having to request permission from a commander. At a cabinet meeting in early August, Reagan approved the new rules of engagement, saying, "Any time we send an American anywhere in the world where he or she can be shot at, they have the right to shoot back." When pressed to clarify how far this right extended, he replied, "All the way into the hangar." Among pilots the new rules became known approvingly as the "Reagan ROE."

As had occurred routinely in the past, the Libyan air force flew several dozen sorties to disrupt the naval exercise. U.S. combat air patrols intercepted more than seventy Libyan planes, including several first-line MiG-23s and French-made Mirages, during the first day of the exercise, and eight more on the morning of the second day, August 19. But a little later in the morning two Libyan SU-22s, second-line Soviet-made fighters known as "Fitters," fired air-to-air missiles at American F-14s. The new Reagan ROE got their first use, and the F-14s made quick work of the Libyan planes. Lasting less than a minute, the aerial battle was "more skeet shoot than dogfight," *Newsweek* commented. Within days T-shirts sold out quickly on American military bases: "USA 2; Libya 0."

Two days later Reagan made a previously scheduled visit to an aircraft carrier, where heightened media attention magnified his message that "there was a new management team at the White House." The *New Republic* concurred: "Nothing has better dramatized the contrast between the Reagan and Carter administrations in managing foreign policy than the shoot-out over the Gulf of Sidra. . . . The Reagan administration has definitely laid to rest what might well be called the post-Iran syndrome."[50] Coincidentally the episode found its pop culture analogue in the current film *Raiders of the Lost Ark,* where theater audiences cheered when the no-nonsense Indiana Jones nonchalantly guns down a sword-wielding Arab standing in his way.

Why Libya would have second-line planes fire upon F-14s when it had more capable MiG-23s and Mirages, and where the order might have come from, is a murky question. It is unlikely to have been an accident. U.S. intelligence monitored conversations between the Libyan pilots and their ground controllers and heard one of the pilots tell his ground controller that he had fired. Kaddafi, out of Libya on a visit to Aden at the time, appears to have been remote from the command structure.

Kaddafi's isolation from the chain of command found a crude symmetry back in the United States. News of the incident traveled within minutes to the Pentagon and then on to Los Angeles, where Reagan was finishing a birthday party for his son Michael at the Century Plaza Hotel in Los Angeles. The local time was about 11:00 p.m. Ed Meese and National Security Adviser Richard Allen were the point of contact for the news, and as no immediate presidential decision was required, they delayed informing Reagan while they waited for more complete information. At 2:30 a.m. (5:30 a.m. in Washington), the Pentagon began briefing the news media on the incident, but *Reagan still had not been told.* Finally, at 4:24 a.m. California time, Meese awakened Reagan with the news.

Meese's decision not to awaken the president earlier caused a firestorm of criticism and contributed to the perception that Reagan was not in charge of his administration. Reagan laughed the matter off with his typical avuncular style, saying, "If our planes were shot down, yes, they'd wake me up right away. If the other fellows were shot down, why wake me up?" Privately he was annoyed, and sent word that he should be awakened immediately in any future incident.[51] Meese's rivals used the affair to lay the groundwork for easing him out of the national security process later in the year.

The tempest over waking the president obscured the more salient aspects of the moment. The Reagan administration was quickly proved correct in its calculation that Libya would not retaliate against the more than two thousand Americans working in Libya with an Iranian-style hostage taking. To the contrary, Libyan officials rushed to reassure Americans that they would take no steps against them or American economic interests. Just to be sure, though, Reagan had warned Kaddafi that any moves against Americans in Libya would be regarded as an act of war and that the United States would respond accordingly. There were predictable rumblings on the Left that the navy had somehow provoked the Libyan attack, with the hope that the Gulf of Sidra would be the 1980s equivalent of the Gulf of Tonkin incident. But Kaddafi unhelpfully squashed that narrative when he admitted a few days later that Libyan planes had shot first.[52]

In the next few weeks after the Gulf of Sidra incident, American intelligence picked up reports from multiple sources (including an intercepted phone call of Kaddafi himself) that Kaddafi was plotting to assassinate Reagan in retaliation. Some of the reports were strikingly detailed, including an attempt to shoot down Air Force One with a surface-to-air missile, attack Reagan's limousine with a rocket-propelled grenade, or fire at him with small arms at his ranch. More than a dozen Libyan operatives were identified by name. Reagan was duly apprised in his daily intelligence briefing but downplayed the matter.

Then on October 6 Anwar Sadat, by then an implacable foe of Kaddafi, was assassinated during a military parade in Cairo. No direct evidence of Libyan involvement in the assassination could be found, though the seemingly organized celebrations that erupted quickly in the streets of Tripoli and statements in Libyan state-run media suggest prior knowledge of the plot.[53] Washington suddenly took a heightened interest in the reports of Libyan hit squads intent on exacting revenge against Reagan and other top government officials. It was a fresh anxiety for Nancy Reagan, who never got over her worry after the March shooting. Reagan started wearing body armor under his shirt to most of his public appearances and began riding to some appearances in an unmarked limousine.[54] Secret Service protection was assigned for the first time to Baker, Deaver, and Meese, since Kaddafi supposedly had been heard to say that if he couldn't get Reagan, he'd get someone else. Reagan sent a secret personal note to Kaddafi through Belgian diplomats threatening serious reprisals, and directed the National Security Council to develop military options against Libya. These did not yet include a full-scale invasion to topple the regime, but they were deliberately leaked to the media to make sure Kaddafi got the message.

Subsequent intelligence suggested that the hit squad story was exaggerated or that several sources had fabricated their stories, and there was criticism that the White House deliberately manipulated the media by hyping the affair. "There are doubts around here," Massachusetts senator Paul Tsongas said. "It's not so much whether there is evidence, but why the Administration is making such a big deal about it."[55] In fact the White House had not wanted to publicize the news, but it leaked, most likely from FBI and CIA sources. Regardless of how much Libyan or other sources may have deliberately manipulated U.S. intelligence or how much the Reagan administration spun the media, the episode was not made up out of whole cloth. In October solid intelligence indicated that Libya was targeting the American ambassador to Italy, Maxwell Rabb. The State Department was so alarmed that it flew Rabb out of Rome without giving him time to pack a change of clothes, and Italy arrested and deported ten suspected Libyan terrorists. Libyan surveillance of U.S. embassies in Athens and Ankara was detected, and in November a gunman in Paris fired six shots at the American chargé d'affaires as he was leaving his apartment.

Libya's brazen behavior was the last straw for Reagan. At the end of the year the United States discontinued all Libyan oil imports and expanded a ban on U.S. exports to Libya. A more serious step was canceling U.S. passports for Libyan travel, a prelude for withdrawing more than two thousand Americans living and working in Libya.

Reagan's assertiveness toward Libya, coming in the aftermath of the long Iranian hostage crisis, might have seemed at the time to mark a turning point for the better in America's involvement in the Middle East, which had been escalating steadily ever since the United States supplanted the British and the French in the Middle East following the Suez crisis in 1956. In fact the Libyan episode marked the beginning of a new level of American agony in the Middle East that continues to this day.

Soon after the Libyan affair Reagan had to engage in a bruising legislative battle to win approval for the sale of advanced AWAC (Airborne Warning and Control) airplanes to Saudi Arabia. The idea for the sale had originated during the Carter administration, but the final commitment for the sale was not yet complete when Reagan took office. The AWACs served the strategic purpose of creating a foothold for the U.S. military in Saudi Arabia, while the Saudis wanted the AWACs as a tangible symbol that the United States was committed to preventing an Iranian-style fundamentalist revolution. Despite Saudi assurances that its AWACs would be used under American supervision for self-defense only, there was concern that the Saudis might use the planes against Israel's interests. The real argument, though, involved a more delicate issue, about which few would speak directly.

The delicacy of the matter arose because Israel had carried off a brazen attack against an Iraqi nuclear reactor in June. The bombing raid, utilizing American-made warplanes and based partly on American intelligence about the reactor, came without prior notification to the United States, and involved flying through Jordanian and Saudi airspace, using Jordanian air force call signs to mislead radar operators. Israel bombed the reactor out of concern that Iraq was on its way to developing nuclear weapons. Israel justified its act with the statement that would become familiar to Americans after September 11, 2001: "Under no circumstances would we allow the enemy [Iraq] to develop weapons of mass destruction." No one in 1981 doubted that Israel was correct in its judgment about Saddam Hussein's intentions—the French-made Osirak facility was not an electricity-generating reactor but a "research" reactor that produced large quantities of weapons-grade material—and most nations were privately relieved at Israel's action. Indeed, Iran had tried to attack the Osirak reactor the previous year.[56] But the Kabuki theater of international law and diplomacy required that the United States join the "outrage" of the international community and express its displeasure at the United Nations. "There was much bitterness in CIA," intelligence expert Angelo Codevilla wrote, "over what the Israelis had done and how they had, indirectly, involved the U.S."[57] There was bitterness also at the State Department, which was hoping for closer U.S. ties to Iraq.

The calculus would change once the Saudis had AWAC airplanes at their disposal. Israel's ability to conduct surprise raids would be constricted—which is why the pro-Israel lobby opposed the sale, and probably one reason why the State Department favored it. Reagan had to twist arms to get the necessary votes; in October the Senate approved the sale by a vote of 52–48. Israeli prime minister Menachem Begin had publicly opposed the sale, to which Reagan responded tartly, "It is not the business of other nations to make American foreign policy."[58] This was the first test of whether Reagan's clout on foreign affairs equaled his strength on domestic policy.

And so as the summer gave way to fall in 1981, it appeared the Reagan Revolution was on a roll both domestically and abroad.

Then things started to go wrong.

CHAPTER 5

STAY THE COURSE

*Can anyone here say that if we can't do it, someone
down the road can do it? And if no one does it, what happens
to the country? All of us here know the economy would
face an eventual collapse. I know it's a hell of a challenge,
but ask yourselves: If not us, who? If not now, when?*
—REAGAN TO HIS CABINET, SEPTEMBER 1981

ONE OF THE most memorable photographs of Reagan shows him at
the signing of the tax cut bill at his California ranch in August 1981.
Seated at an outdoor table dressed in jeans and jacket, he was beaming from
ear to ear. This was not an unusual countenance for Reagan, but this particular scene caught him with his right leg outstretched and his cowboy boot
pointed skyward—a human exclamation point. He was understandably riding high.

But the media, and even some of Reagan's aides such as Richard Darman, thought it symbolic that a thick fog bank, typical summer weather on
California's central coast, descended upon the ranch just as Reagan was putting his signature on the bill.[1] The implication was that Reagan's economic
policy was fogged up. A tongue-in-cheek Reagan blamed the media for the
fog. In retrospect the passage of the tax bill was the high-water mark for
macroeconomic policy reform in Reagan's first term.

In fact a wave of bad news was about to crash on his head. In a portent
of what was to come, a week before Reagan signed the tax bill he received a
briefing over lunch from Stockman on the deteriorating state of the federal
budget. Stockman had concluded that the budget cuts were too small and the
tax cut too big to reach a balanced budget by 1984, or even 1986. His budget

models showed the deficit for the next fiscal year swelling from a previous estimate of $42.5 billion to $60 billion or more, with even worse deficits in 1983 and 1984. (In fact, the 1982 deficit would be $111 billion, nearly twice what Stockman feared.) "On the margin," Stockman said, "every single important number in the budget is going in the wrong direction." He would later say that he knew long before the tax vote that things were going wrong, but that his attitude, as expressed to Richard Darman, was "Win now, fix it later."

Reagan was dismayed at the news, saying, "If these numbers were out, Tip O'Neill would be wearing a halo."[2] Stockman reassured Reagan, promising to put together a "fall offensive" of more budget cuts for Congress to consider. Stockman had two primary targets in mind: Social Security and defense spending. He argued that he had made a large mistake in calculating increases in defense spending back in the early weeks of the administration in January. Reagan's team had settled on the goal of a 7 percent increase in real defense spending for each of the next several years, which Stockman built into his budget projections. But the budget plan he inherited from Jimmy Carter already contained a roughly 5 percent increase in defense spending, and Stockman added 7 percent more on top of Carter's 5 percent.

While a substantial increase in defense spending was essential to Reagan's grand strategy, it is less clear that this enormous infusion of cash was spent wisely. The incoming Reaganites under Caspar Weinberger at the Pentagon seemed to have taken Carter's procurement targets and simply doubled them without much strategic forethought. Carter's proposed 1981 defense budget called for building 14 antisubmarine aircraft; Weinberger upped the number to 48. Carter had requested 214 Air Force and Navy planes; Weinberger, 345. And so it went. Air-to-air missiles—Carter, 2,827; Weinberger, 5,357. Tanks: Carter, 569; Weinberger, 1,080. Helicopters: Carter, 86; Weinberger, 110. The most expensive and perhaps least justified initiative was the determination to build a 600-ship navy, with 15 carrier battle groups instead of Carter's plan for 12, even though the era of battleship warfare was over. Of more certain value was the doubling of the amount Carter proposed to spend to build up the Rapid Deployment Force, which would prove its utility ten years later in the days leading up to the first Gulf War against Iraq.

As with any large government procurement program, abuses and irregularities later emerged, to the embarrassment of Reagan and Congress alike. Defense contractors were found to have charged $7,000 for a coffeepot for C5-A cargo planes; $435 for a standard claw hammer available at hardware stores for $5; $437 for a twelve-foot measuring tape; $640 for a toilet seat;

$17.59 for a three-inch steel bolt; and $1,118 for plastic caps for stool legs. A Pentagon inspector general's study of fifteen thousand spare parts found that contractors had raised the price on two-thirds of the parts by more than 50 percent since 1980; some had risen 500 percent. Some of these outlandish stories represented abuses on the part of uncompetitive private sector con-tractors, but many turned out to reflect peculiarities of Pentagon accounting systems, in which defense contractors spread overhead costs more or less evenly across the entire spectrum of products, which is simpler (and cheaper) than trying to figure out how much overhead should be applied to each item. In fact military hammers didn't really cost $435, but when a sailor unpacked a shipment of mixed goods including extensive tent equipment and hammers and saw the overhead charges applied to hammers, he called his congress-man, touching off a media and oversight hearing frenzy.[3] Likewise, cof-feemakers for civilian jumbo jet airplanes can cost several thousand dollars, as they need to make coffee for several hundred people at a time.

With inflation still expected to run high, nominal defense spending would now more than double over the next five years under this compounded plan.[4] Stockman wanted to claw back some of that increase, but Defense Secretary Weinberger stood squarely in the way. The August lunch meeting marked the beginning of the administration's partial retreat on taxes and of what Richard Darman called "the struggle for the president's mind"—an unfortu-nate story line that was quickly adopted by the news media.[5] Darman was one of the ringleaders (along with Stockman and Chief of Staff James Baker) of the faction that wanted to raise taxes to lower the deficit. Darman and oth-ers in the "pragmatist" faction were frustrated at Reagan's resistance. "The luncheon yielded no intellectual progress," Darman complained.[6]

This episode has long been wrongly reported. In fact, Reagan knew some defense cuts were necessary, but in his typical manner he remained quiet about this fact. In a diary entry for September 8, Reagan wrote: "We have to convince the money market that we mean it & that means some cuts in de-fense. But we have to do that in such a way that the world sees us as keeping our word to restore our defense strength."

As with the economy, the major media adopted an adversarial stance toward Reagan's defense buildup and foreign policy. CBS News led the way, with a five-part documentary in 1981 entitled *The Defense of the United States* that concluded with the liberal cliché "You can't buy peace simply by spending more and more on arms." It was the most elaborate and expen-sive network documentary series ever made to date. Dan Rather intoned:

"Never before in our history have so many of our weapons been behind schedule, over budget, out of order." Defense spending, correspondent Richard Threlkeld said, would destroy the economy. He did not tell viewers that defense budgets under Reagan were a smaller portion of the economy than they had been during the fast-growth years of the early 1960s.[7]

*　　*　　*

WHEN REAGAN RETURNED to Washington in early September from his sojourn at the ranch, his political fortunes had taken a dramatic reversal. Economic indicators were turning negative—the first overt signals that the economy was already in a recession. After a strong first quarter in 1981, the economy was losing steam fast and turned in negative growth in the third quarter. By September the Index of Leading Economic Indicators had fallen for four months in a row, with August's 2.7 percent drop the largest decline in two years. Housing starts remained at their lowest level since 1946, auto sales were off 30 percent from their level in 1978, and General Motors reported a whopping $469 million loss for the third quarter. Business bankruptcies were up more than 40 percent from the previous year. Unemployment was on the rise, and long-term interest rates jumped 1½ points.

Worse news came soon. In December the Federal Reserve reported that industrial utilization—the measure of how fully America's industrial capacity is being used—was down to a shockingly low 75 percent. Unemployment had risen from 7.4 percent to 8.9 percent since Reagan took office. In the last quarter of 1981, real GDP fell at an annual rate of 5.2 percent. Democrats wasted no time in attacking. "It's a shame that it takes the human tragedy of unemployment to show the Reagan economic nonsense for what it is," Tip O'Neill said in October.

Although nearly every public and private sector forecast was predicting (incorrectly, as it turned out) a healthy rebound by the middle of 1982, there were other sour tidings.[8] It appeared the financial markets were getting a case of the jitters. The stock market slumped to its lowest level of the year in mid-September, and interest rates spurted upward again, driving the Dow Jones bond index to a record low. *Fortune* magazine was typical of the financial press: "Rarely has the public mood turned so swiftly. . . . Many people have understandably interpreted the high interest rates and low stock prices as a thundering no-confidence vote in Reagan's strategy for ending inflation. . . . Investors are said to be terrified by a tax cut that far exceeds the spending reductions Reagan hopes to achieve."[9] But *Fortune* went on to speculate sensibly that the real fear of investors was that Reagan wouldn't stick with a worthy policy but would succumb to mounting pressures to reverse course on his tax cut.

Fortune was right to be worried, as the pressure to delay or cancel the third year of the tax cut became relentless—pressure that would soon come not merely from critics but also from fellow Republicans on Capitol Hill and Reagan's own senior staff at the White House. Stockman began leaking to the press his view that the tax cut had been too big, a tactic he later admitted amounted to "out-and-out subversion . . . to force a tax hike." The reports of a higher deficit and the wobbly financial markets were enough to spur the media and Reagan's Democratic critics to pronounce Reaganomics a failure, even before the first installment of the tax cut went into effect on October 1.

Throughout September Reagan responded defensively to this onslaught with the correct but weak-sounding explanation that his plan hadn't taken effect yet. He complained: "They say, 'Well, the slump is because the program isn't working.' Well, it isn't—it doesn't start until October 1." Democrats, Reagan said, "were like Monday morning quarterbacks who are sounding off on Friday night." Reagan delighted in passing around a cartoon at a luncheon with out-of-town editors that contained this punch line: "And so it seems clear to this reporter that Reaganomics has failed, failed to thrive in a climate of optimism, failed to blossom into a viable economic alternative, failed to bear the fruit of prosperity—at least in these first five disappointing minutes."

Reagan was determined to respond to the economic situation by pursuing more budget cuts. In September the White House floated the idea of asking Congress to restore the president's authority to impound up to 10 percent of the 1982 budget (that is, not spend money Congress had appropriated), a power Congress had taken away from the executive branch in the mid-1970s in the aftermath of Watergate. It was a total nonstarter. Reagan was even ready to tackle Social Security again, beginning with another nationally televised speech on the need to cut Social Security, but Republicans on Capitol Hill firmly told him there was no support for the idea. Meanwhile, as Tip O'Neill's biographer John A. Farrell recounts, "O'Neill made a far-reaching decision to politicize Social Security, ordering his Democrats to withdraw from the bipartisan alliance with Republican moderates" that might save Social Security from looming insolvency. (The Social Security trust fund was projected to go into the red within a year.) So when Reagan finally went on national television again in late September to make another appeal for public and congressional support for further budget cuts, he threw in the towel on Social Security, calling for a bipartisan commission to figure out a fix for the failing system. Its chairman was Alan Greenspan.

The speech hinted that there was trouble on the budget: "Our immediate challenge is to hold down the deficit in the fiscal year that begins next week. A number of threats are now appearing that will drive the deficit upward if we fail to act. . . . And without further cuts, we can't achieve our goal of a balanced budget by 1984." In all Reagan announced a package of $57 billion in further spending cuts ($27 billion from social welfare programs), along with abolishing two cabinet departments, Energy and Education, closing some tax loopholes, and curtailing some federal loan guarantees. He invoked a now familiar appeal: "I'm asking all of you who joined in this crusade to save our economy to help again, to let your representatives know that you will support them in making the hard decisions to further reduce the cost and size of government." To his cabinet earlier in the day, Reagan had said: "I know it's a hell of a challenge, but ask yourselves: If not us, who? If not now, when?"

The appeal for spending cuts fell on deaf ears on Capitol Hill. Ted Kennedy gave the Democratic response to Reagan on TV and didn't even attempt to propose compromise or an alternative. Instead he attacked: "This is government of the rich, by the rich, and for the rich." A sign of how badly the momentum for budget cutting had been lost came on the eve of Reagan's appeal, in a widely publicized dustup over the most unlikely item imaginable: a sandwich condiment.

The Gramm-Latta budget plan that finally passed reduced the growth of school lunch program funding by $1 billion below its automatic-pilot baseline, and gave the U.S. Department of Agriculture (USDA), which runs the program, ninety days to come up with ways for school districts to accommodate the lower funding without reducing nutrition. A panel of nutritionists came up with the option to "accept catsup as a fruit/vegetable when used as an ingredient," which might include its use as a condiment. USDA standards required that a federally funded lunch must include five elements: meat, milk, bread, and two servings of fruits or vegetables. Most kids don't eat their vegetables in school lunches anyway, so allowing catsup as a vegetable for funding purposes might reduce food waste as well as save money. (It wasn't just catsup; comparable items included pickle relish.) The budget crunchers at USDA thought this idea allowed states more flexibility, and the tight time line allowed no time for higher review by political appointees at the USDA or at OMB.

When the USDA released the new guidelines in mid-September, a fire-storm erupted. Democrats staged indignant photo ops with small, dreary-looking meals that supposedly met the guidelines, such as a small slice of white bread with a dab of catsup in the middle. Agriculture Secretary John Block attempted to defend the idea, claiming with justification that the guidelines had been misunderstood, but the rout was on and the guidelines were hastily withdrawn. Reagan initially suspected that bureaucrats had deliberately sabotaged the program to embarrass the administration. As is often the case, no one would ever admit to having thought up the idea. (In the 1990s, the Clinton administration proposed classifying salsa as a vegetable in the school lunch program, and no one took any notice.) In the public mind, though, it was "the cold-hearted White House" that wanted to pinch pennies by classifying catsup as a vegetable, which suggested that social spending had been cut too far already. The episode became one of the ill-founded but un-shakable myths of the Reagan years.[10] (Jay Leno was still joking about it years later.) The catsup-as-a-vegetable episode may have been a small thing, but it was perhaps the turning point of the Reagan tide, just as Lyndon John-son's "rat bill," a request for a new federal aid program to eradicate rats in urban areas, signaled a turning of the tide against the Great Society in 1967.[11]

Unable to agree on a budget, Congress passed a "continuing resolution" in November to keep the government running at current levels. Reagan cast his first veto and briefly shut down the government, in a pattern that would repeat itself for much of the next six years (and which was repeated most dra-matically during Bill Clinton's presidency in 1995).

Just as Reagan was digging in for a protracted defense of his policy, he suffered one of the worst embarrassments and most politically damaging self-inflicted wounds of all time. It came from the most unexpected source: David Stockman. On November 10 (Stockman's thirty-fifth birthday), the *Atlantic Monthly* hit the newsstands featuring a cover story by *Washington Post* na-tional editor William Greider, who, as noted, had been meeting with Stock-man throughout the winter, spring, and summer. The article was entitled "The Education of David Stockman." It could have been called "The Con-fessions of David Stockman." Stockman went overnight from *wunderkind* to Deep Throat.

Greider's story reported that Stockman had known as far back as Janu-ary that Reaganomics would create huge deficits, but he had rigged the OMB economic models to conceal this fact. As explained in Chapter 2, this account is misleading at best. More damaging to Reagan and Stockman was not Greider's narrative or spin but Stockman's own words. The whiz kid who had held Washington in thrall to his encyclopedic knowledge of the immense federal budget was quoted as saying, "*None of us really understands what's going on with all these numbers.* You've got so many different budgets out and so many different baselines and such complexity now in the interactive parts of the budget between policy action and the economic environment and all of the internal mysteries of the budget, and there are a lot of them" (emphasis added). The whole process had gone too fast, Stockman explained, and the people involved in the process didn't know what they were doing. By Greider's telling, Stockman had changed his mind about the income tax cut in May.

Greider chronicled Stockman's defection from supply-side economics.[12] "I've never believed that just cutting taxes alone would cause output and employment to expand," Stockman told Greider. It got worse: "Kemp-Roth was always a Trojan horse to bring down the top rate." Greider wrote, "This seemed a cynical concession for Stockman to make in private conversation while the Reagan Administration was still selling the supply-side doctrine to Congress." Pressed on this issue, Stockman appeared to admit that Reaganomics was no more than its liberal critics had made it out to be: "It's kind of hard to sell 'trickle down,' so the supply-side formula was the only way to get a tax policy that was really 'trickle down.' Supply-side is 'trickle-down' theory." Later in the article Stockman seemed to imply that supply-side economics was a "crackpot theory."

At first the *Atlantic* article received only secondary notice in the media, but it exploded when the *CBS Evening News* led with the story two days after the magazine hit newsstands.[13] The *New York Times* put the story on the front page—"Stockman's Views Touch Off Furor"—and the story was the focus of the punditocracy for more than a week. Typical of the media judgment of the episode was Hobart Rowen's column in the *Washington Post*: "Stockman is saying flat out that Reaganomics is a failure, and the economic arguments for it were fraudulent—and he knew it." The *New York Times* editorial page said, "The Reagan Administration's vaunted economic policy cannot work; the Administration knows that; and yet the Administration keeps on flogging it as just the medicine America needs," and went on to compare Reagan's "deception" to Lyndon Johnson's disastrous decision to pursue "guns and butter" in the 1960s.

Ecstatic Democrats claimed vindication and read the entire article into the *Congressional Record* as though it were the equivalent of the *Pentagon*

Papers. Tip O'Neill was triumphant: "The architect of the Administration's program is admitting exactly what I and other critics have been saying for six months." Senator Howard Baker expressed the bewilderment of most Republicans, asking, "How could such a smart guy be so dumb?" Senator Bob Dole, on the other hand, praised Stockman, calling the article "refreshing" and adding, "I think he may have gained some credibility. I think people like candor in this town."

Reagan was furious. "What the hell happened?" he asked at the morning staff meeting the day after the story erupted. Reagan's senior advisers were split on whether to keep Stockman: Ed Meese—and Nancy Reagan—thought he should be fired; James Baker and others in the pragmatist camp argued for a reprieve. After a well-publicized visit to the woodshed, during which Stockman offered his apology and his resignation, Reagan decided to keep him in part because it was felt that Stockman's mastery of the federal budget was indispensable. But keeping Stockman was paradoxically a shrewd political move in the short run; his firing tacitly would have confirmed that Greider's account was accurate.

Stockman would stay on until 1985 with his credibility and clout much diminished. Reagan charitably blamed Greider for the debacle, writing to a friend that "you can bet [Dave's] no longer a friend to that journalistic prostitute he once trusted." But Reagan never treated Stockman warmly afterward, and expressed regret years later that he didn't fire Stockman at the time. (Stockman repaid Reagan's forbearance by writing a bitter and condescending memoir in 1986, *The Triumph of Politics,* in which he argued that Reaganomics was "doomed from the start.")

The *Atlantic* article did severe damage, finishing off what little political momentum Reaganomics had left. The *Wall Street Journal*'s Robert Bartley observed that the *Atlantic* story was well timed to coincide with the onset of the recession. For the rest of his presidency, Reagan was on the defensive about his tax cuts, under mounting pressure to reverse course, and mostly stalemated on further spending restraint.

One aspect of the budget story that was obscured at the time was that some of the worsening budget situation was arising from *improvement* in some economic fundamentals. Inflation was falling faster than expected; while this was good for consumers and the economy, every one-point drop in inflation had the perverse effect of worsening the budget deficit for 1982 by $4 billion. A one-point drop in overall economic activity added $8 billion to the deficit, so the slowing economy along with the drop in inflation was delivering a double whammy to the budget.

In hindsight it is clear that the Reagan administration made a tactical blunder in placing new heavy emphasis on the budget deficit *as an economic factor* and thinking the deficit would be to their political advantage in getting Congress to embrace spending restraint. It lent verisimilitude to the orthodox view that budget deficits, rather than monetary policy, are the preeminent force in causing inflation and high interest rates. The White House put itself in a box from which it could not escape for the rest of Reagan's presidency.[14] From a modern conservative point of view the budget deficit should be viewed not as a primary economic factor but as a measure of the growth of government and of the insatiability of spending urges.

On the other hand, it is hard to imagine that the White House could have been able to feign indifference to the projections of unprecedented and heretofore unimaginable deficits. After all, back in February Reagan himself had said in his first televised address: "We know now that inflation results from all that deficit spending." Reagan would later quip that "I don't worry much about the deficit; it's big enough to take care of itself," but neither he nor his economic team was prepared to mount a sustained argument in favor of downplaying the importance of the deficit, which might have spooked the financial markets. After decades of conservative criticism of deficit spending, such an about-face would have lacked credibility. Herbert Stein, the conservative critic of supply-side economics, pointed out the obvious: "If now the most classical, hard-line president in fifty years accepts indefinite deferral of a balanced budget who will any longer be inhibited by fear of deficits?" In fact, when in December 1981 William Niskanen, a member of the President's Council of Economic Advisers, delivered an academic paper downplaying the role of budget deficits as a driver of inflation and interest rates, all hell broke loose. He was instantly disavowed by the White House, even though he had the facts on his side.[15]

*   *   *

THE STOCKMAN DEBACLE and the media din about the failure of Reaganomics before it even began established the conventional wisdom, which persists to this day, that Reagan's tax cut package was too big and was the chief cause of the subsequent huge deficits and the recession of 1982.[16] In fact the tax cut barely held the line at the end of the day, as previously enacted Social Security tax hikes taking effect in the early 1980s erased the income tax cut for many working Americans. This is a crucial point: five-year tax and spending projections under Carter's last year would have seen taxes and spending rise from about 21 percent of GDP to 24 percent by

1984. Reagan's modest budget cuts had cut the growth rate of spending from 17 percent a year to about 7 percent, and, since Social Security payroll taxes were increasing, the income tax cut would keep most taxpayers' burdens even overall. The recession, however, threw everything off.

To understand the entire arc of the Reagan presidency it is necessary to perceive the full causes of the recession of 1982, including especially the role of monetary policy under the Federal Reserve, but starting with the heretical idea that the tax cut wasn't large enough or implemented soon enough. Keep in mind that the first year's tax rate cut was only 5 percent and took effect for just the last three months of 1981, rather than being retroactive to January 1 as Reagan had originally wanted.[17] On an annual basis it was worth only 1.25 percent—not enough to be a meaningful stimulus in Keynesian terms nor enough of a supply-side incentive to spur large changes in savings and investment. Economist Lawrence Lindsey concluded: "Delaying the tax cuts almost certainly contributed to the very severe recession of 1981–82."[18] While the tax cut was too small and came too late to have much effect in 1981, it was running into the teeth of the Federal Reserve's increasingly tight monetary policy—much tighter than the Reagan plan expected or desired.

Monetary restraint—more specifically, a gradual reduction in monetary growth in order to bring inflation down slowly over the next three years— was one of the four pillars of Reagan's economic plan (the other three being tax cuts, spending restraint, and deregulation).[19] But neither the president nor Congress controls monetary policy, of course; it is the domain of the Federal Reserve. While the Fed is independent, it does not exist in a complete political vacuum. Fed chairman Paul Volcker recognized this, commenting candidly, "No central bank can—or should, in my judgment—conduct policies for long that are out of keeping with basic, continuing objectives of the political system."[20]

In other words, Reagan needed the Fed's cooperation for his economic plan to work. Following the election there had been rumors that Reagan might try to replace Volcker (a Democrat) before his term expired in 1983. Others had recommended that Reagan meet with Volcker to secure a commitment to a steady policy of slow but predictable monetary growth. *Time* magazine commented, "Reagan is unlikely to follow that advice, mainly because he knows that the independent Federal Reserve would never agree to such restrictions on its freedom." Sure enough, in the opening weeks of his administration Reagan said, "We fully recognize the independence of the Federal Reserve System, and will do nothing to interfere with or undermine that independence." He understood this as a matter of principle, but he had also roughed up Volcker in his typically understated fashion.

Reagan had his first meeting with the Fed chairman over lunch on his third day in the Oval Office. Reagan opened the lunch with a question that must have nearly knocked Volcker out of his chair: why do we need a Federal Reserve anyway? Martin Anderson, who had prepared a memorandum for Reagan briefing him for the meeting, recalls Reagan's words as follows: "I was wondering if you could help me with a question that's often put to me. I've had several letters from people who raise the question of why we need a Federal Reserve at all. They seem to feel that it is the Fed that causes much of our monetary problems and that we would be better off if we abolished it. Why do we need the Federal Reserve?" Had Volcker been chewing on one of his trademark cigars, Anderson thought, he would have swallowed it.

Reagan was invoking here the idea of "free banking," which he probably learned about from his reading of conservative and libertarian periodicals such as the *Freeman*. Free banking is essentially the system of privately issued competitive currencies in a system without a central bank. Was Reagan just trying to make small talk or expressing curiosity about Volcker's opinion, or was he sending a subtle signal that he could make a world of trouble for the Fed if it didn't mesh with his policies? Reagan had already expressed some sympathy for the gold standard, which would severely circumscribe the Fed's role if adopted. Now he was hinting that he could consider going far beyond this. To orthodox Keynesian economists, if tax cuts were voodoo economics and the gold standard a medieval superstition, the idea of free banking ranked somewhere below leechcraft.

Volcker needn't have worried about such a radical prospect, but Reagan had subtly reinforced that the chairman needed to restrain his public remarks. Between the election and inauguration, Volcker had made several public comments that suggested skepticism of Reagan's supply-side prescriptions. "Let us not be beguiled into thinking there are quick and painless solutions," he told a New York audience. He also said that "the likelihood of a squeeze is apparent."[21] After Reagan took office, Volcker became more circumspect.

He had good reason to be, aside from any implicit threat from Reagan. The Fed had been highly erratic over the past decade and had remained inconsistent during his brief tenure. Volcker abruptly adopted an explicit tight money policy in the fall of 1979 in an effort to combat inflation, but during the second half of 1980 the money supply grew at its fastest rate in history.

Milton Friedman and other monetarists thought it was a blatant play to help Jimmy Carter win the election.

After the election the Fed tried to put monetary growth back on a gradual downward path, but instead monetary growth surged in the spring of 1981, sparking fears of resumed inflation. Then, in the summer, the Fed slammed on the brakes, with monetary growth now coming in below the bottom end of the Fed's own target range. The Reagan economic plan had hoped for monetary growth of about 6 percent in 1981, but during the second half of the year monetary growth was about zero.[22] The nation's credit markets were now confronted with the kind of tight money conditions that nearly always presaged a recession.

What was the Fed up to? Volcker and the Fed staff remained resolutely mum, much to the frustration of the Reagan administration. The informed speculation then and now is that after the tax cuts passed, Volcker believed the Fed would have only a short window of opportunity to strangle inflation through tight money before the political pressure became overwhelming for the Fed to ease.[23] William Niskanen wrote: "My judgment is that Volcker believed that the consensus for monetary restraint was temporary and that the American political system would not tolerate the slow, steady reduction in money growth recommended by the initial Reagan guidance. He may have wanted to reduce inflation as rapidly as possible, despite the temporary adverse effects on the economy and the destruction of the consensus for sustained restraint."[24]

Volcker knew that the Fed had its own credibility problems. *Fortune* magazine summarized the situation: "The central bank's performance has been so awful over the last 15 years that hardly anyone believes the Fed anymore." Volcker admitted as much in testimony before the Senate Budget Committee: "Americans have not seen for many years a successful fight on inflation, or balanced budgets, or so massive a tax reduction. A lot of bets on the future are still being hedged against the possibility that you, and we, will not carry through."

Reagan himself displayed a clear grasp of this problem, explaining at a lunch with out-of-town editors how the Fed was missing its monetary targets:

> We know that we have to have a consistent monetary policy that doesn't do what we've done over the last few decades, of the roller coaster effect—of when unemployment gets out of hand and it looks like hard times, they flood the market with paper money. And then when that brings on inflation, then all of a sudden you pull in and

tighten it down and you go the other way. This is what's been happening. I do have one little criticism, and yet I can see how it happened. You realize that we can visit with them, but we can't impose on them. They're totally autonomous. But it is true, recently, that they have two lines going up, a kind of a bracket, following productivity in the country, and they are trying to keep the money supply between those two lines. It may fluctuate a little bit, but staying between those two lines. And sometime back, they fell below their bottom line in this. And then they were faced with the prospect of trying to have a stable monetary policy to help in the fight against inflation. They didn't know how to just get back up where they should be without it looking like when on Wall Street they would look at the money supply and see this surge, they'd say, "Oh, oh, here we go again," and start acting as if, well, it was the same old game being played.[25]

The result of the Fed's monetary policy in the second half of 1981 was to pitch the nation into a recession deeper than anyone expected. In part the depth of the recession was due to a fundamental change in economic behavior that was hard to perceive and measure at the time. The change involved a technical detail, what became known to economists as the velocity puzzle. *Velocity* in this context refers to how quickly a dollar is turned over again and again in the economy, and changes in velocity can have a major effect on inflation. Because the velocity of money had been very stable for most of the previous thirty years—rising by about 3 percent a year—monetarists had focused instead on another key cause of inflation, the erratic rate of money supply growth. It was assumed that velocity would continue to increase at about that same rate in the 1980s, or maybe even a little faster, given the proliferation of new forms of credit in the late 1970s.

But in the middle of 1981 the unexpected happened: velocity started *falling* by an annual rate of about 2 percent (and would continue falling for the next several years). This is one reason why inflation fell faster than expected in 1981, much faster than the reduction of the money supply would justify. It also meant that the economy was going to contract a lot more than all the forecasters expected.

Most economists were at a loss to explain why velocity started to decline, which is why this aspect of the story was called the velocity puzzle. Supply-siders were not puzzled, however. They argued that the higher real returns on investment offered by lower tax rates would increase the attractiveness of holding financial assets, as opposed to physical assets such as real estate, commodities, and other hedges against inflation. Many supply-siders had predicted that such a shift would take place and would set the stage for a salutary, noninflationary investment-led economic expansion.

The point to grasp here is that the conventional economic view held that the tax cut must be offset by tight money to avert higher inflation; the supply-side argument was that the decline in velocity meant that tight money was unnecessary or that the tax cut should have been even larger to offset the Fed's tight monetary policy.

But the rotation of capital and the turnaround in the economy would not happen overnight; it would take more than a year to begin. The vindication of the beleaguered supply-siders would have to wait, as there was no way to abate the panic over the sinking economy and the soaring deficit. Thus the political outcry against the Fed's tight money was swift, severe, and bipartisan. Democratic congressman Henry Gonzales of Texas called for Volcker's impeachment at a testy hearing of the House Banking Committee. Democratic Senator Robert Byrd introduced legislation to require the Fed to reduce interest rates; his bill found several eager co-sponsors. Bob Dole, getting an earful from a credit-strapped farmer during a visit back to his home state of Kansas, called Volcker on the phone and handed the receiver to the farmer. "These high interest rates are stretching us to the breaking point," the exasperated farmer complained. Even Reagan briefly buckled, telling a Republican audience in September, "The Fed is independent, but they're hurting us in what we're trying to do as much as they're hurting everyone else."

The press raised its eyebrows over this remark ("It was a remarkable turnabout from an ardent supporter of hard money," said *Newsweek),* but Reagan settled down a few days later, reassuring his cabinet that "I want to see the Fed continue monetary restraint and be the fourth leg of our economic program." Milton Friedman, the godfather of monetarism, admired Reagan's principled restraint: "No other president would have stood by and let Volcker push the economy into recession by restricting the money supply so sharply."[26] Economist Michael Mussa (a member of the President's Council of Economic Advisers during Reagan's second term) wrote: "[T]here can be little doubt that, had Ronald Reagan pulled on his cowboy boots and led a lynch mob from the south lawn of the White House down to Federal Reserve headquarters on Constitution Avenue, he would have been joined not only by members of his administration but also by majorities from both houses of Congress, by the Washington representatives of a vast array of American businesses, and by a fair number of foreign diplomats, particularly from heavily indebted countries."[27] Volcker himself later credited Reagan for his measured response, writing in 1992, "President Reagan must have received lots of advice to take on the Fed himself, but he never did despite plenty of invitations at press conferences. . . . I had the sense that, unlike some of his predecessors, he had a strong visceral aversion to inflation and an instinct that, whatever some of his advisers might have thought, it wasn't a good idea to tamper with the independence of the Federal Reserve."[28]

Indeed, many of Reagan's political advisers and allies urged Reagan to lean on Volcker as the devastating political implications of a recession became obvious. James Baker was heard to say, "This guy is killing us," and White House political director Ed Rollins complained, "There's only one man who can cost the President re-election all by himself, and that's the chairman of the Federal Reserve. We need to control that guy."[29] Jack Kemp and other supply-siders urged Reagan to fire Volcker; one adviser who counseled the president against this course was Alan Greenspan. Reagan agreed, saying in July 1982, "I have to tell you we can't make a scapegoat of the Federal Reserve."

What does all this talk of the Fed and monetary policy mean? First, that the economy was already headed for recession before Reagan's tax and budget cuts passed, both for ordinary cyclical reasons and because of tight monetary policy. In fact the recession became a worldwide phenomenon, in part because countries such as West Germany and Japan had even tighter monetary policy than the United States at the time. Economist Michael Boskin points out, "It was never a 'Reagan' recession: the rest of the world went through one too."[30]

Second, the budget deficit was not the cause of high interest rates, and even a balanced budget in 1982 or 1983 would have done little to bring them down. The cyclical element of the recession can be seen in the fact that half of the decline in GDP came from a fall in exports—the result of an overly strong dollar.

Finally, despite the severity of the recession—the worst since the Great Depression of the 1930s, it was said—it was only half as severe as Keynesian economic models predicted it would be. Keynesian models forecast that GDP would have to fall by as much as $2 trillion to reduce inflation as far as occurred in 1981–82, with unemployment reaching perhaps as high as 20 percent. The actual fall in GDP was about $800 billion, and unemployment reached a high of 10.8 percent in the fall of 1982. The old economic orthodoxy was wrong. Only the supply-siders understood this at the time, and most of their already small number were jumping ship out of discouragement.[31]

Even if all of these factors could have been known at the time, it wouldn't have mattered much. Events that occur on the president's watch belong to him. Democrats were quick to pounce on "the Reagan recession," and they pressed their turning political fortunes with ruthlessness. The most brazen was the campaign chairman of the House Democrats, California congressman Tony Coelho. *Wall Street Journal* reporter Brooks Jackson described Coelho as heading "a modern-day political machine, a sort of New Tammany Hall in which money and pork-barrel legislation have become the new patronage."[32] Coelho, Jackson said, was "a cold-blooded Machiavelli" whose "tactics sometimes resembled a legal version of the old protection racket." Coelho would send letters to GOP-leaning business groups with thinly veiled threats that Democrats might consider their interests harshly if they did not contribute to Democratic candidates. One Coelho letter about a particular House race that Jackson unearthed read: "The NAHB [National Association of Home Builders] has a good relationship with Democrats in the House, and we would like to see that relationship continue and grow. Your action in this race [contributing to the Democratic candidate's Republican opponent] causes us to be concerned that the relationship will be damaged."[33] Coelho's hardball tactic largely succeeded in erasing the traditional Republican fund-raising advantage. Over the next several election cycles starting with 1982, Jackson concluded, "Coelho completely routed the threat of a PAC-financed Republican revolution."[34] But his edgy tactics caught up with him in the end. In 1989 Coelho abruptly resigned from the House under an ethical cloud, amidst allegations that he had accepted favorable treatment on junk bond deals.

*   *   *

FOR THE TIME being, Reagan's high public approval ratings—about 60 percent in the Gallup poll in October 1981—were holding up. But his prospects were on·a knife edge. With much of his staff, his own political party, and his opponents ready to reverse course, one person saved the Reagan Revolution from retreat and rout. That person was Ronald Reagan.

Although Darman and Stockman had complained that there had been "no intellectual progress" with Reagan on taxes and spending in the fall of 1981, perhaps the real issue was that Darman and Stockman had made no progress in understanding Ronald Reagan. Reagan very likely knew, intuitively at least, that a tax increase of some kind would be necessary. Keep in mind that Reagan had acceded to the largest tax increase in California history in his first year as governor when it became clear that the state budget could not be balanced through spending cuts alone.[35] Later in his governorship, when he gave ground on a tax issue about which he had said his position was cast in concrete, he quipped, "That sound you hear is the concrete breaking around my feet."[36] Remember also that in the winter of 1981 Reagan had wanted a "clean bill" on taxes, meaning limited to just the reductions in income tax rates. His original proposal would have resulted in a static five-year revenue reduction of about $500 billion. The goodie-filled tax bill that passed came with a five-year revenue loss of about $750 billion. "Nobody really thought we'd end up with a tax cut as big as the one we got," an unnamed aide told the *New York Times*.

But Reagan surely knew by instinct, both as a politician and from his previous stint as a labor negotiator, that an early concession on a tax increase would be politically catastrophic as well as ensure that he'd get a bad deal. Having got a larger tax cut than he'd asked for, he knew he was in a strong bargaining position. Giving in at the outset would be ruinous; it would amount to a repudiation of his economic program before it had gone into effect. It would give away any leverage for further spending cuts, and probably would have ensured that he'd be a one-term president. Reagan knew that in the coming months he'd have to negotiate on two fronts—with Democrats in Congress and with the faction in his own administration that favored a tax increase. Above all, Reagan wanted to preserve the full income tax cut—the chief target of Democrats—which had not even been implemented yet.

So Reagan played for time, arguing publicly and privately that what the economy needed most was patience. He had an opening position on higher taxes: he was willing to raise tax revenue by $3 billion. Nine months later he would accede to a $98 billion tax increase over the next three years (the largest in history up to that moment), in what many conservatives believed was a betrayal and a defeat at the hands of the Washington establishment. Reagan himself came to regret the deal he eventually struck, calling it the worst mistake of his presidency, and yet a closer look suggests that Reagan played his hand with considerable skill during the extraordinarily difficult months that followed the tax cut triumph of August 1981.

The standard story line of 1982 is that congressional Democrats and the White House staff wore down Reagan's "stubbornness" and compelled him to concede ground on raising taxes. This is the testimony of friend and foe alike. In hindsight the remarkable aspect of this episode was that Reagan held out as long as he did against the near unanimity of the political forces arrayed against him and the steady water torture to which he was subjected.

Capitol Hill Republicans were in a state of panic. Senator William Armstrong of Colorado, one of Reagan's staunchest conservative supporters, worried that growing deficits "will be the death knell of the Republican Party." Dole began openly sniping at supply-siders such as Jack Kemp: "The good news is that a bus loaded with supply-siders went over a cliff," Dole quipped. "The bad news is that there were three empty seats. The extra bad news is that the missing three are now huddling with the President."[37] Stockman was meeting clandestinely with Senate Republicans to craft a tax increase package, with Senator Pete Domenici ready to sponsor an $84 billion tax hike. Other Republicans talked openly of adopting a 4 percent surtax on high income earners for three years. Reagan recorded in his diary: "[Republican] Congressional leaders . . . are really antsy about the deficit and seem determined that we must retreat on our program—taxes and defense spending."

Reagan's own staff and cabinet were just as panicky. Richard Darman and James Baker proposed a "standby" tax that would kick in automatically if the deficit didn't come down. Transportation Secretary Drew Lewis proposed a gas tax hike to fund public works programs that would double as a program to reduce unemployment. Treasury Secretary Don Regan was about Reagan's only ally among his senior appointees in resisting a tax increase.

The media were relentless, with the *New York Times* being arguably the most slanted in its coverage. "President Still Resists Tax Rises" was the *Times*'s incredulous headline of November 6. On January 10 the *Times* ran the headline "On Taxes, the President's Men Versus the President." "It would be difficult for any President to defy so many aides and allies," *New York Times* reporter Steven Weisman wrote hopefully. Even George Will deserted Reagan, writing in 1982 that the nation was "undertaxed."

At one point late in the fall, Reagan attempted to deflect pressure from his staff in his usual semi-direct and affable way by opening a staff meeting with the comment, "You know, everybody in the press says that you guys have a conspiracy to talk me into a tax increase." At the end of the meeting, he said, "By God, they're right!" But his avuncular tactics could be deployed only a few times. At other meetings Reagan is said to have resorted to scowling and scolding, asking Stockman and Baker sharply at one point what they were doing in his White House if they held those views. Behind the scenes Reagan's staff, including many of Stockman's crew at OMB, were sharply divided, carrying on a lively debate between counsels of fiscal responsibility that dictated a tax increase, and the faction closer to Reagan believed "starving the beast" was the only way to limit the growth of government.

Reagan wrote in a letter to *Washingtonian* magazine that "if the deficit continues to grow it will not be because your tax cut was too big, but because spending cuts were too small." He began his November 10 press conference with the declaration that "[w]e will not go back to business as usual. Our plan for economic recovery is sound. . . . I am determined to stick with it and stay on course, and I will not be deterred by temporary economic changes or short-term political expediency." He repeated this again at his December 10 press conference: "I have no plans for increasing taxes in any way."

Reagan understood, as few of his staff did, that the debate over economic policy during a recession was merely a subset of a wider debate about the welfare state. Throughout the fall and winter, as he publicly assailed calls for a tax increase, he attempted to widen the focus back to the fundamental question of reversing long-term trends in the runaway growth of government. He made his argument most fully in his State of the Union speech in January 1982:

> Our current problems are not the product of the recovery program that's only just now getting underway, as some would have you believe; they are the inheritance of decades of tax and tax and spend and spend. . . .
>
> I will seek no tax increases this year, and I have no intention of retreating from our basic program of tax relief. I promise to bring the American people—to bring their tax rates down and to keep them down, to provide them incentives to rebuild our economy, to save, to invest in America's future. I will stand by my word. . . .
>
> In 1960 the Federal Government had 132 categorical grant programs, costing $7 billion. When I took office, there were approximately 500, costing nearly a hundred billion dollars—13 programs for energy, 36 for pollution control, 66 for social services, 90 for education. And here in the Congress, it takes at least 166 committees just to try to keep track of them. . . .
>
> Let's solve this problem with a single, bold stroke: the return of some $47 billion in Federal programs to State and local government, together with the means to finance them and a transition period of nearly 10 years to avoid unnecessary disruption.

Reagan's proposal to devolve programs to the states was called "the new federalism," though Reagan never used that phrase to describe it in his speech. The idea went nowhere, just as Nixon's "new federalism" had gone nowhere a decade before. State governors were not wild about the idea, and Washington is bipartisan in its interest in keeping programs centralized. The media picked up on the no-tax-hike language instead, peppering White House spokesman Larry Speakes the next day with questions about whether James Baker would keep his job.

A few weeks later Reagan submitted to Congress his formal 1983 budget proposal, containing $45 billion in cuts in domestic spending. If adopted as proposed, Reagan's budget would still have delivered a record $91.5 billion deficit. In a ritual that became precedent for the rest of Reagan's presidency, Democrats pronounced the budget plan "dead on arrival." Later in the spring Reagan renewed his offensive on another front, pushing Congress for a vote on a balanced budget amendment to the Constitution. It passed out of the Republican-controlled Senate but was defeated in the House.

The Democrats understood the larger stakes as well. They didn't just want more revenue; they wanted vindication, a tangible repudiation of Reagan's conservatism. The clash of political philosophy behind the budget debate was made most explicit by Detroit mayor Coleman Young, who said in the Democrats' televised response to Reagan's 1982 State of the Union message that the "pursuit of happiness" in the Declaration of Independence meant that the federal government was obligated to secure "the right of a job, the right to eat, the right to human dignity . . . [It is a] Federal responsibility that can't be shifted off to the states, or to the cities."

Before long Democrats distilled their counterargument to Reagan down to one word: *fairness*. The Democratic National Committee rolled out a TV ad campaign with the tag line "It's not fair—it's Republican." The subsidiary slogan was that Reagan was seeking to "balance the budget on the backs of the poor." Tip O'Neill referred to Reagan's "Beverly Hills budget." Protestors constructed a shanty Hooverville in Lafayette Park across from the White House to dramatize the point. A coalition of religious, labor, and community action groups set up similar tent cities called "Reagan Ranches" in several Midwestern cities. The White House responded with a seventy-five-page briefing book on fairness issues.

Once again the media gave Democrats their full cooperation. Helen Thomas's opening question at Reagan's first news conference of 1982 is typical of elite media attitudes: "How's it possible for you to propose deep cuts in the social programs in view of all this suffering?" *Newsweek* carried a cover story with the banner headline "Reagan's America: And the Poor Get Poorer." The story included reporting such as: "[R]esearch demonstrates that

Reagan's 1983 proposed reductions—combined with the effects of this year's reductions—will push low-income families deeper into poverty while virtually eliminating any incentive for them to work. . . . Reagan's attack on the welfare state is, at the very least, a radical approach to a problem that has been dealt with all too meekly in the past. And most radical of all is the Administration's economic-recovery program that asks the poor to take as an article of faith that tax cuts that mostly benefit the very rich eventually will trickle down to all income groups. So far it hasn't worked out that way—and there is scant evidence it ever will." "Television news is pounding home a message of economic pain night after night," Morton Kondracke noted in the *New Republic*, "providing the Democratic Party with better advertising than it could ever buy."

In April CBS News aired a special documentary by Bill Moyers, *People Like Us*, dramatizing the plight of low-income households that Reagan's policies were supposedly hurting. Moyers drew attention to four case studies of "people who slipped through the safety net," including a disabled man who lost his Social Security benefits and two mothers with severely ill children whose federal health care aid was curtailed. Moyers's theme: "In the great outcry about spending, some helpless people are getting hurt." In his diary Reagan called it "[a] thoroughly dishonest, demagogic cheap shot." The White House issued a rebuttal disputing the accuracy of Moyers's claims, but it was like spitting into a hurricane. The media had its theme: Reagan was heartless and uncaring.[38] Unbeknownst to everyone, the president was in the habit of sending personal checks to people who wrote to him at the White House with hard-luck stories. Reagan's own practice mirrored America's: charitable giving during the recession year of 1982 increased by 10 percent, to $49 billion. Meanwhile, despite the well-advertised cuts, the federal government was still spending $6,500 for every elderly, poor, or unemployed person.

And then there was the rise of the "homeless," as vagrants were now called. All around the nation the media reported that the incidence of homeless people living on the streets was rapidly increasing. There was some truth to this, chiefly because of the deinstitutionalization of nonviolent mental patients in the 1970s and the widespread closing of low-cost single-room occupancy (SRO) hotels in the name of urban renewal. Now, however, the media reported that homelessness was becoming a phenomenon of the middle class squeezed by the Reagan recession, even though there was little evidence to back up this claim. It was, in the words of *Atlantic Monthly* writer Gregg Easterbrook, a "media myth."[39] "Middle Class: New Victims of Homelessness," the *Washington Post* declared. To the *New York Times*, the homeless were "the new poor." The House Banking Committee held the first congressional hearing on homelessness since 1933 in an attempt to embarrass the administration. A homeless advocate named Mitch Snyder became a national figure; Snyder claimed that there were three million homeless people in the United States, a figure that surveys showed was inflated by as much as an order of magnitude but which the media accepted uncritically. When the Reagan administration offered hard-pressed cities the use of more than fourteen hundred vacant government buildings to offer temporary shelter to the homeless, only six were used.

Reagan replied as gamely as possible to the unrelenting onslaught. In one challenge to the welfare state, he said that if every church in America were to look after the needs of ten poor families, "we could eliminate all government welfare in this country," and "the actual help would be greater because it would come from the heart."[40] Reagan also complained about sensationally negative media coverage of the economy in remarks to reporters in March: "You can't turn on evening news without seeing that they're going to interview someone else who's lost his job, or they're outside the factory that has laid off workers and so forth—the constant downbeat that can contribute psychologically to slowing down a new recovery that is in the offing. . . . [I]s it news that some fellow out in South Succotash someplace has just been laid off, that he should be interviewed nationwide? Or someone's complaint that the budget cuts are going to hurt their present program?" Not content merely with playing defense, Reagan also made a frontal assault on the Great Society, arguing before a black audience that blacks and the poor would have been better off if the Great Society programs had never happened.

Reagan also referred several times throughout the year to the help-wanted ads in major papers, noting that there were jobs going begging: "I've counted as many as 65 pages of employers looking for people to fill jobs; and they're back the following week trying again." He modified his view on this point as the year progressed, noting that many job openings required specialized training, which led him to endorse a modest new jobs program, the Jobs Training Partnership Act (cosponsored in the Senate by the unlikely duo of Dan Quayle and Ted Kennedy). But on the whole these counterpunches were used to reinforce the charge that Reagan was insensitive and uncaring about the plight of the unemployed. By the fall, Reagan was joking that he wouldn't mention "South Succotash" again.

*   *   *

THE POLITICAL ONSLAUGHT and the continuing decline of the economy in the spring of 1982 began to take its toll on public opinion. "Reagan Evoking Rising Concern, New Poll Shows," the *New York Times* announced in late March. "The American public generally disagrees with President Reagan's unyielding budget positions on taxes and arms spending," the *Times* reported. A slight majority told the *Times*'s pollster that they favored canceling the 10 percent income tax cut scheduled to take effect on July 1. By May, trial heat polls for the 1984 election showed Senator Ted Kennedy beating Reagan, and Walter Mondale running even. A generic July poll that omitted any hypothetical matchup reported that 52 percent opposed Reagan's reelection. Alan Baron, a prominent Democratic political analyst, reported in late spring that at a gathering of about seventy media figures three-quarters expressed the opinion that Reagan wouldn't run for reelection in 1984. Lou Cannon, the dean of Reagan reporters, published a new biography of Reagan in 1982 that ended with Cannon's prediction that Reagan would not run again.

Whether Reagan was worn down into acceding to a tax increase or was following a conscious negotiating strategy from the first is difficult to know, but the unusual way he handled this issue in his memoir, *An American Life,* indicates that the latter might have been the case. Rather than provide an original narrative explaining his account of the 1982 tax hike battle, Reagan in *An American Life* tells the story entirely by reprinting entries from his diary for ten consecutive pages. On the surface no account could seem more candid and contemporary than Reagan's own diary entries, yet there is reason to doubt their probity. He took up the diary at the insistence of his staff "for the sake of history," and he wrote it more out of duty than inspiration. The diary entries are less wide-ranging and intimate than his personal letters to friends and private individuals he knew well. He was probably self-conscious that his "private" diary would become a public document some day; he even used dashes in his mild profanity ("h—l" or "d—n").

On the surface, then, the diary entries support the conventional account of the 1982 tax battle, but a close reading hints that Reagan was consciously maneuvering for advantage. *An American Life* begins its narrative-by-diary with an entry a few days before Christmas in 1981. Some excerpts:

> [M]y team is pushing for a tax increase to hold down the deficits. I'm being stubborn. I think our tax cuts will produce more revenue by stimulating the economy. I intend to wait and see some results.

January 11 [1982]:

Republican House leaders came down here to the W.H. Except for Jack Kemp they are h—l bent on new taxes and cutting the defense budget. Looks like a heavy year ahead.

January 20:

First anniversary [of inauguration]. The day was a tough one. A budget meeting and pressure from everyone to give into increases in excise taxes. . . . I finally gave in but my heart wasn't in it.

January 21:

Met with the U.S. Chamber of Commerce group. They made an impassioned plea that I not raise taxes. They were touching a nerve when they said I would look as if [*sic*] I were retreating from my own program. That's exactly how I feel. After meeting, told Ed [Meese], Jim [Baker] and Mike [Deaver] we had to go back to the drawing board. I just can't hold still for the tax increases.

January 22:

I told our guys I couldn't go for tax increases. If I have to be criticized, I'd rather be criticized for a deficit than for backing away from our economic program.

Although Reagan continued to say, as late as March 1, "don't touch our tax cut," he had quietly authorized James Baker to begin negotiations with congressional leadership about a tax and budget deal. The "Gang of 17," as it came to be known, met at Baker's suburban Virginia house to avoid notice by the media, but the news quickly leaked anyway. (One reason we can be sure Reagan knew about these meetings is that the gang included Senator Paul Laxalt, Reagan's closest friend in the Senate.) The talks made little progress. Let the story resume with more diary entries:

March 26:

It is imperative that we get further budget cuts. So far the Dems aren't budging.

April 19:

Met with Repub. Congressional leadership. The budget was the subject. I think they are relieved to learn that I'm willing to compro-

mise some in return for a bipartisan program. I called Tip O'Neill.
I'm not sure he's ready to give up.

April 23:
. . . the group debating the budget seems unable to arrive at any
kind of consensus. If we can't get a bipartisan agreement to act together in the face of the projected deficit, then I take to the air—
TV—and there will be blood on the floor.

April 26:
The Dems are playing games—they want me to rescind the third
year of the tax cuts—not in a million years!

April 27:
Well, it looks like the three weeks of budget talks got nowhere.

The next day, April 28, Reagan made a rare trip up to Capitol Hill for a
climactic meeting with O'Neill and other Democratic House leaders. Both
sides came spoiling for a fight, and for three hours, fight is exactly what they
did. O'Neill threw the "trickle-down" charge at Reagan's income tax cut and
called the president's proposed budget unfair. Reagan replied, "I've heard all
that crap," and argued, "I don't know where any unfair situation has resulted from my program. We haven't thrown anyone out in the snow to die."
Reagan and O'Neill sparred over who was the legitimate keeper of FDR's
legacy—"big roundhouse exchanges," in Stockman's words. It was as pure a
clash as can be found in American politics, with O'Neill arguing that the
New Deal made modern America possible, and Reagan counterpunching
with attacks on the runaway growth of government.[41]

Democrats hoped they could get Reagan to propose cuts in Social Security, chiefly so they could attack him politically in the upcoming election.
"You're not going to trap me on that," Reagan demurred. (Democrats already had bumper stickers printed: VOTE DEMOCRATIC—SAVE SOCIAL SECU-
RITY.) O'Neill eventually said Democrats would be willing to back $35
billion in domestic policy cuts, but wanted a commensurate amount cut from
defense spending. Reagan countered with $60 billion in domestic spending
cuts and refused to consider defense cuts, arguing that defense spending was
less than 30 percent of total federal spending, down from nearly half the
budget when John F. Kennedy had been president. "Times aren't the same
now as under Kennedy," O'Neill replied.

Majority leader Jim Wright attempted to break the impasse with the offer that Democrats would back larger domestic spending cuts if Reagan would cut in half the third year of the income tax cut. "You can get me to crap a pineapple," Reagan replied, "but you can't get me to crap a cactus." The president left the door slightly ajar, however, offering to consider a slight delay in the third year of the tax cut or other tax measures in return for larger domestic spending cuts. But there was no deal in sight that day. The meeting ended so discordantly, in fact, that neither side wanted to get up first from the table, for fear of being accused by the other of breaking up the meeting. Finally James Baker suggested that everyone stand up to leave at the same time.

Reagan's summary of the meeting in his diary left out all of the colorful detail and language he had used:

> April 28:
> The big thing today was a meeting with Tip, Howard Bohling [Reagan meant Richard Bolling], Jim Wright, Jim Baker, Ed Meese, Don Regan, and Dave Stockman. . . . Three hours later we'd gotten nowhere. Finally I said I'd split the difference with you and they refused that. Meeting over.

While Reagan may have been willing to play out the confrontation a while longer, Senate Republicans lost what little nerve they had and charged ahead with a tax increase package in May and June. This was a remarkable state of affairs, since the Constitution specifies that revenue measures are supposed to originate in the House, and also since the House in June passed by a narrow margin a budget resolution close to Reagan's request.

Democrats on the Senate Finance Committee attempted to put through a rollback of the third year of the income tax cut, but Republicans voted it down. Bob Dole's tax increase bill passed out of the Finance Committee on a straight party-line vote. If there was going to be a tax increase other than income taxes on the rich, Democrats wanted Republicans to own it. The Dole bill consisted mostly of excise taxes on telephones, air travel, cigarettes, and other activities. While the tax bill kept the cuts in marginal income tax rates in place, it contained some odious features, such as withholding on interest and dividend income. (The House had rejected this idea by a vote of 401–4 in 1980 when Jimmy Carter proposed it.)

Although House Republican leaders, including Wyoming's Dick Cheney, agreed to support the tax bill, Jack Kemp led a Republican rebellion against the tax hike. Reagan had called Kemp to the White House to ask him to support, or at least not vocally oppose, the tax package, but the young congressman told the president, "I didn't come to Washington to raise taxes," adding later in a House floor speech that the tax bill wouldn't affect you as long as "you don't use the telephone, don't pay medical insurance premiums, don't suffer losses due to theft or casualty, don't smoke, don't ride in airplanes, or don't have a savings account." He sent Reagan a letter signed by sixty-one GOP House members saying that the Dole tax bill was "impossible to support. . . . Quietly, without debate, the Republican Party is in danger of making a U-turn back to its familiar role of tax collector for Democratic spending programs." (This was the origin of Newt Gingrich's remark that Dole was "the tax collector for the welfare state"—a quote that came back into currency more than a decade later when Gingrich became Speaker of the House while Dole became Senate majority leader.) Dole protested, "We're not trying to make a U-turn. We're just trying to avoid going over the cliff." But he was also happy to disassociate himself from Reaganomics: "I never understood all that supply-side business," Dole told NBC News.

In the background of the Dole-Kemp face-off over taxes was the question of who would succeed Reagan in 1988 (or 1984 if Reagan didn't run again), which makes all the more revealing the great press Dole received for his tax-hiking ways. The *Boston Globe* praised "Pitchfork Bob Dole, the latter day populist from Kansas," for lifting the "fairness issue" from Democrats. Kevin Phillips, engaged in his own crabwalk to the left at that time, said Dole's leadership on the tax hike "moves him right up in the 1984 presidential sweepstakes." *Time* magazine, running photos of Dole striking statesman-like poses, praised him for having "mellowed and matured" and for "shunning rigid ideology." The *New Republic* editorialized, "Who would have thought that Senator Bob Dole would emerge as the loophole-closing hero of 1982?"[42] The *Baltimore Sun* declared 1982 to be "the year of Bob Dole," and Ralph Nader's Public Citizen group hailed Dole for being "the architect of the best tax reform bill in history." Rowland Evans and Robert Novak attacked Dole as the "new McGovern," and as if on cue, George McGovern himself uttered the words conservatives dread to hear about one of their own: "Bob Dole has grown." As the *American Spectator*'s Tom Bethell had become weary of pointing out, "grown in office" is a Beltway euphemism for "moved to the left." The Ripon Society, the last bastion of dwindling Republican liberalism, certified Dole's new status by naming him its Man of the Year.

The relentless leaking from the pro-tax faction in the White House lent credence to the conservative charge that Reagan's staff was manipulating him into agreeing to the tax hike. A memo from congressional liaison Ken Duberstein on July 2, the day after Dole's bill finally passed out of the Finance Committee, backs up this charge. "Don Regan believes," Duberstein wrote Reagan, "that the measure by and large (a) is in harmony with the deficit reduction program contained in the recently adopted budget resolution, (b) does preserve the integrity of our economic recovery program, and (c) has been carefully crafted to insure that the incentives adopted last year will be maintained."[43]

But Reagan's personal letters from this period contradict this, and indicate that he was willing all along to deal on taxes even while he argued publicly against tax hikes. Reagan wrote to George Champion of Chase Manhattan Bank in March: "George the press here in Washington and to a great extent the *[New York] Times* seem bent on portraying our administration as divided and me as standing alone. Believe me this is not the case."[44] To Clymer Wright, a conservative supporter in Texas, Reagan wrote in May: "Yes there is undermining of my efforts and yes there is sabotage of all I'm trying to accomplish. But it's being done by the people who write these articles and columns and not by any White House staff member and certainly not by James Baker. . . . There has not been one single instance of Jim Baker doing anything but what I've settled on as our policy. . . . Some in the media delight in trying to portray me as being manipulated and led around by the nose. They do so because they are opposed to everything this administration represents."[45] In June Reagan wrote to *Manchester Union-Leader* editor William Loeb: "[N]one of our gang has tried to talk me into giving up our tax cuts even though for a time half the columnists were saying they were on a daily basis."[46]

Reagan also met in June with several leaders of the conservative movement, including columnist M. Stanton Evans, Alan Ryskind of *Human Events,* and *Conservative Digest* editor John Lofton—one of a series of periodic meetings Reagan held to keep in touch with his political core. The group suggested to Reagan that his staff was disloyal, at one point putting James Baker, present in the room, uncomfortably on the defensive. Reagan would hear none of it and made a stout defense of his staff. The conservative group left unhappy and disillusioned.

When Reagan came out in support of the Dole tax bill in July, calling it "bitter medicine," conservatives cried betrayal. *Conservative Digest* asked on its cover: "Has Reagan Deserted the Conservatives?" In the article within, Howard Phillips of the Conservative Caucus blasted Reagan, writing: "It's silly for conservatives to waste an ounce of energy anymore trying to get a 72-year-old leopard to change his spots. We've got to write this Administration off. This is not our Administration." Reagan was furious, firing off a letter to John Lofton: "I believe that the July *Conservative Digest* is one of the most dishonest and unfair bits of journalism I have ever seen." (In Reagan's original handwritten draft, he went further, adding "not excepting *Pravda* and *Tass*," the Soviet propaganda organs. Richard Darman talked Reagan into dropping this phrase.)[47]

This controversy between Reagan and his base reveals a paradox about Reagan that is hard to resolve. We know that Baker, Stockman, Darman, and others were relentless leakers who later kept to the media story line that Reagan stubbornly rebuffed their entreaties to raise taxes month after month, yet we also see here and elsewhere Reagan's clearheaded grasp of the larger political stakes in playing along with the outlines of a strategy.

Churchill offers a useful refraction of the problem in his essay "Consistency in Politics":

> [A] statesman in contact with the moving current of events and anxious to keep the ship of state on an even keel and steer a steady course may lean all his weight now on one side and now on the other. His arguments in each case when contrasted can be shown to be not only very different in character, but contradictory in spirit and opposite in direction: yet his object will throughout have remained the same. His resolves, his wishes, his outlook may have been unchanged; his methods may be verbally irreconcilable. We cannot call this inconsistency. In fact it may be claimed to be the truest consistency. The only way a man can remain consistent amid changing circumstances is to change with them while preserving the same dominating purpose.[48]

Reagan's "dominating purpose" was to shrink the size and influence of the federal government. The key to his acceptance of the tax deal was what appeared to be a favorable compromise according to which each $1 of increased taxes would be matched with $3 of spending cuts from Congress. On paper the deal looked like it advanced Reagan's goal of shrinking the federal government, but Congress never delivered on meaningful spending restraint.

By one calculation, the 1982 tax increase (known as TEFRA, for Tax Equity and Fiscal Reform Act) actually resulted in $1.14 of new spending for each extra tax dollar.[49]

Stockman later said he more or less bamboozled Reagan by counting interest savings from lower interest rates among the cuts. Between the idea of the budget resolution and the reality of subsequent appropriations that didn't stay within the budget resolution's caps "falls the shadow," to borrow T. S. Eliot's lyric. It was one of the few compromises that didn't work out in Reagan's favor. It may have looked good on paper—a $98 billion tax increase following a $750 billion tax cut—but with Social Security taxes rising by more than $100 billion over the next three years, as set by the Social Security bailout of 1977, the income tax cut barely kept many workers even. More tax increases were coming too.

Once again Reagan's diary entries show the progression of his practical politics:

> May 20:
> A compromise is never to anyone's liking; it's just the best you can get and contains enough of what you want to justify what you give up.

> July 21:
> Cutting defense sends a message I don't like to allies and enemies alike. But Dave [Stockman's] reports of deficits are too high and send shock waves to the world just as we seem to be gaining ground.

> August 4:
> The tax increase is the price we have to pay to get the budget cuts.

> August 19:
> All day I sat at my desk phoning Congressmen on the tax bill and tonight it passed. . . . Tip O'Neill made a speech to Republicans telling them why they should support me. It seemed strange. Both of us on the same side.

Reagan went on national TV a few days before the final House vote in mid-August to drum up public support. Despite Reagan's appeal, a *Washington Post* poll taken the day after the speech found that 54 percent of the public opposed the tax bill. The bill passed the House by the narrow vote of 208–197.

The tax compromise unquestionably weakened Reagan, who was portrayed in the media as the clear loser to O'Neill. Liberals thought they had the president on the run. "The fun has really just begun," said liberal Democratic representative Thomas Downey of New York. "We're going to need a tax bill every year Reagan is in the White House because of the bender we went on in 1981." Reagan's signature was barely dry on the tax increase when Congress mustered the two-thirds vote required to override his veto of a $14 billion supplemental spending bill that he said exceeded budget targets. A measure of the dispiritedness of congressional Republicans was that fifty-one GOP House members who had pledged the year before to sustain any Reagan vetoes of spending bills voted for the override.

Despite the veto override—the first Reagan suffered—in a larger sense Reagan was able to play from a position of relative strength. As Michael Boskin observed: "It is astounding to any serious economic historian that in the depths of what was called the worst recession since the Great Depression, Congressional demands for action were limited to spending a few billion dollars on highway construction and other related 'job creation' programs. Only a few years earlier, such calls for public service jobs would have demanded ten times that amount."[50] Indeed, in 1975, labor groups had demanded a $100 billion jobs program for a recession only about half as severe. The most ambitious scheme Democrats proposed in 1982 was a $7.5 billion jobs program to employ just 500,000 people, and House Democrats ultimately passed a paltry $1 billion jobs bill that made nary a ripple. That the Democrats made little headway with an old-fashioned jobs program or any similarly substantial government intervention in the economy was a sign of the advance of Reagan's conservative message that Washington was more of a problem than a solution to the nation's economic woes.

* * *

WHILE TAX AND budget issues dominated the headlines for most of 1982, another leg of Reagan's economic policy was unfolding with less public attention but no less controversy in Washington: regulatory reform. This sounds like an arcane subject, fit only for insomniacs, but at a remove from the narrow policy wonk details it is possible to discern another important fault line between left and right, with significant constitutional as well as economic consequences.

Regulatory reform was long overdue: between 1970 and 1980 the federal government enacted more regulatory statutes than had been enacted in the previous four decades combined.[51] Throughout the second half of the 1970s there was a growing consensus that many areas of federal regulation were counterproductive and should be reformed or abolished. By 1980 even the Carter administration believed that federal regulation was partly responsible for the slump in productivity growth.

A decent measure of deregulation began under the Ford administration and accelerated under Carter, with deregulation of the trucking and airline industries, along with the beginnings of deregulation of parts of the energy industry (especially natural gas) and railroads. These deregulations shared a common aspect: they all pertained to basic markets once thought to be natural monopolies to some extent, whereas technological changes and a deepening understanding of competition eroded the theoretical and historic bases for these regulatory schemes.

Reaganites thought these salutary first steps were puny and miserable compared to what ought to be done, and Reagan's corps of deregulators brought a ferocious antiregulatory attitude to Washington. Daniel Oliver, whom Reagan would appoint to be chairman of the Federal Trade Commission (FTC) in his second term, expressed the insurgent mood with the quip that being a Reaganite in a regulatory agency was like being the bride carried across the threshold, whose dominant thought was, "Don't just stand there— undo something!"

Undo they did—at least initially. During the first ten months of 1981, the number of pages printed in the *Federal Register*—the best rough measure of new federal regulatory activity—fell by one-third from a year before, while the total number of new agency rules fell by a more impressive 50 percent.[52] Not surprisingly, Reagan's agency administrators reduced staff levels, though not as drastically as Reagan's critics liked to think. Some agency staff levels, such as at the Environmental Protection Agency (EPA), continued to rise. Vice President Bush was placed in charge of a Presidential Task Force on Regulatory Relief and by the end of 1981 had recommended revision or repeal of 111 existing regulations, the most prominent of which was the unpopular rule requiring automatic seatbelts on new cars.

Antitrust policy was the arena with the most drastic reversal. Between 1981 and 1983, federal antitrust actions fell by one-third, and the Justice Department issued more permissive merger guidelines that enabled a subsequent upswing in corporate mergers in the 1980s. More significant is the fact that by the mid-1980s, the Justice Department began routinely *losing* the antitrust cases it still brought to court. Prior to 1980, the Justice Department seldom lost in court. By the late 1980s many Washington, D.C., law firms began scaling back or abandoning their large antitrust practices. One firm that specialized in antitrust closed up for good.

The revolution in antitrust law had been building for a long time and is a good example of how intellectual change precedes political and legal change. Since the 1960s scholars associated especially with the "Chicago School" of law and economics (and to a certain extent the emerging public choice school of analysis) had developed a powerful critique of the existing understanding of market competition and had undermined the coherence of existing antitrust doctrines. As one scholar put it, the government's evidence of anticompetitive practices was "weak and at times bordered on fiction," and "neither the government nor the Courts seemed able to distinguish competition from monopolizing."[53] Government antitrust policy, and the key supporting doctrines about predatory pricing, mergers, and market concentration, was increasingly seen as arbitrary, capricious, and economically counterproductive—a tool used more for political than economic purposes.[54] Economic historian Jonathan R. T. Hughes, for example, described the Sherman Antitrust Act as "an institutional sumptuary law for business enterprise."[55] The little-known editor of *Regulation* magazine, law professor Antonin Scalia, emphasized the Machiavellian character of antitrust laws by comparing their working to the tradition of the frontier sheriff: "He did not sift the evidence, distinguish between suspects, and solve crimes, but merely walked the main street and every so often pistol-whipped a few people."[56]

Reagan had followed this bold work, mentioning some of the revisionist ideas about antitrust in several of his radio addresses in the 1970s and decrying Carter's antitrust policies as a "witch hunt." As president, Reagan appointed the first economist to head the FTC, Jim Miller, who ended an antitrust action against cereal companies for the supposed offense of offering consumers too many breakfast cereal choices. By 1984 Miller would proudly announce that the FTC's "reign of terror" as the "national nanny" was over. Reagan also appointed Stanford Law School faculty member William F. Baxter to head the new team at the Justice Department antitrust division. Baxter used the insights of the law and economics movement to shake up the whole scene. Yale's Paul Joskow said that "effectively, Baxter put up a sign in his office reading, 'No More Mush.' "

Baxter moved quickly to resolve two of the longest-running and most spectacular antitrust controversies—the IBM case and the AT&T case. The

IBM case had dragged on since the late 1960s without resolution, consuming thousands of hours of lawyers' time and many millions of taxpayer dollars. By 1981, the pretrial phase transcript had reached 104,000 pages. In reviewing the facts of the case, Baxter was appalled to find that career Justice Department antitrust lawyers were "infused with inappropriate zeal" to prosecute IBM for, among other things, predatory pricing of its new flagship 360-90 mainframe computer because IBM lost money on the model. Never mind that IBM was selling few of the machines even at cut-rate prices. "As an example of predation," Baxter said, "it was pathetic." (There was good evidence from several studies that the antitrust suit had led IBM to keep prices artificially high on other computer models to avoid more predation counts.) Baxter summarily dropped the suit in early 1982; the announcement to end the suit caused very little controversy, for an ironic reason we shall come to shortly. The chimera of IBM's supposed monopoly power was subsequently exposed in the computer revolution of the 1980s, when newer firms such as Apple, Hewlett-Packard, Oracle, and others successfully challenged Big Blue for market share. A 1985 study calculated that dropping the IBM suit reduced the cost of mainframe computers by about 20 percent.[57]

The AT&T case, brought in the mid-1970s, was peculiar and impenetrable. Regulated much like an electric utility, AT&T and its local telephone operating companies had built up a complex system of cross-subsidization, whereby long-distance calls subsidized low-cost local telephone service. As the equipment gatekeeper for its local Bell telephone operating companies, AT&T also had a stranglehold on innovations in communication technologies. By the late 1970s, however, advances in technology were drastically reducing the cost of long-distance communication and providing ways for new service providers, such as Sprint and MCI, to provide real competition and lower prices for consumers. Restructuring AT&T was thought the key not only to opening up innovation but also to deregulating telecommunications. Ultimately it was agreed to break up AT&T's operating companies into seven separate regional companies (the "Baby Bells") and require equal access to local markets for all long distance carriers, starting in 1984. The initial effect was to raise the price of local telephone service, though by less than had been predicted, while reducing the price of long-distance calls. This was not initially popular. George Will complained that the government had fixed something that wasn't broken, and indignant congressmen held indignant hearings.[58]

One major blot on Reagan's regulation record was the embrace of "voluntary" import restraints on Japanese auto imports. At the beginning of the 1980s the American auto industry was reeling under pressure from foreign competition—deservedly so, as the quality of American-made autos from the Big Three was noticeably inferior to that of imports from Europe and Japan. The auto market was a study of the decline in American competitiveness and innovation that had occurred in the 1970s. Japanese auto plants turned out each car with about fourteen man-hours of labor, compared to forty-three man-hours for the average American car. The extra time on the Detroit assembly line didn't help. According to Jimmy Carter's deregulation czar, Alfred Kahn, by 1980 Japanese and German cars averaged slightly more than one major repair in their first year, compared to three to four major repairs for the average new American car. Japanese auto imports had soared from 380,000 in 1970 to about 2 million in 1980. The automakers' plight, Kahn said, was "richly deserved competitive retribution for its poor record."

Unable to meet this quality competition head-on, and having lost $4.2 billion in 1980, the Big Three American automakers pressed for the predictable solution: trade protectionism. Amazingly, the automakers' calls for protectionism found wide support, including from the Consumer Federation of America. There was bipartisan support on Capitol Hill in early 1981 for mandatory limits on Japanese auto imports to give American automakers "breathing room" to modernize—a task that the industry estimated would require $80 billion in capital investment in the coming decade. The Reagan administration didn't like the sound of this, but an internal Treasury Department memorandum worried, "Congress may take the question out of our hands if we fail to act." After a heated debate at the White House, Reagan passively agreed to seek a "voluntary export restraint agreement" with Japan. Japan complied, in the same sense that a victim complies "voluntarily" with an armed mugger demanding a wallet. Japan reduced its auto imports by almost 50 percent and maintained import restraints into the 1990s, even after the United States dropped pressure on the Japanese. Japan responded nimbly, changing their import mix to emphasize luxury brands for the first time and raising prices across the board. According to one estimate, the import restraints added more than $1,000 to the price of the average car and cost American consumers more than $5 billion over the next three years. It was, economist Stephen D. Cohen judged, "an excessively costly approach to the domestic automobile problem."[59] Each American auto job "saved" by the policy cost an estimated $160,000. It was not one of the Reaganites' finest free market moments.

While the Reagan administration was successful in capitalizing on the deregulatory momentum it had inherited from the Carter and Ford administrations in basic economic markets such as communications, transportation, and energy, it was much less successful in the realm of social regulation—that is, health, safety, and environmental regulation. A brief excursion into this dichotomy offers another perspective on the deep partisan fault lines of the decade as well as the intractable nature of the administrative state against which the Reagan offensive would eventually stall out. Reagan's team understood that genuine regulatory reform required changes to authorizing statutes through Congress. But Democrats in Congress, for whom the bureaucracy had become a partisan interest, were in no mood to deal. Even modest proposals to stretch out the time line for compliance with the Clean Air Act couldn't get a vote in committee. Proposals to rein in regulatory authority over meat processing, banking, trucking, Davis-Bacon prevailing wage rules, and civil rights were dead on arrival.

So the Reagan administration attempted the next best thing: delivering a measure of relief through administrative means. This accounts for much of the decline in new regulations and the number of pages in the *Federal Register*. The administration also issued new guidelines imposing cost-benefit analysis for all proposed regulations (many areas of social regulation had been hitherto exempt from cost-benefit analysis). To give the review teeth, it established a special department in the Office of Management and Budget, bearing the anodyne title Office of Information and Regulatory Affairs (OIRA), to review and critique agency cost-benefit analyses. Cost-benefit analysis was and remains today a controversial aspect of government regulation. Critics charge that cost-benefit analysis is too subjective and easily manipulated. While there is some merit to this critique, the exercise of having to apply at least some standard of economic reasoning to political decisions deters agencies from promulgating ill-considered rules. Reagan's cost-benefit order undoubtedly played a role in the dramatic reduction in new proposed regulations. The rules that did get through were less likely, as a consequence, to be rejected by OMB. In 1981, OIRA reviewed more than two thousand proposed regulations. Fewer than 3 percent were rejected; 87 percent were accepted without change. OIRA's efforts often succeeded in embarrassing regulators with their analysis of out-of-whack costs and benefits; in one case, a proposed regulation to protect fish in Adirondack mountain lakes would have cost more than $12,000 per fish saved.

Democrats paid lip service to the need for regulatory reform but were wary of Reagan's larger designs to restrain government regulatory authority. Democratic senator Thomas Eagleton, for example, noted the stakes in 1981, telling a reporter, "It was very much of an up-front, dominant issue." He feared that Reagan would try "to massively alter the regulatory process . . . [and] to make lots of substantive changes in organic statutes. Regulatory reform is going to be fought on a much broader front." This meant congressional hearings, and by degrees Congress, especially the Democratic-controlled, oversight-hearing-happy House, began to reassert itself in the bureaucratic struggles that the Reaganites incited. Much of the subsequent fighting between the White House and Congress remained an obscure, back-page, inside-the-Beltway circus to most of the public, but it underscored the nature of the constitutional no-man's-land between executive branch administrative discretion and sensitive congressional prerogatives of pork barrel spending and interest group favoritism.

*   *   *

THE FRICTION OVER the congressional pork prerogatives of regulatory policy was minor compared to the heat various social and cultural policy controversies generated. This should not be the least surprising. Political clashes over pork barrel and regulatory programs are chiefly about money. The clashes over issues that make up the culture war—civil rights, abortion, crime, education, and feminism—involve matters of the heart and are only secondarily about money. There were usually two aspects to cultural issues: moral principles themselves, and the constitutional argument over how such issues should be governed.

As it did with economic regulation, the Reagan administration set out to reverse course on many hot button social policy issues. Perhaps no Reagan policy on social issues sparked more high-decibel liberal denunciations than his stance on civil rights. The civil rights disputes of the Reagan years, which continued to fester throughout the 1990s and right up through the present day, were merely another facet of the fundamental split between left and right over the nature and role of government power and individual rights. As we shall see, Reagan's civil rights policy was hardly an attempt to revive Jim Crow segregation, as Reagan's hyperbolic critics sometimes suggested. Herman Belz noted in his wide-ranging book on the history of affirmative action, "By the standards used to measure civil rights enforcement, the Reagan Justice Department record was comparable to that of the Carter Administration." Nonetheless, Belz added, "[l]iberals attacked the civil rights record of the Reagan Administration with an ideological fervor almost impervious to reality."[60] Reagan's opponents would sometimes resort to veiled threats. William Robinson of the Lawyers' Committee for Civil Rights Under Law said in 1982, "This country is fairly unique in that social change doesn't have to come about through violence. You take away that belief, and things can become much rougher." This intemperate reaction occurred because Reagan and his appointees persisted in picking the scabs of racial liberalism, starting arguments that the left thought or hoped could be kept closed.

A good example is a September 1982 speech in which Reagan attacked the Great Society for having retarded the progress of blacks and the poor, a rousing counterattack during the campaign season in which Reagan's lack of fairness was the centerpiece of the Democratic campaign. (Black unemployment in 1982 stood at 20 percent, twice the national rate.)

> The record is there for all to see. This country entered the 1960s having made tremendous strides in reducing poverty. From 1949 until just before the Great Society burst upon the scene in 1964, the percentage of American families living in poverty fell dramatically from nearly 33 percent to only 18 percent. True, the number of blacks living in poverty was still disproportionately high. But tremendous progress had been made. With the coming of the Great Society, government began eating away at the underpinnings of the private enterprise system. The big taxers and big spenders in the Congress had started a binge that would slowly change the nature of our society and, even worse, it threatened the character of our people. . . . By the time the full weight of Great Society programs was felt, economic progress for America's poor had come to a tragic halt. By 1980 the trend had reversed itself, and even more people, including more blacks, were living in poverty than back in 1969.
>
> It's ironic that if the economic expansion and low inflation of the years prior to the Great Society had been maintained, black families and all Americans would be appreciably better off today. In fact, if we had just maintained the progress made from 1950 through 1965, black family income in 1980 would have been nearly $3,000 higher than it was after 15 years of Great Society programs.[61]

The reaction to Reagan's remarks demonstrated the extent to which the legitimate cause of civil rights had become fully enmeshed with, and corrupted by, the welfare state. Civil rights leaders and the media jumped on Reagan's remarks, tut-tutting that he did not understand the "symbolic importance" of Great Society programs for blacks. NAACP president Benjamin Hooks blasted Reagan: "The problem with the Great Society was not that it failed but that Americans did not give it a chance to work." It was difficult to tell the difference between supposedly objective news stories and editorials about Reagan's speech. The lead of Howell Raines's *New York Times* "news analysis" said that "Reagan provided fresh ammunition for critics who say he is trying to reverse the racial progress of the last 20 years." Raines quoted several Reagan critics, but not one supporter, of his views on the Great Society. The *Times* editorialized: "[T]he Great Society was a necessary, imaginative and productive response to a deeply rooted social conflict. Its legacy is real." The *Washington Post* marched in lockstep, editorializing that Reagan's views were "[a]t best, a joke, at worst a travesty . . . It is point-missing on a truly breathtaking scale."

Like his changes to social spending programs, Reagan's civil rights agenda was modest rather than revolutionary, but liberals saw even a modest retrenchment as contravening the idea that "progress" moves only in one direction. The position of civil rights groups had ultimately been reduced to simple redistributionism on racial lines—equality of result rather than equality of opportunity. The whole field of civil rights law and policy was a classic example of pursuing liberal ends by undemocratic means—chiefly judicial incrementalism and bureaucratic stealth—because they were too unpopular with the public ever to be accomplished out in the open. Liberal civil rights leaders made the peculiar and disingenuous charge that Reagan was upsetting the "consensus" on civil rights, even though the central demands of the civil rights lobby were deeply unpopular with a large majority of Americans.

Now and then, civil rights partisans would tip their hand, such as in 1985 when Mary Frances Berry and Blandina Ramirez, two Carter holdovers on the U.S. Commission on Civil Rights, wrote that "civil rights laws were not passed to give civil rights protections to all Americans, as a majority of this Commission seems to believe. Instead, they were passed out of a recognition that some Americans already had protection because they belonged to a favored group; and others, including blacks, Hispanics, and women of all races, did not because they belonged to disfavored groups."[62] Seldom has the idea of group rights over individual rights, and the desire for the unequal application of the law, been put with greater clarity and directness.

By the early 1980s civil rights policy had become a grand muddle. By degrees a series of convoluted court decisions, consent decrees, and bureaucratic maneuvering had turned the principle of color-blind nondiscrimination on its head. "Affirmative action," the vague phrase John F. Kennedy and Lyndon Johnson had made into a policy, had come in practice to mean reverse discrimination through racial quotas and set-asides (that is, government contracts reserved explicitly for minorities). This turnabout was accomplished mainly through the judicially created doctrine of "disparate impact," which meant that if the racial composition of an employer's workforce did not match the racial composition of the workforce in the area where it was located, the employer was presumptively guilty of discrimination and required to adopt aggressive affirmative action measures—quotas—as a remedy.[63] The blunt and disagreeable fact of de facto quotas in hiring was covered up with semantic disguises, such as "goals and timetables," that fooled no one. Attempts to challenge this constitutionally corrupt practice at the Supreme Court, most notably the *Bakke* case in 1978 and the *Weber* case in 1979, produced mixed and inconclusive decisions that further muddled the law. (In the 5–4 *Bakke* decision, each justice wrote a separate opinion.) By 1980, the Office of Federal Contract Compliance Programs (OFCCP) had imposed on federal contractors a tendentious eight-point statistical test of discrimination and was requiring affirmative action plans from more than three hundred thousand American business firms. The paperwork burden was immense. At a Senate hearing about OFCCP regulations, Johns Hopkins University displayed a two-and-a-half-foot stack of documents weighing sixty-five pounds that the university had produced to comply with OFCCP procedures.

As with economic regulatory policy, the Reagan administration's aim was not to roll back genuine civil rights protections but to draw the line against the egregious use of explicit race-conscious quotas and the legitimization of group rights that racial quotas represent. But just as the Arms Control and Disarmament Agency, the EPA, and numerous other federal agencies resisted Reagan appointees who arrived determined to implement a different governing philosophy, the civil rights establishment regarded the various government offices and departments with purview over civil rights law as wholly owned fiefdoms. The Justice Department's civil rights division, the Equal Employment Opportunity Commission (EEOC), the U.S. Commission on Civil Rights—these and many other agencies were dominated by permanent bureaucrats who fiercely opposed the Reagan administration agenda and leaked damaging information to the media and Congress at every opportunity.

At the Justice Department, Reagan appointed William Bradford Reynolds to be assistant attorney general for civil rights. In the 1970s, Reynolds said, "[T]he idea of equal opportunity got changed in the minds of some to a concept of equal results, and individual rights were translated into group entitlements." These were fighting words for the Left. Reynolds and his deputies set out a two-part strategy for reversing the slow slide to explicit group-based race-consciousness in civil rights law. First, using the Justice Department's prerogative to lay out the executive branch's constitutional interpretation of the law and choose cases to push forward in court, Reynolds looked to set up a number of incremental court challenges to halt the momentum of existing precedents that promoted racial quotas in hiring and contracting. The Justice Department also tried to put the brakes on further court-ordered busing programs—busing being the most unpopular civil rights policy—and intervened in another case seeking to limit the reach of the Fourteenth Amendment's equal protection clause to illegal aliens. Second, the Justice Department and the White House would work to get other government agencies to rationalize civil rights policy and implement racial outreach programs in a less arbitrary way.

Reynolds made clear that he would not try to discard the "disparate impact" method of identifying potentially discriminatory practices by employers, but that policy should focus on remedies for actual victims of discrimination and sanctioning businesses found engaging in clearly biased hiring practices rather than become a pretext for a blatant racial spoils system. For this balanced approach Reynolds became the target of full-throated opprobrium of liberals. NAACP legal counsel Barry Goldstein charged that "[t]he Civil Rights Division is waging an aggressive, unprecedented national campaign to reverse 20 years of well-established principles for remedying racial discrimination and for ensuring that practices and patterns of discrimination cease." *New York Times* columnist Anthony Lewis called Reynolds "lawless and heartless," and ACLU president Ira Glasser said Reynolds was "the moral equivalent of those southern segregationists of a generation ago standing in the schoolhouse door to defend segregation."[64]

Needless to say, Reynolds was controversial within the Justice Department. Career employees did their best to sabotage his initiatives, and even some political appointees found him occasionally too aggressive. "He proposed a constant stream of suicidally radical and unconvincing projects," Charles Fried, Reagan's second solicitor general at Justice, wrote of Reynolds. But Fried noted that perhaps Reynolds's aggressiveness was required in the face of the intransigence of the department's careerists and the civil rights establishment: "Brad exaggerated and bullied, but maybe that was the only way he could even come near his goals. Perhaps more moderate people would not have arrested the drift toward a quota society. Perhaps only someone who was prepared to be eaten alive could have achieved half (the proper half) of what he tried to do."[65] It was a fitting credo for Reaganites in many top positions.

Trying to strike the fine balance between maintaining disparate-impact analysis while avoiding quota remedies generated a number of inconsistencies and confusions within the administration. Even as the administration criticized explicit race consciousness, it continued the practice itself, carefully counting its own appointees by race and announcing with pride at the end of 1981 that out of 2,865 noncareer positions filled, Reagan had appointed 877 women, 80 Hispanics, and 130 blacks. In a press conference in late 1981 Reagan was asked whether he agreed with Justice Department plans to overturn the *Weber* decision that had upheld so-called voluntary affirmative action programs. Not being familiar with the actual terms of the *Weber* case, Reagan said, "I can't see any fault" with voluntary affirmative action; "I'm for that." The White House press office quietly issued a correction a few days later, stating that Reagan did indeed share the Justice Department's reservations about the *Weber* decision.

In other precincts of the government the fight was sometimes more vigorous and political. At the National Endowment for the Humanities (NEH), chairman William Bennett announced with a flourish that the NEH would no longer set race-oriented hiring goals.[66] (Congress later inserted language in the NEH's appropriation bill requiring the agency to resume racial "goals and timetables.") But over at the EEOC, which shares civil rights enforcement responsibilities with the Justice Department, the new Reagan-appointed chairman, Clarence Thomas, sounded more like a conventional civil rights spokesman, saying that "job discrimination is still very, very serious" and that "some employers have seen certain actions of this administration over the past two years as reason to cool their heels in reducing job discrimination."[67] The EEOC got crossways with the Justice Department over positions Justice was taking in a Supreme Court case, and under White House pressure the EEOC withdrew an amicus brief defending quotas.

Despite Thomas's independent positions and his reforms of EEOC management that speeded up case processing, he enraged Democrats and civil rights activists when he announced that the EEOC would follow the Justice Department's view that remedies should be directed toward individual victims of discrimination rather than to classes or racial groups. Thomas subsequently went further than the Justice Department and abolished EEOC's unit that brought discrimination cases solely on the basis of disparate-impact statistics, and restrained the use of "goals and timetable" remedies. These reforms ironically led to a sharp increase in the number of EEOC enforcement actions and settlements (including a record $42 million settlement with General Motors), but Democrats and civil rights activists were not mollified. Thomas was repeatedly summoned to hostile congressional hearings, where he infuriated Democrats with the argument that quotas actually abetted discrimination and retarded the progress of minorities in the workplace.

There were sharp political limits to what could be accomplished. Despite the unpopularity of race-conscious quotas that compelled even black civil rights leaders to denounce them publicly (while demanding them privately), the Reagan administration met widespread resistance from state and local governments and big business to making any substantial reforms. Most large corporations had an institutionalized faction in their human resources departments that supported affirmative action, and having a government-approved affirmative action program provided considerable insulation from civil rights legal challenges. The attitude of many business groups was *Don't rock the boat*. According to one survey of Fortune 500 companies, 88 percent said they would maintain affirmative action quotas even if the law no longer required it, and both the National Association of Manufacturers and the U.S. Chamber of Commerce opposed changes to affirmative action.[68]

*   *   *

WHILE THE REAGAN team was consistently forced to swim upstream in instituting its bold reforms, sometimes the administration complicated its efforts through outright blunders.

Lou Cannon wrote, "The White House pragmatists believed [Reagan] paid more attention to articles in *Human Events*, particularly at the outset of his administration, than to information he received in his [regular] briefings. . . . [A]ides waged a long and losing battle to keep the publication out of his hands."[69] Their frequent failures to intercept *Human Events* sometimes had policy consequences. One such instance involved the July 18, 1981, edition of *Human Events*, which carried James Jackson Kilpatrick's column about the decision of the Internal Revenue Service (IRS) to deny tax-exempt status to Bob Jones University in South Carolina because of the school's racially discriminatory policies. (Bob Jones barred interracial dating and marriage—a controversy that erupted again in the 2000 presidential campaign, when George W. Bush chose the university as a venue for a major campaign speech.) In "Bob Jones and the Taxman," Kilpatrick (one of Reagan's favorite columnists) argued that the IRS had overreached its authority in applying civil rights policy to a purely ministerial tax matter: "Implicit in the government's position is the government's power to abridge the freedom of religion." A federal appeals court had upheld the IRS's view, and the matter was sent up on appeal to the Supreme Court. Reagan clipped out the article, scribbled a note in the margin expressing his displeasure with the IRS position, and sent it off to the Justice Department.[70] It was a sound legal and constitutional principle to object to the IRS's actions, which represented another example of the breakdown of the separation of powers between the executive and legislative branches ("an audacious bit of activism," editorialized *Regulation* magazine, whose editor was Antonin Scalia).[71] But it was also disastrous politics.

Reagan appointees at the Justice Department, eager for ways to challenge the abuse of bureaucratic discretion, lobbied the Treasury Department (since the IRS is part of Treasury) to overrule the IRS policy while the Justice Department would ask the Supreme Court to reverse the appeals court decision in favor of the IRS position. Reaganites at Treasury were just as eager as the Reaganites at Justice to rein in the IRS, and because the two agencies were joining forces, the matter escaped the close scrutiny of the senior White House staff. (Baker and Deaver later tried to make Meese the scapegoat, though both of them had been briefed on the initiative.) Treasury general counsel Peter Wallison announced the Bob Jones policy in haste on Friday, January 8, 1982. "The Treasury Department," Wallison correctly argued, "has concluded that this kind of judgment which may mean life or death for certain organizations is fundamentally a question for Congress."

The reaction was immediate. "Tax Exemption for Discrimination" read the Associated Press headline the following day. NAACP president Benjamin Hooks declared: "For the IRS to take such a position at this time on an issue as settled as this matter is nothing short of criminal." "Appalling," said the head of the American Jewish Congress. "Outrageous and probably unlawful," said the chairman of the Democratic National Committee. "The Reagan administration has intervened on the side of bigotry," columnist Richard Cohen wrote. "Immoral," said Senator Pat Moynihan, who added that Reagan "wants to undo the civil rights movement." "Indecent," said Ted Kennedy; "this is the most anti-civil-rights administration in the history of this land."

Several Republican senators joined the pile-on. The only person publicly celebrating the decision was Bob Jones III: "God answered our prayers and delivered His people from the hands of the IRS tyrants."

The policy didn't last seventy-two hours and would have perished even faster had there not been a weekend to intervene. Before the *Post* and the *Times* could crank up indignant editorials, Reagan went before the press to announce a complete reversal. The White House would now support congressional legislation giving the IRS authority to deny tax exemption to any schools that discriminated by race. Democrats rejected the idea that congressional permission was necessary for the IRS action; they recognized that Reagan's larger position about bureaucratic prerogative would be vindicated by such a concession. Reagan explained that the action had been "misinterpreted," and made the substantive point that administrative agencies should not exercise "powers that the Constitution assigns to Congress" or "govern by administrative fiat." He was emphatic that "I am unalterably opposed to racial discrimination in any form." Peter Wallison reflected: "Reagan really felt that he had been blindsided, because he had made a little note in the margin of his *Human Events* issue, and his administration had turned it into a gigantic scandal. . . . We really shot ourselves in the foot—both feet—on that one."[72] Having celebrated the initial decision, Bob Jones III now complained that "Reagan has become a traitor to God's people."

Even though the White House beat a rapid retreat, Democrats on Capitol Hill couldn't resist prolonging Reagan's embarrassment through a series of committee hearings that roasted Justice and Treasury Department witnesses. Much of it had the show-trial tone of these Ways and Means Committee exchanges between House Democrats and administration witnesses:

REP. STARK: Do you find the advocating of murder and kidnapping of blacks and Jews abhorrent?
BRAD REYNOLDS: Certainly.
REP. BRODHEAD: Mr. Chairman, in my view the performance by these witnesses today is without question the shabbiest performance that I have ever witnessed before any congressional committee. It is absolutely unbelievable, the things that have been said here today. . . . I am appalled.
REP. PICKLE: In my opinion the whole country is frightened and embarrassed about this ruling, and the way it has been handled. . . . [T]he onus is going to be on your backs as the ones who temporarily halted the progress of civil rights in this country.[73]

And so it went. Even in the face of this onslaught, the Reagan administration stuck to its legal position at the Supreme Court about the IRS's lack of authority. Nearly two hundred career Justice Department lawyers signed a public letter deploring the administration's position, prompting a few Reaganites to mutter that they shouldn't let the door hit them on the way out after resigning from Justice, but naturally none took the hint. The Supreme Court finally heard the Bob Jones case in the fall of 1982 and issued its ruling on May 24, 1983: the administration's position was routed on an 8–1 vote, with only Justice William Rehnquist siding with Reagan. It was a typically untethered Court opinion, ruling that the IRS didn't need statutory authority because civil rights was "a fundamental national public policy" and that its importance "substantially outweighs whatever burden" it might place on religious freedom.

The administration suffered other setbacks, forced to back down in its opposition to some features of the reauthorized Voting Rights Act, the composition of the U.S. Commission on Civil Rights, and the Legal Services Corporation. Though it later made some progress at the Supreme Court in limiting the further spread of quotas—both *Memphis Firefighters v. Stotts* (1984) and *Wygant v. Jackson Board of Education* (1986) chipped away at the legal basis for quotas and set-asides—at best the field of civil rights policy seemed a stalemate. Conservatives were disappointed that the administration didn't fight harder or take a clearer line on civil rights, and they had a point: it is hard to imagine liberals becoming more outraged over the issue. In the spring of 1982 Chester Finn described the Reagan civil rights policy as "a fitful and uneven process, in which the nation's long slide into color-coded policies and group entitlements was somewhat slowed but hardly stopped by an administration that seemed uncertain whether it really wanted to apply the brakes and not altogether sure where to find them. . . . The most ideological administration in history seems not to have its ideas sorted out."[74]

Over the longer term, however, the arguments and legal challenges Reagan set in motion would bear fruit after he left office.[75] By the mid-1990s, it was not conservative critics but the civil rights movement that was on the defensive, with civil rights groups actively working to prevent affirmative action cases from reaching the appellate courts and President Bill Clinton defending affirmative action quotas with the slogan "Mend it, don't end it," even as voters in states with the initiative process were voting by lopsided margins to end affirmative action as we know it. Today the matter sits in uneasy equilibrium; race-conscious policy is highly unpopular and is not advancing to new areas, but existing practices and programs remain in force under the improvised rationale of "diversity." The Supreme Court recently upheld—again—the legality of race consciousness, but added dicta that hopefully it won't be necessary in another generation.

There is one interesting footnote to the Bob Jones affair: the initial announcement that started the firestorm came on the same day—Friday, January 8, 1982—that the Justice Department announced the aforementioned settlement of the AT&T antitrust suit and the dropping of the IBM case. Both would have been much bigger and controversial announcements had they not been overshadowed by Bob Jones. Reagan liked to joke that the problem with his administration was that "the right hand doesn't know what the far-right hand is doing." It may have been true in this case, but it worked out for at least one of the right hands in this instance.

There is a broader point to be understood from this brief survey of regulatory and social policy controversies. In these nitty-gritty fields of domestic policy and regulation we can see one of the great ironies of the Reagan presidency at work, one most biographers overlook or mischaracterize: for a president supposedly uninterested in the details of policy, there was a stunning amount of policy activity under way throughout his presidency from the people he appointed, and at many decisive moments, Reagan was in the middle of it, not always to his own benefit.

* * *

TIME WAS THE decisive factor in causing Reagan to give in on a tax increase in the summer of 1982: he had hoped the economy would show signs of improvement in the first half of 1982, but instead the economic news had gotten steadily worse. The mortgage industry's "foreclosure inventory"—the percentage of homes on which a formal foreclosure process was under way—reached its highest level since the 1930s. Business bankruptcies were also running at record levels. Construction and auto manufacturing employment were down by a third. Most ominous was a string of major bank failures, starting with the Continental Illinois Bank and cascading down through several savings and loan associations. The Hartford Federal Savings and Loan Association in Connecticut experienced what news reports called "the first genuine depositor bank panic since the 1930s" in February, when depositors withdrew $3 million in cash in a matter of hours.

Talk of panics and bank failures threw off the frisson of the Great

Depression, and there was ample talk of a 1929-style crash. Alan Greenspan said on ABC's *This Week,* "There are similarities to 1929. I think it's the most risky period we have been in in the post–World War II period." *The New Republic* wondered whether Reaganomics "may actually have produced a new depression, a self-sustaining slump from which there will be no recovery."[76] The 1982 Nobel laureate in economics, free marketeer George Stigler of the Reagan-friendly University of Chicago, dismayed the White House when he came away from a photo op with Reagan and told the media that the United States was in "a depression," a view also endorsed by Harvard economist Richard Cooper, who said "the economic situation is worse today than at any peacetime period since the 1930s."

A contrarian might take these expressions of maximum pessimism as a sign that the worst was over, which in fact was the case. A key turning point came in July and August, when Mexico threatened to default on $90 billion in foreign loans, mostly owed to American banks. The Federal Reserve saw this as a threat to the liquidity of the entire banking system and abruptly reversed its tight money course of the previous eighteen months. With the money spigot suddenly wide open, the stock market staged a huge rally in mid-August, the beginning of one of the greatest bull markets in history. The Dow Jones Industrial Average bottomed out at 776.92 on August 12, 1982; the next day, following the Fed's cut in the discount rate, the Dow soared 11 points. By October, it had crossed back over the psychologically important 1,000 level, and has never looked back.

But the overall economy would lag behind these early signs of a turnaround. While a few leading indicators were turning positive in the second half of 1982, the number that counted most—unemployment—continued to rise. Unemployment moved steadily upward past 9 percent in August, and ran even higher in the industrial heartland: By the end of summer, Michigan's unemployment rate reached 14.3 percent; in Indiana it was 12.4 percent; Ohio, 11.1 percent; West Virginia, 18 percent. In October Reagan admitted that unemployment might worsen.

Reagan's approval ratings sagged badly, with several midsummer polls showing a majority of voters opposing his reelection. One poll found that 49 percent of voters who pulled the lever for Reagan in 1980 said they would not do so again, with the highest defections being among working-class voters Reagan had peeled away from the Democrats. Political observers were predicting a GOP wipeout in the upcoming midterm elections. The leading quantitative models of academic political scientists predicted a forty-five-seat loss in the House for Republicans; some predictions of GOP losses ran as high as seventy seats. Polls of the generic vote showed Democrats with a fifteen-to-twenty-point lead over Republicans, a lead that usually presaged a thirty-seat Democratic gain, which is exactly the figure Reagan's pollster Richard Wirthlin was privately telling the White House to expect.

While Reagan ran out of time for the economy to turn around, he didn't run out of fight. Instead, in the words of presidential scholars Beth Ingold and Theodore Windt, "Reagan launched the most vigorous campaign of any modern President in an off-year election."[77] His overarching theme was "stay the course": *Give my program time to work.* Franklin Roosevelt had employed this theme with great success in the 1934 election when the Great Depression was still close to its depth, arguing that the New Deal needed more time, and more Democrats in Congress, to work. It was the only successful midterm election for a president's party in the previous eighty years.

This appeal to virtue had some resonance with the public. As usual, there was a lot of dissonance in public opinion. Despite the Democratic attack on the "Reagan recession" and "fairness," polls showed that by a three-to-one margin voters blamed Carter more than Reagan for the recession, and while people told pollsters that unemployment was the most important problem facing the nation, the same surveys showed that people personally feared inflation would affect them more than the possibility of unemployment. Reagan frequently invoked "the trouble that originated in the four years before we took office" and portrayed the choice in the election as being "whether we will continue on our sure and steady course to put America back on track or whether we will slide backward into another economic binge like the one which left us with today's pounding national hangover." Despite this aggressiveness, a few GOP candidates avoided appearing with Reagan, a sure sign of a wounded and weakened president.[78]

Although Reagan's stay-the-course theme was somewhat successful in isolating his biggest liability, it was still essentially a defensive strategy, and elections are seldom won on the defensive. Early in the fall Reagan attempted to play up social issues and family values, including abortion, school prayer, and crime, as a way of putting Democrats on the defensive. (One clever Democrat parried by proposing to combine the school prayer amendment and a balanced budget amendment into a single measure that would require schoolchildren to pray for a balanced budget.) This line of attack also had the benefit of keeping faith with conservatives who felt the president had paid too little attention to social issues while making his push for economic policy.[79]

But the Senate Republican leadership refused to force votes on social issues such as restoring school prayer that would have put Democrats on the defensive. To the contrary, the Senate in a late September procedural vote tabled legislation to restore prayer in public schools—an issue that polled very highly for Republicans.

As a result, for the stretch run Reagan reverted almost wholly to "stay the course." Tip O'Neill mocked this approach, saying, "Stay the course? That is unfair. American needs a change." O'Neill charged that Reagan had thrown "millions of people out of work as part of a deliberate plan to slow down inflation." In reply, Reagan lustily bashed what he called Democratic "myths, fairy-tales, and doomsaying."

The last unemployment report before the election, released in early October, was a disaster for Reagan and the Republicans. The unemployment rate clocked in at 10.1 percent, the first double-digit unemployment rate since 1940. The Democrats were ready, with plans laid in advance to have Democratic candidates visit unemployment lines and closed factory locations. A Democratic TV ad was released depicting a current unemployment line morphing into a bread line from the 1930s, with the suggestion that once again Democrats were needed to pull the nation out of a depression. The bottom fell out for Republicans. Fourteen House Republicans who held double-digit leads in their district tracking polls on October 1 went down to defeat.

Republicans lost twenty-six House seats on November 2, while staying even in the Senate. The GOP held the Senate by the narrowest of margins; as had been the case in 1980, a shift of just forty-three thousand votes in five states would have handed Senate control back to the Democrats. On election night Bob Dole appeared on CBS News and validated Dan Rather's theme that Reaganomics had hurt Republicans, much to the annoyance of the White House. A jubilant Tip O'Neill declared that the results were "a disaster for the Republican Party." Among the significant Democratic winners was Bill Clinton, who returned to the governor's mansion in Arkansas after having been written off following his ignominious loss in 1980. In New York Democratic liberal Mario Cuomo won a close race for governor (the *New York Times* welcomed Cuomo as "the reincarnation of the New Deal at a peculiar time," while the *New Republic* called Cuomo "one of the most attractive Democrats to come along in many years"). But in California, underdog Republican George Deukmejian pulled off an upset against Los Angeles mayor Tom Bradley to recapture the governorship for the GOP. In Arizona, former Vietnam War POW John McCain was elected to the House for the first time. (McCain was well known to Reagan, as Reagan had hosted him several times in Sacramento in the mid-1970s following McCain's return from North Vietnam.)

Although the GOP loss in the House was the largest for either party in a first midterm election since 1922, political observers were left scratching their heads that the Democratic gains weren't much larger given the unemployment rate. Kevin Phillips was astounded: "Never before in the post-1954 competitions has the party out of power scored such piddling gains in the face of massive and increasing unemployment." After a close analysis of polling data, political scientist Alan Abramowitz concluded that "Democratic gains were limited because, despite a severe recession, many voters had not given up hope that Reaganomics would eventually work."[80] Robert Rowland and Rodger Payne of Baylor University wrote, "When the historical trend [of off-year election losses] is considered, the Republican loss of twenty-six seats not only seems relatively small, but might be interpreted as a kind of political victory."[81]

Reagan's forward strategy of embracing the election as a referendum on his policy direction appears to have paid a modest dividend. The *New Republic*'s Morton Kondracke summarized the ambiguous outcome: "The 1982 election conferred no great mandate on liberals to run the country, but it did seem to withdraw the 1980 mandate of extreme conservatism." In practical terms, however, it meant that Reagan could no longer command a working majority in the House. Reagan was defiant, saying the day after the election that "we will not compromise on principle—on what we believe is absolutely essential to recovery."

*　　*　　*

THE ECONOMY HADN'T been Reagan's only worry in the midterm election of 1982. Concern about Reagan's handling of foreign affairs was also prominent in the public mind. One poll found that 44 percent of Americans thought the danger of nuclear war had increased since Reagan took office, versus 39 percent who didn't.

A well-organized political campaign on behalf of a nuclear freeze had been rapidly gathering strength. The idea was ostensibly for a "mutual, verifiable" freeze in nuclear weapons by both the United States and the Soviet Union. The freeze campaign tapped into the still-vibrant infrastructure and reserve manpower of the professional anti–Vietnam War protest movement. It also managed to enlist several prominent figures such as Father Theodore

Hesburgh and Billy Graham. "By the spring of 1982," public opinion specialists Michael Hogan and Ted Smith noted in *Public Opinion Quarterly,* "virtually the entire liberal establishment had endorsed the freeze."[82] Four elder statesmen of the liberal foreign policy establishment—Robert McNamara, George Kennan, McGeorge Bundy, and Gerard K. Smith—lent the freeze movement indirect aid with a widely publicized article in *Foreign Affairs* calling for the United States and NATO to commit to a no-first-use policy for nuclear weapons in the European theater. This was tantamount to giving up NATO's nuclear deterrent capability.

A mutual and verifiable freeze by both sides was a seductive idea, but in practice it was likely to mean a unilateral freeze by the United States, since the Soviet Union was impervious to public opinion. In other words, it would merely stop Reagan's arms buildup. And a freeze at that time would have meant Western acceptance of a disadvantageous strategic position, especially in Europe. Conservatives had their own bumper-sticker slogan to counter the idea: "Freeze now, fry later." Even Jimmy Carter criticized the idea (before, typically, endorsing it), noting that Brezhnev had refused his 1979 offer of a freeze and had changed his mind only after the Soviet Union had gotten its SS-20 missiles in place. While freeze supporters pointed to polls showing that 70 percent of Americans liked the freeze, a CBS/*New York Times* poll found that 80 percent opposed a freeze if they thought the Soviets would cheat, and that two-thirds opposed a freeze if it would leave the United States in an inferior position. Polling analyst Everett Carll Ladd argued that the superficial support for the nuclear freeze represented a public desire for the nation's leaders "to do what is possible to draw the world back from the possibility of nuclear war."[83]

But the freeze idea got traction anyway, in part because politicians and the media ignored the subtleties of public opinion on the matter. There were a total of thirty-eight nonbinding nuclear freeze initiatives on state and local ballots across the United States; thirty-five of the thirty-eight passed, mostly by lopsided two-to-one margins. Dozens of city councils across the country (including 177 town meetings in Vermont) also passed nuclear freeze resolutions. In Congress, Republican senator Mark Hatfield, a man of devout pacifist inclinations, joined with Senator Ted Kennedy in sponsoring a profreeze resolution that was widely seen as a vote of no confidence in Reagan's stance on arms control. In its first vote in the House, a freeze proposal was defeated by only two votes, 204–202.

The potency of antinuclear agitation reflected the unease with which

Americans and the world viewed the way in which Reagan was shaking loose the generation-long stalemate of the Cold War.[84] Reagan's presidency had begun with explicit focus on domestic problems, but by degrees his attention was beginning to shift. Could Reagan stay the course on foreign policy as well?

CHAPTER 6

THE GATHERING STORM

⸺◦◦◦⸺

A serious foreign policy requires a comprehensive
central concept; without it, pronouncements are exercises
in rhetoric, and actions are driven by short-term tactical
consideration without coherence or sense of direction.
—HENRY KISSINGER, JANUARY 1982

A TINY CULTURAL SIGN of the changing national mood that followed Ronald Reagan's election occurred in 1982, when the Hasbro toy
company revived the GI Joe action figure. Originally created in 1962, the toy
lost popularity in the aftermath of Vietnam, despite Hasbro's offering new
models that emphasized generic adventure instead of militaristic lethality. It
didn't work. Hasbro discontinued GI Joe in 1978, unconvincingly citing high
oil prices as a constraint on manufacturing. Now GI Joe was back, along
with a cartoon theme song, "Real American Hero." By the end of 1983,
more than two hundred million war-themed action figures would be sold.
The revival of GI Joe coincided with the decline of another cultural totem:
the antiwar TV show *M*A*S*H* ended in early 1983 after eleven years
on CBS.

Reagan's defense buildup, emphasized with high-profile announcements
of the resumption of several major arms programs that Jimmy Carter had
cancelled, such as the B-1 bomber and the neutron bomb, renewed morale in
the military (as well as its private sector suppliers). Recruitment and retention
in the armed forces were up, after lagging in the late 1970s. The quality of
military recruits improved; the number of army recruits with high school
diplomas increased from 54 percent in 1980 to 90 percent in 1984.[1] But a
larger military budget is not a foreign policy, despite Reagan's view of the ne-

cessity of patiently engaging in a buildup before engaging the Soviet Union in new arms negotiations.

While Reagan was patient, Europe was not. The Reagan administration had inherited the two-track intermediate-range nuclear force (INF) initiative of the Carter administration, according to which the United States would deploy 572 Pershing II and cruise missiles in the fall of 1983 if negotiations with the Soviets failed to reduce their growing number of intermediate-range missiles aimed at Europe. The Reagan administration was actually unenthusiastic about the INF program; it would have preferred simply to bolster the U.S. strategic ICBM force and to deploy more missile submarines to the region. Abandoning the missile deployment would have been politically ruinous for NATO and the United States, however. As summer yielded to fall in 1981, European leaders, reluctant to see U.S. missiles deployed on their soil, were growing increasingly anxious about the absence of INF negotiations and the Reagan administration's near silence on the matter. A European peace movement was gathering strength, turning out 150,000 people in West Germany in the spring to oppose the NATO missile deployment plans. Left-leaning opposition parties were starting to make the INF deployment an issue, and even some members of West Germany's ruling Social Democratic Party were turning against the plan. The Polish philosopher Leszek Kolakowski suggested that the European attitude should be summarized with the slogan "Better slave than brave."

In the midst of this growing European nervousness Reagan made a remark that revived the talk of his potential for being a "mad bomber" adventurist. Over lunch with a group of out-of-town newspaper editors on October 16, 1981, Reagan was asked whether he thought there could be a limited exchange of nuclear weapons in Europe without it escalating into a full-fledged intercontinental nuclear war. Part of Reagan's answer was: "I don't honestly know. . . . I could see where you could have the exchange of tactical weapons against troops in the field without it bringing either one of the major powers to pushing the button."

American news outlets largely ignored the remark, probably because it was an unexceptional if syntactically challenged restatement of the well-established American doctrine of flexible response, but it was lavishly covered in the European press, where it touched off a furor. This was the last thing European leaders such as West Germany's Helmut Schmidt wanted to hear. The persistent European fear was that they would become the casualties of a superpower confrontation—a fear the Soviet Union had adroitly exploited with the theme that America "would fight to the last European." Reagan's remark came hard on the heels of a statement from Secretary of State Al Haig that the United States might fire a nuclear "warning shot" against the Soviet Union in the early innings of a European war.[2] Defense Secretary Caspar Weinberger disavowed Haig, and Reagan, at a subsequent press conference, prudently obfuscated the question. Nonetheless, Weinberger had to reassure nervous NATO defense ministers that American nuclear strategy had not come unhinged.

But below the level of Reagan, Haig, and Weinberger, there was incessant chatter, backed up occasionally with some official documents and statements, that the Reagan administration believed a nuclear war could be fought and won. NSC aide Richard Pipes told the *Washington Post* that he thought the probability of a nuclear war was about 40 percent.[3] "Nuclear War a Real Prospect to Reagan Hard-Liners," the *Chicago Sun-Times* reported in a typical headline on October 4. The most sensational comment came a few weeks later, when *Los Angeles Times* reporter Robert Scheer published comments from an assistant secretary of defense named T. K. Jones that the United States could survive and recover quickly from a nuclear war if everyone dug holes in the ground and covered them up with a door and three feet of dirt. "If there are enough shovels to go around," an unguarded Jones told the crafty (and far-left) Scheer, "everybody's going to make it."[4] The remark generated a firestorm of criticism in the media and on Capitol Hill, while Jones became a nonperson in the Pentagon.

These media-blown tempests helped swell the ranks of the European peace movement. The week before Reagan's remark in mid-October, 250,000 had turned out in Bonn; 150,000 turned out in London. In subsequent weeks protest marches would spread to Paris, Brussels, and Rome. Banners depicting Reagan as a wild cowboy were especially popular. At the same press lunch where Reagan talked of a limited nuclear exchange, he dismissed the European peace movement as a "propaganda campaign" that "can be traced back to the Soviet Union." (Both American and European news media assiduously ignored this dimension of the story. The East German Communist Party, for example, provided $2 million a month to West German leftist groups, while the Soviets funneled hundreds of thousands of dollars to Danish peace groups, and likely millions more that were not detected in other countries. The Soviets also actively attempted to foment discord among NATO through forged documents purporting to be secret cables from Haig and other American officials.)[5]

Reagan's complete view of the problem, as expressed several times that fall, displayed a more sophisticated grasp of the strategic problem facing the Western alliance, as well as a clue to his own deepest instincts. The proposed American missiles, Reagan explained, would only re-create in Europe the same kind of deterrence (*stalemate* was the term Reagan used in place of *deterrence*) that existed between the superpowers through their strategic nuclear weapons. All of this, Reagan argued, set the stage for upcoming negotiations on limited-theater nuclear weapons in Europe—the second track of the two-track policy NATO had adopted in 1979.[6]

With new arms control negotiations with the Soviet Union scheduled to begin at the end of November, Europeans and a great many Americans doubted Reagan's sincerity about arms negotiation because he adopted as his opening proposal an idea that was nearly as audacious as his economic plan: the "zero option." The proposal was that if the Soviet Union would dismantle all of its intermediate-range missiles, NATO would forgo deployment of Pershing and cruise missiles in 1983. The idea had come from Weinberger aide Richard Perle, who proposed the deal in an interagency working group. The State Department vigorously opposed the proposal, saying that it was so one-sided—the zero option would require the Soviet Union to give up everything, while the United States and its allies gave up nothing—that the Soviets would never go for it. Although the State Department tried to block the zero option proposal from going up the policy ladder to the White House, Weinberger and Ed Meese took the idea straight to Reagan, who approved it.[7] The president then decided that a high-profile speech presenting the zero option would help calm the political waters in Europe, even though it was exactly this kind of public pre-announcement of the American position by Jimmy Carter in 1977 that had offended the Soviets and derailed the SALT II negotiations for two years.

On November 18, Reagan laid out the zero option for the first time. Before detailing the proposal, he set out, with his usual mixture of tough and conciliatory tones, the case for believing in the Soviet Union's aggressive intentions:

> The defense needs of the Soviet Union hardly call for maintaining more combat divisions in East Germany today than were in the whole Allied invasion force that landed in Normandy on D-Day. The Soviet Union could make no more convincing contribution to peace in Europe, and in the world, than by agreeing to reduce its

conventional forces significantly and constrain the potential for sudden aggression. . . .

Consider the facts. Over the past decade, the United States reduced the size of its Armed Forces and decreased its military spending. The Soviets steadily increased the number of men under arms. They now number more than double those of the United States. Over the same period, the Soviets expanded their real military spending by about one-third. The Soviet Union increased its inventory of tanks to some 50,000, compared to our 11,000. Historically a land power, they transformed their navy from a coastal defense force to an open ocean fleet, while the United States, a sea power with transoceanic alliances, cut its fleet in half.

During a period when NATO deployed no new intermediate-range nuclear missiles and actually withdrew 1,000 nuclear warheads, the Soviet Union deployed more than 750 nuclear warheads on the new SS-20 missiles alone. . . . And the Soviets continue to add one new SS-20 a week. . . . They now enjoy a superiority on the order of six to one.

Having established the Soviets' military advantage over the United States and their aggressive aims in Europe and beyond, Reagan turned to the zero option:

I have informed President Brezhnev that when our delegation travels to the negotiations on intermediate range, land-based nuclear missiles in Geneva on the 30th of this month, my representatives will present the following proposal: The United States is prepared to cancel its deployment of Pershing II and ground-launch cruise missiles if the Soviets will dismantle their SS-20, SS-4, and SS-5 missiles. This would be an historic step.

But Reagan did not limit his proposals to just the zero option. He had three other initiatives to go along with it: talks to reduce the level of conventional forces in Europe, talks to improve communication links between the superpowers to reduce the risk of accidental nuclear war, and most importantly, new talks aimed at reducing the number of strategic nuclear weapons (rather than merely limiting their buildup, as previous SALT treaties had done), which Reagan proposed to call START, for Strategic Arms Reduction Talks.[8]

The speech was given at 10:00 a.m. Washington time so that it could be broadcast in the early evening in Europe (an estimated sixteen million West Germans tuned in). There Reagan's proposal was well received—Helmut Schmidt went as far as publicly taking credit for the idea.[9] But was the zero option a serious proposal? Cynics (and Strobe Talbott) suggested that making an offer the Soviets would refuse was exactly what the Reaganites intended, hoping to scuttle any arms deal. The official Soviet line took the same view.[10] The chief Soviet arms negotiator in Geneva, Yuli Kvitsinskiy, dismissed the zero option as "a formula for unilateral disarmament by our side, and, frankly, an insult to our intelligence."

Not for the last time in his presidency, Reagan's proposal was thought to be merely an opening position, from which concessions would inevitably follow.[11] The idea for the zero option had been batted around European capitals publicly for several weeks as a "possible negotiating position" (in the words of the *Washington Post*), which means it wasn't to be taken seriously. "Unnamed officials" were quoted in the media suggesting that the zero option would be abandoned quickly.[12] Weinberger had actually opposed a NATO defense ministers' resolution in late October calling for the zero option, and White House press secretary Larry Speakes had thrown cold water on the idea a week later with the comment that "the 'zero option' is something to look at under ideal conditions, but not at present." Haig, meanwhile, said that the United States would merely seek "significant reductions" in the levels of Soviet missiles. Weinberger, Haig, and others thought the zero option was a sop to appease the European peace movement and might result in the cancellation of NATO missile deployment in return for only small reductions in Soviet missiles—in other words, a zero level for only one side.

One factor that propelled the timing of Reagan's zero option announcement was the late November trip Soviet leader Leonid Brezhnev was scheduled to make to West Germany—his first visit to a Western nation since the invasion of Afghanistan two years before. The administration expected and feared that Brezhnev would offer some vague freeze proposal, which is exactly what he did. Brezhnev offered to remove some missiles and stop deployment of new missiles (which the Soviets were doing at the rate of about one missile a month) if the United States cancelled its INF deployment. The United States noted, however, that Soviet SS-20 missiles could still strike most of Europe from beyond the Urals, so removing missiles from Eastern Europe offered no change in the balance of terror. Brezhnev mixed this offer with his own tough rhetoric blaming the United States for "intensifying the arms race" and threatening "the emptying of Europe and turning it into its own tombstone." Though Schmidt privately fended off Brezhnev's overtures and reaffirmed West Germany's commitment to NATO's INF policy, the Soviet gambit did produce favorable media coverage. An Associated Press headline, for example, read: "Brezhnev Seen Ready for Euromissile Compromise."

It was clearly the beginning of a significant Soviet peace offensive. It might have succeeded had its early momentum not been blunted by the second act in the Polish drama.

*   *   *

HAVING AVOIDED THE catastrophe of a Soviet invasion by the narrowest of margins in December 1980, Poland's Solidarity movement attempted throughout 1981 to consolidate and extend its bold position, demanding a five-day workweek, higher wages, and an uncensored press. Emboldened by the success of the Gdansk shipyard strike the previous year, local Solidarity chapters increasingly resorted to short work stoppages. Despite government censorship of Solidarity publications (something it had promised not to do in the Gdansk accord), piece by piece Solidarity was winning concessions from the government, but in a chaotic fashion indicating that Lech Walesa's grip on the union was unsure. Solidarity was threatening to displace the Communist Party as the leading force in Poland's governance, which guaranteed that a showdown would ultimately come.

The inability of the Communist Party to get a firm hold over Solidarity led to a change in the nation's leadership in February, with General Wojciech Jaruzelski being elevated from the post of minister of defense to prime minister. Jaruzelski's appointment was initially popular because he was reputed to be a Polish patriot and much of the army was thought to be sympathetic, or at least neutral, toward Solidarity. But as it turned out, Jaruzelski did Moscow's bidding and would eventually receive the Order of Lenin, the Soviet Union's most distinguished medal; Caspar Weinberger later called him "a Russian general in a Polish uniform."[13] Jaruzelski would end up being the key figure in Poland's subsequent upheaval.

In March 1981, the Soviet Politburo summoned the leaders of the Polish government to Moscow for a dressing-down. The Polish regime subsequently attempted to suppress Solidarity activities and arrest leading dissidents, but this only enraged Solidarity and led the union to threaten its ultimate weapon: a general strike. The prospect of a civil war was openly discussed. As the Soviet military once again mobilized for a possible intervention, Solidarity backed down. Both the Pope and, according to some reports, the Reagan administration passed along warnings to Solidarity that a general strike was too large a risk.[14] In hindsight, Solidarity may have missed its best chance to bring down Communist Party rule.[15]

Over the summer Solidarity and the government conducted negotiations ostensibly as "partners" for Poland's future. Despite a few government concessions on censorship, it was a sham. The government's strategy all along had been to weaken and divide Solidarity, and it is likely that some of the firebrands arguing within Solidarity for radical action were agent provocateurs placed there by the government. Despite internal frictions and rising complaints about Walesa's leadership, Solidarity did not break. At the end of summer the talks broke down, and nine hundred Solidarity leaders retreated to Gdansk for their own First National Congress to consider their next steps. As the Soviet navy conducted large-scale exercises offshore from Gdansk in an obvious attempt at intimidation, the Solidarity delegates called for a national referendum to limit the power of the Communist Party in Poland's government, and issued a "Message to the Working Peoples of Eastern Europe" (pointedly including the Soviet Union) calling for their fellow workers to assert their right to have self-governing trade unions. Walesa remarked that this appeal was merely following Marx's advice for proletarians of all nations to unite.

In Moscow, the Politburo was not amused. Brezhnev erupted at a special Politburo meeting, calling the Solidarity message "an insolent stunt." He had been complaining for months that Poland's Communist Party leader, Stanislaw Kania, was "indecisive and soft," telling Kania bluntly in August that "there never had been a case when revolution triumphed over counterrevolution without a battle and without the use of force." Following the September Solidarity meeting Brezhnev blistered Kania's eardrums over the telephone. The Politburo followed up with a public letter demanding that Kania take stern measures "to prevent the imminent loss of socialism in Poland." A few weeks later Kania was ousted and Jaruzelski elevated to the post of Communist Party leader in addition to being prime minister.

Unbeknownst to Solidarity, preparations to use the army to impose martial law had begun to be made as early as the fall of 1980, and they intensified in the middle of 1981. The KGB began printing martial law posters in August, before Solidarity issued its inflammatory appeal for the workers of other Eastern bloc nations to organize. The regime abruptly extended the conscription period for army draftees and sent new "military operational groups" to two thousand cities and villages across the country, supposedly to improve food distribution and keep order. Far from being clandestine, this deployment was prominently broadcast on Polish television news. Yet Solidarity's leadership, increasingly frayed amidst growing criticism of Walesa, remained oblivious to the accumulating signals that the government was readying a crackdown.

When the hammer finally fell on the night of December 12, Solidarity was completely unprepared. Telephone communications were cut, a curfew was imposed, and tanks rolled through the streets throughout the country, surrounding Solidarity offices and other locations of dissidence. Solidarity's leaders, many of whom were conveniently attending yet another conference in Gdansk, were easily rolled up. More than four thousand people were arrested. Lech Walesa was interned, and Solidarity was outlawed in an emergency decree.[16] Jaruzelski's declaration that Poland was in a "state of war" was accurate, for his well-executed crackdown amounted to a coup. Poland had invaded itself.

The manner in which the martial law decision unfolded in both Moscow and Warsaw, and the U.S. reaction to it, opens onto a crucial phase in the last decade of the Cold War. U.S. intelligence had known about the preparations for martial law in detail, thanks to Polish general Ryszard Kuklinski, who had been spying for the CIA for several years. Kuklinski's reports of the coming crackdown were presented to Reagan and Vice President Bush, yet the United States sent no warning to Solidarity that a crackdown was coming. "It remains to this day one of the unsolved mysteries of the Reagan presidency why this invaluable information was never acted upon," Reagan's NSC aide Richard Pipes has written.[17] For many observers besides Pipes (who had recommended to Reagan that he make a statement sometime in the fall), the lack of an American public statement or private warning either to Poland's government or to Solidarity is the "dog that did not bark" in this pivotal Cold War episode.[18]

But the situation was not as clear-cut as hindsight suggests. Kuklinski had been spirited out of Poland in November—"a real cloak and dagger affair," in the words of a U.S. agent who took part—after the KGB had gotten wind that the Americans had a mole in Warsaw. With Kuklinski's information flow abruptly cut off, the United States had no knowledge of the timing of a crackdown. Also, there were some suggestions that U.S. warnings to Moscow in December 1980 had been counterproductive—perhaps even deliberately manipulated by Moscow and Warsaw—because they made Solidarity cautious when it should have been most aggressive.[19] Another concern was that a new warning against the regime might embolden Solidarity into thinking the United States would offer additional support of some kind, as it had before the Hungarian uprising of 1956. (The AFL-CIO was already funneling money to Solidarity. The CIA wisely decided to stay away because, as CIA director William Casey put it, the AFL-CIO would do a better job.) But the principle of Occam's razor probably supplies the main reason. As former CIA agent Douglas MacEachin put it, despite having "plenty of information on what the Polish regime was preparing to do, [the Reagan administration] did not believe they would do it."[20]

The Soviets had the same doubts about whether the Polish government would go through with it. Brezhnev complained at a Politburo meeting at the end of October that Jaruzelski "is not a brave enough man," and contemplated replacing the general with yet another hard-line military officer. Even as Jaruzelski was pressuring the Soviets to commit troops to back up martial law, Moscow doubted up to the last minute whether he would go through with the crackdown. The Soviets sent a senior officer, Marshal Viktor Kulikov, to Warsaw on December 11, the day before martial law was imposed, to buck up Jaruzelski.[21]

If the Soviets thought Jaruzelski was halfhearted, it was a reflection of their own deep indecision about what to do. Although the Soviet military once again worked up contingency plans for securing Poland, the Politburo was set against intervening directly, even if Jaruzelski had flinched. Most of the Politburo minutes that have emerged from Soviet archives present a picture of unrelenting pressure on Poland to crack down amidst an overlay of pervasive doubt and hand-wringing. The minutes of one Politburo meeting even include discussion of whether it might be necessary to allow Poland to slip away from the Warsaw Pact.[22]

These signs of restraint might be taken as early hints that the Moscow gerontocracy perceived that their empire was starting to slip irretrievably away. (Ironically, other Eastern European regimes such as Czechoslovakia and East Germany were eager to intervene.) More likely, however, wider geopolitics was the decisive reason for the Politburo's restraint. As Timothy Garton Ash observed, "Every day that the Soviets did not invade brought encouragement for the opposition to American Cruise and Pershing II missiles in western Europe."[23] Ash added that Solidarity knew this and did not like the Western European peace movement precisely because "it tended to weaken the West's resistance to Soviet imperialism."

Even though Soviet involvement with the coup was obvious from the martial law posters that had been printed in Moscow, the fact that the Soviets had the Poles do their own dirty work provided enough of a fig leaf for Western leaders to downplay the significance of Poland. West Germany's foreign minister, Hans-Dietrich Genscher, said that martial law was a purely internal Polish matter. The day after martial law was imposed, Helmut Schmidt made a previously scheduled visit to East Germany's Stalinist ruler, Erich Honecker, where Schmidt weakly declared that "Herr Honecker is as dismayed as I am that this was necessary."[24] Canadian prime minister Pierre Trudeau said, "All countries should respect Poland's right to settle its own problems its own way." British Labour Party grandee Denis Healey said, "I think we should all pray for the success of General Jaruzelski." Several European Communist parties ironically issued stronger condemnations than their centrist governments did.

Reagan, however, was livid over Poland. The National Security Council met almost daily about the Polish crisis over the next two weeks, in what Richard Pipes characterized as "an emotionally charged atmosphere inspired largely by Reagan's mounting fury." Reagan derided the "chicken littles" in Europe and once again compared the present moment to the 1930s, noting the failure of the democracies to stand up to totalitarian aggression and making reference to FDR's "quarantine the aggressor" speech. This was "the last chance of a lifetime to go against this damned force," Reagan said at the December 22 NSC meeting.[25]

But what could the United States actually do to the Soviet Union? Nearly every option contained a dilemma, and the tougher options risked splitting the NATO alliance. Reagan's advisers divided into two camps. Caspar Weinberger, Jeane Kirkpatrick, William Casey, and William Clark urged tough sanctions. "It is comfortable for the Europeans to do nothing," Weinberger observed. Reagan was determined: "We should let our Allies know they, too, will pay a price if they don't go along; that we have long memories." Secretary of State Al Haig led the call for restraint. The division grew heated at times. Weinberger criticized the State Department's option papers as "an eloquent plea for doing nothing." Reagan mused about declaring the Helsinki Accord "null and void." Haig: "Europe will go bonkers if we do that." Reagan: "Why pretend we have an agreement if they violate it constantly?"[26]

The blunt communications between Reagan and Brezhnev during this fortnight show how raw relations had become. Reagan fired off an indignant message to Brezhnev on the Direct Communications Link (the "hotline") on December 23. "The recent events in Poland clearly are not an 'internal matter,' and in writing to you, as the head of the Soviet government, I am not misaddressing my communication. Your country has repeatedly intervened in Polish affairs during the months preceding the recent tragic events. . . . [N]othing has so outraged our public opinion as the pressures and threats which your government has exerted on Poland to stifle the stirrings of freedom." Reagan reminded Brezhnev that Soviet actions violated several international laws, including the Helsinki Accords, "which you, Mr. President, personally initialed on behalf of your country." Polish reform, Reagan added, was no threat to the Soviet Union. "The United States cannot accept suppression of the Polish people's legitimate desire for such a process of renewal, particularly when it is imposed under external pressure."

Brezhnev's equally indignant reply arrived promptly two days later, on Christmas morning in Washington. "[Y]ou have placed your personal signature upon the fact that gross interference in the internal affairs of Poland is the official policy of the United States," Brezhnev claimed. Soviet communications with Poland, Brezhnev explained, were merely "mutual relations between two political parties" (the Communist parties of the USSR and Poland) "completely equal and friendly"—the equivalent, one supposes, to the Nevada and California Republican parties exchanging campaign plans. "The Polish people do not sit in judgment of others, who would force their values on them. . . . American officials, yes, even you personally, are defaming our social and state system, our internal order. We resolutely repudiate this. . . . But one cannot help but notice that the general tone of your letter is not the way in which leaders of such powers as the Soviet Union and the United States should talk with each other. . . . It is not us, not the Soviet Union, which would bear responsibility should the further undermining of Soviet-American relations take place."

Reagan was incredulous about Brezhnev's reply. He sent a handwritten note to Admiral James Nance, who was presiding over the NSC because Richard Allen had taken a leave of absence in the wake of a typical Washington mini-scandal.[27] Reagan's letter restated his argument in simple terms: "It seems to me we are supporting the *right* of the Polish people to vote on the gov't they'd like to have. Mr B. [Brezhnev] is supporting the right of the gov't to deny the Polish people a voice in their gov't." He also brought up the Yalta agreement's promise of free elections in Poland, saying with droll understatement, "The Soviets violated that pact." Reagan sent a follow-up message back to Brezhnev reminding him of this. In Richard Pipe's words, Reagan's statements and actions "broke with the Yalta syndrome that had tacitly acknowledged Poland as lying within the Soviet sphere of influence."

Against the advice of Michael Deaver and the anxieties of Haig, Reagan went on TV December 23 to give a speech on the Polish crisis. ("My problem is the timing in a speech tomorrow," Haig said in the December 22 NSC meeting, "will bring the specter of the terror of World War III on Christmas Eve.") "The fate of a proud and ancient nation hangs in the balance," Reagan said. "This Christmas brings little joy to the courageous Polish people. They have been betrayed by their own government. . . . I want emphatically to state tonight that if the outrages in Poland do not cease, we cannot and will not conduct 'business as usual' with the perpetrators and those who aid and abet them. Make no mistake, their crime will cost them dearly in their future dealings with America and free peoples everywhere. I do not make this statement lightly or without serious reflection." The president urged Americans to emulate a sign of protest that Solidarity had adopted in Poland, placing a single lighted candle in a window—"a sign that the light of liberty still glows in their hearts." Reagan did so at the White House.

Reagan's December 23 hotline message to Moscow had warned, "Should the Soviet Union persist in aiding the course of continued suppression in Poland, the United States will have no choice but to take concrete measures affecting the full range of our relationship." The largest economic weapon would be to declare Poland in default on $27 billion in loans owed to Western banks (Poland was technically in default already, having stopped interest payments months before). The primary repercussion of default would be on American and European banks, dealing a blow to bank balance sheets at a time when Western credit markets were already straining under high interest rates and tight monetary policy. West Germany claimed that some of its banks might collapse if Poland defaulted.

Henry Kissinger suggested that the United States suspend the INF talks in Geneva, but Reagan and Haig wanted to avoid specific linkage in arms control negotiations. Still, it was embarrassing for the Reagan administration to have Kissinger to its right. Instead of declaring Poland in default or reviving linkage, Reagan announced a few small-bore sanctions against Poland: canceling Export-Import Bank credit insurance, suspending commercial airline landing rights for the Polish airline Lot (Lot had only one flight a week to the United States), and denying access to U.S. water's for the Polish fishing fleet. He later stripped Poland of its most-favored-nation trade status (Poland had been the only Eastern bloc nation with MFN status).

Haig and other critics within the administration argued that sanctions would mostly hurt the Polish people rather than the regime, though, as Timothy Garton Ash wrote, "[T]he only trouble with this argument was that the poor suffering Polish people showed embarrassing signs of *supporting* President Reagan's line" and would have cheered tougher sanctions.[28] Haig also argued that tough sanctions would drive Poland into greater dependency on the Soviet Union, forgetting that such an effect would be a further burden on the Soviet economy. (The Politburo was already complaining before martial law about the food and matériel shipments required to keep Poland afloat.)

Outside the administration, critics across the political spectrum, from George Will to Lane Kirkland, blasted Reagan's Polish sanctions for being weak and "symbolic," though Jaruzelski claimed years later that the sanctions had been more damaging than the West knew.[29] Norman Podhoretz wrote, "Where Poland was concerned, the Administration seemed more worried about hurting a few bankers than about hurting the Soviet empire."[30] *National Review* called the sanctions "marginal deprivations." The Committee for the Free World placed a full-page ad in the *New York Times* calling for a tougher response. *Human Events'* front-page article was savage: "It may seem rather harsh to say so, but the Reagan Administration is beginning to acquire the reputation of one that sounds a bit like Churchill but frequently acts like Chamberlain."[31] More damning than the criticism from Reagan's ideological allies was the praise he received from liberals who normally disdained his every breath. *New York Times* columnist Anthony Lewis wrote a column entitled "Reagan Gets It Right," and Jimmy Carter signaled his approval: "He's comin' toward me all the time."

More significant than the Polish sanctions were Reagan's actions against the Soviet Union. The first step was an embargo on the use of U.S. technology for the three-thousand-mile Yamil gas pipeline from Siberia to Western Europe, a multibillion-dollar project that promised to generate as much as $10 billion a year in hard currency earnings for the Soviet Union. The pipeline was a classic product of détente—a valuable piece of infrastructure built with Western technology and Western credit. Not only was the West selling the rope with which to be hung by the Communists, as Lenin's famous phrase had it, but the West was financing that rope on highly favorable terms, amounting to a subsidy. The United States had worried that the gas pipeline would make Western Europe partially dependent on the Soviets for energy— the pipeline would supply a quarter of West Germany's gas and a third of France's—but had no way to prevent it. Reagan's embargo on the use of U.S. technology prevented hundreds of millions of dollars in sales to Caterpillar Tractor and General Electric. Caterpillar, whose business was already slumping because of the recession, had a $90 million order from Moscow for two hundred state-of-the-art pipe layers, while GE had a $175 million order for turbine equipment, some of which had already been shipped to European warehouses. Both contracts were suspended.

More problematic was Reagan's proposal to extend the embargo to European firms manufacturing pipeline components with American-made parts or under American license. This prospect caused an uproar among NATO allies, including Margaret Thatcher. (British firms stood to lose more than $300 million at a time when unemployment in Britain was 14 percent, and French, Italian, and West German firms stood to lose even more.) Thatcher warned the United States in January that "there was a clear danger of the American Government's present policy damaging Western interests more than those of the East and provoking a major transatlantic quarrel of precisely the sort that it had long been the main objective of Soviet policy to bring about." She additionally complained to Secretary of State Haig that the United States, in disdaining to impose a grain embargo on the Soviets because it would harm hard-pressed American farmers, was in a weak position to ask Europeans to sacrifice. "To say the least," Thatcher wrote, "there was a certain lack of symmetry."[32]

Thatcher found a sympathetic ear in Haig, who argued vigorously against pipeline sanctions in Washington.[33] Reagan was adamant: "They can build their damn pipeline, but not with our technology."[34] Thatcher's opposition, however, gave Reagan pause, and he agreed to allow the State Department to explore whether agreement could be reached on restricting credit to the Soviet Union.

At the root of Reagan's policy was the view that it was time to strike at the Soviet Union's greatest weakness, its faltering economy, and especially its hard currency earnings from trade with the West. Indeed, there were signs that the Soviet Union's foreign currency reserves were dangerously low. In January the Soviets began selling off large quantities of their gold reserves on the world market to raise cash, even though the price of gold was off more than 50 percent from a year and a half before.

The matter was in limbo for five months until late June, when Reagan abruptly decided to extend the embargo to foreign subsidiaries of American firms and their European licensees. Europe reacted angrily. Thatcher said she was "appalled" and denounced the embargo publicly. It was, she said, "a lesson in how not to conduct alliance business." Reagan took the decision in part to prod the allies to quit subsidizing Soviet trade. At the G-7 summit in France a few weeks before, Reagan thought he had won some ground in getting the European allies to pledge to cut back easy credit for the Soviet Union, but the French were dragging their feet and trying to back out.[35]

There is good evidence that Reagan chose to impose the extended pipeline embargo chiefly because he knew it would send Al Haig packing. (Lou Cannon makes this case in *President Reagan: Role of a Lifetime*.)[36] Haig had threatened resignation before, but this time the president would accept it with relish. Reagan had heard rumors that Haig was undermining administration policy in Europe, and in a rare face-to-face confrontation in the Oval Office in early June, Reagan told Haig that he would not stand for this insubordination. It was the culmination of months of rising friction between Haig and others in the administration over matters of policy beyond just the Polish sanctions. "It's amazing," Reagan wrote of Haig in his diary in March 1982, "how sound he can be on complex international matters but how utterly paranoid with regard to the people he must work with." In addition to Haig's abrasiveness, he had offended Nancy Reagan with a bout of ham-handed grandstanding at the G-7 summit a few weeks before, and gotten into a heated shouting match with William Clark, who was not a man given to raising his voice.

Haig agreed that Reagan should have a different secretary of state, but deferred a formal resignation. After the extended embargo was announced, Haig came to see Reagan again, complaining of being undermined by the White House staff and hoping he could talk the president into augmenting his power. Strange to the end, Haig showed Reagan the envelope with his resignation letter but did not hand it over. He didn't need to. Reagan promptly announced Haig's resignation and in the same statement named George Shultz as his replacement (though Reagan briefly considered Kissinger). "This has been a heavy load," Reagan wrote of Haig in his diary that night.

On the specific issue of the pipeline sanctions, Shultz's views were close to Haig's. In November the Reagan administration ended the pipeline embargo, Shultz having gained a few minor concessions from Europe in return for the lifting of sanctions. The conventional wisdom is that Reagan's pipeline policy was a failure, and while this is largely correct, it was not a complete rout. Reagan never could have stopped the Soviet pipeline project entirely, but he did slow its completion by at least a year and increased the cost to the Soviets. By the time the pipeline finally came online in the mid-1980s, gas prices, following oil prices, had fallen by half in real terms. The pipeline was less of a boon than the Soviets had hoped.

Yet the Polish crisis was significant far beyond the internal debate over sanctions policy and the pipeline embargo. The Polish crisis roused the administration from the foreign policy drift and improvisation of Reagan's first year in office. In the months following the beginning of the Polish crisis, Reagan's national security team began a process that generated several policy guidelines and decision directives that brought clarity and purpose to Reagan's anti-Soviet principles. A year later, a grand strategy was in place to turn the tide of the Cold War.

*   *   *

THE OLD WASHINGTON adage "personnel is policy" played the key role in jump-starting Reagan's foreign policy in the aftermath of Poland. Replacing Haig with Shultz completed a necessary turnover in foreign policy staff that enabled Reagan's foreign policy apparatus to function more deliberately. The infighting and disagreement did not cease—it never does—but a focused effort began to bear fruit.[37]

Shultz was a close friend and academic colleague of Milton Friedman, and was pictured on the cover of *Time* magazine after his appointment wearing an Adam Smith necktie, considered a certain marker of an intellectual—if not movement—conservative. (Ed Meese hardly ever wore any other tie.) But movement conservatives were wary of Shultz nonetheless. He had little background in foreign policy and was thought to be sympathetic to Kissinger-style détente. Some conservatives warned that Shultz would turn out to be "Reagan's Cy Vance," referring to Carter's secretary of state. "Shultz," Richard Viguerie complained, "is part of the elite, big-business establishment."

Reagan, however, liked Shultz and was comfortable with him. The new secretary of state was "normally as excitable as a cigar store Indian," in the words of *National Review,* but he was thought to be a team player. He therefore seemed a good corrective to the frenetic Haig; Shultz was the last person who would grab a microphone in a crisis to declare, "I'm in charge." Beyond Shultz's stolid virtue, what may have recommended him most to Reagan was a similarity that escaped notice: Shultz had been a labor mediator. In Shultz, the former union leader Reagan discerned someone who instinctively understood and could emulate Reagan's bargaining approach to Soviet relations. Shultz would prove adept at this over the next few years.

Shultz represented one side of Reagan's extraordinary equipoise, which balanced hard-line anti-Communism with a genuine idealism for reducing nuclear weaponry and reaching agreements with the Soviet Union. Reagan had the NSC to bolster his hard anti-Communism; he needed a supple hand at State to finesse the diplomacy. Conservatives nervous about Shultz should have taken cheer from some of his congressional testimony, such as this terse exchange with far-left California senator Alan Cranston in a Senate hearing:

SENATOR CRANSTON: Can you tell us what the United States, for its part, has done to contribute to the tension that exists between the United States and the Soviet Union?
SECRETARY SHULTZ: Nothing.

More important than Shultz at the time, however, was Judge William Clark, who officially became national security adviser in January 1982 after Richard Allen was forced to resign. The job of national security adviser had acquired a public mystique starting with Henry Kissinger, who made the post a locus of grand strategy and a virtual co-equal with the secretary of state. The real job of the national security adviser is to coordinate the State Department, the Pentagon, and other agencies that have foreign policy responsibility, but in practice this means mediating their inevitable clashes. Above all, the job requires pushing issues and decisions to the president. This can't be done very well unless the national security adviser has direct and regular access to the president. Having Richard Allen report to Reagan indirectly through Ed Meese clogged up the whole apparatus, and foreign policy decisions were not being made. Clark demanded direct daily access to Reagan when he became national security adviser. In effect, the Baker-Deaver-Meese troika became a foursome. Clark rescued the national security interagency process from the doldrums it had suffered for the previous year. "Clark was the James Stewart of the Reagan Administration," Michael Ledeen wrote. "Tall, lanky, a man of few words and little visible emotion, but whose demeanor bespoke an inner calm and an underlying loyalty to his leader . . . [H]e had qualities that, in retrospect, made him the best of Reagan's national security advisers."[38]

In the fullness of time there would be considerable friction between Shultz and Clark, rooted in institutional as well as personal differences of opinion. This did not prevent the national security working group from producing a series of NSDDs (National Security Decision Directives) for Reagan's signature that finally provided guidance for executing foreign policy toward the Soviet Union; in fact, the dynamic tension probably helped for a time. Clark had been widely criticized in 1981 when, during his confirmation hearings to be deputy secretary of state, he displayed scant knowledge of foreign affairs. This, ironically, was to Reagan's benefit: a more conventional foreign policy figure never would have helped to promulgate the audacious Cold War strategy that now took shape.

In August 1982 Reagan issued a formal request for a top-to-bottom review of American policy toward the Soviet Union. Richard Pipes had long wanted to produce a background policy paper explaining a new strategy for Soviet relations, but the NSC's dysfunctions and opposition from the State Department prevented much progress in 1981. Pipes, among others, had argued that the time had come to reorient America's Soviet policy from containment to transformation. The Soviet Union's expansionism, he wrote in an early NSC paper, would not cease until the Soviet system either collapsed or was thoroughly reformed. Pipes discerned that Soviet economic weakness could be exploited, and that a reformist faction might come to the fore in Soviet leadership in the near future. The Soviet Union was ripe for change, provided the West raised the cost of Soviet imperialism and actively encouraged internal reform.[39]

Reagan read an early draft of Pipes's analysis and indicated his agreement with it. Even as the policy review process was under way, Reagan began incorporating the evolving strategy into his public rhetoric, first in short phrases that were easily overlooked, but starting in 1982 in a more prominent way. Over the course of his presidency Reagan made five historic speeches about Cold War relations.[40] The first was his speech in June 1982 in Westminster Hall in London. There is an obvious symmetry to this speech: its debt to Churchill's 1946 "Iron Curtain" speech at Westminster College in Missouri, made in the presence of Harry Truman, is evident. Churchill's speech might be said to have been the official announcement of the beginning of the Cold War. Here, at another location named Westminster, Reagan began to lay out an understanding of how it might end. Reagan quoted or referred to Churchill directly throughout the speech. He associated himself with Churchill's understanding of the Soviet Union and the Cold War, but then went on to suggest that a turning point was at hand. An extended excerpt is necessary to capture the sweep and boldness of the speech:

> We're approaching the end of a bloody century plagued by a terrible political invention—totalitarianism. Optimism comes less easily today, not because democracy is less vigorous, but because democracy's enemies have refined their instruments of repression. Yet optimism is in order, because day-by-day democracy is proving itself to be a not-at-all-fragile flower. From Stettin on the Baltic to Varna on

the Black Sea, the regimes planted by totalitarianism have had more than 30 years to establish their legitimacy. But none—not one regime—has yet been able to risk free elections. Regimes planted by bayonets do not take root. . . .

[Churchill] also had that special attribute of great statesmen—the gift of vision, the willingness to see the future based on the experience of the past. It is this sense of history, this understanding of the past that I want to talk with you about today, for it is in remembering what we share of the past that our two nations can make common cause for the future. . . .

What, then, is our course? Must civilization perish in a hail of fiery atoms? Must freedom wither in a quiet, deadening accommodation with totalitarian evil? Sir Winston Churchill refused to accept the inevitability of war or even that it was imminent. He said, "I do not believe that Soviet Russia desires war. What they desire is the fruits of war and the indefinite expansion of their power and doctrines. But what we have to consider here today while time remains is the permanent prevention of war and the establishment of conditions of freedom and democracy as rapidly as possible in all countries."

Well, this is precisely our mission today: to preserve freedom as well as peace. It may not be easy to see, but I believe we live now at a turning point.

In an ironic sense Karl Marx was right. We are witnessing today a great revolutionary crisis, a crisis where the demands of the economic order are conflicting directly with those of the political order. But the crisis is happening not in the free, non-Marxist West, but in the home of Marxist-Leninism, the Soviet Union. It is the Soviet Union that runs against the tide of history by denying human freedom and human dignity to its citizens. It also is in deep economic difficulty. The rate of growth in the national product has been steadily declining since the Fifties and is less than half of what it was then. The dimensions of this failure are astounding. . . .

While we must be cautious about forcing the pace of change, we must not hesitate to declare our ultimate objectives and to take concrete actions to move toward them. . . . The objective I propose is quite simple to state: to foster the infrastructure of democracy, the system of a free press, unions, political parties, universities, which allows a people to choose their own way to develop their own culture, to reconcile their own differences through peaceful means.

This is not cultural imperialism, it is providing the means for genuine self-determination and protection for diversity.

Now, I don't wish to sound overly optimistic, yet the Soviet Union is not immune from the reality of what is going on in the world.

A central feature of Churchill's "Iron Curtain" speech and his Cold War strategy was the importance of Anglo-American unity. It was not an accident, as the Marxist cliché goes, that Reagan made this speech in London, in the presence of Margaret Thatcher (who, being unfamiliar with teleprompters, was impressed that Reagan spoke without a single note).[41] Notably, the day after his London speech Reagan delivered a far more conventional address to the West German Bundestag, a speech that featured none of the bold language about Communism's weakness.[42] Reagan had already demonstrated the importance of Anglo-American unity by backing—against considerable opposition from senior members of his cabinet—Thatcher's military campaign against Argentina to retake the Falkland Islands in the south Atlantic, a campaign that was climaxing as Reagan arrived in England.

Reagan's rhetorical larceny in the Westminster speech—the idea that it was Soviet Communism, not the capitalist West, that faced a revolutionary crisis—"infuriated the Russians more than anything Reagan had said or done since taking office," according to Pipes. Reagan was delighted; "So, we touched a nerve."[43] The reaction in the Western media was not so far removed from the Soviets' shock. The *New York Times* headline read: "President Urges Global Crusade for Democracy: Revives Flavor of the 1950s in a Speech to Britons." "Reviving the flavor of the 1950s" was not meant as praise. George Ball, one of the elder statesmen of Democratic Party foreign policy figures, was dismissive: "Crusade for democracy? I thought we had gotten over that a long time ago."

While Reagan's Westminster speech is the most vividly recalled aspect of his June 1982 European trip, perhaps the most important event did not involve a speech: his private visit with Pope John Paul II in Rome on June 7. The media focused on the embarrassment of a jet-lagged Reagan falling asleep briefly during the Pope's public welcoming remarks, but naturally they were unaware of what was taking place behind closed doors between Reagan and the Pope, who met alone without advisers or even translators for nearly an hour. The Pope later told his closest aides that Reagan had assured him that he was committed not merely to ending the arms race but also to abolishing nuclear weapons outright. The Reagan administration had already begun sharing intelligence information about Poland with the Vatican (though the Pope surely had better Polish intelligence than the CIA) and discussed actions the United States was taking to provide clandestine aid to Solidarity, but biographer George Weigel's considered judgment is that "the claim that the two men entered into a conspiracy to effect the downfall of European communism is journalistic fantasy."[44]

They didn't need to concoct a conspiracy: both men had a long record of deploring the state of the Captive Nations.

*   *   *

THE NEW UNDERSTANDING of the Cold War that Reagan began articulating in his Westminster speech found formal policy expression in NSDD 75, which Reagan finally signed six months later in January 1983. With NSDD 75 the Reagan Doctrine was born (though this was not yet the public title). The directive declared that henceforth U.S. policy toward the Soviet Union would consist of three elements. The first element was to contain and over time reverse Soviet expansionism, and the third element was negotiations to reach agreements that would enhance American interests. The second element was the most significant:

> To promote, within the narrow limits available to us, the process of change in the Soviet Union toward a more pluralistic political and economic system in which the power of the privileged ruling elite is gradually reduced. The U.S. recognizes that Soviet aggressiveness has deep roots in the internal system, and that relations with the USSR should therefore take into account whether or not they help to strengthen this system and its capacity to engage in aggression.

Beyond these three central elements, there was lots of Reaganite language, such as "U.S. policy must have an ideological thrust which clearly affirms the superiority of U.S. and Western values of individual dignity and freedom, a free press, free trade unions, free enterprise and political democracy over the repressive features of Soviet Communism." The directive called specifically for "exploiting Soviet weaknesses and vulnerabilities," trying to pry Eastern European nations out of the Soviet grip, and putting pressure on the Soviets to withdraw from Afghanistan. Several measures were outlined to end or reduce Western economic support for the Soviet Union.

The directive ended on a sober and prophetic note:

> The policy outlined above is for the long haul. It is unlikely to yield a rapid breakthrough in bilateral relations with the Soviet Union. In the absence of dramatic near-term victories in the U.S. effort to moderate Soviet behavior, pressure is likely to mount for a change in U.S. policy. There will be appeals from important segments of domestic opinion for a more "normal" U.S.-Soviet relationship.

While NSDD 75 suggested it was a long-term strategy, the Reagan team displayed some awareness that circumstances in the Soviet Union might be conducive to rapid change. The lengthy supporting analysis that went into generating the final language of NSDD 75 noted, "Economic problems, the loss of ideological commitment, a growing malaise in society and the succession process now underway should impinge more on the consciousness of the leaders in the Kremlin in the coming decade than they did in the past."[45] But the analysis drew back from concluding that the Soviet Union could potentially collapse in the next decade: "the prospect for major systemic change in the next few years is relatively low."

*   *   *

WHILE REAGAN WAS outlining a forceful new approach to taking on Soviet Communism, the American Left demonstrated that anti-anti-Communism was still its decisive sentiment.

In the fallout from the Polish crisis, the *Nation* magazine organized a forum of left-leaning intellectuals and activists in New York. The forum did decry Solidarity's suppression—after all, Solidarity's frequent appeals to "worker self-management" threw off overtones of syndicalism that appealed to the leftist romanticism for "authentic" socialism—but it found a way to balance the scales through the gambit of moral equivalence between East and West. The predominant theme was: "Let Poland be Poland, but let El Salvador be El Salvador." American interference in El Salvador, it was argued, was no different from Soviet interference in Poland; American support for the Contras in Nicaragua was much the same as Soviet intervention in Afghanistan. Revisionist Cold War historian Ronald Steel had articulated this viewpoint in the *New York Times*, writing: "The Administration is trying to punish the Russians for what the Polish military regime is doing. This is as logical as Soviet punishment of the United States for the actions of the junta we support in El Salvador."[46]

There was one problem: famed literary critic Susan Sontag didn't stick to the script. In her comments at the forum Sontag said: "Imagine, if you will, someone who read only the *Reader's Digest* between 1950 and 1970, and someone in the same period who read only the *Nation* or the *New Statesman.* Which reader would have been better informed about the realities of Communism? The answer, I think, should give us pause. Can it be that our enemies were right?" Communism, Sontag concluded, was just "facism with a human face." (This represented a surprising reversal on Sontag's part; in 1969 she had written: "It is self-evident that the *Reader's Digest* and Lawrence Welk and Hilton Hotels are organically connected with the Special Forces napalming villages in Guatemala."[47])

Sontag's fellow leftists were outraged. She was attacked for being "divisive" and for "hijacking" the forum. The *Nation* quickly ran a string of rebuttals, with the magazine's editors noting that "there are few takers for the equation she makes between Communism and fascism." She was called a "turncoat" and a "converted sinner." Daniel Singer verged on self-parody by dismissing Sontag's observations with the comment "Susan Sontag, as far as I know, does not come from a working-class family." Her speech, Singer said, "could easily be printed in, say, *Commentary.*" (In another sign of self-parody, in the middle of the indignant responses to Sontag was an advertisement for a *Nation* magazine cruise on the Volga River. *We're not Soviet sympathizers! We just like to vacation there.*)

The moral equivalence between East and West revealed in the Sontag affair found broad assent within mainstream liberalism and the media—an example of how far-Left opinion has a magnetic effect on supposedly mainstream liberal opinion. The moral ambivalence of the Left was the fundamental source of the fierce undertow against Reagan's foreign policy designs throughout his presidency.

The malignancy of liberalism's moral ambivalence is best seen in the stark divergence of opinion over two closely related strands of Reagan's anti-Communist policy. There was broad bipartisan support for modest aid to the rebels fighting Soviet forces in Afghanistan (in fact Congress sometimes appropriated more Afghanistan aid than Reagan asked for), but Democrats and some Republicans fiercely opposed aid to the Contra rebels fighting against the pro-Soviet Sandinista regime of Nicaragua.

In the case of Afghanistan the fact of Soviet aggression could not be ob-fuscated. Aid to the Afghan rebels began modestly under Jimmy Carter but was augmented significantly under Reagan, culminating in his second term with Stinger missiles that enabled the Afghan resistance to target high-altitude Soviet helicopters and airplanes. This direct challenge to the Soviets' power in their own backyard proceeded with little criticism or opposition in Washington, even though the nitty-gritty work of distributing weapons and training the *mujahadeen* (as the Afghan holy warriors came to be called) was farmed out to the Pakistani military and intelligence services and hence was out of direct U.S. control.

But the challenge to Soviet proxies in Nicaragua and to the guerilla movement that Nicaragua and Cuba were supplying in El Salvador drew strenuous opposition from the earliest days of the Reagan administration, and indeed nearly became the undoing of the Reagan presidency in the Iran-Contra scandal, as we shall see. Aid to the Nicaraguan Contras was the sin-gle most controversial issue of the Reagan presidency.

El Salvador and Nicaragua need to be understood as a single problem, even though the Reagan administration sometimes proceeded as though each nation required a separate policy response. Policy toward El Salvador was beset with multiple difficulties. The chief American concern was the leftist rebel insurgency that, if successful, might herald a domino effect in Central America (most of the nations in Central America had a leftist guerilla insur-gency of some dimension) culminating in the destabilization of already shaky Mexico. The well-armed Salvadoran rebels were exacting a frightful death toll on the Salvadoran army (casualty rates were as high as 12 percent ac-cording to some estimates), and the CIA thought both El Salvador and Guatemala were in imminent danger of collapse.

A military junta currently governed El Salvador, and it had an abysmal human rights record. Roving gangs of far-right death squads meted out vigi-lante justice not only to leftist rebels but even to innocent moderates who stood in their way, including a Catholic bishop, several American nuns, and relief workers. Even if the leftist guerillas didn't succeed, it was feared the far right might. Reagan administration policy tried to thread the needle of get-ting the military junta to manage a transition to a popular democracy. Mak-ing the democratization of El Salvador a policy goal became necessary to maintain congressional support for aid.

Without fanfare Reagan dispatched fifty-five American military advisers and $25 million in military aid to El Salvador shortly after taking office. So skittish was the Pentagon that the American officers were permitted to carry only sidearms; one officer was sent back to the United States for carrying a rifle. Reagan made the move quietly because the American public was nervous and typically confused about the region. Polls consistently found a large majority (69 percent in a 1983 poll, for example) agreeing with the statement that a pro-Communist government in El Salvador "would be a security threat to the United States."[48] Yet majorities also expressed opposition to military aid to El Salvador. Reagan assiduously avoided talking publicly about Central America in his first year of his presidency, and equivocated when the media raised the subject. When asked about El Salvador at an early press conference, Reagan was defensive: "We're there at the request of the government. We're supporting a government which we believe has an intention of improving the society there for the benefit of the people, and we're opposed to terrorism of the right or left."

Reagan's modest military aid to El Salvador summoned all the reflexes of the Left, which saw this first increment of American military involvement as a sign of another Vietnam. Indeed, for the Left, Central America in the 1980s would become, in the words of Robert Leiken, a liberal who got caught up in the maelstrom, "the most passionate issue since Vietnam." Walter Cronkite's first question in a March 1981 TV interview with Reagan was: "How do you intend to avoid having El Salvador turn into a Vietnam for this country?" The "most trusted man in America," whose turn against the Vietnam War in 1968 was a heavy blow to Lyndon Johnson, was sending a clear signal that he had prejudged prospective American action in Central America. The successful elections in El Salvador in March 1982 (turnout was estimated at about 80 percent, in the face of persistent threats against voters from the guerillas) did little to dampen the controversy or vindicate Reagan's Central America policy.

For the Left, Reagan's aid to El Salvador wasn't merely imprudent or risky—it was an unjust cause. Just as the Left openly sided with the Vietcong in the 1960s, some American leftists, especially the organization CISPES (Committee in Solidarity with the People of El Salvador), supported a guerilla victory and extolled the virtues of the guerillas. Hollywood lefty Ed Asner, for example, said that "the rebel forces are now the most effective institution in El Salvador committed to health delivery."[49] (CISPES also received funding from the New World Foundation, whose chairman at the time was Hillary Rodham Clinton.)[50]

The Left's affection for the Salvadoran guerillas became a full-blown love affair when it came to the Sandinistas in Nicaragua. During the 1980s thousands of Americans made pilgrimages to Nicaragua (as many as forty thousand Americans a year, the Sandinistas claimed) and came back, like the Potemkin tourists of a previous generation, extolling the virtues of the regime. Paul Berman wrote that "[b]ackwater Nicaragua was the world center of the New Left," and *Washington Post* reporter Edward Cody quoted an unnamed American tourist saying, "Nicaragua seems to be a way station on a trip back through the 1960s." University of Massachusetts professor John Brentlinger, author of a large book on Nicaragua, wrote that Nicaragua is "a deeply spiritual country trying to become independent and build a new version of socialism."[51] The *Boston Globe* editorialized that Nicaragua was "a serious, popular, mostly well-intentioned and frequently competent national experiment not altogether unlike our own revolution."[52] The Reverend Jesse Jackson proclaimed that "the Sandinistas are on the right side of history." Such sentiments could fill a small encyclopedia.[53] The usual trendy enclaves of Burlington, Vermont, and Berkeley, California, adopted Managua as a sister city, and the Boston city council declared Ernesto Cardenal Day in honor of the Sandinistas' minister of culture. So fashionable became the Nicaraguan cause that it became de rigueur to pronounce the nation's name with an affected Spanish accent: "knee-car-AH-gew-ah."

A few steps removed from the rabid anti-Americanism of the far Left was the guilt reflex of moderate liberals, who argued that the Sandinistas weren't really Marxist-Leninists inclined to ally with the Soviet bloc, or if they were, it was the United States' fault for having pushed Nicaragua toward the East. This argument was especially popular among "Watergate babies"—Democratic politicians first elected in 1974, in the immediate aftermath of Vietnam—such as Representative Michael Barnes of Maryland, who would later say that Reagan's belligerence "has pushed the Sandinistas further away from the negotiating table and into the willing embrace of the Soviets." But otherwise sensible Democrats such as Lee Hamilton, the chairman of the House Foreign Affairs Committee, also embraced this view. The National Security Agency monitored telephone calls between Sandinistas and Democratic congressmen discussing how to undermine Reagan's policy.[54] This was near the heart of the phenomenon that Jeane Kirkpatrick called "the blame America first crowd."

But the liberal argument, as Peter Rodman wrote, "got the sequence of events startlingly wrong."[55] In 1981, long before Reagan began to take steps against the Sandinistas, Humberto Ortega, brother of the regime's president

Daniel Ortega, declared openly: "Our revolution has a profoundly anti-imperialist character, profoundly revolutionary, profoundly classist; we are anti-Yankee, we are against the bourgeoisie, we are guided by the scientific doctrine of the revolution, by Marxism-Leninism." Indeed, the Sandinistas were probably more enthusiastic about Marxism-Leninism than the Soviet Politburo was at that time, and were certainly more enthusiastic about the Soviet Union than the American Left was. Sandinista foreign minister Miguel d'Escoto, upon being awarded the Lenin Prize in Moscow, said, "I believe the Soviet Union is a great torch which emits hope for the preservation of peace on our planet."[56]

Even liberals who were not bewitched by the Sandinistas found fault with the Reagan administration's hostility toward the regime, blaming the revolutionary ferment in the region on poverty and oppression rather than ideology. Senator Christopher Dodd (D-Conn.), the most fervent opponent of Reagan's Central America policy, put it this way in a speech attacking Reagan: "If Central America were not racked with poverty, there would be no revolution. If Central America were not racked with hunger, there would be no revolution. If Central America were not racked with injustice, there would be no revolution. In short, there would be nothing for the Soviets to exploit. But unless those oppressive conditions change, the region will continue to seethe with revolution—with or without the Soviets." This understanding of the matter raises the question of why most poor nations did not experience revolutionary conditions, never mind the inconvenient fact that nearly all revolutionary movements of the era drew their inspiration from Marxism-Leninism and their weapons from Moscow and Havana.

Nonetheless, to the extent that poverty and despotism create fertile soil for revolutionary movements, Reagan was eager to assert his core principles as a remedy. Rather than appease his foreign and domestic critics with more foreign aid, Reagan decided to pick an ideological fight with liberalism and especially the premise of the international community that Western colonialism and exploitation were the principal causes of what it liked to call the "North-South" divide between rich and poor nations. If conservative economic policy was fit for the United States, it was fit for export too. Here we see an example of how Reagan carried his central principles into all reaches of policy.

Reagan first showed that he intended to take Reaganomics global in the fall of 1981, when he upended the carefully prepared agenda of the North-South Summit in Cancún, Mexico. The summit was the culmination of a process several years in the making by the so-called G-77 nations of the developing world, in a plain counterpoint to the G-7 industrialized nations, which held their own annual summit. In 1980 an international commission chaired by former West German chancellor Willy Brandt had issued a report calling for a "New International Economic Order" that would would require "a large scale transfer of resources to developing countries" and "a start of some major reforms in the international economic system," including international regulatory and perhaps even taxing authority.[57] (High on the Third World wish list was transferring control of the International Monetary Fund and the World Bank to the United Nations, from which it would become even easier to extract cash on favorable terms.) This was simply fancy dress for class conflict theory at the international level. Although Peter Bauer's pathbreaking work on Third World economic development was just beginning to burst onto the intellectual scene, it was still axiomatic in 1981 that the wealthy nations, with their multinational corporations, were responsible for Third World poverty, and therefore owed large amounts of foreign aid almost as reparation.[58]

The Cancún summit in October 1981 was supposed to be the opening round of "global negotiations"—essentially a settlement conference—to determine how much the North would cough up to the South. The *Wall Street Journal* accurately described the Cancún meeting as the Third World's "most spectacular reach for the American wallet." The Reagan administration signaled in advance that it might not agree to such an agenda at Cancún; moreover, Reagan's budget proposed cutting foreign aid. A few days before the summit convened, Reagan fired a preemptive shot in a speech to the World Affairs Council in Philadelphia:

> To listen to some shrill voices, you'd think our policies were as stingy as your Philadelphia Eagles' defense. There is a propaganda campaign in wide circulation that would have the world believe that capitalist United States is the cause of world hunger and poverty. . . .
> Others mistake compassion for development and claim massive transfers of wealth somehow miraculously will produce new well-being. And still others confuse development with collectivism.[59]

Reagan went on extol open markets, private enterprise, individual initiative, low taxes, and limited government as the true path to prosperity for the developing world. (He also took a shot at the Soviet Union for having "nothing to offer.") The fastest-growing nations, Reagan observed, were the ones providing more economic freedom to their people. Although Reagan's view would be amply vindicated in Peruvian economist Hernando de Soto's subsequent research (not to mention the growth in the developing world in the latter half of the 1980s and 1990s), his speech got a rude reception. The Third World, *Fortune* magazine observed, is "accustomed to lecture others, not to being lectured at themselves." Media and diplomats in the developing world immediately pronounced that Reagan risked being "isolated" at Cancún and blasted American intransigence. In a White House planning meeting before departing for Cancún, Reagan made clear that he was inclined to up the ante, telling Secretary of State Haig, "Shouldn't we ask the countries at the beginning of the session what happened to all the aid we've given in the past?"

However, the State Department feared being blamed for scuttling global development talks, and thus Reagan relented slightly at Cancún, agreeing to enter global negotiations on development but with the caveat that aid programs should emphasize private sector initiatives. In early 1982 Reagan attempted to jump-start his ideas with a full-fledged Caribbean Basin Initiative (CBI). The CBI was more than just John F. Kennedy's Alliance for Progress with a new name. Reagan called for expanded free trade between the United States and Latin America, along with investment tax incentives and a dollop of foreign aid directed mostly to the private sector. It represented a logical extension of his 1980 campaign call for a "North American accord" that eventually found fulfillment in the North American Free Trade Agreement and the Central America Free Trade Agreement.

But the CBI was a sideshow at best. Any aid or development program takes a long time to work even under the best circumstances, and the administration's political-economic initiatives would prove inadequate against the revolutionary determination of the Sandinistas and the political whirlwind in Washington. Even before Reagan took office the Sandinistas had assembled an army twice the size of Somoza's hated national guard and begun shipping large quantities of Soviet-bloc weapons to the guerillas in El Salvador.[60]

*   *   *

THE STORY OF Ronald Reagan's handling of Central America features several ironies. As usual, his senior staff was divided over how to proceed. Defense Secretary Cap Weinberger was openly wary that any American involvement in the region could lead to a Vietnam-style "involuntary escalation," and the Joint Chiefs of Staff were concerned that a Central American campaign would undermine Reagan's broader rearmament effort. But the most significant figure in the administration who shared this wariness was Reagan himself. This is the first irony of the Central American story. Although liberals liked to say that Reagan was "obsessed" with Nicaragua (the *New York Times*'s Anthony Lewis used this term), he was more than reluctant to get the United States involved in the region. Hence in the early months of his administration Reagan attempted to placate the Sandinistas much as Jimmy Carter had.

In the summer of 1981 Reagan and Haig dispatched Assistant Secretary of State Thomas Enders to Managua to attempt a deal with the Sandinistas. Enders offered to emulate the deal President Kennedy made over Cuba in 1962: the United States would not interfere with Nicaragua—and would even resume economic aid—if Nicaragua would cease its role in El Salvador and Guatemala. Nicaraguan President Daniel Ortega, complaining that Enders was "arrogant," rejected any deal with the United States outright, telling Enders that the Sandinistas were "interested in seeing the guerillas in El Salvador and Guatemala triumph." Ortega later told Fidel Castro that he saw Enders's message as a sign of U.S. weakness and as a green light for the Sandinistas to consolidate their rule in typical Marxist-Leninist fashion, which they proceeded to do, jailing political opponents, shutting down the independent newspaper *La Prensa,* and postponing elections until 1985. "Enders' trip to Managua," Robert Kagan wrote in his magisterial treatment of American policy in Nicaragua, "had itself been a sign of the administration's weakness. . . . It was not fear of the United States that prompted the Sandinistas to take a hard line in their foreign and domestic policies, but rather their lack of fear."[61]

The Sandinistas had read American public opinion correctly and knew that Reagan faced more political constraints in his policy toward Central America than toward the Soviet Union.[62] Herein lies the second irony of the Central American story: the powerful Soviets feared Reagan more than did the rulers of Nicaragua, a weak nation with fewer than four million people. But there was foxy wisdom at work, for if the Soviet Union fell, Nicaragua would instantly become irrelevant to world politics and of little concern to the United States—as in fact happened in the fullness of time.

Although Reagan had signed a finding in March 1981 authorizing the CIA to conduct covert operations to interdict arms shipments to El Salvador, the president was skeptical when the National Security Planning Group (NSPG) came to him on October 16 with a plan to arm a resistance movement in Nicaragua. In his diary he called this "the most profound decision I've ever had to make."[63] He expressed doubt that the plan would work and worried about civilian casualties. Even after the NSPG improvised modifications aimed at reducing direct U.S. involvement and lowering civilian casualties, he still wouldn't approve the plan because, in Thomas Enders's estimation, Reagan was "profoundly averse to violence."[64] The *Washington Post* later quoted an unnamed White House source as observing, "Ronald Reagan has the reputation of being a gunslinger, but he [was] the most cautious, conservative guy in those meetings." Instead, in a bizarre gesture Reagan sent Haig to Mexico to hold a secret meeting with Cuba's vice president, but Haig's mission went nowhere, since the Cubans, like the Sandinistas, could see that the United States was playing a weak hand.

With all avenues for a negotiated settlement at a dead end, on December 1 Reagan finally authorized the covert action program. Over the next year the United States sent $20 million in military aid to a small force of five hundred Nicaraguan exiles trained by—follow the bouncing ball—Argentina. Reagan's advisers and the CIA considered it a low-intensity option, "the *least* controversial means of applying pressure on the Sandinistas to change its policy toward El Salvador," in Robert Kagan's words.[65] There was little chance that the small Contra force could succeed in toppling the Sandinista regime; CIA director William Casey explicitly affirmed this in public testimony.

In ordinary usage, *covert* implies top secret, but the obvious contradiction is that in modern American politics, "covert" operations are highly public, making them a bit of a farce.[66] It was never likely that U.S. aid to the Nicaraguan Contras would remain secret; in fact the general idea was reported the day after the first meeting with Reagan in November 1981, and detailed information about the Argentinean connection was splashed on the front page of the *Washington Post* in March 1982, touching off the usual flurry of mock surprise, even though congressional leaders had been fully briefed from the beginning.

Properly understood, covert action suggests a strategy that limits the responsibility of the United States—just as the Contra situation demanded. Legally the United States could not openly back the overthrow of the recognized, sovereign government in Managua. The Contras naturally had other ideas, and their pressure wouldn't have been effective unless there was a prospect that they might topple the Sandinistas. Critics of Reagan's policy suspected that removing the Sandinistas was Reagan's real aim, despite the administration's denials. Congressional resistance to Reagan's policy reached a critical mass in December 1982, when House Intelligence Committee chairman Edward Boland (D-Mass.) succeeded in attaching an amendment to the Pentagon's 1983 budget appropriation banning any U.S. support "for the purpose of overthrowing the Government of Nicaragua."

Boland's amendment, the first of several bearing his name in the 1980s, was the beginning of much mischief, and was the third irony of the unfolding story of Reagan's Central American odyssey. Congressional liberals were unenthusiastic about Boland's amendment and initially opposed it; they wanted to kill off Contra aid entirely. Representative Tom Harkin of Iowa and Senator Christopher Dodd of Connecticut offered budget amendments in their respective chambers that would have barred *all* U.S. aid to the Contras from *any* source. Boland rejected the Harkin-Dodd terms, saying, "I believe that it sets a bad precedent." In the Senate, the liberal Republican senator John Chafee, not a great enthusiast of Reagan's foreign policy, asked on the Senate floor: "Are we going to tie the hands of the President? After all, it is the President who sits at the top of the heap in this. . . . I do not believe we have ever imposed a draconian restriction such as proposed by the Senator from Connecticut." These early hesitations about the propriety and prudence of trying to tie the president's hands in the conduct of foreign policy would loom large in Reagan's second term.

The Reagan administration embraced Boland's compromise amendment (it ultimately passed the House 411–0; the unanimity of this vote should be taken as the first sign of a policy muddle to come) because they felt confident that Contra aid was well within its limits. They would come to rue this decision.

A THIRD SKIRMISH line in the Cold War erupted in 1982 in the Middle East. In early June, Israel invaded Lebanon, ostensibly to protect itself from PLO attacks originating from Lebanese territory near Israel's northern border. In recent years the PLO had exploited the chronic instability and occasional civil war in Lebanon to establish a home base from which to continue its low-intensity war against Israel. The rising tempo of the PLO's cross-border provocations could no longer be answered with tit-for-tat retaliations. Prime Minister Menachem Begin had led the Reagan administration to believe that Israel would confine its military operation to clearing out the area adjacent to Israel's border, but when Israeli forces advanced quickly to the outskirts of Beirut and settled in for a protracted siege, Washington felt deceived, and suspected that Israel intended to wipe out the PLO or at least expel it from Lebanon. Reagan signaled his displeasure to Begin in a face-to-face meeting in the Oval Office—Reagan had come to share Washington's near-universal dislike of the diminutive Israeli leader—but Begin was intransigent. As U.S. diplomats attempted to arrange a cease-fire, Israel continued to pound PLO strongholds in Beirut with artillery and from the air.

Israel ultimately drove the PLO from Beirut to Algeria, and the war had several lasting consequences that were felt far beyond the region. The ferocity of the Israeli offensive exacted a high toll on Israel's moral authority. In previous wars Israel could legitimately claim to be responding to Arab aggression, but the siege of Beirut turned Israel into the brutal aggressor in the eyes of the world. Reports of massive civilian casualties—exaggerated it turned out—led to media comparisons of Israel to the Nazis. (This comparison even appeared in the American press.)[67] The invasion also shattered Israel's internal unity over defense and foreign policy. For the first time, large-scale antiwar protests occurred in Tel Aviv, with Lebanon portrayed as Israel's Vietnam.

The war strained U.S.-Israeli relations to the breaking point. Reagan, who had strong pro-Israel sentiments, had to intervene personally to get Israel to stop the intense shelling of West Beirut in August, telling Begin over the telephone that Israel's actions amounted to a "holocaust." Begin, a survivor of Stalin's gulag, did not react well to the comparison.[68] After a series of cease-fires failed to hold, Reagan decided in August 1982 to send a contingent of eight hundred U.S. Marines into Lebanon as peacekeepers. The decision split the administration, with Secretary of State Shultz strongly backing the mission and Weinberger and the Pentagon opposing deployment. It was a decision Reagan would come to regret and was the source of some of the harshest judgments about his presidency. Lou Cannon argued that Lebanon was "the greatest disaster of the Reagan presidency" and that "Reagan's actions in Lebanon demonstrate his deficiencies when confronted with cabinet conflicts he could not resolve by reliance on his basic script."[69]

While Reagan's interventions failed to quell Lebanon's instability or advance the Camp David peace process, they did have some significant consequences for the wider U.S.-Soviet confrontation. PLO leader Yasir Arafat had been predicting for more than a year that Israel would invade Lebanon, and it is likely that Arafat was hoping to draw Israel and Syria (which had signed a recent defense pact with the Soviet Union) into direct conflict.[70] He got his wish. Armed with the latest Soviet tanks, warplanes, and antiaircraft missile systems, Syrian forces engaged Israel on the ground and in the skies over Lebanon. The outcome was one-sided. Israel destroyed Syria's entire air defense system and shot down ninety-two Syrian warplanes, including dozens of MIG-23s, the Soviets' best, without the loss of a single Israeli plane. On the ground Israel enjoyed considerable success destroying Syrian T-72 tanks.[71] This represented a startling turnabout from the 1973 Arab-Israeli war, where Israel experienced considerable losses.[72]

Syria grumbled openly about the poor performance of their Soviet-supplied weaponry, and the Soviet press blamed Syrian incompetence for the result. Behind the scenes, however, Soviet military leaders were stunned, and recognized that the result could not be attributed solely to poor training of Syrian pilots and soldiers. Reports filtered out that Soviet military commanders had warned the Politburo that they were falling dangerously behind American military technology. General Nikolai Ogarkov, the chief of the Soviets' General Staff, remarked candidly to American reporter Leslie Gelb: "In the U.S. small children play with computers. Here, we don't even have computers in every office of the Defense Ministry. And for reasons you well know, we cannot make computers widely available in our society." The CIA judged that the Soviet Union had less than 10 percent as much computer capacity as the United States and the gap was widening. Ogarkov added presciently: "We will never be able to catch up with you in modern arms until we have an economic revolution. And the question is whether we can have an economic revolution without a political revolution."[73] American military strategists reached the same conclusion, though expressing themselves more laconically. General David Jones, chairman of the Joint Chiefs of Staff, told the *Washington Post* that "we don't have to be quite as pessimistic as we have been in the past about these [weapons] systems."

The Soviet Union was curiously quiescent throughout the Lebanese crisis, in marked contrast to its saber-rattling during the 1973 Arab-Israeli war. To the contrary, a diplomatic note from Brezhnev to Reagan refrained from implying any Soviet action should the United States fail to restrain Israel, and the Soviets appeared deliberately slow in resupplying Syria's equipment losses.[74] Both Syria and the PLO publicly complained about the lack of meaningful Soviet support during the Israeli action. Suddenly the sense of Soviet ascendance in the region that had been so palpable in 1980 was on the wane.

A key reason for Soviet reticence may have been that sclerosis had taken hold of Soviet leadership. As recently as 1977 Brezhnev had declared, "Our aim is to gain control of the two great treasure houses on which the West depends: the energy treasure house of the Persian Gulf and the mineral treasure house of central and southern Africa."[75] But by mid-1982 Brezhnev was near death and the Politburo was struggling over his succession. Reagan had lost patience with Brezhnev, marking up a five-page letter from him in May 1982 with sarcastic notes in the margin, culminating with the summary comment at the end, "He's a barrel of laughs."

When Brezhnev finally expired in November 1982, Reagan rejected advice to go to the funeral in Moscow, sending Vice President Bush and Shultz instead. (Reagan went to the Soviet embassy to sign a condolence book and offer a prayer for Brezhnev's soul. "There's a strange feeling in that place," Reagan wrote in his diary; "no one smiles.")[76] Yuri Andropov, longtime head of the KGB, had become Brezhnev's heir apparent in the spring when he leapt over several more senior Politburo members to be named Communist Party secretary, so it was no surprise when he immediately took the reins. But as Shultz recalled upon meeting the seventy-one-year-old Andropov after Brezhnev's funeral, "He looked more like a cadaver than did the just-interred Brezhnev."[77] Shultz's impression was not deceiving; within a few months Andropov would need to be visibly propped up in public appearances.

Andropov's past as head of the KGB raised concern in the West. He had presided over the crushing of the Hungarian revolt in 1956, was an instigator of the expulsion of Aleksandr Solzhenitsyn and the internal exile of Andrei Sakharov, and was suspected of having given the order for the assassination attempt against Pope John Paul II the previous year. Western intelligence services also thought Andropov was one of the prime movers behind the recent reductions in Soviet cultural exchanges and travel to the West, as well as an architect of the crackdown in Poland. Surely he would be a hard-liner and embrace expansionist policies. In his first major speech he made certain to hit all the high notes of the Communist liturgy, such as "The principle of proletarian internationalism was and remains the core of the foreign policy of our Leninist party."[78]

Yet the Western press hurried to portray Andropov as a cosmopolitan liberal, and by implication the ideal partner with whom to make peace. Princeton Sovietologist Stephen Cohen wrote that Andropov was "the most reform-minded senior member of Brezhnev's Politburo." The *Washington Post* reported that the new Soviet leader "collects abstract art, likes jazz and Gypsy music," and wears Western-tailored suits. The *Wall Street Journal* said that Andropov "likes Glenn Miller records, good scotch whisky, Oriental rugs, and American books" such as, improbably, Jacqueline Susann's *Valley of the Dolls. Time* reported that he listened to Chubby Checker albums, the *Christian Science Monitor* that he was a poet "of a comic variety." The *New York Times* said that Andropov was fluent in English, though no American diplomat or reporter could recall having ever spoken with him in English.[79] These traits meant, according to the *Times*'s Harrison Salisbury, that Andropov was "different" from the other crude, shoe-banging Soviet leaders; he was "cosmopolitan." It was "Uncle Joe" and "the Spirit of Glassboro" all over again.[80]

There was scant evidence for any of this—so little was known about Andropov personally, in fact, that the CIA couldn't even say whether his wife, Tania, was still living. Edward Jay Epstein called it "a portrait worthy of 'Saturday Night Live': the head of the KGB as one wild and crazy guy." It may have been deliberate misinformation; the flattering news stories were thinly sourced to a handful of dubious émigrés and defectors.

Henry Kissinger was not fooled for a minute. "How," the ubiquitous Dr. K. asked, "did the man who headed the Soviet secret police for 15 years suddenly emerge as a closet liberal?" Richard Nixon regarded Andropov as potentially "the most formidable and dangerous adversary" of any recent Soviet leader. In fact, despite some reformist instincts, Andropov was deeply hostile to the United States. He had once defined détente as being exemplified by the "friendly and cooperative relation" between the Soviet Union and Finland. But such was the will to believe that Cold War tensions could be lifted through acts of goodwill and mutual understanding that these tall tales of Andropov received prominent embrace in Western media.[81]

Shultz wrote, "I was uneasy about this new Soviet leader." He was right to be. Just a year earlier Andropov had told the Politburo that Reagan was readying a nuclear war against the Soviet Union. He was now taking the reins as the most dangerous and fateful year in the entire Cold War struggle unfolded.

CHAPTER 7

THE YEAR OF LIVING DANGEROUSLY

*We are launching an effort which holds the promise of
changing the course of human history.*
—RONALD REAGAN, MARCH 23, 1983

*Who is the scriptwriter? Reagan just could not invent
that SDI scheme! Washington's actions are
putting the entire world in jeopardy.*
—YURI ANDROPOV, LATE MARCH, 1983

IN HINDSIGHT 1983 emerges as the most significant and eventful year of the Reagan presidency. It was the year that both the Cold War and domestic affairs—chiefly the economy—reached decisive turning points.

A gloomy outlook greeted Reagan as the new year arrived. His public approval rating had slumped to 35 percent—the lowest ever for a postwar president at the beginning of his third year—and polls showed him trailing the two leading Democratic candidates for 1984, Walter Mondale and John Glenn. Reagan was discouraged, joking to his pollster, Richard Wirthlin, "Maybe I should get shot again." A number of Reagan's closest aides, including national security adviser Bill Clark, thought Reagan should not run for reelection.[1] Nancy Reagan was inclined to agree. *Time* magazine's White House correspondent, George Church, wrote that "Reagan does not feel the driving personal ambition that would make re-election a psychological necessity"—surely one of the greatest lingering misperceptions of Reagan among the media.[2] In February, Reagan observed his seventy-second birthday; he was now older than Dwight Eisenhower when Ike left the White House at the end of two terms in 1961.

The economy had performed so poorly for so long that there was little optimism to be found. The *New York Times* reported on January 1: "The typical consensus forecast [for 1983] calls for only modest gains in industrial production, an unemployment level that may still be hovering around 10 percent next Christmas, and still further drops in both business investment and exports."[3] Reagan's new chief economic adviser, Martin Feldstein, told the president to expect a weak economic outlook for 1983 and 1984, and in the official budget forecast predicted an anemic 2 percent increase in GDP for the year. "The mood in the White House was as foul as the weather," wrote William Niskanen, Feldstein's colleague on the Council of Economic Advisers. The *New York Times* said that "the stench of failure" hung around the White House, the *Wall Street Journal* discerned "a whiff of panic" in the administration's mood, and in a column entitled "The End of Reagan?" William F. Buckley Jr. wrote that "Mr. Reagan shows signs of slipping." On ABC News, White House correspondent Sam Donaldson reported, "[T]here is a consensus in Washington that unless he changes his game plan, economically the grade for the next two years will almost certainly be an F." Naturally there was a cacophony of calls to abandon Reaganomics; failure to do so, the *New Republic* warned in a typical example of the conventional wisdom, "could push us into another Great Depression."

The 1983 deficit was now expected to reach $200 billion—more than 6 percent of the GDP, a peacetime record. The tax and budget deal of the previous year wasn't achieving much. Reagan was already backing away from $26 billion in proposed budget cuts for fear that the inevitable scare stories would make such cuts politically impossible, but he was reportedly furious at news leaks that he was considering more tax increases. He fought back against his more timorous advisers by suggesting that perhaps the third leg of his income tax cut, scheduled to take effect on July 1, should be moved up to January 1.[4]

The battle lines over fiscal policy were obvious—it was going to be a rerun of 1982. On January 20 nearly five hundred Wall Street and business leaders signed a two-page ad in the *Washington Post* urging Reagan to do something about "the structural deficit." This was code for *Raise taxes again.* When Reagan submitted his FY 1984 budget to Congress at the end of January, Capitol Hill Democrats immediately pronounced it dead on arrival in what was becoming an annual ritual. Reagan's budget proposed a modified freeze on domestic spending, but some conservative Republicans in Congress, such as Newt Gingrich, wanted the freeze extended across the board to

defense spending, an ominous prospect to the White House.[5] The most startling item in Reagan's budget was a standby contingency tax increase that
would take effect automatically in 1985 if the deficit did not fall sufficiently.
Congress was unenthusiastic about the standby tax and fortunately saved
Reagan from this dreadful idea: Republicans feared it let Democrats off the
hook to restrain spending, while leading Democrats clung to the position that
the third year of Reagan's income tax cut needed to be rescinded.

Reagan deliberately sanded down the ideological edges of his February
State of the Union speech to Congress, and Democrats gave him a mock standing ovation when he said, "We who are in government must take the lead in
restoring the economy." "He sounded like a changed man," the *New Republic* observed, while Stephen Roberts of the *New York Times* thought that "the
President seemed monumentally uncomfortable and unenthusiastic."

The final 10 percent cut in income tax rates was scheduled to come into
effect midyear, but so gloomy was the mood from the brutal recession that
few held out hope it would spur a significant change in the nation's fortunes.
"The economy," said Alan Greenspan, then a private sector economist, "continues to drift along." He expected business activity to be "extremely slow-
paced." The *New Republic* speculated that the United States had entered a
"permanent recession."

Despite this near-universal pessimism, the end of the recession had in fact
arrived, though the lingering effects of the downturn would continue to ham-
per the economy. One of the earliest signs of the rebound came in late 1982,
when the Federal Reserve's industrial production index showed its first
monthly gain in more than a year. General Motors quietly began recalling
laid-off autoworkers. By the second quarter, retail sales were up 10 percent
and the economy as a whole was growing at an 8.7 percent annual rate—
higher than is typical for the early phase of an economic recovery. Over the
course of the year unemployment, interest rates, and inflation would all drop
rapidly while real after-tax per capita income would grow by 5.3 percent.
Most significantly for supply-side theory, business investment began to take
off, rising 8.4 percent even though Chase Econometrics, one of the leading
private sector forecasting firms, had projected a 5 percent *decline* for 1983;
the next year private sector investment would rise a robust 23.5 percent,
when Chase had predicted only a 1.5 percent increase. In a sign of the rise of
the high-tech sector, Apple Computer would reach $1 billion in sales for the
first time in 1983. In late March, Reagan wrote in his diary, "Our program is
working even better than we expected two months ago." The stock market

took notice, rising 20 percent by May—a gain it held through the end of the year, making it the best year for the stock market since the 1960s. Reagan began quipping, "Pretty soon they won't be calling it 'Reaganomics' anymore."

Not that the news media noticed the signs of a dramatic turnaround. One study of network news coverage in 1983 found that 85 percent of TV news stories about the economy were negative. *Fortune* magazine editor Paul Weaver observed: "It is hard not to conclude that their [the networks'] opinion of [Reagan] and his program was so low that they were determined to do everything within their legitimate discretion, and perhaps then some, to prevent their reportage from suggesting that the policies worked, or that a recovery was in full swing, or that the President might be in line for some credit for the expansion of the economy."[6] *Time* magazine's William A. Henry wrote that "the most antagonistic major news organization was CBS, which had challenged the morality of Reagan's approach almost from its outset."[7] Reagan took notice of this in his diary, writing in March 1983: "CBS evening news an almost total attack on our admin. They are beginning to look like a deliberate campaign."

Much of the public proved remarkably impervious to the media myopia and the pessimism in Washington. For the first time in more than a decade, a majority of Americans told pollsters at the beginning of 1983—before most economic indicators turned positive—that they were optimistic about the year ahead. By midyear, Reagan's approval ratings were becoming as buoyant as the economy, rising back to the crucial 50 percent mark.

With the economy recovering, Federal Reserve chairman Paul Volcker worried that inflation would heat up again and wanted to tighten the money supply to ward off this prospect. The supply-siders understood that an economy undergoing a fundamental rotation needed more money growth rather than less, and that such money growth would not fuel inflation. Volcker argued for deliberately slowing the economy in his regular meetings with Reagan, but Reagan demurred, while Treasury Secretary Don Regan told Volcker to stop being such a "nanny." Regional Federal Reserve banks pressed Volcker to cut interest rates—filing twenty-one requests in 1983—but the chairman wanted to tighten monetary growth through a modest interest rate hike, which he barely carried by a 7–5 vote of the Fed governors in May.[8]

In the meantime, Reagan faced a dilemma. Volcker's term as chairman was up in the fall of 1983. Treasury Secretary Regan and other senior advisers, including James Baker and Ed Meese, wanted the president to dump Volcker and appoint a new chairman. After initially siding with the critics (and having that fact leak to the media in the spring) and leaning toward appointing Alan Greenspan as the new chairman, Reagan reversed course and reappointed Volcker in June, largely because the financial markets were still skittish about inflation and viewed the Fed chairman as an inflation fighter. Volcker also enjoyed support in Congress and among major business groups.

Other aspects of Reagan's agenda were also improving. Oil imports from OPEC had fallen by more than two million barrels a day by the end of 1982, contributing to a drop in both energy prices and OPEC's clout. In the spring Reagan vetoed a bill that would have reestablished federal authority to ration gasoline.

Reagan's retreat on Social Security was completed in early 1983 when the commission he had appointed to find a solution to the program's looming insolvency came in with its plan. The commission, headed by Alan Greenspan, reflected a typical bipartisan compromise—raising payroll taxes, temporarily reducing cost-of-living increases, and compelling more people to join the system (public employees and nonprofit organizations had been exempt). The result removed a political albatross for Reagan and Republicans, but at the cost of deferring for another generation fundamental debate about reforming the national Ponzi scheme. "I'm afraid our bi-partisan commission has failed us," Reagan wrote in his diary, though what did he expect from a bipartisan commission? To the consternation of many conservatives, Reagan was looking less and less like the nemesis of the New Deal than like its rescuer.[9]

*   *   *

WHILE ECONOMIC AND fiscal policy was settling into an equilibrium of sorts, social issues that had been largely overlooked during the first year of the administration began to emerge from the shadows. The ratification period for the Equal Rights Amendment expired in 1982, and attempts in Congress to extend the ratification period or pass a modified amendment flopped. Behind the bitter fights over civil rights and the broader argument about constitutional construction lay the issue that might be called the Big One: abortion.

It has become commonplace in the years since Reagan to complain—or praise in a backhanded way, depending on the point of view—that he did little to reverse *Roe v. Wade* or the abortion culture.[10] This overlooks White House lobbying on Capitol Hill in support of a constitutional amendment to restrict abortion in 1982 and collateral measures to limit federal funding of abortion. Both measures were blocked by a filibuster from Republican senator Bob Packwood. The administration acted on its own where it could, especially through two controversial regulations known as the "Baby Doe rule" and the "squeal rule." The Baby Doe rule required hospitals to guarantee medical treatment to infants born handicapped, in an effort to stop the rare and unspoken practice of allowing deformed newborns to die—de facto infanticide. The administration also required federally funded family planning clinics to notify parents when they supplied contraceptives to minors. Liberals derided this measure as the "squeal rule" and immediately went to court seeking an injunction against it.

To mark the tenth anniversary of the *Roe v. Wade* decision, in the spring of 1983 Reagan published a long article in the *Human Life Review* (later republished as a small book in 1984) entitled "Abortion and the Conscience of a Nation." His political advisers were nervous about publishing such an article so close to his reelection campaign. He replied: "I might not be re-elected. We're going with it now."[11] Reagan was the first sitting president to publish a book, and seldom has any president since Lincoln spoken so openly and forcefully about such a contentious moral issue. He was just as direct and unequivocal as Lincoln: "Make no mistake, abortion-on-demand is not a right granted by the Constitution." *Roe* was an act of "raw judicial power," Reagan said, comparable to *Dred Scott:* "This is not the first time our country has been divided by a Supreme Court decision that denied the value of certain human lives." Some of Reagan's language was bracing: "The abortionist who reassembles the arms and legs of a tiny baby to make sure all its parts have been torn from its mother's body can hardly doubt whether it is a human being." The media said such a controversial article by a sitting president was "rare" and "unusual."

Reagan's article appeared a few weeks before the Supreme Court issued its first decision on abortion during his presidency, in the case of *Akron v. Akron Center for Reproductive Health.* By a 6–3 vote, the Court struck down the Ohio city's attempts to place restrictions on second- and third-trimester abortions and require a twenty-four-hour waiting period. Reagan announced that he was "profoundly disappointed" by the ruling, but he and other conservatives were cheered that Justice O'Connor joined the two other dissenters (Rehnquist and Byron White, who were the two dissenting votes in the 1973 *Roe* case).[12] O'Connor's strongly worded dissent took dead aim at *Roe,* criticizing the ruling for forcing courts "to pretend to act as science review boards." *Roe* "is clearly on a collision course with itself . . . [T]here is no justification in the law or logic for the trimester framework adopted in

Roe." It was widely noted that five of the six justices who voted to strike down abortion restrictions in the ruling were over seventy-five, which, one wire service news story observed, "could give President Reagan a chance to appoint more sympathetic successors."

A new social concern fraught with political implications began to emerge from the shadows in early 1983. For the previous three years the infectious disease community had been tracking the mysterious rise of cases of severe immune system breakdown predominantly among homosexuals. By 1983 this obscure disease was on the way to becoming a mass epidemic, though scientists now think the disease had been spreading slowly in Africa as far back as the 1930s. (The first identified death from AIDS in Africa is thought to have occurred in 1959.) "Something unusual and frightening was happening," *Newsweek* magazine wrote in an April cover story that broke the news to many Americans for the first time. There were more than thirteen hundred cases identified in the United States, with a mortality rate that approached 100 percent. The cause of the disease was as yet unidentified, though its transmission through blood contact had been established. French researchers announced in May that they had isolated a retrovirus, though it would be another year before American researchers confirmed the French finding.[13] By then the number of diagnosed AIDS cases had grown to more than six thousand, with thirty-five hundred recorded deaths.

The fact that AIDS cases were overwhelmingly concentrated among homosexuals raised the issue of sexual behavior (*Newsweek* reported that one early survey of gay AIDS patients found that they averaged more than a thousand sexual partners) and ensured that it would become America's first fully politicized disease. Pat Buchanan expressed the views of many social conservatives: "The poor homosexuals—they have declared war against nature, and now nature is exacting an awful retribution." Initially gay rights groups and the gay media denied reports of a new sexually transmitted disease ("Disease Rumors Largely Unfounded," read a *New York Native* headline in 1981) and resisted calls to close the bathhouses in San Francisco that were obvious AIDS hotbeds.

Inevitably homosexual AIDS patients became a new high-profile victim constituency group for Democrats, while Reagan would come under withering criticism for not paying more attention to the epidemic in its early stages, and most of all for not spending more on research into the disease. To be sure, in 1983 the National Institutes of Health was spending only $7.9 million on AIDS research, but eventually government funding for AIDS research would come to exceed spending for more common forms of lethal disease such as breast and prostate cancer. Leftist attacks on Reagan over AIDS would come to compete with civil rights agitators to reach the furthest hyperbole, such as gay activist Larry Kramer's moniker "Adolf Reagan": "Hitler knew what he was doing. How could Ronald Reagan not have known what he was doing?"[14]

The spring of 1983 also brought to fruition the work of yet another bipartisan commission, this one recommending reforms for public education. The National Commission on Excellence in Education generated disproportionately prominent headlines and public chatter because of its sensationally titled report, "A Nation at Risk." The summary judgment was ominous: "a rising tide of mediocrity" in public schools was so severe that "if an unfriendly foreign power had attempted to impose on America the mediocre educational performance that exists today, we might well have viewed it as an act of war."

Liberals and the education lobby naturally embraced the report as a justification for increased federal spending on education. The National Education Association, for example, argued that public schools required "additional billions of dollars—and a big boost from the Federal Government—to achieve their sweeping objectives." The education establishment—which Reagan's second-term secretary of education, William Bennett, would vividly label "the Blob"—missed the fact that the commission's policy recommendations were largely Reaganite. It called for a *lesser* federal role in education; indeed, it was emphatic that states and localities should take the lead. As usual, Reagan stuck to his principles, telling *USA Today,* "We think there is a parallel between Federal involvement in education and the decline in quality over recent years. Improving the quality of education doesn't require a big Federal program.... The road to better education cannot be paved with more and more recycled tax dollars collected, redistributed and overregulated by Washington bureaucrats." Reagan added, "I know this idea is not too popular in some sophisticated circles, but I can't help but believe that voluntary prayer deserves a place in our Nation's classrooms." Quite a contrast from the consensus surrounding the No Child Left Behind Act of the George W. Bush years.

*   *   *

AT THE BEGINNING of the year an unnamed White House aide told the *New York Times:* "There is nothing about our political difficulties that an economic recovery and an arms agreement with the Soviets wouldn't solve."

While the economic cloud was finally lifting, prospects for an arms agreement appeared remote. Late in 1982 Reagan got his long-sought chance to say *nyet* to the outline of a bad arms control agreement—but not to the Soviets. He had to say *nyet* to his own arms negotiators. This aggravated the domestic arms control controversy on the eve of the Euromissile deployment.

Negotiations over European-theater missiles had begun in Geneva in late 1981 and went nowhere. Here a significant personal drama occurred. Reagan had chosen Paul Nitze, one of the grand wise men whose career spanned the entire Cold War era, to lead the U.S. negotiating team. Nitze, a Democrat, brought enormous prestige to the post. During World War II under President Roosevelt, he participated in a review of the effectiveness of Allied bombing and in the interrogation of Albert Speer, Hitler's prodigious minister of armaments, in the closing days of the war. He worked with Dean Acheson, George Marshall, and George Kennan in the drafting of the Marshall Plan, and was a principal author of NSC 68, the seminal 1950 report to President Truman that articulated new directions for U.S. strategic doctrine for the Cold War. After serving in the Kennedy and Johnson administrations, where he was in the thick of the Cuban missile crisis and the Vietnam War, Nitze joined Nixon's negotiating team that concluded the first SALT Treaty with the Soviet Union in 1972. But later in the 1970s, like many other hawkish Democrats, he broke with Jimmy Carter and opposed the SALT II Treaty. Nitze became a charter member of the Committee on the Present Danger, the bipartisan lobby group that in the late 1970s advocated a tougher U.S. stance vis-à-vis the Soviets. In between government assignments, Nitze made a fortune as an investment banker and as the developer of Aspen, Colorado.[15] A man of sophistication and charm, he could also be direct and blunt, more than once calling Soviet negotiators liars to their faces. He was the very kind of man who by elite acclamation should be president, and the kind of man to whom, it might be thought, Reagan would show deference. Not a bit.

In Geneva Nitze opened with Reagan's zero option, though everyone assumed that the United States would fall back on a compromise position at some point. The Soviets called for the United States to forgo basing any Pershing II missiles in Europe while maintaining the Soviets' existing advantage. Judging that the formal negotiating sessions were going nowhere, Nitze daringly decided that the only chance for a breakthrough was through a personal initiative outside the Geneva meeting room.

Nitze enjoyed surprisingly cordial relations with the chief Soviet negotiator, Yuli Kvitsinskiy, and so he proposed that the two of them meet informally to see if they could break the deadlock. After weeks of prenegotiation, in July 1982 Nitze and Kvitsinskiy met up in the mountains outside Geneva and strolled down a logging road in what became known as the "Walk in the Woods." Nitze told Kvitsinskiy that while the United States remained committed to the zero option, he knew it was not possible to reach zero at that moment. Nitze instead proposed a complicated interim agreement, the core element of which was a ceiling of seventy-five medium-range missiles for each side: SS-20s for the Soviets, but slower and short-range cruise missiles for the United States. While this represented a large reduction in the number of Soviet SS-20s, it meant that the United States would forgo basing the Pershing II missiles in Europe, which were the heart of the NATO European theater arsenal. And even with equal numbers of launchers (the term of art for the farce of arms control as it was practiced up to that date), the Soviets would still boast about a four-to-one advantage in nuclear warheads, since each SS-20 carried three warheads, while cruise missiles carried only one. Verification would be a difficult sticking point. Kvitsinskiy expressed skepticism that Moscow would go for it, but said he would present Nitze's formula.

Nitze did the same in Washington, where it touched off a firestorm. It was not so much the substance of the proposal, which some of Reagan's advisers thought was broadly acceptable, as bad timing and freelance tactics. In departing from his negotiating instructions without consulting Washington, Nitze had "signaled premature retreat" and represented "political and intellectual cowardice," in the harsh judgment of Richard Perle.[16] In late August Reagan expressed his displeasure to Shultz that Nitze had exceeded his instructions, while Weinberger reported separately that the president was furious with Nitze. When the matter finally came before Reagan in early September 1982, he wondered why the United States would want to give up preemptively its chief bargaining chip, the Pershing IIs. If the United States could give up Pershings, he asked Nitze, why couldn't the Soviets give up their SS-20s? Nitze said that he did not think it realistic to go back to the zero option position in Geneva. Reagan replied: "Well, Paul, you just tell them you're working for one tough son of a bitch."[17] As he had long wanted to, Reagan had said *nyet* to a weak arms deal—but to his own people, not face-to-face with a Soviet leader. That prospect now seemed far away.

All the while Nitze heard nothing from Kvitsinskiy in Moscow. It turned out that Moscow had rejected the proposal out of hand, which Nitze found out when he returned to Geneva in late September to convey Reagan's thumbs-down. It is understandable why the Soviets did so. Moscow thought that the lack of progress on arms talks served its political objective of splitting Europe and the United States over missile deployment—especially if the impasse could be blamed on the United States.[18] The Soviets worked hard to position the negotiations for this very result, and it looked for a while as though it might work. The State Department frankly doubted that West Germany would stick with the commitment to accept the Pershing II missiles at the end of 1983.

The "Walk in the Woods" formula remained closely guarded in Washington in the summer and fall, and when it eventually leaked out early in 1983 the news sparked outrage—against Reagan. Reagan's rejection of Nitze's proposal, the *New York Times* and other critics charged, showed that he was not serious about arms control. It did not matter to Reagan's political opponents that the Soviets also had rejected the putative deal. The story line that Reagan had rejected a potential breakthrough was a fillip for the peace movement and sent the controversy over nuclear weapons to a new level of intensity.

One sign of the ferocity of the political divide over foreign policy came to sight in January 1983, when Reagan and Shultz decided to name thirty-six-year-old Ken Adelman as director of the Arms Control and Disarmament Agency (ACDA). The appointment set off a furor in the Senate because Adelman had expressed a frankly realistic—that is to say, heretical—view of arms control. "Perhaps nowhere in life is the disparity greater between exalted expectations and a dismal track record than in arms control," Adelman reflected. "No area of science, medicine, or even public policy would continue to elicit so much hope after so many years of unsuccessful effort. Arms control must be approached as one of the intangibles of life, a rite seemingly needed to satisfy some deep longing in our collective soul."[19] The *Atlantic Monthly*'s James Fallows put the matter directly: "Certain agencies in Washington are ceded to certain interest groups. . . . Liberals think of [ACDA] as, by rights, their agency." Picking someone who hadn't drunk the arms control Kool-Aid was, Fallows suggested, like appointing an atheist chaplain.[20] The Adelman nomination laid bare the Beltway establishment's irritation that the Reagan administration thought it could appoint people who reflected its philosophy of governance to key positions in agencies that were de facto organs of Democratic Party policy preferences. One of the favorite epithets for Adelman was that he was "the James Watt of arms negotiations."

Adelman's confirmation hearings before the Senate Foreign Relations Committee became a protracted struggle, with one Democratic staffer admitting to James Fallows that "we pursued every scum angle we could think of" to derail the confirmation. James Baker became nervous and wanted to drop Adelman, but Reagan refused to budge. The committee voted against Adelman 9–8 (with liberal Republican senator Charles Mathias joining all eight Democrats on the committee against Adelman) but sent the nomination on to the full Senate anyway. Democrats considered a filibuster but lacked the votes to sustain it. Adelman was finally confirmed by the full Senate 57–42.

The Reagan administration had endured foreign policy confirmation controversies before Adelman, most notably the Senate's rejection of Ernest Lefever to be assistant secretary of state for human rights in 1981, but the Adelman contretemps took on added significance because it occurred against the backdrop of a raging debate over American nuclear policy. Behind the partisan debate over nuclear weapons was the fundamental ideological divide between how liberals and conservatives see the world. Fallows put his finger on the problem with his observation that when liberals looked out at the world during the Cold War, they saw 1914—the fear that a misunderstanding or miscalculation would lead to an uncontrollable war. Conservatives, especially since the Soviet military buildup of the 1970s, saw the Cold War and the arms control process as 1938—a repeat of the Munich appeasement. Reagan had explicitly compared Jimmy Carter to Neville Chamberlain in 1979 (a rhetorical attack his political advisers had opposed) and spoke often of the lessons of Munich and appeasement. During the Senate debate over Adelman, for example, the Utah Republican Jake Garn said, "I guess Ronald Reagan is a warmonger just like Winston Churchill."

But to a surprising extent that has only recently become better known, Reagan sympathized with the liberal fear that an accident or miscalculation could lead to an unlimited nuclear war. The great irony of Reagan is that he fully shared the liberals' dread of nuclear weapons. The difference is that he was not inclined to surrender either to platitudes or to the Soviet Union. What he was willing to do was fuse both viewpoints. Even as he was pursuing his arms buildup and his tough anti-Soviet rhetoric, Reagan was continuing to express interest in negotiating with Moscow.

The problem with the arms control process was that the asymmetries between American democracy and Soviet Communist rule gave the advantage to the Soviets. Seymour Weiss, an arms control expert and former State Department director of political and military affairs, explained the problem well: "Historically arms control negotiations tend to have a kind of tranquilizing effect upon the American public, whether or not there are any results. Negotiations of the sort that we're talking about are bound to stretch out over a period of years. . . . [The Soviets] can and do sit at the table and say 'Nyet' and hold to their position, whereas the dynamics in our own society creates pressure to get an agreement, to make concessions while our own defense programs are brought to a halt." So Reagan was playing against the clock as well as against an ideological disposition.

Reagan was unperturbed. In fact, he was about the throw down the gauntlet in ways that upset nervous European allies and sent liberals into fresh paroxysms of outrage. It was a remarkably gutsy performance, given that much of his defense program was living on a knife-edge, with Congress closely divided over military spending and key weapons systems such as the MX missile. Moreover, Reagan's public approval ratings on foreign policy were just as bad as his numbers on the economy: two-thirds of the respondents in one January Harris poll thought Reagan was doing a poor job on arms control, and 57 percent agreed that Reagan might start a nuclear war.[21]

However, Reagan was not without some concurrent surprises in his Soviet diplomacy.

*   *   *

UNSEEN BY PUBLIC eyes, Reagan in February held his first meeting with a senior Soviet official, Ambassador Anatoly Dobrynin, upstairs in the private residence of the White House. The meeting arose at Shultz's suggestion, and reportedly against the wishes of National Security Adviser Bill Clark. Clark is often portrayed as having opposed any high-level contacts between Reagan and the Soviets, but this is not true. In 1982 Clark pondered arranging a Reagan-Brezhnev meeting, and also considered his own back-channel overture to Dobrynin. Clark's hesitation was about the State Department, whom he distrusted to manage summit diplomacy.

Shultz thought the time had come to contemplate the first steps toward a summit meeting, and Reagan cautiously agreed. Dobrynin spoke with Reagan for two hours (most commentators on this meeting say it was an unusually long meeting for Reagan because of his "short attention span"), with both men repeating general professions of peaceful intent toward each other's nations. Reagan employed one of his favorite talking points—the fact that the United States had not used its nuclear monopoly in the late 1940s for purposes of conquest. Dobrynin replied that the USSR had also shown restraint by not using its conventional military superiority to conquer the rest of Europe after America substantially demobilized. "Sometimes we got pretty nose to nose," Reagan wrote in his diary.

Reagan's purpose in this meeting was to convey the simple message that he was ready to do business seriously with the Soviet Union, so rather than trump Dobrynin's weak argument, the former labor negotiator pressed Dobrynin for concrete proof of benign Soviet intentions. He asked the Soviet ambassador to allow seven Pentecostal Christians who in 1978 had taken sanctuary in the American embassy in Moscow to emigrate from the Soviet Union. (Reagan had done one of his radio commentaries about their plight in 1978.) It was a simple thing, Reagan said, more akin to a personal favor than a policy concession. Most importantly, Reagan assured Dobrynin, if the Soviets granted his request, he would not take public credit or seek to embarrass the USSR. Reagan had previously brought up the Pentecostals in a personal letter to Brezhnev in 1981, also promising then that he would say nothing publicly about the matter. Brezhnev never responded.

The new Soviet premier, Yuri Andropov (who, unbeknownst to Westerners, had begun dialysis for kidney failure and was approaching death's door), had told Dobrynin before the meeting, "Reagan is unpredictable. You should expect anything from him."[22] Presented with this proposal, Dobrynin reacted cautiously but positively. Although the Politburo did not like the idea, Dobrynin and his allies in the foreign ministry were able to push it through. The Pentecostals and their extended families were allowed to leave for Israel four months later. Reagan said nothing but reciprocated by approving a new long-term grain deal with the Soviets.

Even as Reagan was taking his first steps to thaw out relations with the Soviet Union, he was readying several bold public initiatives that kept everyone—Soviets and Democrats alike—in a high state of agitation. The first item on Reagan's agenda was finding a way to outflank the nuclear freeze movement. For several months religious groups had been supplying moral authority to the movement. Even the theologically conservative Southern Baptist Convention passed a nuclear disarmament resolution in 1982, as did the American Lutheran Church and the United Presbyterian Church. The U.S. Conference of Catholic Bishops, meanwhile, issued a highly dovish draft statement condemning nuclear weapons just a week before the 1982 election, leading *National Review* to dub the bishops "an adjunct of the Democratic National Committee." This early draft rejected the idea of nuclear deterrence, the very cornerstone of American strategic doctrine, and suggested that nuclear weapons could not fit within classic Christian "just war" teaching.[23] The final statement drew back from the worst of these views after European Catholic bishops defended nuclear deterrence in a series of pastoral letters of their own, but the damage had been done. (These pro-deterrence clerical statements received little attention from the media.)

The secular agitation for the freeze expressed itself as unalloyed nihilism. The existence of nuclear weapons, Jonathan Schell wrote in a surprise runaway bestseller, *The Fate of the Earth,* threatened nothing less than human extinction and the destruction of planet Earth itself. Not even the ability to travel to other solar systems offered Schell any hope, because "wherever human beings went, there also would go the knowledge of how to build nuclear weapons, and, with it, the peril of extinction." Schell's solution? World government to replace national sovereignty. Survival trumped all other considerations. Implicit in this line of argument was that there was nothing worth defending with nuclear weapons, even if built only as a deterrent. Schell wrote: "The nuclear powers put a higher value on national sovereignty than they do on human survival."

Better Red than dead.[24]

The freeze agitation threatened the centerpiece of Reagan's efforts to address the nation's vulnerability in strategic nuclear weaponry—the MX missile. The MX was a highly accurate ten-warhead missile designed to replace the aging three-warhead Minuteman missile and to survive a Soviet first strike. But after the rejection of Jimmy Carter's outlandish plan to shelter the missiles in a vast network of scattered silos linked by an underground railroad, the United States still had not come up with a basing system for the MX. When the Reagan administration announced in late 1981 that it would place a hundred MX missiles (half the number, by the way, that Carter had proposed to deploy—a significant fact that got lost in the discussion) in superhardened existing missile silos, which would do nothing to reduce the vulnerability of America's land-based ICBMs, congressional support for the MX eroded badly. Leaders of both parties told the White House that Congress might not approve MX funding unless a better basing mode could be found.

Nearly a year later the Pentagon unveiled the best idea it could come up with: base all the MX missiles closely together, on the controversial theory that fratricide among incoming nuclear warheads would make it unlikely that the Soviets could take them out with a first strike. The idea was called "dense pack," and it was as unconvincing as the name, as the scathing editorial cartoons quickly made clear. The Joint Chiefs of Staff publicly expressed their lack of enthusiasm for the idea, and near the end of 1982 the House of Representatives voted to cut off funding for the MX.

Another crucial appropriation vote was scheduled for May 1983, and to quell the congressional rebellion, Reagan appointed former national security adviser Brent Scowcroft to head a commission to come up with a basing solution before the vote. Reagan gamely tried to stem the tide of anti-MX sentiment by prominently renaming the missile. He started referring to MX as the "peacekeeper missile." Reagan was willing to trade away the MX missile in an arms control deal with the Soviets but didn't think he'd be able to get a deal unless the MX was built and deployed.

This was the background against which Reagan traveled to Orlando, Florida, on March 8, just three weeks after his meeting with Dobrynin, to speak before the National Association of Evangelicals.[25] The appearance called for a domestic policy speech—which therefore did not go through the usual State Department and NSC review—and indeed, most of it was about domestic concerns. But it shall forever be remembered for calling the Soviet Union an "evil empire"—a phrase the State Department never would have let through in a foreign policy speech. Shultz in his memoirs delicately noted that he had no prior knowledge that Reagan would use such language, adding that the "evil empire" phrase "had not been planned or developed through any careful or systematic process. . . . [M]any of our [European] friends were alarmed."[26]

Some White House staffers dubbed it the "Darth Vader" speech. Communications Director David Gergen called the "evil empire" phrase "outrageous." In fact, he and others had excised the line from Reagan speechwriter Tony Dolan's early draft of Reagan's 1982 Westminster speech before it ever reached the president. Gergen backed down this time when he discovered that Reagan himself had insisted on including the phrase and had actually toughened that section of the speech with some flourishes of his own.

The speech provoked outrage and contempt among liberals, who never seemed to notice or object to the much more extreme language the Soviets routinely used to describe the United States in official pronouncements. Historian Henry Steele Commager said, "It was the worst presidential speech in American history, and I've seen them all." The *New Republic* huffed that "the speech left friends and foes around the world with the impression that the President of the United States was contemplating holy war." *New York Times* columnist Anthony Lewis complained that the speech was "outrageous" and "primitive." "What is the world to think," Lewis wrote, "when the greatest of powers is led by a man who applies to the most difficult human problem a simplistic theology?" One remarkable aspect of the reaction is that U.S. critics used harsher language than the Soviets, who merely called the speech "provocative" and "bellicose." The Soviet newspaper *Pravda* made a point of quoting negative Western media reaction, which made it unnecessary for them to tax their own phrasemaking vocabulary.

The reaction in the diplomatic community and among some European leaders matched the media's apoplexy. Helmut Schmidt, who had been ousted as West German chancellor in October, was reported to have said that Reagan had thrown away twenty years of patient diplomacy with the Soviets. Told of this remark, Reagan replied (according to Cap Weinberger's recollection), "What did patient diplomatic effort for 20 years get us? It got us an expanding Soviet Union and a continual expansion of their ability to enslave peoples and deny freedom. And it left us so vulnerable we couldn't do anything when Afghanistan was invaded. That's not much of an accomplishment."[27] Shultz wrote later, "How conscious of the implications of their words the president and his speechwriters were, I don't know." But Reagan told an interviewer a few weeks after the speech that his choice of language had been conscious and deliberate: "I made the 'Evil Empire' speech and others like it with malice aforethought." The "evil empire" phrase stuck in the craw of liberalism and rankled as much as, if not more than, Reagan's "welfare queen" theme.

Regard for the "evil empire" speech has risen with the passage of time and especially since the demise of the Soviet Union. Incarcerated Soviet dissidents such as Natan Sharansky testified that the "evil empire" speech bolstered their morale: "Finally, the leader of the free world had spoken the truth." Seweryn Bialer, one of the West's leading Sovietologists and a critic of Reagan, returned from a visit to the Soviet Union shortly after the speech to report that "President Reagan's rhetoric has badly shaken the self-esteem and patriotic pride of the Soviet political elites." A number of former Soviet officials admitted after 1991 that Reagan had been right all along.[28] A rare clearly worded CIA report noted, "By describing the Soviet Union as 'the focus of evil,' President Reagan has singlehandedly deployed the one weapon for which the Soviets lack even a rudimentary defense: the truth." Even Strobe Talbott, one of Reagan's toughest critics, admitted, "He may have been impolitic, but he was not wrong."[29]

The fireworks over the "evil empire" phrase distracted from the central argument of the speech, which was Reagan's challenge to evangelicals not to embrace the idea of "moral equivalence" between East and West, which the nuclear freeze enthusiasm wittingly or unwittingly abetted. He did this by connecting the issue with the core of the dispute over the domestic issues of greatest concern to evangelicals—abortion, school prayer, and traditional values. Reagan attacked "modern-day secularism" as the source of contemporary liberalism. In a long passage that the president himself added to the speech, Reagan addressed the injunction a federal judge had issued against the parental notification rule on birth control. Hitting back hard with deliberate language, Reagan noted that while the well-intentioned purpose of health clinics that dispensed birth control was to prevent illegitimate births, it was significant that the bureaucrats referred to minors as *sexually active* rather than using the older moral term *promiscuous*. "I've watched TV panel shows discuss this issue, seen columnists pontificating on our error, but no one seems to mention morality as playing a part in the subject of sex." This was "really only one example of many attempts to water down traditional values and even abrogate the original terms of American democracy," Reagan explained. At the root of all these policy disputes, he argued, was a rejection of the Judeo-Christian tradition. Above all, Reagan inplied, liberalism didn't take seriously the idea of sin.

This was the pivot from which Reagan introduced the Soviet Union and the problem of the nuclear freeze. The Soviet Union didn't believe in sin or morality either, he said. Another of the passages Reagan wrote himself was:

> A number of years ago I heard a young father, a very prominent young man in the entertainment world, addressing a tremendous gathering in California. It was during the time of the Cold War when Communism and our own way of life were very much on people's minds. And he was speaking to that subject. And suddenly, though, I heard him saying, "I love my little girls more than anything." And I said to myself, "Oh no, don't. You can't—don't say that." But I had underestimated him. He went on: "I would rather see my little girls die now, still believing in God, than to have to grow up under Communism and one day die no longer believing in God."

Better dead than Red.

Reagan closed with a quotation from C. S. Lewis's *Screwtape Letters* and the admonition that "in your discussions of the nuclear freeze proposals, I urge you to beware the temptation of pride—the temptation of blithely declaring yourselves above it all and label both sides equally at fault, to ignore the facts of history and the aggressive impulses of an evil empire, to simply call the arms race a giant misunderstanding and thereby remove yourself from the struggle between right and wrong and good and evil."

The "evil empire" thread distracted from the fact that, from a liberal point of view, the speech was even worse than they thought. He didn't merely challenge the legitimacy of the Soviet Union; he turned the ideal of moral equivalency on its head by tracing a linkage between the corruption of Soviet Communism and the weakness of domestic liberalism. And Reagan was just warming up.

*　　*　　*

THE DUST HAD not yet settled from the "evil empire" speech when Reagan kicked up a fresh cloud two weeks later with an even more dramatic new theme: the Strategic Defense Initiative.[30] Speaking from the Oval Office on March 23, he issued his call to make nuclear weapons obsolete by reviving ballistic missile defense—the very thing an earlier generation of American strategists thought destabilizing and detrimental to deterrence, and therefore bargained away with the Anti-Ballistic Missile (ABM) Treaty in 1972. Mutual assured destruction, Reagan argued in the penultimate passage of the speech, is "a sad commentary on the human condition. Wouldn't it be better to save lives than to avenge them?"

Friends and critics alike ascribe Reagan's expansive conception of an impermeable missile defense—a veritable *Star Trek*–like shield that "could intercept and destroy strategic ballistic missiles before they reached our own soil"—to his Hollywood-fueled imagination, especially one of his early movie roles as Lieutenant "Brass" Bancroft in *Murder in the Air*. In this 1940 movie (one of six Reagan made that year), Reagan's character safeguards a new secret weapon, the Inertia Projector, that utilizes electric currents to destroy enemy aircraft.[31] *Murder in the Air* was released in July 1940, on the eve of the German blitz on London, so this imaginative dream was plainly salient but seemingly farfetched: "The bomber will always get through" was Stanley Baldwin's infamous dismissal of Churchill's repeated calls in the 1930s for developing air defenses such as radar. The equivalent in the 1970s and 1980s from missile defense skeptics was "The missile will always get through." Here again Reagan's imagination might be compared with that of Churchill, who in 1926 anticipated not only the development of nuclear weapons and ballistic missiles but also the possibility of advanced defenses against them. "It might have been hoped," Churchill wrote in his melancholy essay "Shall We All Commit Suicide?" "that the electro-magnetic waves would in certain scales be found capable of detonating explosives of all kinds from a great distance."

The emphasis on Reagan's unconventional imagination in conceiving of missile defense as the pathway to supplanting the suicidal barbarity of mutual assured destruction does a disservice to the richness of the full story and to what it reveals about Reagan's force of will and his disregard of the conventional wisdom. It is one of the best refutations of the commonplace view that Reagan was wholly dependent on his staff and aloof from important policy decisions. The emergence of robust missile defense, later named the Strategic Defense Initiative (SDI), owed to a confluence of many factors, but the decisive factor was Reagan himself.

The idea of ballistic defense was not new; the United States had worked on the idea back in the 1950s and deployed the rudimentary Nike-Zeus system in the early 1960s. Although the United States formally gave up on serious missile defense by embracing the doctrine of mutual assured destruction and signing the ABM treaty in 1972, the idea never completely died out in the defense establishment. A few political leaders, especially Wyoming senator Malcolm Wallop, pushed the idea on Capitol Hill in the late 1970s, and researchers grasped that breakthroughs in computing technology, optics, and space-based lasers used for antisatellite purposes could be employed for ballistic missile defense as well. Reagan's first budget revisions in 1981 included a significant increase in spending for Pentagon research on missile defense.

Meanwhile, the difficulties with the MX missile basing were undermining American strategic planning and weakening the rationale of mutual assured destruction. The blunt truth was that the United States simply could not find a basing mode for a new ICBM; the Soviets, with their more extensive territory (not to mention lack of democracy), did not have this problem. Between the restiveness on Capitol Hill and the popularity of the nuclear freeze movement, Reagan was slowly losing the initiative on defense. The Joint Chiefs of Staff (in particular Naval Chief Admiral James Watkins) saw missile defense as a way of salvaging the MX missile, while Reagan's political advisers thought missile defense could be used to deflect the nuclear freeze and would provide a bargaining chip to use in arms control talks with the Soviets.

The idea to embrace a high-profile revival of missile defense began to take shape in a series of White House meetings in late 1982 and early 1983. The famed physicist Edward Teller appeared on William F. Buckley's PBS program *Firing Line* in August 1982 and, in the course of advocating missile defense, complained that the White House was not listening to him. Reagan saw the broadcast and invited Teller to the White House the following month. Teller thought the meeting went poorly. The problem was that Reagan couldn't hear him very well—Teller's thick accent made him hard to understand in any case—and the meeting went off the rails when it turned to a funding request for Lawrence Livermore Lab (funding requests in meetings with Reagan were a White House staff no-no). Teller also advocated a space-based X-ray laser system that would require a nuclear detonation to operate, and employing nuclear weapons to counteract nuclear missiles made Reagan uncomfortable. He wanted a non-nuclear technology.

The idea of missile defense limped along until February 11, 1983, when Reagan met with the Joint Chiefs of Staff to review options for American strategic doctrine. General John Vessey, the chairman of the Joint Chiefs, raised the idea of missile defense and asked Reagan: "Wouldn't it be better to protect the American people rather than avenge them?" Such a defense, Vessey added, would be "more moral." The Joint Chiefs had not developed the idea very thoroughly; it was merely one of several defense initiatives for Reagan to consider. They thought that it would become a matter for extended study in the usual maw of the Pentagon and National Security Council before eventually becoming a modest weapons development program aimed principally at defending America's ICBM force from missile attack, thereby enhancing deterrence. Neither the Joint Chiefs nor any of the Pentagon experts believed at that point that missile defense could be extended to protect the bulk of America's population.

The Joint Chiefs underestimated Reagan, who pounced on the idea and suggested that the Pentagon proceed full speed ahead. Reagan had scheduled a major speech to defend his defense budget for March 23, and he decided he would use the occasion to announce the missile defense initiative. He wanted to describe the initiative in the most expansive terms—as a means of protecting the American people from nuclear annihilation and making nuclear weapons obsolete. "If there is one thing I do not mean by this, gentlemen," Reagan told his advisers two days before the speech, "it is some kind of a string of terminal defenses around this country."[32] Reagan's science adviser, George Keyworth, duly complied with Reagan's wishes and drafted much of the language that Reagan would eventually use on March 23.

All of this occurred at dizzying speed within the last five days before Reagan's speech. As the draft speech circulated through the usual channels, nearly everyone around Reagan got cold feet. The Joint Chiefs of Staff, having elevated the idea to Reagan directly, were uncomfortable. Deputy National Security Adviser Robert McFarlane, while supporting the idea generally, tried to talk Reagan out of it. Edward Frieman, a member of the White House

Science Council, said, "I almost fell out of my chair when I saw it." (Frieman had just produced a report skeptical of the potential for comprehensive missile defense.) No one on the Science Council aside from Keyworth supported it; one member submitted his resignation because of it. Richard Darman, according to Keyworth, was "violently opposed." Secretary of State Shultz objected strongly to language describing the initiative as "a revolution in our strategic doctrine." The line came out, but the implication remained; Shultz was not mollified. He called Keyworth a "lunatic" in an Oval Office meeting in front of Reagan. He warned Reagan that the Soviets would react badly, that the idea as presented would be "destabilizing." Shultz complained strongly to Bill Clark and Robert McFarlane: "I feel you guys are leading the president out on a limb, and people will saw it off. The Chiefs should have their necks wrung."[33] To his own staff, Shultz complained, "We do not have the technology to say this." His chief arms negotiator, Richard Burt, was dismayed, telling Shultz, "Not only is a nuclear-free world a pipe dream, but a speech like this by the president will unilaterally destroy the foundation of the Western alliance."[34] Lawrence Eagleburger huffed, "The president seems to be proposing an updated version of the Maginot Line."

For once Shultz found the Pentagon on his side. Caspar Weinberger did not stand in the way of Reagan's proposed speech despite his lack of enthusiasm for it, but his chief deputies, Richard Perle and Ron Lehman, traveling with Weinberger at a NATO meeting in Portugal, spent most of the night on March 22 on the telephone to Washington trying to derail the speech. Lehman thought it would upset the NATO allies. He was right: Margaret Thatcher wrote later, "I differed sharply from the President's view that SDI was a major step towards a nuclear-free world—something which I believed was neither attainable nor desirable." The specter of the United States protected behind a missile shield could perversely have the result long sought by Soviet foreign policy if it led to the decoupling of American and European security. But she would eventually change her mind: "Looking back, it is now clear to me that Ronald Reagan's original decision on SDI was the single most important of his presidency."[35] Perle thought it would backfire and damage Reagan's arms buildup. Like Reagan, Perle didn't care much for mutual assured destruction ("mutual assured suicide," Perle called it), but thought Reagan's speech was too abrupt a way to introduce a potential revolution in America's strategic thinking. He also thought the idea technically frivolous, saying it was "the product of millions of American teenagers putting quarters into video machines."

Aside from Clark and Keyworth, then, Reagan had almost no support for the idea. Keyworth dutifully drafted an alternative "wimpy" speech that reflected the State Department's perspective, and forwarded it to the president. Reagan rejected it. Only two hours before Reagan was to go on the air, Shultz told him, "I have to say honestly that I am deeply troubled." Reagan was unmoved but gave Shultz permission to share the speech in advance with Dobrynin. The Soviet ambassador responded to Shultz's news, "You will be opening a new phase in the arms race." Back at the Politburo, Andropov reacted harshly, saying, "Engaging in this is not just irresponsible, it is insane. . . . Washington's actions are putting the entire world in jeopardy." It was one more sign to Andropov that the United States was planning to attack, and it abetted the Soviet fear that, despite their own missile defense program, they could not match a determined American effort. "It wasn't SDI per se that frightened Soviet leaders," Robert Gates wrote; "after all, at best it would take many years to develop and deploy an effective system. It was the *idea* of SDI and all that it represented that frightened them."[36] Years later Gorbachev's foreign minister, Alexander Bessmertnykh, confirmed Gates's assessment, saying that "SDI frightened us very much" and "had a long-lasting impact on us." Although Soviet scientists were skeptical SDI could work, Bessmertnykh said it prompted Soviet leaders to reconsider their position.[37]

American media and Capitol Hill were nearly as apoplectic as Andropov. The *New York Times* called it "a pipe dream," while the *Chicago Sun-Times* said Reagan's speech was "an appalling disservice." Liberals were incredulous, seeing that the idea of missile defense represented a new frontier for the arms race. But the dismay was not limited to liberals. Senate Budget Committee chairman Pete Domenici was livid, according to David Stockman, because missile defense represented a potentially significant increase in defense spending at a time when Senate Republicans were trying to hold the line against cutting the Pentagon's budget. (And Stockman didn't like SDI either.)

Senator Ted Kennedy and other Democrats thought they had hit on an effective ridicule for the idea by dubbing it "Star Wars."[38] It is questionable whether attempting to denigrate Reagan's idea by associating it with the most popular movie franchise in history was an effective tactic. Even as common-sense Americans understood Luke Skywalker and the Force to be fantasy, at the same time Americans like audacious imagination. SDI, by whatever name, polled very strongly after Reagan elevated it to the front burner of American public discourse. The idea should not have come as a surprise to anyone who had paid attention to Reagan or to the signals his administration had been giving off since before they arrived in Washington. Reagan had prominently criticized the ABM Treaty and professed support for ballistic missile defense in the 1970s. The 1980 Republican platform had called for a renewal of ballistic missile defense. Cap Weinberger had brought up the subject of reviving such defenses in his Senate confirmation hearings in 1981.

Reagan's introduction of missile defense is nowadays considered a political and diplomatic masterstroke that contributed significantly to the arms reduction breakthroughs of the late 1980s and the eventual end of the Cold War. However, the ultimate irony of Reagan's grand conception of SDI was that it arguably *set back* progress toward near-term deployment of a partial, practical missile defense system. A close reading of Reagan's March 23 speech shows that he never directly claimed that an impenetrable shield for the whole nation could be built. (That would come later; in a 1986 speech, Reagan would lay out the possibility that SDI "might one day enable us to put in space a shield that missiles could not penetrate, a shield that could protect us from nuclear missiles just as a roof protects a family from the rain.") But his capacious description of the initiative made that implication inescapable. Calling it "a vision of the future that offers hope," Reagan asked: "What if free people could be secure in the knowledge that their security did not rest upon the threat of instant U.S. retaliation to deter a Soviet attack, that we could intercept and destroy strategic ballistic missiles before they could reach our own soil or that of our allies? I know it is a formidable, technical task, *one that may not be accomplished before the end of this century.* . . . I call upon the scientific community in our country, those who gave us nuclear weapons, to turn their great talents now to the cause of mankind and world peace, to give us the means of rendering these nuclear weapons impotent and obsolete" (emphasis added). Even more disorienting was Reagan's subsequent suggestion that he would be willing to share missile defense technology with the Soviet Union in the fullness of time.[39] What was this?

This was not at all what the Joint Chiefs and the advocates of missile defense had in mind. The Pentagon wanted a point defense for America's ballistic missile arsenal that would complicate Soviet strategic planning. But what began as a gambit to help the MX missile, blunt the momentum of the freeze movement, and create a bargaining chip for arms negotiations became a much larger thing in Reagan's hands. Frances FitzGerald's account of the SDI story nails it: "The President surely saw what would have been obvious to anyone in his position: You can't tell the American people that you will make them half safe."[40] And so the idea of an *effective* missile defense to bolster deterrence had morphed into a program that sought *perfect* missile defense to put the nuclear genie back in the bottle.

This meant that the technical requirements for a comprehensive missile defense system were increased by orders of magnitude. By saying that the task might take "decades," Reagan transformed strategic defense from a near-term deployment project using off-the-shelf technology of proven effectiveness to a research program that sought to anticipate and conquer all possible Soviet countermeasures that might be devised over a similarly long time horizon. There is no surer way of slowing a new government initiative than to turn it into a research project.

Although neither Reagan nor his advisers ever said anything about devising a system that would be fully seamless against Soviet missiles, the Pentagon panel appointed after Reagan's speech to scope out SDI research and development chose an overall effectiveness target of 99.75 percent. In a manner that aped the arms control process, the national debate over SDI transformed quickly from a political and strategic debate into a largely technical debate. The air was thick with arcane discussion of possible Soviet countermeasures such as decoy warheads, reflective missile coatings, spinning rockets, and so forth. SDI research became the ideal means to throw up political and bureaucratic roadblocks to the actual deployment of a system, even though several aspects of effective missile defense were feasible at the time.[41] The Office of Technology Assessment issued a report concluding that the prospects for effective missile defense were "so remote that it should not serve as the basis for public expectations or national policy." Opponents of SDI in Congress used the technical debate to constrict appropriations for the program. Reagan himself would later acquiesce to some of the delaying tactics of the bureaucracy, leading SDI supporter Angelo Codevilla to compare Reagan to Stanley Baldwin.

The technical debate obscured the fact that the root of liberal outrage was that Reagan was challenging arms control orthodoxy.[42] Questioning the doctrine of nuclear deterrence was, Reagan aide David Abshire said, "like a Christian questioning the Trinity."[43] "The opponents of SDI," Colin Powell said later, "did not want us to aggressively pursue the research because, Lord forbid, we might be able to do it, in which case all of their thinking about mutual assured destruction would be down the tubes."[44] That the Soviet Union was aggressively pursuing its own missile defense program, and was obviously alarmed at Reagan's SDI announcement, seemed to have little or no effect on Reagan's critics, though it was usually a debate-ending rejoinder to ask (as Reagan often did), "If SDI can't possibly work, why are the Soviets so worried about it?"

In fact Reagan's speech deeply shook the Soviets. Andropov, hospitalized at the time of the speech, summoned his top aides to his bedside, where he worried that Reagan's initiative might mean that "[t]he USSR will just stop being a superpower." Soviets said missile defense as Reagan described it was not technically feasible, but Andropov looked down the road:

> It looks like it can't be done now as such a system can be broken by various means. However, in 10 to 15 years' time the situation might change. But what if not in 10 to 15 years, but in five years? One can't set hopes upon the forecasted time. . . . The situation is too serious, and I am not going to disregard both of the possible scenarios, even the possibility to create an efficient anti-missile defense system. Irrespective of the fact of whether the system is practicable or not, it is a real factor in today's U.S. policies. And we can't ignore it.[45]

While the technical debate over SDI's feasibility would rage on for the rest of Reagan's presidency, few at the time perceived that it was a political masterstroke. Christopher Hitchens noted that SDI "had the effect of making liberal noises about a nuclear 'freeze' seem tinny and irrelevant."[46] It was awkward for the Left to oppose defending the homeland from foreign missile attack.

Liberal peace activists and the media wasted no time looking for a way to put Reagan back on the defensive. The ideal media sensation came to hand when a ten-year-old Maine schoolgirl, Samantha Smith, wrote a letter to Yuri Andropov expressing her worry about "Russia and the United States getting into a nuclear war." The Soviet propaganda machine made the most of it, releasing a supposed personal reply from Andropov in April that included contrivances such as "It seems to me, and I take it from your letter, that you are a courageous and honest girl, resembling in some way Becky, Tom Sawyer's friend from the well-known book by your compatriot Mark Twain. All kids in our country, boys and girls alike, know and love this book." Andropov concluded the letter with an invitation for Smith to make an all-expense-paid two-week trip to the Soviet Union so she could see firsthand how peaceful they were. "It was almost as if," the *Omaha World-Herald* observed, "Andropov had taken a line from 'Yes, Virginia, there is a Santa Claus.'"

Andropov's transparent gesture propelled Smith into instant celebrity status. Print and TV network reporters descended upon Smith's hometown of

Manchester and set up a stakeout outside her home. *New York Times* senior foreign correspondent John Burns filed several stories, and *People* magazine produced its usual spread. Smith was booked on the *Tonight* show with Johnny Carson (twice), the *Today* show with Jane Pauley, and *Nightline* with Ted Koppel. Reporters from France, England, Australia, Bulgaria, and Germany rang up for telephone interviews with the schoolgirl "diplomat," as the media called her. There was talk of nominating her for the Nobel Peace Prize. The media reported that Smith had sent a letter to Reagan as well, but it did not yield a White House invitation.[47] The subtext of most stories was incredulity that Reagan couldn't grasp the wisdom of a ten-year-old girl that was perfectly obvious to the adolescents in the news media. Only a few media accounts acknowledged the plain truth of the matter—that the Soviet Union was using Smith as a propaganda gesture.[48]

Along with her parents—and a media contingent of sixty-eight—Smith made her two-week trip to the Soviet Union in July. *ABC World News Tonight* sent Sam Donaldson to report on Smith's visit to a youth camp and Red Square, though a hoped-for audience with Andropov never came off because of the Soviet leader's ill-health. Soviet spokesman Vladimir Pozner, a fixture on American television in the 1980s (especially *The Phil Donahue Show*), gleefully announced that "there are many Soviet citizens who have written and who write to President Reagan. He has chosen not to reply which is, of course, his prerogative."[49] Smith returned home and dutifully reported that the Soviets were peace-loving people.

The story didn't end there, and it didn't end happily. The *Today Show* had Smith on for an encore where she challenged Ken Adelman on U.S. military spending. She addressed an international youth conference in Japan. A book project was hatched. She hosted a ninety-minute TV show in 1984, *Samantha Smith Goes to Washington,* in which she interviewed presidential hopefuls. But in 1985, on her way back home from London, where she had been filming a TV sitcom, Smith and her father were killed in a plane crash. Smith is remembered as a symbol of youthful idealism; CBS News offered a retrospective on her as recently as 2004. It is just as easy to see her as a victim of the media's insatiable appetite for instant celebrity and sentimental story lines.

*   *   *

REAGAN COMPLETED THE trifecta of outrages against liberal dogma in April when he broke his long silence on another contentious point of his foreign policy—Central America. Congressional opposition to Reagan's Central

America policy was rising as the initial Boland Amendment compromise on aid to the Nicaraguan Contras was unraveling. Nearly every congressional committee appearance by administration foreign policy principals was contentious or inflammatory—even behind closed doors and away from the cameras. With the administration unable to speak directly and publicly about its ostensibly covert support for the Contras, the liberal and leftist opposition was free to mount an unanswered attack against the Contras along with propaganda favorable to the Sandinistas. As Lou Cannon put it, "The contras were introduced to the American people by those who opposed their existence rather than by Reagan."[50]

By coincidence Pope John Paul II had visited Central America in March, where a dramatic confrontation with the Sandinistas provided fresh evidence of the ideological character of the Nicaraguan regime. The Pope had previously told the three Catholic clergy serving in the Nicaraguan government that they had to relinquish either their government posts or their holy orders, but the three, thoroughly infused with Marxist liberation theology, pointedly refused. The Pope confronted one of the recalcitrant clergymen at the arrival ceremony at the Managua airport, and a photo of the Pope wagging his finger in reproach appeared prominently in the media around the world. More notable was the heckling the Pope endured during a large open-air Mass later in the day. The Sandinistas had placed their supporters close to the altar, and when the Pope began to criticize liberation theology in his sermon, the Sandinista mob began to shout while the sound engineer turned down the Pope's microphone. As millions in the region watched on live television, John Paul angrily shouted *"Silencio!"* and managed to regain a measure of control. "Millions were shocked at the vulgarity of Sandinista misbehavior," John Paul's biographer George Weigel wrote; the Sandinista claim that the heckling had been a spontaneous reaction was "a clumsy lie."[51] The Pope's rough treatment was an example of the routine harassment of Catholic clergy who didn't fall into line supporting the Sandinistas.

As Nicaragua festered, further American aid to El Salvador was in jeopardy. Congress had required that aid be contingent upon the State Department's certifying at six-month intervals that El Salvador was making progress on human rights and other political reforms. Progress was halting, to say the least, amidst the pressure from the extreme Left and Right in the beleaguered nation. "What this amounted to," Shultz rightly complained, "was congressional micromanagement of the U.S. economic and security assistance." The uncertainty over the U.S. commitment was making the Salvadoran government tentative in its own actions; if the United States might pull the plug (as it had in Vietnam), Salvadoran commanders figured, then they had better conserve ammunition. Critics in Washington predictably argued that American military assistance "was not being used." American military advisers in El Salvador passed word back to the Pentagon that the military situation was deteriorating. The Joint Chiefs of Staff believed that the guerilla insurgency might succeed in toppling the government by the end of the year.

Beset by political opposition, the Reagan administration was racked with infighting over Central American policy. The National Security Council and the Pentagon wanted to increase the number of American military advisers in El Salvador from the current 55 to 160 or more, and step up covert action against Nicaragua. The State Department thought this looked like the same slippery slope as the Vietnam analogy, and favored instead a two-track approach that would seek regional negotiations involving all the nations of Central America while military assistance and covert action continued. The cooler heads in the State Department (which included Shultz) worried that a confrontational policy in Nicaragua would lose the already tenuous congressional support, but hardliners in the White House accused State of having an appeasement mentality. Shultz and National Security Adviser William Clark bickered often ("Bill Clark was very difficult for me to deal with," Shultz said of this period). The divisiveness was so severe that when, in February, UN Ambassador Jeane Kirkpatrick traveled to Central America, delivering a personal letter from Reagan to the various heads of state communicating Reagan's resolve to contain Nicaragua and stabilize El Salvador, the State Department cabled ambassadors in the region that she should be ignored.[52]

By the spring Reagan had come around to the State Department's two-track policy. On April 27, he went before a joint session of Congress to give his first major speech on Central America. Reagan explained the significance of Central America in strategic terms, noting that El Salvador was closer to Texas than Texas was to Massachusetts, and that two-thirds of America's foreign trade passed through the Panama Canal and the Caribbean. He said, "The Caribbean Basin is a magnet for adventurism," and he mentioned a place that would become more familiar a few months later—the tiny island nation of Grenada, where a large new military airfield was being built.

Reagan went on to describe in detail Nicaragua's substantial military buildup and active role in the subversion of its neighbors, though he did not, significantly, mention the Contras by name or U.S. support of their efforts. He praised the progress of democracy and reform in El Salvador amidst the ruinous tactics of the guerillas. "The goal of the professional guerilla move-ments in Central America," Reagan bluntly summarized, "is as simple as it is sinister: to destabilize the entire region from the Panama Canal to Mexico."

But before laying out the administration's request for additional military and development aid to go along with a push for negotiations, Reagan felt it necessary to disavow any intention of deposing the Nicaraguan government ("We do not seek its overthrow") and to address directly the Vietnam syn-drome: "Now, before I go any further, let me say to those who invoke the memory of Vietnam, there is no thought of sending American combat troops to Central America." This represented a necessary rhetorical gesture against the relentless liberal refrain that Reagan wouldn't be happy until American troops were fighting in the jungles of Central America.

The concession to liberal opinion was counterbalanced with a pointed appeal to liberalism's old Cold War tradition. Reagan restated the Truman Doctrine and associated his outlook with that of the thirty-third president:

> President Truman's words are as apt today as they were in 1947, when he, too, spoke before a joint session of the Congress: "At the present moment in world history, nearly every nation must choose between alternate ways of life. The choice is not too often a free one. . . . I believe that it must be the policy of the United States to support free peoples who are resisting attempted subjugation by armed minorities or by outside pressures. . . ." The countries of Cen-tral America are smaller than the nations that prompted President Truman's message. But the political and strategic stakes are the same. Will our response—economic, social, military—be as appro-priate and successful as Mr. Truman's bold solutions to the problems of postwar Europe?

The irony of invoking the Truman Doctrine was deliberate. Truman's 1947 speech was highly controversial at the time but had the effect of flum-moxing Republicans, who were divided between traditional isolationists and the more commercially minded internationalists. Reagan turned this circum-stance on its head, as it was now liberals and Democrats who, in the after-math of Vietnam, were bitterly divided over foreign policy.

This division was laid bare in the immediate sequel to Reagan's speech. Senator Christopher Dodd gave the official Democratic response, in which he demonstrated that the Vietnam syndrome held him and much of his party in thrall: "We cannot afford to found so important a policy on ignorance—and the painful truth is that many of our highest officials seem to know as little about Central America in 1983 as we knew about Indochina in 1963. . . . [I]t is a proven prescription for picking a loser. The American people know that we have been down this road before and that it only leads to a dark tunnel of endless intervention." Dodd proved himself fully credulous over the Salvadoran guerillas' willingness to negotiate for "power sharing," which had always been a formula for slow-motion surrender to Leninist dictatorship. (The liberal advocates of negotiations for power sharing in El Salvador curiously never suggested that the Sandinistas in Nicaragua consider power sharing.)

But Dodd's response didn't go down well with some Democrats. House majority leader Jim Wright of Texas said Dodd's language was "florid," "hyperbolic," "inappropriate," and "as destructive as the McGovern view of Vietnam." "It is a dangerous exercise for people to club the president in a delicate matter of foreign policy," Wright added, though, as we shall see, this is exactly what Wright himself would later do after he succeeded Tip O'Neill as Speaker of the House in 1987. Wright was especially skillful at talking out both sides of his mouth about Central America, and though he supported Reagan's aid package to El Salvador, he voted with most House Democrats a week later to cut off aid to the Nicaraguan Contras.

Wright's straddle exposed the fissure through the heart of the Democratic Party, which was partly along generational lines. Those Democrats like Dodd who had come of age during or after Vietnam rejected the containment consensus of the Cold War, while older Democrats who came of age during World War II and the early years of the Cold War were much more likely to see matters as Reagan did. The most significant of the latter group was Senator Henry ("Scoop") Jackson, who had been saying publicly for months that the subversion of Mexico, and the concomitant problems this would pose for the United States on its border, was the object of Soviet policy in Central America. Jackson told the *New York Times* in March, "Mexico is the ultimate objective of those forces seeking to destabilize countries in Central America." The same day he appeared on ABC's *This Week with David Brinkley*, pointing out that with a revolutionary Mexico "any U.S. government would be faced with the demands to bring our troops home from Europe and to reduce our commitment in the Pacific."

Although Reagan's televised speech boosted public approval of his Central America policy substantially, that summer the Senate joined the House in voting down further Contra aid and approved aid to El Salvador at only about half the level he sought. Reagan's policy was in trouble, and Jackson thought he had a solution. He suggested that Reagan attempt to reforge a consensus by setting up a twelve-member bipartisan commission on Central America policy. Reagan jumped at the idea, but startled observers across the political spectrum by recruiting Henry Kissinger to be the commission's chairman. The Left issued its usual complaints about Kissinger, but so did the Right. Senator Jesse Helms said, "There may be someone in this broad land further down on my list of choices, but I can't think of anyone." At the very least the establishment of the Kissinger Commission, which was directed to deliver its recommendations the following February, kicked the can down the road for a few months.

*   *   *

Overseas, meanwhile, America's key NATO allies were going through an equally rancorous debate as the fall missile deployment date approached. "Every week there is new evidence that the West European leaders might be wavering," Strobe Talbott reported in *Time* magazine in early 1983. "If NATO were forced to postpone deployment, either because of the German election results or a further breakdown in NATO solidarity, then the game would almost certainly be over, and the U.S.S.R. would have won the whole pot."[53]

West Germany was the key: if it backed out, other nervous NATO governments would likely follow, calling for a postponement that would give the Soviets the upper hand in the Geneva negotiations and little incentive to reach any agreement. As chancellor, Helmut Schmidt was one of the key instigators of the original NATO decision to deploy missiles, but elements of his party, the center-Left Social Democrats (SPD), began pushing to rescind the missile deployment. This weakening of SPD resolve proved to be Schmidt's undoing: in the fall of 1982 the small but pivotal Free Democratic Party (FDP), Schmidt's coalition partner in the government, removed its support for Schmidt and entered into coalition with Helmut Kohl's center-Right Christian Democratic Union (CDU), making Kohl the new chancellor. However, the coalition had a razor thin majority of just seven votes in the Bundestag, and in January 1983 Kohl called an election for March, explicitly seeking a mandate from West German voters for the NATO missile deployment.

In the campaign that followed the Soviet Union made clear that it preferred an SPD victory (the SPD party platform now officially embraced neutralism and endorsed the Soviet negotiating position over Euromissiles). "In the year from November 1982 to November 1983 the Soviet Union pulled all available levers of West German politics," wrote Jeffery Herf, the preeminent American observer of West German politics during this crucial period.[54] The Soviet press took the unsubtle line that an SPD victory was necessary to save "Europeans from a nuclear Auschwitz." Soviet officials including Andropov and Foreign Minister Andrei Gromyko issued open threats of additional missile deployments if the NATO deployment went forward. Vice President Bush visited West Germany in the middle of the campaign to offer tacit support for Kohl and was greeted with thousands of peace protestors; when Soviet foreign minister Gromyko turned up for a visit, there were, tellingly, no peace protests putting symmetrical pressure on the other superpower.

The missile question dominated the election campaign, sparking several wrenching debates in the Bundestag and among West German elites that were extraordinary for their direct confrontation with Germany's Nazi past and for their arguments over fundamental views of the causes of war and peace. (In all, the Bundestag debated the missile deployment thirty-seven times between 1979 and the fall of 1983.) Leading figures argued bitterly about the lessons of the 1938 Munich agreement between Neville Chamberlain and Hitler, the intractable nature of totalitarian governments, and the purported moral equivalence of the United States and Soviet Union. Novelist Günter Grass and other German Leftists compared the missile policy to the 1943 Wannsee Conference where the Nazi "final solution" was decided.[55] Kohl bluntly charged that the SPD was a security risk for West Germany, showing that the fault lines of West German politics resembled those of American politics.

Kohl's coalition won a substantial victory on March 6, capturing 45.8 percent of the vote, which along with the FDP's 6.9 percent provided an ample margin of sixty seats in the Bundestag. Washington breathed a sigh of relief. "The election of March 6 was a turning point in postwar history," Jeffrey Herf argues. "The outcome was a defeat for the Soviet Union's diplomatic offensive and for missile opponents in West Germany."[56] Freed from the responsibility of having to govern, however, the SPD moved further to the left in the aftermath of the election. Opposition to the missile deployment, now defeated at the ballot box, would become more vocal and move to the streets. Kohl's government braced itself for a "hot autumn," and refused to disclose publicly where the new American missiles would be based.

A similar debate occurred in Britain at the same time. In April Thatcher called a new election for early June. The opposition Labour Party announced its fifteen-thousand-word campaign program, "New Hope for England." It called for unilateral nuclear disarmament, which meant canceling the deployment of U.S. cruise missiles, along with steep cuts in defense spending and the renationalization of British industry. Several political observers in the U.K. dubbed the Labour platform "the longest suicide note in history." A letter to the London *Times* by a prominent university physicist arguing in favor of not merely disarmament but outright surrender to the Soviet Union was debated seriously for weeks. Thatcher, riding high in the aftermath of the successful Falkland Islands campaign the year before, had her Conservative Party issue its own election manifesto, reaffirming without equivocation her reformist philosophy.

In between the West German and British elections there occurred the most important G-7 summit of the decade in Williamsburg, Virginia, in May. Despite being in the closing weeks of an election campaign, Thatcher attended anyway. Although the summit focused on economic interests, it was decided to issue a strong resolution reiterating Western resolve for the missile deployment. The French and the Canadians objected to the strong draft statement that the United States and Britain proposed; Canada's Pierre Trudeau advocated "speaking more softly" to the Soviet Union. This prompted one of Reagan's pencil-throwing gestures (it was always said that the way to detect if Reagan was angry was if he threw his pencil or his reading glasses down on the table), and Thatcher spoke sharply to Trudeau. "I thought at one point Margaret was going to order Pierre to go stand in a corner," Reagan wrote in his diary. When Kohl proposed compromise language that Thatcher found weak, the Iron Lady showed her legendary spine, telling Kohl: "I'm in the middle of an election. I bent over backwards for your election. Now it's your turn. I have taken a strong position, and I want a strong statement here."[57] French president François Mitterrand proposed new compromise language that Reagan and Thatcher found surprisingly strong, and with Mitterrand's course correction Trudeau's opposition wilted, but the Williamsburg summit made clear that the Western alliance remained solid on all fronts.[58] The Soviets noticed; at a Politburo meeting a few days later, Moscow Communist Party secretary Viktor Grishin complained, "The resolution of the 'Big Seven' that they will put the missiles in Europe has an offensive character."

Two weeks later Thatcher crushed Labour in the election, gaining for her party the largest parliamentary majority in forty years. It was a good omen for Reagan as he pondered his own reelection prospects a year ahead.

*   *   *

SUCH WAS THE state of play as Reagan left Washington at the end of June for the first of three summer trips to his California ranch. Summer passed with its usual languor in Washington, with only the semicomic interruption of Interior Secretary James Watt trying to ban the Beach Boys from playing on the Mall on July 4 because, according to Watt, rock and roll music attracts "an undesirable element." Instead Watt's decision attracted the undesirable attention of Beach Boys fan Nancy Reagan, and the ban dissolved into the Potomac humidity. Reagan good-naturedly sent Watt a plaster model of a foot with a hole in it. Watt would be gone from Interior before the fall leaves changed, following the September announcement of an Interior Department advisory committee in which Watt violated the pieties of diversity in describing his appointees: "I have a black, a woman, two Jews, and a cripple." Crude and obsolete language, to be sure, but Watt's real sin was transgressing the chief dialectical convention of modern liberalism, which is that while we are to be always conscious of race and ethnicity, we are never to be explicit or direct about it. Watt was explicit. For that he had to go. Even Gerald Ford and Bob Dole said so.

Otherwise the summer of 1983 passed without major incident. Pioneer 10, a U.S. space probe launched in 1972, became the first man-made object to leave the solar system, while astronomers at the Jet Propulsion Lab announced the first direct evidence of a solar system around another star. Sally Ride became the first female astronaut to fly in the space shuttle in late June, followed by the first black astronaut, Guy Bluford, in August. Libya invaded Chad again, and the United States responded by holding military exercises in the Egyptian desert. Iran and Iraq escalated their three-year-old war, with heavy losses on both sides. Poland finally lifted martial law.

The media tried but largely failed to make hay out of the controversy over the stolen 1980 Carter campaign debate briefing book that came to light in the spring.[59] At a mid-July press conference, Reagan was asked: "Would you deny the possibility that all of this is little more than *Washington Post–National Enquirer*–style summer theater?" Reagan: "Oh, you're tempting me."

On July 1 the third and final phase of Reagan's income tax cut went into effect. Some 1.1 million new jobs had been created through mid-year, and the pace of job growth was accelerating, with 345,000 new jobs generated in June. In July automakers reported a 48 percent jump in sales over the previous year. A new $2 billion grain deal with the evil empire was unveiled, and three weeks later Reagan approved the sale of Caterpillar pipe-laying equipment to the Soviets. In August, 675,000 unionized telephone workers went on strike against AT&T, then on the eve of its historic breakup. There was little disruption in phone service, and the strike was settled in three weeks. National Public Radio, facing bankruptcy, received a bailout from the Corporation for Public Broadcasting.

Unknown to everyone including most of Reagan's senior staff, Reagan sent a handwritten letter to Andropov in July, in response to a letter he had received from Andropov in which the Soviet leader expressed the desire to eliminate the nuclear threat and improve relations. In the spring Reagan had indicated a new flexibility in arms control, offering as a concession a proposal for an "interim agreement" by which the United States would reduce its planned European missile deployment if the Soviet Union would agree to reduce its intermediate-range warheads to an equal number. The Soviets rejected it, insisting that the independent British and French nuclear warhead arsenals be included in any arms deal. The Geneva arms control talks adjourned on July 14 and were scheduled to resume on September 6.

However, Andropov's letter encouraged Reagan. After months of harsh anti-Reagan rhetoric from the Soviets, it appeared possible they were turning a new page. "Historically," Reagan wrote back, "our predecessors have made better progress when communicating has been private and candid. If you wish to engage in such communication you will find me ready. I await your reply." In other words, Reagan was ready for a summit.

Andropov didn't grasp the opening, replying a month later with a repetition of an offer to redeploy Soviet missiles that the United States had already rejected. Reagan was disappointed but in a conciliatory mood, according to Shultz, as the president returned to his California ranch to relax for the last few weeks of summer. By degrees it appeared superpower relations were easing, with the prospect of a summit becoming more likely. Late in the spring, in the aftermath of his private meeting with Dobrynin, Reagan wrote to a friend that "we have more contact with the Soviets than anyone is aware of and whether to have a meeting or not is on the agenda at both ends of the line."[60] "There is a faint hint of tango music in the air," Strobe Talbott wrote in *Time*. "Neither side," *Newsweek* reported on August 29, "wanted to spoil a perceptible thaw in U.S.-Soviet relations."

*   *   *

THE AIR OF incipient comity in late summer was shattered on August 31, when midafternoon Washington time a Korean Airlines 747, Flight 007, en route from New York to Seoul, disappeared from air traffic control radar screens in the Far East. It took air traffic controllers and American intelligence agencies several hours to piece together what had happened. By 10:30 p.m., American intelligence was growing more certain that the unthinkable had occurred: the Soviets had shot the civilian airplane out of the sky. Sixty Americans, including a congressman, were among the 269 passengers. Bill Clark telephoned Reagan at the ranch with the initial unconfirmed report of the incident. Reagan, true to form in a crisis, reacted calmly, telling Clark that the United States should be careful not to overreact to what was arguably an atrocity akin to the sinking of the *Lusitania* in 1915. "Let's pray that it's not true," he told Clark. When Reagan received confirmation the next morning—on another telephone call from Clark during a horseback ride—he immediately packed and returned to Washington.

In the course of its overnight flight after refueling in Alaska, KAL 007 apparently strayed off course over Soviet territory near military installations on Sakhalin Island. How and why KAL 007 veered off course remains controversial. In those days polar routes to the Far East had to take a circuitous southern zigzag to avoid Soviet territory, though this required more jet fuel and added to the length of the flight. Did the Korean pilots deliberately cut corners in an attempt to save time and fuel? Unlikely; the Soviets had forced down another wayward Korean Airlines 747 in 1978, killing two passengers in the process. The leading theory is pilot error—that the pilots misprogrammed the in-flight navigational aids and the autopilot upon taking off from Alaska and never noticed they were off course.[61] Conspiracy fetishists and grassy-knollers on the Left, such as Seymour Hersh, claimed that the Soviets confused KAL 007 with an American spy plane (or that KAL 007 was itself on an espionage mission); U.S. spy planes—none of them 747s—had deliberately approached Soviet airspace in the region around this time, and there had been a spy flight that night, code-named Cobra Ball. But Cobra Ball was hundreds of miles away from the KAL 007 flight track, and U.S. intelligence was able to demonstrate that the Soviets had tracked the Cobra Ball flight and KAL 007 separately. In fact, the Cobra Ball flight was back on the ground in Alaska by the time the Soviets fired on KAL 007.

American intelligence intercepts proved that the Soviets tracked the plane for more than two hours, and that the fighter aircraft that finally fired on the 747 observed the plane from a variety of close positions for about twenty minutes. The pilot later claimed that Soviet airmen were not trained to recognize civilian aircraft, though the 747, with its distinctive hump, is one of the most easily recognized airplanes in the world, and moreover the Korean plane had its civilian running lights on. Most damning were the intelligence intercepts of the pilot receiving orders from the ground to fire on the plane: "Invader has violated state border. Destroy target." It was later learned that the order had been cleared with senior defense officials in Moscow, the head of whom was subsequently promoted.

As international reaction reached a fever pitch—Reagan alternately called the act an "atrocity," a "crime against humanity," and a "massacre"—for five days the Soviets denied that they had shot down the plane. A few cool heads in the Kremlin wanted to admit that a mistake had been made and apologize for the loss of life, but Andropov, who was hospitalized at the time, rejected the idea. Faced with this intransigence, the Reagan administration took the unusual decision of releasing the intelligence intercepts of the communications between the ground and the Soviet pilot. Reagan played a portion of the Russian-language tape in a televised address (much of which Reagan wrote himself), dramatically narrating the events it described. Presented with this embarrassing proof, the Soviets retreated to the line that KAL 007 had been a spy plane and an American provocation, and therefore justifiably shot down.[62] (There was one other indirect casualty of the KAL 007 incident: Senator Scoop Jackson died on September 1 of a heart attack a few hours after blasting the Soviet Union for its "dastardly, barbaric act against humanity" at a Seattle press conference. Jackson had been in poor health, but it was hard to dismiss this cold warrior's sudden death as a pure coincidence.)

The dilemma for Reagan was what concrete steps should be taken in reaction. Weinberger and others wanted Reagan to cancel further arms talks and Shultz's imminent Madrid meeting with Soviet foreign minister Gromyko. Don Regan wanted economic sanctions or a boycott; at the very least, the recent grain sales deal should be cancelled. Members of Congress wanted a mass expulsion of Soviet diplomats based in the United States, many of whom were KGB spies anyway. Reagan didn't like any of these options and settled for a number of weak-sounding measures such as slowing cultural exchanges and extending limits on landing rights for Soviet civilian airliners that had been in place since the Polish crisis the year before.

Many conservatives were not happy. "Conservatives Dismayed by Limp Response to Soviets," read the *Human Events* front-page headline in mid-September. "The President," *Human Events* blasted, "for whatever reason, is acting for all the world like Ramsey Clark." *New York Times* columnist William Safire said Reagan "has sounded off more fiercely than Theodore Roosevelt and has acted more pusillanimously than Jimmy Carter." The *Washington Times* lamented that Reagan "did no more than pelt the swaggering offender with the adjectives of pious outrage."[63] George Will wrote: "Thank God it is not December or some dunce would suggest dimming the national Christmas tree." A Gallup poll showed a small majority of the public thought Reagan hadn't been tough enough, though, in typically cognitively dissonant fashion, large majorities opposed cutting off arms talks or instituting sanctions. Reagan was defensive: "I know that some of our critics have sounded off that somehow we haven't exacted enough vengeance. Well, vengeance isn't the name of the game. . . . Short of going to war, what would they have us do?"

States and private entities undertook a number of anti-Soviet steps of their own: Ohio and New Hampshire banned Russian vodka from their state liquor stores, and in California longshoremen refused to unload Russian timber from a freighter. Other symbolic steps were more colorful. One video game operator changed the display to show as the target "Andropov, Communist mutant from outer space."

Shultz kept his previously scheduled meeting with Gromyko in Madrid on September 7, and it was one of his finest moments, as it prompted the first tiny crack in Soviet diplomatic intransigence. By prior agreement Shultz was to host Gromyko at the American ambassador's residence, but when Gromyko's limousine pulled up, in front of a gallery of several hundred reporters and photographers, there was only a low-level State Department aide to greet Gromyko at the door. Shultz was pointedly absent. The meeting table was left spare, with not even a glass of water for Gromyko. Shultz opened, as he deliberately did in every meeting with Gromyko, with a particular case of Soviet human rights abuse (in this instance, jailed dissident Anatoly Sharansky) as well as KAL 007. Gromyko insisted that he would not discuss either subject, and rose from the table as if to walk out. Shultz rose from the table but made no effort to persuade Gromyko to stay; to the contrary, he called Gromyko's bluff: "Fine—go," Shultz said sharply.

Gromyko remained standing and kept talking; he didn't want the blame for having ended the meeting abruptly. At length he backed down and sat down. No real progress was made in the two hours of acrimonious back-and-forth that followed, and after the meeting ended Shultz went before the media outside and said, practically before Gromyko's limousine was out of the driveway, that the Soviet's responses were "totally unacceptable." Shultz's veteran State Department interpreter told him that in nearly two decades of participating in high-level meetings with Soviet officials, he had never seen such a blunt encounter.[64]

With Gromyko scheduled to appear at the United Nations two weeks after the KAL 007 incident, New York governor Mario Cuomo and New Jersey governor Tom Kean denied permission for Soviet planes to land at civilian airports in either state, much to the annoyance of Shultz and the State Department, which relished the thought of watching Gromyko squirm in his seat as the United States played the tape of the incident in the UN General Assembly. Instead, Gromyko cancelled his scheduled UN appearance, blasting the United States for not living up to its obligations as host of the United Nations. The United States offered to let Gromyko land at an air force base in New Jersey; the deputy U.S. ambassador to the United Nations, Charles Lichenstein, sarcastically added, "We won't even shoot it down if it strays from its designated path." Gromyko declined.

Lichenstein's sequel cheered conservatives. If the UN membership thought the United States was inadequately discharging its host duties, Lichenstein said, the United Nations was welcome to leave for a more accommodating locale: "We will be at the dockside, bidding you a fond farewell as you set off into the sunset." Both the State Department and White House press secretary Larry Speakes disavowed Lichenstein's off-the-cuff comment and said it did not reflect American policy, but Reagan, in a typical let-Reagan-be-Reagan moment, defended it when queried by a reporter: "I think the gentleman who spoke the other day had the hearty approval of most people in America in his suggestion that we weren't asking anyone to leave, but if they choose to leave, goodbye. . . . Maybe all those delegates should have six months in the United Nations meetings in Moscow and then six months in New York, and it would give them the opportunity to see two ways of life. And we'd permit them." On Capitol Hill, twenty-four House Democrats sent a letter to Reagan demanding that Lichenstein be fired because of his remarks.

Reagan's measured reaction to KAL 007 was shrewd. With this one rash act, the Soviets threw away three years' worth of effort through the European peace movement to split the NATO alliance and prevent the Euromissile deployment. The Soviets' uncompromising reaction further isolated them; in addition to their intransigence, they increased the intensity of their personal attacks on Reagan. Cartoonists in the state-controlled press had previously depicted Reagan as a six-shooter-toting cowboy; now they depicted him as Hitler and added swastikas to their images. At home liberal complaints about Reagan's "evil empire" theme fell temporarily mute, and the incident blunted congressional opposition to Reagan's next defense budget plan, especially the MX missile. Columnist Mary McGrory wondered whether Andropov was acting as "chairman of Reagan's re-election committee." A few liberals persisted in casting blame on the United States. George McGovern told the *Washington Post:* "We ought to be very thankful that this man Andropov seems to be a reasonable guy and somewhat restrained [given that] the Reagan-Weinberger approach is one of intense confrontation."

Reagan's restraint was in service of his larger object of achieving a genuine arms reduction deal, though he knew intuitively that such a breakthrough was now further away. In fact, a few weeks later Reagan offered new arms control proposals whose emphasis on flexibility represented a substantial concession to the Soviet negotiating position. He started using language of a "build-down" of nuclear arms. Andropov was not interested, this time rejecting Reagan's entreaties with old-style anti-American vituperation. Reagan said to Shultz in mid-October, "If things get hotter and arms control remains an issue, maybe I should see Andropov and propose eliminating all nuclear weapons."[65] Reagan had no idea just how much hotter things were going to get over the last two months of the year.

*   *   *

WHILE THE WORLD'S attention was focused on the KAL 007 incident and the imminent Euromissile deployment, the Middle East continued to fester. The United States remained deeply involved in Lebanon, working diplomatically to arrange a pullback of Israeli and Syrian troops dug in around Beirut, while simultaneously trying to mediate the various Lebanese factions. In April a powerful truck bomb at the U.S. embassy in Beirut had killed sixty-three (including seventeen Americans, among them eight CIA agents); construction to harden the embassy against just such an attack had not been completed. It was a rare occasion when Reagan's political sense failed him; he compared the unfinished work to protect the embassy against terrorist attacks to a home-remodeling project that was behind schedule. U.S. intelligence quickly concluded that Iranian-backed terrorists, with help from Syria, were responsible for the bombing. Lou Cannon commented: "The destruction of the U.S. embassy was seen in retrospect as a signal that the holy war declared against America by Shiites in Iran four years earlier had been extended to Lebanon."[66] Reagan and his foreign policy team did not grasp this fact with sufficient seriousness.

Reagan disliked dealing with the Middle East, partly because it was a peripheral front in the Cold War, and partly because he didn't understand the religious fault lines of the region. To William F. Buckley Reagan wrote in a letter: "Bill, the Middle East is a complicated place—well, not really a place, it's more a state of mind. A disordered mind."[67] To another correspondent Reagan wrote at about the same time: "Sometimes I wonder if the Middle East was the cradle of the world's three great religions because they needed religion more than any other spot on earth."[68]

Reagan had floated a comprehensive Middle East peace plan in the fall of 1982 that for the first time included a U.S. endorsement for Palestinian autonomy on the West Bank. Even Jimmy Carter approved, but Yasir Arafat did not, so the plan withered, as have nearly all Middle East peace initiatives. In the spring of 1983 the United States brokered a formula between Israel and Lebanon for the withdrawal of Israeli forces. The deal was contingent on Syria withdrawing after Israel, and the State Department was naively confident that the Saudis would pressure Syria to go along. Fat chance; Syria not only gave a flat no but purposely humiliated the State Department by declaring Philip Habib, the U.S. Middle East envoy, to be persona non grata in Damascus. The Israelis didn't want to wait for hell to freeze over to withdraw; their pullout over the summer left a vacuum in Beirut, which various indigenous and Syrian-backed militias rushed in to fill.

With Lebanon's own armed forces weakened and split along religious lines, Reagan followed Shultz's view that the contingent of American marines, supplemented by French and Italian forces, was necessary to keep the fragile peace in Beirut. Congress agreed, with Tip O'Neill providing important support in the House for a resolution authorizing the deployment for a further eighteen months under the terms of the constitutionally dubious War Powers Act. The irony of the Lebanon affair is that it was the supposed hard-liners around Reagan—especially Weinberger and Clark—who were most opposed to continued deployment of American forces in Lebanon. Weinberger and Clark began arguing for the redeployment of marines to ships offshore, which was a mere fig leaf for withdrawal.

The multiple diplomatic missions to Syria's implacable Hafez Assad served only to increase tensions within the Reagan administration; Shultz and Bill Clark were clashing, with Deputy National Security Adviser Robert McFarlane (who had willy-nilly become Reagan's special envoy to the Middle East) caught in the middle. Assad concluded that the United States could be pushed out of Lebanon if the cost in blood was increased. Late in the summer, marines hunkered down in a vulnerable position as the Beirut airport began taking increasing fire from various militias now occupying the high ground that the Israelis had vacated. By degrees the American-led multinational contingent came to be seen less as a peacekeeping force than as an adjunct to the Lebanese government, whose Christian leader, Amin Gemayel, was not acceptable to many Muslim factions, let alone the Syrians. By mid-September, four marines had been killed and twenty-eight wounded from the constant hostile mortar and small-arms fire. The Reagan administration responded by authorizing air strikes and the presence of navy ships (including the World War II–era battleship *New Jersey*) to shell the hillside positions. With Pentagon military leaders increasingly uncomfortable—and intelligence analysts warning that the marines could be a target of terrorist attacks— Weinberger made the case for withdrawal to Reagan on October 18. Worried that precipitous American withdrawal would plunge Lebanon into chaos, Reagan demurred.

*   *   *

LEBANON WAS NOT the only foreign crisis on Reagan's mind. Even as Lebanon was festering, affairs involving the USSR-Cuba-Nicaragua axis reached a flash point on the flyspeck Caribbean island of Grenada, the scene of a bizarre and unlikely Marxist revolution that in 1979 had deposed the democratically elected government through a military coup.[69] Reagan had been mentioning the tiny island ominously for more than a year, warning, for example, in an overlooked line of his March 1983 SDI speech: "On the small island of Grenada, at the southern end of the Caribbean chain, the Cubans, with Soviet financing and backing, are in the process of building an airfield with a 10,000 foot runway. Grenada doesn't even have an air force. Who is it intended for? The Soviet-Cuban militarization of Grenada, in short, can only be seen as power projection into the region." Shortly after this speech came an incident Reagan had mentioned in his April 27 speech on Central America policy: the Libyan transport plane, loaded with arms, that Brazil interdicted when the aircraft stopped to refuel en route to Nicaragua. The plane's manifest said its cargo consisted of medical supplies, but Brazil's inspectors found a planeload of arms. Reagan noted in his speech that had the Grenadian airfield been ready, the Libyan plane could have refueled there instead. This turned out to be only the tip of the iceberg: Grenada experienced occasional nighttime power outages that coincided with Soviet and Cuban ships unloading and distributing cargo to various locations on the tiny island.

The real worry over Grenada went unpublicized, however. Among the escalating war of words over the Euromissile deployment, the Soviets had threatened an analogous deployment if NATO went ahead. Cuba had been out of bounds since the 1962 agreement that ended the Cuban missile crisis, and Nicaragua was too risky as well as too valuable as a base for destabilizing the mainland of Central America. Might the Soviet Union deploy missiles to Grenada, hoping to trade them for the removal of our Euromissiles, just as they had bargained NATO missiles from Turkey in 1962? More than a few intelligence analysts thought the possibility plausible.[70] A Mexican journalist, José Pérez Stuart, noted the presence of a KGB general and nearly a hundred Soviet technicians on the island in September. At the very least the United States thought it likely that the Soviets would deploy advanced MiG fighter planes to Grenada, which would fall short of a Cuban-missile-crisis-level provocation, but would still complicate the military posture of the region.

But a funny thing happened on the way to consolidating Grenada as a clone of Cuba and a base for the Soviets. In mid-October Grenada's revolutionary Marxist leader Maurice Bishop was ousted in a coup led by an even more radical faction that thought Bishop's Leninism was insufficiently pure. (Had there been doubts about Bishop's fidelity to Marxist revolution?) Bishop had held a secret meeting with Bill Clark in Washington in the spring of 1983, where Clark attempted to persuade Bishop to move away from Cuba. Taking over for Bishop was the deputy prime minister, Bernard Coard, who seems to have learned his radical Marxism in Western universities, having attended Brandeis on a full scholarship, as well as the University of Sussex in Britain, which may help explain the unusual fervency of the Grenadian revolution. Castro was upset by Coard's coup; he issued a head-turning public condemnation, calling Coard "the Pol Pot of the Caribbean." News quickly filtered out that Coard had summarily executed Bishop and several of his cabinet ministers and political supporters by firing squad. Further chaos and a possible civil war were thought likely. The British governor-general on Grenada, Sir Paul Scoon, had gone into hiding, but managed to get out word of the deteriorating scene.

At the White House the concern turned from a possible Soviet missile intrigue to a more existential problem: the status and safety of American citizens on Grenada, particularly the several hundred American students who attended medical school on the island. Around the time of the Iranian hostage crisis in 1979–80, the New Jewel Movement that had promulgated the original Grenadian revolution threatened to take American medical students as hostages, and why not, since it had proven so successful in Iran. Grenada refused American diplomatic requests to send an airplane or a passenger ship to evacuate American citizens. The NSC began making contingency plans for a military rescue operation, and a naval flotilla bound for

Lebanon was diverted to the southern Caribbean just in case. When the Grenadian government refused a State Department request to send an envoy to see to the safety of American citizens, planning for a military intervention intensified.

As head of crisis management, Vice President Bush chaired the National Security Council meetings evaluating the situation. The State Department reported that neighboring Caribbean nations were extremely worried about Grenada and hoped for firm U.S. action, eventually asking the United States to support a military intervention. Bush and Weinberger were reluctant; Bush wanted to see if the United States could arrange some kind of multinational force that included other Latin American nations. Reagan rejected the idea, saying it would delay action and would likely leak out, eliminating the element of surprise. Shultz, significantly, was strongly in favor of intervening, which helped tip the deliberations of the NSC. But the decisive voice was Reagan's. Shultz recalls Reagan asking: "What kind of country would we be if we refused to help small but steadfast democratic countries in our neighborhood to defend themselves against the threat of this kind of tyranny and lawlessness?"[71] On Friday, October 21, it was tentatively decided to launch an invasion the following Tuesday, October 25.

To keep up the appearance of business as usual, Reagan and Shultz went on a previously scheduled weekend golf outing to Augusta, Georgia, while final planning for the invasion, code-named Operation Urgent Fury, quietly continued in Washington. In the early morning hours on Sunday came the awful news that a terrorist suicide truck bomb had blown up the Marine barracks in Beirut, killing 241 marines—the largest loss of uniformed men since the Vietnam War. The enormous truck bomb packed the equivalent of twelve thousand pounds of TNT, making it one of the largest non-nuclear explosions ever recorded. A simultaneous suicide bomber killed fifty-eight French soldiers two miles away. The Iranian-backed Hezbollah was undoubtedly behind the bombing; American intelligence noted that the Iranian embassy packed up and moved out within hours of the blast.

Reagan returned to Washington directly, where his advisers wondered whether to call off the Grenada invasion. The Beirut bombing was a hard blow emotionally for Reagan—he later called that Sunday "the worst day of my presidency"—but he was unwavering about the Grenada mission. Weinberger still opposed the invasion, and the Joint Chiefs of Staff warned Reagan about the political fallout. It is impossible to overstate the extent to which the lingering shadow of Vietnam hung over the military leadership at this late date, despite Reagan's forceful attitude and generous Pentagon budgets. John Poindexter, then deputy national security adviser, said, "We used to say that [Joint Chiefs chairman] General John Vessey was a charter member of the Vietnam Never Again Syndrome." Admiral William Crowe, the chief of naval operations, said, "Anytime anyone has proposed the use of military force, Vietnam was right there, in the middle of the table."[72] Reagan told the Joint Chiefs to leave the politics to him. Mindful of the insufficient forces of Jimmy Carter's Iranian hostage rescue fiasco in 1980, he ordered the Joint Chiefs to increase their forces. Reagan was suspicious that the so-called construction workers at the Grenada airport were well-trained Cuban soldiers.

On Monday evening Reagan summoned congressional leaders to the White House to inform them of the imminent action. Tip O'Neill said he understood the rationale but thought an invasion premature. He complained, "Mr. President, I have been informed but not consulted," and left the White House family quarters in a huff, according to Shultz. (O'Neill would later briefly claim that "Grenada was really about Lebanon.") House majority leader Jim Wright thought the situation didn't yet merit the use of force. Democratic Senate leader Robert Byrd said he opposed the operation, and would say so once it became public. House GOP leader Bob Michel offered his strong support, but Senate GOP leader Howard Baker was surprisingly tepid, calling the operation "bad politics." The president's advisers were nervous; Reagan told them to relax: "You can always trust Americans." Reagan also spoke by phone early in the evening with Margaret Thatcher, who was furious that the United States was taking preemptive action in a British Commonwealth territory.

In the ordinary sense Operation Urgent Fury was a walkover. American forces rolled up the Cuban soldiers—who were far more numerous, well trained, and well armed than expected—and seized control of the Point Salines airstrip and other key targets. But beneath the surface a number of fiascos rekindled doubt that the Pentagon had truly reformed itself amidst Reagan's defense buildup or had learned from the Iranian hostage rescue debacle. Instead of a simple offensive, Operation Urgent Fury was unduly complicated, involving army Rangers, navy SEALs, marines, the Eighty-second Airborne Division, and Delta Force. Several of the discrete operations miscarried and were salvaged only by superior backup firepower from the air. Initial Delta Force and Ranger forces were pinned down in several locations, while a SEAL team assigned to rescue Governor-General Scoon was surrounded and trapped for nearly ten hours. There were problems with incompatible radios between units. In one notorious incident, a commander used a credit card to place a long-distance call over a public telephone to reach another American officer to request fire support. An American airplane mistakenly bombed a mental hospital, killing twenty-one patients. Overall intelligence was very poor; some army units had to land with photocopied tourist maps. The CIA had no presence on the island, a legacy of the deliberate shrinkage of the CIA's clandestine service during the late 1970s. One advance SEAL reconnaissance team drowned at sea, while another had its raft motor fail, leaving it adrift far from land, depriving follow-on forces of crucial intelligence. The exact whereabouts of the American students, who were scattered at various locations, was not known, and U.S. forces had to improvise. All the students were safely secured eventually, but it could have ended badly. It took two days for U.S. forces to subdue the island. An after-action review later concluded that a stronger Cuban defense force might have thrown American forces back into the sea. Nineteen American soldiers were killed and 115 wounded.

As the Joint Chiefs expected, there was a political uproar at home. The news media were furious that they had been excluded from covering the operation and barred for several days from sending any reporters to Grenada. CBS News president Edward Royce complained: "We are saddened to bear witness to this new, unchecked censorship, leading to an off-the-record war." NBC News anchor John Chancellor declared on air, "The American government is doing whatever it wants to without any representative of the American public watching what it is doing." The *Los Angeles Times* huffed about "the public's right to know." Richard Nixon gamely commented that while news reporters indeed accompanied troops ashore on the D-Day landings in 1944, "[I]n those days the media was on our side." Conservative columnist Joe Sobran remarked on the good sense of the White House; after all, he wrote, you don't take the enemy with you on your military ventures. The public overwhelmingly agreed; letters to news organizations ran as high as eight to one in favor of excluding the media.

In a typical display of moral confusion, the *New York Times* editorialized that "the cost is the loss of the moral high ground: a reverberating demonstration to the world that America has no more respect for laws and borders, for the codes of civilization, than the Soviet Union." (The *Times* returned to the subject with an extra helping of snark a month later: "So the invasion is finally justified because Americans needed a win, needed to invade someone. Happy 1984.")

Leading liberals adopted the *Times*'s line. Senator Carl Levin of Michigan complained: "The Soviet Union has no right to impose its will upon the people of Poland. How then, at the same time, can we insist that we have a right to impose our way of life upon another people in this hemisphere?" Representative Ted Weiss said, "Ronald Reagan has adopted the tactic of the Japanese attack on Pearl Harbor as the new American standard of behavior" and introduced an impeachment resolution in the House, which the Congressional Black Caucus endorsed almost unanimously. Representative Charles Rangel charged Reagan with having "embarked upon a frightening course of gunboat diplomacy." Jesse Jackson called for "reparations" to the people of Grenada (who, polls showed, were grateful for the U.S. intervention, by a margin of nine to one). The Southern Christian Leadership Conference said the invasion made the United States into "the villain of the Western Hemisphere," and the National Conference of Black Lawyers said it was a "violent and criminal" act.

Liberals who should have known better went the same way. Presidential front-runner Walter Mondale charged that Reagan's invasion "undermines our ability to effectively criticize what the Soviets have done in their brutal intervention in Afghanistan, in Poland, and elsewhere."[73] Could it really be that liberals were unable to distinguish between Hitler's invasion of France and the Allied invasion of France on D-Day? So it seemed. George Will noted tartly, "The logic of Mondale's position is that all uses of force, by Castro or Reagan, Hitler or Lincoln, are censorable, regardless of the aims or outcomes."

Standing out among Democrats with a more nuanced view was Senator Pat Moynihan, who thought that a rescue operation of U.S. citizens was justified, but not a full-scale invasion to replace the sitting government, as though such a discrete operation could be calibrated on a tiny island. The invasion was, he argued, a violation of the UN Charter and the charter of the Organization of American States (OAS).[74] It was "an act of war," he said, adding, "I don't know that you restore democracy at the point of a bayonet." Moynihan's neoconservative friends and admirers were startled: was this the same Moynihan who had spoken so resolutely against the Soviet threat, and the corruption of the UN, while UN ambassador just a few years before? The same Moynihan who had said that "so long as the ideas underlying Jimmy Carter's UN policy are dominant in the Democratic Party, Democrats will be out of power—and rightly so." "Moynihan was the obvious heir to Scoop Jackson," one unnamed neoconservative told *Policy Review.* "Now with Scoop's death and Moynihan's defection, the Jackson Democrats have nowhere to go."[75] *National Review* said that Moynihan's "metamorphosis" had made him "a national disaster." The *New Republic*'s Morton Kondracke observed, "The new Moynihan seems to put primary emphasis on the American government's obeying rules, rather than gaining geopolitical advantage in the struggle of systems that the old Moynihan considered the central concern of the contemporary world." One of Moynihan's own former staffers wrote: "Those who are looking for unflinching resolve in opposition to the Soviets should stop thinking of him as one of their number."[76]

In fact Moynihan had been edging to the left since Reagan's election in 1980. Some of his tergiversations could be attributed to his contrarian temperament, and some to the political calculation of self-preservation. Although reelected comfortably in 1982, he continued to fear a challenge from the Left in a Democratic primary in New York. That Moynihan felt compelled to move toward the Left (partly under the advice of his new young political director, Tim Russert) showed how strong the leftward undertow in the Democratic Party had become (as Senator Joe Lieberman would find out twenty years later). To be sure, Moynihan's disagreement with the Grenada invasion (and also Reagan's Nicaragua policy) derived from his view that the Soviet Union and Marxism were in decline. As he said in a 1982 speech, "The truth is, the Soviet idea is spent. . . . [I]t summons no loyalty. History is moving away from it with astounding speed. . . . It is as if the whole Marxist-Leninist ethos is hurtling off into a black hole." Moynihan therefore thought "[O]ur grand strategy should be to wait out the Soviet Union; its time is passing."[77]

While this view marked out Moynihan from other liberals and conservatives who saw the Soviet empire as a durable state, it evaded the underlying dilemma practical statesmen must face: a blind fealty to international law will be to the disadvantage of law-abiding nations in the face of a major power bloc that refuses to abide by it equally. Liberalism in the 1980s had no serious answer to the lawlessness of the Soviet Union and its allies other than to continue to "negotiate" while Marxist revolution marched on to the ruin of more countries like Grenada. Reagan had been right that, as he put it in 1982, Grenada "bears the Soviet and Cuban trademark." In fact the whole Eastern bloc syndicate was represented. Among the non-Grenadians captured on the island and eventually deported were forty-nine Soviets, ten East Germans, three Bulgarians, fifteen North Koreans, and seventeen Libyans, along with nearly eight hundred Cubans. American forces uncovered an arms cache that would have sufficed to supply a ten-thousand-man force. A million rounds of ammunition were found in a false floor of the vacated Cuban embassy.

Documents captured on Grenada offered Americans for the first time an inside look at a Marxist-Leninist revolution in progress. Political scientists Paul Seabury and Walter McDougall, who produced an edited volume of the captured documents, described them as having been written in "the suffocating prose of badly educated sociology students."[78] Included in the voluminous cabinet memos, government directives, diplomatic cables, and letters to foreign governments were intensive plans for external propaganda, transforming the island's schools into indoctrination factories, complete censorship, and establishing neighborhood informant networks on the Cuban model to detect dissidents, who were then arrested and jailed. (About 1 percent of Grenada's population was jailed on politcal charges at the time of the U.S. invasion.) The documents were compelling evidence that the Cold War was far from moribund and that Marxist revolutionary ardor was hardly a spent force. Although it may have been true that genuine belief in Marxism-Leninism was on the wane in the Soviet Union, the Soviet propaganda and indoctrination apparatus operated in Grenada as if it was 1917. "Grenadians were given the whole Soviet world view," said Michael Ledeen, who reviewed the captured documents for the State Department. "They were not simply becoming a Communist country. They were becoming a part of the Communist movement."

Though the documents do suggest some friction between the Soviets and Cuba, the diplomatic and military ties with the Soviet bloc were extensive and important. Among the documents was a memo of a Moscow meeting between Grenada's top military commander and Soviet chief of staff Marshal Nikolai Ogarkov, who boasted that "over two decades ago there was only Cuba in Latin America, today there are Nicaragua, Grenada, and a serious battle is going on in El Salvador." (Reagan would later quote this statement in his speeches about Central America.) Equally revealing were the records of the Marxist junta's friendly contacts with the office of Democratic congressman Ron Dellums of California, a member of the House Armed Services Committee, and of substantial efforts to influence political opinion in the United States with the enthusiastic cooperation of Dellums and his staff. Small wonder that Dellums described the American invasion as a "crime against humanity executed by people who deserve to be condemned as war criminals."

Liberal outrage over Grenada fell suddenly mute when the evacuated students arrived back in the United States a few days later. Upon climbing down the airplane steps, the first students knelt down and kissed the ground. There had been commentary in the press that the students had not faced any serious danger, but that was not how they told it. One student, Jeff Geller, came to the White House a week later (nearly four hundred of the evacuated students accepted the White House invitation) and told a temporarily chastened White House press corps: "Prior to this experience, I had held liberal political views which were not always sympathetic with the position of the American military. . . . Well, let me say I learned a lot from this experience. To you, President Reagan, thank you for bringing us back to the United States." Young Americans for Freedom produced a poster with a photo of the students celebrating their repatriation with the headline: "What's the difference between students in Grenada and hostages in Iran? President Ronald Reagan."

The public agreed. Reagan's pollster, Richard Wirthlin, had been conducting a rolling poll during the span of days that included the Beirut barracks bombing and the Grenada invasion. Reagan's approval rating had slumped during the forty-eight hours following the Beirut catastrophe but rebounded after Grenada. Suddenly Speaker O'Neill and other leading Democrats changed their tune, with O'Neill now saying that Reagan was "justified" in taking action. The ultimate political success of Grenada led Reagan and others to proclaim (not for the last time) that the Vietnam syndrome was over.

The success of the Grenada invasion also blunted the blow from the Beirut bombing and postponed the political backlash over Reagan's Lebanon policy. When Reagan went on TV three days after Grenada to talk about both issues, he couldn't help poking at the de facto isolationism of contemporary liberals: "You know, there was a time when our national security was based on a standing army here within our own borders and shore batteries of artillery along our coasts, and, of course, a navy to keep the sea lanes open for the shipping of things necessary to our well-being. The world has changed. Today, our national security can be threatened in faraway places. It's up to all of us to be aware of the strategic importance of such places and to be able to identify them."

Reagan was greeted as a hero when he later visited Grenada, where free elections resumed in 1984. Nicaraguan President Daniel Ortega compared Reagan's trip to Grenada to Adolf Hitler's entry into Vienna after the German occupation of Austria in 1936. There is evidence that the Sandinistas were genuinely frightened, however. Grenada marked the first time that American military force had been used to roll back a Communist government. If it could be done once, it might be done again—or at least so thought the Sandinistas. When word reached Reagan that Castro was musing that Cuba might be next, Reagan said to Robert McFarlane, "That's fine. They might be."[79] The Nicaraguans took no chances. Sandinista *comandante* Tomás Borge called up the American ambassador with the message that if the United States ever wanted to evacuate Americans from Nicaragua, all the United States had to do was call and the Sandanistas would help facilitate it.

The significance of the Grenada invasion cannot be overstated. It conveyed what Churchill liked to call a "moral effect" out of proportion with the small scale of the enterprise. The military operation ranked alongside Reagan's firing of the air traffic controllers in 1981 for its sobering effect on world perception of Reagan's toughness. It removed the last lingering doubts in Europe about America's staying power, which, despite Reagan's rhetoric and defense buildup, persisted. In the spring of 1983, Stephen Haseler, leader of Britain's Social Democratic Party, put his finger on the matter: "There have not been, to put it bluntly, any clear-cut American *victories*, specific events which are widely seen to 'tilt the ground' decisively in America's direction."[80] With Grenada, America finally had an unambiguous win for the scoreboard.

*   *   *

IN THE MIDDLE of the growing crises of Lebanon and Grenada in mid-October, Bill Clark decided to step down as national security adviser. Clark had been talking with Reagan about leaving since January. The constant friction between Shultz and Weinberger, and the relentless undercutting Clark received from James Baker and Mike Deaver, who abetted a ferocious media campaign against Clark, had worn him to the breaking point, and, in his own view, diminished his ability to serve Reagan adequately in the post. The NSC process was becoming dysfunctional again. Clark wanted to return to his quiet life as a rancher in California and had never intended to stay in Washington beyond two years. Reagan had prevailed upon him to stay on as national security adviser at the end of 1982, and now convinced him to replace James Watt as secretary of the interior, which Clark found more agreeable. Conservatives inside and outside the White House were dismayed at his departure from NSC. Jeane Kirkpatrick said, "It is an unmitigated disaster for him to leave. That decision shouldn't have been made. And, once made, it should have been rescinded."

Clark's departure set in motion another power struggle. Baker and Deaver saw an opportunity to solidify their power over Meese, and Reagan initially decided to name Baker his new national security adviser and Deaver to be Baker's replacement as chief of staff. But when confronted with ferocious opposition from Clark, Meese, Casey, Kirkpatrick, and Weinberger,

Reagan changed his mind, much to the annoyance and disappointment of Baker and Deaver. ("You don't have enough confidence in me to make me chief of staff!" an angry Deaver shouted at Reagan in the Oval Office.) The opposition contained an element of payback. A few months before, Baker and Deaver had attempted to enlist Clark in an intrigue to ease out Meese, but miscalculated; Clark sided firmly with Meese and scuttled the plan. Casey, Meese, and others urged Reagan to select Kirkpatrick as Clark's NSC replacement, but Shultz objected.

Faced with these irreconcilable factions, Reagan chose Clark's deputy, Robert McFarlane, as the compromise pick to be national security adviser, which ensured that the Pentagon–State Department and Weinberger-Shultz feuds would continue. McFarlane, a Marine veteran, had a quiet demeanor that led some to dismiss him as "a quintessential staff man." New Right activist Paul Weyrich disparaged McFarlane as having been "created by God to disappear into crowds," but this was unfair and inaccurate. Michael Ledeen, among others, discerned McFarlane's "distinctly hawkish instincts" that comported with Reagan's hard line side. But he lacked Clark's personal ties to Reagan that made Clark so effective.[81]

"It was an unhappy day all around," Reagan wrote in his diary of the staff discord. Later in his memoirs, Reagan wrote, "My decision not to appoint Jim Baker as national security adviser, I suppose, was a turning point for my administration, although I had no idea at the time how significant it would prove to be."[82]

*   *   *

IN THE AFTERMATH of the harsh rhetoric of the spring and summer, the KAL 007 incident, and the invasion of Grenada, the year now reached its climax—and what is said to have been the most dangerous moment in U.S.-Soviet relations since the Cuban missile crisis of 1962. As the deployment of U.S. missiles in Europe approached, some evidence suggests that the Soviets believed the United States was on the brink of launching a surprise nuclear attack and that the Soviet Union may have pondered a preemptive attack of its own.

It almost happened by accident. In the middle of the night in Moscow on September 26, a launch warning alarm went off at Serpukhov-15, an underground early warning command center. Soviet satellites linked to their early warning computers flashed that five American Minuteman ICBMs were in flight heading for Soviet territory. An American surprise nuclear attack was under way. The commanding officer on duty, forty-four-year-old Lieutenant Colonel Stanislav Petrov, later said, "I had a funny feeling in my gut" that it was a false alarm. He delayed passing the warning up the chain of command while he cross-checked with ground-based radar, which showed nothing. Soviet early warning officers were trained to expect that any American attack would be massive. "When people start a war, they don't start it with only five missiles," Petrov recalled thinking. Nonetheless, senior Soviet commanders later sharply questioned and second-guessed Petrov for not promptly alerting Moscow. Eventually the false alarm was traced to defective computer software that misread a satellite reading of a reflection of the sun on cloud tops.[83]

That was not the only worrisome glitch in the Soviet nuclear command and control system. At the time of this incident, the Soviets were still redesigning a remote firing control system comparable to the president's nuclear suitcase, known as the "football." To remedy the lack of command mobility for Soviet leaders, Moscow was developing an automated launch system for its massive ICBM force—the Soviets called it the "Death Grip" system—that would ensure the destruction of the United States even if the United States decapitated the Soviet command structure in a first strike.

From November 2 through 11—at the same moment the American Pershing and cruise missiles were to begin arriving in Europe—the NATO member countries scheduled an extensive military exercise spanning an area from Norway to Turkey and involving more than three hundred thousand military personnel. Code-named Able Archer, this exercise differed from periodic NATO exercises of the past in that it was to involve NATO heads of state, including President Reagan, in nuclear-release simulations. The Soviets feared Able Archer was a pretext for a surprise American attack.

That the Soviets found this threat plausible perhaps came from reflecting on their own war planning; in June 1982 the Soviets had conducted a full-scale simulation of their European war plan, which consisted of a seven-hour nuclear war against the United States and Western Europe. The Soviet war plan called for using exercises as a cover for building up to an actual offensive attack. Surely, Moscow thought, the West would use the same ruse. (In addition, the Soviets conducted nineteen nuclear weapons tests in 1983, along with multiple tests for several new types of missiles.)

There are several tantalizing aspects to this episode that remain controversial among scholars and inside observers. The first concerns Andropov's paranoia about an American attack, which his defense minister, Dmitri Ustinov, fully shared.[84] Although available minutes of Politburo meetings from

1983 show the Soviets fearing that the West was gaining political advantage, there were voices of sobriety arguing that the United States would never launch a suicidal first strike. At a Politburo meeting in May, where Andropov rambled about "Reagan's anti-Soviet, militaristic intentions" and claimed that "an anti-Soviet coalition is being formed out there," Andrei Gromyko argued, "The United States, as is known, is talking about the fact that they can only strike in response to aggression. I think that they without enough reason wouldn't dare to use nuclear missiles. Against the first strike are also Canada, England, France, and West Germany."[85] Anatoly Dobrynin, undoubtedly reflecting the awareness of perceptive Soviet leaders, said that "the existing political and social structure of the United States was the best guarantee against an unprovoked first strike against us."[86] While Dobrynin noted that every Soviet leader since Khrushchev had worried seriously about an American attack, "I personally never believed that any president was ever planning a nuclear attack."

But Dobrynin was isolated from Politburo deliberations and only learned inadvertently that Andropov had urgently ordered his intelligence services in the United States to look for signs of an imminent attack. KGB agents were tasked with monitoring U.S. military bases at home and abroad; counting the number of windows with lights on at the Pentagon, as if this would be an indication of serious war planning; monitoring blood banks and meatpacking plants in Britain and the United States to see if supplies were being stockpiled; and befriending Western bankers and clergymen, supposing that financiers and religious leaders somehow would have advance knowledge of a decision for war. Agents received reprimands from Moscow if they didn't submit semiweekly reports on the metrics for "abnormal activity" in Western government and defense bureaus. "It can be assumed," one of the KGB communiqués to its agents read, "that the period of time from the moment when the preliminary decision for [a nuclear first strike] is taken up to the order to deliver the strike will be of very short duration, possibly 7 to 10 days."[87] Near the end of Able Archer on November 8 or 9, Moscow sent an urgent message to KGB officers in the West stepping up surveillance demands to their maximum level, erroneously reporting that U.S. and NATO military bases had gone on high alert.

A number of persistent American actions lent a small amount of verisimilitude to Soviet paranoia. Beyond the overt episodes, such as the Grenada invasion and the arming of the Contras and the Afghan *mujahadeen,* both the U.S. Navy and Air Force had conducted psychological operations (psy-op) missions to probe Soviet military weaknesses and responses. In one unpublicized episode, navy attack submarines shadowed Soviet submarines and according to a prearranged plan pinged with active sonar every Soviet sub at the same time to demonstrate our tracking capabilities. The navy had also worked out ways of avoiding Soviet ocean surveillance systems and had conducted surprise exercises close to Soviet territory.[88] In the murkier field of covert intelligence, the CIA had confounded the KGB's aggressive attempts to steal advanced Western technology—as many as five thousand Soviet military components used stolen or copied Western technology, according to a 1985 assessment—by surreptitiously supplying false or defective blueprints and computer programming code. One sabotaged software package led to an enormous explosion of the Siberian natural gas pipeline. Before long the Soviets grew to distrust the products of their own intelligence nets.[89]

These capabilities were no doubt unsettling to the Soviets. As a CIA analyst reviewing the period wrote: "The Soviets had learned a disturbing lesson about what Washington *could* do in a wartime situation or other crisis. . . . Moscow did not know what the U.S. *would* do."[90] When U.S. overseas military bases went on a higher state of alert in late October following the Beirut bombing, the Soviets took it as one more sign of possible attack and accordingly raised the alert status of Warsaw Pact forces in Poland and East Germany. The urgent message to overseas KGB posts ordering a superalert followed in early November.[91] The alert status of forces on Soviet territory remains a matter of speculation. It was known at the time that Soviet combat flight operations had been suspended between November 4 and 9 (the middle of Able Archer) and that the Soviet Fourth Air Army had increased its readiness status. According to some accounts, Soviet forces began preparations for a retaliatory nuclear strike. Senior Soviet officials, including Gorbachev, subsequently said that they were unaware of heightened alert status, though these demurrals should not necessarily be taken at face value.[92]

Even without the behind-the-scenes drama over Able Archer, in public comments throughout the fall a common theme emerged: U.S.-Soviet relations were at their most dangerous level since the Cuban missile crisis. Soviet spokesman Georgi Arbatov told a reporter that "the situation is worse now than at any time since the Cuban missile crisis."[93] George Kennan said that the situation had "the familiar characteristics, the unfailing characteristics, of a march toward war—that and nothing else." French president François Mitterrand said, "[T]he present situation is comparable to the Cuban Missile Crisis." Russian scholar Suzanne Massie, who was shortly to begin quietly advising Reagan on Soviet affairs, recalled meeting in Moscow with a high-ranking KGB official who masqueraded as a cultural specialist. "You don't know how close war is!" he told Massie. Massie returned to Washington to convey the message that "the heated Soviet reaction was much more than the usual Soviet truculence, that they felt cornered, and that it was an extremely dangerous time."[94] Some American observers adopted the Soviet line. Princeton Sovietologist Stephen Cohen said: "All evidence indicates that the Reagan administration has abandoned both containment and détente for a very different objective: destroying the Soviet Union as a world power and possibly even its Communist system. [This is a] potentially fatal form of Soviet-phobia . . . a pathological rather than a healthy response to the Soviet Union."

Here we should take note of an important asymmetry between the strategic outlook of the Soviet Union and the West. For the West, the lesson of Munich was the dominant background against which superpower relations were conducted. Never again would the Western democracies capitulate to the political demands of totalitarians or allow an imbalance of military capability to tempt a dictatorship. For the Soviets, the looming background for their approach to superpower relations was not Munich in 1938 but Hitler's surprise attack of June 1941. Marshal Sergei Akhromeyev, the Soviet chief of staff at the time, commented: "Soviet military doctrine can be summed up as follows: 1941 shall never be repeated."[95] In 1941, the Soviets had missed or misinterpreted the signs of Hitler's impending invasion; now they proceeded according to a worst-case scenario.

The new U.S. national security adviser, Robert McFarlane, recognized the Soviets' apprehension about Able Archer, which contributed to the ultimate decision not to have Reagan participate in the NATO exercise (the White House instead scheduled Reagan for a trip to the Far East). "I had serious misgivings about approving the drill as originally planned; there was concern with how Moscow would perceive such a realistic drill," McFarlane told political scientist Beth Fischer, one of the first scholars to delve into this crucial episode.[96]

But there is another aspect of this episode that bears scrutiny, and it concerns Reagan's attitude toward his commander-in-chief responsibilities. Although Reagan had been briefed, as are all incoming presidents, on how to operate the command authority card he kept in his pocket for activating the nuclear "football" to transmit launch codes, he had waited *at least a year and a half into his presidency* before he participated in a complete briefing and rehearsal of the actual operating plan for a nuclear war. SIOP (Single Integrated

Operating Plan) was the protocol for targeting and decision making in the event of a war with the Soviets, and it was customary for presidents to participate in SIOP rehearsals as the plan was periodically modified. So strong was Reagan's aversion to thinking about nuclear war that he kept finding excuses to avoid scheduling a full SIOP briefing, much to the dismay of his aides.[97] Beth Fischer noted, "Reagan was nearly the first modern president not to receive the SIOP briefing."[98] A week after sitting out Able Archer, which was merely a European-theater version of a full-dress SIOP exercise, Reagan received an update of the SIOP plan, and he described it in his diary as "sobering."

A complete SIOP briefing is undoubtedly a grim exercise. It includes explaining the various preprogrammed strike options from which a president might have to choose under intense pressure, including the targets to be destroyed and the number of casualties that would be inflicted. These plans are among the most closely held military secrets, but most strike options involved the simultaneous launch of as many as 4,200 warheads.[99] Above all, the SIOP thought process made clear that it would be very difficult to control escalation, but to have any hope of limiting a nuclear war, a president would need full command of the SIOP options. A conventional analytical mind like Richard Nixon or Jimmy Carter or Bill Clinton probably found SIOP exercises to be an abstract potentiality and duly compartmentalized them to mitigate their mental horror, though we do know that the hardheaded Henry Kissinger once recoiled from the subject, saying in an SIOP meeting in 1973 that "to have the only option that of killing 80 million people is the height of immorality." For the anecdotally oriented, highly imaginative Reagan, a dress rehearsal was probably as vivid as the real thing, and we know that back in the late 1970s Reagan lamented that the strategic situation of the United States paralyzed the president between unacceptable choices—surrender or self-destruction.

While some of Reagan's own aides privately doubted whether, in the face of a real Soviet attack, he would give the order to retaliate, both our allies and the public discounted Reagan's repeated indications of his sincere abhorrence of nuclear weapons. Even with the benefit of hindsight, the opening of classified materials, and the publication of several fine studies on the subject, it remains difficult to square in the same person the seemingly contradictory positions of, on one hand, pursuing a large arms buildup and employing aggressive rhetoric about an adversary and, on the other, a sincere desire for productive negotiations to *abolish* nuclear weapons.[100]

An additional dimension of Reagan's outlook deepens the mystery, and this centers on his occasional mention of the biblical Armageddon. As far back as his governorship in California, friends and acquaintances recall Reagan remarking about how biblical prophecies of the end times were falling into place.[101] During the 1980 campaign Reagan had said to evangelical broadcaster Jim Bakker, "We may be the generation that sees Armageddon." Liberals who found Reagan's mention of Armageddon to be disturbing would have been apoplectic had they known of his more private thoughts. After Israel bombed the Iraqi nuclear reactor in June 1981, he wrote in his diary: "I swear I believe Armageddon is near." In February 1983 he wrote to his former speechwriter Peter Hannaford: "Lately I've been wondering about some older prophecies—those having to do with Armageddon. Things that are news today sound an awful lot like what was predicted would take place just prior to 'A' Day." Reagan knew this was extraordinarily sensitive, as he added: "Don't quote me."[102] Reagan's speculations about the details of the "end times" are a matter of conjecture. It is certainly possible to infer that avoiding Armageddon was prominent in Reagan's underlying statecraft. Is it also possible that part of his aversion to rehearsing nuclear war stemmed from fearing that such a task might implicate him in the role of the anti-Christ?[103]

Matters reached a head when a disturbing report came in from London. British intelligence had recruited the KGB's Oleg Gordievsky as an agent, and Gordievsky told of the Soviet fear of an imminent Western attack and the heightened alert status. Although Soviet defectors tended to embroider their information to increase their prestige and value to the West, U.S. intelligence had noticed a sharp increase in urgent signals traffic from the Warsaw Pact during the Able Archer exercises as well as other signs of Soviet discomfort. The CIA had assumed that this activity was a calculated response intended to show that the Soviets were paying attention, but after examining Gordievsky's claims along with other information, the agency concluded that the situation was more serious than initially thought.[104] For one thing, the CIA had predicted several months before that the Soviets would step up KGB intelligence gathering if they suspected a possible Western attack and, more ominously, that "[i]f [the Soviets] acquired convincing evidence that a U.S. intercontinental strike was imminent, they would try to preempt."[105]

When CIA director Bill Casey brought these findings to Reagan in December, the president was shocked, saying to McFarlane, "I don't see how they could believe that—but it's something to think about."[106] Reagan had been thinking about it, noting in his diary on November 18 that the Soviets were "so paranoid about being attacked." He thought the idea ridiculous: "What the h—l have they got that anyone would want." Still, the fear that the two superpowers could blunder through miscalculation into a nuclear war had been growing in Reagan's mind, making him, as he explained in his memoirs, "even more anxious to get a top Soviet leader in a room alone and try to convince him we had no designs on the Soviet Union." Spurred by these events, a decisive change of tone and direction started to take shape in the White House, though it should be understood that such a shift had always been Reagan's intention. Reagan instructed his foreign policy team to begin drafting a major speech charting a new direction for U.S.-Soviet relations.

To the now-popular view that the world violence and tense atmosphere of the fall shook Reagan into a more accommodating posture must be added the idea that it was beginning to dawn on Reagan and a few of his advisers that a turning point had been reached. At the end of November, Herbert Meyer, vice chairman of the National Intelligence Council within the CIA, wrote a remarkable memorandum to CIA director Casey, titled "Why Is the World So Dangerous?" Meyer's answer was breathtaking: "Present U.S. policies have fundamentally changed the course of history in a direction favorable to the interests and security of ourselves and our allies. . . . [I]f present trends continue, we're going to win the Cold War," probably within twenty years. Meyer thought this prospect made the world a *more* dangerous place in the short run, as surely some perceptive Soviet leaders, "more likely at the third or fourth echelons," recognized that their future was bleak, and as such, some actions, including possibly launching a war, "may no longer be too risky to contemplate." "From now on the Cold War will become more and more of a bare-knuckles street fight." The next few years would be "the most dangerous years we have ever faced."

Meyer admitted that he could offer little hard proof for his conclusion, saying that it required "a leap of the imagination." His most audacious speculation was astounding for its prescience:

> It has long been fashionable to view the Cold War as a permanent feature of global politics, one that will endure through the next several generations at least. But it seems to me more likely that President Reagan was absolutely correct when he observed in his Notre Dame speech that the Soviet Union—"one of history's saddest and

most bizarre chapters"—is entering its final pages. We really should take up the President's suggestion to begin planning for a post-Soviet world; the Soviet Union and its people won't disappear from the planet, and we have not yet thought seriously about the sort of political and economic structure likely to emerge.[107]

*   *   *

WHATEVER REAGAN'S PRIVATE doubts about Soviet paranoia and the need for real negotiations, one thing he thought would bring war closer would be the failure to go through with the Euromissile deployment. And there was still one last piece of high political drama before the deployment would be completed. On the eve of the deployment, Hollywood decided to insert itself into the middle of events. ABC television produced a two-hour drama depicting an all-out nuclear war as it would be experienced in Lawrence, Kansas. Hollywood had offered up many nuclear war films before, but never before had a movie depicted the aftermath of a nuclear explosion so graphically or been tied as closely to immediate circumstances.[108]

The Day After was calculated to play off the controversy over the nuclear freeze. After two decades the movie does not hold up well, and not just because of the women's feathered hairstyles. Even its $7 million budget—three times the average cost for a TV movie at that time—couldn't make up for flat acting and the plodding didacticism of its dialogue. Small wonder that the *New York Post* called it "a 100 mega-yawn bomb." Typical was the clichéd use of the barbershop conversation:

CUSTOMER #1: I really don't think either side wants to be the first one to use a nuclear device.

CUSTOMER #2: It's not a question of who, but where. Over whose real estate? Say we explode a nuclear bomb over their troops, on our side. The fallout would drift over to their side.

CUSTOMER #1: They're crazy. How do they think it's going to stop with just one bomb?

BARBER: I'll tell you what crazy is. Crazy is not staying out of other people's business. We shouldn't be over there in the first place.

CUSTOMER #2: The thing that bothers me is that damn launch-on-warning.

CUSTOMER #3: What's that?

CUSTOMER #2: That's when one side tells the other side that they're going to fire their missiles as soon as they think the other guy's missiles are already on the way.

CUSTOMER #3: You know—use 'em or lose 'em.

CUSTOMER #4: What do you really think [are the] chances of something like that happening way out here in the middle of nowhere?

CUSTOMER #3: Nowhere? There's no "Nowhere" anymore.

The movie featured lots of skeletons vaporizing in mushroom clouds, reminded us that cockroaches would be the only guaranteed survivors, and made sure to include John Lithgow, playing the part of a college professor, gravely intoning Einstein's famous dictum that while he didn't know how World War III would be fought, he knew that World War IV would be fought with sticks and stones.[109] Though the movie was politically shallow, ABC attempted to lend it gravitas by hosting a town-hall-style news show immediately after the broadcast, featuring luminaries such as Robert McNamara, Henry Kissinger, and George Shultz.

ABC tried to deny that the movie had any political motive or angle and removed direct references in the film to the Pershing and cruise missile deployment. This fooled no one; the movie's screenwriter, Ed Hume, gave it up, saying, "It's sympathetic with disarmament," while ABC vice president Alfred Schneider incautiously told the *New York Times,* "Graphically you are showing the core of the argument of those who are for the nuclear freeze." *National Review* criticized ABC for making "a $7 million contribution to the faltering Soviet campaign against the deployment of the Pershing II," and Janet Michaud, executive director of the Campaign Against Nuclear War, confirmed *National Review*'s assessment when she said that "ABC is doing a $7 million advertising job for our issue." But just to be sure, nuclear freeze groups spent several hundred thousand dollars on advertising and set up toll-free phone banks to sign up recruits.

Controversy over the movie raged for weeks before its air date on November 20 (it was theatrically released in Europe shortly after), no doubt to ABC's delight, since this was ratings sweeps period. A nine-year-old girl in Kansas City sent a letter to Reagan suggesting that the United States and Soviet Union exchange workers who would dismantle the nuclear arsenal of the other nation. Somehow the Associated Press thought this frivolous missive worthy of a national wire story. The mayor of Lawrence, Kansas, wrote to the president offering to host a summit between Reagan and Andropov. Nuclear freeze groups obtained advance copies of the movie and organized their favorite device, the teach-in, in hundreds of churches and community centers around the country. ABC prepared a half million copies of a viewer's guide that, like the movie, implied that nuclear deterrence was a failure. The publicity about the movie generated the second-largest TV audience in history, with an estimated one hundred million tuning in to the broadcast.

The White House was deeply concerned about *The Day After.* Reagan's senior staff got an advance screening more than a month ahead of the broadcast date (Reagan watched it alone at Camp David) and found the experience devastating.[110] Reagan wrote in his diary that it was "profoundly depressing." David Gergen told the Associated Press that the film could be "potentially the most emotionally powerful thing ever shown on American television." White House aides held a series of meetings to come up with a response, and contemplated having Reagan give a TV address to rebut the movie's effect. Attacking ABC directly wouldn't work, the White House thought, so Reagan's aides worked the phones to friendly journalists and had the Republican National Committee distribute talking points to party officials in all fifty states.

The White House needn't have worried to this extent. Reagan aides who had seen the advance screening noticed that the movie had less of an emotional effect on TV; the regular commercial breaks for advertisements greatly mitigated the force of the broadcast. The irony is that ABC had difficulty selling advertising for the movie—except to Alan Cranston's pacifist-oriented presidential campaign—but in the end advertisers couldn't resist the cheap rates (ABC discounted ad prices by 75 percent) offered to reach a Super Bowl–sized audience.[111] Many of these ads for hearty American totems such as pickup trucks and baked goods may have had a calming effect on viewers; the normality of American commerce underscored the hyperbole of the film's tendentious plot. Polls taken before and after the movie's broadcast showed that it had no effect on public opinion about American defense policy.[112] The freeze movement had made its last throw, and lost.

Two days later the West German Bundestag ratified the deployment of Pershing missiles by a final vote of 286–226. The first missiles were uncrated two days after the vote; in all, 108 Pershing and 96 cruise missiles were deployed in West Germany; Britain took 160 cruise missiles; Italy took 112; tiny Belgium and the Netherlands each took 48. The NATO alliance had shown its durability and resolve in the face of massive internal and external pressure. The *New Republic* offered a significant editorial concession to Reagan's leadership: "It is hard to think of a single Democratic candidate for President who would have toughed it out the way Mr. Reagan did."[113]

The Soviets walked out of the Geneva talks the next day, with Marshal Ogarkov charging at a rare Soviet press conference that the United States "would still like to launch a decapitating nuclear first strike." Gromyko blustered to Italian foreign minister Giulio Andreotti that "we will turn Italy into a Pompeii." A few weeks later, the Soviets walked out of two parallel negotiations—on strategic nuclear weapons (START) and the talks to reduce conventional forces in Europe. For the first time in fourteen years, there were no arms control talks under way between the United States and the Soviet Union. Reagan reacted coolly, telling aides, "They'll be back." Meanwhile, he was preparing to send Congress a forceful report on the Soviets' consistent cheating on past arms control agreements.

It was too much for the *Bulletin of Atomic Scientists,* which moved the hands on its "Doomsday Clock" from 11:48 to 11:57.[114] The European press was full of editorials decrying "the new Cold War," as though the old one had ended. *Time* magazine chose Reagan and Andropov as their "men of the year," though in Andropov's case, Kremlinologist Dimitri Simes noted, it was the first time a ghost had been selected for the honor. By year's end Andropov had not been seen in public for nearly six months. The Soviets continued to insist that he was merely suffering from a severe cold, surely the longest-running rhinovirus in medical history. He failed to show up in late December for the annual Communist Party Central Committee meeting, a public spectacle analogous to the president's annual State of the Union appearance in Congress. There was increasing speculation that a succession struggle was under way and some thought that the military was running the country.

In his interview for the year-end issue of *Time,* Reagan reflected this concern:

> There is one new development that I have worried about for some time. That is the extent, lately, to which military leaders in the Soviet Union are, apparently without any coaching or being briefed by the civilian part of government—at least there is no evidence of that— taking it upon themselves to make statements, and rather bellicose statements. There has not, in the past, been evidence of top military leaders going public with attacks on the U.S. and seeming to enunciate policy on their own. We have to be aware of this and pay a little attention to this, to see if they have become a power on their own.

Time also asked Reagan about his "evil empire" statement:

QUESTION: When you made the remark containing the phrase "focus of evil," which certainly nettled the Soviets, did you feel that it was appropriate? Would you make it again?

REAGAN: No, I would not say things like that again, even after some of the things that have been done recently.

CHAPTER 8

REALIGNMENT MANQUÉ

Democrats preferred not to face the evidence that their guiding light of half a century—the New Deal of Franklin Roosevelt and its successor mutations from Truman through Carter and Mondale—had been all but snuffed out by the voters as the preferred framework for governmental policy at the national level.
—JACK GERMOND AND JULES WITCOVER,
WAKE US WHEN IT'S OVER

Those Democrats who are seriously interested in the future of their party should be ready to consider the fact, however unwelcome, that it is the Republicans who in recent years have been appealing to masses of voters who have considered themselves disenfranchised.
—HENRY FAIRLIE, *THE NEW REPUBLIC*, APRIL 25, 1983

NINETEEN EIGHTY-FOUR, the year George Orwell made ominous, is remembered politically as the year of Ronald Reagan's triumphant landslide reelection, in which he won forty-nine states and 59 percent of the popular vote. The magnitude of this win—the fourth-largest landslide in history—obscures the fact that, in contrast to his 1980 victory, Reagan had short coattails. Republicans picked up only fourteen House seats and lost ground in the Senate. In this respect Reagan's landslide was like Nixon's solitary landslide in 1972, and unlike the landslides of FDR in 1936 and Lyndon Johnson in 1964, both of which translated into significant party gains that enabled major policy changes in their aftermath. This anomaly attracted little notice among journalists at the time, and with few exceptions has escaped the scrutiny of political scientists and historians since.[1]

Reagan had better instincts about the matter. At a campaign stop on November 3 in Little Rock, he said:

> I'm telling you quite frankly that if a gypsy were to look into her crystal ball and say, "Mr. President, you can either win easily on Tuesday, or win with fewer votes, but with a Congress that will help you," I would choose the latter, because if we're to solidify our gains, the gains we've made in these past 4 years, we'll need a Congress that will allow us to move forward—a Congress that won't insist on going back to the bad old days and the bad old ways.

This kind of sharp partisan argument was rare, however, and with the outcome of the election beyond doubt by late October, it received little national media attention. Reagan's political team, meanwhile, never incorporated such partisan appeals into the campaign strategy or advertising messages; instead, like Nixon's team in 1972, they campaigned for a personal victory for the president, and a personal victory is exactly what they got. It was a sound, prudent, and sensible political strategy from a conventional point of view. It was also a mistake of historic proportions. The strategy of the 1984 Reagan campaign to run a defensive campaign—the political equivalent of the four-corner stall in basketball—represents one of the greatest lost opportunities in American politics to break the opposition party and bring about a lasting and fundamental realignment. A closer look at the political dynamics of that infamous year shows how and why.

*   *   *

THERE WAS A Groundhog Day element to the beginning of 1984. Once again, Congress and the White House were facing a bleak budget cycle, with a deficit projected for the next fiscal year approaching 5 percent of GDP—a peacetime record. A grim fact was inescapable: the Reagan administration was not having much luck containing the growth of federal spending. Reagan's proposed budget for fiscal year 1985 projected an 8 percent increase in total spending at a time when inflation was less than 4 percent. Much of this was driven by automatic entitlement programs beyond the easy reach of the president, but there was no mood in Congress to reform these programs. Many conservatives were restless. Republican senator William Armstrong of Colorado complained: "What's the sense of having a Republican administration and a Republican Senate if the best we can do is a $200 billion deficit?"

Democrats attempted to make the budget deficit an issue for the upcoming presidential campaign, but Republicans, fearful of playing into the hands of the fairness issue, declined to put up much of a fight about reducing federal spending. Some of Reagan's top aides, such as James Baker, Richard Darman, and David Stockman, felt defensive about the record deficit, since Reagan's 1980 promise to balance the budget by 1984 now looked ludicrous. On January 2, the president's chief economic adviser, Martin Feldstein, sent Reagan a memo (which was promptly leaked to the *Washington Post*) calling for tax increases of up to $50 billion a year for the next three years. Conservatives and supply-siders stepped up their public demand that Feldstein be fired. Senator Bob Dole wanted to reprise his role in the 1982 tax increase, proposing a dollar-for-dollar package of spending cuts and tax increases. Reagan wasn't going to bite on that sucker's deal again. Newt Gingrich complained: "People like Dole and Domenici spend all their time running around trying to feed the liberal welfare state they inherited."

Yet the deficit issue was a lost opportunity. One poll from the time found that 59 percent of the public thought Congress was more responsible than the president for the budget deficit, suggesting the vulnerability of Congress should Reagan have decided to attack. And the White House had a tool in hand for carrying on such an argument. Early in the year the President's Private Sector Survey on Cost Control, chaired by legendary businessman J. Peter Grace, produced a forty-seven-volume, twenty-three-thousand-page report detailing $424 billion in potential savings without cutting any social programs.[2] Calling the federal government "the worst-run enterprise in America," the Grace Commission, as it was known, itemized more than twenty-seven hundred examples of poor management and idiotic waste. The Department of Health and Human Services (HHS) was paying Medicare benefits to more than eight thousand dead people; the army spent $4.20 to issue each payroll check, compared to $1 in the private sector; the Government Printing Office wasted $96 million a year in postage sending publications (including such indispensable titles as *How to Serve Nuts*) to incorrect addresses; the Justice Department failed to deposit seized drug money in interest-bearing accounts; the Veterans Administration spent more than $100 to process a single medical claim, compared to $3 to $6 for private insurance companies. If all the Grace Commission's recommendations were followed, the deficit would fall by half.[3]

Reagan mentioned the Grace Commission findings in his State of the Union speech in January but did not return to the theme in the fall campaign.

The White House staff was never enthusiastic about the Grace Commission. At the announcement of one early meeting, an anonymous White House aide (probably Darman or someone in his office) told the *Washington Post* that he hoped the meeting would be held in Siberia. David Gergen, who left his job as White House communications director at the beginning of 1984, remarked to the media in March, "The [Reagan] Administration in the second term must either raise taxes and stretch out defense increases or face an end to recovery." But the president didn't get the memo. "Stockman & Feldstein plus others want a tax increase," Reagan noted in his diary on January 9. "I think they are wrong as h—l."

The rapidly expanding economy overshadowed deficit anxiety. Unemployment was still above 7 percent but had fallen for thirteen months in a row by the start of the year. Moreover, the recovery had gained so much speed in 1983 that by the end of the year, four million new jobs had been generated, the largest one-year jump in employment in the nation's history. It was more jobs than Canada had created since 1965, more than the British economy had generated between 1950 and 1982, and as many as Japan had created during the entire decade of the 1970s. The Index of Leading Economic Indicators rose in eleven of the twelve months of 1983. As the new year opened, it appeared economic growth was still gaining speed. First-quarter 1984 growth came in at an annual rate of 7.2 percent (for the full year, real GDP growth would clock in at 6.8 percent, the fastest rate of growth in thirty-four years); housing starts were at their highest level in six years, up 28 percent over a year earlier. Inflation remained tame, running at less than 3 percent.

Looking ahead to the election, Dan Rather gratuitously pointed out on the *CBS Evening News* that by the end of a second term Reagan would be seventy-eight, the same age at which Churchill was "senile" but presiding over the decline of the British Empire in the mid-1950s. But more Americans took in Reagan on the cover of *Parade* magazine lifting weights in the White House gym shortly before his seventy-third birthday in February. *Parade* skipped over the fact that the president had begun wearing a hearing aid in one ear. Since the assassination attempt in 1981, Reagan had added nearly two inches to his chest from his daily workouts on a weight machine. The bulletproof vest he wore under his shirt for public appearances added to his upper-body profile. Reagan's mood matched the vigor of the economy. He wrote in his diary in late January: "I'm embarrassed even writing this but I feel good at the same time. There is a respect for the U.S. abroad that wasn't there just a few years ago." A few days later, on January 29, Reagan formally announced his candidacy for reelection.

With the economy clearly heading into a vigorous boom during the second half of 1983, Reagan was now a strong favorite for reelection. A *New York Times*/CBS News poll taken early in the new year found that for the first time in nearly a decade a majority of Americans thought things were going well and would improve in the future.[4] Reagan's approval rating was up sharply; one poll had his approval rating at 56 percent, the highest for a fourth-year president since Eisenhower in 1956. "This recovery was unprecedented," public opinion specialists Charles Ostrom and Dennis Simon wrote in *Public Opinion Quarterly*. "For the first time in the history of the Gallup poll, a president fell below 40% and then rose to *sustain* a level above 50%."[5]

The coming year would see a number of milestones. Pete Rose got his four-thousandth hit, and Reggie Jackson hit his five-hundreth home run. Milk cartons became bulletin boards for photos of missing children. Chrysler, rejuvenated from its near-death condition in 1979 thanks to large, federally guaranteed bank loans (which had been repaid ahead of schedule), brought the first minivan to the market, the Dodge Caravan. Bruce Springsteen rejected a large offer from Chrysler to allow his hit single "Born in the USA" to be used in an ad campaign for the Caravan. Reagan would make reference to "Born in the USA" in his fall campaign, much to the annoyance of the very Left-minded Springsteen. Cell phones were starting to become available, but at a retail cost of several thousand dollars. Clarkson University in New York became one of the first institutions of higher education to require that all incoming freshmen purchase a computer. Sometime around midyear, McDonald's sold its fifty-billionth hamburger. The median price of a new home reached $100,000 for the first time. *The One Minute Manager,* a 106-page speed read that was perfect for the short attention span of fast-paced yuppie junior executives, was a surprise bestseller. *Newsweek* declared 1984 to be the "Year of the Yuppie." Major publications such as the *New Republic* began imitating a fashion that began in academia of using *she* instead of *he* as a generic pronoun. *The Cosby Show,* starring comedian Bill Cosby, was the top-rated TV show; in portraying blacks as middle-class professionals, it was distinct from *The Jeffersons* in the 1970s, and was taken as a sign of the declining salience of race in American culture, despite the histrionics of Jesse Jackson. In Hollywood, twenty-seven-year-old first-time director James Cameron was readying a high-concept time travel story to be called *The Terminator,* and the production studio was considering O. J. Simpson for the starring role. Simpson was rejected because, according to a studio executive, "People wouldn't have believed a nice guy like O.J. playing the part of a ruthless killer." Instead they cast Austrian bodybuilder Arnold Schwarzenegger, fresh off his first major movie role in *Conan the Barbarian.*

*   *   *

WHILE *THE TERMINATOR* represented the latest iteration of the recurrent phobia about technology and progress that stretched back at least to Mary Shelley's *Frankenstein,* the rollover of the calendar to 1984 made it inevitable that another such dystopian vision would become topical—George Orwell's famous novel of that year. A brief excursion into the intellectual contortions that the book's anniversary prompted offers a useful window into the decayed Cold War–weary state of Western thought on the eve of Reagan's reelection campaign.

Intellectuals on the left tried to leverage Orwell's socialist sympathies to suggest that he would have been a Cold War dissenter (even though Orwell may have originated the term), an implausible case that would collapse completely in the 1990s when it emerged that Orwell had quietly named names of Communist sympathizers to Britain's counterintelligence service.[6] There was the predictable refrain that *1984* was "really about us too," but it takes a high degree or moral obtuseness to equate the situation in the United States with Communist totalitarianism. The West German author Johanno Strasser was up to the job, writing: "Whoever reads Orwell's book again nowadays cannot comfort himself so easily any more with the thought that all this has nothing to do with the reality in which we live. . . . Is this not the world that is planned and developed in the head offices of large corporations and in government bureaucracies? . . . [W]e must read Orwell quite differently nowadays. The menace hovering over the eighties is not total dominance by some fanatical party elite, but rather the progressive undermining of democracy by the silent dictatorship of forces inherent in our society."[7] Other writers pointed to Watergate as an example of Orwell's nightmare come to life in the West, conveniently forgetting that America's constitutional order quickly and peaceably righted itself.

This is exactly the kind of obfuscating exegesis that Orwell set himself against during his lifetime. Writing in *Harper's,* Norman Podhoretz argued that Orwell would have become a neoconservative: "If he were alive today, he would find the very ideas and attitudes against which he so fearlessly argued more influential than ever in left-wing centers of opinion: that the freedoms of the West are relatively unimportant as compared with other values; that war is the greatest of all evils; that nothing is worth fighting or dying for; and that the Soviet Union is basically defensive and peaceful."[8]

Ordinarily these kinds of arguments cannot be resolved, but in this case popular culture trumped *arguendo Orwell* in the most unlikely of venues—the Super Bowl. Apple Computer placed a lavishly produced sixty-second ad during the third quarter of Super Bowl XVIII in late January, directed by Ridley Scott, fresh off his feature film triumphs *Alien* and *Blade Runner*. The ad featured an auditorium of gray-clad men with shaved heads listening hypnotically to an Orwellian Big Brother figure on a large theater screen:

> Today, we celebrate the first glorious anniversary of the Information Purification Directives. We have created, for the first time in all history, a garden of pure ideology. Where each worker may bloom, secure from the pests purveying contradictory thoughts. Our Unification of Thought is more powerful a weapon than any fleet or army on earth. We are one people. With one will, one resolve, one cause. Our enemies shall talk themselves to death and we will bury them with their own confusion. We shall prevail![9]

The trance is broken when a woman in orange shorts and white tank top (the only character in color) runs to the front of the auditorium and throws a sledgehammer through the theater screen, whereupon the voice-over narrative says, "On January 24, Apple Computer will introduce Macintosh. And you'll see why 1984 won't be like *1984*."

The ad almost did not air. Some of Apple's board of directors were nervous about the ad and wanted to scrap it, but Apple's management went ahead. It was an obvious slap at IBM (though Apple denied this): Big Blue's new mainframe was supposed to be the technological equivalent of Orwell's Big Brother. Though the ad ran nationally only this one time, *Advertising Age* would later name the spot "Commercial of the Decade." Ironically, in 1984 there began to come into view the liberating effect of technology, which would play a role in the downfall of the Soviet tyranny that had inspired Orwell's dark vision.

That the argument over Orwell's meaning and legacy was not merely a literary and intellectual sideshow was made evident in February when the Oxford Union hosted a debate on the question of the moral equivalence of East and West: "Resolved—that there is no moral difference between the world policies of the United States and the Soviet Union." Ordinarily an Oxford debate would pass without much notice in the wider world (excepting the infamous wrongheaded resolution from 1933 that "this House will in no circumstances fight for King and Country"), but one of the debaters against the resolution happened to be the defense secretary of the United States, Caspar Weinberger. Against the wishes of the State Department and some White House political advisers, Weinberger accepted the Oxford Union's invitation, thereby ensuring that the event would receive wide attention.

Weinberger showed up in the Oxford Union standard black tie, while his principal opponent, the Marxist historian E. P. Thompson, disdained formal wear and appeared in his professor's garb instead. Thompson told Weinberger that he considered black tie another mark of class distinction, and Weinberger scored the first debating point before the formal program began by replying, "On the contrary; my father used to say that black tie was the most democratic of all costumes, because everybody wore exactly the same thing."

Thompson and his team, which included a rising Oxford student named Andrew Sullivan, made the usual leftist point that U.S. support for authoritarian rulers such as Ferdinand Marcos in the Philippines was no different from Soviet rule over Eastern Europe, along with the standard refrain about militarism. Weinberger effectively parried by noting that a debate such as this was not possible in the Soviet Union, and that democratic nations could control their foreign policies through the ballot box. The audience voted Weinberger the winner, rejecting the motion by a vote of 271–232. The frivolous posturing of 1933 was not going to be repeated. It was a significant win in the arena of public argument.

*   *   *

THERE WAS AN obvious irony to Weinberger's core argument that democracies can change their foreign policy through the ballot box. This was exactly what most concerned Reagan's political team. Polls showed continuing nervousness among voters about Reagan's foreign policy acumen. One Gallup poll early in the year reported that 49 percent disapproved of Reagan's handling of foreign policy, with only 38 percent approving. (The same polls, however, showed that a majority of voters agreed with Reagan's assessment of the Soviet Union as an "evil empire.") A bumper sticker popular with the Left read: REAGAN '84/ WAR '85. Pollster Daniel Yankelovich commented: "Reagan has proved that he can be tough, but he has not yet proved that he can be a peacemaker. It is unlikely that this issue will escape bitter and partisan debate in an election year."

Reagan, however, was about to move on to a new phase of his diplomatic strategy that would begin to assuage public anxiety. On January 16, he gave a major televised speech (broadcast at 10:00 a.m. so that it could be viewed in prime time in Europe) in which he broke noticeably with the tough tone of his speeches from the previous year. Its overall rhetorical emphasis was on conciliation and flexibility. For example: "We must and will engage the Soviets in dialogue as serious and constructive as possible. . . . We will negotiate in good faith. Whenever the Soviet Union is ready to do likewise, we'll meet them halfway."

As Reagan explained in his diary entry for that day, "The speech was carefully crafted by all of us to counter Soviet propaganda that we are not sincere in wanting arms reductions or peace." The reference to "all of us" is significant, because Reagan wrote the peroration at the end of the speech that was its most memorable part: an imaginary conversation between an American couple and a Soviet couple in which the fundamental political differences between the two regimes dissolved into irrelevance.

> Just suppose with me for a moment that an Ivan and an Anya could find themselves, oh, say, in a waiting room, or sharing a shelter from the rain or a storm with a Jim and Sally, and there was no language barrier to keep them from getting acquainted. Would they then debate the differences between their respective governments? Or would they find themselves comparing notes about their children and what each other did for a living? Before they parted company, they would probably have touched on ambitions and hobbies and what they wanted for their children and problems of making ends meet. And as they went their separate ways, maybe Anya would be saying to Ivan, "Wasn't she nice? She also teaches music." Or Jim would be telling Sally what Ivan did or didn't like about his boss. They might even have decided they were all going to get together for dinner some evening soon. Above all, they would have proven that people don't make wars. People want to raise their children in a world without fear and without war. . . . Their common interests cross all borders.

This vintage Reagan fable is clearly problematic—while Ivan would tell Jim what he didn't like about his boss, would he feel as free to tell Jim what he didn't like about his *rulers*? It was this and other qualities that led observers across the political spectrum to interpret the speech as a pure election-year gambit to address Reagan's political vulnerabilities on foreign affairs. "Ronald Reagan is making fools of the American people," the *New Republic* editorialized about the speech. "Politics is all that the President's reasonableness is about. . . . The public knows when it is being pandered to."[10] The *Nation* huffed: "No Nielsen [rating] will say whether it played in Novosibirsk, but the show must have got good numbers in Nebraska."[11] Henry Kissinger would write a while later that "the administration is now involved in an essentially irrevocable process indistinguishable from what used to be called détente."

This interpretation of the speech was understandable, given that Reagan's "evil empire" phrase was still reverberating in countless media treatments of Reagan and the Soviets (and would continue as a dominant media theme for the rest of Reagan's presidency). No one outside a tight circle of aides knew of Reagan's growing worry over the possibility of an accidental war and his sincere—and intense—desire to engage a Soviet leader in face-to-face talks. The January 16 speech had, in fact, been in the works at least since November and is said to have been intended for delivery before the end of the year, but was delayed at the recommendation of Mrs. Reagan's astrologist.[12]

Moreover, a close reading of the speech indicates that Reagan saw that his grand strategy of waiting patiently for the rebuilding of American credibility had paid off and that he was ready to move on to a new phase. The speech opened with a recitation of the Soviet arms buildup of the 1970s, now matched by the United States. Reagan then said: "America's recovery may have taken Soviet leaders by surprise. They may have counted on us to keep weakening ourselves. They've been saying for years that our demise was inevitable. They said it so often they probably started believing it. Well, if so, they can see now they were wrong." To reverse Reagan's famous formula, now that the strength part of the equation had been addressed, it was possible to move on to the peace side of the ledger.

The Soviets, not for the first or last time, adopted the same line as the Western press and dismissed the speech as a political stunt, despite Reagan's various direct overtures to open a quiet back-channel means of resuming diplomacy. The following day the Conference on Disarmament in Europe opened in Stockholm, where Soviet foreign minister Andrei Gromyko delivered what George Shultz called "a truly brutal speech" excoriating the United States: "The incumbent U.S. administration is an administration thinking in categories of war and acting accordingly. Naturally, those who have assumed a course of war have no interest in reaching arms limitation agreements." In a previously scheduled five-hour face-to-face meeting at the Soviet embassy, Shultz told Gromyko that his language was "outrageous," "beyond the pale," and "unacceptable." "It was an ugly dialogue," Shultz recalled, but Gromyko blinked on a couple of points: he agreed to return to Mutual Balanced Force Reduction (MBFR) talks on conventional forces, and he also opened the door a crack to resuming missile negotiations. Shultz sensed that the Soviets were looking for a way of coming back to the table without losing face. Despite the lingering bitterness, "[T]his had been my best meeting with Gromyko by miles," Shultz judged afterward.[13]

The question of where U.S.-Soviet relations were headed was made freshly acute just a few weeks later, on February 9, when Yuri Andropov died. Reagan again declined to make the trip to Moscow for the funeral; some of his political advisers thought it would seem like a crass election-year gesture, while Reagan said simply, "I don't want to honor that prick."[14] So Vice President Bush had to pack his bags again. The Left used Andropov's death as an occasion to blame Reagan for the tense state of relations. The *Nation* editorialized: "If Yuri Andropov's fifteen-month leadership of the Soviet nation was anything more than a blip on the world historical screen, it was because of the extraordinary explosion of American enmity in that period." George McGovern, then in the midst of making a nostalgic run for the Democratic presidential nomination, channeled the *Nation* with this encomium to the former KGB chief: "It is a modern tragedy that one of the Soviet Union's most intelligent and realistic leaders has served and died during the Administration of the most ill-informed and dangerous man ever to occupy the White House. We can only hope and pray that a realistic leader will come forward in the Soviet Union and that the American people will end Ronald Reagan's reign of error in 1984."

Seventy-three-year-old Konstantin Chernenko was quickly anointed as Andropov's successor. His background was every bit as unnerving as Andropov's: Chernenko had been a commissar in Stalin's NKVD secret police organization between 1938 and 1941, where, according to some accounts, he presided over several mass executions. Though not quite as obviously frail as Andropov had been, he suffered from emphysema and had trouble standing through Andropov's lengthy funeral ceremonies. A popular joke around Moscow had it that Chernenko's staff held a mirror to his nose every morning to determine if he was still breathing. Kremlin watchers assumed Chernenko was a caregiver, with a younger generation of Politburo members maneuvering for the top job after him. He didn't seem a likely reformer. Chernenko had told the Central Committee in June 1983: "There are some truths which are not subject to revision, problems that have been solved long ago and unequivocally." But Vice President Bush and the American delegation that met with Chernenko found him lucid, loquacious, and forthcoming about negotiating with the United States.

Ten days later Reagan received a letter from Chernenko, warmer in tone than any of Andropov's letters but containing no new concrete ideas. Reagan scribbled in the margin: "I think this calls for a very well thought out reply and not just a routine acknowledgment that leaves the status quo as is." Reagan wrote in his diary on March 1 of his "gut feeling" that the time had come for a face-to-face meeting with his Soviet counterpart, and the next day he wrote, "I'm convinced the time has come for me to meet with Chernenko along about July." The State Department produced a seven-page letter for Reagan's signature with the standard Foggy Bottom talking points about negotiating flexibility and proposals for "confidence-building" agreements. Reagan transmitted the letter to Chernenko on March 7 but included a handwritten postscript in which he assured Chernenko that "neither I nor the American people hold any offensive intentions toward the Soviet people" and proclaimed his desire for a summit.[15]

Chernenko—or rather the Foreign Ministry writing in his name—wrote back less than two weeks later, slamming the door on a summit and resuming the frosty tone of Andropov's communiqués. Moscow also rebuffed efforts to open a back channel for quiet diplomacy, rudely treating several American intermediaries whom Shultz had been led to believe would be received seriously. Jack Matlock, then serving on the NSC, observed, "The Soviet leadership had obviously decided not to deal seriously with Reagan during the 1984 election year lest they inadvertently help his campaign for reelection." In fact, the KGB was instructed to do whatever it could to impede Reagan's reelection and attempted a number of dirty tricks worthy of Nixon's campaign goons, including producing carefully doctored tapes of Reagan purporting to threaten U.S. nuclear strikes on our European allies. In May the Soviet Union stepped up the pressure, announcing that it would boycott the Summer Olympics being held in Los Angeles—retaliation for the U.S. boycott of the Moscow Summer Olympics in 1980.

Reagan's overtures for a summit and a back channel for quiet diplomacy had been orchestrated with the strictest secrecy inside the White House to prevent leaks to the media. Meanwhile, Walter Mondale had criticized Reagan for being the first president in decades not to have held a summit with a Soviet leader, saying in January, "If I were President, I'd get on that hot line and I'd say this: 'Dear Mr. Andropov, please meet me in Geneva this afternoon, and let's sit down and do some work to bring some easing of tensions.' " No one outside the White House knew how hard Reagan was trying to do exactly that.

*   *   *

SOVIET RELATIONS WERE not Reagan's only foreign policy vulnerability heading into the election. In February Reagan decided to cut his losses in Lebanon. The Lebanese government and its army were collapsing under the pressure of Syrian-backed Shiite militia violence, and in the aftermath of the Beirut barracks bombing the previous October, U.S. Marines were living underground in dispersed locations, an ineffective fighting force. As the *New Republic* commented, "[T]he President sent in too few Marines to fight and too many to die." American attempts at retaliation for the bombing came to nothing, while Syria killed one American airman and captured another in a halfhearted aerial bombing raid. Reagan suffered the embarrassment of having the airman's release brokered by Jesse Jackson.[16]

More important politically was that the American presence in Lebanon was increasingly unpopular at home. Polls showed rising public opposition to keeping marines in Lebanon, and congressional Democrats, most of whom had voted back in September to authorize the policy for eighteen months, opportunistically changed their mind. Congressional Republicans were also nervous and communicated their anxiety to the White House. (One of the Republicans most vocally apprehensive was freshman Arizona congressman John McCain, who had voted against the House resolution backing the Lebanon deployment.) House Speaker Tip O'Neill, whose support of the mission had been crucial just three months before, now promised to support a House resolution calling for the "prompt withdrawal" of the United States from Lebanon. Reagan initially reacted sharply: "He may be ready to surrender, but I'm not."

But Reagan's foreign policy team had almost unanimously reached the opposite conclusion, including Shultz, who had hitherto been the strongest voice in favor of the American military presence. Lou Cannon records Shultz remarking in a National Security Council meeting, "If I ever say send in the Marines again, somebody shoot me."[17] Reagan reluctantly agreed with his national security team's recommendation that the marines be "redeployed" to navy ships offshore. This term of art fooled no one. "Redeployment" was understood as a euphemism for withdrawal. The last marines left Beirut on February 26.

There is no doubt that ending the unpopular deployment was a short-term political boon to Reagan, but the president understood the costs of withdrawal. Before reversing course Reagan had warned, "If we get out, it means the end of Lebanon. . . . If we cut and run, we'll be sending one signal to terrorists everywhere." The *New Republic,* for once nearly as hawkish as the conservative press, warned that "as with Vietnam and Iran, the United States will also suffer long-term consequences, in terms of shaken confidence among allies and encouragement to U.S. enemies."[18] Over on the right, *Human Events* lamented that "this country has virtually given up the struggle to create a viable, pro-Western Lebanon. . . . The results are likely to be a bitter blow to the West." Indeed, Islamic radicals took to heart the lesson that delivering a blow to American forces would suffice to drive them from the region. In the fullness of time Osama bin Laden and the post-2003 insurgents in Iraq would show that they had learned the lesson.

But the United States didn't have to wait that long for its troubles in Lebanon to intensify. Two weeks after the last marine departed the shores of Beirut, Islamic terrorists kidnapped Jeremy Levin, CNN's Beirut bureau chief. A larger blow hit the following week, when the CIA's station chief, William Buckley, was kidnapped. Over the coming weeks the CIA frantically tried to locate and rescue Buckley, without success. The agency couldn't even manage to track down top Islamic militants implicated in the kidnappings. Twelve more Americans would be kidnapped in Beirut over the coming months; it was a slow-motion Middle East hostage crisis for Reagan.

Reagan had thought he was extricating himself from Lebanon. He would soon recognize that he could not.

* * *

CENTRAL AMERICA WAS the other festering foreign policy problem. In January the Kissinger Commission issued its report, which affirmed three things of particular concern to Reagan: that Central America was a "vital interest" to the United States, that El Salvador should receive increased military assistance, and that Nicaragua was a destabilizing force in the region (the members of the commission had visited Managua and been shocked at the Sandinistas' brazen portrayal of their strategic orientation).[19] Despite the last conclusion, however, the report avoided addressing the "highly controversial question" of Contra aid. Instead, the most eye-grabbing part of the report was its recommendation that the United States devote at least $8 billion in economic aid to Central America over the next five years—a Central American Marshall Plan. The idea was dead on arrival in a supposedly deficit-conscious Congress, though it had the value of calling the bluff of liberals who claimed that addressing economic "root causes" should be the cornerstone of U.S. policy.

In the end the Kissinger Commission report, despite the group's prominent Democratic members, did little to soften liberal opposition to Reagan's Central American policy. Senator Ted Kennedy, for instance, demanded that El Salvador invite the Communist insurgents into a coalition government. Liberal opposition to aiding El Salvador prompted one of Shultz's better-controlled outbursts of anger. Before a House committee in March, Shultz rebuked Democrats who opposed aid: "I really don't understand you people. Here we have an area right next to us which a cross-section of Americans, a bipartisan commission, have studied very carefully, and concluded is in the vital interest of the United States. Now there are problems there, we all know that, and what you're telling me is, 'Because there are problems, let's walk away.' "

Events on the ground would prove decisive. In late March El Salvador held another round of elections, and the centrist government of José Napoleón Duarte—with considerable campaign assistance from the CIA—narrowly held off the surprisingly popular right-wing candidacy of Roberto d'Aubuisson, who was implicated in supporting the death squads that were wreaking havoc on American designs. A d'Aubuisson victory would have provided liberals an excuse to cut off U.S. military aid to El Salvador, but on May 10 House majority leader Jim Wright defied Tip O'Neill and corralled fifty-five Democratic votes in support of continued aid.

Just two weeks after the House approved aid to El Salvador, it voted 241–177 *against* funding the Contras. "Central America has turned into a political game, and Democrats tend to play it irresponsibly," the *New Republic* observed in an editorial. Tip O'Neill referred to the Contras as "marauders, murderers, and rapists." While the Contras were unquestionably guilty of savage violence and disagreeable deeds, it is nonetheless striking that similar behavior by the American-supported Afghan *mujahadeen* did not receive similar scrutiny from liberals in Congress. For that matter, the deplorable human rights record of the Sandinistas got a complete pass from most liberals. (The occasional liberal who spoke out against Sandinista human rights abuses, such as Paul Berman or human rights activist Nina Shea, was greeted with ferocious denunciations from the Left.)

The continuation of Contra aid depended entirely on the Senate. At the end of 1983 a House-Senate conference committee on the budget had restored Contra funding that had been cut off by the House in the spring, but support for Contra aid remained paper-thin. Then, in mid-March, Barry Goldwater, with Pat Moynihan's support, got $21 million in Contra aid approved in the Senate Intelligence Committee by a surprising 14–0 vote. The full Senate would approve Contra aid in early April by a vote of 76–19.

The Contras had become a serious fighting force inside Nicaragua. Their numbers had grown from about one thousand in 1981 to about six thousand by the end of 1983, and they had staged a number of successful sustained offensives (in part because the CIA was resupplying them by air drops), briefly capturing entire towns and holding swaths of territory deep inside Nicaragua. After the U.S. invasion of Grenada—and stiff warnings from the Americans—the Soviets were suddenly less forthcoming with promises of further aid to the Sandinistas and failed to deliver previously promised MiG fighter planes. Late in 1983, the Sandinistas capitulated to a key American demand, agreeing to hold elections late in 1984. Unable to contain his revolutionary bravado, however, a senior Sandinista leader made a speech confessing that the elections were "a nuisance" because "what a revolution really needs is the power to act," such power being "the essence of the dictatorship of the proletariat." Elections, another Sandinista directorate member admitted, "were a tactical tool, a weapon."[20] Such transparency would have made Lenin blush.

The White House did not think time was on its side, and the usual factions debated fiercely how to press the issue to a faster conclusion. Despite Contra successes, there was little chance that they could topple the Sandinistas without direct American intervention, which Reagan privately (but never publicly) ruled out. The State Department wanted to pursue direct negotiations with the Sandinistas, despite a high-ranking Nicaraguan defector who had reliably informed Washington that Sandinista policy regarded "the negotiations process as a tool to buy time for the revolution." Shultz actually made a stop in Nicaragua to meet with Daniel Ortega, though he was not optimistic about success. A group of Central American nations had proposed a regional framework for negotiations that became known as the Contadora process, but the proposal for a freeze on arms shipments and limits on the size of military forces was unacceptable to the Sandinistas. While Contadora was a substantive dead end, it aided the American aim of isolating Nicaragua diplomatically.

The Pentagon proposed massive military exercises near Nicaragua and Cuba. Reagan, showing his usual good sense, asked in an NSC meeting, "How do we stop Castro with *exercises*?" But he approved the plan anyway until Shultz, who was not consulted, threatened to resign after he found out about it following a leak to the *New York Times*.

The CIA had more luck pressing for aggressive covert operations, sponsoring small but effective motorboat attacks on docks and oil storage facilities in Nicaraguan ports. The CIA also began mining Nicaraguan harbors with nonlethal mines designed to frighten foreign ships away. The mines were designed more to damage the courage of shipping insurers than the hulls of the ships themselves. At least seven ships in the Pacific Ocean port of Corinto—Nicaragua's largest—had struck mines, including a Soviet oil tanker, and export goods were beginning to stack up on the docks for want of shipping. But in this success lay the seeds of political catastrophe for Reagan.

In early April, the morning after the Senate approved aid to the Contras, the CIA's mining of Nicaraguan harbors leaked to the press. In their best imitation of Claude Rains in *Casablanca,* senators in both parties professed themselves outraged that the CIA would engage in such behavior, and the Senate voted 84–12 a few days later to condemn the mining. "It's an act of war!" indignant senators complained. Intelligence Committee chairman Goldwater fired off an angry letter to CIA director William Casey that opened with the decorous phrase "I am pissed off!" Moynihan ostentatiously resigned as vice chairman of the Intelligence Committee.

It was typical Capitol Hill theater. Casey had fully briefed the Senate Intelligence Committee on the mining operation, and there had been no objections. Twice in March, according to committee transcripts, Casey had told the committee that "magnetic mines have been placed in the Pacific harbor of Corinto and the Atlantic harbor of El Bluff, as well as the oil terminal at Puerto Sandino." Senators now claimed that Casey had either mumbled or misled them by not saying exactly *who* was laying the mines. Goldwater's excuse was slightly better: he had missed the briefings.

Nicaragua brought a lawsuit against the United States at the World Court, whereupon the administration announced that it would not recognize the World Court's jurisdiction—a position allowed under treaty, but which looked bad in the higher court of international public opinion. (Very few media accounts noted that prior to Nicaragua's case, no Communist nation had ever accepted the World Court's jurisdiction. Some legal scholars argued that the Reagan administration had a strong argument that the mining activities were legal under international law.) More embarrassments were to follow in the months ahead, including disclosure in the fall of a purported assassination manual that the CIA had produced for the Contras.[21]

The result was a collapse in political support for Contra aid. In June the Senate reversed course and rejected further Contra aid by a lopsided 88–1 vote. This time Reagan could not rely on the Senate to bail out his policy in a House-Senate conference committee. More trouble was coming from the House, where a new, much more restrictive Boland Amendment (call it Boland III on your scorecard) was heading toward easy passage. This version of the Boland Amendment prohibited any military assistance to the Contras, direct or indirect, from the CIA or the Pentagon: "During fiscal year 1985, no funds available to the Central Intelligence Agency, the Department of Defense, or any other agency or entity of the United States involved in intelligence activities may be obligated or expended for the purpose or which would have the effect of supporting, directly or indirectly, military or paramilitary operations in Nicaragua by any nation, group, organization, movement or individual." Did these restrictions extend to the president and the White House staff? Such an interpretation would be constitutionally dubious, as it would imply a restriction on the president's ability to conduct diplomacy—for example, forbidding the president from asking a foreign government to provide aid to the Contras. The Boland Amendment was attached to a stopgap twelve-hundred-page continuing resolution necessary to keep the federal government running, and Congress sent it to Reagan in mid-October. Vetoing the bill because of the Boland Amendment would have involved shutting down the government three weeks before the election.

One reason Reagan didn't take the risk of vetoing Boland in the fall was that a fallback strategy had begun to take shape early in the summer. With their Nicaragua policy in tatters and current funds about to run out, Reagan and his national security team huddled to decide how to go forward. In a long National Security Council meeting at the White House on June 25, Shultz argued that continuing good-faith efforts at negotiations with Nicaragua was the only possible way to salvage Contra aid. Reagan sided with Shultz, though he was realistic about the prospects for negotiations, saying it "is so farfetched to imagine that a Communist government like that would make any reasonable deal with us, but if it is to get Congress to support the anti-Sandinistas, then it can be helpful."

At the same meeting, Jeane Kirkpatrick and Cap Weinberger said they wanted a more public fight against Democrats on behalf of Contra funding, but also wondered whether Contra funding from other countries (possibly Israel) might be arranged. Shultz objected that brokering funds from private sources or third countries was "very likely illegal"; he added, in fact, that James Baker (who was not present at this meeting) thought it would be "an impeachable offense."[22] Vice President Bush and others disagreed.

Everyone knew they were treading on sensitive ground. Reagan allowed that "if such a story gets out, we'll all be hanging by our thumbs in front of the White House until we find out who did it." He later said this comment referred to leaking, rather than the substance of the issue itself. Normally quiet in NSC meetings, Reagan was an active participant this time. He gave Shultz the green light to pursue the Nicaraguan negotiations (with some limits on terms), and he also encouraged the independent Contra funding track.

Unknown to everyone in the June 25 meeting except Reagan, Robert McFarlane had already arranged outside funding for the Contras. Reagan had told McFarlane sometime earlier—later McFarlane could not place the exact date—to find a way to keep the Contras together "body and soul." National Security Council staffer Colonel Oliver North had seen to the details: Saudi Arabia would transfer funds to the Contras' Miami bank accounts. Reagan and McFarlane kept the details closely held. Attorney General William French Smith subsequently advised that he saw no legal obstacle to discussing Contra funding with other nations, though neither he nor any other administration lawyer produced a written opinion on the matter.

Reagan was correct that negotiations were fruitless; the Sandinistas rebuffed American overtures. Efforts to gain Contra funds from more Third World countries, unfortunately, would soon become more successful.

* * *

THE POLITICAL THEATER over Nicaragua was not limited to embarrassments for the administration. The spring also witnessed a spirited counterattack on the Democrats when Newt Gingrich publicized a sympathetic letter that ten House Democrats, including majority leader Jim Wright, had sent to Daniel Ortega in April.

The "Dear Comandante" letter, as it became known, began: "We address you in the spirit of hopefulness and goodwill." It made plain that the Democrats opposed President Reagan's policy and sought symbolic concessions from the Sandinistas that would enable their opposition at home to be more successful. "We regret the fact that better relations do not exist between the United States and your country," the letter read. "We have been, and remain, opposed to U.S. support for military action directed against the people or government of Nicaragua." The letter also criticized "those responsible for supporting violence against your government, and for obstructing serious negotiations for broad political participation in El Salvador"—obvious euphemisms for Reagan and on behalf of a coalition government in El Salvador. The letter asked Ortega to take steps to "strengthen the hands of those in our country who desire better relations."

Gingrich called a debate on the House floor, where he charged that the letter was illegal and possibly unconstitutional. "This statement crosses the bounds from legitimate opposition to American policy to a deliberate communication of that opposition to a foreign government," he argued. By offering essentially to negotiate with the Sandinistas, Gingrich added, the letter arguably violated the seldom-enforced Logan Act, which prohibited diplomacy by anyone other than the executive branch. Only one signatory to the letter, New York representative Steven Solarz, defended the communication, saying it was meant chiefly to encourage free elections in Nicaragua, for which the Sandinistas had repeatedly expressed scorn. Typical of conservative commentary was Pat Buchanan: "In the war between Western democracy and Castroism for Central America, Jim Wright and the Democratic leadership are on the side of the Sandinistas."

Gingrich's attack on the "Dear Comandante" letter was merely one skirmish line in the intensifying bitterness and partisanship in the House. In 1984 Gingrich and about a dozen other House Republicans began using the special-orders period at the end of the day and in the evening, when House members may give longer speeches to be included in the *Congressional Record,* to launch a sustained attack on Democrats. Typically there were no Democrats present to engage in debate, so the attacks went unanswered. However, because C-SPAN broadcast the special orders, the Republican criticism was reaching a wider public audience and was beginning to attract notice. By rule, C-SPAN cameras were tightly fixed on the individual speaker in the House well and did not convey that the House chamber was virtually empty during special orders. House Speaker Tip O'Neill, annoyed at Gingrich's tactics, ordered C-SPAN cameras to pan the House during Special Orders to show up the Republicans.

Republicans cried foul, charging O'Neill with a "dirty trick" and an "arrogant and arbitrary abuse of power." Invoking "personal privilege,"

Gingrich took the House floor to rebut O'Neill's claim that Republicans had unfairly used special orders to attack Democrats without notice. Gingrich had in fact sent letters to House Democrats informing them of the arguments and issues Republicans would present during special orders, and inviting them to debate. O'Neill lost his temper and made a rare trip to the well of the House to take on Gingrich, where he promptly blundered. O'Neill charged that Gingrich's tactics were "[u]n-American . . . It's the lowest thing I've heard in my 32 years here!"

But O'Neill's personal language was a violation of House rules. Republican House whip Trent Lott pounced; he interrupted with a parliamentary inquiry. The House parliamentarian sided with the Republicans, informing the House chair (O'Neill's fellow Massachusetts Democrat Joe Moakley) that O'Neill's words had to be "taken down." It was a stunning rebuke to O'Neill, who sat down red faced as nearly the entire Republican caucus gave Gingrich a standing ovation.

The episode quickly became known as "Camscam," and Gingrich's triumphant face-off against O'Neill made the news on all three broadcast networks that night and the front page of the *Washington Post* the next day. One Republican who conspicuously did not join the ovation was minority leader Bob Michel, who played golf regularly with O'Neill and disliked the partisan rancor that Gingrich and his insurgents had brought to the House. This was precisely the problem with Gingrich's point of view—the Republican minority had been too accommodating for too long. "Democrats have been in the majority for almost 60 years, cheerfully fighting in public," Gingrich told the *Washington Post*. "Majorities worry about gathering the energy of conflict in order to dominate." Now, Trent Lott said, Republicans were "absolutely united" in their anger over the heavy-handed way Democrats ran the House and resolved to be more aggressive in opposition.

As the *Washington Post* laconically commented, "During the fiery arguments on the floor yesterday, the GOP's center of gravity appeared to be moving toward that view and away from House Republican leader Michel." It was a genuine watershed moment in the political course of the 1980s; the friction between the parties, and *within* the parties, in the House would grow steadily worse over the next few years. The following year, in fact, there would be two near-fistfights on the House floor as partisan rancor reached a new high.

*   *   *

ALTHOUGH REAGAN'S REELECTION seems a forgone conclusion, there is still much to be learned from a closer examination of the election campaign as it unfolded. Campaigns tell us much about the disposition of the two parties and the ever-changing center of gravity in American politics. The internal arguments of a party can be more significant than their clashes with the other party. Political scientist Theodore Lowi wrote early in 1984: "The ideological cores of the two parties are a great deal more distinct and further apart than at any time before." Harvard political scientist Harvey Mansfield thought the two parties had now become distinct, as partisans of entitlement (Democrats) or opportunity (Republicans): "Americans have not yet chosen—they have not yet been compelled to choose—between these parties." Would the voters perceive this fundamental choice in the 1984 election?

The question for Republicans was whether they would extend the Reagan Revolution in the face of internal and external pressures—especially the federal budget deficit—to reverse course or at least trim their sails. This internal fight within the GOP would play out in the fight over the placement of a single comma in a key sentence of the party platform at its convention in August.

The challenge confronting Democrats, meanwhile, was whether they were capable of reforming themselves in light of Reagan's challenge to their governing philosophy. This would unfold in a more protracted manner in the Democratic primaries and requires unbundling the personalities and ideas that contested for the Democratic soul. The threshold question for liberals was whether Reagan's election was a fluke, whether the old New Deal coalition could successfully reassert itself under the banner of fairness coupled with fanning fears of Reagan's ostensibly dangerous foreign policy. Nearly every Democrat thought the answer to these questions was, to one degree or another, a resounding yes.

Eight Democrats would contest for the nomination to face Reagan, but for the true-believing New Dealers, former vice president Walter Mondale was the obvious man to carry the party's banner. Mondale was a purebred liberal of the old school—the *New Republic*'s Henry Fairlie correctly pegged him as "a renovated Hubert Humphrey"—who did not believe that America had turned away from liberalism in any fundamental way. *Time*'s William A. Henry observed that "Mondale insisted on trying to lecture the public out of its rejection of paternalistic government." Mondale had been the clear front-runner from the moment in 1982 when Ted Kennedy announced he would not run—an event that left many liberals bereft. Arthur Schlesinger Jr.

lamented: "His withdrawal leaves the country without the all-out challenge to Reaganism that the miserable state of our affairs demands."[23]

To be sure, Mondale lacked Kennedy's supposed charisma and rousing public presence. Mondale was only fifty-six, but he seemed much older. "I got the bags under my eyes the old-fashioned way," he boasted at one point; "I earned them." Everything about Mondale seemed to prompt relentless put-downs. "Mondale," Jeffrey Hart quipped, "sounds like the name of a Los Angeles suburb." Eugene McCarthy had the ultimate dismissal, saying Mondale "has the soul of a vice president." *National Review*'s Richard Brookhiser wrote that Mondale's nose looked like a failed design for a can opener. Mondale's plodding, nasal speech and haggard visage caused Sidney Blumenthal to write that he "has the vibrant exhaustion of one who has spent too many nights in Holiday Inns. His speech is half battle cry and half dirge."

In an ironic reversal of what was said to explain Reagan's success (that his telegenic personality obscured his retrograde politics), Mondale's lack of public personality was said to undermine the appeal of his liberal ideas. This is unfair to Mondale, who is one of those unfortunate political figures (like Richard Nixon and Al Gore) for whom public exposure in the modern media age is unkind. Mondale came across as monochromatic in a Technicolor world. The *Wall Street Journal*'s conservative editorial page editor, Robert Bartley, who knew Mondale personally from serving with him on the board of the Mayo Clinic, wrote: "The great mystery of the man is how and why he contrived to keep his personal wit and humor, readily apparent in even short conversation as vice president, from showing itself on the campaign trail."[24]

Although a deficit of public personality is a handicap in modern American politics, Mondale's real problems were substantive. He attempted to couch his old-school liberalism in the patina of consensus, and in doing so lost the élan of liberalism as it was expressed by FDR and John F. Kennedy. Mondale, by contrast, embraced jejune slogans such as "daring to be cautious." Jack Germond and Jules Witcover found it telling that Mondale once *bunted* in a staff softball game. The *New Republic*'s Richard Strout chided Mondale when his campaign "formally unveiled 'leadership' as a political issue for the fall, the way General Motors might unveil a new car, after extensive market research and design." Following the 1980 election Mondale announced with great flair that he was taking a year off to reexamine his beliefs, "a gesture so goofy," *Time* magazine's William Henry wrote, "that few people took it seriously enough even to mock it." Especially since Mondale's reexamination yielded no new beliefs or ideas.

Mondale set about to secure the Democratic nomination the same way FDR or Lyndon Johnson would have done it, by appealing to the discrete and insular interest groups that constitute the modern Democratic Party. In *Time,* Evan Thomas wrote that Mondale "approaches great national issues not with overarching vision, but like a train conductor punching tickets." But Mondale did not betray the slightest recognition that it was precisely the metastasizing of interest-group liberalism that had contributed, as much as inflation and Jimmy Carter's ineptitude, to the declining electoral appeal of the Democratic Party. By adroitly catering to the various liberal interest groups—especially organized labor—Mondale secured unprecedented early endorsements and organizational support in key primary states. The AFL-CIO endorsed Mondale in the fall of 1983, months earlier than it had ever issued an endorsement.

But Mondale's solicitousness got out of hand, with plaintive professions of sympathy piling up faster than the national debt. Before the National Organization for Women (NOW) he professed to be a feminist; NOW responded by giving him the first presidential endorsement in its history. Before labor unions, he endorsed domestic-content mandates for manufacturing, which was a clever euphemism for trade protectionism. Before education groups such as the National Education Association (NEA), he promised more federal spending. Before ethnic minority groups, he pledged fealty to affirmative action and quotas (though calling them "verifiable measurements" instead of quotas). At one point Mondale professed himself to being the candidate of "the sad," even though depressed Americans were not (yet) an organized constituency. It was all too much for *Wall Street Journal* political reporter Albert Hunt, who wrote that he wouldn't be surprised if Mondale "soon endorses government-subsidized kosher lunches for gay left-handed unemployed schoolteachers."[25] Sidney Blumenthal worried that "the longer the [nomination] process lasts, the more likely it is that he may be seen as the public affairs director of the AFL-CIO." A bumper sticker read: HONK IF MONDALE HAS PROMISED YOU SOMETHING.

Mondale and the Democratic Party establishment that fell in behind him thought he had the nomination sewed up months before any votes were cast in primaries or caucuses. But Mondale's close embrace of liberal interest groups became the opening by which Democratic rivals successfully attacked him. Senator John Glenn said that Mondale had turned the Democrats into "a party that can't say no to anyone with a mailing list." South Carolina senator Fritz Hollings, whose own presidential campaign proved abortive because too many voters confused his name with a trucking company, complained that Mondale "is a good lapdog; he'll lick every hand." When challenged in a candidate debate to name a single issue on which he differed from the AFL-CIO, Mondale couldn't come up with an answer. It took his campaign two days to supply one.

Yet the charge of pandering is unfair because Mondale *believed* in the agendas of the liberal interest groups. So did most of his Democratic rivals, who were merely frustrated that Mondale had monopolized their support. None of his rivals, with one partial exception to be considered shortly, offered much of an alternative to Mondale's liberalism. The three slightly conservative Democrats in the race—Glenn, Florida's ex-governor Ruben Askew, and Hollings—got nowhere, showing that the Scoop Jackson wing of the party was extinct. (Glenn was the Democrat Reagan's political team feared most.) To Mondale's left were California's Alan Cranston and Jesse Jackson, who generated the most excitement in the race, partly because of his talent at rhyming schemes: "From the outhouse to the courthouse . . . from the slave ship to the championship . . . from disgrace to amazing grace!" While this field displayed some width on the Democratic ideological spectrum (Glenn and Hollings had voted for Reagan's tax cuts, and they had supported higher military spending as far back as the Carter years), they were united in supporting the nuclear freeze—in fact, the chief point of contention on foreign policy was trying to claim to have supported the freeze first.

Political scientist Theodore Lowi observed: "In 1984 at least, the leading Democratic alternatives to President Reagan looked like the same Democrats who gave us the collapse of liberalism in the 1970s. Despite the talk about new ideas inside the Democratic Party, these are difficult, if not impossible, to find." Liberal intellectuals, however, sensed that something was wrong with business as usual. Just as the rise of neoconservatism had given a boost to Republicans in the 1970s, now leading thinkers on the Left were casting about for a commensurate version of neoliberalism. Just as neoconservatives had journals (*Commentary* and the *Public Interest* most especially), nascent neoliberalism found a journalistic home at the *Washington Monthly,* whose maverick editor, Charles Peters, attempted to push a "neoliberal manifesto."[26]

For a while, would-be neoliberals peppered their speeches with the term *high-tech,* which acted as a rhetorical talisman. A handful of liberals labeled themselves "Atari Democrats" after the market-leading computer game maker, but the label became an embarrassment when Atari moved to Taiwan and cut more than seventeen hundred jobs in the United States. A spate of books and articles grudgingly acknowledged that the old-time liberal religion of large-scale government intervention was dead; the liberal economist Robert Kuttner wrote that "Keynesian full employment remains intellectually out of fashion for liberals" and that liberal thought on social and economic problems "is an ideological shambles."[27]

Beyond a welcome attitude of self-criticism, was there anything really neo about neoliberalism, or was it merely the old liberalism repackaged for the high-tech age? Economist Melville Ulmer observed, "[T]he more acceptable to the public did the Reagan program appear in action during the past two years, the more resolutely did the entire spectrum of liberals move to the Left. . . . [E]ach upward notch in the present business expansion elicited new and more flamboyant assaults on Reaganomics, and new and bolder stratagems for the future."[28] The most prominent of the new stratagems was industrial policy. This amalgam became the flavor of the month for liberalism, and the rage for know-it-all newspaper editorial writers. The core of industrial policy was . . . well, it was hard to say. It lacked a central idea, beyond an implicit distrust of markets and a residual confidence in bureaucrats and government economic planning.

Some liberals, including economist Lester Thurow, wanted the government to invest in sunrise industries in the high-tech sector. Others, such as investment banker Felix Rohatyn, wanted the government to revive struggling basic industries such as steel, rubber, auto, and manufacturing. Rohatyn proposed a federal Reconstruction Finance Corporation that would invest billions to "turn losers into winners." Robert Reich, whose bestselling book *The Next American Frontier* "occupies a position with liberals not dissimilar to that of *Das Kapital* with Marxists," according to Ulmer, went beyond Rohatyn in proposing the formation of a National Planning Board and an Industrial Redevelopment Bank to direct capital into more-promising enterprises. To the threat of inflation, the industrial policy advocates blithely offered wage and price controls. The liberal economists such as Kuttner, Reich, and Thurow were writing as though Milton Friedman and Friedrich Hayek had never existed, let alone won Nobel Prizes for their robust challenges to liberal orthodoxy.

In other words, at best industrial policy was merely a spiffed-up version of the old Keynesian interventionism, based on the hubris that government planners can allocate capital and resources better than the market and regulate any undesirable outcomes. At worst, it was a fancy dress for extending subsidies to favored industries. Under any understanding, it was hardly a crowd stirrer. Kuttner commented that industrial policy "has too many contradictory meanings, too slender a constituency, and in any case it is one lousy bumper sticker."

There were some specific, narrower variations that came to the fore in this discussion. Some liberals were intent on passing plant-closing legislation that would require companies to adopt long lead times before closing or relocating an old factory—"fugitive industries," such companies were revealingly called in the liberal lexicon. Feminists were pushing the idea of comparable worth, which would have involved the government in superseding the labor market in the setting of wage levels between jobs that the market valued differently; for example, librarians should be paid like truck drivers because the labor market unfairly undervalued female-dominated occupations. Liberal commentator Mickey Kaus referred to comparable worth as "one of the really bad ideas from the comic book era of interest-group liberalism."

For a party that was supposedly looking for a way to move beyond New Deal liberalism, its leading policy ideas seemed frozen in amber from 1933 and betrayed a lack of perception of how the American economy was rapidly reforming itself through the dynamic process Joseph Schumpeter had called "creative destruction." Contrary to liberal rhetoric about deindustrialization, 1.1 million of the 4 million new jobs generated in 1983 were in the manufacturing sector. In the industrial heartland, where the 1982 recession had been most severe, unemployment had fallen dramatically in some hard-hit places: unemployment in the state of Michigan dropped from 17.3 percent to 11.9 percent; in Youngstown, Ohio, from 20.3 percent to 13.7 percent; in Rockford, Illinois, from 19.8 percent to 11.1 percent; in Dubuque, Iowa, from 13.6 percent to 8.3 percent. Private sector capital investment soared 30 percent during 1984, to $715 billion.

Meanwhile, as the United States was reinvigorating its industrial sector, liberals cast their gaze across the ocean to Japan and its vaunted Ministry of International Trade and Development (MITI). The refrain that America needed to emulate the Japanese became louder as the decade went on, and MITI was held out as proof that centralized industrial policy worked. Japan was a bad example, as the collapse of its "economic miracle" at the end of the decade made evident. Even in 1984 the signs were evident to the discerning eye. Japan's economic growth, which had run as high as 10 percent a year in the 1970s, had slowed to a more normal 3 percent per year by 1983. While Japan's exports to the United States were dominated by conspicuous consumer goods from cars to televisions to computers, the fact was that exports made up a smaller share of Japan's total economy than they did for most

European nations. As many of Japan's basic industries started to erode, Theodore Eismeier of Japan's Institute for Policy Science concluded, "The best evidence suggests that the Japanese miracle has been more a matter of private than public initiative, and that the attempted outguessing of the market that has received so much laudatory publicity has in fact had relatively little to do with Japan's singular record of postwar growth."[29]

For a while in 1983 and early 1984 it appeared that Democrats might embrace the one economic reform idea that would have enabled them to outflank Reagan and redefine liberalism: tax reform. A handful of Democrats, especially Representative Richard Gephardt and Senator Bill Bradley, proposed a sweeping tax reform plan that would have flattened income tax rates and simplified the tax code. The Bradley-Gephardt plan proposed a new top income tax rate of 30 percent (down from about 46 percent at that time) while eliminating a wide range of deductions and exemptions. For most middle-class Americans, it would have involved a tax cut. Reagan's political team was alarmed, not wanting to cede the tax issue to Democrats. But Reagan needn't have worried. Bradley and Gephardt tried to talk Mondale into making tax reform a centerpiece of his campaign, but Mondale rejected the idea. Imposing high tax rates on the rich held too much sway. He couldn't see a way of combining tax cuts with his central campaign theme—fairness. He had no interest in reforming liberalism, telling a *Washington Post* reporter: "I think there's always been this neo-liberal approach that disdains what I view to be a fundamental and sacred objective of the Democratic Party, which is to pursue fairness."[30]

On foreign policy Mondale retained the residue of the older Cold War liberalism, but it was nearly impossible to detect in his public pronouncements. Mondale's public posture reflected the demoralized state of liberalism in its post-Vietnam paralysis, and at nearly every step of the way Mondale caved to the dovish base in the party. Instead Mondale jumped on the nuclear freeze bandwagon and attacked the Strategic Defense Initiative. He resisted calls in his party to cut defense spending, but he wanted a much lower rate of increase than Reagan did. On defense the Democrats now assumed the position Republicans had long occupied on domestic policy: whereas Republicans were low-budget liberals in the 1960s and 1970s, Democrats were now low-budget hawks, promoting schemes for smaller aircraft carriers, cheaper airplanes, and no new strategic weapons systems. Reagan delighted in pointing out that he was spending a smaller share of the federal budget on defense than John F. Kennedy had. Most Americans were outraged by inaccurate stories of $435 Pentagon hammers, but they weren't ready to buy the low-budget liberal alternative.

*   *   *

THE ONE PARTIAL exception to the lockstep old-school liberalism of Mondale and his rivals was Colorado senator Gary Hart, and he brought drama to the campaign as well as the only real threat to Mondale's coronation parade. On the surface Hart looked to be the ideal champion for neoliberalism, and from time to time he even appeared to be a genuine departure from Mondale's New Deal liberalism. Hart seemed to have a clue that the old interest-group liberalism had become debilitating in practice as well as in theory. He wrote in a campaign book, *A New Democracy,* that "American liberalism was near bankruptcy." His signature campaign theme was that the party needed "new ideas and new leadership." At one point Hart said that his generation of Democrats was not "a bunch of little Hubert Humphreys" and that they "were not automatic regulators, new-agency creators, and higher tax-and-spend people."

But this novelty collapsed on closer inspection. Arthur Schlesinger called Hart's attempted neoliberalism "a hoax from the start." Richard Reeves wrote that Hart "was offering not much more than the idea that he was open to new ideas," and Henry Fairlie scoffed that "Hart runs so hard to appear up to date that, when he catches up with it, he is as out of date as last year's *Time* covers."

Hart's "new ideas" theme turned out to be more a skillful way of exploiting Mondale's weaknesses and making a generational appeal to baby boomers than any genuine innovation in liberal thought. He was surprisingly vague and superficial when pressed for details about the substance of his new ideas, a point Mondale adroitly hammered in a debate when he invoked a currently popular TV commercial for Wendy's hamburgers. "You know, when I hear those 'new ideas,' " Mondale smirked, "I'm reminded of that ad, 'Where's the beef?' " Hart lamely replied the next day by putting a copy of his book *A New Democracy* between the two halves of a hamburger bun. Even on his signature economic theme—industrial policy (which he never defined with any clarity)—Hart appeared insincere. In 1979 he had voted against federal loan guarantees for Chrysler, an example of pro-industry government intervention if there ever was one.

Other "new ideas" bordered on silly. He proposed to engage the Soviet Union by challenging the Kremlin "to a crusade to eliminate hunger for every child on this planet in the 1980s," and calling for the United States and the Soviets to establish somewhere in Europe a joint missile-tracking center where, *Time* magazine reported, "each side could see pictures of what the other's satellites were showing and explain any activity that looked threatening." He said the United States wouldn't need to defend Persian Gulf oil shipping routes because, as president, he would achieve energy independence. When the *Washington Post* asked Hart whether he considered Cuba a totalitarian nation, Hart answered, "I don't know."

He proposed instituting a White House Council on Emerging Issues, to go along with the Council of Economic Advisers. When asked the hypothetical question of what he would do if a Czech airliner strayed over a U.S. military installation, Hart replied that he would instruct American pilots to look in the aircraft windows to see whether the occupants were wearing military uniforms before ordering the plane to be shot down. This drew a hearty snort from former fighter pilot and astronaut John Glenn, who was appalled at Hart's childlike grasp of military realities. Somehow Hart enjoyed a reputation as a serious person on military affairs, yet his Senate record revealed him to be a standard-issue liberal, opposing every weapons system currently in production in favor of hypothetical systems always years away. Hart cast votes against or voiced opposition to the MX missile, the Apache helicopter, the Bradley armored vehicle, the Patriot surface-to-air missile system, the B-1 bomber, the F-18 fighter, the F-15 fighter, and radar-guided air-to-air missiles— in other words, nearly every system that would be integral to American military operations over the next two decades, culminating especially in the two Gulf Wars.

The more Hart talked the more it became apparent that he did not represent any real departure from liberalism; in fact, as the campaign went on he appeared increasingly fraudulent. One of his leading boosters, actor Warren Beatty, explained his enthusiasm for Hart thusly: "He stands for 'new ideas.' And 'new ideas' mean, 'You pay, motherfucker.' "[31] When Hart did exclaim directly about issues, he was usually to the left of Mondale. He explicitly backed racial quotas, and on foreign policy he was distinctly McGovernite (he had been McGovern's campaign manager in 1972)—"eager," George Will wrote, "to get U.S. forces out of Oklahoma and prepared to sacrifice economic growth for the convenience of lesbian snail darters." Morton Kondracke called it "jacuzzi-generation foreign policy."

Just as Jimmy Carter in 1976 had the insight that in the aftermath of Watergate a significant block of voters would swoon over a candidate who taught Sunday school, Hart perceived correctly that many baby boomers would respond to a generational appeal. (Mondale received less than 30 percent of the Democratic primary vote from voters under thirty.) Like Carter, Hart ran against or aloof from the Democratic Party establishment. He engaged in a calculated imitation of the vigorous and youthful imagery of John F. Kennedy, right down to thrusting his hands in his coat pockets. "The Kennedy nostalgia," Morton Kondracke reported, "was heavily contrived—tested out, in fact, in focus groups supervised by Hart's pollster, Dottie Lynch." Johnny Carson mocked Hart on the *Tonight* show: "I like his slogan, 'Vote for me, I have Kennedy hair.' " George Will observed that "Hart is Jay Gatsby in politics: He is his own work of art."

Hart's Peter Pan act worked early on. Eight days after finishing a distant second to Mondale in the Iowa caucuses (garnering only 14.8 percent of caucus-goers' votes), Hart scored a stunning upset in the New Hampshire primary.[32] An NBC News survey a week before the Iowa caucuses had found that 87 percent of Democrats had never heard of or had any opinion about Gary Hart, and even the morning of the New Hampshire primary, a *New York Times* poll had Mondale winning with 57 percent of the vote and Hart finishing fourth with 6 percent. Such is the magic of small states such as Iowa and New Hampshire, where personal appeals have more leverage with voters than a big campaign organization. In a telling indication of the problems with Mondale's campaign, half of Democratic voters in New Hampshire told exit pollsters that Mondale had made too many promises to special-interest groups.

In the two weeks after New Hampshire, Hart trounced Mondale in Florida, Maine, Vermont, Massachusetts, Rhode Island, Washington, Wyoming, Oklahoma, and Nevada, even though he had barely campaigned in some of these states and his organization was thin. Hart was suddenly the front-runner, and campaign contributions instantly surged. Fresh opinion polls showed him drawing even with Reagan in a head-to-head matchup. So many things were going wrong that Mondale contemplated dropping out of the race; a campaign aide prepared a memo for the logistics of withdrawing. Had the 1984 primaries been as front-loaded as they are today, it surely would have meant Mondale's quick end. But in 1984 Mondale still had a small window of time to recover.

Presidential candidates who rise from obscurity tend to be like half-baked soufflés: they collapse just as quickly. With success came intensified media scrutiny, and soon it emerged that Hart was . . . *weird*. It turned out his given name was Hartpence; he had shortened it to Hart in college, but gave contradictory accounts of why he had done so. He had radically changed the style of his signature well into adulthood. And there was an odd discrepancy about his age: Hart claimed to be forty-six, and his campaign biography said he was born on November 28, 1937, but in fact he was born in 1936. He had studied for a divinity degree at Yale but, curiously, omitted this fact from his various biographies such as those in *Who's Who* and the *Congressional Directory*. Hart's only new ideas, one of his campaign aides quipped, were his name and his age. While it was not apparent to voters who only saw Hart on TV, Hart made little or no eye contact with audiences; Hart's speaking style is to look over the heads of crowds. Rumors about his womanizing—he had been separated from his wife twice—reached the news media; the stately David Broder made an oblique reference to this gossip in a column that speculated whether Hart's interest in feminist issues derived from his "many women friends."

Hart's bizarre explanations for these biographical oddities set off a media feeding frenzy and unnerved a lot of Democrats. "What the public held against Hart," Ronald Steel wrote later, "was not his lack of solutions, but his lack of authenticity." Numerous leading media outlets including the *Wall Street Journal*, the *Washington Post,* and the TV networks ran prominent features on Hart's peculiarities. On the *CBS Evening News* in early March, shortly before the next round of big primaries, Dan Rather led a segment thus: "Who is this man, this Gary Hart?" On NBC the following night, Roger Mudd asked: "How old is Gary Hart? And why did he change his name?" NBC wasn't done. Two nights later, NBC's John Dancy offered another Hart segment that began: "Who is Gary Hart, anyway, and what does he believe?" Tom Brokaw dismissed Hart as "this season's hit rock-'n'-roll single." Roger Mudd practically taunted Hart in an interview: "Why do you imitate John Kennedy so much?" CBS's Bruce Morton kept up the theme: "Gary Hart is the hottest political property around, at least this week. But who is he?" ABC was not left out, with Jack Smith delivering a devastating syllabus of Hart's strangeness: "He's even fudged the year of his birth." The troubled state of Hart's marriage became fodder for media analysis. The only thing missing was an analogue to Chappaquiddick. (That would come three years later.)

The hypothesis must be entertained that the media, having been caught off guard by Hart's surprise emergence, were out to exact retribution. The *New York Times* and the three TV networks don't like it when they proclaim before the first primary that Mondale is the all-but-certain nominee, only to have the pesky voters defy them. Who gave Hart permission? "His candidacy had made a fool of Washington insiders," *Time*'s William A. Henry wrote. "No one, no matter how long his memory, was able to recall anything in politics to compare with the mania of exuberance about Gary Hart that swept America. Prairie fire, Hart's delighted partisans called it." (Curious that Hart's boosters used the same catchphrase Reagan had been using for twenty years.) The media did their best to put the fire out.

Hart compounded the fresh doubts about his character with several miscues in the next round of primaries, which happened to be in the big unionized, Mondale-friendly states, including Illinois, New York, Pennsylvania, and Michigan. Mondale's campaign was suddenly rejuvenated and skillfully exploited Hart's vulnerabilities. The most devastating hit was the "red phone" TV spot, which never mentioned Hart. Instead, the camera panned in slowly on a blinking red telephone, meant to evoke the mythical hotline to Moscow, with a voice-over saying: "The most awesome, powerful responsibility in the world lies in the hand that picks up this phone. The idea of an unsure, unsteady, untested hand is something to really think about. Vote as if the future of the world is at stake, because it is. Mondale. This President will know what he's doing, and that's the difference."

Mondale's superior organization and party support sufficed to put him over the top by a small margin at the end of the primary season in June, though it wasn't pretty or convincing. "Mondale still had no coherent message to present to the electorate on why he should replace President Reagan," Germond and Witcover wrote. A Mondale speechwriter admitted, "We had a hell of a time putting down on paper what this campaign was going to be all about."[33] Hart had won more primaries (the score was sixteen for Hart, eleven for Mondale), but Mondale won slightly more total votes (39 percent to Hart's 36 percent). After the last primary, Mondale said, "I never want to be called a front-runner again as long as I live."

Although Hart's challenge made Mondale a marginally better candidate, Mondale headed toward the convention with the albatross of the third-place finisher—Jesse Jackson. Jackson won 18 percent of the primary vote but did disproportionately well in states with a large black vote (and, not coincidentally, depriving Mondale of likely votes). Well and truly could it be said that the "Jackson wing" of the Democratic Party now meant Jesse, not Scoop. Jackson, whom the *New Republic* called "the great ambulance chaser of American politics," expressed every leftover radical sentiment of the 1960s New Left inventory. During the long primary season he referred to the United States as a "repressive regime," said the Sandinistas were "on the right side of history," referred to his boyhood home state of South Carolina as an "occupied zone," claimed that George Washington ran a "military dictatorship," said "Reagan is closer to Herod than he would be to the family of Jesus," and in an especially careless moment even for him referred to New York City as "Hymietown." His all-time chart topper may have been his remark about Cambodia's genocidal Khmer Rouge: "Unfortunately sometimes the best of people lose their way." When the primaries ended, he went to Nicaragua to embrace the Sandinistas and then to Cuba to visit with Fidel Castro, where Jackson toasted Che Guevara and taught Castro to sing "We Shall Overcome." Yet none of his rival Democratic candidates ever called him out for his egregious statements and attacks.

This restraint is usually attributed to the Democrats' fear of offending the crucial black constituency Jackson purported to lead, but the deeper problem was that the self-styled Rainbow Coalition of minorities-as-victims was merely an extreme variation of the fairness theme central to Mondale and other mainstream liberals.[34] This put liberals in the awkward position of not being able to push back without risk of contradicting or rendering incoherent their own principles. Jackson's noisy, media-hogging presence on the Democratic stage was symptomatic of a wider radical strain at the heart of the most motivated Democrats, and it was going to require a large measure of appeasement to tame. Mondale thought he saw a way to do so to his advantage: he would put his legendary caution to the side and go with an unconventional pick for a running mate—a woman or a minority.

To the delight of the stakeout brigades in the media, Mondale had prospective running mates come calling at his Minnesota home. Hart ridiculed it for resembling "the old Hollywood World War II movies, where you had one of everything in the lifeboat." Mondale's prospect list included a few white males, including Texas senator Lloyd Bentsen, Arkansas senator Dale Bumpers, Georgia senator Sam Nunn, Florida governor Bob Graham, New York governor Mario Cuomo, and—Mondale's first fallback choice—Massachusetts governor Michael Dukakis. But he spent far more time considering such figures as Los Angeles mayor Tom Bradley (black), Philadelphia mayor Wilson Goode (ditto), and San Antonio mayor Henry Cisneros (Hispanic). Notably missing from the list was Jackson, who dismissed Mondale's public vetting process as "a PR parade of personalities." Jackson was behaving with extreme truculence, demanding more delegates to the convention as well as a prime-time speaking slot and consultations on cabinet posts, even as he continued to trash Mondale publicly.

One of the key segments of Jackson's Rainbow Coalition was the feminist movement, and feminist leaders had been browbeating Mondale for months to choose a woman as a running mate. The president of NOW threatened a floor fight at the Democratic convention if Mondale didn't pick a woman running mate, and she expected that President Mondale would appoint women to half of his cabinet posts. A *Washington Post*/ABC News poll before the convention found that seven out of ten delegates favored a woman running mate (though a Gallup poll found that among Democratic voters at large, 59 percent preferred Hart to be Mondale's running mate). Jesse Jackson embraced the idea, as did House Speaker Tip O'Neill. Three women emerged as serious possibilities: San Francisco mayor Dianne Feinstein, Kentucky governor Martha Lane Collins, and—O'Neill's recommendation—New York congresswoman Geraldine Ferraro. Feminist groups vetoed consideration of a fourth woman, Louisiana congresswoman Lindy Boggs, because she wasn't fully pro-choice on abortion.

Mondale settled on Ferraro, who had already impressed the party establishment as chair of the Democrats' platform committee in 1984. A former prosecutor, Ferraro came from a House district in Queens that had gone for Reagan in 1980. But she had bucked the Reagan tide, running with the slogan "Finally . . . a tough Democrat." As an Italian Catholic, she was thought to have appeal with religious and ethnic constituencies where Democrats were showing weakness. But a closer look at her House voting record, as reflected in the vote tally ratings of various interest groups, revealed that she was to the left of 99 percent of the House membership.

While Ferraro was a historic choice that excited the media and the Democratic Party base, it also reinforced the impression that Mondale was in thrall to liberal interest groups. Then there was the Democrats' choice of city for their nominating convention: San Francisco, the city least representative of the suburban, growth-oriented political culture of the Sunbelt. To the contrary, it reinforced all of the liberal stereotypes of what the post-1960s Democratic Party had become. "Democrats," *Newsweek* observed on the eve of the convention, "will be hard pressed to put on a show inside the convention center to rival the one San Francisco puts on outside." The day before the convention opened, ten thousand marched in a gay pride parade down Market Street, bearing placards like FREEZE NUCLEAR FAMILIES/ABORT PHYLLIS SCHLAFLY and LESBIAN/GAY LIBERATION THROUGH REVOLUTIONARY SOCIALIST FEMINISM. But for the huge numbers and well-known local leadership including Sister Boom-Boom, the transvestite "mother superior" of the Sisters of Perpetual Indulgence (Boom-Boom had received twenty-three thousand votes in the last election for city supervisor), one might have thought the spectacle was a Republican dirty trick. A Republican observing the street scene said, "In 1972, Nixon paid his dirty-tricksters to do this—now they're doing it for us," and a *New Republic* editor remarked, "Sister Boom-Boom on TV is the best thing that ever could have happened for the Republicans."

Inside the convention hall the political equivalent of the Sisters of Perpetual Indulgence was threatening floor fights if Mondale didn't yield to platform demands. Most voters and even political junkies in the media tend to ignore party platforms, though this is a mistake, as they are an excellent barometer of the state of a party's mind amidst the crosscutting pressures of intra-party divisions and the larger public opinion. The overarching principles of the platform were "the Democratic commitment to an activist government" and "the Democratic tradition of caring." The platform opposed a balanced budget amendment and pledged to repeal the third year of Reagan's income tax cut, defer income tax indexing, raise corporate income taxes, and adopt a more progressive tax system.

Overall one would have thought from the platform, as well as the proceedings from the convention podium, that the nation had returned to the conditions of the Great Depression. New York governor Mario Cuomo electrified the delegates with his superbly delivered keynote address, in which he appropriated the imagery of Charles Dickens's *A Tale of Two Cities* to revivify the core liberal idea of class division. So successful was the speech that several journalists wrote the following day that the convention should dump Mondale and nominate Cuomo in his place. In the biting words of conservative Democrat Joshua Muravchik, however, a close reading of Cuomo's text leads to the view that Democrats have a "penchant for hollow rhetoric," while historian Ronald Radosh called it "the swan song of the old liberalism."[35] *Time*'s William A. Henry acerbically commented: "Cuomo and all the Democrats were affirming that the central concern of government was ministering to life's losers."[36] Among Cuomo's aphorisms was praise for the nuclear freeze movement because the freeze understood "that peace is better than war because life is better than death."

On foreign policy, Mondale had to beat back popular proposals calling for cuts in defense spending and a "no first use" policy for nuclear weapons, but he did have to acquiesce to a plank eschewing intervention in Central America and other hot spots. Neither in speeches nor in the platform did the Democrats offer any coherent alternative national security policy. Mondale also caved to Jesse Jackson's opposition to including a statement in the platform condemning anti-Semitism. Jackson and his allies derided such a statement as "unnecessary" and "very divisive." Jews were virtually the only interest group that Mondale stiffed.

Feminists wanted a revived commitment to the Equal Rights Amendment and a nod to the policy of comparable worth. Gay rights activists demanded, and got, a gay rights plank. Jesse Jackson pushed for a platform plank that mentioned racial quotas explicitly with the implication that some quotas were acceptable. (Jackson's exact draft language—and this is important when we consider in due course the Republican equivalent—was: "The Democratic Party opposes quotas which are inconsistent with the principles of our country.") Mondale compromised on language endorsing "the use of affirmative action goals, timetables, and other verifiable measures."

Jackson also wanted a Fairness Commission to deliver higher numbers of black delegates to future conventions. The composition of the delegates was already skewed away from the rank-and-file profile of the party; most had gone to college or graduate school and enjoyed household incomes twice the national average. *Time*'s William Henry remarked, "If times were as bad as their party said, for most of the delegates that knowledge would have to be an article of faith."[37] *Congressional Quarterly* noted how the unrepresentative profile of the delegates contributed to the party's ever-leftward tilt; there were no longer "those centrists and conservative forces that are the source of party strength in many regions of the country. Nobody at this convention called for the construction of the MX missile, nobody defended income tax indexing, nobody publicly disputed the gay-rights plank in the platform. The people who used to do that, with a few notable exceptions, no longer attend Democratic conventions." According to a *Washington Post* poll of convention delegates, just 22 percent agreed with the statement "The United States should take all steps, including the use of force, to prevent the spread of Communism"; by contrast, 63 percent of Democratic voters at large agreed with this statement. Joshua Muravchik lamented, "In 1984 the McGovernization of the Democratic Party was completed."[38]

Mondale compounded his party's liberalism-*über-alles* with the pledge to raise taxes in his acceptance speech: "Let's tell the truth. Mr. Reagan will raise taxes, and so will I. He won't tell you. I just did." According to Dan Rostenkowski, who was on the stage with Mondale at the conclusion of the speech, Mondale quipped: "Look at 'em; we're going to tax their ass off."[39] Throughout the campaign Mondale also called for the repeal of income tax indexing.

Republicans couldn't believe it. Reagan's chief campaign strategist, Stu

Spencer, said, "I was in ecstasy. The political graveyard is full of tax increasers." His campaign colleague Lee Atwater said, "I thought I was dreaming. I thought I had fallen asleep and was dreaming." Newt Gingrich, in San Francisco to hold daily press conferences attacking the proceedings, promptly canceled the next day's session, explaining that Republicans thought it best not to get between Mondale and the American people. "He hadn't read the public right," was Reagan's subdued reaction.[40] Many Democrats, caught by surprise, were as dismayed as Republicans were gleeful. Displaying the shrewdness that became evident a decade later, Bill Clinton urged that Mondale pledge to put any new revenue from a tax increase into a trust fund to reduce the deficit, or else voters would think that Democrats would just spend the money on more social programs. Clinton's suggestion fell on deaf ears.

Mondale's choice of words on foreign policy also reinforced liberal stereotypes. He complained about Reagan's arms buildup and the lack of negotiations with the Soviets: "But the truth is that between us, we have the capacity to destroy the planet. Every president since the bomb went off understood that and talked with the Soviets and negotiated arms control. Why has this administration failed? Why haven't they tried? Why can't they understand the cry of Americans and human beings for sense and sanity in control of these God-awful weapons? Why, why? Why can't we meet in summit conferences with the Soviet Union at least once a year?" Mondale's nasal twang made this paragraph sound weaker and whinier than it reads.[41]

*   *   *

REAGAN AND HIS campaign strategists enjoyed the luxury of sitting back and watching the internecine fighting and ideological nervous breakdown of the Democrats. The economic winds were blowing at Reagan's back (second quarter growth in 1984 came in at a sizzling 7.4 percent with inflation at 3.2 percent; as of July 1, the U.S. economy had experienced the strongest four quarters of growth in a generation), and he had addressed his vulnerabilities on foreign policy with his January 16 speech on Soviet relations. Consequently, the polls looked strong during the first half of the year except for the brief Gary Hart boomlet. Some polls showed Reagan ahead by more than 20 points; "It looks so good it's frightening," a top campaign aide said in March. While Hart and Mondale were prolonging the Democrats' prenomination agony in early June, Reagan was in Normandy, France, observing the fortieth anniversary of the D-Day landings with the kind of imagery and adulation for which he was the unequaled master among modern American presidents.[42]

Reagan's 1984 campaign stands in marked contrast to his aggressive

1980 effort. The conventional wisdom of political science is that elections featuring an incumbent are always referendums on the incumbent, compelling the incumbent to run a defensive campaign. But with the exogenous factors such as the strong economy along with the disarray of the Democrats, Reagan had more latitude to go on offense than many other incumbents. This is the strategy Franklin Roosevelt followed in the 1936 election—his object was not just reelection but the delegitimization of the Republican Party. Reagan had the opportunity to follow this approach; in fact, he was always at his best when on offense against liberalism, and seldom worse than when he assumed a defensive posture.

Instead of emulating FDR, however, the president's team went into a defensive crouch, deliberately adopting a generic campaign based on Reagan's record and personality, and especially on the renewed sense of optimism among Americans—"It's morning again in America," went the opening line of a Reagan ad that became the campaign's signature theme. Generally absent was any articulation of his principles. "There is to be no discussion of issues in this campaign," one of Reagan's political strategists informed the senior White House staff early in the year.[43] The political strategists would later blame the White House staff for the lack of specific new ideas to use in the campaign. "They don't have a goddamn thing in the pipeline," Stuart Spencer said in a tape-recorded campaign strategy meeting in June.[44] Maybe, Spencer thought, Reagan could talk about "acid rain and all that stuff," while others thought he might try talking about women's issues. Above all, abortion, Social Security, and—amazingly—tax reform must never be mentioned. The plain mistake here, on the part of both the White House staff and campaign strategists, was to think in terms of narrow issues rather than broad long-term partisan strategy.[45]

In any event, as Jane Mayer and Doyle McManus wrote in their book on Reagan's second term, *Landslide*, "[T]he Reagan campaign resorted to the political equivalent of mood music." William F. Buckley Jr. called it "the blandification of Ronald Reagan." After the election, Lou Cannon noted that "Reagan originated nothing in the campaign that produced his lopsided victory. He proposed no new programs and discussed no new ideas."[46] James MacGregor Burns wrote of FDR's 1936 reelection: "Roosevelt had fought the campaign on a highly personal basis. And he had built a winning coalition around himself—not the Democratic party, not the Democratic platform, not the liberal ideology—but around himself."[47] As it happens, Burns's view of FDR's 1936 campaign is mostly wrong—but substitute Reagan for FDR and it would be spot-on for 1984.

The bitter fruits of this defensive strategy would become most evident in the fall during Reagan's extremely poor showing in his first head-to-head debate with Mondale in Louisville, Kentucky, on October 7. Despite five debate practice sessions, the decision to cram Reagan with facts and figures to try to rebut Mondale's unfairness charge deprived Reagan of his chief asset as a critic of liberalism.[48] The conventional thinkers of his team had, in other words, turned him into a low-budget liberal, conceding the premises of liberalism about the role of government—a role he could not convincingly act. Reagan knew he'd done poorly and was furious with himself afterward. RNC chairman Paul Laxalt said, "He was brutalized by a briefing process that didn't make any sense." The media missed this aspect of the matter entirely, instead marching in lockstep on the theme that Reagan's age had caught up with him. (The *Wall Street Journal* opened the floodgates with its page-one feature: "New Question in Race: Is Oldest U.S. President Now Showing His Age?") Not surprisingly, when Reagan showed up in the second debate in a mood to attack, he did much better. In fact it was precisely the media's superficial coverage of the campaign that set up Reagan's showstopping one-liner in the second debate: "I am not going to exploit, for political purposes, my opponent's youth and inexperience."

According to Lou Cannon, Reagan chafed at the bland scripts his campaign team prepared for him and wanted to go harder after Mondale and the Democrats.[49] On a few occasions Reagan slipped the leash and got off some good general shots at Mondale and Democrats. "[Mondale] sees an America in which every day is tax day, April 15," Reagan quipped. "Well, we see an America in which every day is Independence Day, the Fourth of July." In his nomination acceptance speech at the Republican convention in Dallas he said, "America is presented with the clearest political choice of half a century. The distinctions between our two parties and the different philosophy of our political opponents are at the heart of this campaign." Except that they weren't. Reagan never made a serious or sustained case against the Democratic Congress, never argued that he couldn't govern unless the Democratic Congress was turned out. Although he had called repeatedly in his previous policy speeches for giving the president a line-item veto to control spending, he did not make this a campaign issue in the fall of 1984. He never mentioned his Strategic Defense Initiative or attacked Democrats for their opposition to this popular idea. (To the contrary, Reagan personally intervened to prevent the GOP platform from including a plank calling for the near-term deployment of missile defense.) Political scientists Marc Landy and Sidney Milkis, authors of *Presidential Greatness,* observed that "Reagan's 1984 campaign was a marvel of anti-partisanship. . . . Congressional Republican challengers, eagerly grasping after Reagan's coattails, were hard put to claim that they were more 'pro-morning' than their Democratic adversaries who were obstinate in their refusal to endorse the afternoon."

It is useful to contrast the language Reagan used in his standard stump speech in 1984 to appeal for Democratic votes with the language FDR used in 1936. On the surface their language seems similar—both appealed to members of the other party to "join us." FDR:

> There are two ways of viewing the government's duty in matters affecting economic and social life. The first sees to it that a favored few are helped and hopes that some of their prosperity will leak through, sift through, to labor, to the farmer, to the small businessman. That theory belongs to the party of Toryism, and I had hoped that most of the Tories left this country in 1776. But it is not and never will be the theory of the Democratic Party. This is no time for fear, for reaction or for timidity. *And here and now I invite those nominal Republicans who find their conscience cannot be squared with the groping and the failure of their party leaders to join hands with us.* (Emphasis added)

Notice especially that in equating Republicans with Toryism, FDR is arguing the Republican Party out of the mainstream of American politics. He also appeals to the class of "nominal Republicans" to switch parties.

By contrast, Reagan's approach to the other party was more ambiguous and less partisan. His appeals to Democratic voters were soft, never offering any positive reasons for voting Republican (or for Democrats and independents to *become* Republicans), nor did the president attempt to argue the Democratic Party out of the mainstream of American politics, as FDR had tried to do to the GOP. For example, a passage from Reagan's standard campaign stump speech reads:

> To all those Democrats, and I hope there are many here, who have been loyal to the party of FDR and Harry Truman and JFK, people who believe in protecting the interests of working people, who are not ashamed of America's standing for freedom in the world—we say to you: Join us. Come walk with us down that new path of hope and opportunity. I was a Democrat most of my adult life. *I didn't*

leave my party and we're not suggesting you leave yours. I am telling you that what I felt was that the leadership of the Democratic Party had left me and millions of patriotic Democrats in this country who believed in freedom. (Emphasis added)

Indeed, Reagan seldom referred to the Republican Party by name in his stump speeches, a fact not lost on perceptive observers on the left. Sidney Blumenthal noted in the *New Republic,* "The ancient ADAer never evoked the glorious past of the Grand Old Party. He ran for reelection as the true heir of Roosevelt."

Reagan's transpartisan appeal left open the possibility of a reformed Democratic Party being worthy of returning home at some future date, which turned out to be the successful strategy of Bill Clinton eight years later. Political scientist Charles Kesler observed: "Reagan, in short, was reluctant to create the serious political division that was required to shatter and humiliate the Democratic Party, and to reform the Republican Party." Harvey Mansfield wrote in a similar vein: "Reagan's failure to demand anything of the American people may have improved his own chances of re-election, but by reducing the size of the task, it softened the argument for voting for his party." Landy and Milkis offered a harsher judgment: "Indeed, his conduct was so politically feckless as to raise doubts about the degree to which Reagan himself was a Reaganite."[50]

The Republicans' reluctance to go for the jugular is all the more astonishing in retrospect given the large opening that the Democrats' disarray presented. As was the case with McGovern's candidacy in 1972, many members of Congress and other lower level Democrats dissociated themselves from the national ticket. Peter Schramm observed: "Democratic candidates showed great creativity. Some were able to be out of town, visiting relatives, or even checking their poultry farms in the northern part of the state, when Mondale was in town."[51] A few local Democratic organizations built wooden platforms wide enough for candidates to appear out of camera view from Mondale if they wished. Some went so far as to obfuscate their party preference deliberately. In Iowa, the very liberal Democratic congressman Tom Harkin accused his Republican opponent of being a "big spender." New York congressman Tom Downey, another of the most liberal House members, sent out a mailer showing a photo of himself with Reagan, along with the slogan "Return Tom Downey to Congress where he can continue to work with President Reagan." Downey was narrowly reelected. Here the paradox of the

1984 campaign can be most fully appreciated: when one party eschews partisan appeals, it enables the other party to do the same thing.

*   *   *

REAGAN'S DEFENSIVE STRATEGY obscured the lingering divisions within the Republican Party, which manifested themselves at the party's convention in Dallas. UN Ambassador Jeane Kirkpatrick gave a rousing keynote speech in which she coined the phrase "San Francisco Democrats," defined as those who always "blame America first." Behind the scenes, party moderates had opposed the selection of Kirkpatrick for the keynote and tried to limit her time at the podium. A compromise was struck whereby a dual keynote address was given by U.S. Treasurer Katherine Ortega in an attempt to appeal to Hispanic voters. Which party was flirting with quotas now? Her address was as forgettable as she was obscure.

Six Republican senators from the liberal wing of the party convened a rump platform session in Dallas to argue for a more liberal Republicanism, and seldom has the slang term *rump* been more appropriately employed.[52] This effort naturally attracted laudatory media. The *Los Angeles Times* editorialized that the liberal senators were "six of the most constructive Republicans in the U.S. Senate" and "are among the true party conservatives, not least for seeking to conserve the virtues that have made the Republican Party great."

Like the Democrats' platform fight over racial quotas, there was a revealing platform fight in Dallas that illuminated the split between the moderates, or old-guard pragmatists, and the conservative young Turks who wanted a more aggressive ideological party appeal.[53] The moderates argued in the platform committee hearings for an open-ended plank that could accept tax increases to curb the federal deficit "as a last resort." There was a certain coyness here, as moderate Republicans such as Bob Dole surely thought the last resort was inevitable.[54] As such, the proposed plank was a huge concession to Mondale's argument about the need for a tax increase.

Supply-siders vehemently disagreed, and there followed the Republican equivalent of the Democrats' fight over the deliberately ambiguous language about racial quotas in their platform. A compromise statement was offered: "We therefore oppose any attempts to increase taxes which would harm the recovery and reverse the trend toward restoring control of the economy to individual Americans." *Hold on a moment,* a few gimlet-eyed observers said. Note in this language an ambiguity of Talmudic subtlety: it is possible to imply that there might be forms of tax hikes that *would not* harm economic growth. The supply-siders were on guard against the evasive locutions such as "revenue enhancement" and "loophole closing" by which politicians describe tax increases.

Texas congressman Tom Loeffler proposed a change in punctuation to clarify the party's position: "We therefore oppose any attempts to increase taxes, which would harm the recovery . . ." Adding a comma after *taxes* sealed off this thin opening by making it categorically clear that it was Republican philosophy that *any* tax increase would harm economic growth and that therefore the Republican Party opposed *all* tax increases. The moderates objected, but Loeffler's amendment passed, aided in part by the platform committee chairman, Mississippi congressman Trent Lott.[55]

There were similar language fights elsewhere in the platform process. The 1980 Republican platform had endorsed the goal of U.S. military superiority over the Soviet Union, but now Senator John Warner, chairman of the platform committee on national security, pushed to delete the word *superiority*, arguing that it was not necessary for deterrence. While Warner won this change in his committee, the young Turks struck back in the full platform committee, inserting language asserting that the United States shall be "stronger than any potential adversary" so that "in case of conflict, the United States would clearly prevail." The young Turks won other victories over the old-guard establishment, including beating back attempts by a handful of moderates to revive Republican support for the Equal Rights Amendment and reiterating or even expanding pro-family planks from the 1980 platform. These victories ensured, though did not immediately achieve, the conservative future of the Republican Party.

The significance of the intraparty divisions was lost on the media, which portrayed the Republican convention as a uniformly extremist affair. The biased coverage of GOP conventions is not exactly a man-bites-dog story. In a survey of CBS and NBC News coverage published in *Public Opinion* magazine after the convention, William C. Adams found that "together, both CBS News and NBC News called the Republican Party, its platform, or its dominant leaders by conservative labels 113 times. They called the Democrats by liberal labels 21 times and moderate labels 14 times. . . . Republicans were measured in ideological terms, with their distance to the right discussed and calibrated. Democrats were seldom evaluated by such criteria. The terms 'right-wing' and 'right-winger' appeared repeatedly in covering Republicans; the terms 'left-wing' and 'left-winger' were never used by CBS News or NBC

News reporters covering Democrats." A separate study by Michael J. Robinson of the Media Analysis Project at George Washington University found "eight times as many references to the far right as to the far left in network coverage of the campaign."[56]

Overall, Robinson concluded after the election, the three TV news networks were three times more critical of Reagan than Mondale. The media were nearly as frustrated as Mondale that they couldn't get voters to come around to their point of view. A few days before the election, *New York Times* columnist James Reston wrote, "Not since the days of H. L. Mencken have so many reporters written so much or so well about the shortcomings of the President and influenced so few voters."[57] *Newsweek,* for example, wrote before the election that "[Reagan] is neither especially acute nor especially driven, neither especially knowledgeable nor especially well prepared for the most powerful job in the world."

*   *   *

IF THE REAGAN team's generic campaign strategy failed to take advantage of the strong Republican position and the Democrats' severe vulnerabilities, its most prominent theme—"Morning in America"—did manage to bring out the worst of liberal pessimism. Democratic representative Richard Gephardt said in response to the slogan: "It's getting closer and closer to midnight." The Democrats had stopped playing FDR's favorite anthem, "Happy Days Are Here Again," so Republicans played it at their convention.

The Democrats' reaction to "Morning in America" was remarkably tone deaf, as there was a palpable resurgence of patriotism among Americans in 1984. The full depth and dimensions of this were revealed by the way the nation turned a cosmopolitan event—the Olympic Games—into a patriotic rallying point. It was somehow fitting in the Age of Reagan that the 1984 Los Angeles Olympic Games were the first wholly managed as a private sector effort, and LA Olympic organizer Peter Ueberroth thought it would be a great marketing tactic to have the Olympic torch conveyed from Greece to Los Angeles by a circuitous relay involving thousands of runners who would each carry the torch for a few hundred yards. The torch procession took eighty-two days to wend its way through the United States, attracting large crowds even in the middle of the night.

On June 4, the *New York Times* carried a front-page story about how the torch procession had become a surprising cultural phenomenon. "More than Olympic Flame Crosses America," read the *Times* headline. Filing his story from Loose Creek, Missouri, *Times* reporter Andrew Malcolm observed that "something unusual and unplanned is also happening as the Olympic torch makes its way slowly across the nation. . . . For, unseen by most of the country, as the flame moves through places like Useful, Linn and Knob Noster, Union, Sedalia and Festus, it seems to be igniting some special feelings less tied to the Olympics and more to patriotism. They show themselves in many ways, often producing tears for spectators and participants alike."

Although the *Times* reporter didn't make the connection, it is plain that many people associated the torch with the Statue of Liberty, which during 1984 was shrouded in scaffolding during renovations, with its torch temporarily removed. The Olympic torch did nicely as a substitute and a catalyst, and it had the advantage of being mobile; after all, much of the U.S. population had never seen the Statue of Liberty in person. Flag-waving crowds everywhere would spontaneously begin singing "God Bless America" and "The Battle Hymn of the Republic." "I never expected it," one relay official told the *Times*. "But there's all these feelings pent up. And a special chemistry. And when people see that torch, they relate it to patriotism. There's a hunger for that in the land. And for a hero." Eventually all three TV networks, the major news weeklies, and large metropolitan papers followed the *Times*'s lead and took notice of this outpouring of patriotic sentiment over the torch. Reagan made sure to attend the opening ceremonies in Los Angeles in July.

The point is, there was more than just national pride at work in the American mind in 1984. For all of the legitimate caveats and reservations that can be made about American exceptionalism, there is no avoiding the conclusion that Americans were feeling exceptionally exceptional in 1984, perhaps in overcompensation for the years of doubt and decay in the 1960s and 1970s. Whatever its exact nature and meaning, the phenomenon was not fully lost on the Democrats; the Mondale campaign made sure there was an American flag placed on each seat for the final night of the San Francisco convention. They were a McGovernite party at heart, but they were shrewd enough not to want to look like one.

Reagan's skillful exploitation of the nation's improving mood contrasts sharply with the harshness of Democratic rhetoric. Indeed, the artless harshness of Democratic partisanship played into Reagan's hand. Tip O'Neill let fly with this: "The evil is in the White House at the present time. And that evil is a man who has no care and no concern for the working class of America and the future generations of America, and who likes to ride a horse. He's cold. He's mean. He's got ice water for blood." Geraldine Ferraro, taking heavy fire from Catholics for her pro-abortion views, fought back by saying that Reagan was not a good Christian, while Mondale argued that God was not a Republican. Senator Alan Cranston said, "Reagan is a trigger-happy President [with a] simplistic and paranoid world view leading us toward a nuclear collision that could end us all."

Just as the Democratic attack on "Republican unfairness" misread the reality and mood of a majority of Americans, their line on Reagan as a warmonger failed to gain traction for the same reason. A careful reading of public opinion polls would have revealed the subtle and dissonant state of Americans on the question of war and peace, but ideology and partisan enthusiasm blinded liberals and the media from perceiving that Reagan's theme of "peace through strength" easily trumped the Democrats' emphasis on peace through talk. Reagan's pollster, Richard Wirthlin, detected this subtlety in his polls and crafted a strategy to gain the initiative over the Democrats.

One result of Wirthlin's more subtle reading of the dissonance in American opinion was a memorable campaign ad that gently deflected the worry about Reagan on foreign policy and attacked Democratic weakness at the same time: the "Bear in the Woods" TV spot. Narrated with the relaxing dulcet voice of Hal Riney (who also voiced the "Morning in America" ads) over an image of a grizzly bear on the prowl, the ad said: "There is a bear in the woods. For some people, the bear is easy to see. Others don't see it at all. Some people say the bear is tame. Others say it's vicious and dangerous. Since no one can really be sure who's right, isn't it smart to be as strong as the bear? If there is a bear?" The spot climaxes with the bear backing off from the silhouette of a man (Reagan?) whose firearms are not apparent.

The "Bear in the Woods" ad coincided with the release of a surprise summer hit movie, a film about a Soviet-sponsored invasion of the United States called *Red Dawn,* in which a band of high school students mounts a guerilla campaign against the brutal occupation. (Alexander Haig provided technical and plot advice for the film.) The very premise of the movie made most critics sneer. The *New York Times*'s Janet Maslin called it "rabidly inflammatory" and "incorrigibly gung-ho." Vincent Canby, writing also for the *Times,* wrote that *Red Dawn* "provides an unusual glimpse into the mind of a certain kind of contemporary archconservative . . . [I]t exposes for all to see the cockeyed nightmares of those on the lunatic fringe." *TV Guide,* once owned by Reagan's friend Walter Annenberg, called it "infantile right-wing fantasy" and the "cinematic embodiment of the paranoid delusions of militarists, survivalists, and television evangelists; definitely a film for the Reagan era." The *Financial Times* wrote: "*Red Dawn* is a slice of gung-ho anti-Communism cut fresh and quivering from the American body paranoiac." Once again it was difficult to distinguish American media from Soviet media. *Pravda* called *Red Dawn* "a monstrous anti-Soviet concoction filled with so many bloody scenes, a film so primitive, and so relentlessly false." Soviet television didn't bother with the heavy lifting of original criticism; it simply quoted American reviewers. As is often the case with movies the critics widely dislike, *Red Dawn* did big box office over the summer, and therein lies another parable of establishment liberalism misreading the public.

The tactic of portraying Reagan as a warmonger might have gained some traction in August when, during a microphone check before the president's regular Saturday radio broadcast, Reagan quipped: "My fellow Americans, I am pleased to tell you today that I've signed legislation that will outlaw Russia forever. We begin bombing in five minutes." Reagan forgot—not for the first time—the Washington adage that all microphones should be assumed to be live, and despite the audible guffaws from the people in the room making it clear it was a joke, the news media played it up with grim satisfaction. Snap polls showed a hiccup in public support for the president.

Then, inexplicably, the Soviets gave Reagan an assist. After saying that it could not deal with Reagan and tasking the KGB to do everything possible to impede Reagan's reelection, the Kremlin suddenly began sending feelers to resume some kind of contact. The Soviets had probably concluded that Reagan was a sure bet for reelection and wanted to begin figuring out a face-saving way to resume arms negotiations. A Soviet diplomatic blunder in late June may have contributed to their about-face. The Soviets proposed a new round of arms talks focusing on "the militarization of space"—an obvious gambit to undermine SDI—expecting the United States to refuse and hand the Soviets a propaganda club. But when the United States quickly accepted, with the proviso that space weapons ought to include missiles that travel through space, the Soviets clumsily backed away from their own offer.

In early September the Kremlin accepted Reagan's invitation for Andrei Gromyko to visit the White House following Gromyko's annual address to the United Nations, even though the Soviets knew that Reagan would press hard on human rights. Reagan prepared for the meeting as though it were a full-blown summit, having meetings with Richard Nixon and Henry Kissinger. Reagan recorded in his diary three days before the meeting: "Henry K. came by with more insight re Gromyko. I found we are tracking very close on the approach to take." The State Department produced a set of talking points for Reagan, but he spent the weekend at Camp David writing several pages of talking points of his own, much to the surprise of Shultz and Foggy Bottom.

Gromyko and Reagan sat down in the Oval Office on Friday, September 28, and the media demand for photographs was so immense that photographers had to be brought through in shifts. After the media were finally excused, Reagan and Gromyko got down to three and a half hours of talks culminating with lunch in the formal dining room. As he had with Dobrynin and in his correspondence with other Soviet rulers, Reagan put forward his view that the Soviet Union was philosophically and practically an expansionist power, but that the United States did not seek conflict or to change the Soviet system (although NSDD 75 came close to declaring regime transformation to be the goal of U.S. policy). Gromyko naturally demurred, and asserted that while he believed in the Marxist dialectic that all the world would eventually become socialist "as a historical process," the Soviet Union did not seek to spread its ideology by force. He also refused to be drawn into discussion of human rights in the Soviet Union, which he said were none of the United States' business.

But for all the appearances, the meeting was not the usual standoff. *Washington Post* reporter Don Oberdorfer observed: "It quickly became apparent that Gromyko had not come to Washington to negotiate the details of agreements but to size up Reagan for the Soviet leadership on a philosophical level, which the Soviets themselves call the 'level of principle.' " Oberdorfer added the obvious point: "Reagan was most comfortable at precisely this level of broad generality: the fundamental reasons for the West's belief that it was threatened by the Soviet Union's ideology and actions."[58] Despite the sour statement Gromyko later issued wondering "whether Washington is going to correct its line of policy," he is thought to have recognized Reagan's sincerity about improving relations. For his part, Reagan made a curious diary entry about the encounter: "I figured they nursed a grudge that we don't respect them as a superpower." It was to be Gromyko's last visit to the White House.

Gromyko met briefly with Walter Mondale later the same afternoon to avoid the impression of favoring Reagan and to cause as much mischief as possible. Mondale, according to the *New York Times,* told Gromyko that if elected he would unilaterally freeze all new weapons development for six months as an incentive for the Soviets to hold a summit. The Soviet press heralded Mondale's attitude in what was tantamount to an endorsement, but the effort could not match the boon Reagan received from the home field advantage of the Oval Office.

Gromyko's White House visit removed the last possibility that Mondale could effectively exploit fears of Reagan's foreign policy, and the die was cast for the election. After late October, when Reagan dispatched Mondale with his memorable one-liner in the second debate about his opponent's "youth and inexperience," there was no drama about the outcome. Relentless polling showed that very few voters—perhaps 10 percent or less—changed their mind in the course of the fall campaign. When it appeared that a fifty-state sweep of the electoral college might be possible, Reagan made a last-minute visit to Minnesota in an attempt to wrest Mondale's home state away from him. Mondale closed out the campaign in a state of disbelief and denial; he couldn't perceive how political conditions had changed. "I don't believe that the American people are selfish," he said repeatedly before the election, as if charitable sentiment was possible only through partisan liberalism. Margaret Warner of *Newsweek* commented: "To him, those were the possibilities: to be selfish or vote for his kind of Democrat. He could not recognize that something was changing in the relationship between individuals and government."[59]

Mondale managed to hang on to his home state by the slight margin of eight thousand votes (making Minnesota the only state that never voted for Reagan even once), while Reagan swept the other forty-nine states, collecting the largest electoral college margin ever. Reagan racked up 59 percent of the popular vote—the fourth-largest popular vote landslide in presidential history, and a figure that no candidate has come close to matching since. He carried nearly every demographic except blacks, Hispanics, and Jews. He carried 61 percent of independents, a quarter of registered Democrats, and three-quarters of young first-time voters. Despite the presence of a Catholic woman as a running mate on the Democratic ticket, Reagan carried 56 percent of the Catholic vote and 54 percent of the women's vote. The gender gap facing the GOP was—and still is—an unshakeable media theme, though one wonders whether the media have it backward: Reagan pulled 62 percent of men, suggesting that the gender gap is as much a problem of Democrats failing to attract the votes of men as Republicans falling short with women.[60]

Despite the magnitude of Reagan's landslide, he had no coattails. Reagan received seventeen million more votes than Republican House candidates. Before the election Reagan's campaign manager, Ed Rollins, said: "If we don't gain Republican seats in Congress, the Reagan Revolution is over."[61] Most analysis predicted a twenty-to-twenty-five-seat gain for Republicans in the House, but on election day the GOP picked up a paltry fourteen seats, compared to thirty-three in 1980, most of which gain had been lost in the 1982 mid-term election. Nine of the Republican House pickups were in two states—Texas and North Carolina—where the Republican Party ran integrated campaigns, presenting a united front to voters. Nationally the popular vote for the House was almost exactly equal (Republicans actually received a majority of total votes cast in contested seats), but because of gerrymandering Democrats would enjoy a comfortable 253–182 margin in the House. Ninety-six percent of House incumbents were reelected; the incoming Ninety-ninth Congress had one of the lowest numbers of new representatives in decades. One of the newcomers was Tom Delay of Texas, elected in a Houston district once held by Vice President George H. W. Bush.

Action on the Senate side was more interesting. Judge Mitch McConnell in Kentucky upset incumbent Democratic senator Dee Huddleston after trailing by more than ten points in preelection polls. Illinois's liberal Republican senator Charles Percy, who had been a thorn in the side of Reagan's foreign policy, lost to a liberal, Representative Paul Simon. Other notable newcomers to the Senate included John Kerry in Massachusetts and Albert Gore Jr. in Tennessee, who won the seat vacated by retiring Republican Howard Baker. Victor Ashe, the Republican candidate Gore defeated, said of Gore: "He's bright, intelligent, and will be on the national ticket within a decade."[62] Republicans ended up losing two Senate seats, narrowing their advantage to 53–47.

The election result left the ideological divisions in Congress more raw than ever, especially in the House, where a dispute over an Indiana congressional district is said to have been a turning point in the partisan fury of the people's chamber. A Republican had been certified as the winner after two recounts of a close contest, but House Democrats voted to seat the Democratic candidate instead. House Republican whip Trent Lott said, "I think we ought to go to war," while Representative Henry Hyde said, "This has put a breach in the House like nothing I've seen in my ten years here." House Republicans would continue to be, in the words of the *National Journal*, "the Rodney Dangerfields of American politics—no respect."

The Republicans' middling results on the congressional level also enabled Democrats and the media to deprecate the magnitude of Reagan's landslide. Speaker Tip O'Neill said: "There is no mandate out there." A *New York Times* headline conferred its blessing on O'Neill's line: "Poll Finds Reagan Failed to Obtain Policy Mandate." Political scientist Theodore Lowi wrote that Reagan's victory "was a personal triumph—broad, nationwide, but shallow. The majority was large but weak." It was, he added, not a victory of "a conservative majority, but of a Reagan majority." Representative Tony Coelho: "The people gave him a personal victory. But they let us keep effective control of the House to counteract his extremism." Coelho went on to tell Hedrick Smith of the *New York Times:* "If the White House had not been so selfish and had not worried about trying to carry fifty states and if they had gone out after key Senate races and key House seats, we would be in much worse shape. Reagan did not win a party landslide and that is what his party needed."[63]

Newt Gingrich displayed his instinct for the political jugular with his comment that "Reagan should have prepared for reelection by forcing a polarization of the country. He should have been running against liberals and radicals. . . . Reagan should have focused more on changing the nation than on governing." Ed Rollins later acknowledged the strategic error of the campaign: "We'd run an issueless campaign. There was no second-term plan." Marc Landy and Sid Milkis concluded: "Morning in America dimmed into the twilight of de-alignment."

But dismissing Reagan's landslide as a mere "personal victory" ironically enabled many liberals to ignore their own mounting troubles and set them up for future disappointments. The cliché that voters liked Reagan's personality more than his policies reassured dispirited liberals, who clung to the belief that all liberalism needed to do was ride out Reagan. A careful look at opinion research would have exposed liberalism's wishful thinking: one study in *Public Opinion Quarterly* found that Reagan's job approval rating was consistently higher than his personal approval rating, and that issue by issue, a solid majority of voters sided more with Reagan than Democrats.[64] More ominous for liberal Democrats was the fact that Reagan and Republicans were noticeably more popular among younger voters, those under age thirty. Reagan's highest approval ratings—a stunning 82 percent favorable in the fall of 1984—came from voters under age twenty-four, and Reagan's best receptions on the campaign trail occurred on college campuses, a fact that astonished everyone who recalled Reagan's adversarial relationship with "the kids" on campus in the 1960s. In fact, *Rolling Stone* magazine reported that a survey of its readers revealed a majority had voted for Reagan.

Most liberals who took note of these trends simply lashed out at the young. Alvin Schorr wrote in the *Los Angeles Times* that conservative young people were "cowards" lacking the "venturesomeness and excitement" of their 1960s predecessors. Ellen Goodman took Reagan's showing among the young as a sign of "youthful selfishness," and Arthur Schlesinger attributed it to a "cyclical retreat" from idealism to "privatism."

Schlesinger's "cycles of American history" thesis provided the warm blanket that chilled liberals needed. The following year Richard Reeves would offer this prediction in his book *The Reagan Detour:* "The Reagan years would be a detour, necessary if sometimes nasty, in the long progression of American liberal democracy. . . . [I]deas and issues will inevitably bring liberalism and the Democrats back into fashion and power—sooner rather than later."[65] A little bit of class warfare would do the trick, Reeves thought. As if on cue, a few days after the election the American Catholic bishops released a new pastoral letter on the economy that sounded like a clerical echo of the Democratic Party platform, calling for large government interventions on behalf of economic equality. The fairness issue was not going to go away, even though voters had repudiated it.

But a few liberals understood that the size and nature of Reagan's landslide clearly indicated significant problems for the Democratic Party. Pat Moynihan said: "I'll tell you what chills the blood of liberals. It was always thought that the old bastards were the conservatives. Now the young people are becoming the conservatives and we're the old bastards."[66] Incoming Democratic Party chairman Paul Kirk, a former aide to Ted Kennedy, said forthrightly that Democrats needed to "shed the interest-group image." Kevin Phillips said Mondale's crushing defeat was "the death knell for the smokestack wing of the Democratic Party." Moderates and thoughtful liberals founded the Democratic Leadership Council (DLC) in an effort to wrest the party back toward the center. One early enthusiast of the DLC was Bill Clinton, who said the council's purpose was to create "a new middle ground of thinking on which someone can not only run for President but actually be elected."[67]

Clinton said that the Democratic Party "knows it has to change" and told journalist Peter Brown, "If we lead with class warfare, we lose." About Jesse Jackson, Clinton added presciently, "I have never believed Democrats need to distance themselves from him. I think Democrats need to *disagree* with him."[68] Sister Souljah acquired a bull's-eye on her back, with a use-by date of 1992.

*   *   *

EVEN IF THE 1984 election failed to be the decisive realignment that conservative partisans had hoped for, Harvey Mansfield judged that "[t]here were incremental changes favorable to the Republicans portending a future realignment, together with the continued, perhaps intensified division for now between a Republican presidency and a Democratic House of Representatives." Running a campaign aimed at propelling party realignment would have required a high-risk audacity that is rare among political figures, and almost nonexistent among political strategists and operatives. Reagan conceivably could have lost had he attempted a high-risk strategy. The temptation to run a campaign playing to Reagan's personal popularity and virtues along with the strong economy was overwhelming, especially when the overwrought pessimism of Democrats presented such an easy target.

In his election night victory speech (in which he deliberately neglected to mention Mondale because of his bitter feelings about Democratic attacks on him), Reagan signed off with what became a signature line of his fall stump speech: "You ain't seen nothin' yet." Then he left to spend most of the remainder of November at the ranch, contemplating how to make good on this boast.

INTERMISSION

REAGAN AT THE RANCH

―――❦―――

*Some place along the line, a fella has to have time to sit
on a hill and think, or maybe just sit on a hill.*
—RONALD REAGAN, JUNE 1979

TWENTY MILES NORTH of Santa Barbara, California, and seven
miles up Refugio Canyon Road from the Pacific Ocean, past fragrant
citrus groves, nut tree orchards, and a rustic church camp, through dry creek
beds, around steep, hair-curling switchback curves, and near the twenty-five-
hundred-foot summit of the Santa Ynez coastal mountains, is the left turn
that is the key to understanding Ronald Reagan.

It is the location of Rancho del Cielo, the "Ranch in the Sky."

The difficulty of reaching Reagan's remote mountain location might be
taken as a metaphor of the difficulty of reaching past the supposed personal
remoteness of Reagan himself. Yet contemplating Reagan's most cherished
private space reveals important clues to his public character. It was no accident that Reagan retreated to the ranch after securing his reelection: he
would spend nearly one-eighth of his presidency—354 days spread over
forty-seven separate trips—there, far more than Nixon spent at his Western
White House in San Clemente. His total would have exceeded a calendar
year but for crises that cut short ranch trips or prevented his scheduled departure, which happened four or five times during his presidency. Reagan
liked to pass Thanksgiving at the ranch, but he never spent Christmas there
during his presidency, out of deference to the staff and Secret Service agents,
who would have been forced to be apart from their families if he did so.

Lou Cannon noted: "There is more of Reagan in this ranch than in all the speeches he ever gave." For all its remoteness, seclusion from the world is not the sole effect the ranch conveys. To the contrary, the expansiveness of the views from Rancho del Cielo matches the capaciousness of Reagan's outlook for America. The vista from the western ridge of the ranch includes the Channel Islands off the coast and stretches south to Santa Barbara, more than twenty miles away. The eastern ridge of the ranch looks out over the long Santa Ynez Valley northwest toward Santa Maria. It offers some of the most exquisite views in all of California, easily matching the coastal vista from William Randolph Hearst's famous castle farther north up the coast at San Simeon.

From the ridges and promontories of the 688-acre Rancho del Cielo all the expansive possibilities of California can be imagined. California has always conveyed its own distinctive subset of the American dream, in a way that Reagan's home state of Illinois cannot. (The Illinois dream? The Indiana dream? The Oklahoma dream? Not likely.) Imagination, California's great historian Kevin Starr has written, is the first premise of lifestyle, and Reagan, our most imaginative president, drew inspiration and sustenance from the landscape. Reagan liked to say, "This place casts a spell. I suppose it's the scriptural line [from Psalm 121], 'I look into the hills from whence cometh my strength.' I understand it better when I'm up here." Michael Deaver recalls a moment in the spring of Reagan's first year in office when the president asked him about the absence of ranch time in his long-range schedule: "Look, Mike, you can tell me to do a lot of things, but you're not going to tell me when to go to the ranch. I'm seventy years old and I figure that ranch is going to add some years onto my life, and I'm going to enjoy it."

Reagan came from a flat place—Dixon, Illinois—in the flattest region of the country, and probably didn't see his first mountains until he left his radio broadcasting job in Des Moines to head to Hollywood when he was twenty-six. He was slightly claustrophobic, which is one reason he liked high, open places with big views. This relatively late experience with mountains makes all the more significant Reagan's frequent references to John Winthrop's famous sermon about the "shining city on a hill"; while Reagan saw that America was the ever-emerging city on a hill, his mountaintop ranch represented his own microcosm of the dream. "We relax at the ranch," he liked to say, "which if not Heaven itself, probably has the same ZIP code."

Winston Churchill made note of the transcendent beauty of California on his leisurely trip up the coast in 1929 (he passed through Santa Barbara on his way to visit Hearst in San Simeon), writing in the London *Daily Telegraph*:

"A more beautiful region I have hardly ever seen. . . . The Pacific laps the long-drawn shores, and assures at all seasons of the year an equable and temperate climate. The cool ocean and the warm land create in their contact a misty curtain which veils and mitigates the vigour of the sun. By a strange inversion, you ascend the mountain to get warm, and descend to the sea level to get cool. Take it for all in all, the western slopes of the Rocky Mountains offer a spacious, delectable land, where man may work or play on every day of the year."[1] Churchill was confused about his geography—California's central coast mountains are known as the Santa Lucia range, not the Rockies— but he would have understood Reagan's fascination with and longing for Rancho del Cielo.

A survey of Reagan's activity at the ranch dispels the widespread view that he was a lazy man or that his ranch was merely another "set," an affectation acquired from his frequent movie roles as a western cowboy. Although Reagan went to the ranch chiefly for recreation and relaxation, the fulfillment of both purposes depended upon its being an authentic working ranch. At the ranch Reagan rose early, often shortly after sunrise, which was earlier than he would rise in the White House. (When told before assuming office in 1981 that his national security staff would be in the Oval Office at 7:00 a.m. for his daily briefing, Reagan replied, "Well, they'll have an awful long wait, then, because I'm not coming to the office until 9.") In the first light of morning, Reagan, wearing a bathrobe, would eat breakfast and read the morning newspaper along with a limited number of official papers—his "homework"— that an aide would bring up from Santa Barbara first thing every day. Always mindful to watch his weight and stay trim, he ate a light breakfast, usually fruit or toast.

Daily life at the ranch revolved around horseback riding and the collateral chores to maintain and improve the ranch. At about 9:00 a.m. Reagan would change into his jodhpurs and boots and walk up the hill to his tack room and barn to prepare his and Nancy's horses for their morning ride. Jodhpurs? Aide Ed Harper recalls Reagan explaining, "You know, my PR guys tell me I should wear jeans when I ride a horse. I never have. I don't wear jeans, I wear jodhpurs. And they say, 'Well, you know, that kind of looks like you're uppity or something.' That's the way I am. I've always worn them, I'm going to continue to wear them. I'm not going to wear jeans. That would be phony for me."[2] (Reagan did sometimes wear jeans, though typically if he was doing physical chores such as brush clearing.)

Reagan's tack room and workshop, like his desk back at the White House, were perfectly arranged. He kept tools hung in the proper order on Peg-Boards just as they might be arranged in a hardware store display case, and his multiple chain saws were cleaned, oiled, and lined up neatly on the wall.

Reagan's favorite mount was a large white Arabian named El Alamein, a gift from Mexican president José López Portillo.³ Reagan liked to say, "There is nothing quite so good for the inside of a man than the outside of a horse"—he said it so often, in fact, that it could be thought of as the central creed of Reagan's equestrian liturgy. Most reporters were ignorant that the phrase actually comes from Xenophon's *Art of Horsemanship.*

Once the horses were groomed and saddled, Reagan would clang an old railroad bell outside the barn (it had belonged to Nancy's grandfather), a signal to let Nancy know that the horses were ready for the ride. The Secret Service says the biggest challenge for any president is providing recreation that is both safe and secure. Outdoor activities, such as Gerald Ford's skiing or Jimmy Carter's whitewater raft trips, are a nightmare for security and communications planning. Although horseback riding confined to the president's private land offered advantages for security planning, riding is inherently dangerous. (In fact, Reagan's fall from a horse onto his head in 1992 is thought to have contributed to the onset of his Alzheimer's disease.) Reagan, who rode English saddle, was a "consummate horseman," in the words of John Barletta, his most frequent Secret Service riding companion. Riding was arguably more dangerous for the Secret Service detail than for Reagan. One agent broke an arm from a riding fall.

Even though the ranch was isolated, it presented considerable security challenges. With more than four miles of perimeter, it was impossible to seal off the ranch from potential intruders. A one-thousand-square-foot modular building was brought to the ranch to serve as a Secret Service command post and discreetly set up behind the tree line (Reagan would sometimes wander up there on Sunday afternoons and ask if he could watch football games on TV with his off-duty agents). Checkpoints had to be manned twenty-four hours a day along the access road to the ranch. Bulletproof glass was installed on Reagan's old adobe ranch house (the weight of the large picture window in the dining room caused the wall below it to sag), and a steel-lined secure room was built in an interior closet, to be Reagan's last refuge in a worst-case scenario. Motion sensors and emergency perimeter lighting were set up throughout the ranch, some concealed in fake boulders supplied by Disney's special-effects department. False alarms from jackrabbits, deer, and coyotes were frequent. Two Secret Service marksmen manned a countersniper's nest at the highest point of the ranch whenever Reagan was present. Air traffic over the area was banned. At several points credible threats against

Reagan, including one involving the famous terrorist Carlos the Jackal, generated a state of high alert at the ranch.

Even these thorough measures proved unavailing on rare occasions. One morning after a thick fog bank lifted, the Secret Service command post was astounded to spot a backpacker with a small tent pitched in the meadow barely a hundred yards from Reagan's house. The backpacker had wandered onto the ranch in the middle of the night and somehow avoided tripping any of the numerous motion detectors set around the perimeter. The Secret Service quietly ushered the unwitting camper off the grounds, telling him only that he was trespassing on private property. One threat the Secret Service could not counter was a Soviet missile submarine that would take up position off the California coast when Reagan visited the ranch.

The command post set up a large topographical wall map that divided the ranch into tiny grids and established numbered checkpoints along every riding route Reagan might take. Reagan's Secret Service code name was Rawhide, and seldom has a president matched up with his code name so fully. A horseback ride involved having a detail of four mounted agents along with a Humvee carrying secure communications equipment and the military aide with the ubiquitous nuclear launch codes known as the "football." Agents were in constant radio contact with the command post, where an agent would mark the riding party's location with a pushpin on the wall map. It was in the middle of a ride on September 2, 1983, that Reagan stopped to take a call from National Security Adviser William Clark confirming that the Soviet Union had shot down Korean Air flight 007. An angry Reagan made his way back to the barn, remarking bitterly about how those "damn Russians" had "killed all those innocent people." (His Secret Service horseback-riding partner, John Barletta, recalls that this was one of only two instances when he ever witnessed Reagan visibly angry.)[4]

Riding brought out Reagan's playful side. Once or twice he pulled a practical joke on new Secret Service agents riding with him for the first time by suddenly galloping away over the side of a steep hillside out of sight, then doubling around behind the panicked agents who thought the president of the United States had just ridden off a cliff. When the TV networks installed cameras with powerful telephoto lenses on a nearby peak to peer down on the ranch, Reagan wanted to fake a heart attack and fall off his horse as a prank. The Secret Service talked him out of it, warning that the hair-trigger news networks might rush to broadcast the story, potentially crashing the stock market and alarming allies. Nancy Reagan turned the tables on the media voyeurs by displaying a JUST SAY NO sign (the slogan of her antidrug campaign) whenever in camera range. (After vigorous White House complaints, the networks eventually agreed to remove the cameras and respect the president's privacy.)

Riding was also reconnaissance for Reagan; he looked for places to clear brush, trim trees, and blaze new trails. Over the years he had blazed dozens of riding routes through the square-mile ranch. Following the morning ride and lunch, he would often head out in the afternoon with several ranch hands to cut brush and trim trees. When Reagan was shot in 1981, and again when he had hip replacement surgery in 2001, surgeons remarked on his remarkable fitness. *He has the body of a much younger man,* doctors said. "I have never in my life seen a chest like that on a man his age," said Dr. Benjamin Aaron, the surgeon who extracted the bullet from behind Reagan's heart on March 30, 1981.

His ranch hands didn't need a doctor's word to know this. Reagan regularly outlasted his ranch hands at physical tasks, sometimes continuing to saw, chop, and cut when everyone else took a drink break. The Secret Service was reluctant to allow Reagan to continue to operate a chain saw and were even more anxious about his use of a wood chipper (known as "Gipper's chipper") but relented when they recognized that he knew how to handle yard equipment better than they did. They drew the line, however, at another of his ranch activities: shooting at coyotes that menaced his small herd of cattle. Reagan shot at a coyote early one morning in November 1980, shortly after his election, and set his new Secret Service detail into a full-scale panic. "I guess I should have told you I was going to do that," Reagan said to an agent. The Secret Service regretfully informed him that they had to confiscate his ammunition.

Reagan's trimming and cutting had a practical purpose beyond clearing riding trails. His main ranch house was without modern heat and depended wholly on two fireplaces for warmth. He prided himself on chopping the wood supply for the house, and always kept an ample stack outside the front door. Reagan's fondness for brush clearing also pleased the Secret Service, since the potential for a catastrophic fire, a frequent occurrence in this part of California, ranked high among their security worries. When a friend remarked once that Reagan couldn't possibly ever hope to clear all the brush on the ranch, Reagan looked surprised and said, "That's rather the point, isn't it?" ABC's Sam Donaldson once joked on the air, "I suspect just before he gets there, they haul up truckloads of brush and wood for him to chop because, if he chopped as much as they say he does, there wouldn't be any trees left on the ranch." The remark got back to Reagan, who ordered his ranch foreman to pile up in one place all the brush he had cut during his current stay and then sent a photo of it to Donaldson. Reagan's note read: "Dear Sam: Here's the proof I chopped it all with my own little hatchet."[5]

Like Churchill, who built a substantial brick wall at his country estate of Chartwell, Reagan was an energetic and unorthodox builder at the ranch. He decided to build a rail fence around his pond (which he had previously dug himself with a rented tractor) with cut-up telephone poles, and called the phone company himself to inquire about how he could purchase some poles. (The employee who took the call at Pacific Bell thought the familiar-sounding voice on the phone had to be a hoax.) Reagan dug most of the large holes to sink the fence posts himself with a pick and shovel rather than a mechanical auger. He built a stone patio in front of the main house with stones he had rounded up on the ranch. Over the fireplace mantel was Reagan's custom taxidermy: two "jackalopes," jackrabbit heads fitted with deer antlers.

Reagan had first heard about the ranch in 1974 from his longtime friend William Wilson. The story goes that the first time Reagan went to see the ranch when he was considering its purchase, Nancy wanted to turn the car around when they reached the first switchback. For one of the rare instances in their marriage, Reagan refused to defer to Nancy's urgings, telling her firmly, "We're going to make this ranch work!" Make it work he did; Reagan remodeled the house substantially by himself with the assistance of two ranch hands, Willard "Barney" Barnett and Dennis Leblanc, tearing down walls and enclosing a screened porch to make an anteroom. Still, Nancy didn't care for the ranch during the first few years. But she came to treasure it during Reagan's White House years because it was the one place where she and her Ronnie could find a relative degree of privacy.

The ranch was a counterpoint to the glamour and high style of the Reagan White House in Washington. In fact, Mikhail Gorbachev was unimpressed with Rancho del Cielo when he and his wife, Raisa, visited in 1992 after both men had left office. Surely, Gorbachev thought, the former leader of the United States of America would have a more lavish private residence than the modestly appointed twelve-hundred-square-foot adobe ranch house that Reagan proudly showed off to his guests. Not even the square mile of land comprising the ranch—raw land being about the only commodity the Soviet economy had in surplus during its terminal phase—could make up for his surprise at its modest character. (One detail did make an impression on Gorbachev, though: Reagan had his own gasoline pump, installed outside his barn.) Reagan also hosted Queen Elizabeth, Margaret Thatcher, and Canadian prime minister Brian Mulroney at the ranch during or after his presidency.

Unlike Nixon, who had made his home in San Clemente into a working Western White House, Reagan did not want his ranch to become a surrogate White House overrun with staff and crowded with official activity. Reporters were ambivalent about following Reagan out to California in the summer; they loved escaping the humid Washington summer for the cool ocean breezes of Santa Barbara, but precious little news emanated from Rancho del Cielo. Sam Donaldson said, "When he was up at the ranch, the hardest decision the reporters had to make was where to go for dinner. There was no real news, just the routine 'ranch report' every day." Hence reporters had to make news with what scraps they could find, generating such riveting headlines as "Plague-Bearing Rat Found at Reagan Ranch."

In the absence of frantic presidential activity, which is the crack cocaine of the Washington press corps, the media naturally reverted to criticism of Reagan's supposedly lax ways. *Time*'s Roger Rosenblatt wrote of Reagan's twenty-eight-day ranch stay in August 1981: "A pleasant image for the public to dwell on, but it also raises some questions and a bit of a stir: Is so long a holiday fitting and proper for a President, the leader of the free world? Can Washington survive without being the center of Government for so long a stretch? Is there life without news?"[6] Rosenblatt quoted a typically unctuous academic scribbler, Professor Louis Masotti of Northwestern University, who complained: "We don't have a foreign policy, and the real issues of transportation, urban policy and open lands have not been addressed. I don't know how a President in this day and age can take a month off." Reagan knew better. "Presidents don't have vacations," he wrote in his diary; "they just have a change of scenery."[7]

Reagan usually found time for a nap in an outdoor hammock late in the afternoon after the day's chores were done. In the evening, if he finished his official paperwork he would delve into the mixture of western and sports books that rested alongside serious conservative works on the ranch house bookshelves, such as Whittaker Chambers's *Witness* and Churchill's World War II memoirs. The Reagan aide who told Carl Bernstein that "it's true that he's got more horses than books" clearly never saw these bookshelves. Often Reagan would watch TV with Nancy in their living room, which served as their most private inner sanctum; their favorite viewing was *Jeopardy!* and *Murder, She Wrote.*

Reagan would go for his last horseback ride at the ranch in 1995, a few months after he announced his Alzheimer's disease to the nation. It fell to his Secret Service riding companions to tell him that it was no longer safe for him to ride at the ranch. John Barletta recalls being choked up with emotion as he went to Reagan to break the sad news, but Reagan, ever the reassuring figure, put his hand on Barletta's shoulder and said, "It's okay." Even in adversity, life was always okay for Reagan at his own city on a hill.

PART II

THE NEW COLOSSUS

CHAPTER 9

THE FULCRUM: THREE DAYS IN GENEVA

———⟫•⟪———

Russian policy does not change. Its methods, tactics,
maneuvers may be altered but the pole star of this policy,
the domination of the world, is fixed.
—KARL MARX, 1867

As everybody has always known, any move for
disarmament is going to be slow, tortuous, and
certainly gradual, even at best.
—PRESIDENT DWIGHT EISENHOWER, 1955

THE CONVENTIONAL WISDOM among journalists, political scientists, and historians is that second presidential terms are a disappointment and often a disaster, especially if the second term arrives through a landslide. FDR's second term foundered quickly on the shoals of the ill-conceived court-packing scheme, which derailed the momentum of the New Deal and led to a rout at the next midterm election. Eisenhower had a recession, minor scandals, and foreign policy embarrassments in his second term. Johnson, in winning a landslide for what would have been JFK's second term, was engulfed in the Vietnam War and the domestic calamities of the 1960s. Nixon had Watergate. Bill Clinton was impeached. George W. Bush had Hurricane Katrina, the unpopularity of the Iraq War, and the implosion of the financial markets.

Reagan became the first president to serve two full terms since Eisenhower, but despite the favorable revisionism of the past few years, his second term is still defined by the unmitigated disaster of the Iran-Contra scandal and only partially redeemed through his summits and arms control break-throughs with the Soviet Union. And it is assumed without examination that little of note was accomplished in domestic policy, especially the budget deficit.

This summary judgment is wrong. Even allowing for the stain of Iran-Contra, Reagan's second term was one of substantial accomplishment, and not just in superpower relations. In domestic policy he enjoyed a number of triumphs, and even where a hostile Congress, including leading members of his own party, stymied his initiatives, he and his administration pressed the conservative case. The flood tide of pent-up problems ran full, but never engulfed Reagan as it did Johnson and Nixon. His resolution in defending the principles of his economic policy established the template against which his successors would be measured. His opposition to income tax increases is remembered, but less well recalled is his steadfast opposition to trade protectionism, which Congress was eager to enact throughout his second term. Though Reagan lost many battles, he did not lose the initiative, and herein lies a fundamental lesson of politics. Even when losing, a political ideology that remains on the offensive creates a favorable political environment; Reagan helped create the political environment that made it possible for his party to achieve the rarity of winning the White House for a third straight election in 1988.

The conventional view of a lackluster second term owes to the hyper-critical herd mentality of the adversarial media at the time and the laziness of the initial historians and writers who failed to look afresh at the record. The media had their theme: Reagan was a lame duck already. *Newsweek* wrote in early 1985, in a sentence that reads poorly in hindsight, that "second-term presidents are afflicted with a kind of political Alzheimer's disease, a progressive and incurable loss of potency leading sooner or later to terminal lame duckery." *Time* magazine reported in January 1985 that Reagan had "no blueprint, no grand design," and was governing "as if by whimsy." Since the election, the *New Republic* wrote, "[T]he administration seemed in a state of torpor. . . . [Reagan] has little on his mind beyond tax reform and trips to Rancho del Cielo."

On the surface it may be hard to perceive Reagan's second-term energy because the initiatives in domestic affairs had less drama—though no less substance—than those of 1981. But the rightward tilt of the second Reagan administration is evident even from the staff changes the president made. Most notably, James Baker and Donald Regan surprised the Washington establishment by swapping jobs, with Baker going to Treasury and Regan moving to the White House as chief of staff. Reagan had got along well with Regan during the first term, in which the treasury secretary had distinguished himself as a stalwart supporter of Reagan's economic policy, especially against the in-house tax increasers. Conservatives welcomed Regan's ascension—for the time being—if for no other reason than that moving Baker to the Treasury also meant the removal of the Rasputin-like Richard Darman from the White House. (They would soon find, however, that the personal strengths that had made Regan an effective corporate CEO and treasury secretary made him ill-suited to be White House chief of staff.)

Conservatives were also thrilled when Pat Buchanan was named communications director in February 1985. In striking contrast to his predecessor, David Gergen, Buchanan refused to return reporters' phone calls for several months after taking up his post, on the straightforward theory that the media were Reagan's enemy. Mike Deaver, whom Regan (along with most movement conservatives) regarded as an "insidious manipulator," would soon depart to launch his own lobbying and public relations company, his personal struggle with alcoholism unknown at the time. Other personnel moves cheered conservatives, especially the new secretary of education, William Bennett, but also Donald Hodel at Interior and John Herrington at Energy.

The only real sad news for conservatives—and Reagan—was that Jeane Kirkpatrick resigned from the UN post; she was worn out by constant State Department infighting as well as the abyss of Turtle Bay. "The conservatives who worry that I'll go soft will lose a lot of sleep," Reagan wrote in his diary of Kirkpatrick's resignation. But overall, Reagan's second-term cabinet was decidedly more conservative than his first-term cabinet. At his first cabinet meeting after the election, Reagan passed out his "Time for Choosing" speech from 1964 to remind his people why they were there.

*　　*　　*

AS HE APPROACHED his second inauguration in late January, Reagan's approval rating rose to 68 percent. It would go higher in the months ahead, to levels never seen before in a second-term president. "In my fifty years in public life," Tip O'Neill said to Reagan in a gracious moment, "I've never seen a man more popular with the American people." Reagan came out swinging rhetorically after a gauzy, soft-focus inauguration. His second inaugural address, moved indoors under the Capitol rotunda on account of brutally cold weather (the traditional inaugural parade down Pennsylvania Avenue was canceled), did not match the urgency or hard-edged clarity of his momentous first inaugural. It contained a bland version of his usual conservative themes, leavened with generic oratory such as: "My friends, we live in a world that is lit by lightning. So much is changing and will change, but so much endures, and transcends time. History is a ribbon, always unfurling; history is a journey." Solid Jerry Ford territory.

His policy-oriented State of the Union address three weeks later (delivered on his seventy-fourth birthday) was another matter. Reagan resumed his fundamental attack on liberalism: "Four years ago we began to change, forever I hope, our assumptions about government and its place in our lives," Reagan began. "But it's only a beginning. We're not here to congratulate ourselves on what we have done but to challenge ourselves to finish what has not yet been done. . . . This government will meet its responsibility to help those in need. But policies that increase dependency, break up families, and destroy self-respect are not progressive; they're reactionary." He touted tax reform as the centerpiece of a "second American revolution."

As important as what Reagan said was what he did not say: he spent less than thirty seconds discussing the federal budget deficit. And he did not give ground: "There are some who say that growth initiatives must await final action on deficit reductions. Well, the best way to reduce deficits is through economic growth. . . . To move steadily toward a balanced budget, we must also lighten government's claim on our total economy. We will not do this by raising taxes." Reagan also asked Congress to give him the line-item veto, a power held by forty-three governors in the United States.[1]

Senator Bob Dole, the new Senate majority leader, told NBC News after the speech, "I wish the president had spent a little more time on the deficit." Dole along with other Senate Republicans favored a tax increase and cuts in defense spending. "I never thought growth would deal with the deficit," Dole said. "Mondale's view of it was all right. He was the wrong salesman." Reagan was not about to budge on the budget. The day before his State of the Union speech, Reagan told his staff that he wanted to resume his Saturday radio addresses, suspended during the 1984 campaign, "to educate the people on such things as who really is responsible for the deficit and the budget."[2] Despite a grim budget deficit forecast, Reagan was going to stick to his guns. When Stockman had presented his initial budget forecast shortly after the election, Reagan wrote in his diary, "I can't help but be suspicious that Dave made it so tough hoping we'd turn to a tax increase. Well I won't." Stockman would be gone by the summer, replaced by a more reliable conservative as head of OMB, James Miller. Miller became the anti-Stockman; he actually opposed tax increases in public, and he became known as "the

Abominable No-Man." He once boasted that his budget employees "are the kind of people that run over dogs." Unlike Stockman, who was welcomed into clandestine Capitol Hill tax increase intrigues, Democratic congressional leadership would try to exclude Miller from budget negotiations.

One conservative observer summarized the dynamic of Reagan's State of the Union address to *National Review* thus: "Bob Dole was run over by a truck, Ronald Reagan was driving it, and Jack Kemp was riding shotgun." In case people weren't paying attention, a few weeks later Reagan threw down a marker against revived congressional talk of a tax increase, borrowing a line from Clint Eastwood's latest Dirty Harry movie, *Sudden Impact:* "The scene in the Senate Budget Committee this past week was a disappointing one, I think, for the American people. They seem to be in full-scale retreat from spending cuts and are talking about raising people's taxes again. Well, let them be forewarned: I have my veto pen drawn and ready for any tax increase that Congress might even think of sending up. And I have only one thing to say to the tax increasers: 'Go ahead, make my day.' " Reagan's instinct was correct that using the popular film line—which the American Film Institute would later select as one of the ten most memorable lines in movie history—would ensure its prominence on the nightly network news. (When Eastwood was elected mayor of Carmel, California, the following year, Reagan repeated the line, adding, "I have to confess that I'm amazed that a Hollywood actor who co-starred with a monkey could ever make it in politics.")

Congressional Republicans got the message but came to Reagan with a proposal to cut defense spending and freeze cost-of-living increases for Social Security. Reagan described his attitude in his diary as "stubborn as h—l" against both ideas; "suggesting a cut in S.S. [Social Security] is to give the Dems the issue they want for '86." He had already taken note in his diary of a fund-raising letter Tip O'Neill had sent out attacking Reagan for wanting to "destroy Medicare and Social Security." Reagan described it as "the most vicious pack of lies I've ever seen." He wasn't going to walk into that political trap again. He did, however, show he was serious about cuts to other programs when, in early March, he vetoed a popular farm relief bill that had grown well beyond his budget target.

*   *   *

THE IDEOLOGICAL DIVISION between the parties sparked new political clashes. In the Senate, Reagan's opponents mugged several of the president's appointees for purely ideological reasons The most conspicuous case involved Ed Meese, who had been named in January 1984 to succeed the quiet and unassuming William French Smith as attorney general following Smith's resignation. The entire hive of liberal activist groups, 165 in all, erupted to oppose Meese's confirmation, led by the ACLU (whom Meese had referred to as "the criminals' lobby"), Common Cause, the National Organization for Women, and the NAACP. The *Nation* voiced the real worry of the activist Left, namely, that Meese's "record inspires the worst fears that individual liberties will be sacrificed to military and police practices," while the *New Republic*'s TRB wrote that "Meese is bound to be a terrible Attorney General, if what you like in an Attorney General is some kind of passion for justice." Alan Dershowitz said that Meese had "a radical mission to roll back our most fundamental Constitutional protections." Benjamin Hooks of the NAACP said: "By this action, Mr. Reagan is putting another anti–civil rights devil in charge of the agency responsible for protecting minorities."[3]

The Left peddled every vicious rumor and charge imaginable, hoping something would stick. Rather than fight Meese directly on ideological grounds, however, Senate Democrats seized upon allegations of financial irregularities and influence peddling to derail Meese's nomination. Not being a wealthy man, Meese had faced considerable financial distress when he came to Washington with Reagan in 1981 and was unable to sell his southern California home in a declining market. He fell behind on mortgage payments to one lender, while another lender stretched out payment terms in ways not customary for most borrowers. Meese did not correctly disclose a personal loan from a private individual on the complicated ethics forms he filled out without legal assistance in 1981.[4] When it emerged that a few people on or near to the other side of these transactions later received appointments to low-level administration positions (such as the part-time Board of Governors for the U.S. Postal Service, which paid $10,000 a year), the Washington scandal machine went into high gear.

The uproar over the Meese case fit with a prominent Democratic campaign theme of 1984—the "sleaze factor." It was the kind of scandal that never would have been such during the New Deal or the Great Society but became typical of the post-Watergate hothouse ethics climate. As a practical matter, Washington's hyperethics now make it difficult for nonwealthy people to participate in government, while exposing people of means to a minefield. Michael Ledeen wrote in the *New Republic:* "Had the media been of a fairer turn of mind, they might have reported that the stories of Meese and his California home reflected the man's real condition: Meese had to borrow money, tried to sell his house during a tough time for the real estate market, and got some help from—imagine!—his friends."[5] Meese reluctantly called for the Justice Department to appoint an independent counsel to review the whole matter, delaying his confirmation vote by a year.

When independent counsel Jacob Stein reported shortly after the election that Meese was guilty of no wrongdoing, the Left's opposition pivoted quickly to a new charge: while Meese might not be guilty of criminal wrongdoing, he had created the *appearance* of impropriety. This was a strange new standard, the reverse of the position liberals took during the McCarthy era against allowing innuendo to tar reputations or threaten government employment. The *New Republic*'s TRB, hitherto critical of Meese, agreed: "This hoary formulation has always struck me as an unfair cop-out, since the accusation itself—when picked up by the national media—is what creates the appearance. If an official has not done anything actually wrong, he shouldn't be pilloried or punished."[6] Nonetheless, the appearance-of-impropriety charge was pressed lustily in the Senate Judiciary Committee, especially by Senators Howard Metzenbaum and Joe Biden. The charge was especially rich coming from the multimillionaire Metzenbaum, who had been dunned by the IRS for back taxes more than once while in the Senate, and who had to return a suspicious $250,000 "finder's fee" for his part in a hotel sales transaction.

The charge against Meese fizzled when a glaring double standard became impossible to overlook. After the original charges had been made against Meese in the winter of 1984, Geraldine Ferraro, in the course of her vice presidential campaign, had run afoul of similar ethics problems involving her husband's complicated business dealings and incorrect or incomplete disclosure on the required congressional ethics forms. Despite a number of clear technical violations, the House Ethics Committee exonerated Ferraro of any wrongdoing. The campaign against Meese collapsed, and he was finally confirmed in February 1985.

The mugging of William Bradford Reynolds had a different outcome. In March Reagan appointed Reynolds, then the head of the Civil Rights Division in the Justice Department, to be associate attorney general, the number three post at Justice. Reynolds immediately ran into a buzz saw of opposition from civil rights groups. Ralph Neas of the Leadership Council on Civil Rights said that Reynolds was a "rigid ideologue and an extremist who has done everything possible to weaken the civil rights laws of this country." The NAACP's Benjamin Hooks led a street protest against Reynolds outside Senate offices, where he attacked "the Department of Injustice" for "catering to the worst instincts of the American public" while hiding behind "mushy-mushy, goody-goody words: 'color blind,' 'sex blind,' 'equity, fairness and justice.' " NOW president Judy Goldsmith called Reynolds "the Scrooge of the Justice Department." The media gave the activist groups' charges full credibility. The *Washington Post* editorialized: "His nomination sends an unmistakable message to both black and white Americans. It is not a pleasant message; it has to do with how much the government—and the majority—any longer care about trying to redress the society's historic racial wrongs."

Much as liberals charged Meese with the appearance of impropriety, Reynolds's opponents carefully avoided substantive charges and instead accused him of having too much zeal. (Strange that activist liberal appointees are seldom criticized for bringing too much zeal to their jobs.) It mattered not that the Civil Rights Division under Reynolds had brought *more* enforcement actions during the first four years of the Reagan administration than occurred during Jimmy Carter's four years—177 civil rights prosecutions (compared to 167 under Carter), 53 employment discrimination suits (51 under Carter), 53 voting rights cases (47 under Carter), and 110 objections to discriminatory redistricting plans (26 under Carter).[7] In fact, Reynolds's substantive record counted against him, since it was compiled according to the wrong theory, from the Left's point of view.

The Senate Judiciary Committee hearings for Reynolds, repeatedly delayed so that opposition could organize, were more of a show trial than a confirmation hearing. (Senator Joe Biden actually slipped at one point and referred to the hearing as a "trial.") Its McCarthyite flavor can be captured from a single broadside from Howard Metzenbaum: "I do not understand. You are intelligent, you appear to be a decent human being and yet you come down in some of these cases on the side of the bigots. . . . I get the feeling maybe you don't like blacks, maybe you're bigoted. I've never seen so many instances in which one man is involved on the wrong side." In late June, the Judiciary Committee killed Reynolds's nomination. Once again, it was Republican senators who enabled a liberal political victory. Senators Arlen Specter and Charles Mathias both voted with Democrats in committee. Reagan was furious. "That some members of the committee chose to use the confirmation process to conduct an ideological assault on so superbly qualified a candidate was unjust and deeply wrong," Reagan said in a statement. Referring to the role of Specter and Mathias, he wrote in his diary, "Well there are 2 Sens. that I won't have to help campaign."[8]

The irony of the opposition to Reynolds was that by being turned down for promotion, he remained in the very post in the Civil Rights Division where his actions had so angered the Left. But the imperative of taking a political scalp trumped this kind of rational calculation, in large part because the

Meese and Reynolds fights were merely warm-up acts, a prelude to a broader argument over jurisprudence and the future course of the Supreme Court.

Meese wasted no time picking fights with liberalism upon finally taking office. He transformed the Justice Department into something of a school of continuing legal education. The department held a series of seminars with outside speakers and academics to stimulate the department's thinking about the many controversies it had on its plate. The *New York Times* noted the significance of Meese's activities: "The flame of ideological fervor only flickers at some agencies, but it burns bright at the Justice Department, where Mr. Meese and his lieutenants have appointed a flock of young conservatives to help carry out the Reagan goals, and not just those having to do with the Justice Department." (Two of Meese's many lieutenants were young lawyers John Roberts and Samuel Alito.)

Whereas Reagan's first attorney general, William French Smith, had been a quiet manager of the Justice Department, Meese and his lieutenants relished stirring up a public fight. In his first speech to Justice Department employees following confirmation, Meese said he wanted to place a new emphasis on federalism, a concept that was "not a dead letter." In several subsequent speeches over the next year, Meese laid out the issues sharply, arguing that the Supreme Court had improperly undermined federalism, questioning the constitutionality of independent regulatory agencies, and drawing a distinction between the Constitution and constitutional law as promulgated by the Supreme Court.[9] This last argument represented a revival of the constitutional axiom, dating back to Andrew Jackson and Lincoln, of "coordinate review"—that is, the view that all three branches, not just the Supreme Court, are entitled to interpret the Constitution.[10] Most importantly, Meese argued that the Court should not behave as if it were a policy-making body. To the American Bar Association Meese argued: "Too many of the [Supreme] Court's opinions, on the whole, have been more policy choices than articulations of long-term Constitutional principle. The [Court's] voting blocs, the arguments, all reveal a greater allegiance to what the Court thinks constitutes sound public policy than a deference to what the Constitution—its text and intention—may demand."

In pursuing these heterodox themes Meese was saying nothing that Reagan hadn't said in general terms both during and before his presidency. During the 1980 campaign Reagan told the *Wall Street Journal:* "I think for a long time we've had a number of Supreme Court Justices who, given any chance, invade the prerogative of the legislature; they legislate rather than make judgments, and some try to rewrite the Constitution instead of inter-preting it."[11] Both as governor and during his long march to the presidency in the late 1970s, Reagan had referred to the older understanding of feder-alism and deplored the way in which the federal government had made the states administrative appendages of Washington. The 1980 Republican plat-form pledged to appoint judges "who share our commitment to judicial restraint."

Liberals thought the emphasis on federalism was an oblique attempt to roll back the *Roe v. Wade* abortion decision and return abortion policy to the states, but in fact the resuscitation of the idea of federalism was part of a more ambitious effort to revive constitutional argumentation. Meese soon framed his entire effort under the banner of "original intent"—that is, the proposition that constitutional issues should be interpreted as they were un-derstood by the Framers of the Constitution. While this debate has emerged as a fundamental fault line between Left and Right in contemporary America, Meese was the first prominent Republican to advance such an argument seri-ously since Coolidge. Indeed, he reopened one of the central arguments in American politics, a fundamental quarrel that liberals had thought was more or less closed.

To understand why original intent proved so incendiary to liberals, we must recognize the process by which they rejected a restrained or limited con-stitutionalism. The judicial activism that contemporary conservatives decry has its roots in the Progressive movement from a century ago. The Progres-sives, the precursors to modern American liberals who redefined the very meaning of liberalism, thought that the Constitution was obsolete for mod-ern conditions, particularly in its restrictions on the power of the central gov-ernment (such as the commerce clause and the contracts clause) and the protections of individual liberties—especially property rights. Frank Good-now, a prominent academic writer of the period, wrote that "we should abandon the idea that the political theory at the basis of our constitutional system is either permanent or absolute." He offered a perfect early expres-sion of the idea of the "living Constitution" when he said that "constitutions, which are practically unamendable, should be seen rather as statements of general principles whose detailed application should take account of chang-ing conditions, and should be so interpreted by judicial decision as to be sus-ceptible of a continuous and uninterrupted development."[12]

These ideas trickled down rapidly to practical politicians of both parties, including Republican Theodore Roosevelt, who was initially the leading advocate of a Progressive view of the Constitution. In his Special Message of December 8, 1908, Roosevelt called for "judges who hold to a twentieth century economic and social philosophy and not to a long outgrown philosophy, which was itself the product of primitive economic conditions."[13] But without question the most significant figure in changing America's constitutionalism was Democrat Woodrow Wilson, the only academic ever elected president of the United States and, significantly, the first president ever to criticize the Constitution openly.[14] In *Constitutional Government,* Wilson wrote that the increased role of the national government could be accomplished "only by wrestling the Constitution to strange and as yet unimagined uses. . . . As the life of the nation changes so must the interpretation of the document which contains it change, by a nice adjustment, determined, *not by the original intention of those who drew the paper,* but by the exigencies and the new aspects of life itself" (emphasis added).

Needless to say, Franklin Roosevelt and the New Deal extended and deepened this argument such that, in the fullness of time, the Supreme Court came around to accepting the Progressive point of view as the basis for much of its jurisprudence starting in the 1930s.[15] Once the Supreme Court adopted, most decisively by 1937, a permissive attitude toward expansive central government, the last political resistance to the idea of the living Constitution fell away. Liberals never thought it would come back in any serious way.

*　　*　　*

FROM THIS BRIEF survey we can appreciate that the liberal rejection of original intent is much older than the 1973 *Roe* decision or the fuss over the Warren Court's judicial activism in the 1960s. And in seeing the underlying philosophy at work, we also come to understand why original intent, however understood, is incendiary for liberals—the idea of a restrained or limited constitutionalism strikes at the heart of any liberal agenda for political intervention into social affairs.

There had been lively argument over this constitutional fault line among scholars and lawyers for a long time, but it was chiefly confined to the ivory tower. The idea of original intent is not without its conceptual and philosophical difficulties, which liberal intellectuals hastened to point out in learned law review articles. Meese now brought the matter back into the political arena. The public fight Meese started over original intent, legal scholar Jonathan O'Neill wrote, "constituted the most direct constitutional debate

between the executive branch and the Court since the New Deal."[16] Meese
and his Justice Department compatriots were attempting nothing less than to
wrest the Constitution away from a self-appointed legal elite and return it to
the people.

The reaction from liberals ensured that Meese's initiative would not dissipate into the mists. In a highly unusual step, two sitting Supreme Court justices, John Paul Stevens and William Brennan—both, ironically, appointed by
Republican presidents—made public speeches disputing Meese. Brennan attacked original intent as "doctrinaire," "little more than arrogance cloaked
as humility." Echoing a point that Woodrow Wilson had made decades earlier, he said: "Those who would restrict claims of right to the values of 1789
specifically articulated in the Constitution turn a blind eye to social progress
and eschew adaptation of overarching principles to changes of social circumstance. . . . The genius of the Constitution rests not in any static meaning it
might have had in a world that is dead and gone, but in the adaptability of its
great principles to cope with current problems and current needs." Brennan
even argued that the death penalty should be struck down as unconstitutional—despite the fact that the text of the Constitution explicitly recognizes
the death penalty ("capital crimes") several times. There is much other mischief in Brennan's formulation about the "values" of 1789, as opposed to
principles of individual rights and self-government that the Founders—and
Lincoln—thought were timeless. Legal scholar Stephen Calabresi comments:
"To say that the genius of a constitution lies in the fluidity of its meaning is a
little bit like saying that the genius of the brakes on your car is the way they
can be used for acceleration."[17]

Meese set out to translate his critique into initiatives directed at specific
Supreme Court doctrines and precedents. For example, he challenged one of
the leading totems of the Warren Court era—the *Miranda* decision on self-
incrimination that led to the adoption of the "you have the right to remain
silent" recitation that is overdramatized in every television police drama. He
also pushed forward a proposal to have Reagan rescind or modify President
Lyndon Johnson's Executive Order 11246—the order that set in motion affirmative action quotas in federal government contracting. In August 1985, at
Meese's instigation, the White House floated a draft executive order that
would have ended the quotas and timetables that had grown up under Johnson's infamous decree. The split within the business community, as well as
the disagreement among Reagan's own cabinet, shows how deeply the tangled regime of quotas and no-win discrimination law had become entrenched.

Inside the White House, sentiment for the proposed change split exactly on the pragmatist-ideologue axis of Reaganites versus establishment Republicans. Labor Secretary William Brock assailed the proposed change as "politically crazy." Siding with him were Transportation Secretary Elizabeth Dole, Treasury Secretary Baker, and Secretary of State Shultz, who had played a role in expanding racial goals and timetables as labor secretary in the Nixon administration. Siding with Meese were William Bennett, Interior Secretary Don Hodel, and Energy Secretary John Herrington. At length Brock and the establishment faction won; Meese quietly withdrew the proposed revision a few months later.

But Meese did not give up on his attempts at significant reform. Meese's Justice Department also set out after *Roe v. Wade.* In 1985 Charles Fried, the new solicitor general at Justice, filed a brief with the Supreme Court calling for *Roe* to be overturned. Fried argued that *Roe* "had no moorings in the text of our Constitution, in familiar constitutional doctrines," or in "the historical facts." The case before the Court, *Thornburgh v. American College of Gynecologists and Obstetricians,* concerned restrictions that the Pennsylvania legislature had enacted requiring doctors to advise potential recipients of abortion about the possible psychological and physical side effects, the gestational age of the fetus, and several other factors. In another defeat for the pro-life cause, the Court upheld *Roe* and struck down the Pennsylvania law, though by a narrow 5–4 vote (*Roe,* remember, had been decided by a 7–2 vote in 1973). Justice Sandra Day O'Connor once again joined the dissenters, writing in her separate dissent that "[t]his Court's abortion decisions have already worked a major distortion in the Court's constitutional jurisprudence," indicating her willingness to revise or overrule *Roe.* While the pro-life movement rued another loss, the closeness of the vote gave hope that with one or two more appointments to the Court the tide could be turned.

This is exactly what liberals feared and why the reaction to Meese's constitutional arguments was so ferocious. There were more than a hundred vacancies on the federal bench at the time Meese became attorney general, and it was no secret that Meese and Reagan wanted to appoint judges with a conservative judicial philosophy. (By the end of his second term, Reagan would appoint 379 federal judges.) The Meese Justice Department had the most vigorous vetting process ever to secure this end, especially for prospective Supreme Court appointments.[18] Democrats in the Senate began blocking some Reagan appointees to appellate court seats, most significantly Jefferson Sessions, Bernard Siegan, and Lino Graglia. Sessions would later gain a measure of revenge by being elected to the Senate from Alabama, where he would take his place on the Senate Judiciary Committee a few seats down from Ted Kennedy. Siegan and Graglia were both formidable academics who had written powerful critiques of modern jurisprudence: Graglia had targeted affirmative action, while Siegan was a champion of property rights. Liberals feared their intellectual firepower on the bench, and Ted Kennedy led the opposition to their appointments in the Senate Judiciary Committee. The new slogan became that too many of Reagan's nominees were "out of the mainstream." Harvard Law School professor Laurence Tribe wrote to the Senate Judiciary Committee that Siegan was "not a judicial conservative but an ideologue of the right, one who would deploy the Constitution in service of a conservative economic philosophy."[19] While Reagan and Meese were successful in getting a number of impressive conservatives confirmed to appellate seats (such as Alex Kozinski on the Ninth Circuit and Richard Posner on the Seventh Circuit), the new skirmish line over jurisprudence was clear, and would explode in spectacular fashion over the next few years as Supreme Court vacancies arose.

The initial skirmish would come in 1986, when Chief Justice Warren Burger surprised everyone by announcing his retirement from the Court to become chairman of the commission to celebrate the bicentennial of the Constitution in 1987. Reagan and Meese were thus faced with two decisions: whom to appoint to the vacant seat, and whom to appoint as the new chief justice. The short list of potential nominees that Meese and Reynolds recommended to Reagan was very short indeed; it had only two names—Robert Bork and Antonin Scalia. Bork, then currently serving on the D.C. Circuit Court of Appeals (as was Scalia), was most every conservative's beau ideal of an original intent judge, having been in the forefront of reviving the idea in the 1970s, and had been widely favored as Reagan's first appointment in 1981, when the president decided to appoint O'Connor instead. Thus it came as something of a surprise when Reagan tapped Scalia for the open seat rather than Bork. Several factors tipped Reagan toward Scalia. At forty-nine, Scalia was ten years younger than Bork. Reagan and Meese didn't know whether there would be another opening on the Court and wanted to appoint someone who could serve for a long time. Bork was a heavy smoker, raising concerns about his longevity. Reagan met with both Bork and Scalia, but the gregarious president took an instant liking to the gregarious jurist. That Scalia would be the first Italian American on the Court was an added political plus.

Another factor was Reagan's decision to designate William Rehnquist to be the new chief justice. Even though Rehnquist was already on the Court, liberals announced their opposition to his elevation to the chief's chair, and his confirmation hearings followed the now-familiar pattern of dredging up supposed improprieties and controversial statements from Rehnquist's past. When his nomination finally came to the Senate floor for a vote, thirty-one Democrats and two Republicans (Charles Mathias and Lowell Weicker) voted against Rehnquist's confirmation to be chief justice, the highest number of negative votes for a Supreme Court nominee in the twentieth century, and remarkable in that he was already a member of the Court.

By contrast, Scalia sailed through on a 98–0 vote. Political observers suggested that liberals didn't want to cast votes against the first Italian American nominee to the Court (even Mario Cuomo publicly supported Scalia's confirmation), but it is also likely that, having spent their fury attacking Rehnquist, they had little left to make a fight over Scalia, who would go on to become a demonized figure for the Left.

The fight over jurisprudence and judicial appointments would take on a two-steps-forward, one-step-back quality for the next two decades. It was foreign developments that dominated public attention in 1985. After the tense year of 1983 and the pause for the 1984 election, things were about to shake loose in dramatic fashion.

*   *   *

IN MAY 1983, the Polish intellectual Leszek Kolakowski, author of *Main Currents of Marxism*, arguably the finest critical history of this malignant and overpowering fad, speculated about the possible unraveling of the Soviet Union: "We can imagine that the Soviet rulers, under the combined pressure of self-inflicted economic disasters and social tensions, will accept, however grudgingly, a genuine verifiable international disarmament plan and concentrate their efforts on a large-scale economic recovery, which they cannot achieve without a number of social and political reforms. This might conceivably usher in a process of gradual and non-explosive disintegration of the empire." At the time, such a thought was fanciful. And as Kolakowski went on to warn, "Such a path, though the most desirable, is fraught with dangers as well. Everybody knows the great risk all despotic regimes incur when they try, under duress, to grow milder."[20]

This is the lens through which the subsequent events of the next five years should be viewed. The full story, amply told elsewhere, contained enormous personal and political drama whose outcome in hindsight seems simple and straightforward.[21] Underlying factors—what the Soviets used to call "the correlation of forces"—were important, but the vital fact was Reagan's force of personality and will, along with a new generation of Soviet leaders who recognized that they had reached the end of the road but who had only limited understanding of how to turn around from their dead end.

With reelection bolstering his position, Reagan was ready to resume his diplomacy with the Soviet Union. Barely a week after the election, Reagan and Chernenko sent each other letters that crossed in the diplomatic mail. The letters ironically said the same thing: both wanted to restart direct arms negotiations. Chernenko was more specific: could Shultz meet Gromyko in Geneva in two months to get things started? It was the first of several small Soviet concessions that revealed their growing weakness. Reagan and Shultz immediately accepted.

The Soviets were transparent in their strategy: they held out the prospect of steep cuts in warheads as an enticement for Reagan to abandon SDI. Reagan was on to this ploy and was wary. "I stand firm we cannot retreat on that no matter what they offer," he wrote in his diary. In a meeting with his arms control team, Reagan emphasized that "we wanted a good agreement or no agreement." Shultz and Gromyko met in early January and, after the usual bluster and clashes over human rights, directly agreed to restart formal negotiations in March on American terms, namely, that all arms issues—space, strategic, and medium-range missiles—be treated under one umbrella instead of separately. It was a significant Soviet concession and tended to confirm the impression that Soviet strength and confidence were ebbing. Reagan intuitively grasped this, writing in a letter two weeks later, "I feel . . . that the Soviets came to the table because they finally decided it was in their best interest to do so."[22]

The depth of interest in the resumption of formal contact between the United States and Soviets is attested by the ridiculous presence of eight hundred journalists, including all three anchormen of the American TV networks (Dan Rather, Peter Jennings, and Tom Brokaw), at the Shultz-Gromyko meeting in Geneva, even though a news blackout during their meeting meant the broadcasters had no news to report until the end. This was remarkable for a meeting intended only to reach agreement on the *structure* of new negotiations, not on weapons themselves. The *Wall Street Journal*'s Dan Henninger characterized the press coverage of the meeting as "Armageddon for Dummies." Dan Rather asked Shultz at the conclusion: "When you were sitting in the room with Mr. Gromyko, as a person, as a human being, did you sense that you were sitting across the table from a friend and fellow inhabitant of the planet?" Perhaps it is not a coincidence that it was in 1985 that the big three TV networks saw their share of the prime-time viewing audience dip below 50 percent for the first time—a sign of the inroads made by cable TV.

Meanwhile, the Reagan administration faced an immediate problem that would affect upcoming negotiations. The United States and the Soviet Union had been unofficially observing the terms of the unratified SALT II Treaty, but the United States was about to exceed one of the limits of the treaty with the launch of the next Trident missile submarine. Staying within SALT II would require dismantling an older Poseidon missile submarine, but there was ample evidence of Soviet cheating on the limits of both SALT I and SALT II. The Defense Department naturally wanted to bust out of the SALT II limits and publicly blast the Soviets for cheating. The original agreement was scheduled to expire at the end of 1985 anyway; why bother to keep adhering to its terms? The State Department predictably took the opposite view: the arms control advocates argued that even with cheating, SALT II constrained the Soviets from deploying hundreds or thousands of new ICBMs.

There was a parallel controversy over the 1972 ABM Treaty; a strict interpretation would have impeded the progress of SDI. Many within the Reagan administration favored a liberal interpretation of the treaty's terms, which, as it happened, was the construction the Soviets had long given to the agreement. Not surprisingly, the Soviets now did an about-face on the legal interpretation of the treaty. Like SALT II, this argument divided Defense and State.

Much was made at the time and subsequently about the sharp divisions between the two departments, their chiefs, Weinberger and Shultz, and especially their influential deputies, Richard Perle and Richard Burt. Certainly the arguments were fierce and the leaks to the all-too-eager press manipulative. (The media used to call the airplane carrying the State-Defense delegations the "ship of feuds.") There were substantive arguments on both sides, but the differences were rooted more in the perspectives that arise from the parochialism of Defense and State (the Soviet government had a similar split between the Foreign Ministry and the Communist Party Central Committee), though an element of personal rivalry should not be discounted. In any case, the philosophical differences between the two purported camps were much smaller than media accounts suggested. Shultz would later write that Richard Perle and arms control director Ken Adelman turned out to be among the most helpful members of the American delegation at the subsequent U.S.-Soviet meetings.

Reagan ended up splitting the difference on the SALT II decision. He would announce in June that the United States would no longer be bound by SALT II's limits, but that he would dismantle two older Poseidon submarines to stay within the limits for the time being. The decision pleased no one. And even as the administration debated the ABM Treaty, the House of Representatives passed a resolution calling on the administration to adhere to a strict interpretation of the treaty, siding with the new Soviet position.

Before the formal U.S.-Soviet arms negotiations could begin, a major development altered the course of the Soviet Union. On March 11, Reagan was awakened at 4:00 a.m. with the news that Konstantin Chernenko was dead. It was not a surprise: Chernenko had been "working" from a hospital bed for most of the previous two months, and some "meetings" of the Politburo lasted less than fifteen minutes. With the death of Chernenko, the Politburo had run out of septuagenarians to prop up, and a younger cohort was straining at the leash.[23] The transition to the next generation occurred with surprising swiftness. Mikhail Gorbachev was named the new general secretary the same day that Chernenko's death was announced, the first time that had ever happened.[24]

This was only one sign that the ascension of Gorbachev signaled a meaningful changing of the guard, and perhaps new prospects. For sixty years, from 1922 to 1982, just three men had been general secretary of the Central Committee of the Communist Party—Stalin, Khrushchev, and Brezhnev. Now, within the space of three years, the job had turned over three times. Gorbachev, at fifty-four years old, was the youngest member of the Politburo (average age sixty-seven) by five years.

Western observers had thought Gorbachev was the most likely successor for Chernenko, but in many respects his rise seemed improbable. He had worked in the central government in Moscow for only six and a half years. Prior to that he had been the first Party secretary in Stavropol, out in the boondocks. But he caught the attention of Moscow for increasing agricultural output (from dismal to merely mediocre, one supposes), so he was brought to Moscow and made minister of agriculture in the Politburo. *Time* magazine commented on this anomalous rise: "A rough American parallel would be the appointment of a little-known Governor of, say, South Dakota to be officially Secretary of Agriculture and unofficially a member of the President's inner circle of top advisers."

It is tempting to suggest that Gorbachev rose because he was the least incompetent among Party apparatchiks; anyone who could make the dysfunctional Soviet agricultural system work better might be able to get the rest of the system to work better. His charisma plainly helped. Here was the first Soviet leader who, among other things, had a presentable spouse, Raisa, a philosophy professor at Moscow University. In fact, she was the first Soviet first lady who weighed less than her husband. The Western press would swoon over her almost as much as him. One British paper called her "Soviet realism's answer to Princess Diana," while another called her "the Bo Derek of the Steppes." *National Review* called Gorbachev and his circle "the Kremlin's equivalent of New Coke"—not necessarily all that different from the old version, but perhaps more skilled or more vigorous in their faithfulness to Leninism.

Gromyko told Shultz that "Gorbachev has a nice smile, but he has iron teeth," and Arthur Hartman, the U.S. ambassador to Moscow, thought Gorbachev would be very difficult to deal with. Some European leaders shared this apprehension; West Germany's Helmut Kohl said that he feared Gorbachev would be a skilled propagandist on par with Joseph Goebbels. But Shultz noted in his first encounter with Gorbachev at Chernenko's funeral, "He was articulate and spontaneous. He seemed to be thinking out loud. . . . I could sense instinctively in our hour-and-a-half meeting that he was out of a completely different mold." Shultz intuited that Gorbachev would make a clean break with the past. In this he joined Margaret Thatcher, who had met Gorbachev the previous December and professed her liking for him, adding significantly, "We can do business with him." Reagan remained to be convinced. When Armand Hammer, a thoroughly dubious source, tried to convince Reagan that Gorbachev was "a different type than past Soviet leaders," Reagan wrote in his diary (June 24, 1985), "I'm too cynical to believe that."

He had good reason for skepticism. Although Gorbachev had increased agricultural output in the Stavropol region by expanding the use of private plots and allowing farmers more input in local planning, he derived no wider lessons for economic reform. Indeed, as Politburo minister he did not replicate nationally the policies that had worked locally, probably because of bureaucratic opposition. During the three years Gorbachev was agriculture minister, grain production fell from 230 million tons to 155 million tons. While he may have had genuine reformist sentiments, he was not a liberalizer economically or politically. He had no intention of abandoning central planning. Russian economist Vassily Selyunin, who was warning Moscow at the time Gorbachev came to power that the Soviet economy was heading for inevitable collapse, said that "Gorbachev never accepted that you won't have a market unless first you privatize property."[25]

Moreover, even as Gorbachev complained in Politburo meetings that Soviet industry was in the "cave age" compared to Western industries, and detailed the shocking inefficiency and waste of the Soviet economy, it turned out that all he really had in mind to fix these problems was more intelligent management by the state. "Throughout the 1980s," observed Jack Matlock, the American ambassador to the USSR late in the decade, "Gorbachev believed in more government rather than less."[26] Gorbachev and others were correct in perceiving that the nation was in a crisis and that "things can't go on like this" (as Gorbachev claims he told his wife the night before his elevation to general secretary); in a December 1984 speech, only a portion of which was published at the time, he had said that the Soviets needed "serious scientific recommendations on the application in contemporary conditions of such economic levers as price, cost, profit, credit, and certain others."[27] But fellow students from his time in university in the late 1940s and early 1950s recalled Gorbachev as someone who didn't merely learn the Marxist patter by rote but "fully engaged with the arguments of Marx and Lenin," in the words of Oxford University historian Archie Brown. He was feisty in defending socialism in his meeting with Vice President Bush and Shultz following Chernenko's funeral, telling the American delegation, "Thank God there is socialism, because with socialism the people of [former] capitalist countries have gained more rights." And in his first Politburo meeting as general secretary he made sure to reiterate his Marxist-Leninist bona fides: "I am deeply devoted to the idea of collective work. . . . We should not change our policy. It is the right, correct, genuinely Leninist policy." Anatoly Dobrynin unintentionally testified to Gorbachev's confusion and incoherence by quoting him at the time of his ascension: "What we need is more dynamism, more social justice, more democracy—in a word, more socialism."[28]

Still, Western observers and intelligence agencies were picking up unmistakable signs that certain elements within Soviet leadership recognized that fundamental change was necessary; these signs went beyond the reflexive wishful thinking of credulous Western Kremlinologists who were always ready to declare the USSR on the cusp of liberalization. Many members of the younger generation of Soviet leadership were openly contemptuous of the moribund, cliché-driven thinking of the old guard. An especially good source is the copious diary and memoirs of Anatoly Chernyaev, a senior analyst in the International Department of the Communist Party, the office charged with nurturing the international revolution, and later a foreign policy adviser to Gorbachev. His entry for March 12, 1985—the day of Gorbachev's ascension—read in part: "People are tired of the social stagnation, of the demonstration of official stupidity. . . . If Andropov hadn't found Gorbachev, who would we be left with? The pretenders for Chernenko's place were: [Viktor] Grishin, [Grigory] Romanov, and Gromyko. One can imagine what kind of a fate would have been waiting for Russia if any of them had taken lead, especially after Chernenko. It's terrible to imagine!"[29]

Gorbachev set out in his first weeks in office to purge the Politburo and upper ranks of Soviet leadership. He fired dozens of regional Communist Party officials, promptly cashiered his chief rival in the Politburo, Grigory Romanov, and added new members to the Politburo to shore up his position further.[30] More government ministers and Party committee functionaries were replaced in Gorbachev's first year than in the Andropov and Chernenko years combined, and in abolishing five ministries entirely by the end of 1985, Gorbachev actually eliminated a substantial number of government jobs rather than reshuffling people under a new organizational chart. With great fanfare he announced a bold-sounding reform program under the banner of *perestroika*, which was variously translated as "restructuring" or "renewal." A related rhetorical banner, *glasnost*, which meant "transparency" or "openness," would follow shortly.

Just as *perestroika* didn't entail much real economic liberalization, so too *glasnost* did not represent much genuine political liberalization. Gorbachev was forthright about its limits, telling the French-USSR Friendship Society, "We openly say that nobody will be allowed to act against socialism." Censorship was relaxed, but dissidents were still being jailed or sent to psychiatric hospitals. Andrei Sakharov's harsh internal exile continued. Alain Besançon, an expert on Russian politics, wrote that the word *perestroika* "functions as a kind of fetish, a magic formula whose meaning is purposefully vague and whose true significance is that given it by the party . . . Substantially he is not doing much more than Brezhnev did in similar circumstances." *Perestroika* was not even a reprise of Lenin's New Economic Program of the 1920s, though it was often claimed to be such. The heart of *perestroika* initially was a call for discipline, belt-tightening, and harder work in the factories. Gorbachev passed a new law in the spring of 1986 outlawing independent income from any source outside a person's official job, and some local officials took it upon themselves to crack down on the backyard gardens and greenhouses that supplied much of the nation's fresh produce. When output predictably fell, enforcement of these new edicts was quietly dropped.

The most dramatic social initiative was the crackdown on rampant alcoholism among the Soviet population. Gorbachev stepped up criminal penalties for drunkenness. More than 125,000 people were reported to have been arrested on alcoholism-related charges over the next two years. He also raised the price of vodka by 200 percent and reduced its production by more than 50 percent. "If we do not solve this problem," Gorbachev said, "communism will be out of the question." He went so far as to host a Kremlin reception without hard liquor, but as Anatoly Chernyaev noted drolly in his diary, "[T]he buzz was not the same."

The anti-alcohol campaign was not successful. Illegal stills and the black market stepped in to keep the liquor supply ample. Thousands of people poisoned themselves drinking perfume, aircraft fuel, deodorant, and other alcohol surrogates. Chernyaev pointed out the difficulty of the policy in another diary entry: "On the way home I stopped by a grocery store to get some vegetables. Everyone there, from the manager to the saleswomen, is drunk. The anti-alcoholism law is nothing for them. Try to fire them. Who are you going to find to replace them?" It is unlikely that overall alcohol consumption changed at all, though the government now received far less revenue.

As a political and economic reformer, then, Gorbachev was more Inspector Clouseau than Machiavelli or Bismarck. At best, as NSC aide and Russian expert Richard Pipes put it, "Soviet reformers undertook to transform the Soviet Union from a totalitarian into an authoritarian regime."[31] British historian Robert Skidelsky concurred: "Through the fog of his delphic oratory and his contradictory zigzagging actions, it is difficult to understand what he thought he was doing." Gorbachev wasn't even for the incoherent or oxymoronic hybrid sometimes called market socialism; he thought Yugoslavia and China had gone too far in the direction of capitalist market economics. Margaret Thatcher, by now an authority on economic restructuring, commented to Shultz: "Gorbachev thinks there are problems with the way the system works; he thinks he can make changes to make it work better. He doesn't understand that *the system is the problem*."

The fundamental dilemma was whether Gorbachev and his cadre of leaders were capable of ending Communist Party control of the nation's social and economic life. They were not. The Soviet dilemma was essentially insoluble given the requirement of preserving Party dominance.

Shultz, the former Chicago economics professor, tried to explain the problem to Gorbachev several times. In a meeting in Moscow shortly before the first Reagan-Gorbachev summit, Shultz attempted to persuade Gorbachev of the virtues of open, liberal societies. Shultz called it "classroom in the Kremlin." He pressed two themes on Gorbachev. The first was that the industrial age was giving way to the information age, and only open societies could take full advantage of these changes: "The Soviet economy will have to be radically changed to adapt to the new era." The second was that observing human rights was in the Soviets' *economic* self-interest; political freedom and economic freedom go together. Shultz's State Department advisers tried to dissuade him from this course, fearing it would offend Gorbachev. Instead, Gorbachev listened with rapt attention to Shultz's case, after which he beamed at Shultz and said, "You should take over the planning office here in Moscow."[32]

While Gorbachev was in a muddle on the home front, the story in foreign affairs was different. Here the major irony of Gorbachev's statecraft emerges. He rose for his skill at domestic issues; he had little foreign policy experience, although he had traveled to the West, to Canada, France, and Britain. His lack of experience was probably to his benefit. From his first moments he was skeptical about the direction of Soviet foreign policy and began signaling that a serious change might be due. A few days after taking office he publicly stated, "People abroad who hold the same views as we may rest assured—in the struggle for peace and social progress the party of Lenin will, as always, closely cooperate with fraternal Communist workers' and revolutionary democratic parties." That sounded like good news for Managua, Havana, and the African clients. But he was saying something else privately. At his meeting with East European Communist leaders in the days after Chernenko's funeral, Gorbachev told them bluntly that they should no longer expect Soviet military interventions to keep them in power.[33] This statement implicitly repudiated the Brezhnev Doctrine (the 1970s-era declaration that socialism was irreversible—at least in nations within the Soviet bloc).

The significance of this cannot be overstated, because it also represented the first step toward abandoning the core idea of Marxist class struggle as a unitary global phenomenon, directed from Moscow and carried on through the international Communist movement and, where necessary, armed struggle. There was, in fact, an official bureau in the Kremlin assigned to coordinate the international Communist movement—that is, the activities of all the Communist parties scattered around the world. Gorbachev was skeptical, ordering a "frank, unembellished analysis" of the operation, "without the Hallelujah-ness," as he put it. In this area too, Gorbachev cleaned house, kicking Gromyko upstairs to the largely ceremonial post of chairman of the Soviet Presidium and surprising everyone by installing Eduard Shevardnadze, a regional Communist Party boss, as his new foreign minister, rather than picking Gromyko's chief deputy, Georgy Korniyenko.[34] Korniyenko would have represented continuity (that is, stagnation) in foreign policy; Shevard-nadze, a genuine outsider in every sense, could make a fresh start. Gromyko, Gorbachev's chief supporter in his elevation to general secretary, was report-edly stunned at the move. The old guard of the Brezhnev era was being turned out.

One point of foreign policy where Gorbachev went beyond skepticism was Afghanistan. It was later learned that he had not known ahead of time about the invasion of Afghanistan in 1979 and did not approve of it. He quickly concluded that it was costing the Soviet Union too much in resources and lives and needed to be reversed. Gorbachev took the extraordinary step of reading aloud to the Politburo samples from the "torrent of letters" sent to Moscow from families of soldiers serving in Afghanistan, many of the letters bravely signed rather than sent anonymously. There were even a few from military officers, including a general, who complained that he was unable to explain to his soldiers why they were there. Less than a month into Gorba-chev's rule, Chernyaev recorded in his diary, "It is obvious that there are no alternatives. We must pull out." By fall, the decision was made. Chernyaev's diary entry for October 17, 1985, reads:

> I was at the Politburo today. There was a historical statement about Afghanistan. Gorbachev has finally made up his mind to put an end to it. [Gorbachev] outlined his talk with [Afghan president Babrak] Karmal. He, Gorbachev said, was dumbfounded, in no way expected such a turn, was sure that we need Afghanistan more than he does, and was clearly expecting that we will be there for a long time, if not forever. That is why I had to express myself with the utmost clarity: by the summer of 1986 you will have to learn how to defend your revolution yourselves.

This decision was kept secret for the time being. Gorbachev didn't want to hand the West a preemptive concession. In fact, in coming months the So-viets would increase their forces and step up military action in Afghanistan.

Despite their ideological gulf, Gorbachev shared one of Reagan's core traits: an aversion to the use of military force—a trait that would become especially significant in 1989. Above all there was one decisive fact about Gorbachev of immense significance: he understood that the arms race was counterproductive. He was also plainly worried that Reagan's SDI would make it worse for the Soviet Union. When House Speaker Tip O'Neill called on Gorbachev during an April visit to Moscow, Gorbachev gave a two-hour monologue directed against SDI. That same month Gorbachev made a splash with an offer to freeze further deployment of Soviet intermediate-range missiles in Europe if the United States and NATO would freeze their ongoing deployment. The United States and NATO swiftly rejected the offer for the reason they had rejected the same offer from Brezhnev in 1982: it would cement in place an asymmetry in forces and reduce the incentive for the Soviets to agree to real reductions. The Soviet Union had 414 SS-20 missiles deployed in Eastern Europe, each carrying three warheads. At that point in the NATO deployment, the West had only 63 Pershing II missiles and 80 cruise missiles, with a total of 143 warheads. Gorbachev was proposing to freeze in place a nearly nine-to-one Soviet advantage.

But Gorbachev and Reagan were fast becoming pen pals. Reagan sent a letter to Gorbachev with the American delegation to Chernenko's funeral expressing "my hope that we can in the months and years ahead develop a more stable and constructive relationship between our two countries" and inviting Gorbachev to come to Washington. Gorbachev wrote back ten days later with a long letter reciprocating Reagan's sentiments about improving relations and agreeing to the general idea of a meeting, though demurring on Washington as a location. He included a remonstrance for "talk[ing] in two languages, one for private contacts, and the other for the audience"—a clear shot at the "evil empire" rhetoric. (Over the summer he would complain that the United States was waging "a campaign of hate" against the Soviet Union.) Curiously, Gorbachev added that it would not be necessary for such a meeting to be concluded with the signing of a major agreement. Clearly Gorbachev was interested in sizing up Reagan, but the abandonment of a substantive precondition was another small concession that Reagan would skillfully exploit.

So the door was open for the first meeting of the respective heads of state in six years. There were a number of roadblocks that needed clearing away, and new obstacles would arise over the summer. But here the narrative should pause to add a coda to the scene as it stood at this moment. In years since the end of the Cold War it has been fashionable in the West to heap praise upon Gorbachev for being the key person in the story. *Time* magazine would go so far as to name Gorbachev "person of the decade" in the 1990s. George Kennan would later declare Gorbachev's ascension a "miracle." Gorbachev certainly deserves his full share of credit for this beneficent outcome. Yet it must also be borne in mind that before Gorbachev's ascension, a frequent criticism of Reagan's policy toward the Soviet Union was that it would surely strengthen the hand of Soviet hard-liners and prevent the emergence of moderates. Columbia University's Robert Legvold, for example, wrote critically of Reagan's Soviet policy in 1982, "[I]t is conceivable that vigorous, sometimes bellicose anti-Soviet policies on the part of U.S. authorities could vindicate and strengthen their hard-line rivals. This is precisely what some Soviets hint might happen."[35] But it was Gorbachev, a moderate and a reformer (even if a confused one), who came to power in 1985. And some of Reagan's advisers perceived that such might be the outcome of their deliberate policy. In January 1984 Reagan's recently departed National Security Adviser William Clark wrote him to say that he thought administration policy would "very likely influence the rise of a less dangerous Soviet leader than the dying Andropov." Reagan's critics, operating from a nonfalsifiable point of view, pivoted without pause to the argument that Gorbachev ascended *in spite of* Reagan's belligerence. It is ironic the sclerotic Soviet intelligentsia demonstrated more ability to entertain new thoughts than did Western liberals and Sovietologists.

*   *   *

THE ROAD TO a summit would be neither smooth nor easy. On March 24, just two weeks after Gorbachev became general secretary in Moscow and took up the hopeful exchange of letters with Reagan, a Soviet soldier shot an American officer, army major Arthur D. Nicholson, who was lawfully exercising his liaison duties according to postwar treaties in Potsdam in East Germany. Worse than the shooting was the Soviet refusal to allow American medics to come to Major Nicholson's aid. By the time Americans were allowed to reach Nicholson, he had bled to death from his wound. Shultz called it a "barbaric cold-blooded murder." The Soviets naturally claimed that Nicholson was engaged in espionage. Shultz protested strongly to Dobrynin, demanding an apology and restitution for Nicholson's family. The Soviets refused. Weinberger wanted Reagan to halt arms talks and progress toward a summit until the Soviets relented—the very kind of linkage that Reagan had mostly rejected from the beginning of his presidency. Reagan sent a stiff note to Gorbachev: "Certain recent events have cast doubt on the desire of your government to improve relations." He blasted Soviet behavior in Afghanistan and turned the tables on Gorbachev's criticism in his last letter about Reagan's speaking in "two languages." "Soviet words and actions," Reagan concluded, "do not always seem to us to be speaking the same language."

Even as the prospect of direct summitry with the Soviet Union took center stage, Reagan's de facto anti-Communist rollback policy continued to affect peripheral theaters. By far the most urgent peripheral venue remained Central America. On March 1 Reagan recorded in his diary: "The Nicaragua problem continues to fester." Since the cutoff of American military aid late in 1984 the Contras had been in retreat. As Robert Kagan put it in his magisterial history of the U.S.-Nicaraguan struggle of the 1980s, "[W]eakness in the American political system in 1984 had translated into weakness on the battlefield in 1985."[36] Half of the Contra forces had left Nicaragua for sanctuary in Honduras. Armed with the latest Soviet helicopters, the Sandinistas massed as many as sixty thousand troops near the Honduran border and announced plans to resettle twenty-four thousand villagers in order to clear out a free-fire zone as a prelude to a push to crush the Contras.

The Contras were managing to hang on with other foreign sources of support—a fact that both the Reagan administration and members of Congress acknowledged publicly and repeatedly in late 1984 and the early months of 1985. Saudi Arabia continued to be the principal source of funds (Israel having rebuffed two American requests to supply Contra aid). King Fahd delighted Reagan in an early February visit to Washington when he indicated willingness to increase Saudi aid. In all Saudi Arabia would provide $32 million in Contra aid. Robert McFarlane deliberately withheld details of Saudi aid from Shultz and Weinberger.

Reagan's landslide reelection and the slight Republican gains in the House revived prospects that American aid to the Contras might get through the new Congress. But it was the result of the Nicaraguan election, held the same week as the U.S. election, that had the most political impact on Capitol Hill. While the Sandinistas won the balloting by a comfortable margin, few regarded the result as fair or legitimate. Prior to the election the Sandinistas had ratcheted up press censorship, tapped the telephones of their political opponents, and actively prevented opposition candidates and parties from campaigning, in some cases organizing mobs to disrupt opposition political rallies.[37] The Sandinistas' unwillingness to permit a free and fair campaign led Arturo Cruz, the most significant opposition leader, to withdraw as a candidate despite obvious and widespread popular support. In the aftermath of the election, the Sandinistas tightened press censorship further, driving several remaining opposition editors into exile. Shortly after the first of the year Cruz turned up in Washington to announce, for the first time, his support for the Contras, and to urge Congress to resume Contra aid. This announcement shook up a number of moderate Democrats on Capitol Hill, since Cruz had earned a reputation as a democratic opposition leader through his earlier alliance with the Sandinistas to oust the dictator Somoza.

Nevertheless, most Democrats remained opposed when Reagan sought to have $14 million in escrowed funds for military aid released to the Contras. At the White House there was a vigorous debate about whether Reagan should press hard against the Democrats' opposition to Contra aid, making them politically accountable for a failed and inconsistent policy. Reagan expressed some sympathy with the idea of making Congress "feel the heat" if they didn't "see the light." Pat Buchanan and other hard-liners wanted Reagan to make a televised speech. Michael Deaver, not yet departed from the White House, and other political advisers were against the idea, as were key Capitol Hill Republicans such as Bob Dole. (Reagan should give a speech on the budget instead, the monomaniacal Dole told the White House.) Reagan ultimately decided against making a high-profile speech. Opinion polls continued to show public unease with U.S. support for the Contras, but on the same day (March 1) that Reagan noted in his diary that Nicaragua was "festering," he told the annual Conservative Political Action Conference (CPAC) that the Nicaragua Contras were "freedom fighters" and "the moral equivalent of our Founding Fathers and the brave men and women of the French Resistance. We cannot turn away from them."

A few weeks later it occurred to columnist Charles Krauthammer that Reagan's repeated pronouncements on behalf of guerilla forces from Nicaragua to Afghanistan, from Southeast Asia to southern Africa, as well as his invasion of Grenada, amounted to a grand strategy. Writing in *Time* magazine on April 1, Krauthammer called it "the Reagan Doctrine." Reagan himself spoke of the idea explicitly on only one occasion, late in his presidency. In a speech on October 25, 1988, Reagan said: "We stand with ordinary people who have the courage to take up arms against Communist tyranny. This stand is the core of what some have called the Reagan doctrine. . . . Some have called our support for at least one of these movements bizarre, but I say it's as natural as what makes us Americans—that there is something in our spirit and our history that calls on us to say these battles are our battles and these freedom fighters are our brothers and sisters." Even without Reagan's explicit embrace in 1985 or 1986, the slogan caught on.

Faced with the deteriorating situation in Central America, moderate Democrats sought a compromise policy on Contra aid that would maintain enough pressure on the Sandinistas to make diplomatic concessions. Perhaps, some moderate Democrats proposed, humanitarian assistance to the Contras would be enough to keep them sufficiently solvent to maintain pressure on Managua. Reagan thought he could live with this as a first step, and he proposed converting the $14 million in previously appropriated military aid into humanitarian aid.

As a vote on the new formula approached, a full-scale public relations and lobbying battle unfolded, highlighting the deep ideological divisions over Central America. More than 150 liberal organizations and church groups mobilized to oppose Contra aid, and it brought out some of the usual self-destructive liberal reflexes. George McGovern commented that if he had to choose between the Contras and the Sandinistas, "[W]ith the interests of both Nicaragua and the United States in mind, I would go with the Sandinistas." Protesters outside the White House chanted, "Hey, hey, Uncle Sam, we remember Vietnam!" The Sandinistas retained a New York law firm to produce a dossier of Contra human rights abuses, which was effectively marketed to the media. The State Department's Office of Public Diplomacy and several private conservative groups countered with their own substantial efforts to expose Sandinista perfidy and support Contra aid. Secretary of State Shultz forcefully proclaimed his own version of the Reagan Doctrine while testifying before Congress, saying that the United States should neither accept nor respect the Brezhnev Doctrine.[38] Weinberger did Shultz one better, saying, "I simply cannot understand why a Communist regime so close to our borders has so much support in Congress."

Contra aid passed the Senate narrowly on a 53–46 vote on April 23, but over in the House, Speaker O'Neill mounted a heavy effort to defeat the proposal. "An aide to O'Neill later said he hadn't seen the Speaker work so hard on a vote in ten years," Robert Kagan reported. The measure failed in the House by two votes, 213–215. A weaker substitute proposal that would have provided some Contra aid through the Red Cross, designed to give Democrats cover against charges of undermining Reagan, failed by a wide margin as Republicans refused to be drawn into such a transparent ploy. It appeared that Contra aid was dead.

Then the Sandinistas committed a colossal blunder. The day after the House vote, the news broke that President Daniel Ortega was leaving imminently for Moscow to consult with the new Soviet leader, Gorbachev. (One of the discordant notes that made reading Gorbachev's intentions difficult was that Soviet military aid to Nicaragua increased substantially *after* Gorbachev came to power.) This was Ortega's eighth trip to the Soviet Union in five years, but as columnist Mary McGrory wrote, "If ever they give an Oscar for bad timing, there is no need to ask for the envelope. Ortega will be the winner going away." Democrats who had led the fight against Contra aid were embarrassed and chagrined. Several said they would have voted in support of Contra aid if they had known Ortega would take such a boneheaded step. New York representative Charles Schumer called Ortega's trip "a personal rebuke to Congress."

Overnight Democratic moderates turned on their leadership. Democratic representative Tommy Robinson of Arkansas blasted O'Neill and majority leader Jim Wright for having "a Neville Chamberlain mentality," while Virginia Democratic representative Dan Daniel sounded like Weinberger in saying that "we can no longer temporize or compromise with Communists on our doorsteps." In early June a new $27 million Contra aid package passed the House, with seventy-three Democrats joining nearly all Republicans in supporting the measure by a 248–184 vote. As Robert Kagan wrote, Democrats "voted more out of anger and fear than out of conviction, anger at Ortega and fear of the political consequences of voting against aid to the contras."[39] Tip O'Neill was bitter in defeat: "They're afraid. They're afraid of Ronald Reagan." Although this package was also limited to "humanitarian aid," it was widely understood that the Contras would receive private support for arms and ammunition.

This was not the only such legislative victory for the Reagan Doctrine. In the spring and early summer of 1985 Congress also approved $5 million in military aid to anti-Communist guerillas in Cambodia, renewed military aid for the anti-Soviet resistance in Afghanistan, and, perhaps most significantly, voted to repeal the Clark Amendment, a ten-year-old ban on CIA assistance to anti-Communist rebels in Angola. (For many Democrats, supporting aid to anti-Communist guerillas in Africa and Asia was a way of covering themselves politically for their opposition to Contra aid.) While Reagan's own foreign policy team was divided on the matter, with Shultz opposing aid to Jonas Savimbi's UNITA faction, there was strong support among conservatives for stepped-up aid. Conservatives also wanted the United States to support anti-Communist guerillas against the Marxist government of Mozambique, but in this case Reagan resisted because his administration was quietly trying to draw Mozambique out of the Soviet orbit with carrots instead of sticks, with some signs of success.

Despite these compromises and crosscutting difficulties, in general Reagan continued to have the initiative in foreign policy. In the spring he had been frustrated by congressional resistance—during a May meeting with Republican congressional leaders Reagan complained, "We've got to get where we can run a foreign policy without a committee of 535 telling us what to do"—but things were starting to look up. What could go wrong? Plenty.

*   *   *

THREE FOREIGN EVENTS beset Reagan over the spring and summer of 1985. The first was a political tempest in a teapot that was quickly forgotten. The other two would combine to bring his presidency near to crashing down the following year.

Early in 1985 Reagan agreed to visit Europe to mark the fortieth anniversary of the end of World War II, but this time he thought it important to include West Germany prominently in the observances. West German chancellor Helmut Kohl had been conspicuously missing from the D-Day observances the year before, a slight that had disappointed Kohl. But West Germany was coincidentally hosting the G-7 economic summit in May 1985, simplifying the organization of some suitable observance of postwar reconciliation. Or so the White House thought. Reagan accepted Kohl's suggestion to lay a wreath at a cemetery in honor of Germany's war dead; at the same time, Reagan declined an invitation to visit the Dachau concentration camp site, on the sensible grounds that it went against the intention of observing and bolstering the birth of a new democratic Germany. (An additional factor was Nancy Reagan's dislike of the idea.)

In the abstract the timing had seemed right to reciprocate German efforts to atone for midcentury misdeeds and end West Germany's de facto probation from the community of leading nations. West Germany's first postwar chancellor, Konrad Adenauer, had laid a wreath at the Tomb of the Unknown Soldier at Arlington National Cemetery in Virginia on a 1953 visit to the United States. "It had been a long and hard road," Adenauer wrote in his memoirs of the occasion, "from the total catastrophe of 1945 to this moment of the year 1953 when the German national anthem was heard in the national cemetery of the United States. . . . It showed the world that that epoch was over and that an era of friendship had begun in which the Federal Republic was accepted once more in the circle and company of free peoples." And the decision to avoid a visit to a death camp seemed sensible. By 1985 about 60 percent of the West German population had been born after World War II. How would current-generation Americans feel if each African head of state insisted on a pointed visit to a slave plantation as a part of every diplomatic itinerary?

As subsequent legend has it, Reagan's advance team, visiting the recommended cemetery at Bitburg in the winter, failed to notice the markings on the headstones denoting that nearly fifty of the grave sites were occupied by members of Hitler's dreaded SS corps, which carried out some of the worst Nazi war crimes. One of the interred was an SS sergeant who had been decorated specifically for killing ten Americans; another group had been implicated in the massacre of an entire French village. The SS markings had been covered up by snow, Mike Deaver later offered as an excuse.[40]

The news of this planning blunder provoked a firestorm of outrage, and there was an unrelenting chorus that Reagan had to cancel the visit. The ensuing controversy reopened and rubbed raw the precise wounds of German memory that Reagan had been hoping to close up once and for all. The news media echoed the understandable criticism by Jewish groups. The U.S. Senate passed a resolution calling for Reagan to cancel the Bitburg appearance by a vote of 82–0; a similar resolution in the House received 390 votes. Protestant and Catholic clergy joined Jews in urging Reagan to reverse course. Opinion polls showed that a majority of Americans opposed the visit. Even the American Legion abandoned Reagan and protested the visit. The matter penetrated pop music. The Ramones, one of the pioneers of punk rock, whipped out a single, "My Brain Is Hanging Upside Down (Bonzo Goes to Bitburg)."

Many in Reagan's administration—and his wife, Nancy—agreed with the critics.[41] "Bitburg is killing us," Don Regan said. Shultz said, "Hitler is laughing in hell right now." The Soviet press had a field day, blasting Reagan for coddling "German revanchism." Reagan compounded the controversy with some ill-chosen remarks that the young German draftees in the SS "were victims, just as surely as the victims in the concentration camps," a remark George Will characterized as "stark intellectual chaos" and Charles Krauthammer called "grotesquely wrong." By a fluke of prior scheduling, Reagan had to host one of the world's best-known Holocaust survivors, Elie Wiesel, at a White House award ceremony a week into the furor. In a live televised broadcast of the ceremony, Wiesel scolded Reagan, saying, "That place, Mr. President, is not your place. Your place is with the victims of the SS."

The criticism brought out Reagan's stubborn streak. He wrote in his diary, "There is no way I'll back down and run for cover." A few days later he returned to this theme: "I'm not going to cancel anything no matter how much the bastards scream."[42] Reagan was angry when he discovered that his senior staff (especially McFarlane) had been working back channels with the West German government to scuttle the Bitburg visit. Reagan's stubbornness found counterbalance in the timidity and fearfulness of Chancellor Kohl, who both wrote and pleaded with Reagan in an emotional telephone call that cancellation of the Bitburg visit would bring down his government.[43] Shultz thought Kohl was being massively insensitive to the problems the episode was causing Reagan and that Kohl displayed startling weakness for a national leader.

Ultimately it was decided to amend the itinerary, with Reagan making his principal appearance at the site of the Bergen-Belsen concentration camp, and with the visit to the Bitburg cemetery shortened to a mere eight minutes, with no staged photo opportunity beside Kohl. Thousands of Germans lined the motorcade route, many carrying signs expressing their appreciation of Reagan's politically costly gesture. Not backing down in the face of political disaster actually served Reagan well at home: public approval of the Bitburg visit *went up* by 10 percent in the aftermath, from 49 to 59 percent. Reagan felt a measure of vindication, writing in his diary: "I always felt it was the morally right thing to do."

Yet Reagan equivocated on his clear moral sentiments in the second foreign crisis of 1985, and it contributed to the flood tide that eventually threatened to engulf him. Reagan was awakened early on the morning of June 14 with the news that terrorists had hijacked TWA flight 847 in Athens, Greece. It was the beginning of a prolonged and bizarre hijacking, which would see the commandeered plane first taken to Beirut and then making two round-trips to Algiers and back, with the news media covering the story live and up close. On the second stop in Beirut, the hijackers shot an American navy man, Robert Stethem, and dumped his body on the tarmac. There were more than fifty Americans on the flight, and a hundred other passengers. The most riveting scene of the drama involved a hijacker putting a gun to the head of pilot John Testrake as he spoke to TV reporters out the window of the cockpit. The live TV coverage placed additional pressure on the Reagan administration as it pondered its responses. Reagan cancelled his plans to travel to his ranch for the rest of the month, as the media-crisis cycle was set in motion.

The hijackers demanded the release of 766 Shiite prisoners whom Israel had captured in southern Lebanon, along with a handful of Islamic terrorists held in Kuwait. The irony—and the beginning of much trouble—was that Israel had been planning soon to release most or all of these captives even before the hijacking, and had informed the U.S. embassy of its intentions. Now, however, no one wanted to be seen giving in to terrorist threats. At a National Security Council meeting on the second day of the affair, Reagan suggested that the United States call on the hijackers to release the hostages, after which the United States would see that Israel released their prisoners. Shultz and others objected that such a course would be too transparent a concession to terrorists, and the president immediately backed off. At a press conference on June 18 (day four of the hijacking), Reagan enunciated a clear principle: "America will never make concessions to terrorists—to do so would only invite more terrorism—nor will we ask nor pressure any other government to do so." Israel fell into line too, stating publicly that it would not yield to terrorist demands even if the United States asked.

After the third and final landing in Beirut on the fourth day, the hostages were removed from the plane and dispersed among terrorist cells (most of them connected to the Iranian-backed Hezbollah Shiite faction) throughout the city, transforming the matter from a hijacking to a kidnapping and making a rescue attempt—difficult in the best circumstances—impossible. Reagan's foreign policy team debated a number of options, from bombing the Beirut airport to "declaring war on terrorism."[44] The situation underscored the weakness of a superpower in the face of what was becoming known as "asymmetrical warfare."

In the midst of the drawn-out affair, Reagan watched the new hit movie from Sylvester Stallone, *Rambo: First Blood Part II,* in which the former Green Beret John Rambo single-handedly dispatches a company of North Vietnamese troops holding U.S. POWs. The next day Reagan remarked, "After seeing *Rambo* last night, I know what to do the next time this happens." In fact he was reluctant to use force to retaliate against terrorists for fear of putting the hostages' lives in jeopardy.

The only realistic course was to pursue patient diplomacy, and there ensued over the next ten days a five-way dance involving Syria's Hafez Assad, Israel, Algeria, Iran, and Lebanese opportunists, especially Nabih Berri, a Shiite leader well known to Americans from his time living in the United States. Given the intense media circus surrounding the hijacking, it was inevitable that Jesse Jackson eventually stuck his nose into the matter, contacting Berri directly. At length the United States applied pressure on Berri and the kidnappers through Syria, and the hostages were finally let go on June 30, whereupon Israel released the sought-after Arab prisoners. The hijackers, unfortunately, escaped with impunity. Reagan felt compelled to take the distasteful step of telephoning Assad to thank him for his "help."

There was more to the story than Assad and Nabih Berri, however. Behind the scenes, Iran had, as a result of Assad's intervention, brought decisive pressure on the Hezbollah kidnappers to release the hostages. Reagan and Shultz had hoped that the seven previously kidnapped Americans could also be freed in the course of resolving the TWA 847 affair, but they could not make this happen. Two days before the TWA 847 hostages were released, Reagan met in Chicago with the family of a Catholic priest named Lawrence Jenco, who had been kidnapped in Beirut in January. The meeting went badly, with Jenco's family criticizing Reagan for not doing enough to secure Jenco's release. Reagan emerged shaken and upset.

Three weeks later, on July 17, while Reagan was recuperating in Bethesda Naval Hospital from a colonoscopy that had discovered a malignant polyp, he made an enigmatic entry in his diary: "Some strange soundings are coming from the Iranians. Bud M. will be here tomorrow to talk about it. It could be a breakthrough on getting our 7 kidnap victims." The initiative that exploded into the Iran-Contra scandal a year later was about to be set in motion.

* * *

THE "STRANGE SOUNDINGS" Reagan mentioned were reports from Israeli sources that a moderate faction within the government of Iran wished to open a quiet channel of communications with Washington. It was an intriguing possibility. Several factors complicated American policy toward Iran. In the fall of 1980, Iraq's Saddam Hussein, thinking Iran vulnerable, opportunistically attacked its neighbor. This conflict needs to be understood in the context of the Cold War as well as for its direct implications for Persian Gulf stability. When Iran proved more ferocious in its defense than Hussein had expected, the United States, fearing an outright Iranian victory and the potential spread of Iranian-style Shiite radicalism, tilted ever so slightly toward Iraq, going so far as to share limited intelligence with Iraq about Iran's military disposition. But the United States didn't want Soviet-leaning Iraq to prevail outright, which might have opened the region to further Soviet intrigues and made Iran vulnerable to a Soviet takeover. And so a war with frequent large-scale savage battles ground on with no end in sight. No one was enthusiastic about this state of affairs. Henry Kissinger commented that it was too bad both sides couldn't lose.

There was a catch to the purported Iranian opening—a big one. Iran wanted American weapons and spare parts, which it desperately needed in its war with Iraq. The Israeli government at the highest levels, including Prime Minister Shimon Peres, quietly passed along the idea to the Reagan administration. This posed multiple dilemmas. Such an act would violate at least two emphatically stated U.S. policies and damage American credibility if the veil of secrecy was pierced. The United States had sought to isolate Iran through an international arms embargo and pressed its European allies vigorously; though, surprisingly, the United States had looked the other way on some Israeli arms sales to Iran in the early 1980s, which should have been a red flag to be wary of this proposed strategy. The intrigue deepened when the Israelis introduced as key players into the mix two Middle Eastern figures seemingly created in a Hollywood central casting office. One was the flamboyant arms dealer Adnan Khashoggi, a Saudi well known for being a one-man intelligence and diplomatic operation. The second figure was as obscure as Khashoggi was famous—an Iranian expat named Manucher Ghorbanifar.

Khashoggi brought Ghorbanifar to the attention of the Israelis in 1985, and it was Ghorbanifar who first broached the idea that the United States might be able to broker the release of the hostages in Lebanon through arms sales to Iran. While Ghorbanifar was new to the Israelis, he was not a stranger to the CIA: he had failed two CIA polygraph tests in the early 1980s, and in 1984, the CIA issued a "burn notice" to allied intelligence services declaring him to be untrustworthy.[45] Israel's Mossad should have received this CIA notice, and either lost track of it or chose to ignore it (perhaps, it was speculated later, because Ghorbanifar was in fact an Israeli agent).[46] Israel was convinced Ghorbanifar could deliver, and passed its endorsement along to Washington.

On August 6 Robert McFarlane formally brought to the National Security Planning Group the Israeli request to sell a hundred American-made TOW missiles to Iran. Vice President Bush, Chief of Staff Regan, Weinberger, and Shultz were present. Weinberger and Shultz were in rare agreement, with each man saying that the proposed arms sale was a bad idea and possibly illegal under the Arms Export Control Act. Regan and Bush were cautiously but favorably disposed to the idea. As was typical when his advisers disagreed, Reagan made no decision at the meeting. He cryptically recorded in his diary, "Rumors have it that 5 of our 7 hostages are going to be released."

In the words of the Tower Commission, which Reagan later appointed to sort out the ensuing mess, "what followed is quite murky." Indeed, there are few written records of the sequence of key meetings that followed, and there are multiple conflicting accounts of each step along the way.[47] Michael Kinsley would later summarize the kaleidoscope of implausible characters and unbelievable events as including the full range of "pies in faces, missing pants, stubbed toes, confused identities, mistaken embraces, role reversals, strange noises, and other classic elements of lowbrow comedy."

Several days after the August 6 meeting Reagan telephoned McFarlane to give his approval for the plan to go forward. Reminded of Shultz and Weinberger's vehement opposition, Reagan said he'd take the heat. Reagan later could not recall this conversation and said he thought he had merely approved replenishing Israel's TOW missile inventory after the fact. Regardless, by degrees the tacit decision had been made to pay ransom—the customary Middle Eastern practice that most of our European allies followed—to gain the hostages' release, though this fact was never directly acknowledged as such. In fact the United States had already attempted in the winter of 1985 to ransom the hostages the old-fashioned way—with cash—though the initiative had come to nothing. The decision in the late summer to pay ransom with arms was subsumed within the strategic possibility of repairing relations with Iran in a prospective post-Khomeini era (the CIA believed the ayatollah was in poor health and would not last much longer), and the involvement of two intermediaries—Israel and Iran—made it superficially plausible for Reagan to suppose that he wasn't dealing directly with Hezbollah terrorists.

Two weeks later Israel shipped ninety-four TOW missiles to Iran, and right away the deal the United States thought it had to gain the release of all seven American hostages in Lebanon began to unravel. No hostages were released. To the contrary, Iran passed word that it wanted four hundred more missiles, for which only *one* hostage would be released rather than all seven. Following a vigorous argument, Israel shipped another 408 TOW missiles to Iran on September 15 in a complicated and hazardous operation that involved the CIA putting out the story that the unusual shipment transiting through Europe was "oil equipment." The United States had hoped for the release of CIA agent William Buckley, but as Buckley was already dead by this point (a fact the United States would not determine until later), Hezbollah instead freed the Reverend Benjamin Weir, who upon release displayed all the hallmarks of Stockholm syndrome, publicly expressing sympathy for his captors and blasting the Reagan administration. "The Iranians had chosen well," Michael Ledeen bitterly reflected about the man he called "Rev. Weird"—"a hostage who would do their propaganda work in the United States."

Through the same questionable intermediaries, particularly Ghorbanifar and his Iranian government contacts, came word that Iran wanted to deal further, but the cost was going up. Iran wanted more advanced American weapons, and also wanted the release of seventeen Shiite terrorists currently jailed in Kuwait. McFarlane said, "I have a bad feeling about this whole operation." It was starting to look like out-and-out extortion. Why, then, did it continue?

*   *   *

HERE IT MAY be useful to pause and, as Churchill reflected in the context of understanding the Munich disaster of 1938, "set down some principles of morals and action which may be a guide in the future." Ronald Reagan's critics often liked to assail him through his Hollywood background, suggesting he was merely imitating his heroic but mythic on-screen roles. One irony of the Iran-Contra disaster is that had Reagan emulated the hard-bitten attitude of submarine commander Casey Abbott in *Hellcats of the Navy,* one of his last major film roles, his administration might have avoided the Iran-Contra train wreck. In the role of Commander Abbott, Reagan made the difficult but necessary decision to sacrifice an adrift crewman to save his submarine and its vital mission. "You think I enjoy letting men drown?" Reagan's character asks a junior officer who questioned his decision. "Someday you may have a command of your own. If you want to take a chance and risk an entire crew, a ship, and a mission for one man, that'll be your decision to make. This one was mine."

Reagan could not bring himself to regard the hostages as inevitable casualties whose sacrifice all great powers must tragically endure in an unruly world. He also drew back from violent covert operations against Hezbollah for fear the hostages would be killed in retaliation. The Soviet Union, though, had shown how to get results with direct tactics: after three Soviet diplomats were kidnapped in Beirut, the KGB kidnapped a relative of a Hezbollah leader and, as Bob Woodward narrated, "castrated him, stuffed his testicles in his mouth, shot him in the head, and sent the body back to Hezbollah."[48] The Soviet hostages were promptly released and no more were taken. (Reagan did, at one late point, muse in his diary about "being ready to kidnap Khomeini.")

For Reagan, sentiment trumped principle, as the imperative of rescuing imperiled Americans overwhelmed the imprudence of treating with terrorists and rogue nations. Three more Americans had been taken hostage in Lebanon in the winter and spring of 1985—Father Lawrence Jenco, a Catholic relief worker, and David Jacobsen and Thomas Sutherland, both of American University. Periodically their captors would release photos of the captives that made evident their poor condition. McFarlane and his NSC successor, John

Poindexter, recalled that Reagan asked at almost every daily briefing, "Anything new on the hostages?" In a December 1985 meeting Reagan said, "I don't care if I have to go to Leavenworth; I want the hostages out."[49]

The arms intrigue was not the sole effort made to gain the hostages' release. Reagan got Japanese prime minister Yasuhiro Nakasone, with whom he enjoyed good relations, to send a special emissary to Tehran to plead for the hostages' release in August ("very hush hush," Reagan noted in his diary), thinking Japan's trade clout with Iran would carry weight. The State Department attempted to leverage diplomatic pressure from Egypt and Syria and even the Palestinians. It was to no avail, and may have been an error. Placing such a high value on the hostages increased the bargaining position of Iran and Hezbollah. As Shultz later put it, "To let the terrorists sell hostages to us one by one was to create a hostage-taking industry." Indeed, it was the conscious decision of the George H. W. Bush administration upon taking office in 1989 to downplay the status of the hostages that contributed to their eventual release in 1991.

It is tempting to say in hindsight that Reagan should have stuck to his announced policy of not dealing with terrorists, though not even the Israelis faithfully hew to this clear principle. "No case of this kind can be judged apart from its circumstances," Churchill wrote of the infamous Munich accord. "The facts may be unknown at the time, and estimates of them must be largely guesswork." Were there any real Iranian moderates sympathetic to improving relations with the United States, and if so, would arms sales to a faction help or harm their position? One Iranian source told the United States that the arms sales were counterproductive because they strengthened the most radical elements. ("What's an Iranian moderate?" ran one mordant joke. "One who has run out of ammunition.") How real was the danger, later briefly touted by a central figure in the affair, that the Soviet Union was poised to begin a major intrigue against Iran? Perhaps, as was argued once or twice at the time, the idea of attempting an opening to Iran should have been pursued directly, without regard for the hostages in Lebanon. In the absence of decent intelligence about these and other questions—a chronic problem for the United States in the Middle East, as the nation would become acutely aware following September 11, 2001—one repairs to Churchill's simple principle from the time of Munich: honor, which points to the path of duty. However human the motives, Reagan's choice to violate his own policy of an Iranian arms embargo and deal with terrorists was leading down a path to dishonor.

It should also be observed, finally, that Reagan's decisions in this matter offer yet another disproof of the theme that he was easily led or manipulated by his staff. If this had been true, the vehement opposition of his secretaries of state and defense would have derailed the misadventure. It is a commonplace of Reagan literature that the Iranian arms initiative never would have happened if James Baker and the rest of the first-term troika had still been in place. This is far from certain. Reagan's later sketchy memory of the decision making involved continues to attract controversy, skepticism, and speculation about whether it was an early sign of his Alzheimer's disease.[50] From his diary entries for the late summer and fall of 1985 it is clear that the dominant foreign matter on his mind, and the focal point of his attention and that of his key advisers, was the upcoming summit with Gorbachev. Through all the murkiness of the decisions made throughout the entire affair, however, one fact is clear—the Iran arms-for-hostages initiative carried on because Ronald Reagan wanted it to.

*   *   *

IN ADDITION TO the role of Reagan's deep sympathy for the plight of the hostages, an institutional factor needs to be entered onto the historical balance sheet, along with the object lesson it provides in the way seemingly disparate events become interconnected. By degrees and for reasons both understandable and precarious, the National Security Council had become the focal point for keeping alive both the Contra supply operation and the Iran hostage initiative. Understandable, because the traditional bureaucracies, especially the State Department and to a lesser extent the CIA, could not be relied upon to carry out policies for which they had no enthusiasm or to which they were actively opposed. Precarious, because the NSC should not be an operational organ of the executive branch, though given the erratic congressional restrictions on aiding the Contras, utilizing the president's staff to conduct foreign policy seemed the only viable (and legal) option. (Was this very far removed from how Nixon had used Kissinger's NSC to bypass the State Department?) And in this operational mode, the two arenas had the fortune and misfortune of coming together under the purview of one Lieutenant Colonel Oliver North.

North, U.S. Naval Academy class of 1968, a highly decorated Marine officer in Vietnam whose fellow soldiers described him as "absolutely fearless," brought undeniable courage, fervor, and talent to his post in the NSC starting in 1981. For all his considerable virtues, he also had the defects of courage that Aristotle wrote had no name; indeed, North epitomizes Aristotle's caution that "he who exceeds in confidence in a fearful situation is called reckless."[51] North would eventually become the vortex of the multiple fearful situations Reagan faced in the 1980s. His work on behalf of the Contras was only the tip of the iceberg. North, using a number of private citizens as contractors, sought to develop a virtual off-the-shelf covert-operations apparatus within the NSC that would come to be called "the Enterprise."[52]

Throughout 1984 and 1985 North was fully immersed in the practical details of securing private financial support to keep the Contras together "body and soul," as Reagan had wanted, within the strict confines of the Boland Amendment restrictions on direct U.S. aid. North was tireless and effective in securing private donations to arm the Contras. Beer magnate Joseph Coors bought the Contras an airplane. North helped broker substantial funds from other private donors, including oil tycoon Nelson Bunker Hunt, heiresses Ellen Garwood and Barbara Newington, and even the *Washington Times* newspaper (which kicked in $100,000)—more than $10 million in all in 1985 and 1986, though much of the private funds seemed to go to middlemen and fund-raisers rather than into the Contras' coffers.[53] North arranged for Reagan to meet or personally thank most of these private donors. In addition to the Saudis and their $32 million given from 1984 to 1986, the major sources of third-party funds were Taiwan ($2 million) and the sultan of Brunei (though his $10 million contribution got wired to the wrong bank account in Switzerland due to a typographical error by North's secretary, Fawn Hall, and never did reach the Contras).[54] Perhaps the most unusual source of small arms for the Contras was the Florida city of Hialeah, whose largely Cuban American city council decided to send weapons confiscated in drug raids to the Contras.

North was not just a fund-raiser. He arranged procurement of arms from third countries and collaborated closely with the Contras on strategy. But he was starting to attract unwanted attention from the media and congressional Democrats. In early August North's semi-clandestine role came out from behind the curtain when the *New York Times* reported, "Rebels fighting to overthrow the Nicaraguan Government have been receiving direct military advice from White House officials on the National Security Council, senior Administration officials and members of Congress have disclosed. A senior Administration official said the direction had included advice and 'tactical influence' on the rebels' military operations as well as help in raising money from private sources."[55] The story was a remarkably detailed account of North's activities, but at the request of the White House, the *Times* did not publish North's name. The article was, however, a harbinger of the storm to come:

> The officer would not agree to an interview today. But another senior N.S.C. official said in a recent interview that the National Security Council had taken a leading role in directing the Administration's Nicaragua policy last year because of confusion at the State Department. However, the official did not acknowledge that the office had been directing the rebel forces.
>
> "There was so much fighting over there" at the State Department "that the action items were grabbed up by the N.S.C., mainly the trade embargo and contra aid."
>
> Often in past administrations, covert actions like the aid to the Nicaraguan rebels have been isolated from the White House, giving the President and his staff what came to be known as "plausible deniability" of the programs. . . .
>
> Still, within the White House the program was not managed as most N.S.C. programs are, a former senior White House official said today. "It was not handled through the crisis management apparatus," he said.

Everyone who followed Central American issues on Capitol Hill knew that North was the unnamed officer in the *Times* story, and it was no surprise when the *Washington Post* three days later outed North: "In a city of largely invisible staff workers," the *Post*'s front-page story reported, "Marine Corps Lt. Col. Oliver L. North of the National Security Council staff has emerged as an influential and occasionally controversial character in the implementation of the Reagan administration's foreign policy."[56] Several members of Congress raised questions about North and his NSC activities (prominent among them the freshman senator from Massachusetts, John Kerry), and McFarlane and North began altering NSC documents that Congress requested in an effort to determine if the Boland law was being violated.

Although North had been involved in an earlier effort to use money from Texas businessman H. Ross Perot to ransom the hostages in Lebanon, in September North was drawn directly into the matter afresh when he was sent to Lebanon to receive and debrief the first released hostage, Benjamin Weir. Three weeks later there occurred the second major terrorist incident of the year, the hijacking of the cruise ship *Achille Lauro* in the eastern Mediterranean. North's heroic role in this episode would elevate his status further while drawing him deeper into Middle Eastern intrigues.

The four well-armed Palestinians who boarded the *Achille Lauro* in Italy on October 7 originally intended to disembark in Israel and embark on a terror spree there, but when a ship steward inadvertently discovered their arms cache, the terrorists improvised by taking over the ship. While the United States and the Italians deliberated about mounting a paramilitary assault on the ship, the PLO brokered a deal. The terrorists would guarantee the well-being of the passengers and take the ship to Egypt, where they would be given safe passage out. When the United States learned that the terrorists had killed an American Jewish passenger, Leon Klinghoffer, disappointment at the deal turned to rage. North recognized an opportunity when Israeli intelligence sources in Egypt passed along detailed information about the flight plan for the terrorists to leave Egypt (including even the tail number of the aircraft). He called up John Poindexter and said, "I think we do an Admiral Yamamoto"—a reference to the successful aerial interception in April 1943 of the Japanese officer who had planned the Pearl Harbor attack.

It was a thrilling moment when U.S. F-14 warplanes from the aircraft carrier *Saratoga* intercepted the Egypt Air 737 and forced it to land at a NATO base in Sicily. "America as well as friends abroad are standing 6 inches taller," Reagan wrote in his diary that evening. The following day Reagan said publicly, "They can run, but they can't hide." The triumph of bagging the terrorists came to a bitter end, however, when Italy invoked its jurisdiction over the terrorists and then, wishing to appease the PLO, let the ringleader of the four terrorists, Abu Abbas, go free.[57] The other three hijackers served less than ten years in prison.

North's central role in the episode drew him into close contact with some of the same Israeli figures who were instrumental in the Iranian arms sales. The release of just a single hostage in September was enough to make the White House acquiesce to the prospect that an Israeli shipment of a hundred HAWK anti-aircraft missiles could produce the release of all the remaining hostages. This time the CIA and the National Security Council were drawn directly into the matter of the Israeli shipment, which would occur in mid-November. And the point person for the United States was North.

Shipping a hundred missiles from Israel to Iran was no easy logistical feat. The plan required sending the first eighty missiles to a European country and then transferring them to a CIA-supplied airplane for the final leg to Iran. But when Portugal balked at allowing the Israeli plane to land—*after*

*the plane was already airborne, following North's instruction for it to depart
from Israel*—an alternative arrangement was hastily improvised involving a
smaller plane with less cargo capacity, an itinerary through Cyprus, and the
intervention of a senior CIA officer who told the Cypriot government that the
"humanitarian" flight contained (once again) oil equipment. The NSC-CIA
involvement was conducted without a presidential finding to provide proper
legal authorization.[58]

After additional delays and snafus the shipment finally arrived in Iran
four days later but carried only eighteen HAWK missiles instead of the promised eighty. Although the Iranians were told that this was the first of five shipments, they angrily complained that they had been double-crossed. They had
paid for this shipment in advance and were furious that the missiles not only
were older, less-capable HAWKs (one of which failed when tested) but also
bore Israeli markings. Might as well be a pig in a mosque, as far as the Iranians were concerned. No hostages were released. The United States and the Israelis blamed each other for the botched operation.

Meanwhile, North had a "neat idea," as he later put it. There was about
$800,000 left over from the Iranian-Israeli payment to the United States for
the eighteen HAWK missiles. Why not, North thought, send it to the Contras? (North would later claim that Ghorbanifar first suggested the idea.) The
combination of the ironic prospect of using Iranian money to support the
Contras along with gaining the release of the American hostages in Lebanon
was sufficient reason for North to want to keep the initiative alive, despite
the HAWK fiasco.

The next steps would have to wait, however. At that precise moment in
November, everyone in the senior ranks of the White House was absorbed in
a much more important matter—the first Reagan-Gorbachev summit.

*   *   *

THE REAGAN-GORBACHEV Geneva summit in November 1985 was the
first such meeting in six years, and the longest interval the two superpowers
had gone without a summit since the decade between 1945 and 1955, when
the Cold War first took shape. Reagan was probably fortunate not to have
held a summit with Andropov or Chernenko, as neither man was capable of
breaking out of the rut of by-the-numbers Soviet diplomacy. With the Soviet
leadership now undergoing its most thoroughgoing transformation since the
1950s, there was perhaps an opportunity for the United States.[59]

Reagan, like Churchill, placed great stock in personal diplomacy. When

Churchill began to perceive, as early as 1944, the postwar difficulties that would become the Cold War, he said that if he could dine with Stalin once a week, "there would be no trouble at all." Reagan held the same view. Repeatedly over the years he expressed the thought that he could resolve the Cold War if he could just sit down with his Soviet counterpart and discuss matters rationally. He admitted that the Soviet leader would need to understand the futility of the arms race and Communist ideology, and that "to be candid, I doubted I'd ever meet anybody like that."

Gorbachev would later express the same sentiments. After his third face-to-face meeting with Reagan in 1987, Gorbachev would tell the Politburo:

> [P]erhaps for the first time, we understood so clearly how important the human factor is in international politics. For us, Reagan appeared as a representative of and a spokesman for the most conservative part of the most conservative segment of American capitalism and the military-industrial complex. But it turned out that, on top of all that, it is also important that policy makers, including the leaders of states, of governments, if they are really responsible people, they also represent human qualities, the interests and aspirations of common people, and that they can be guided by purely normal human feelings and aspirations. And in our day and age, this turns out to be of enormous importance.

At the same time, it must be recognized that Westerners placed an inordinate emphasis on summits for their own sake, despite the fact that none of the previous summits going back to the end of World War II had produced a noticeable change in Soviet global ambitions. In fact they probably reduced the effectiveness of Western containment strategy; Nixon and Kissinger later admitted that they found it difficult to maintain the stick half of a carrot-and-stick approach to the Soviets while they were having regular summits. What would be different this time? Conservatives were deeply skeptical, with good reason.

Previous summits had been organized around the premise that reaching some kind of technical agreement, especially on arms, could ease fundamental tensions. But armaments are a *symptom,* not a *cause,* of international tensions. Churchill repeatedly urged Britain's leaders to look to "the political and economic causes which lie behind the maintenance of armies and navies." "Disarmament has nothing to do with peace," he observed in the

1930s. "When you have peace, you will have disarmament." Reagan echoed this, and cited some of the same examples as Churchill, such as the Washington Naval Agreement of 1921. "Do arms limitation agreements—even good ones—really bring or preserve peace?" Reagan asked in 1979. "History would seem to say 'no.' " Hence Reagan's single most important argument to Gorbachev in their first meeting was "[W]e do not mistrust each other because we are armed; we are armed because we mistrust each other."

Gorbachev's suggestion in his first letter to Reagan back in March that it would not be necessary to conclude some kind of formal agreement was, therefore, highly significant, because it meant that the summit could be a more freewheeling exchange of arguments, dealing with fundamental rather than technical differences. The Soviets also surprisingly agreed, in the preparatory meetings between Shultz and Shevardnadze, to the proposed four-part American framework for future bilateral negotiations, which meant including human rights, regional conflicts, and cultural exchanges as subjects for full discussion, rather than limiting the discussion solely to arms control. In agreeing to the new American framework, the Soviets conceded the moral and political high ground, and Reagan would make the most of it over the next three years, relentlessly putting the Soviets on the defensive. In a sense, then, Geneva was positioned to be the first genuine summit, in the highest sense of the term, between the United States and Soviet Union in their history. Would it—did it—live up to this potential?

A week before the summit, *U.S. News and World Report* quoted an unnamed European diplomat saying that "Gorbachev will swallow Reagan within half an hour." Even American conservatives were nervous about how Reagan would perform. "Conservatives Jittery as Summit Approaches," ran a *Human Events* front-page headline on November 16. "The president can't get any pluses out of the summit," an unnamed senior White House aide told the *New Republic,* perhaps in a deliberate effort to lower expectations. "The best he can do is break even." One conservative congressman told *National Review* of his sellout fears: "The summit was orchestrated to make Reagan think that his highest second-term achievement will be the Nobel Peace Prize." A group of conservative senators and the Heritage Foundation produced a set of principles they suggested Reagan follow in Geneva—a document that Gorbachev would mention with disdain in one of their sessions. And right before Reagan departed, a mildly chastising letter to the president from Defense Secretary Weinberger was leaked to the media. Weinberger's opponents in the White House and State Department publicly accused him of trying to sabotage the summit. (Weinberger was not included in the delegation to Geneva.)

The contrast between how Reagan and Gorbachev sized up each other and how each approached the meeting provides the first major clue as to why this typical condescension about Reagan was so wide of the mark. To the delight of Reagan's more hard-line advisers, he almost completely ignored the suggested talking points and positions contained in the thick briefing book that the State Department prepared for him. "I'm getting d—n sick of cramming like a school kid [for Soviet meetings]," Reagan had written in his diary in September. "Sometimes they tell me more than I need to know." Throughout the summit NSC aide Jack Matlock was struck "by the number of statements Reagan made that went far beyond the thinking of the Defense Department, State Department, and his own NSC staff." He didn't just wing it. In preparation he dictated four pages of his own notes about how he viewed Gorbachev and, more importantly, how he saw Gorbachev's constraints and objectives playing out at the summit. It was, according to Matlock, "one of the few statements that Reagan dictated spontaneously to explain his views." (Reagan also quietly consulted Nixon and Gerald Ford for their insights on how to approach the summit. "Dick [Nixon] had a h—l of a good idea on the arms negotiations," Reagan wrote in his diary.)

Here we see again the canniness of the former labor negotiator in evidence. Reagan would hit hard on human rights, but he wanted this confined to the negotiating room. "Front page stories," Reagan wrote in the notes he prepared for the summit, "that we are banging away at them on their human rights abuses will get us some cheers from the bleachers but it won't help those who are being abused." Repeatedly he noted the imperative of not showing up Gorbachev, of not making him seem weak or the loser in the summit, since the general secretary would "need to show his strength to the Soviet gang back in the Kremlin."[60] The United States should let Gorbachev maintain his toughness on human rights, Reagan said, and try to press him to yield on Soviet aggression in Afghanistan and elsewhere. Regarding other tertiary issues that the Soviets were likely to bring up, such as trade, Reagan said, "[H]ow about just hanging back until we get some of the things we want instead of giving consideration up front to what they want?"[61] One of the more significant steps Reagan took was to prohibit the State Department from trying to negotiate with the Soviets a summit-concluding communiqué in advance, as had been the past practice. The State Department already had a draft in the works and had discussed it with Soviet diplomats. Reagan had to be stubborn and forceful on this point, insisting that he didn't want something "pre-cooked." It is clear that Reagan was looking beyond this summit, knowing that success in Geneva would mean subsequent summits where the real progress would be made.

Ironically, then, it was Reagan, the seventy-four-year-old, term-limited chief of state, who could afford to play for time. Gorbachev was in a bigger hurry. Gorbachev was, by numerous accounts, nervous about meeting Reagan. On his very first day as general secretary back in March, he had requested from a top adviser a study of how to handle Reagan. His aide, Alexander Yakovlev, perceived better than many American observers that Reagan, having set in motion a significant military buildup, was now ready to engage in serious diplomacy.[62] Yakovlev was also frank in his perception of the weaknesses of the Soviet position going into any summit—an implicit acknowledgment that Reagan had captured the initiative. There was little downside political risk for Reagan in a summit, but Soviet refusal to meet or failure to make progress in a summit would hand the United States a propaganda victory. Like Yakovlev, Chernyaev noted in his diary that it was important for Gorbachev "not to get worked up about regional problems" or yield to Reagan on Soviet "solidarity" with the "fighters for independence" (that is, Afghanistan, Nicaragua, and so forth)—the exact pressure points Reagan planned to target. Above all, Yakovlev suggested Gorbachev not provoke Reagan or "intensify the threat," which would "play up to the hawks" in the United States.

Gorbachev had his own hard-line faction in Moscow to worry about; the remnants from the Brezhnev era openly opposed making any progress and wanted to use a summit for propaganda purposes only. Georgi Arbatov, head of the U.S.-Canada Institute, had sent Gorbachev a memo in the winter arguing that he must deliberately wreck any summit, and Korniyenko, Gromyko's disappointed deputy at the Foreign Ministry, did his best to derail things in Geneva. This may have played a role in Gorbachev's floating the idea of a 50 percent cut in nuclear weapons in September. The proposal put pressure on Reagan as well as his own hawks in the Kremlin. Gorbachev further telegraphed his arms negotiating position several weeks before Geneva, when he visited Paris, denounced SDI, and said no arms reductions would be possible unless Reagan agreed to curtail missile defense. Taken as a whole, these signs indicate the extent to which Gorbachev yielded the advantage to Reagan before the first handshake.

The two and a half days that followed in Geneva turned out to be the point at which Reagan pressed against the fulcrum that ended the Cold War. Even with an open agenda and asymmetries of political position heading into a summit, just how would the two sides conduct a real argument without running the risk of blowing up the meeting at the outset? The format—plenary sessions with senior advisers, interspersed with one-on-one meetings between Reagan and Gorbachev—favored Reagan more than anyone perceived ahead of time. As Ken Adelman observed later, "[E]very single time [they met] Reagan took him to the cleaners."[63]

Many observers such as Edmund Morris have noted the visual triumph Reagan scored by standing coatless and hatless in the early Geneva winter on November 19 as a tightly bundled Gorbachev rolled up to the Maison Fleur d'Eau, where the first negotiating session would take place. Reagan bounded down the steps—"like a Labrador retriever," to borrow Adelman's phrase—to greet Gorbachev. Reagan's mastery of the situation continued behind closed doors in his first one-on-one meeting with Gorbachev. Scheduled to last only thirty minutes, it ran for an hour, worrying some of Reagan's aides (though not Shultz). Reagan and Gorbachev spent much of the time exchanging long speeches along the lines of *Gee, it's good that we're finally talking. Can't we clear away misunderstandings and learn more about each other?* and so forth.

Reagan, the host, waited for Gorbachev to offer the first opening. This was clever, for the anxious Gorbachev said that the question of ending the arms race was of critical importance and then moved on to defend the Soviet Union's "national interest" in the course of development in the Third World. Reagan pushed back, saying it was not acceptable for the Soviet Union to promote Marxist revolution in the Third World because it trampled the principle of self-determination. But perhaps they could continue this in the main plenary session, Reagan suggested. Gorbachev didn't want to let go of the point, however. He tried to defend Marxist revolution through the expedient of moral equivalency, arguing that "there had been those who considered that the American Revolution should have been crushed," but then, strangely, he went on to deny that the Soviet Union deliberately sought to spread revolution beyond its borders. Next he abruptly changed the subject, telling Reagan that Russian scientists were predicting a major earthquake in California in the next few years. Was he trying to establish goodwill while also defusing a potential clash before it got out of hand? In any event, what he got was a display of Reagan's reserves: Reagan proceeded to give Gorbachev a short tutorial about the history and nature of the San Andreas Fault.

Gorbachev failed to disarm Reagan. In the first plenary session that immediately followed the private, get-acquainted meeting, Gorbachev began with a broad appeal for improving the level of trust between the two super-powers, saying that he welcomed cultural exchanges, expanded trade, and other such initiatives. He denied that the Soviet economy was in trouble and therefore vulnerable to an American-led arms race, and also denied that the Soviet Union sought to foment revolution beyond its borders. Some of Reagan's advisers seated around the table couldn't believe that Gorbachev was committing the elementary negotiating mistake of bringing up well-known weaknesses—the very weaknesses Reagan wanted to target. "I observed him from across the table with growing disbelief," Jack Matlock wrote; "he was leading with his chin."

When Reagan's turn came, he agreed with the central theme of building trust but laid out a comprehensive case for the deep distrust with which Americans regarded the Soviet Union. He cited specific Soviet bad behavior going back to World War II, accused the Soviets of cheating on past treaties, and noted that the Soviets had their own missile defense research program. On this last point Reagan drew a line: America's SDI was a purely defensive weapon and not a tool for achieving first-strike capability over the Soviets.

Gorbachev was annoyed, but time for the first plenary session had come to an end. After a lunch break, the argument intensified. Gorbachev contin-ued to argue from a defensive posture, saying he thought it more useful to discuss solutions to their conflicts rather than causes. But then he shot back at Reagan's arguments from the first session, denying not only Soviet intent to spread revolution worldwide but also any aim of using Afghanistan as a base from which to dominate the Persian Gulf. At this point he seemed to blink for a second time: he had provided an oblique invitation for the United States to help the Soviets withdraw from Afghanistan. But Gorbachev used most of his time to bore in on SDI; he grew agitated and raised his voice as he attacked it as an American attempt to gain strategic superiority over the So-viet Union.

Reagan would have none of it. He calmly recited a long list of reasons and historical events demonstrating why the West distrusted the Soviet Union. He cited specific facts and figures on the progress of Soviet arms buildups amidst Western restraint. He was sarcastic at times: noting that the Soviets had installed Afghanistan's current leader, Reagan added, "Actually he was their second choice, since the first one did not work out as they wished"—a reference to the fact that Soviet special forces had assassinated the previous Soviet-backed leader as a prelude to the 1979 invasion. Above all, he was unyielding about SDI. It was for now a research program to see if it was even possible, Reagan argued. Besides, how could a wholly defensive weapon contribute to an arms race? There were two ways to end the arms race, Reagan concluded: reduce offensive weapons, or keep building up and develop defensive systems against them.

Gorbachev, clearly frustrated, asked Reagan how they should instruct their arms negotiators to proceed. Reagan suggested they shoot for Gorbachev's goal of a 50 percent cut in nuclear weapons; the issue of the respective nations' different force structure would have to be worked out. (So much for the view that Reagan was ignorant of such details.) But wouldn't SDI represent the offensive militarization of space? Gorbachev countered. No, Reagan said; besides, if the United States succeeded in developing SDI, "it should be shared." Reagan then went with one of his homespun anecdotes: "Our UN Ambassador [Vernon] Walters was asked by some Chinese, what happens when a man with a spear that can penetrate anything meets a man with a shield that is impenetrable? He responded that he didn't know, but that he did know what happens when a man with no shield meets that same opponent who has the spear. Neither of us want to be in situation of having no shield." Gorbachev became exasperated, at which point Reagan suggested they adjourn the second plenary session and take a walk outside.

There followed the most famous encounter of the summit, prefaced by a genial Reagan learning, during the stroll down to the nearby boathouse, that Gorbachev had seen several of his movies, including *Kings Row,* generally considered Reagan's best acting effort. Once seated by the roaring fireplace (a deliberate touch), Reagan dropped his previous argumentativeness and turned practical, offering Gorbachev a working paper, already translated into Russian, proposing a framework for reducing nuclear weapons. Gorbachev said he could support the idea of a 50 percent cut in warheads, but only so long as it was coupled with limitations on space-based weapons. Reagan repeated his view that defensive weaponry shouldn't be considered part of the arms race, and suggested the question be set aside while they got on with the job of cutting nuclear arms. After all, Reagan pointed out, if both countries reduced or eliminated nuclear missiles, no one would need missile defense.

Gorbachev countered again: what if both countries refrained from developing space weapons? Reagan rejected the term *space weapons,* saying there was no way to know whether SDI would be land- or space-based. And once more he reminded Gorbachev that the system wouldn't be offensive in nature and therefore should pose no obstacle to reducing nuclear warheads. Reagan used a fresh anecdote to make his point: he'd noticed, he said, that when European nations agreed after World War I to ban chemical weapons, "all had kept their gas masks."

While it might appear that Reagan and Gorbachev were going around and around the same arguments, Reagan's anecdotal approach was starting to make an impression on Gorbachev. Here we begin to see the germ of a personal relationship between the two men. Gorbachev replied that "he could understand the President on a human level" and see why missile defense "had captivated the President's imagination." As a *political* leader, however, he could not accept Reagan's point of view. The Soviet Union, he argued, could not have any long-term confidence that an American missile defense system wouldn't be used to obtain a first-strike advantage, despite Reagan's reassurances. The Soviets would eventually have to respond by building up a large enough number of ICBMs to overwhelm any defensive system.

It was now Reagan's turn to relent slightly. Without yielding an inch on SDI, he allowed that both men had made "strong statements" from which it would be difficult for either to back away. But he suggested that Gorbachev should consider taking up the idea to share research on missile defense. Both sides could open their laboratories for verification. Gorbachev changed the subject and returned to Reagan's point in only a roundabout way, suggesting that SDI would violate the ABM Treaty. Again Reagan had a rejoinder: he said that the ABM Treaty should be superseded by a new agreement built around his idea of sharing missile defense technology.

As in the second plenary session, Gorbachev grew exasperated. "With some emotion," as the official Memorandum of Conversation put it, he wondered why the United States would not believe the Soviet pledge never to launch a first strike, and further asked what purpose would be served by starting an arms race in a new sphere of defensive weapons. Reagan rebutted that missile defense would be useful against other possible aggressors, such as Libya, and besides, why fear weapons that destroy only other weapons rather than entire cities?

Gorbachev surely expected—as many of Reagan's aides hoped—that at some point Reagan would offer some kind of concession to negotiate about SDI. But the nearest Reagan came to a concession was his offer to reach agreement on sharing research and opening laboratories; Gorbachev made a tactical mistake not to take him up on the offer. To adapt Reagan's own metaphor, he was breaking Gorbachev's irresistible spear on the immovable object of his SDI shield.[64]

Gorbachev concluded the private session with a heartfelt plea for Reagan to believe his professions of wanting a change in Soviet-American relations, which was based on the Soviet assessment that it was necessary "precisely now" to make a change; "later it would be too late." Remarkably, Gorbachev ended this peroration by asking Reagan "not to regard this as weakness" on the part of the Soviet Union. Reagan surely recognized from his old labor negotiating days that he had gained the upper hand. On the walk back from the boathouse, he invited Gorbachev to hold their next meeting in Washington; Gorbachev accepted, but proposed that Reagan then come to Moscow. Reagan accepted. Advisers to both men were astounded; this had been expected to be a point for negotiation.

The second day of the summit must have given off feelings of déjà vu, as both men cycled through the same fundamental arguments from the first day's sessions, even though it had been clear the first time through that neither intended to yield. This made for a more heated atmosphere in the meeting room.

The second day began, like the first, with a private one-on-one meeting between Reagan and Gorbachev. Reagan opened this private discussion with the subject of human rights. Knowing the extreme Soviet sensitivity to "interfering with internal affairs," he made a practical rather than principled argument. He did not wish to raise this issue in the main meeting, Reagan said, implying that he did not seek to embarrass Gorbachev. But he pointed out that ethnic constituency groups in the United States cared deeply about human rights and were exerting pressure on public opinion and Congress; Soviet concessions on immigration would make it easier for Reagan to get agreements through Congress. As was the case with the Pentecostals the Soviets released from the U.S. embassy in Moscow in 1983, Reagan would not publicly claim credit, nor ask that the Soviets acknowledge American pressure in this area. It was a remarkable concession from Reagan's thoroughly Jeffersonian/Lincolnian view that human rights were a matter of universal application.

Even with this concession from Reagan, Gorbachev would have none of it, and quickly attempted to shift the conversation to the expanded cultural exchanges under discussion at the summit. But Reagan escalated, mentioning that Jews were persecuted in the Soviet Union, and even citing specific cases, including a Jewish pianist denied emigration to Israel and also denied the opportunity to play with major orchestras in the Soviet Union. Gorbachev was clearly annoyed and responded with the familiar Communist accusation that human rights violations were rampant in Western democracies. The

Memorandum of Conversation reveals that Gorbachev derived his talking points from the National Organization for Women:

> Gorbachev interjected that he was familiar with the state of things in the U.S. The President had said that there was no discrimination on the basis of sex. This was not true. According to U.S. law a woman could make 60 percent of the salary a man made for the same job. The President had spoken of equality. But so much time had passed since the American Revolution, and women still did not have the same rights as men. He knew this to be the case. He was informed. He had a legal education. . . . [I]f we are referring to changing laws, with other interests in mind, this could not be done. The Soviet people set their laws. Any other approach shows a disrespect for the Soviet people. The U.S. had its own system, and the Soviet Union had its own. The president would defend the United States, and he, Gorbachev, would defend the Soviet Union. Such a discussion could take a very long time.

It is one of the more unremarked-upon aspects of political discourse during these years that it was impossible to distinguish *Pravda* editorials and official Soviet rhetoric from the routine attitudes of American liberals and the *New York Times* editorial page. Though such arguments were certain to offend Reagan, he kept his cool, explaining that Gorbachev was wrong about American law, and adding that there were limits to the ability of law and bureaucracy to eradicate all discrimination and racial prejudice. He began relating anecdotes from his California governorship, likely in an attempt to wear down Gorbachev. Gorbachev interrupted, "without listening to the translation"—the first hint that his command of English was perhaps better than he let on—to chide Reagan for hiding behind the American political process.

The meeting ended in a standoff. "When the two leaders emerged," Shultz recalled, "they were not smiling. The atmosphere had been highly charged." Shultz took this as a good sign; the Soviets were attempting to argue rather than stonewall.

Reagan opened the third plenary session with a detailed position on the structure of strategic arms reductions, criticizing the Soviet classification of delivery systems that would maintain an overall Soviet advantage. But Gorbachev didn't want to drop his central focus on SDI; he parried Reagan's details and resumed his insistence that "space weapons" be included in any arms reduction package. Gorbachev resorted to the argument, which he attributed to "a Soviet scientist" rather than his own authority, that Reagan favored SDI chiefly because it would feed "a trillion dollars" into the American military-industrial complex. In other words, Reagan really just wanted to line the pockets of arms merchants. One wonders whether Gorbachev really believed this hoary chestnut or was looking for something—anything—to shake Reagan from SDI. It had the opposite effect.

"President Reagan exploded," as Shultz put it. Don Regan's characterization is that Reagan and Gorbachev "went at it like two taxi drivers after a fender-bender." Simultaneous translation enabled a fast-paced argument. At one point Gorbachev grew so insistent and heated that he interrupted Reagan twice to demand a direct answer. At another point Gorbachev said, "Do you take us for idiots?"

Around and around they went. Reagan pointed out that even if a missile shield was possible, it would be years before it was ready; in the meantime, the United States and Soviet Union could reduce arms. Why stop at 50 percent, Reagan added; why not cut to zero? Now Reagan was exceeding what his own advisers and the Pentagon thought either possible or wise. ("Nuclear weapons have kept the peace in Europe for forty years," more than one of Reagan's advisers argued to him before and after Geneva.) Gorbachev answered that the Soviet Union would have to proceed on the assumption that the United States would develop space weapons to gain strategic advantage.

Reagan and Gorbachev could only circle this block so many times. Gorbachev gave up first. After a long pause (as much as thirty seconds, according to some accounts), he said, "I don't agree with you, but I can see you really mean it." Reagan generously replied that perhaps the discussion had gone too far off track. So, Gorbachev asked, where were they now? They agreed that they wanted to stop the arms race, he noted, but this would not happen if the United States pursued "space weapons."

Now it was Reagan's turn to relent ever so slightly. Perhaps the two countries could cut by 50 percent while conducting missile defense research to see if it was even possible, he said. Then they could sit down someday and negotiate about deployment. Was that not a fair deal?

Gorbachev accused Reagan of condescending to the Soviet Union, of thinking the Soviets "simple people." Another tactical mistake, as it allowed Reagan to strike a magnanimous posture, a virtue that came easily to him. Reagan denied that he had shown disrespect. What was the matter with research? he asked.

Now the summit reached a crucial moment. Gorbachev insisted that it had been clear for months that progress on arms reduction depended on stopping "space weapons," and threatened to leave the summit saying that nothing positive had come out of Geneva because Reagan was unwilling to yield on this point. Reagan held firm, saying the United States "would tell a different story," that Soviet suspicions about what were purely defensive systems were preventing a reduction of nuclear weapons. "An opportunity was thus being lost; public opinion would find that difficult to understand." In response to Gorbachev's objection that space weapons would be impossible to negotiate over or verify, Reagan revived an idea that President Eisenhower had presented at his summit with the Soviets in 1955—an "open skies" verification system, in which each side could conduct aerial surveillance on the other. It was a proposal the secretive and paranoid Soviets were guaranteed to choke on.

Shultz had sensed before the summit that Gorbachev would blink; now, with the third plenary session reaching the end of its scheduled time, Gorbachev suggested that both sides analyze what had been said and return to the subject in the last session in the afternoon. He then added that he saw "no obstacles to movement towards a solution which might serve both sides' interests." Gorbachev had just opened the door for a general agreement in Geneva while kicking the SDI can down the road for future negotiations.

Reagan may have sensed that he was winning the summit. Before the final plenary session, he walked into a meeting with his staff grinning and hiding one arm behind his back inside his suit coat. Someone noted the empty coat sleeve and asked, "Mr. President, where's your arm?" Reagan grasped the empty sleeve in mock surprise and said, "Well, it was here before I met Gorbachev. I don't know where it is now."

Sure enough, the tone of the last plenary session was markedly different from that of the other three. Reagan began with an upbeat assessment of areas of agreement between the two leaders, though he did not minimize clear differences on key points. He ended by reading a draft statement calling for the goal of a 50 percent reduction in nuclear warheads while leaving open further discussions about "space weapons." Gorbachev initially demurred in joining Reagan's optimism, saying that a summit communiqué along the lines Reagan suggested was not justified: "It was impossible to report to our peoples and to the world that there had been a rapprochement of positions."

But Gorbachev embraced the goal of a 50 percent reduction in nuclear weapons, spoke favorably of expanding cultural exchanges, and then suddenly reversed course on the subject of a summit communiqué, inviting Reagan to restate his position. At this point Reagan asked Shultz to lay out options for a communiqué. This was about the only occasion in the entire summit when either nation's supporting cast entered the discussion in a meaningful way; Reagan and Gorbachev had dominated the sessions to an extent that surprised everyone on both sides.

The real issue remaining to be settled was whether Reagan and Gorbachev would appear together at a final public meeting the following day. Gorbachev softened at this point and suggested that each side's diplomats work out a joint statement overnight summarizing in general terms the points of agreement and disagreement. Over dinner that evening, however, word came to Shultz that the Soviets were obstructing the communiqué on nearly every agreed point. An angry Shultz confronted Gorbachev at the dinner table; the Soviet leader relented and sent word that his foreign ministry should stop haggling.

The following day Reagan and Gorbachev appeared onstage together to issue the summit communiqué and make brief statements. In addition to stating the goal of a 50 percent cut in nuclear weapons along with an interim agreement on European theater missiles, the high point of the communiqué was the statement that "a nuclear war cannot be won and must never be fought." It was the exact phrasing that Reagan had used in several speeches preceding the summit, and while it may not have seemed remarkable on the surface, it represented a significant change from the previous Soviet position that the United States and USSR should agree to a no-first-use policy on nuclear weapons, which the United States and NATO had always rejected because it undercut Western deterrence against a conventional attack.

Ultimately the Soviets had given in to the United States on almost every point. The final irony is that the Soviets viewed the agreement on a communiqué as a political and diplomatic victory. "And in the end," Anatoly Chernyaev wrote in his diary, "Reagan did crack open after all, and even agreed to sign a joint statement." Reagan's refusal to allow for a "precooked" draft communiqué before the summit paid handsome dividends.

From Geneva Reagan went to Brussels to brief NATO's senior representatives and then continued across the Atlantic, where he arrived for a dramatic speech to a joint session of Congress at 9:00 p.m. Eastern time to report on the summit. Although Reagan had noted in his closing remarks at the summit that "the real report card on Geneva will not come in for months or even years," his immediate marks were positive. Conservatives who had been apprehensive about the summit were generally pleased. *Human Events* breathed a sigh of relief: "President Reagan appeared to have more than held his own with the media's new superhero. He signed no Yalta-type agreements, stood up to Gorbachev's rough assaults, and refused to surrender the Strategic Defense Initiative." *National Review,* which had pronounced itself "skeptical and anxious" before the summit, now editorialized: "All in all, the summit was a tactical success for the President. . . . The Russians, not used to having their temper tantrums ignored, seem to have left the Summit a bit shaken."[65] Conventional media reached the same conclusion. Frances Fitz-Gerald, no enthusiast of Reagan, wrote, "For Reagan the summit was an unmitigated triumph." The president's public approval rating shot up to a new high; in fact, Reagan would end 1985 with an approval rating of 68 percent, the highest ever for a post–World War II second-term president, and higher than in the aftermath of the assassination attempt in 1981.

The enthusiasm was warranted. First, what did *not* happen during the summit is as important as what did. Everyone, including many of Reagan's aides, had wondered when and how he would play SDI as a bargaining chip. But Reagan had merely twirled the chip and put it back in his vest pocket. Second, Gorbachev, Jack Matlock judged, had committed a strategic error by his "adamant refusal to consider SDI in any form." It was, Matlock thought, an error "even more profound than Andropov's refusal to make a deal on INF before American deployments started in Europe."[66]

If it was not immediately clear that the Geneva meeting would turn out to be the fulcrum of the end of the Cold War, it was because no one could know whether Reagan and Gorbachev would grow to trust each other. Reagan, who six months before had professed himself "cynical" about whether Gorbachev could be different, now began to revise his opinion. He liked Gorbachev, as Reagan liked anyone who could return a smile. Perhaps all that is needed to recognize this is the famous photo of Reagan and Gorbachev flanking the fireplace in their first private meeting; Reagan is flashing his best smile, and Gorbachev is beaming back just as brightly. "A professional actor is pretty good at spotting an act," Matlock observed, and Reagan had found Gorbachev to be authentic, "not some ventriloquist's dummy that just repeated set phrases," as previous Soviet leaders had been. It is less clear that Gorbachev held reciprocal sentiments about Reagan at this point. He came away from Geneva, he said later, thinking Reagan was "a political dinosaur, stubborn and ill-informed."

In a letter to one of his longtime conservative supporters two days after returning from Geneva, Reagan wrote of Gorbachev: "He is a somewhat different breed even though he believes in their system."[67] Reagan found it especially interesting that Gorbachev mentioned God and quoted a Bible verse. "He aroused my curiosity," Reagan wrote another friend in a letter. "I think in our next meeting I may question him on that subject."[68] It apparently did not occur to him that Gorbachev was probably briefed on how to play to Reagan's piety. To Suzanne Massie he wrote a few weeks later: "I'm not going to let myself get euphoric but still I have a feeling we might be at a point of beginning. There did seem to be something of a chemistry between the General Secretary and myself. Certainly it was different than talking to Gromyko."[69] Arms negotiator Max Kampelman recalls Reagan remarking at an NSC meeting that "Maggie [Thatcher] was right. We can do business with this man." Many of Reagan's advisers, however, were nervous about his talk of abolishing nuclear weapons.

A few days after returning from Geneva, Reagan repaired to his Santa Barbara ranch, where he bypassed the usual State Department–NSC process and wrote directly to Gorbachev. His long letter offered Gorbachev an opening on SDI, suggesting that there could be negotiations "in practical terms" to relieve the Soviet anxiety that the United States intended to use SDI to gain first-strike capability. The second item Reagan brought up was Afghanistan, suggesting that the United States would be keen to help the Soviets withdraw "in a manner which does not damage Soviet security interests."

Reagan and his advisers, looking ahead to the next summit sometime the following year, no doubt thought these two gambits were modest and practical steps to pursue in the aftermath of Geneva. Gorbachev had bigger ideas and was preparing to outflank Reagan in dramatic fashion.

*   *   *

REAGAN RETURNED TO Washington after Thanksgiving to confront the ruin of the arms-for-hostages initiative. By early December, McFarlane, worn out from stress and unfounded rumors that he was carrying on an extramarital affair, decided to resign as national security adviser, though he would continue to be involved in the Iran matter after his departure. His deputy, Admiral John Poindexter, was appointed as his successor. At McFarlane's last meeting as national security adviser on December 5, he and Poindexter presented Reagan with a plan to resume the Iran initiative, along with a formal finding for Reagan to sign authorizing the plan. That evening Reagan wrote in his diary, "It is a complex undertaking with only a few of us in on it. I won't even write in the diary what we're up to."

But two days later Reagan did spell it out, following a second meeting in which Shultz and Weinberger expressed anew their strong objections and Meese and especially CIA director William Casey supported the plan. "[The complex plan] calls for Israel selling some weapons to Iran," Reagan wrote on December 7. "As they are delivered in installments by air our hostages will be released. The weapons will go to the moderate leaders in the army who are essential if there's to be a change to a more stable govt. We then sell the Israelis replacements for the delivered weapons. None of this is a gift— the Iranians pay cash for the weapons—so does Israel." But when a follow-up meeting with McFarlane, North, Ghorbanifar, and key Israeli figures in London a few days later went badly, it looked like the idea was dead. McFarlane reached the same conclusion as the CIA—that Ghorbanifar was untrustworthy or worse. Reagan wrote in his diary on December 10 that "the Iranian 'go-between' [Ghorbanifar] turns out to be a devious character. Our plan regarding the hostages is a 'no go.' "

The whole idea should have died right then and there, but it didn't. Despite Reagan's diary entry suggesting that the plan was dead, others in the NSC meeting that day came away with the impression that Reagan wasn't yet ready to give up. Oliver North thought he saw a way to keep the idea alive: cut out Israel as the middleman and deal directly with Iran. He convinced Poindexter to keep the wheels in motion.

*   *   *

THE DAY BEFORE Christmas there occurred a personnel change in the Soviet Union that escaped the notice of the Western media but held important consequences for the future of reform in the evil empire. Gorbachev sacked the first secretary of the Moscow Communist Party Committee, Viktor Grishin, another of the Brezhnev old guard who had been Gorbachev's other chief rival (along with Romanov) to be general secretary back in March. Anatoly Chernyaev wrote in his diary that Grishin's dismissal was "a day of rejoicing for all of Moscow," as Grishin was "a worthless individual." In selecting a replacement, Gorbachev reflected that "we needed an experienced, energetic man, who could look at things critically." For this important post in the nation's capital Gorbachev picked someone he described as a "bulldozer" and who, like himself, had until recently been a provincial Party boss far from the inside circles of Moscow—Boris Yeltsin.

CHAPTER 10

I LIFT UP MY LAMP:

The Road to Reykjavik

What happened at Reykjavik seemed almost too much for
people to absorb, precisely because it was outside the bounds
of the conventional wisdom. Ronald Reagan was attacking
that accepted wisdom across the board.
—George Shultz

O NE OF THE visual high points of the Reagan years came in the summer of 1986, when Reagan presided at the unveiling of a renovated Statue of Liberty in New York Harbor during the week of the July 4 holiday. It was the one-hundredth anniversary of the great French gift to America, and it had just completed a year-long cleaning and repair courtesy of America's favorite corporate executive, Lee Iaccoca. The unveiling naturally became a major spectacle on par with the opening ceremony for the 1984 Los Angeles Olympics, complete with fireworks, light shows, and big bands. The removal of the scaffold-shrouded Lady Liberty was a perfect emblem of Reagan's dominant theme of America's restored confidence and optimism.

Time magazine essayist Lance Morrow wrote that "Ronald Reagan has found the American sweet spot. . . . The 75-year-old man is hitting home runs."

> Reagan inhabits his moment in America with a triumphant (some might say careless or even callous) ease that is astonishing and even mysterious. . . . He proceeds, amiably and formidably, from success to success. . . . The most obvious reason for Reagan's popularity is

the relative success of his presidency and the grace with which he has accomplished it. . . . Whether Reagan will ultimately be judged a great President remains to be seen, but he has shown himself to be one of the strongest leaders of the 20th century. . . . He has restored the authority of the American presidency. He has given Americans an optimism, a pride in themselves and in their country that they have not possessed since the death of John Kennedy. And he is the first President since F.D.R. to alter the debate over what the role of government should be. As one keeps score in the art of the possible, that is not bad at all.[1]

Morrow's effusion was remarkable because he had been among the media elite voices at the outset of the 1980s who embraced the Spenglerian outlook of American decline, along with the doubt that presidential leadership could prove adequate to the challenge of the times. Reagan had made believers of the American people—his popularity rating reached a two-term high of 68 percent in the summer of 1986—and even, as the Morrow essay shows, among skeptics in the media. Through much of 1986 Reagan enjoyed the political initiative in both domestic and foreign policy, racking up new achievements and watching the Democrats relent or reverse course in several areas that had been stuck in political gridlock. At the time of the Statue of Liberty celebration in July, the number of Americans who told pollsters the nation was on the "right track" reached 70 percent, nearly the highest level of Reagan's presidency.

As the 1986 midterm election approached, it appeared Reagan might well break the jinx that had struck every second-term president since at least Woodrow Wilson. He would achieve one of his most cherished goals in domestic policy—another round of fundamental tax reform—and come close to an extraordinary arms control breakthrough with the Soviet Union. Following the reopening of the Statue of Liberty, he signed a bipartisan immigration reform bill that offered amnesty to millions of illegal immigrants. But it was not to last. Before the year was out, Reagan would be knocked from his saddle, his presidency nearly destroyed by events that would cast a shadow over his remaining time in office and color executive controversies for decades to come.

*   *   *

AS REAGAN APPROACHED his seventy-fifth birthday ("but that's only 24 Celsius!" he quipped) and his sixth State of the Union message in early

1986, the natural rhythm of the congressional calendar meant the economy and budget politics would be front and center again for the first few weeks of the year. By January 1986, the economic expansion was entering its thirty-seventh month—four months longer than the average post–World War II expansion. Job growth topped nine million since the trough of the recession in November 1982. The unemployment rate stood at 6.9 percent, down from the recession high of 10.6 percent.

One notable development was the sharp fall in the price of oil, which reached about $14 a barrel in 1986, down from more than $30 when Reagan took office in 1981. This was a double-edged sword: while it added a point or more to the economic growth rate and benefited American consumers (unleaded gasoline fell to as low as 82¢ a gallon by the end of 1986), the collapse devastated the economies of Texas and Oklahoma. Gold, silver, copper, and other commodities experienced similar price declines. Naturally the hand-wringers of the energy crisis from the 1970s saw this price decline as *bad* news. C. Fred Bergstrom, a Carter administration economist and perpetual trade pessimist, told *BusinessWeek:* "It's bad news whether you're an Iowa farmer, or a Saudi oilman, or a Filipino timber producer."[2]

It was also bad news for the Soviet Union, whose hard currency earnings, dominated by oil and natural gas exports, were devastated. "Overnight," one energy expert wrote, "the windfall oil and dollar profits the Soviets had been enjoying were wiped out."[3] The topic came up in a sharp and curious exchange between Reagan and Gorbachev in the Reykjavik summit in October that was overlooked at the time and ever since. Reagan asked Gorbachev why the Soviet Union hadn't honored the terms of a recent grain purchase agreement. Gorbachev replied: "You can tell [American farmers] that the money with which the Russians could have bought grain ended up in the United States and Saudi Arabia because of the sharp drop in oil prices." Reagan said back: "The oil business in the United States suffered greatly from the drop in oil prices. Many countries suffered because of the OPEC actions." Gorbachev shot back: "We know that. *We know who began this process of cutting oil prices, and whose interests it is in*" (emphasis added).

Inflation was running about 4 percent; the short-term federal funds rate was 7.5 percent, down from 14 percent at its peak in 1981 and 10 percent at the end of the recession in 1982. While the steady downward trend in interest rates was encouraging, real interest rates (the interest rate above the inflation rate) were still at record levels, a sign of continuing anxiety about the economy.[4] There was a steady drumbeat of criticism that the economic boom was neither real nor sustainable. The large federal budget deficit, along with the growing foreign trade deficit, was thought to be exerting upward pressure on interest rates and putting a damper on long-run economic growth. For the fiscal year just ended (1985), the budget deficit had been $212 billion, and the deficit was projected to grow larger in 1986.

But as the economic expansion of the mid-1980s matured, those who doubted its sustainability for political reasons grew louder and shriller. Establishment liberalism reacted badly to the new wealth and business models that were created with dizzying speed. The 1980s saw whole new forms of corporate finance and capital formation on a scale that dwarfed previous decades, largely in response to tax cuts that increased returns to risk capital. There was a wave of corporate mergers and acquisitions in the mid-1980s that shook up corporate boardrooms, Wall Street, and Main Street alike.

Following the Reagan administration's rationalizing of antitrust policy, corporate merger activity accelerated. There were thirty corporate mergers or acquisitions of more than $1 billion in value in 1985; by contrast, there had been only twelve mergers or acquisitions of this size during the entire decade of the 1970s. This was merely the tip of the iceberg. Corporate raiders began buying up controlling interests in underperforming publicly traded corporations, sometimes breaking up companies into constituent parts for resale at a higher value, or sometimes installing new management to juice up performance. Buyouts, mergers, and restructurings swept entire industries, especially chemicals, oil, food, consumer products, retailing, and mass media. General Electric bought RCA (parent company of NBC television), Capital Cities Communications swallowed up ABC, and General Motors bought Hughes Aircraft and Electronic Data Systems (which in turn made Ross Perot GM's largest individual shareholder). In some cases, public companies were taken private, such as Beatrice Foods. There were forty-six private buyouts in 1985 and thirty-nine in 1986, up from zero in 1979 and only one in 1980. By the end of the 1980s, $1.3 trillion in corporate assets changed hands, and 143 of the Fortune 500 of 1980 had changed owners.

Much of this activity was highly leveraged with capital raised through unrated debt instruments—so-called junk bonds. According to one study, there were fifty-nine leveraged buyouts financed with junk bonds in 1985 and ninety-six in 1986, with another eighty-five leveraged restructurings of large corporations (and many more of smaller public companies) during those same two years, for a total value of more than $100 billion. Corporate raiders such as Carl Icahn, Ivan Boesky, and T. Boone Pickens were unpopular in corporate boardrooms because they threatened to upend the comfortable sinecures many executives had arranged for themselves at shareholder expense.

One irony of the corporate restructurings of the 1980s is that much of what occurred represented the *de*-conglomeration of big American corporations. Many of the big corporate combinations from the late 1960s and early 1970s, such as ITT, were unwound in sensible ways. Liberals had decried these combinations back then and now decried their reversal. Liberals and much of the media misunderstood what was taking place and depicted corporate raiders and leveraged buyout activity as parasitical in nature, no more than financial flimflammery designed to make paper profits, often at the expense of laid-off workers or looted assets. (This would become the motif of Oliver Stone's depiction of the financial world in *Wall Street,* which fortuitously came out shortly after the stock market crash of October 19, 1987.) To be sure, there were spectacular instances of insider trading and other financial manipulations that violated securities laws (and which sent raider Ivan Boesky, junk bond pioneer Michael Milken, and several other Wall Street figures to prison, many of them prosecuted by U.S. attorney Rudy Giuliani). But in fact the frantic activity of finance capital in the 1980s was the epitome of Joseph Schumpeter's classic conception of creative destruction and contributed significantly to the economic dynamism of the decade. Robert Collins's absorbing history of the decade cites an unpublished judgment of the noted economic historian Louis Galambos that what occurred in the 1980s was "the most formidable transformation" in the history of American business.[5] One study estimated that companies bought out before 1985 saw their profit margins improve by 20 to 30 percent, while 60 percent of bought-out companies improved total operating performance.[6] Reagan's Council of Economic Advisers took a look at the phenomenon and concluded that there was "powerful evidence" that takeovers benefit the economy. The average stock market value of acquired companies went up 30 percent in 1984. Goldman Sachs estimated that takeover activity accounted for three-quarters of all stock gains in 1984 and 1985.[7]

That liberals and the political class generally (including many Washington Republicans) would misunderstand this is not surprising, given that the political marketplace in Washington was more comfortable shifting wealth rather than creating it. It was consistent with the logic and experience of Washington that the machinations of financiers were no different from the financial machinations of politicians and regulators. Where financiers saw opportunity for profit, politicians and the media saw only greed. The froth of the marketplace, it was charged, caused corporations and investors to take a short-term viewpoint that eroded America's international competitiveness (especially versus the Japanese) and contributed to America's growing trade deficit. Felix Rohatyn, the liberal financier who had opposed Reaganomics from the beginning, said, "I think we're living the last days of Pompeii." Some liberals and media second-guessers found a dark side to the venture-capital-sponsored entrepreneurial start-ups, even in the high-technology sector, which did so much to propel the economy in the 1980s. Big companies, Robert Reich argued, suffered when talented individuals left to start their own companies.

Naturally, politicians of both parties proposed to intervene. Democratic senator Howard Metzenbaum complained: "The climate created by the [Reagan] Administration encourages companies to expand through merger rather than through their own growth." Over in the House, Representative Timothy E. Wirth (D-Colo.), chairman of the House Subcommittee on Telecommunications, Consumer Protection, and Finance, wrote menacingly to the chairman of the Securities and Exchange Commission: "There remains a great deal of public and congressional concern about current takeover activity." More than fifty bills were introduced to regulate mergers and acquisitions, but none got very far. Wirth complained: "The economic ideologues at the White House are dominating what debate there is within the Administration, and they believe the market can do no wrong." Sure enough, when the Federal Reserve floated a proposal to restrict the amount of debt financing that could be used for mergers and acquisitions, the administration issued a rare public rebuke of the Fed. "The board's proposal would destroy the market for corporate control, which disciplines inefficient management and enables stockholders to maximize returns on their investment," said Douglas H. Ginsburg, head of the Justice Department's antitrust division.

The decade-of-greed meme helped advance the thesis that the nation's current economic growth was phony or temporary, and was the predicate for the relentless insistence that a tax increase was the only responsible course. This view found bipartisan agreement. Reagan found himself once again assailed as much by his own party as by the Democrats over his refusal to consider an increase in income taxes. In his diary he described a "heated discussion" in late January with *Republican* senators who wanted a tax increase. He pushed back, asking Congress to pass a balanced budget constitutional amendment and a line-item veto. (A filibuster by Republican senator Mark Hatfield had stopped a line-item veto proposal in 1985.) The next budget cycle looked to repeat the previous four years, with Reagan's proposed budget declared dead on arrival on Capitol Hill ("Why do I even bother sending them?" he asked his aides this time) and Reagan returning the serve by saying that "any tax increase the Congress sends me will be DOA, dead on arrival."

The budget cycle for 1985 had seen a near miss at a serious budget deal that caused political friction between Reagan and congressional Republicans. In the spring of 1985, Republican Senate leader Bob Dole and Budget Committee chairman Pete Domenici put together a package of budget cuts to reduce the deficit by $56 billion. The package had two main components: cuts in defense spending and a one-year freeze on cost-of-living adjustments (COLAs) for Social Security. Reagan swallowed hard on the defense cut but gave his initial assent to the package. It was a difficult vote for Republican senators to cast, and it required Vice President Bush to cast a tie-breaking vote to get it through 50–49 in early May. Dole called it "the moment of truth" for Congress. As could be expected, Dole attracted bipartisan and media praise.

The prospects for getting the Dole package through the House were doubtful; Tip O'Neill and House Democrats were unlikely to go along with the Social Security COLA freeze unless Reagan agreed to a tax increase. In the decisive meeting with O'Neill, Reagan slammed the door once again, telling O'Neill, "Do you think I am ever going to have a tax bill? Never! Do you think I am going to let Mondale say, 'Look, I told you I was right?' Never!" But he went further and declared his opposition to the Social Security COLA freeze, effectively pulling the rug out from under Senate Republicans. Reagan had promised in his second debate with Walter Mondale during the 1984 campaign that he would not touch Social Security. He did not wish to go back on that campaign pledge and was wary that Democrats were setting him up for a political trap. (His instincts were correct: despite quashing the proposal, Democrats would pound GOP Senate candidates in 1986 for attempting to cut Social Security.) Dole was furious, complaining to journalist Hedrick Smith: "We were left hanging out there. We marched up the hill and across the ravine, just right up to the cliff, and they [the White House] pushed us over."[8] Senator Warren Rudman said, "People feel they flew a kamakaze mission and ended up in flames and got nothing for it." The compromise budget that subsequently passed for FY 1985 saw the deficit increase by $8 billion over FY 1984.

But that was not the end of the budget story in 1985. Two new dynamic elements came into play that promised to forever upend the status quo of budget politics. The first was the Gramm-Rudman Emergency Deficit Control Act (named for Senators Phil Gramm of Texas and Warren Rudman of New Hampshire). The second was tax reform.

If Congress lacked the discipline or ability to contain spending, the senators behind Gramm-Rudman thought, then it was time to try a mechanism for automatic budget cuts. Gramm-Rudman empowered the comptroller general and the Congressional Budget Office to enact budget "sequestrations" with the aim of balancing the budget by 1991. But although Gramm-Rudman was advertised as an across-the-board spending cut, it applied only to discretionary spending, which accounted for less than half of total federal spending. Gramm-Rudman would not affect Medicare, Social Security, and other welfare-state entitlements, which were among the fastest-growing parts of the federal budget. In other words, Gramm-Rudman didn't get at the largest driver of the problem of federal spending growth. More problematic was that discretionary spending included defense; this meant that Gramm-Rudman would cut automatically into the defense budget, which was already under pressure from Democrats and some Republicans. Gramm-Rudman was an irresponsible, divisive, meat-ax approach to budget discipline, but it passed in early December 1985. Democrats thought the prospective defense cuts would compel Reagan to accept a tax increase. The White House saw it just the opposite way: Reagan's ability to sustain a veto of any tax increase would force Congress to accept spending cuts.

Historian John Ehrman, who called Gramm-Rudman "one of the most disgraceful and irresponsible laws ever passed," aptly summarizes the case against it:

> The cynicism behind Gramm-Rudman was in the open for all to see. The law was passed not because congressmen and senators believed in it, but because they saw it as a way to relieve themselves of their responsibilities for making fiscal decisions. For the immediate term, members of Congress from both parties saw it as an easy way to do what they could not build enough support to accomplish in budget votes.[9]

Reagan nonetheless hailed Gramm-Rudman as a "step toward putting our fiscal house in order," but also noted that there might be "constitutionally suspect provisions" in the law. The Supreme Court eventually agreed, striking down the law in June 1986, ruling by a 7–2 vote that Gramm-

Rudman violated the separation of powers by having the comptroller general, an officer who answers to Congress, exercise a function properly belonging to the executive branch alone. Congress quickly enacted a new version to keep the main Gramm-Rudman budget sequestration mechanism intact. Reagan, facing the prospect that Gramm-Rudman II would constrict the defense budget, signed the successor measure with reluctance. "Bill signing moments are usually happy events," he said, flanked by chagrined congressional leaders. "This one is not."

The customary bloodletting over budget politics would be fundamentally altered by tax reform. At the end of 1985 chances for tax reform appeared close to dead, and with the partisan rancor growing as the 1986 midterm election neared, the likelihood that there would be a revival of tax reform seemed dim. And yet by the end of September Congress would pass one of the most sweeping income tax reforms in decades. The passage of income tax reform was a Capitol Hill epic, a tangled tale involving twists and turns and surprises worthy of a suspenseful Hollywood drama. It was the kind of fundamental reform that political scientists and journalists believe is impossible to achieve. It was at once a rare triumph for bipartisanship and a substantive win for Reagan. (This story is superbly told in one of the best journalistic accounts from the period, Jeffrey Birnbaum and Alan Murray's *Showdown at Gucci Gulch*.)

Reagan had directed the Treasury Department to develop a tax simplification plan for unveiling after the 1984 election, partly in an effort to head off a possible Democratic initiative in the area. No one thought this was serious or had much chance of going forward. One of the tax code's primary problems was that its inequities were often the unintended consequences of previous reform attempts to increase the "fairness" of the tax code. Unwinding this tangle was conceptually daunting and politically complicated. Most congressional leaders thought cutting the deficit was a more important priority than tax reform. Birnbaum and Murray wrote that "tax reform seemed no more than a joke" at that point. Reagan laid out two main criteria for tax reform in his 1985 State of the Union speech: reform had to be "revenue neutral," and the top individual income tax rate had to come down to 35 percent, "and possibly lower," from the current 50 percent.

On paper the trade-off of removing loopholes, exemptions, and tax breaks in exchange for lower tax rates appeared simple. But the largest exemptions, such as for home mortgage interest, were politically untouchable as well as deeply embedded in the economy. Changing some of these deductions would produce windfall gains and wipeouts in certain asset classes. Any substantive change would involve stepping on someone's special interest, ensuring a fierce fight on Capitol Hill. Nonetheless, the Treasury Department went after the idea with zeal. Treasury was especially sensitive to how proposed changes would affect economic growth, and merely lowering individual rates further was not necessarily the sine qua non of a pro-growth tax code. The Treasury plan unveiled in late November proposed a top individual rate of 35 percent, with two lower brackets at 25 and 15 percent (down from fourteen brackets in the existing code). The mortgage interest deduction was preserved, but Treasury proposed eliminating the deductibility of state and local taxes, a sensitive issue for high-tax states such as New York and New Jersey. There was an obvious political aspect to this idea: deductibility of state and local taxes put the federal government and low-tax states in the role of subsidizing liberal states with high taxes. This fact was not lost on liberal governors in high-tax states such as New York. Governor Mario Cuomo complained that it was "wrong, insulting, unfair, and denigrating." Pat Buchanan responded tartly for the White House: "We do not believe in a neo-socialist approach to government that redistributes wealth. This plan will force people to take a second look at government and see what they are getting from it."

The plan's real surprise was the change in corporate income taxes. In order to reduce individual income tax rates—the Treasury proposal would have lowered average individual income tax bills by about 8.5 percent—corporate taxes would have to go up by nearly $150 billion over the next five years, a 36 percent increase. Reagan had said as recently as 1983 that the corporate income tax should be abolished, on the understanding that corporations are simply conduits for taxes from individuals. "You can't tax things, you only tax people," Reagan said. A number of Reagan's advisers noted the heresy. William Niskanen, chairman of the Council of Economic Advisers, trashed the plan in front of Reagan, saying, "Walter Mondale would have been proud." It didn't help that George McGovern stepped forward and supported the idea: "It is a fair, common-sense reform." Within days of his State of the Union speech touting tax reform, Reagan began edging away from a full embrace of his own Treasury proposal. Some big business leaders, however, were surprisingly warm to the idea, hoping that a simplified tax code would be worth it. John H. Bryan, chairman of Sara Lee, said: "If we can get rid of these tax shelters and special breaks for corporations and pull those [tax] rates down, it could be the most powerful stimulus for economic growth we could ever have."

With the changing of the Treasury guard under James Baker, the department went back to the drawing board to revise the whole plan. Reagan actively participated in a series of meetings, deciding what he could and couldn't support in a revised proposal. By April Baker was ready with a new reform plan, which became known as Treasury II. The new plan preserved the previous 35 percent top individual rate but also preserved a lot of popular individual deductions and special-interest breaks, requiring complicated transition rules and other ways of ensuring that the plan would be revenue neutral. It lowered the corporate tax rate from 46 to 33 percent but eliminated a number of popular corporate deductions. Many corporations would still pay higher taxes, though some prominent companies, such as Procter & Gamble, supported the change. Treasury II also proposed cutting the capital gains tax to 17.5 percent. Although the plan would remove millions of lower-income earners from the tax rolls completely, the top rates would also benefit upper-income taxpayers even more.

Reagan gave a prime-time televised address in the spring of 1985 to unveil the new plan formally, explaining its key features in the context of his familiar rhetorical themes of the "second American revolution" and "freedom, fairness, hope, and opportunity." In both his speech and his written message to Congress, Reagan portrayed tax simplification as a continuation of his 1981 tax cut policies. Liberal Democrats might have been expected to be cool to the idea of giving Reagan more reformist momentum, but exactly the opposite happened. The Democratic response to Reagan's speech came from Representative Dan Rostenkowski, the chairman of the Ways and Means Committee and the key figure for crafting any tax changes in the House. He was an unlikely reformer, described by Birnbaum and Murray as "the kind of beef-eating, ward-heeling machine politician who considered the blow-dried world of TV to be sissy stuff."[10] Rather than pick a fight with Reagan, Rostenkowski embraced Reagan's plan, in outline if not in detail. Rostenkowski and other Democrats were fearful of letting Reagan capture the mantle of reform, traditionally a Democratic Party virtue. There were just enough benefits for lower-income groups for the idea to be attractive to Democrats, and if tax reform was popular, they hoped to share in the credit.

Rostenkowski tried to turn Reagan's meta-narrative of tax reform on its head, portraying Reagan as standing up to big business. "It's a Republican president who's bucking his party's tradition as protectors of big business and the wealthy," Rostenkowski said. "His words and feelings go back to Roosevelt and Truman and Kennedy. But the commitment comes from Ronald

Reagan. And that's so important and welcome . . . If the president's plan is everything he says it is, he'll have a great deal of Democratic support."

Rostenkowski was not wrong to hint that some Republicans might not be enthusiastic about a tax plan that increased taxes on business and eliminated so many special-interest tax breaks. Once the markup of a tax bill began in the Ways and Means Committee, everyone knew the special-interest lobbyists would be fully mobilized to block changes affecting their industry or group. The sum total of these inevitable concessions to political pressure threatened to narrow the scope of real reform and rate reduction. Birnbaum and Murray wrote that "Rostenkowski's decision to answer Ronald Reagan with a yes incited the income-tax equivalent of world war."

Sure enough, in the Ways and Means Committee markup process shifting coalitions emerged to vote to preserve or even, in a few cases, expand existing tax breaks. As committee hearings ground on through the summer and into the fall, lobbyists for banking, oil and gas, timber, insurance, labor, restaurants, municipal bonds, and everything in between rolled over Rostenkowski. The deduction for state and local taxes was restored. The White House was not happy with the erosion of the process, and though it maintained public silence about the progress of the bill, behind the scenes Baker and Darman were working closely with Rostenkowski to try to keep the measure alive and intact. Rostenkowski went to Reagan in early November to say that he couldn't hold the line on the 35 percent top rate; would Reagan accept 37 percent? Reagan delivered a flat no, saying that "we need the kind of tax reform we originally proposed, and not some of the waterings-down that are taking place as they discuss it up there."

After a personal plea to his fellow Democrats, Rostenkowski managed in mid-November to pass a bill out of committee that contained a 38 percent top rate, fewer family-friendly deductions, and a higher capital gains tax rate. Now it had to pass the full House. Economics columnist Robert J. Samuelson wrote correctly that "the 'reform' bill before the House Ways and Means Committee does not simplify the tax code so much as rearrange its complexity." George Will wrote that it was "a plan for replacing today's rococo tax code with one that is merely baroque." Despite the cut in the tax rate, most supply-siders were deeply disappointed; too many provisions in the House bill were seen as having negative effects on investment incentives. "The net effect of the [House] bill," Paul Craig Roberts concluded, "would be to make the U.S. a poorer country. . . . It is extraordinary that President Reagan has invested so much political capital in a bill with so little promise."[11]

The White House was lukewarm at best toward many features of the bill but decided to back final passage and hope the Senate could fix it. But it didn't back it very hard, declining to issue a letter of support from Reagan. Noting this silence, House Republicans lined up overwhelmingly to oppose the bill on the floor. Kemp, originally enthusiastic, now blasted the bill: "The hard truth is that the Democratic bill is anti-family, anti-growth, and anti-investment." There was little optimism that the Senate could improve the product. The Senate Finance Committee was even more prone to special-interest manipulations than House Ways and Means, and Finance Committee chairman Senator Bob Packwood seemed unexcited about the whole subject. Republican representative Bill Frenzel said, "The phrase 'the Senate will fix it up' is the moral equivalent of 'I'll respect you in the morning.' "

Nearly the entire Republican membership in the House joined with a handful of Democrats to derail the bill on a procedural vote in early December 1985. It was Reagan's turn to ride to the rescue. In mid-December he went to the Capitol to urge House Republicans to reverse course and support the bill. "The crowd was ready to take on the president," Birnbaum and Murray reported, "but in classic Reagan style, he disarmed them." Reagan had just come from a memorial service for 248 servicemen killed in a plane crash a few days before. It changed the whole mood in the room, no doubt as Reagan intended. Reagan agreed that the House bill fell short, but offered his assurance that he would fight hard to fix the bill in the Senate, or veto the final product if it remained unacceptable. Despite a barrage of criticism, some Republicans began to change their minds and agreed to back the bill. House Speaker Tip O'Neill demanded a commitment of fifty Republican votes before he would bring the bill back up for consideration; Republican whip Trent Lott was able to round up only forty-eight firm votes. Reagan told O'Neill he'd find two more. O'Neill brought the bill back to the floor, where the next surprise occurred. From the Speaker's podium O'Neill declared the bill passed by a voice vote, as is customary House procedure, expecting Republicans would move for a roll-call vote, as is also customary. *But no Republican did.*[12] The most far-reaching overhaul of the nation's tax code was passed without a recorded roll-call vote.

Now it was on to the Senate, where the Senate Finance Committee ran into the same special-interest buzz saw that had bedeviled House Ways and Means. Chairman Packwood had watched Rostenkowski's ordeal in the House and recognized that he had a once-in-a-lifetime opportunity to craft historic legislation. He sought to achieve Reagan's central goal of a 35 percent top rate, and he tried manfully to limit special-interest predation of the bill in the committee, but to no avail. The committee ended up preserving tax breaks the House bill eliminated, and approving a number of new tax breaks on top of that. The tax reform train was going in reverse, and by the beginning of May 1986 Packwood had no choice but to pull the bill. Lobbyists in the committee room and in the hallways outside the hearing room let out a cheer.

Instead of working small backroom deals to patch the bill back together, Packwood set himself upon an audacious course. He decided to start from scratch, with a radical bill that would cut the top tax rate as low as 25 percent while ripping up nearly every tax break from the roots. The mistake of the Treasury and House bills, he reasoned, was that they didn't cut the top rate low enough; at a maximum rate of 25 percent, there would be less reason to protect cherished deductions. His fellow Finance Committee members, embarrassed that the bill had collapsed, were enthusiastic when Packwood presented the idea behind closed doors. Packwood's bold stroke changed the dynamic of the issue. Jack Kemp became effervescent; the man who had warned Reagan about the peril of "economic Dunkirk" in 1980 now said that Packwood had pulled off the tax reform equivalent of MacArthur's Inchon landing.

Beltway insiders were still skeptical that the revived effort could succeed, but Packwood pulled a fast one. He announced on a Friday to lobbyists and reporters that there would be no further committee business over the weekend. He then assembled the committee secretly the next day to hammer out the details of a bill with a 27 percent top rate. Despite some predictable last-minute efforts from oil-state senators to preserve oil and gas tax preferences, Packwood was able to pass the bill out of the Finance Committee a few days later with a unanimous 20–0 vote. K Street was stunned. The full Senate debated the bill, beat back most attempts to amend or derail it, and passed it by a lopsided 97–3 vote on June 24. Moynihan described its passage as "the most ethical event I've ever seen in this place." As William Niskanen put it, "The power of an idea, for a brief period, overwhelmed the most parochial interests. . . . For a time my wavering faith in our political process was restored."[13] The House-Senate conference committee labored all summer to harmonize the differences between the two bills and, after working out numerous technical problems that required the top rate to be set at 28 percent, passed the final bill out of both houses and sent it to Reagan for his signature on September 27.

While the reform was a boon for individuals, corporate taxes went up by

$120 billion over the next five years. The bill affected real estate significantly by sharply reducing depreciation deductions. Multifamily housing starts plummeted, and other forms of commercial real estate investment slowed, contributing to the distress of the already reeling savings and loan industry. The new law raised the capital gains tax from 20 to 28 percent. Supply-siders were divided on the effect of the bill, with many predicting that these changes on the business and investment side would slow capital formation and economic growth over the next few years. Indeed, in the first three years after the tax reform act, revenues from capital gains taxes fell 44 percent, compared with a three-year gain of 49 percent when the rate was cut from 28 to 20 percent in 1981. Others such as Jack Kemp were more enthusiastic, though he later changed his mind. George Gilder said that the tax bill represented the "greatest victory of the Reagan Revolution."

The political effects of the 1986 tax reform act were profound. Cutting the top individual rate to 28 percent cemented in place Reagan's fundamental victory in reorienting tax policy, and as such can be understood as the last act in the tax revolt that had begun in earnest with the passage of California's Proposition 13 in 1978. Despite subsequent increases in the top marginal rate (to 33 percent under President George H. W. Bush in 1990 and to 39 percent under President Bill Clinton in 1993), the 1986 tax reform foreclosed the possibility of using the income tax code for purposes of punishing the rich or redistributing wealth in any significant way. The liberal principle of progressivity was not completely banished, but no longer would the tax code be seen as a plaything for changing society wholesale. Although liberals still reflexively talked of raising taxes on the rich (which usually seemed to include the middle class when tax increases got passed), no one—not even Ted Kennedy—proposed going back to a top rate of 50 percent, let alone the higher pre-1980 tax rates. It also introduced a slight bias toward considering the growth implications of tax changes, an element almost totally absent from tax reform efforts in the decades before 1980. Although the hard work of crafting the reform belonged to Congress and especially Rostenkowski and Packwood, Birnbaum and Murray judged that "[t]he most important player in tax reform was Ronald Reagan himself. . . . Without his backing, tax reform could never have happened." Reagan also captured the mantle of reform away from Democrats. This was a matter of dismay to some Democrats. Gary Hart, eyeing another White House run in 1988, rued that "[tax reform] got away from us and it's theirs now." Democratic pollster Brad Bannon said that tax reform was "very dangerous" because it "reinforces the idea that

Republicans represent change, while Democrats defend the status quo." David Broder offered the right coda: "The historical irony is that what seemed most radical in Reagan's original program—his drive for deep cuts in tax rates—has become the accepted political philosophy of both parties."[14]

*   *   *

THOUGH TAX AND budget policy is the central preoccupation of most of Washington's professional class, its essential dullness ensured that the chief drama for the public continued to be in foreign affairs.

In a remarkable comment to the Politburo in October 1986, Andrei Gromyko said that "the deployment of the SS-20 was a major error in our European policy." The strategy to split the United States from Europe had almost worked, but in large part because of Reagan's steadfastness the Soviet missile push had ended up strengthening the NATO alliance. But, Gromyko added, "We cannot just flip-flop 180 degrees." Could the Soviet Union get something from the United States in return for reversing course on their intermediate-range missiles? The obvious goal would be to stop Reagan's SDI and halt further NATO deployment of intermediate-range missiles in Europe.

Gorbachev had reached this conclusion months before and embarked on a bold strategy to shake up arms negotiations while advancing the Soviet diplomatic goal of driving a wedge into the NATO alliance. On January 15 Gorbachev startled the world with a proposal to abolish nuclear weapons by the year 2000. Gorbachev made clear that the second summit promised seven weeks earlier in Geneva would not take place unless progress was made toward this goal. That Gorbachev announced the idea publicly was unusual. Typically the United States and Soviet Union exchanged new proposals privately to give each side time to react before going public. Gorbachev was clearly trying to seize the initiative and put Reagan on the defensive. Reagan wrote in his diary that "it is a h—l of a propaganda move. We'd be hard put to explain how we could turn it down," but he deflected the recommendation of his aides that he publicly label Gorbachev's proposal a publicity stunt. In spite of the obvious difficulties, Reagan liked what he heard—a fact that gave heartburn to a number of Reagan's hardheaded advisers.[15]

In proposing to eliminate all nuclear weapons within fifteen years, Gorbachev had moved way ahead of his own Foreign Ministry and arms negotiators, most of whom assumed it was mere propaganda. Khrushchev had suggested the same thing in 1959, but he didn't mean it. Although Gorbachev's proposal contained a four-stage outline of how it would work, it lacked necessary specificity. Ken Adelman recalls that "our negotiators probed for days how this would work. Was Gorbachev talking about missiles? Launchers? Warheads? Would he include battlefield systems? What type of aircraft? Allied systems? The Soviets had no answer to these, the obvious questions that had to be answered if this was a serious proposal."[16] Gorbachev's own negotiators in Geneva didn't seem to take the idea any more seriously than the American delegation did.

There were numerous problems with the details of Gorbachev's proposal, which, if implemented, would have provided an advantage to the Soviets on account of asymmetries between U.S. and Soviet arsenals. However, the proposal did contain several significant concessions. It dropped the previous Soviet requirement that the British and French nuclear arsenals be included in any intermediate deal concerning arsenals in Europe, restricting discussions to the Soviet SS-20s and the American Pershing and cruise missiles. It also offered the possibility of an INF deal that included the key U.S. demand that had always been resisted—on-site inspections. It was clear, however, that despite these prospective concessions, any chance for a breakthrough depended on the United States giving up SDI. Despite the difficulties of Gorbachev's proposal, Shultz and others thought it signaled a new agility on the part of the Soviets.

While Reagan's advisers, scattered in their disparate redoubts in the Pentagon and State Department, NSC, CIA, and the Arms Control and Disarmament Agency, scrambled to reach consensus on how to proceed, Reagan picked up his pen and wrote a seven-page letter responding to Gorbachev. He spent four of the seven pages reiterating his rebuttals to Gorbachev's claim that SDI represented an attempt to gain first-strike advantage or to develop space strike weapons. The remaining three pages tackled regional conflicts, meaning chiefly Afghanistan. "Regarding regional conflicts," Reagan wrote, "I can see that our respective analyses of the causes are incompatible. There seems little point in continuing to debate these matters," but then he went on for three pages doing precisely that. The solution to Afghanistan was simple, he said: get out. But the sunny Reagan emerged at the end: "Agreement as to who is to blame is not necessary to find a solution." *Let's speed things up and get to the next summit.*

Gorbachev's gambit occurred just as the internecine fighting in Washington—within Reagan's own team and between the White House and Congress—was reaching a new level of intensity. Reagan and his advisers faced a number of decisions about how to proceed on several aspects of a potential arms agreement. The divisions amongst his advisers festered, and Reagan was reluctant to make up his mind or offer concessions. The infighting frequently spilled out into the public square through relentless leaks, which annoyed Reagan to the point of contemplating mandatory polygraph exams.[17]

Two related issues in particular divided Reagan's advisers. The first was whether to continue to abide by the limits of the unratified SALT II treaty; the second concerned the interpretation of the 1972 ABM Treaty, which would constrain the potential development and deployment of SDI. On the issue of SALT II, Reagan had announced again in 1985 that the United States would abide by the treaty's limits, but with mounting evidence that the Soviets were not abiding by the treaty themselves he was not enthusiastic about this position. He had never liked SALT II, and when the Arms Control and Disarmament Agency reported in March 1986 (in a legally mandated annual compliance review) on continuing Soviet violations of the treaty, Reagan wrote in his diary that "[f]rankly I'm ready" to declare that the United States would no longer observe SALT II.[18]

A vigorous debate within his administration took place between Shultz and Weinberger, who argued their respective positions with some acrimony in front of Reagan more than once. Obeying SALT II while the Soviets violated it was a sign of weakness, Weinberger argued; killing the treaty would show the Soviets that the United States meant business about getting on with an agreement for real reductions, as promised in Geneva. Shultz countered that if SALT II was scuttled completely, the Soviets would be in a better position to deploy large numbers of new ballistic missiles in the absence of an agreement (the Joint Chiefs of Staff concurred with this view).

Reagan came down on the side of Weinberger and against SALT II, announcing on May 23 that the United States would no longer abide by the treaty. Reagan's decision touched off an uproar. In the face of the documented Soviet violations, there was an avalanche of criticism from Capitol Hill, Europe, and the news media, directed primarily at Reagan. Not for the first time, Reagan's domestic critics unabashedly took up the same line of argument as the Soviets: Reagan's step was deliberately meant to kill further arms control. The Soviets would walk out of Geneva again and start building missiles as fast as they could. Reagan could kiss the next summit good-bye. Thatcher and Kohl, about to face the voters again, would be undermined. Robert McNamara lamented, "The entire structure of strategic arms control carefully laid down over a period of 15 years by four presidents will be destroyed." The *New York Times* editorialized that Reagan's decision was "entirely wrong" and "deplorable"—"Now the Kremlin, burned across Europe by Chernobyl, can dust off its propaganda caricatures of the President as nuclear cowboy."[19] Senator Al Gore took to the *Times*'s op-ed pages to pronounce Reagan's decision a "blunder" that would "be judged by history as his most serious mistake." The *Chicago Tribune* huffed that Reagan's decision meant that "it is highly unlikely there will be a new nuclear arms treaty before Mr. Reagan leaves the White House"; moreover, "this administration never had, and still does not have, any honest enthusiasm for striking a deal with the Soviets."[20]

Partly this was the outrage of the process-oriented arms control community at having finally lost the key battle they had been waging since Reagan took office. Reagan had spoken of Soviet noncompliance with SALT I and SALT II and the possibility that the United States might break the SALT II limits since his first year in office. The arms control community persuaded Reagan during his first term that keeping faith with the arms control process was the key to maintaining congressional political support for his arms buildup. Now that Congress was starting to trim defense spending in Reagan's second term, that argument lost its effectiveness.

Democrats nonetheless thought they saw a political opening, and contemplated a suite of legislation to compel Reagan to conform to SALT II, even though SALT II had never been ratified and lacked legal force. It was another example of Congress contesting the executive branch for control of foreign policy. Richard Perle commented tartly, "Either the Congress will stand with the Administration or the Congress will stand with the Soviets." Congress chose the Soviets. One proposed amendment would ban spending money on arms that broke the SALT II ceiling. The House, on a vote of 256 to 145, approved a nonbinding resolution calling on Reagan to continue adherence to the weapons limits set in SALT II. Thirty-seven Republicans defied the administration to vote with the Democratic majority. The House also voted to scale back Reagan's budget request for SDI research funding.

The second issue was the interpretation of the 1972 ABM Treaty, and as with SALT II, the same two-front political controversy came into play. A strict interpretation of ABM might constrain the development and testing of SDI, while such development could go forward under a broad interpretation. The Soviets, who had insisted on ambiguous language susceptible to a broad interpretation back in the 1972 negotiations, naturally demanded that the United States now abide by a strict interpretation. Adding to the intensity of the argument in Washington was the fact that the Soviets were violating the

ABM Treaty, especially with the construction of a large phased-array radar installation in Krasnoyarsk, Siberia. Reagan noted sardonically that it was the USSR that was most aggressively pursuing missile defense in ways that violated even a broad interpretation of the ABM Treaty.

Article V of the ABM Treaty seemed straightforward, stating: "Each Party undertakes not to develop, test, or deploy ABM systems or components which are sea-based, air-based, space-based, or mobile land-based." However, during the 1972 ABM negotiations, the Soviets had insisted upon a codicil, known as Agreed Statement D, that left open the possibility of developing missile defense systems "*based on other physical principles* and including components capable of *substituting* for ABM interceptor missiles" (emphasis added). This seemed to imply that the ABM Treaty was meant to apply only to antimissile missile technology (whether ground- or space-based) as it was known or understood in 1972, but not necessarily to space-based particle beam weapons or other advanced ideas under consideration in Reagan's SDI research program. Agreed Statement D called for consultation and agreement prior to deploying any such new system, and in any event the ABM Treaty allowed each side to exit the treaty with six months' notice to the other side, a step a number of conservatives were publicly urging by 1986 (and which President George W. Bush finally exercised in 2001). The consultation clause was the mechanism by which Reagan thought successful development of SDI could be shared with the Soviets and other nations.[21]

The State Department's legal counsel, Abraham Sofaer, reviewed the treaty and issued an opinion that the broad interpretation allowing SDI research and development (though not deployment) was amply justified—a conclusion that received wide agreement among Reagan's normally fractious advisers. Congressional Democrats again signaled their displeasure. Senator Carl Levin (D-Mich.) demanded to see the State Department's internal analysis, which he pronounced "fatally flawed." The matter would fester well into 1987, when the Pentagon began talking up the possibility of a "phased deployment" of missile defense as soon as 1994, which set off a fresh round of congressional opposition.[22] If this weren't enough, European governments were nervous about the administration's ABM interpretation. A new stalemate had settled in. With no date set for the promised Washington summit, Reagan was content for the moment to wait for the Soviets to move.

Far from scuttling arms control, the Reagan administration's decision to pull the plug on SALT II and proceed with an SDI-friendly interpretation of the ABM Treaty were key turning points on the road toward reaching real arms reduction agreements. Reagan's statements and arms control decisions in the first half of 1986 angered Gorbachev, but ironically bolstered Gorbachev's resolve to break with the past and find a new path to an arms control agreement. Largely undetected or unperceived by American eyes, Gorbachev's impatient reformist inclinations were starting to overturn the Soviet order.

*   *   *

THE UNITED STATES continued to have an uneven grasp of what was going on inside the Soviet Union and elsewhere behind the Iron Curtain under the new man in the Kremlin. In one of the greater (but entirely typical) embarrassments of the time, the CIA's 1986 *Handbook of Economic Statistics* estimated that East German real per capita income was higher than West German per capita ($10,440 versus $10,220). Pat Moynihan mordantly observed that any taxi driver in West Berlin could have told you this was nonsense, but the CIA didn't have any taxi drivers on their payroll, preferring sophisticated Ivy League graduates instead. This misprision turned out to be a cause of alarm and dismay in the Eastern bloc. East Germany's chief spymaster, Markus Wolf, later confessed: "For a time in the late 1970s and 1980s the quality of the American agents was so poor and their work so haphazard that our masters began to ask fearfully whether Washington had stopped taking East Germany seriously."[23]

So it is not surprising that Western observers overlooked or dismissed Gorbachev's subtle doctrinal departures at the Twenty-seventh Party Congress— the Party convention held every five years—that opened in early March in Moscow. In his closing Political Report to the Congress—the Soviet rough equivalent of the president's State of the Union message to Congress— Gorbachev included much of the familiar Marxist nonsense, including a new five-year economic plan and realizing the "full potential of socialism." But he also pointedly omitted a number of the boilerplate tropes of Communist doctrine about "victory over Western imperialism" and "class struggle," adding that both domestic and foreign policy had reached a "turning point." His call for "new thinking" extended to giving the green light to discuss human rights freely with the West, implicitly ending the uniform stonewalling on the issue that had been prior Soviet practice. "Continuity in foreign policy," he said, "has nothing in common with the simple repetition of what has gone before, especially in the approach to problems that have accumulated."

A few weeks earlier Gorbachev had made a move testifying to his bona fides on human rights: he released Anatoly Sharansky, who left the Soviet Union for Israel, but not without first visiting Reagan at the White House to thank Reagan for his efforts on behalf of Soviet refuseniks. Sharansky told Reagan that he was a hero to the prisoners in the Soviet gulag. "The prisoners read the attacks on me in TASS & Pravda and learn what I'm saying about the Soviets," Reagan wrote in his diary, "and they like me." Sharansky's release was the beginning of a liberalization toward dissidents. In December 1986 Gorbachev would telephone Andrei Sakharov to inform him that his internal exile in Gorky was over and that he could return to Moscow. Hundreds of other political prisoners would be released in 1987, and the number of exit visas for Jews wishing to emigrate started to increase, from about one thousand in 1986 to eight thousand in 1987. And a few weeks after the Party Congress Foreign Minister Shevardnadze summoned the entire Soviet ambassador corps to Moscow, where Gorbachev reinforced this point in a rare appearance at the foreign ministry.

Gorbachev's speech, by its very length (five hours), lent itself to conventional appraisal. *National Review* commented that "Kremlinologists were stunned by the most ideological, jargon-laden keynote speech given at a Soviet Party Congress since the days of Stalin." The Heritage Foundation's evaluation bore the headline "Gorbachev and the 27th Soviet Party Congress: Say 'Nyet' to Change."[24] To be sure, although Gorbachev was the first to say the economy needed *"radical* reform," he offered no fundamental political or economic proposals and appeared only to be making a generalized case for continuing his purge of the Brezhnev old guard. Still, Gorbachev's speech was highly controversial among the Soviet *nomenklatura* and some members of the Politburo.[25] There had been a fierce political struggle in the Soviet bureaucracy, similar to the conflicts between State, Defense, and the NSC in Washington, in the drafting of various Party Congress declarations and statements. Boris Ponomarev, an eighty-one-year-old senior Party apparatchik whose career stretched back to Stalin's time, objected to an advance draft of Gorbachev's Party Congress speech, complaining to Chernyaev: "What is 'new thinking'? We already have correct thinking. Let the Americans change their thinking." Another Politburo critic charged that Gorbachev had fallen under the influence of "highly politicized research organizations of a pro-Western character."[26] (There may be truth to this charge. According to one account, in the weeks leading up to the Party Congress Gorbachev had been reading certain Western books, including Churchill's memoirs, that were only available in Russian translation to Soviet elites.)[27] Within weeks of the Party

Congress there began to be rumors in intelligence circles, occasionally breaking into the media, that Gorbachev was the subject of assassination plots. Chernyaev wrote in his diary that "anonymous letters addressed to Gorbachev are coming from military people, with threats to deal with him like Khrushchev if he goes on being in favor of disarmament."[28]

Deputy CIA director Robert Gates reflected later that Gorbachev's Party Congress speech "should be marked as the beginning of the end of the Cold War."[29] At the time, however, Gates and the CIA still regarded the Soviet Union as, in Gates's own words, "a despotism that works." "The idea of *replacing* the Soviet system is nowhere to be found in any Gorbachev speech, writing, or private conversation yet available to the West," Gates added. It should be noted that even with Gorbachev's incipient changes, what the United States observed of Soviet deeds, as opposed to words, in 1986 was a superpower still rapidly deploying new mobile SS-25 missiles, flight-testing another new mobile missile, launching new missile submarines, and beginning production of a new line of strategic bombers and aircraft carriers. Despite plunging hard currency reserves, the Soviet Union in early 1986 extended $3 billion in loans and grants to Nicaragua, Vietnam, and Angola. And despite Gorbachev's conclusion the year before that the Afghanistan war should be ended, the first half of 1986 witnessed an escalation of Soviet forces in Afghanistan, including the deployment of elite Speznaz units.

The United States was not letting down its guard and took its own steps to let the Soviets know that the United States wasn't taking the spirit of Geneva too far. Right after Gorbachev's Party Congress speech, the United States expelled a hundred Soviet diplomats—more than a third of its total corps—from the United Nations in New York for the entirely sensible reason that they were all spies. U.S. Navy ships deliberately provoked the Soviets by sailing into Soviet territorial waters in the Black Sea.

These steps paled compared to Reagan's belated decision in May 1986 to provide Stinger antiaircraft missiles to the Afghan resistance. Whether to provide Stingers had been hotly debated within the administration since early in the first term. Factions at the CIA, State Department, and the Pentagon opposed supplying Stingers to the *mujahadeen* for various reasons.[30] Pressure from Capitol Hill, including from Senator Bob Dole and Representative Charles Wilson (D-Tex.), pushed the matter to the Oval Office, where CIA director William Casey's endorsement swayed Reagan to approve Stingers. According to an early CIA assessment, Stingers "changed the course of the war" instantly. By the end of the Afghan war, it was estimated that the resistance had shot down at least 275 Soviet aircraft with Stingers. The Soviets virtually grounded their previously lethal Mi-24 "Hind" helicopter gunships and Afghan fighters, and suffered the loss of at least two large transport planes. The cost of the war, already intolerable in Gorbachev's reckoning, went up significantly.

In short, the Cold War was still chilly in the spring of 1986.

*   *   *

ONLY LATER WOULD it become evident that, as Cold War scholar Raymond Garthoff put it, "[t]he Reagan administration was unaware that it was essentially marshalling forces to knock down an open door." Gorbachev's potentially promising political developments might have ground along in slow motion or met with fatal bureaucratic resistance were it not for an exogenous event that brought into stark relief how far the Soviet effort at openness and reform needed to go.

In the February 1986 issue of an obscure publication based in the Ukraine, *Literaturna Ukrania,* local writer Lyubov Kovalevska had criticized the nuclear power complex located in Chernobyl, noting poor workmanship, a demoralized workforce, and chronic mismanagement. The Ukrainian energy minister Vitali Sklyarov dismissed worries about the plant, saying that "the odds of a meltdown are one in 10,000 years." Perhaps so, but 1986 turned out to be that one year in ten thousand.

Chernobyl nuclear reactor #4 was only three years old in 1986, but like most Soviet technology it was based on an obsolete design long ago discarded in the West. Most notably, the Chernobyl plant did not enclose its reactors in concrete containment buildings—a standard feature in Western reactors to guard against the release of radioactivity in case of an accident. Even this design flaw might not have been calamitous but for the incompetence of the plant managers, who inexplicably decided on April 25 to disable the plant's automatic safety features so they could run an unusual test of the turbine generators. In the early morning hours of Saturday, April 26, the out-of-control reactor exploded, exposing the surrounding countryside and nearby town of Pripyat to a major radioactive cloud. The reactor core burned out of control for the next two days.

Local authorities began evacuating the immediate vicinity (though not the nearby metropolis of Kiev), but although Moscow had been notified immediately after the accident occurred, there was no public warning as the wind began blowing the radioactive plume into Western Europe. The first hint that something extraordinary had happened came from Sweden, where on Monday, April 28, operators of a nuclear power station were alarmed at readings more than a hundred times normal levels on their radiation detectors, though there was no evidence of a malfunction at any Swedish reactor. Sweden alerted the United States, whose first guess was that the Soviets had botched an underground nuclear test.

Further analysis of the isotopes in the air made clear that its source had to be a reactor somewhere. Tracing the wind patterns of the previous few days drew attention to the Ukraine and finally to Chernobyl. A KH-11 spy satellite was sent on a fly-by on the morning of April 29 to have a look and sent back photos of the still-glowing remains of the reactor core. Moscow, facing insistent questions from foreign diplomats on Monday afternoon, finally acknowledged something had happened, in a terse four-sentence announcement at the top of the 9:00 evening TV newscast.[31] News censors prohibited any further news, issuing a one-sentence directive to state-controlled media: "It is forbidden to publish anything but this TASS bulletin." There was no statement from Gorbachev or any other public official. In Kiev, the May Day parade went ahead as scheduled, while (unannounced to the local population) Communist Party officials evacuated their families from the region.

When Gorbachev finally appeared on Soviet TV more than two weeks after the event to address the Chernobyl accident, he used the occasion to attack the West for having "whipped up anti-Soviet hysteria," and Boris Yeltsin chimed in with an attack on Western "bourgeois media" for "concocting hoaxes" and panic. It didn't wash; the fact that Soviet citizens (and Eastern Europe) got most of their information about Chernobyl from the West underscored the high difficulty of maintaining a closed society in an age of information and made a mockery of *glasnost*. The Soviet reaction had implications for arms control: as the *London Times* put it, "Who would trust the Soviet Union to allow proper international verification of its nuclear missile sites when it does not even tell its own citizens of a fatal accident at one of its own nuclear power stations?"

Moscow's stonewalling and refusal of U.S. and European technical assistance led to wild rumors that as many as fifteen thousand people had died and were being buried in mass graves; a United Press International story, based on a single phone conversation with a doubtful source, claimed there were two thousand dead in Kiev alone. Soviet authorities cut Western media telex lines and blocked satellite links in an effort to control the news, adding further fuel to the rumors.[32] A Japanese physicist made headlines with the estimation that Chernobyl released thirty to forty times as much radiation as the Hiroshima and Nagasaki bombs of 1945. A more sober study from the United States estimated that Chernobyl released more radioactivity than all previous nuclear tests combined.[33]

In fact, the initial death toll was thirty-one, and worries about long-term illness and mortality in the tens of thousands from radiation exposure turned out to have been overestimated. A long-term tracking effort the United Nations set up after Chernobyl reported in 2005 that the death toll from radiation exposure was fewer than fifty—mostly rescue workers exposed to high levels of radiation in the immediate vicinity of the reactor right after the disaster occurred.[34] At the time, however, the general anxiety about all things nuclear contributed to an overreaction. The Soviet Union belatedly evacuated 350,000 people from the region and vacuumed the streets of Ukrainian cities for months. Europe banned food exports from the Soviet Union. Several European nations advised mothers to give powdered milk to their children. Scandinavian countries weighed whether they should destroy their livestock herds for fear of contamination. Whiskey distilleries in Scotland worried that their water sources might be contaminated. The West German newspaper *Bild Zeitung* captured the mood with its banner headline: "Atom Angst."

But even if the radiation risk was overestimated, the Chernobyl accident did bring home in dramatic fashion the risks of even a small-scale nuclear war. Up until that point, a few Soviet war planners (such as Deputy Defense Minister Dmitri Yazov) supposedly believed the USSR could win a nuclear war. But now, since even a single SS-18 missile could produce the equivalent of a hundred Chernobyls, Soviet military strategists were forced to rethink their predictions of a favorable outcome to a major nuclear strike. Twenty years later Gorbachev wrote that the Chernobyl accident "was a historic turning point" and "perhaps the real cause of the collapse of the Soviet Union," reinforcing Gorbachev's view that "the system as we knew it could no longer continue."[35] It was a scandal that the Soviet leadership received more timely and accurate information on the disaster from Western sources than from their own bureaucracies. The aftermath of Chernobyl dominated the Politburo's agenda for the next three months. Gorbachev was furious that the relevant ministers in the government all denied responsibility for Chernobyl. (Six managers of the Chernobyl plant were later sentenced to terms in labor camps.) According to one subsequent account, Gorbachev erupted angrily at a ministerial meeting days after Chernobyl: "For the past 30 years, we have been told that everything was safe, and now you are blaming it all on local employees. We must be completely open with the general secretaries of our sister parties, instead of telling them what they can read in the newspapers. They build nuclear power plants on the basis of our projects, but in East Germany alone, 50 percent of the equipment we deliver is defective."[36] Peter Rutland, an American Soviet studies specialist, judged that "Chernobyl played a crucial role in transforming *glasnost* from a sterile political campaign into a genuine movement for change."[37]

*   *   *

AT ROUGHLY THE same time the Chernobyl disaster was distracting Gorbachev, Reagan was coping with a major distraction of his own—the festering sore of Libya's Kaddafi, whose renewed aggressiveness was a matter of intense focus for Reagan in early 1986.[38] Two days after Christmas in 1985 seven Palestinian terrorists with automatic weapons simultaneously struck the airports in Vienna and Rome, killing twenty people, including five Americans. The Abu Nidal organization claimed credit, though Italian and Austrian intelligence turned up evidence of a Libyan connection. The United States also had evidence that Kaddafi was trying to buy the American hostages in Lebanon. In January Reagan ordered all remaining Americans out of Libya, cut diplomatic relations and future American travel to Libya, and directed the Pentagon to prepare options for a retaliatory strike if Kaddafi sponsored another terror attack. The Reagan administration considered, but ultimately rejected, the idea of sponsoring or joining an Egyptian invasion of Libya to remove Kaddafi and his regime. The administration also had to back off a plan to support Libyan dissidents who might target Kaddafi for assassination after the idea was leaked to the *Washington Post*.

In late March the United States commenced a new round of naval exercises in international waters in the Gulf of Sidra, off the Libyan coast, beyond what Kaddafi had boastfully called the "line of death." In the weeks running up to the new naval exercises, Kaddafi's warplanes had continually harassed U.S. operations but, mindful of the rout of 1981, always backed down at the brink. After two and a half days the U.S. Navy had destroyed two Libyan attack boats and Libya's advanced radar and missile batteries (where, intelligence reports indicated, six Soviet technicians were wounded) and effectively grounded the Libyan air force. In Washington, for a change, Democratic leaders praised Reagan. "The administration's handling of this matter is on the right course," Tip O'Neill said.

In early April British intelligence in West Berlin intercepted and decoded a Libyan transmission indicating that a terrorist attack against Americans was imminent. U.S. intelligence sent a frantic warning to army commanders, who dispatched MPs to search popular West Berlin nightspots for suspicious activity. MPs were minutes away from the La Belle discotheque on the night of April 5 when a bomb exploded in the club, killing 2 and injuring 229 others, including 78 Americans. U.S. intelligence intercepted a second Libyan transmission after the attack boasting of its success to Tripoli.[39]

Reagan had his smoking gun and ordered the prompt execution of the retaliatory strike that had been in preparation for several months, code-named Operation El Dorado Canyon. Because there were not enough carrier-based attack planes available in the Mediterranean to carry out the multiple-target battle plan, land-based F-111 fighter-bombers would be necessary. To use the F-111s based in Britain required Margaret Thatcher's permission. This she readily granted, noting the legal basis in Article 51 of the UN Charter authorizing retaliatory strikes as a measure of self-defense. The French and the Spanish, whose territory the planes would need to fly over, were a different matter. Both refused to grant overflight rights, but French president François Mitterrand had the cheek to tell Weinberger, "If you're going to do this, don't make it a pinprick. Make it a real attack."[40]

The refusal of France and Spain to grant overflight rights meant that the F-111s had to fly 2,800 miles for seven hours around the Iberian peninsula and through the Straits of Gibraltar, refueling three times in flight under conditions of strict radio silence. The raid commenced simultaneously over Tripoli and the coastal town of Benghazi at 2:00 a.m. local time on April 15, catching Libya off guard despite intense media speculation in Washington and in Europe that an attack was imminent.[41] U.S. A-6 attack planes from the aircraft carrier *Coral Sea* inflicted heavy damage on a military airfield and army barracks in Benghazi, while the Tripoli target package, attacked by the British-based F-111s, included Kaddafi's headquarters and residential complex. The United States denied deliberately targeting Kaddafi himself, though his demise as a collateral casualty would have caused no regrets or second thoughts in Washington. (The White House press office had prepared a statement that would say Kaddafi's death was "a fortuitous by-product of our act of self-defense" in the event he was killed.) It was a near miss: two 2,000-pound bombs landed within thirty yards of where Kaddafi was thought to have been sleeping; his adopted infant daughter was killed and two of his young sons were seriously injured. There was an ironic payback for France's lack of support: due to a navigation and equipment error, an errant bomb damaged the French embassy in Tripoli. One American F-111 was lost off the Libyan coast along with its two-man crew.

The raid was intended more for political than military effect, and it seemed initially to have achieved its objective. Reagan went on TV at 9:00 p.m. Eastern time on April 15 to declare, "Today, we have done what we had to do. If necessary, we shall do it again." Polls showed that more than 70 percent of the American public approved, and a *Newsweek* poll found that 56 percent thought the raid would reduce terrorist activity. Even the dovish *New York Times* columnist Anthony Lewis approved: "This American military action did have its reasons . . . there was a rational relationship between ends and means."[42]

Opinion in Europe, however, was exactly the opposite. In Britain, Thatcher was attacked in the press for being "Reagan's poodle" and a *Newsweek* poll found 66 percent of Britons disapproved of the raid, while 71 percent thought it would make terrorism worse.[43] Three-quarters of West Germans expressed their disapproval, and Italian prime minister Bettino Craxi said that Reagan's attack, "far from weakening terrorism, risks provoking explosive reactions of fanaticism and criminal acts." However, European nations, after dragging their feet for fear of damaging business relations with Libya, finally adopted a tougher regime of sanctions chiefly to forestall further U.S. military action. OPEC, meanwhile, pointedly refused Kaddafi's demand that it impose an oil embargo against the United States. The Soviets conveyed their displeasure by canceling a planned trip to the United States by Foreign Minister Shevardnadze.

The raid was thought to have shaken Kaddafi, and he took immediate retribution. Two days after the attack Libyan agents in Lebanon bought three of the hostages held by Hezbollah—an American and two British citizens—and promptly executed all three. Libyan agents also killed an American embassy employee in Khartoum, while Turkish authorities broke up a plot to attack Americans in Ankara with weapons brought into Turkey in a Libyan diplomatic pouch. Though Kaddafi remained in seclusion for nearly two months after the attack, it soon became apparent that, while he cooled his public rhetoric, he did not relent in his support for anti-American terrorism, culminating in the bombing of Pan Am Flight 103 over Lockerbie, Scotland, in December 1988. America's national security community had miscalculated in thinking that a successful attack on Kaddafi would prompt an internal revolt to topple him (the same mistake that would be made about Saddam Hussein at the end of the first Iraq War in 1991). The White House considered and rejected a second attack, deciding to see if the new sanctions regime would work.

                                    *   *   *

WHILE REAGAN AND Gorbachev contended with their own problems, the formal arms control negotiations in Geneva were at a standstill. Gorbachev's arms negotiators showed little flexibility or imagination in the ongoing sessions. The initiative that finally began to get things in motion again came from an unexpected source—Cap Weinberger. In June Weinberger proposed that Reagan answer Gorbachev's January proposal to abolish nuclear weapons with the counterproposal that the two nations abandon their entire arsenal of intercontinental ballistic missiles.

The idea had been percolating around the Pentagon for some time. ICBMs—the "fast flyers," in the terms of the trade—were considered the most destabilizing weapons of the superpower nuclear arsenals. The arms control specialists such as Nitze thought the idea "ridiculous." The Soviets would never agree to give up completely their single greatest strategic advantage over the United States while the United States kept its "slow flyers" such as the cruise missile. But Reagan liked the idea, and Shultz and Weinberger were in rare agreement. In late July Reagan proposed the idea to Gorbachev in another personal letter. Included in Reagan's proposal was a U.S. offer not to withdraw from the ABM Treaty for seven and a half years, and as such represented a small concession to the Soviet position. The Soviets had been seeking a fifteen- to twenty-year ABM Treaty commitment.

As Nitze and other arms control veterans predicted, Gorbachev was not impressed. In a letter hand-delivered to Reagan in the Oval Office on September 15, Gorbachev contemptuously dismissed Reagan's proposal as "a bypass route to securing military superiority." "Is the U.S. leadership at all prepared," he asked, "and really willing to seek agreements which would lead to the termination of the arms race and to genuine disarmament?" "The overall character of U.S. actions," including Reagan's letter, Gorbachev sternly concluded, "all give rise to grave and disturbing thoughts." After Gorbachev ran through a detailed catalogue of complaints about U.S. positions in his letter of September 15, he then switched gears and sought to break the impasse with the suggestion that "we have a quick one-on-one meeting, let us say in Iceland or in London, maybe just for one day, to engage in a strictly confidential, private, and frank discussion." It was not to be the full summit promised in Geneva, but a step toward reaching an agreement that "I could sign during my visit to the United States." Reagan accepted, conditional on a proviso to be discussed shortly.

Gorbachev's reaffirmation that the sequel to Geneva would certainly still take place, rather than suggesting that Reagan's intransigence or the failure of the proposed one-on-one meeting might cause him to call off the full summit, was a revealing concession. Gorbachev and his foreign policy advisers had been steaming over Reagan's July letter and the associated U.S. positions. Anatoly Chernyaev's notes from Politburo meetings during this period have Gorbachev saying, "[M]ost likely nothing can be done with this [U.S.] administration. . . . I am convinced that in the U.S. governing circles they do not want to allow a relaxation of tensions, a slowing down of the arms race." Dobrynin argued that the Soviet Union had little to gain, and potentially much to lose, from an early meeting with Reagan.

Despite these misgivings, it is also evident from Politburo records that Gorbachev was determined to forge ahead and either get Reagan to budge or use the failure of a face-to-face meeting to launch a withering propaganda offensive. "In order to move Reagan, we have to give him something," Chernyaev's notes quote Gorbachev. "Something with pressure and breakthrough potential has to be done. . . . We must emphasize that we are proposing the liquidation of nuclear weapons. . . . If Reagan does not meet us halfway, we will tell the whole world about this. That's the plan." Gorbachev thought the timing of the proposed meeting, weeks before the midterm elections in the United States, would put additional pressure on Reagan to make concessions. "The Americans need this meeting," Gorbachev said on the eve of his departure for Iceland, "otherwise they would not have agreed to it. . . . Reagan needs this as a matter of personal ambition, so as to go down in history as a 'peace president.' The elections are just around the corner."

It is clear from Chernyaev's notes and other records that Gorbachev's determination to make an arms breakthrough either by concession or by propaganda attack derived from his sense of Soviet weakness. Days before the Reykjavik summit commenced, Gorbachev told his foreign policy advisers, "If we do not compromise on some questions, even very important ones, we will lose the main point: we will be pulled into an arms race beyond our power, and we will lose this race, for we are presently at the limits of our capabilities. . . . If they impose a second round of arms race upon us, we will lose! If the new round begins, the pressure on our economy will be inconceivable." He mentioned an embarrassing recent mishap where a Soviet submarine caught fire and sank in the Atlantic: "Because of the submarine which just sank, everybody knows, everybody saw what shape we're in."[44]

But there was a serious obstacle to the proposed minisummit in Iceland. In late August, following a two-year investigation, the FBI arrested a Soviet agent, Gennadi Zakharov, based at the United Nations in New York, on espionage charges. Because Zakharov was a UN employee and lacked diplomatic immunity, he was subject to prosecution and was jailed without bail. Following the tit-for-tat protocol of the spy game, the Soviets retaliated a week later, arresting Nicholas Daniloff, the Moscow correspondent for *U.S. News and World Report*. Daniloff was no U.S. spy, but he had unwittingly exposed himself to legitimate Soviet charges when he had passed along material to the U.S. embassy from a Russian source and was carelessly mentioned in a CIA telephone call from Moscow that the KGB had tapped. The Soviets had set up Daniloff, and his arrest was plainly intended to spur a swap for Zakharov. The traveling White House press office in Santa Barbara, apparently without consulting the NSC or State Department, issued a statement indicating that the United States might consider a swap.

Reagan, vacationing at his ranch, was furious, and sent a direct message to Gorbachev denying that Daniloff was a spy for the United States. Reagan found Gorbachev's response "arrogant," which made him "mad as h—l," as he put it in his diary. Gorbachev publicly called Daniloff a spy, though some behind-the-scenes accounts hold that Gorbachev suspected the Daniloff arrest was a deliberate attempt by hard-liners to derail the proposed summit. Most of Reagan's staff was against a swap, with some calling for a suspension of all ongoing contacts with the Soviets. Reagan himself was open to a swap if a face-saving way could be found for both sides. Maybe, he thought, the United States could get some Soviet dissidents released as part of a deal. As a first step, however, he approved the expulsion of twenty-five Soviet diplomats from the United Nations to signal the Soviets that the United States would not abide every American journalist in Moscow being made a potential hostage every time the United States caught a real Soviet spy.

So when Soviet foreign minister Shevardnadze came to the White House to present Gorbachev's proposal for a minisummit he received a frosty reception. The normally genial Reagan retained a fierce countenance for the entire meeting; in fact, he wouldn't shake Shevardnadze's hand. "Ronald Reagan usually cannot help smiling," Shultz recalled, "but he was not smiling that day. . . . The president did nothing to relieve the tension. I knew Ronald Reagan was an accomplished actor, but this was no act." "I enjoyed being angry," Reagan wrote in his diary that night.

Eventually Shultz and Shevardnadze resolved the Zakharov-Daniloff standoff through a swap in which Zakharov pled guilty and was released on probation to the Soviets in return for the release of dissident Yuri Orlov (and others to be named later) as well as Daniloff. Zakharov's guilty plea along with Orlov's release was thought to have provided enough of a fig leaf for

Reagan to claim that it was not a straight-up swap—spy charges against Daniloff were dropped—but this fooled no one. The news media, which had followed the Daniloff case intensely since it involved one of their own, was scornful ("Mr. President, why did you cave?" Sam Donaldson bellowed at a Rose Garden appearance), but Reagan's real worry was with conservatives, whose criticism of the Daniloff deal was deafening. "When an administration collapses, quickly and completely, like a punctured balloon, as the Reagan administration has done in the Daniloff debacle," George Will wrote, "a reasonable surmise is that the administration, like a balloon, had nothing in it but air." Reagan summoned Will to the Oval Office to tell his side of the story.

It was not so much the spy swap per se that bothered conservatives; they feared that the Daniloff resolution was a prelude to a bad arms deal at the Reykjavik summit. The *New York Times* noted in a new story that "Mr. Reagan seemed aware of the perception in conservative circles that he had become a convert to détente." Reagan told Shultz that he should avoid reading *Human Events*, which was attacking Shultz and the State Department relentlessly.[45] *National Review* worried, "For reasons we cannot fathom, Mr. Reagan now seems more driven to reach an arms-control agreement with the Soviets than he did during his first term, when a re-election challenge loomed." From his ranch Reagan telephoned *National Review* publisher William Rusher to reassure him that it wasn't so. Lyn Nofziger said, "A lot of us were afraid that Reagan would be conned into giving away the store." Reagan invited Nofziger to the Oval Office, where he told him, "Don't worry; I still have the scars on my back from the fights with the Communists in Hollywood. I am not going to give away anything."[46]

William F. Buckley displayed more insight into what was actually happening. Conservative loss of confidence in Reagan was "premature," Buckley wrote, because there was "reason to believe that Reagan is moving in on the Soviet Union, taking special advantage of Soviet weaknesses it does not pay him to advertise. . . . Reagan may be calculating that there are forces moving within the Soviet Union that even Gorbachev can't control, and that these are crying out for relief from exorbitant demands by the military. . . . So it may be that Reagan is approaching the Iceland Summit knowing that he really has the cards." But how would he play them?

*   *   *

THE MEDIA STORIES and subsequent historical accounts of the Reykjavik summit on October 11 and 12 suggest that Gorbachev caught an unprepared Reagan by surprise, a diagnosis that misses the major irony of the way Reagan approached summits and international meetings of all kinds. The man who was said to depend heavily on scripted meetings and events to conduct his presidency in Washington strongly disliked the "precooked" and stage-managed summits, preferring a more open-ended and spontaneous format such as occurred in Geneva. With his instinct for argument, Reagan probably sensed that he had an advantage under such a format. This open-endedness made possible the unexpected—the planned one-day summit stretched out into a second dramatic day as the two sides' diplomatic groups worked furiously around the clock. That Gorbachev also eschewed the previous scheme of choreographing summits in advance meant that Soviet-American relations had entered a new phase equivalent to open-field running.

The documentary record reveals that Reagan and his team went into Reykjavik amply prepared for all the issues that were on the table in the various bilateral negotiations under way at the time. The State Department had a checklist of more than thirty items for discussion, with negotiating positions worked out and with advance briefings provided to NATO allies (who were, in Shultz's words, nervous bordering on "deep desperation" about Reagan's positions). Reagan arrived in Iceland two days early, and spent the entire day before the meeting reviewing briefing papers and going through rehearsal sessions, with Jack Matlock role-playing Gorbachev's anticipated positions.

The trouble was that Reagan's team wasn't quite sure just what Gorbachev was up to. "We go into Reykjavik next week with very little knowledge of how Gorbachev intends to use the meeting," NSC aide Stephen Sestanovich wrote to Reagan in a memo. Sestanovich outlined three possibilities, ranging from general uncertainty to seeking some concrete concessions from Reagan for Gorbachev's "domestic reasons." "There is no agreement within the government on which of these readings is correct"; it was likely, Sestanovich advised, "that you will have to smoke him out during your discussions."[47]

Reagan didn't have to smoke long. When Reagan and Gorbachev sat down alone together for their first session the morning of Saturday, October 11, Reagan, as the nominal host, invited Gorbachev to go first. Gorbachev said that he was willing to discuss "all questions" that Reagan wished to raise (meaning human rights and regional issues) but indicated that he was most eager to present fresh arms proposals.[48] Gorbachev allowed as how "our dialogue has been disrupted several times, it has suffered many bumps and bruises, yet on the whole it is moving ahead." But the arms talks were at a standstill, Gorbachev observed, because "there are 50–100 variants swimming around in the air," and only the two men's direct and urgent attention could break through the impasse. Reagan agreed, and moved to propose a specific goal of 5,500 nuclear warheads for each side as an interim target—a compromise figure between earlier U.S. and Soviet positions.

Gorbachev didn't respond to Reagan's specific targets; instead, he affirmed that "I would like to precisely, firmly and clearly announce that we are in favor of such a solution to the problem which would ultimately provide for complete liquidation of nuclear weapons." Reagan immediately embraced this sentiment but brought up the "difficult question" of verification, trying out on Gorbachev for the first time the Russian proverb *Doveryai no proveryai*— "Trust but verify." "Gorbachev smiled and said he knew the proverb," the U.S. State Department transcript reads. It was a refrain Gorbachev would grow tired of hearing over the next eighteen months. Gorbachev deferred a specific response to verification, instead repeating more generalities about the need for this meeting and the subsequent summit to succeed.

Gorbachev's rhetorical strategy was clear: he was bringing maximum political pressure to bear on Reagan to reach the outline of an agreement in Reykjavik, rather than just formulating new instructions for their diplomats in Geneva. This was no longer a meeting to prepare a summit; it had become a full-blown summit. Reagan parried by bringing up the second substantive point on his agenda: missile throw weight. A mere reduction in the number of missiles is inadequate if their payload capacity—a key Soviet advantage—is not also limited. Without a limit on throw weight, an arms agreement "would not reduce the destructive force of nuclear missiles, and we do not agree to this." Because of the asymmetry of each side's strategic forces, not all 50 percent cuts were created equal.

Gorbachev was mistaken to think he could put Reagan on the defensive through his sentimental appeals to the necessity of success, for Reagan had kept the initiative with his two specific points (again belying the view that he was ill-prepared or unable to command the details of arms control). Gorbachev attempted to regain the initiative by inviting Shultz and Shevardnadze to join the meeting, upon which Gorbachev read out a more specific outline of his new arms proposals. There were three main parts to Gorbachev's proposal, each representing a partial or complete concession to the U.S. position. Gorbachev indicated a Soviet willingness to accommodate American concerns about Soviet land-based missiles if the United States would give on its submarine missile arsenal. He also allowed, for the very first time, the possibility of on-site inspections to verify an agreement. Second, on intermediate

missiles in Europe, the Soviets were now willing to agree to Reagan's zero option and repeated their offer to drop French and British nuclear arsenals from
an arms treaty. This concession was substantively not that significant, as the
French and British nuclear arsenals were tiny compared to the Soviets' (even
after a prospective 50 percent cut); as Chernyaev had advised Gorbachev,
"It's impossible to imagine any circumstances under which they would push
the button against us. Here we are only frightening ourselves and raise anew
the obstacle that has blocked European disarmament for a decade."[49] But
given the past Soviet intransigence over the issue, it was a remarkably potent
political concession. Gorbachev's concession on these points in his January
1986 proposal could be dismissed as a propaganda ploy, but now that he was
offering these concessions at the summit table Reagan saw that they were for
real. There was one small snag, concerning which Gorbachev was prepared
to give way: the original zero-option proposal included mobile Soviet missiles
that were based in Asia but which could be moved back to or targeted on Europe on short notice. The United States preferred that all intermediate-range
missiles be destroyed. This component was missing from Gorbachev's current
proposal.

The third point of Gorbachev's proposal was the crux of the matter: SDI
and the ABM Treaty. In the Geneva negotiations the United States had proposed committing to a seven-and-a-half-year pledge not to break out of the
ABM Treaty; the Soviets had wanted a twenty-year commitment. In a partial
concession to the American proposal, Gorbachev proposed a ten-year commitment, with the crucial proviso that all SDI research and development be
confined to "laboratories." This would be the single word on which the entire meeting turned.

There were good reasons why confining SDI to the laboratory was such
a significant point for both sides. The Soviet Union likely believed that the
United States was further along with SDI technology than in fact it was,
probably because the Soviets were straining so hard to develop missile defense capability themselves, but also because of effective U.S. disinformation.
(An early field test of SDI technology, in June 1984, was faked with the intent
of rattling the Soviets.)[50] Confining the program to the laboratory, everyone
understood, would effectively kill it given the politics of congressional funding in Washington and the limited interest in the technical community in a
laboratory-only research project. Reagan himself had quipped that the surest
way to kill any new proposal in Washington was to turn it into a research
project. As a Soviet memo to Gorbachev shortly before Reykjavik succinctly

put it, "If there is no testing, there will be no SDI." The irony is that the SDI program in the United States *was* largely confined to laboratories at this point for political and bureaucratic reasons. Despite all the talk in the Pentagon about beginning to deploy the first elements of missile defense in the 1990s, there was little serious effort to do so—a fact that became clear in retrospect, as the first missile defenses were not installed until well after the year 2000.[51] Reagan would not have given up much *substantively* had he agreed to Gorbachev's proviso (indeed, many of his advisers wanted to trade away SDI at a propitious moment); the political significance of the outcome was another matter altogether.

Reagan responded optimistically that he was encouraged by Gorbachev's proposal, but he bored in on the ABM proposal. It was a rerun of their argument in Geneva. Reagan counterproposed modifying the ABM Treaty such that each side would share their missile defense research and development while they reduced strategic nuclear weapons, culminating in sharing a system if and when it was fully developed. Gorbachev said SDI was tantamount to attempting to gain a first-strike advantage. How, Reagan parried, could the United States have a first-strike advantage if it had reduced or eliminated offensive nuclear weapons? Gorbachev ignored the point, imploring Reagan to consider the new Soviet proposal in a generous spirit. Both men remained calm and relaxed as they adjourned for lunch separately with their own advisers.

Huddling after the first session in a secure room at the U.S. embassy, Reagan's senior advisers were excited and incredulous at the Soviet concessions. Paul Nitze was nearly euphoric: "This is the best Soviet proposal we have received in 25 years." "Gifts at our feet," Shultz later wrote. "We had not made any concessions but had received more movement from the Soviets than anyone thought possible. . . . The whole nature of the meeting we had planned at Reykjavik had changed." Even Richard Perle, the "prince of darkness" on arms control, was impressed. Reagan was excited too but, ever the essentialist, he spotted the nub: "I'm afraid he's going after SDI." Other observers would put it more bluntly: it was an ambush. But that would be Reagan's burden to sort out. In the meantime, his advisers and staff organized a working group, chaired by Nitze, to carry on the task of negotiating the details of the nuclear arms reductions with Soviet diplomats in a marathon all-night meeting.

Reagan and Gorbachev sat down along with Shultz and Shevardnadze for a second meeting at 3:30 p.m. Reagan led off the afternoon session. He expressed enthusiasm for the proposed 50 percent cut in strategic nuclear weapons but disappointment in Gorbachev's intermediate-range missile proposal. The heart of his reply, however, was a passionate defense of his cherished SDI, which he correctly perceived to be Gorbachev's primary aim. He reprised arguments he had made in the Geneva summit the previous year, much to Gorbachev's visible annoyance. To Reagan's suggestion that the United States could share its SDI technology with the Soviets, Gorbachev huffed that it was incredible to suppose that a nation that wouldn't sell its oil-drilling equipment, machine tools, or even dairy equipment would share its most advanced defense technology. "Sharing SDI would be a second American revolution," Gorbachev retorted, "and revolutions do not occur all that often." "Tempers flared," Shultz wrote later.

The second session was not without some progress, however. Gorbachev indicated he would agree to limits on intermediate-range missiles in Asia if it would preserve the zero option for Europe. Done, said Reagan. Gorbachev pressed for a specific formula of equal reductions in both sides' strategic arsenals, but Reagan insisted this was a matter for the working group to settle on account of the asymmetry of the two sides' force structures. Reagan ended the second session on a typically Reaganesque note: he handed Gorbachev a list of dissidents the United States wanted released from prison or allowed to emigrate. "We will examine these lists carefully," Gorbachev said, "as we always do." "I know that," Reagan replied.

The working group on military issues convened at 8:00 p.m. to work through the details of how a 50 percent reduction in strategic weapons could be constructed fairly for both sides. The session pitted Nitze against one of the most remarkable figures in the Soviet military hierarchy, Chief of the General Staff Sergei Akhromeyev. Akhromeyev, sixty-three, was the last active-duty soldier from World War II still in uniform in the Soviet Union, and the only five-star marshal (equivalent to a U.S. five-star general) in the Soviet forces. This was new. Akhromeyev had never been involved in U.S.-Soviet arms talks before; no one in the American delegation knew him. (Five years later Akhromeyev would be implicated in the attempted coup against Gorbachev; the day after the coup failed, he committed suicide.) The United States, amazingly, had no one from the Joint Chiefs of Staff at Reykjavik.

Nitze and Akhromeyev argued their respective positions tenaciously, debating and disagreeing about the nature and capability of different kinds of weapons delivery systems (bombers versus rockets versus cruise missiles, sea-launched, air-launched, etc.). How different Nitze must have found this session from his previous arms negotiations. What is remarkable is how intent both sides were on reaching a workable agreement despite their many differences, rather than repeating stodgy talking points from position papers while waiting for the next meal break to arrive. The key point—the point that would lead to so much confusion and controversy later—was the difference between the American and Soviet positions on what constituted offensive strategic nuclear weapons. At length the outline of an agreement calling for both sides to reduce strategic nuclear warheads to six thousand apiece, with a sublimit of sixteen hundred delivery systems (or launch platforms) being the key element, began to take shape. The Soviets resisted the sublimits but agreed that sublimits could be subject to follow-up negotiations in Geneva, indicating a willingness to bargain on this point.[52] A separate agreement on a large reduction in intermediate-range missiles in Europe and Asia, with the possibility of Soviet acceptance of Reagan's zero option, also came into view. For the United States it meant ICBMs; for the Soviets the term included airplane-borne bombs and cruise missiles. Each definition was plainly derived from the other side's strengths. But the Soviets made clear that everything hinged on SDI. "We've made more progress than in years," Akhromeyev rightly celebrated after more than ten caffeine-fueled hours of talking with Nitze and the American team until 6:30 a.m., "but we've left much for the President and the General Secretary to do."

After receiving extensive briefings from their two negotiating teams, Reagan and Gorbachev sat down again at ten the next morning for what was supposed to be their final meeting. In between the hammer-and-tongs arguments over the terms of an arms agreement were some extraordinary moments and subtle exchanges that have gone unnoticed in the many accounts and analyses of the Reykjavik summit.

Reagan stood his ground on SDI and firmly attempted to head off Gorbachev: "I am convinced that I cannot retreat from the policy I have declared in the field of space and defensive weapons. I simply cannot do it." Reagan also expressed his fundamental dislike of the ABM Treaty because of its failure as a bulwark to deterrence: "And anyway, damn it, what kind of agreement are you defending? I do not understand the charm of the ABM Treaty, which in fact signifies guaranteed mutual destruction." Reagan tried to reframe the issue as one of abandoning mutual assured destruction in favor of a transition in which nations relied on strategic defense instead, and he pushed to press ahead on the areas of arms reduction where an agreement was in sight.

Gorbachev kept his cool but turned up the pressure, offering additional concessions on reducing Soviet conventional forces. In replying with some frustration to Reagan ("These are not serious arguments. . . . Mr. President, we should not engage in banalities"), he made a curious argument:

I want you to understand that a unique situation has now been created for the American administration. A year ago it was not the case that the Soviet Union had advanced major compromise proposals, and certainly not 2–3 years ago. I simply did not have that capability then. *I am not certain that I will still have it in a year or 2–3 years.* What will happen if we do not make use of this opportunity? Reykjavik will just be mentioned in passing, nothing more. A shame that it all was missed. (Emphasis added)

If this was Gorbachev's oblique attempt to suggest that he was out in front of the Soviet military establishment—that he might face Khrushchev's fate for his proposed concessions—Reagan missed it. He responded: "I am in the same position. It is possible that before long I will not have the powers that I do now."[53]

Their stated differences over the wording of potential agreements on nuclear testing and intermediate-range missiles led to another curious moment in their dialogue. Reagan invoked Marx and Lenin on the theme of global socialist revolution, which drew a sarcastic snort from Gorbachev. Reagan was undeterred, adding a significant observation:

[Marx and Lenin] both said that for the success of socialism it must be victorious throughout the world. They both said that the only morality is that which is in keeping with socialism. And I must say that all the leaders of your country—*except you, you still have not said such a thing*—more than once stated publicly, usually at party congresses, their support for the proposition that socialism must become worldwide, encompass the whole world, and become a unified world communist state. Maybe you have not managed to express your views on this yet, or *maybe you do not believe it.* But so far you have not said it. But all the others said it! (Emphasis added)

If this was Reagan's opening for Gorbachev to break decisively with the Soviet tradition of proclaiming world revolution or to expand on his revisionist positions at the Twenty-seventh Party Congress, Gorbachev didn't take it. He pushed back instead: "So you are talking about Marx and Lenin again." After a pro forma endorsement of self-determination (an implicit rejection of global revolution), Gorbachev exhibited the lingering Soviet irritance at Reagan's rhetoric:

GORBACHEV: I was very surprised when I heard that just before our meeting in Reykjavik you stated in your speeches that you remained loyal to the principles set forth by you in your speech at Westminster Palace. And in that speech you said that the Soviet Union is the Evil Empire, and called for a crusade against socialism in order to drive socialism onto the scrap heap of history. I will tell you, that is quite a terrifying philosophy. What does it mean politically? Make war against us?
REAGAN: No.
GORBACHEV: But that is exactly what you said before Reykjavik. What kind of hint is that to me? I did not want to recall this at all, but you were the first to start talking about that kind of problem.

Reagan was happy to continue in this vein all day, and shortly Gorbachev was trying to return to the terms of an arms agreement, but not before Reagan got the best of him by touting the superiority of American pluralism, concluding by stating, "I would even like to try to convince you to join the Republican Party." "An interesting idea," Gorbachev said, desperate to change the subject. In the years since the Berlin Wall came down there have been numerous nominees for the moment the Cold War ended. This was very nearly it.

Soon the outline of the standoff and the bluff positions of each side were clear. Gorbachev gambled that Reagan wouldn't want to let slip the chance for a historic arms agreement solely on account of SDI. But Reagan was standing his ground stoutly, correctly betting that the Soviets had more to lose from a failure to reach agreement. As Reagan refused to budge on SDI, Gorbachev threatened to pack up and go home. Then he changed the subject to human rights, unpersuasively arguing that "people in the Soviet Union are very concerned about the human rights situation in the United States."

As the session passed its scheduled end point, Gorbachev asked: "Well, Mr. President, 'X-hour' is approaching. What are you going to do?" Shultz proposed going forward to flesh out the areas of agreement on arms reductions alone. "That is not acceptable to us," Gorbachev said. But then

Gorbachev blinked: "Maybe, if the President does not object, we will declare a break for one or two hours and during that time, possibly, our ministers will try to propose something. I think we can slow down a little. After all, we do not want everything to end with a façade." The unheard-of was about to occur: the summit that was not even supposed to be a summit was going into overtime.

Shevardnadze made it clear to Shultz when they met after Reagan and Gorbachev adjourned the session that U.S. refusal of Gorbachev's terms limiting SDI was a deal breaker. While Shultz was arguing with Shevardnadze, members of the U.S. working group hurriedly came up with a counteroffer that upped the ante. What if, the new American proposal read, the United States agreed to the ten-year ABM nonbreakout commitment instead of the five years currently on the table, during which time both sides would eliminate *all* strategic nuclear weapons systems? The Soviets were interested. What they failed to perceive was that the new U.S. proposal would cut the legs out from under Gorbachev: if all ballistic missiles were eliminated, why bother worrying about a U.S. missile defense system?

When Reagan and Gorbachev met again at 3:30 p.m., the weakness of Gorbachev's negotiating position became the focal point. Gorbachev had no good answer to Reagan's repeated argument that without offensive ballistic missiles neither the USSR nor anyone else had anything to fear from a U.S. missile defense system. Reagan mentioned again that SDI was akin to keeping gas masks after poison gas was banned by treaty following World War I, a point Gorbachev found unconvincing. "If you feel so strongly about the ABM Treaty," Reagan asked, "why don't you dismantle the radar you are building at Krasnoyarsk in violation of the treaty?" Gorbachev ignored Reagan's question and, knowing he could not get Reagan to give up SDI, returned to his final redoubt: confining SDI research to the laboratory.

Gorbachev had taken a huge gamble at Reykjavik, and it was failing on account of Reagan's stubbornness. This session alternated between tough argument and giddy moments of empathy and imagination:

REAGAN: I can imagine both of us in 10 years getting together again in Iceland to destroy the last Soviet and American missiles under triumphant circumstances. By then I'll be so old that you won't even recognize me. . . .
GORBACHEV: I don't know whether I'll live till that time.
REAGAN: Well I'm certain I will.
GORBACHEV: Sure you will. You've passed the dangerous age for men, and

now you have smooth sailing to be a hundred. But these dangers still lie ahead for me. . . . I still have to meet with President Reagan, who I can see really hates to give in.

After a short break to allow both sides to work on the wording of a compromise proposal Reagan and Gorbachev met for the fifth time at 5:30 p.m. Despite an official news blackout, word had began to leak out to the press, chiefly from Soviet sources in an attempt to ratchet up pressure on Reagan, of the potentially historic breakthrough. The TV networks in the United States interrupted Sunday programs with special news bulletins heralding the potential breakthrough under way in Iceland. Reagan began by reading the modified U.S. proposal calling for two five-year periods during which time both sides would eliminate their entire strategic nuclear arsenals and would commit to remaining within the terms of the ABM Treaty. Gorbachev objected that the U.S. proposal allowed testing of ABM technology outside the laboratory: "What I'm asking is, did you omit the mention of laboratories deliberately or not?" Reagan: "Yes, it was deliberate. What's the matter?"

Strangely, Gorbachev backed off at this point, asking detailed questions about how different kinds of weapons systems were to be classified. There followed another remarkable turning point. Gorbachev had decided to double down, and it was at this point that the enthusiasm and idealism of both men began to take wing. When Gorbachev probed an ambiguity in the U.S. wording about "offensive weapons" and "ballistic missiles" (the U.S. proposal used the terms interchangeably) and began to suggest ways to resolve the ambiguity and reach an agreement on a ten-year formula to eliminate all offensive weapons, Reagan sensed an opening and audaciously charged in:

REAGAN: Let me ask this. Do we have in mind—and I think it would be very good—that by the end of the two five-year periods all nuclear devices would be eliminated, including bombs, battlefield systems, cruise missiles, submarine weapons, intermediate-range systems, and so on?
GORBACHEV: We could say that, list all those weapons.
SHULTZ: Then let's do it.
REAGAN: If we agree that by the end of the 10-year period all nuclear weapons are to be eliminated, we can turn this agreement over to our delegations in Geneva so that they can prepare a treaty which you can sign during your visit to the U.S.
GORBACHEV: Well, all right. Here we have a chance for an agreement.

The unheard-of had occurred: the president of the United States and the general secretary of the Communist Party of the Soviet Union had just agreed to seek the total abolition of *all* nuclear weapons, not just strategic nuclear missiles. This went well beyond anything Reagan's advisers had ever contemplated, even the entrenched idealists of the Arms Control and Disarmament Agency. It was not what was reflected in any of the written proposals that were on the table, though it was about to take on a life of its own. Gorbachev might conceivably go along with this radical idea, as the USSR and the Warsaw Pact nations enjoyed a huge advantage in conventional forces. Shultz would later come in for harsh criticism for having joined the disarmament parade, but as he noted, Reagan had long spoken publicly of abolishing nuclear weapons. When news of this moment in the negotiation emerged from Reykjavik the U.S. defense establishment and the European allies were astonished and alarmed.

In fact it was not clear from Reagan's statement and Gorbachev's acquiescence that "all" nuclear weapons meant *all* nuclear weapons, but the failure to clarify this didn't matter, as the dialogue soon returned to the central stumbling block of SDI. The climax of the summit could no longer be avoided or put off for another hour. During the afternoon break Reagan asked his team if it was possible for SDI to survive under the Soviet demand that it be confined to the laboratory. Several members of Reagan's team, including Nitze and Shultz, thought the laboratory restriction was not a serious obstacle to SDI and wanted to accept Gorbachev's language. Confining SDI to a laboratory, Shultz thought, was like "giving away the sleeves on your vest." Others, especially Richard Perle, held the opposite opinion. Reagan telegraphed his decision with the rhetorical question: "If we agree to Gorbachev's limitations, won't we be doing that simply so we can leave here with an agreement?"

With the die cast, the only question remaining was how the final showdown would play out. Reagan and Gorbachev went around and around again, with Shevardnadze at one point making an emotional plea to keep a deal alive. Reagan was unmoved. Gorbachev finally gave up: "All right, then, let's end it here. What you propose is something we cannot go along with. I've said all I can." Reagan was furious, asking, "Are you really going to turn down a historic opportunity for agreement for the sake of one word in the text?" The American immovable force and the Soviet irresistible object rehearsed their fixed positions yet one more time before both started shuffling papers in a prelude to breaking up the meeting. Reagan stood up first: "Let's go, George."

There was no need for an official announcement to the waiting media outside Hofti House; the stiff body language and grim visage of the two leaders as they emerged told the story. Both men apologized and offered near-despairing regrets, with Reagan saying, "I don't know whether we'll ever have another chance like this and whether we will meet soon." Gorbachev replied: "I don't know what more I could have done." Reagan replied with some bitterness: "You could have said 'yes.' " Reagan slumped hard in the backseat of his car. He once again had the chance to say *nyet* to a bad arms deal, but no longer relished it.

Naturally, the media rushed to broadcast that the summit had collapsed in spectacular failure, a perception abetted by Shultz's downcast press conference a few minutes later, an appearance Shultz himself later regretted and described as "worn, exhausted, and depressed." Others described it as "funereal"; the *Washington Post* added that "American officials, including arms negotiator Max M. Kampelman, stood at the edge of the stage, their faces drawn and sad." Some of Reagan's own people shared the sour mood; Jack Matlock, who thought Reagan should have accepted Gorbachev's terms, wrote: "I felt crushed. Ten years in laboratories would not have killed SDI. . . . How could Shultz have let this happen?"[54] Some of the hard-liners, such as Adelman, thought the negotiation had spun out of control into never-never land. After the exhilaration of the previous all-nighter and the morning's additional progress, the mood on Air Force One returning to Washington was somber, with one or two conspicuous exceptions. Reagan's old friend and U.S. Information Agency director Charles Wick told Reagan he had just won the Cold War, though the logic of his optimism was not transparent at that moment. The London *Telegraph* headline was more typical of the immediate reaction: "Arms Talk 'Disaster.' " The promised Washington summit seemed to be off.

Few in the media took sufficient notice that Gorbachev struck a sharply contrasting note in his own press conference in Reykjavik right after the meeting broke up. "In spite of all its drama," Gorbachev said, "Reykjavik is not a failure. It is a breakthrough, which allowed us for the first time to look over the horizon."

*   *   *

THE SUMMIT'S UNEXPECTED scope, quick-paced drama, and abrupt, disappointing end created a contradictory landscape back in Washington and in European capitals. The initial media story line of failure soon gave way to confusion about how Reykjavik should be understood. The reaction among

Reagan's liberal critics and the media alternated between outrage at Reagan's stubborn and foolish refusal to give in on SDI and alarm at the seeming recklessness with which Reagan came close to committing to total or near-total nuclear disarmament. George Ball, the wise man of the Johnson administration, expressed the liberal reaction: "I think a real opportunity was missed in Reykjavik. SDI is not only a fantasy, it is a fraud. If the President persists in his SDI fantasy, there is no possibility of success in arms control. All the President is doing with his fixation on Star Wars is to make arms control more difficult to achieve."

But others noted that the sudden talk of total nuclear disarmament was rash. Europeans, especially Margaret Thatcher, were appalled that Reagan had nearly traded away the chief means of deterrence against the massive Soviet conventional forces with little prior consultation. Thatcher described the possible Reykjavik deal as "as if there had been an earthquake under my feet." Thatcher arranged to travel to the United States at the first opportunity to see Reagan in person to express her alarm: "Somehow I had to get the Americans back onto the firm ground of a credible policy of nuclear deterrence."[55] After intense private discussions with Thatcher at Camp David in November, Reagan agreed to a British-drafted statement reaffirming nuclear deterrence, implicitly backing away from the full breadth of Reykjavik.[56] Thatcher conveyed her annoyance to Gorbachev as well. Britain's ambassador to the Soviet Union met with Gorbachev in December and delivered what Gorbachev described as "a thrashing to me and Reagan" for a perfunctory approach in Reykjavik.[57] Thatcher's dismay represented a notable irony: she had been unenthusiastic about SDI at its inception in 1983 but was now thankful it had proven the stumbling block to what she thought was a disastrous course. Nuclear weapons, for all the existential dread they inspired, had kept the peace in Europe for forty years, as Churchill had vividly expressed in calling postwar European peace "the sturdy child of terror." Suddenly, in a strange embrace of the satirical *Dr. Strangelove*, people started learning to love the bomb. Many of the same European and American elites who had wrung their hands about the lack of progress in superpower arms talks now urged Reagan and Gorbachev to slow down. West German foreign minister Hans-Dietrich Genscher admitted publicly that many European politicians had embraced Reagan's zero option in 1981 only because they were confident the Soviet Union would reject it, and Thatcher admitted in her memoirs that "I had gone along with it [the zero option] in the hope that the Soviets would never accept." Unsurprisingly, the French also complained.

Writing in *Foreign Affairs,* James Schlesinger called Reykjavik "a near disaster" and lashed out at the "casual utopianism" that led to "impulsive" proposals: "Surely we must be more cautious in casting aside the existing structure of Western security before we are assured that an alternative truly exists. . . . [Reagan] has clearly done more to weaken deterrence than did the U.S. Catholic bishops in their 1983 pastoral letter."[58]

As previously noted, there was ambiguity about whether Reagan's improvised proposal meant the complete elimination of all nuclear weapons or just missiles and similar strategic systems. But even this more modest proposal was problematic. Ken Adelman wrote: "Even if a dramatic deal had been struck by the two leaders, it would not have stuck." Republican House whip Dick Cheney called Adelman to ask, "What the hell have you guys done?" Democratic senator Sam Nunn criticized Reagan from the right: "It is obvious that this proposal has not been thought through adequately. Prior to the Reykjavik summit, the Joint Chiefs of Staff were not asked to study the implications of the President's proposal for a total elimination within ten years of all ballistic missiles, let alone to consider the elimination of all strategic arms." Nunn was correct about the Joint Chiefs of Staff. Two weeks after Reagan returned from Iceland, the chairman of the Joint Chiefs of Staff, Admiral William Crowe, met with Reagan in the Situation Room to express the Joint Chiefs' alarm about eliminating ballistic missiles. Crowe feared he'd be dismissed from his job for objecting to Reagan's course. Among other implications, without strategic nuclear weapons the United States would need to spend at least another $100 billion a year on conventional defenses, a figure that would choke Congress. Shultz and other senior administration figures began to backtrack, Shultz saying in a speech a few days after Reykjavik that even after a comprehensive disarmament agreement the United States and Soviet Union might each keep a small number of ballistic missiles as an "insurance policy to hedge against cheating and other contingencies."

Richard Nixon was aghast at the whole scene, writing in his book *1999: Victory Without War,* "No summit since Yalta has threatened Western interests so much as the two days at Reykjavik. No deeper blow has ever been dealt to allied confidence in the United States than by the incorporation of the nuclear-free fantasy into the American negotiating position." Freshman senator Al Gore said Reagan's performance at Reykjavik was "bumbling . . . a fiasco." Senator Gary Hart, gearing up for another presidential campaign, complained: "Building Star Wars is more important to this Administration than meaningful arms control." Conservatives naturally had the opposite opinion. A *Human Events* headline read: "Conservatives Very Relieved by Close Call at Reykjavik," though noting in its copy that Reagan "barely escaped with a full set of clothes." *National Review* said Reykjavik should be "added to the list of occasions for which America can be grateful that Reagan sits in the White House," and George Will declared it to be Reagan's "finest hour." Reagan, in a televised speech to the nation the day after returning from Iceland, said: "We prefer no agreement than to bring home a bad agreement."

Political scientist Aaron Wildavsky put his finger on the deeper source of the uproar over Reagan's performance in Reykjavik:

> The contempt hurled at President Reagan over the principles nearly agreed to at Reykjavik reveal the intellectual bankruptcy of his critics. . . . One cannot but feel that much of the violent reaction to Reykjavik had no more substantial basis than the extreme pique felt by arms control intellectuals at not being consulted in advance. That was Ronald Reagan's real sin in Iceland. For what, after all, was wrong with Reykjavik except that it lacked the imprimatur of the foreign policy establishment?[59]

The centrality of SDI to the Soviets was humiliating to the leading establishmentarians who had been deeply skeptical, if not outright opposed, to the idea that the specter of SDI would cause the Soviets to reduce their arsenal. The idea, Robert McNamara had told Strobe Talbott, "was flawed at its very core."[60] But as Richard Perle pointed out: "The speech announcing SDI was made in March 1983, and Reykjavik was in October 1986, so in a little over three years, for a modest investment at that point of five or six billion dollars—for that modest investment—[Reagan] had produced a situation in which the leader of the Soviet Union was prepared to cut their strategic forces in half, and all they asked for in return was that we wouldn't proceed with SDI."[61]

Over in Moscow Gorbachev was saying one thing to the Politburo but within closer circles thinking something else. The politics of the Politburo demanded that he blast Reagan. Gorbachev told the Politburo on October 14 that Reagan "exhibited extreme primitivism, a caveman outlook, and intellectual impotence." But this was about the last time Gorbachev employed such strong personal denunciations of Reagan. In a subtle shift, he attributed Reagan's stubbornness to the demands of the "military-industrial complex" in the United States, which mirrored his own negotiating constraints from the

Soviet military. Far from concluding, as the U.S. political class did, that Reykjavik had been a debacle, Gorbachev repeated that he saw it as a success. Privately he concluded that a permanent turning point had been reached at Reykjavik (a thought he confirmed years later in conversation with Shultz in California). Gorbachev had been impressed by Reagan's improvisations and willingness to agree to deep cuts in nuclear arms. His foreign policy adviser, Chernyaev, wrote, "I believe it was then [in Reykjavik] that he became convinced that it would 'work out' between him and Reagan. . . . A spark of understanding was born between them, as if they had winked to each other about the future."[62]

Most importantly, far from being a roadblock, Reagan's stubbornness on SDI was quickly swept aside as a secondary matter. In fact, Gorbachev and his inner circle were looking for a way to back away from their hardened position on SDI. The United States had not been sure of Gorbachev's aims coming into Reykjavik. But Reagan's advisers had correctly picked up on one important point. "Since mid-summer," Stephen Sestanovich observed before Reykjavik, "the Soviet line on strategic defense has apparently begun to waver just a bit." Sestanovich was mostly guessing. No one knew that Chernyaev had recommended to Gorbachev that he drop his insistence that SDI be curbed; reductions in nuclear arms "needn't hinge on an agreement over SDI," he advised, adding presciently, "otherwise it will be another dead end."[63] Gorbachev had rejected this going into Reykjavik for domestic political reasons—if he didn't try to scuttle SDI, his own defense establishment would raise hackles. In fact, some Soviet sources suggest the tactic of demanding the takedown of SDI in exchange for deep cuts in nuclear weapons was added late in the Soviet planning process, after Gorbachev had already decided on presenting Reagan with a bold disarmament proposal. "That was the price the military asked for this deep cut," Gorbachev aide Alexandr Bessmertnykh said later. There is even some evidence and testimony that the Soviet military was willing before Reykjavik to give in on SDI as a fallback position but that this view was not communicated to Gorbachev in Iceland.[64] Now that Reagan had made clear he would not pay the price, would the Soviets change their view?

The United States didn't have to wait long for an answer. During one of the working-group meetings in Reykjavik, Richard Perle had come up with an inventive solution to the laboratory problem: "What if we put the laboratory in space?" It was shrugged off at the time as a mere witticism, but within days after Reykjavik the Soviets began backtracking in their public definition of laboratory testing in a manner not far removed from Perle's mirthful contrivance. Two weeks after Reykjavik a senior Soviet scientist speaking at the United Nations in New York allowed that some SDI tests could be done in space because Soviet scientists considered manned space stations to be "orbital laboratories."[65] This generated a head-turning *Washington Post* headline: "Soviet Scientist Says 'Modest' SDI Testing Is Compatible with ABM Pact." The Soviets had just blinked again.[66]

As Shultz reflected afterward, "I knew that the genie was out of the bottle: the concessions Gorbachev made at Reykjavik could never, in reality, be taken back." Reykjavik had broken the deadlock. The next few meetings between U.S. and Soviet diplomats in Geneva went poorly (aggravated by the fresh U.S. decision to expel another fifty-five Soviet diplomat-spies from the United States and a public reaffirmation that the United States was dumping SALT II limits), but by February 1987 the Soviets had dropped their demand to limit SDI as a condition for reaching an agreement on intermediate-range missiles in Europe. The road to an early agreement that could be signed at a summit in Washington was now wide open. The broader idea of large cuts in strategic missile forces would take longer to work out, but, as Aaron Wildavsky noted, "American foreign policy has unfolded exactly as Reagan said it would. At the outset, the president said he would help build up the military establishment; later, having given the Soviets greater reason to cooperate, he would seek mutually advantageous agreements—oversimplified, naturally, but that is what policy guidance from the top is about."[67]

*   *   *

THIS FAVORABLE COURSE of events would take months to play out. In the short term there was much back-and-forth among political pundits about how Reykjavik would affect the upcoming midterm election. At the Politburo meeting right after Reykjavik Andrei Gromyko said that the collapse of the summit "will be a grave blow to the Republican Party on the eve of the elections, and this also works to our advantage." To the contrary, Reagan's popularity went up. A *Newsweek* poll found that "Ronald Reagan emerged from Reykjavik a winner. Among Americans who kept abreast of the summit, two out of three support Reagan's decision to reject the Soviet offer. Most blame Mikhail Gorbachev for the failure to reach agreement, and an overwhelming majority believes the President is more committed to arms control than the Soviet leader." Between European alarm at the prospect of no nukes and Reagan's rising popularity at home, Soviet fallback hopes of scoring a propaganda victory through the failure to reach an agreement were dashed. Gorbachev had overplayed this hand too.

Democratic campaign strategists breathed a sigh of relief that Reykjavik collapsed. Representative Tom Downey of New York said openly what many Democrats thought privately: "If he had come back with an agreement, they would be carving his face on Mount Rushmore." Democrats were still wandering in the opposition wilderness. After watching a Democratic House retreat in late winter, Kevin Phillips wrote: "I have a sense that Democrats are as confused and befuddled and divided as the Republicans were after 1964." It was during this election that Tip O'Neill's maxim "All politics is local" became nationally famous, in part because he argued that there were no national issues at stake in the election. Given the sharp partisan divisions over judges, civil rights, and Central American policy (to name a few), this was nonsense, but it was a clever way of circumscribing Reagan's personal popularity.

Republicans girded themselves for election losses nonetheless. Despite the passage of tax reform, Reagan's personal popularity, and the president's other legislative victories, surveys and polls throughout 1986 showed a steady erosion in Republican support. A Harris poll of party identification in the spring found Democrats ahead of Republicans 39 to 31 percent, after having been even after the 1984 election. Reagan agreed to an aggressive schedule of campaign appearances around the country in the fall, traveling twenty-four thousand miles, making fifty-four appearances in twenty-two states, and raising $33 million for Republican candidates.

Midterm elections in the sixth year of a presidency usually go badly. The average sixth-year loss since Woodrow Wilson was forty-one seats in the House and seven in the Senate. So it was somewhat surprising that Republicans lost only five House seats. However, the GOP lost eight Senate seats—one more than the historical average—and thereby lost control of the Senate, ensuring a decisive shift in the balance of power in Washington. The election was closer than it appeared: nationally Republican Senate candidates got a higher share of the two-party vote (49 percent) than they did in the 1980 election (47 percent). But many of the first-term Republicans swept in on narrow margins on Reagan's coattails in 1980 were swept out by similarly small margins in 1986, among them Paula Hawkins in Florida, Jeremiah Denton in Alabama, Slade Gorton in Washington, and Mark Andrews in North Dakota. Some important new faces were heading to the Senate. John McCain was elected to succeed Barry Goldwater in Arizona and to plot his own chapter as a southwestern maverick. Tom Daschle defeated a Republican incumbent in South Dakota, and Harry Reid was elected in Nevada, where Reagan's friend Paul Laxalt was retiring to contemplate his own White House run in 1988.

There is some polling evidence that Reagan's campaigning helped close the gap in many of these races and held down GOP losses. But it can also be argued that the result was an echo of the defensive strategy from Reagan's 1984 reelection campaign. Robert Novak understood it this way, writing, "The electoral catastrophe of 1986 can be blamed in no small part on the policy vacuum created by the issue-less 1984 re-election campaign."

Liberals exulted that they were on the comeback trail. *New York Times* columnist Anthony Lewis celebrated with a column entitled "The End Begins: Radical Right Movement Has Crested." Outgoing Speaker O'Neill said of the election result: "If there ever was a Reagan Revolution, it's over." But the *Washington Post*'s David Broder cautioned: "The biggest mistake Democrats can make is to believe that the 1986 election confirmed them as the majority party in the country." On the state level, there had been little change in the two-party balance in state legislatures or in governorships. There were other signs of conservative strength. Vermont voters rejected adding an Equal Rights Amendment (a clone of the failed federal amendment) to Vermont's state constitution, and in California, three liberal judges (including chief justice Rose Bird) appointed by Governor Jerry Brown were overwhelmingly recalled from the state supreme court after having repeatedly overturned death penalty verdicts.

The notion that there were no national issues at stake in the 1986 election was belied on Election Day when a Beirut newspaper published a sensational story that the United States had been quietly selling arms to Iran in exchange for the release of the American hostages held in Lebanon. The story added the incredible detail that former national security adviser Robert McFarlane had secretly visited Tehran in the spring. It was the spark that ignited the most acrimonious partisan conflagration of the Reagan years, and it nearly snuffed out the lamp on top of Reagan's shining city on a hill.

CHAPTER II

"TEMPEST-TOST":

THE IRAN-CONTRA CLIMAX

———✦———

The nature of foreign negotiations requires caution, and their
success must often depend on secrecy; and even when brought
to a conclusion a full disclosure of all the measures, demands,
or even concessions which may have been proposed or
contemplated would be extremely impolitic; for this might
have a pernicious influence on future negotiations, or
produce immediate inconveniences, perhaps danger and mischief,
in relation to other powers.
—PRESIDENT GEORGE WASHINGTON, ON HIS REFUSAL TO SHARE
DOCUMENTS WITH CONGRESS ABOUT THE
NEGOTIATIONS FOR JAY'S TREATY

Whoever allowed this combination of events to proceed could
not have designed his work more destructively. . . . It was a ticking
time bomb, ingeniously contrived and placed close to the President.
It was only a matter of time before it detonated.
—JAMES SCHLESINGER ABOUT IRAN-CONTRA, DECEMBER 1986

THE STORY OF the Iran-Contra scandal is not easily told in an integrated chronological narrative.[1] The matter exacerbated partisan divisions and raised deep constitutional issues in a way that must not only
dominate any serious evaluation of the Reagan administration but also hold
special significance in light of the second Iraq War and other aspects of the
post-9/11 struggle against terrorism.

The seeds of the Contra half of the scandal were sown in the initial decision in 1981 to arm the Contras for the purpose of arms interdiction and pressure on the Sandinista regime while ostensibly eschewing the aim of overthrowing the Sandinistas, even though this was the real aim of the Contras themselves. The stop-start-stop-start actions Congress exhibited in the intermittent Contra funding bills, combined with the five Boland Amendments limiting or prohibiting Contra aid, not only disrupted policy but also obscured public perception of the deep partisan divide at the root of the matter. In other words, both Central American policy and political accountability were a muddle. The frequent congressional reversals on Contra aid were an object lesson of why foreign policy can't be conducted by a committee of 535.

Nineteen eighty-six would see yet another reversal of congressional mood about Nicaragua policy. In 1985 Congress had reluctantly passed, and the White House had reluctantly accepted, a modest package of "humanitarian" (nonmilitary) aid to keep the Contras on life support while they found resources for arms elsewhere. To keep the CIA and the White House out of mischief, the aid was to be dispensed by a special State Department office. Democrats in Congress later complained when the aid was doled out slowly, inefficiently, and with poor accountability. How did they think it was going to work?

Everyone knew the White House was encouraging funds from overseas and private American sources and that Oliver North was involved in the effort. Congressman Lee Hamilton, chairman of the House Foreign Affairs Committee, cautioned the White House that it "would be well advised not to push the law *too far*," but the law kept changing. In the fall the White House won some legal modifications from Congress in the annual intelligence authorization bill that weakened the latest iteration of the Boland Amendment. Among other changes, soliciting aid from foreign nations got an explicit green light, as did certain other forms of humanitarian aid to the Contras that plainly could be used for lethal purposes, such as trucks and aircraft. The whole matter was becoming a farce. As Robert Kagan summarized, "In the ever-shifting legal terrain shaped by Congress, donations like those of Saudi Arabia, not explicitly prohibited by Congress when first solicited by McFarlane in 1984, possibly illegal when next proffered in 1985, were now, perhaps, possible under the new legislation."[2]

It was hardly a way to run a foreign policy with continuity. Still, there was good reason throughout the second half of 1985 to suppose that the Sandinistas had the Contras stalemated at worst, and perhaps checkmated in the fullness of time. Shrewd diplomacy on the part of the Sandinistas, such as stringing along the Contadora regional negotiating process, would have bolstered the Democratic opposition to Reagan on Capitol Hill and constricted Reagan's latitude. Instead the Sandinistas made a series of fresh blunders that strengthened Reagan's hand in Washington.

In the spring of 1985 Nicaragua's bulging armed forces—as many as sixty thousand under arms by that point—began a series of incursions into Honduras to attack Contra base camps, and a series of smaller sorties against Contra positions in Costa Rica. This posed a problem for the United States. Even though everyone knew the Contras were operating out of Honduras, the Honduran government did not wish to acknowledge this publicly or draw attention to it, so its response was muted, and as a consequence so was the U.S. response. In fact, given the wavering U.S. support for the Contras, Honduras wondered whether it should kick the Contras out. Nicaraguan incursions into Honduras continued intermittently through the summer and fall of 1985. In November, a Nicaraguan helicopter the Contras shot down near the Honduran border was found to contain Cuban army soldiers.

Inside Nicaragua, the Sandinistas cracked down hard on their increasingly popular political opponents. The Sandinistas declared a state of emergency—the legal pretext for suspending constitutional rights of assembly and judicial appeals, closing down the Catholic radio station, and suspending the right to travel abroad. Effectively this made the country an Eastern European–style national prison. The government arrested and jailed more than a hundred political opponents, including all seven directors of an independent trade union. According to one estimate, the Sandinistas had jailed as many as seven thousand political prisoners and were manipulating rationing as a political tool. The remaining independent newspaper, *La Prensa*, was subjected to heightened censorship, and the regime deployed its political goon squads to disrupt anti-Sandinista public demonstrations, including the most potent symbol of the opposition, Catholic mass. Pope John Paul II ratcheted up the tension by making Nicaraguan archbishop Obando y Bravo a cardinal, a rare and significant promotion for Latin America. The cardinal openly supported the Contras and made an offer to mediate negotiations between the Sandinistas and the Contras, which the Sandinistas summarily rejected. The hostility between the regime and the Church intensified when the government expelled Bishop Pablo Antonio Vega in the summer of 1986.

Even sympathetic American liberals were dismayed at the Sandinistas' course. Daniel Ortega came to New York in the fall to address the United

Nations (and attracted criticism for buying expensive designer sunglasses in a Manhattan boutique). TV's quintessential bleeding-heart liberal, Phil Donahue, pleaded with Ortega on his show, telling Ortega that his actions were "a tremendous public relations victory for the Reagan administration" and that the Sandinistas' crackdown "looks like the work of a fascist government . . . You've snatched defeat from the jaws of victory! You've got the whole Catholic Church angry with you. . . . Let them speak! Your revolution is popular!"[3]

Other liberals were not as mulish as Donahue. The defection of a number of prominent liberals from the anti-Contra ranks had a decisive effect on the weakening of Democratic opposition to Contra aid in Congress. The *Los Angeles Times* noted in a front-page article at the end of 1985 that there was "a serious fraying of the Democrats' once-solid front against the Reagan Administration's policies in Central America."[4] Three defections in particular raised hackles on the left. The most significant was Robert Leiken of the Carnegie Endowment for International Peace. Leiken had made his bones as an anti–Vietnam War activist in the 1960s and had opposed aid to the Contras in the early 1980s, but following a series of visits to Nicaragua in 1984 Leiken broke with the Left and published an article in the *New Republic* harshly critical of the Sandinistas and favorable to the Contras. "Each succeeding trip to Nicaragua drains my initial reservoir of sympathy for the Sandinistas," Leiken wrote, "and disabused me of some of the remaining myths about the Sandinista revolution."[5]

The second such figure was Bruce Cameron, a human rights lobbyist for Americans for Democratic Action. After Cameron, who was so far left in the 1960s that he had openly supported the Vietcong, came out in favor of Contra aid he was immediately fired from the ADA and removed from two boards of human rights organizations he had helped found. Other human rights activists who publicly criticized the Sandinistas, such as Nina Shea, were subject to threats and intimidation.

The third notable figure on the left was Paul Berman. In a series of articles in *Mother Jones* magazine, Berman highlighted the essential Leninism of the Sandinistas: "[T]he Sandinistas never gave up on Lenin's idea of the vanguard party. . . . [N]o one seriously believes the Sandinistas mean to go so far with democracy as actually to engage in some form of power sharing, not even if the country and the revolution would be better off for it. So they are going to keep their near-monopoly of power, and they are not going to share it. . . . I think that American friends of the Sandinistas manage sometimes not to notice these ideas."[6] The purge mentality revealed in the reaction to Leiken, Cameron, and others was revealing. Leiken told the *Los Angeles Times,* "There is a purity test and I failed it. It's very difficult for most liberals in Washington to move away from their fixed positions. There are so many vested interests involved: fellowships, positions, organizations."[7] Leiken, Cameron, and a handful of other Democrats were crucial in shifting moderate congressional Democrats toward Contra support.

The Sandinistas' ideologically fueled intransigence explains why they were not more supple in their diplomacy, which George Shultz described as "remarkable ineptness." It should have been an easy matter to string along the Contadora process and make suitably conciliatory noises, thereby giving ample political cover to congressional Democrats who opposed Contra aid in favor of negotiations. The Reagan administration would have been hard-pressed to continue Contra support had the Sandinistas displayed even superficial openness to negotiations, a modicum of interest in power sharing, and the slightest bit of military restraint. At one point the State Department even committed to disbanding the Contras if the Sandinistas agreed to a treaty. But the Sandinistas continued to reject successive drafts of a regional treaty put forth by their neighbors. Early in 1986 the Sandinistas suggested postponing further negotiations or scuttling Contadora altogether. This ham-handed intransigence on the part of the Sandinista leadership is explained by their fantastical Leninism. They actually wanted a direct U.S. intervention in Nicaragua because, as one Sandinista official told Robert Leiken in Managua, it would "vastly accelerate the Latin American revolution against U.S. imperialism." An astounded Leiken said he had considered this Sandinista to be "a moderate."[8]

The bad faith of the Sandinistas began to change the political landscape in Washington. Even Ted Kennedy began to speak harshly of the Sandinista regime. Early in 1986 Reagan and his foreign policy team decided they wouldn't have to settle again for a weak package of humanitarian aid. On January 10 Reagan sent to the Hill a $100 million request for the Contras, with $70 million allocated for military aid. In addition, he demanded that restrictions on CIA and Pentagon direct assistance to the Contras be lifted. Tip O'Neill remained staunchly opposed, confiding to a friend, "I believe [Reagan's] policies are absolutely immoral. It appears he won't be happy until American troops are in Central America."[9] This became a favorite liberal refrain; Representative Marty Russo of Illinois said during a visit to Argentina that "Reagan's not going to be happy until he gets into a war in Central

America." Despite the weakening position of the Sandinistas, O'Neill and the House Democratic leadership appeared strong enough to beat back Reagan's Contra request.

Privately Reagan was adamant in his opposition to direct U.S. military involvement in Central America—he repeatedly noted his strong feelings on this in his diary—but his public rule of never say never kept him from disputing the Democrats when they waved the bloody shirt. Instead Reagan and his team decided to hit back: he turned White House communications director Pat Buchanan loose to launch a partisan attack. In early March Buchanan wrote in the *Washington Post* that Democrats had become, "with Moscow, co-guarantor of the Brezhnev doctrine in Central America." How the Democratic Party came down on Contra aid, Buchanan charged, "will reveal whether it stands with Ronald Reagan and the resistance—or Daniel Ortega and the communists." Democrats cried foul, and denounced the White House for a return to "Red-baiting McCarthyism."

Reagan didn't leave the rough stuff just to Buchanan. First in a weekend radio address and then in a prime-time televised speech to the nation on March 16, Reagan denounced the totalitarian and expansionist nature of the Sandinista regime. In a flourish redolent of John F. Kennedy's speeches about Cuba, Reagan pointed to a map of Central America in describing the flow of arms and mischief emanating from Nicaragua. He mentioned evidence of Sandinista revolutionary intent that was gleaned from documents captured in the Grenada invasion in 1983, and again embraced the Contras as freedom fighters deserving American support.

Reagan then turned up the heat directly on House Democrats:

Now comes the crucial test for the Congress of the United States. Will they provide the assistance the freedom fighters need to deal with Russian tanks and gunships, or will they abandon the democratic resistance to its Communist enemy? In answering that question, I hope Congress will reflect deeply upon what it is the resistance is fighting against in Nicaragua. Ask yourselves: What in the world are Soviets, East Germans, Bulgarians, North Koreans, Cubans, and terrorists from the PLO and the Red Brigades doing in our hemisphere, camped on our own doorstep? Is that for peace? Why have the Soviets invested $600 million to build Nicaragua into an armed force almost the size of Mexico's, a country 15 times as large and 25 times as populous. Is that for peace? Why did Nicaragua's dictator,

Daniel Ortega, go to the Communist Party Congress in Havana and endorse Castro's call for the worldwide triumph of communism? Was that for peace?

Not content with a statement of the case as he saw it, Reagan made a clever appeal to bipartisanship in foreign policy that highlighted how such bipartisanship was a thing of the past—a breach that, by implication, was the responsibility of a faction of Democrats. As he had in his 1983 and 1984 speeches about Central America, Reagan invoked Harry Truman and the Truman Doctrine:

> If we fail, there will be no evading responsibility—history will hold us accountable. This is not some narrow partisan issue; it is a national security issue, an issue on which we must act not as Republicans, not as Democrats, but as Americans. Forty years ago Republicans and Democrats joined together behind the Truman doctrine. It must be our policy, Harry Truman declared, to support peoples struggling to preserve their freedom. Under that doctrine, Congress sent aid to Greece just in time to save that country from the closing grip of a Communist tyranny. We saved freedom in Greece then. And with that same bipartisan spirit, we can save freedom in Nicaragua today.

Just to be sure no one missed the point, Reagan closed with a quotation from Clare Boothe Luce: "'Through all time to come, this, the 99th Congress of the United States, will be remembered as that body of men and women that either stopped the Communists before it was too late—or did not.'" Representative Mike Barnes, a staunch opponent of any Contra aid, said, "We just didn't have the votes if Reagan ever presented it that way."[10] Reagan's aggressiveness presented Democrats with a dilemma. While most opposed Contra aid, they were wary of being blamed if they blocked Reagan wholesale and the region slipped into chaos. By raising the stakes, Reagan upset the delicate political equilibrium.

However, despite his speech and the political offensive, public opinion still wasn't moving in Reagan's favor on the issue. "The numbers aren't with us on this," pollster Richard Wirthlin told the White House, "and they aren't changing." An ABC News poll after the speech found that 60 percent of Americans still opposed Contra aid, though public sentiment was clearly

fluid, as other polls showed an uptick in approval for Reagan's general handling of Central America. "Our people do not support what we're trying to
do in Nicaragua," Reagan ruefully noted in his diary. Polls in Central American nations, however, showed strong support for the Contras. Gallup found
69 percent support for the Contras in Costa Rica, 55 percent in Honduras,
54 percent in Guatemala, and 52 percent in El Salvador.[11]

On the eve of the House vote, the *New Republic* widened the fissures
among liberals with a long editorial endorsing military aid and criticizing liberal opposition:

> What is at stake in this civil war is any hope for a democratic
> Nicaragua. The end of the contras means the end of hope. And a ban
> on military aid will mean, sooner or later, the end of the contras.
> One would think that House Democrats, who for years have been
> urging, pushing, encouraging, threatening, and finally celebrating the
> return of democracy to the Philippines, would be eager to see democ-
> racy returned to Nicaragua. But they are not. Why? They put up a
> case that we find, for an issue of this gravity, stunningly weak.[12]

Thirteen contributing editors to the magazine signed a letter of protest
against the editorial, demonstrating the level of rancor over the issue.

Three days after Reagan's TV address the House voted on his request.
Tip O'Neill took the unusual step of making an impassioned speech from the
well of the House against Contra aid, and cast his vote when the roll opened,
which the Speaker rarely does. Reagan lost the initial House vote in March
by the close vote of 222–210, with sixteen House Republicans voting against
him. However, O'Neill had scored only a short-term tactical victory. A majority supported Reagan's proposal, but O'Neill was able to persuade a handful of moderate Democrats to stick with him for the moment in hopes of a
last-minute diplomatic concession from Managua. Instead, the next day
Nicaragua launched a fresh attack on the Contras across the border in Honduras. Honduras rushed five thousand troops toward the border, and when
Nicaragua shot down a Honduran helicopter inside Honduran territory it appeared a war between the two nations might break out. After hesitation by
the timorous Honduran government, which initially denied in public that a
Nicaraguan attack had taken place, the Hondurans requested U.S. assistance.
When U.S. helicopters began transporting Honduran troops to staging areas
near the border, Nicaragua got the message and backed off.

Democrats who opposed Reagan were once again embarrassed and angry with the Sandinistas. Tip O'Neill called Ortega "a bumbling, incompetent Marxist-Leninist Communist." A last-ditch effort to revive the Contadora process fizzled when the Sandinistas refused to consider a fresh round of concessions. It was a foregone conclusion that when the Contra aid package came up for reconsideration in the House in late June, it passed 221–209, with several of the previous Democratic no votes switching sides. Over in the Senate, which voted several weeks after the House, a number of Democrats also switched sides, most notably New Jersey's Bill Bradley. Virginia's new Democratic senator, Chuck Robb, said, "Americans won't stand behind a party that won't stand up for American values and interests abroad."

Although the restoration of military aid for the Contras represented a significant political victory for Reagan, his Nicaragua policy was still incoherent. Even with fresh military aid in the pipeline, the Contras would not be strong enough to overthrow the Sandinistas by force. No one held out much hope that Contra pressure would succeed in compelling the Sandinistas to allow a genuinely pluralistic democracy. The United States still maintained diplomatic relations with Nicaragua, eschewing the step of breaking relations and recognizing an exile government, which would have made U.S. policy more robust and direct. Several conservatives openly advocated such a course, but it was a nonstarter with Reagan and the State Department, as was the desire of some conservative leaders for direct U.S. military intervention to topple the Sandinistas. Reagan repeatedly expressed his opposition to direct intervention in his diary.[13] U.S. policy looked to be playing for time.

The slowness of the legislative and administrative process meant that cash and arms wouldn't begin reaching the Contras until late in the fall. Furthermore, the Boland Amendment's restrictions on CIA involvement would remain in force until October. Oliver North was intent on keeping the Contras alive in the interim with his private supply effort, abetted by the diversion of funds from the Iran arms-for-hostages effort, which entered a new phase in the spring of 1986.

*   *   *

DURING THE FIRST week in January 1986 Oliver North's idea to have the United States deal directly with Iran was complicated by a new Israeli proposal to act as middleman once again. This time, the United States would need to supply one thousand TOW missiles to Israel in advance, rather than replenishing Israeli inventory after the fact. The deal included something new: Iran wanted some U.S. intelligence information to aid in their war against Iraq, and also supposedly against Soviet incursions into Iranian air space. Here was the tantalizing hook that baited American interest and made the release of the hostages not so much a goal to be reached as an obstacle to be overcome in the interest of larger strategic questions.

All five American hostages were to be freed in the deal, after which Israel would also release a number of Hezbollah prisoners in their custody. In a series of National Security Council meetings in early January, over the continuing objections of Shultz and Weinberger but with the support of Casey and Vice President Bush, Reagan authorized the initiative to go forward. Reagan's later claim that he did not regard the initiative as primarily a straight arms-for-hostages deal is superficially buttressed by the terms of the finding, which placed the hostages third behind the objectives of encouraging a more moderate government in Iran (the United States, incredibly, believed a report that Khomeini was going to step down within weeks) and gaining counter-terrorism intelligence.

Later in January North headed to London to meet with Ghorbanifar, who was still the key middleman despite McFarlane's negative account of their December meeting and despite having dismally failed a new CIA polygraph examination (in which, according to several accounts, the polygraph registered that he was lying about his own name). In February a second meeting ensued in Frankfurt, West Germany, between North and an Iranian official whose exact position in Iran's government remained uncertain; from this meeting further confusion ensued. The one thousand TOW missiles were sent to Iran in two shipments in late February on Israeli airplanes. *But no hostages were released.* The Iranians complained through Ghorbanifar that the intelligence they received from the United States was "garbage," and furthermore, they wanted more and better missiles—three thousand more TOWs, along with HAWKs and Phoenix missiles suitable for shooting down high-altitude Soviet aircraft. North and his CIA adjuncts complained bitterly of having to put up with "rug merchant tactics" and wanted desperately to cut out Ghorbanifar as their principal point of contact with Iran, wondering whether he had correctly communicated U.S. demands that hostages be released as a part of the deal.

But Ghorbanifar's Iranian connections seemed good enough that, lacking an alternative channel, North and Poindexter decided there was no choice but to continue to work through him. North was mesmerized by the tantalizing prospect of a U.S. representative meeting directly with someone at the highest level of the Iranian government—it was suggested that it would be Akbar Hashemi Rafsanjani, speaker of the parliament—to work out the deal. North was also enthusiastic about the prospect of diverting significant profits from further arms sales to the Contras—as much as $12 million. In a five-page memo outlining the arms transactions North included a paragraph explicitly detailing the diversion plan; North passed the memo up the line for approval to Poindexter and, he hoped, President Reagan, but no copy with Reagan's signature was ever found.[14]

Out of this mess of mixed communication and doubtful motives was hatched the mission of sending Robert McFarlane to Tehran as the personal representative of President Reagan; it was hoped he could broker the release of all the hostages before any further arms were shipped. Ghorbanifar assured a wary McFarlane that he would meet with Rafsanjani, President Ali Hosayni Khamenei, and possibly the Ayatollah Khomeini's son Ahmed. On May 25 North and McFarlane traveled to Tehran equipped with phony Irish passports, suicide pills for use in the event of capture, and one pallet of HAWK missile parts.

McFarlane knew right away that something was amiss when there were no officials of any rank at the airport to meet their arriving plane. He and North were hustled off to a downtown hotel, narrowly avoiding arrest by Iranian Revolutionary Guards only after a parking-lot scuffle had taken place. When McFarlane was finally able to meet with low-level Iranian officials, it became immediately clear that Iran had taken no steps to secure the release of the hostages in Lebanon and was more interested in abusing the visiting Americans than in striking a deal. Ghorbanifar had misled both sides about what the other was prepared and able to deliver. McFarlane, disgusted, was ready to leave immediately.

But a second meeting was convened the next day, and then a third, at which time a more senior figure, an adviser to Speaker Rafsanjani, turned up. The mood improved slightly, with the outline of a possible deal once again seemingly in sight. The United States would dispatch another plane with additional missile parts if Iran would broker the hostages' release while the plane was en route. North and McFarlane were nearly ready to relent to an Iranian counteroffer to trade two hostages for the shipment of arms, with two more hostages to follow after the arms had arrived. But after more meetings and fresh contortions, this deal fell apart too. McFarlane and North packed up and left. The failure of McFarlane's mission, Reagan wrote in his diary, "was a heartbreaking disappointment for all of us." Some good came

of the errant venture, North thought. They received full payment for the partial shipment of weapons they had brought along, so at least the Contras
would be getting some support out of the deal (more than $3 million, in fact).
The Iranians complained, with reason, that they had been ripped off.

Once again the arms-for-hostages gambit should have ended. It didn't.
The administration was now so desperate about the hostages that a military
rescue operation was considered, but rejected for want of adequate intelligence. As spring gave way to summer a CIA agent, George Cave, and an
Israeli named Amiram Nir, both of whom had been part of the North-
McFarlane mission to Tehran, continued communicating with Iranian contacts about reviving the arms-for-hostages exchange. Ghorbanifar, whom all
sides thoroughly distrusted by this point, somehow remained in the middle of
the affair.

In late July a breakthrough seemed to have occurred: Iran released a
hostage—Father Lawrence Jenco, who had been held since January 1985.
But this goodwill gesture on the part of the Iranians turned out to be another
of Ghorbanifar's manipulations: unbeknownst to the United States, he had
told Iran that the United States would make good on the remaining HAWK
arms shipment from May if Iran arranged the release of a hostage. North and
Poindexter were furious. Poindexter noted bitterly in a memo that Ghorbanifar had "cooked up a story that if Iran could make a humanitarian gesture
then the U.S. would deliver the rest of the parts and then Iran would release
the rest of the hostages." But it was enough to restart the escapade, and they
honored the U.S. end of Ghorbanifar's deal, sending 240 HAWK missiles to
Iran on August 4. With Reagan's approval, North headed back to Europe in
early August to resume negotiations with Iran to swap arms for hostages.

North and his intermediaries had become thoroughly disgusted with
Ghorbanifar, and they opened a new channel to Iran through Ali Hashemi
Bahramani, the supposedly moderate nephew of Iranian parliament Speaker
Rafsanjani. North hosted Bahramani in Washington and even extended
him the privilege of a late-night tour of the White House. While North
began to negotiate another sequence of arms-for-hostages deals in early September, two more Americans were taken hostage in Beirut: Frank Herbert
Reed and Joseph Cicippio. North's new Iranian contacts said they were
taken by a Lebanese faction with whom Iran had little influence. A month
later yet another American, Edward Tracy, would be seized. Still negotiations proceeded.

Among the requests the new set of Iranian interlocutors presented was one of particular irony: couldn't the United States please take out Iran's arch-enemy, Saddam Hussein? In one conversation that was taped, North assured Bahramani that "he [President Reagan] knows that Hussein is a shit." The translator asked North, "Do you want me to translate that?" North: "Go ahead. That's his word, not mine." Despite North's professed sympathy for removing Hussein, Iran wasn't going to get the United States to do its dirty work against Iraq (yet), but after the usual back-and-forth with the Iranians another deal was struck in early October, the same day Reagan departed Washington to face off with Gorbachev in Reykjavik. Iran would get five hundred TOW missiles; the United States would get one hostage. There was talk that perhaps more hostages would be freed if Kuwait released some or all of the seventeen Shiite prisoners currently being held.

The TOW shipment arrived in Iran on October 28; five days later hostage David Jacobsen was released in Beirut. North and his team flew off to Mainz, West Germany, to follow up with Bahramani and press for more hostages to be released. Bahramani promised that more hostages would be let go shortly, but also conveyed the worrisome news that a student faction in Iran had published leaflets about the arms-for-hostages transactions that had all the essential details. There had already been talk in the Middle Eastern rumor mill that the Americans had been dealing with Iran over arms and hostages, and it now appeared that the entire covert house of cards was on the brink of collapse.

On November 3 the story blew wide open. The Lebanese newspaper *Al-Shiraa* published a detailed account of what had taken place, including McFarlane's secret trip to Tehran in May. The next day—Election Day back in the United States—the Iranian government confirmed the story, but also sent word to North that they hoped the operation would continue. Amazingly, Poindexter and North still wanted to carry on with more arms transactions in spite of the public disclosure; Shultz forcefully put an end to this nonsense. The news immediately set off a mad scramble inside the White House as a media frenzy erupted.

As Poindexter and North began covering their tracks, including preparing false chronologies of events and destroying documents, Reagan made the first of several serious mistakes. Three days after the *Al-Shiraa* story broke, Reagan denied it, saying there was "no foundation" to the report of McFarlane's secret trip and stating, "We will never pay off terrorists because that only encourages more of it." At a White House appearance the next day with freed hostage David Jacobsen, Reagan and Jacobsen pleaded with the press to stop pursuing the matter, as their agitation threatened to prevent the release of other hostages. North and his crew were at that moment in Geneva meeting again with the Iranians hoping for yet another deal.

There was no way Reagan's position was going to hold or the media frenzy die down. Early the following week Reagan delivered a televised speech to the nation and held a follow-up press conference. While admitting that the initiative had been a "high-risk gamble," Reagan said that "[t]he United States has not made concessions to those who hold our people captive in Lebanon, and we will not." In his mind the indirect connections between the United States and the hostage takers by way of Iran was enough for him to believe he had not contradicted U.S. policy. But he did admit to the two-step dynamic of the operation: "During the course of our secret discussions, I authorized the transfer of small amounts of defensive weapons and spare parts for defensive systems to Iran. My purpose was to convince Tehran that our negotiators were acting with my authority, to send a signal that the United States was prepared to replace the animosity between us with a new relationship. These modest deliveries, taken together, could easily fit into a single cargo plane." This last claim was untrue, though Reagan repeated it again at his press conference a few days later. He also denied at the press conference that Israel had been involved. An hour after the press conference ended, Reagan put out a correction, admitting that "there was a third country involved in our secret project with Iran."

The damage control effort was not off to a good start. A *Los Angeles Times* poll found that only 14 percent of Americans believed Reagan's denial that he had swapped arms for hostages, and over the next few weeks Reagan's overall approval rating plummeted from 67 percent to 46 percent. It was the largest one-month decline in the history of the Gallup poll; by February 1987 Reagan had fallen further, to a 40 percent approval rating. The Iran initiative not only appeared to defy policy; it defied common sense. If there was one country Americans hated more than the Soviet Union, it was Iran. Reagan himself had described Iran a few months before as an "outlaw state, run by the strangest collection of misfits, looney tunes and squalid criminals since the advent of the Third Reich." Republican governor William Janklow of South Dakota said, "There are not five people out there who want to send arms to Iran. The only way we want to give them arms is dropping them from the bay of a B-1 bomber." Another pithy sound bite that accurately captured the cognitive dissonance of the story came from an unnamed Reagan appointee: "It's like suddenly learning that John Wayne had secretly been selling liquor and firearms to the Indians."

The media feasted on anonymous sources in the State Department, Pentagon, and CIA who had opposed the operation and who relished the opportunity to trash North and the NSC. Congress was in an uproar and announced plans for hearings. The White House briefly considered invoking executive privilege against congressional demands for documents and testimony, but backed off for fear of a political firestorm.[15] As senior administration officials prepared for the weekend news talk shows and hastily arranged congressional hearings, it became apparent that there was deep confusion about what actually had taken place and whether correct legal procedures had been followed. The proximate issue was the circumstances of the HAWK missile shipment of September 1985; there was much that seemed amiss, from the CIA's knowledge and involvement to whether Reagan had approved it. And the only people who knew, chiefly Poindexter and North, were busy covering their tracks. Speculation grew that Shultz was going to resign; in fact, he had passed word to Reagan that he would resign unless Reagan fired National Security Adviser Poindexter. Reagan noted archly in his diary, "I don't like ultimatums."

Outgoing senator Barry Goldwater bluntly expressed the problem: "I think President Reagan has gotten his butt in a crack on this Iran thing," calling it "probably one of the major mistakes the United States had ever made in foreign policy." Washington was abuzz with the phrase that the Iranian escapade could be a "new Watergate," a fact Reagan noted bitterly in his diary: "This whole irresponsible press bilge about hostages and Iran has gotten totally out of hand. The media looks like it's trying to create another Watergate." He had no idea the other shoe was about to drop.

*   *   *

AT THE SAME time the secrecy of the Iranian arms dealing was starting to unravel, the veil over North's Contra supply operation was coming undone too. On October 5 the Sandinistas shot down a cargo plane carrying weapons for the Contras that had been chartered by North's operation. The pilots were killed, but one of the crew, Eugene Hasenfus, survived and was captured. The Sandinistas paraded Hasenfus in front of the media, and his photo appeared on the front page of U.S. newspapers the next day. Under interrogation Hasenfus admitted the CIA's involvement in his mission, identifying by name a CIA agent operating in El Salvador. The U.S. government, including Reagan, denied any U.S. involvement. "There was no government connection with that at all," Reagan told reporters. Administration officials, including North and Assistant Secretary of State for Latin America Elliott

Abrams (though Abrams was unaware of North's fund diversion from the Iran arms sales), had testified in various congressional hearings that they were not involved in the private Contra supply efforts. The latest Boland Amendment's restrictions on CIA involvement with the Contras were to be lifted as of October 17, but the capture of Hasenfus indicated that someone in the U.S. government had jumped the gun and violated a law still in force. The most worrisome red flag was that the downed plane had been chartered from Southern Air Transport—the same company that the CIA had used to make one of the arms shipments to Iran.

As the controversy boiled over into its third week and concern mounted among lawyers at the White House, State Department, and CIA, Attorney General Ed Meese launched an internal investigation to clear up the discrepancies in the stories being told, along with other unresolved factual and legal questions. Assistant Attorney General William Bradford Reynolds was reviewing National Security Council documents from Oliver North's files on Saturday morning, November 22, when he came across the North memo from the previous April that summarized the TOW missile transaction of September 1985. When Reynolds came to a paragraph stating that "$12 million [of the proceeds] will be used to purchase critically needed supplies for the Nicaraguan Democratic Resistance," he said, "Holy shit!"

Meese confronted North the next day. North, who by that time had shredded hundreds of documents, was surprised that he had missed one. But he improvised on the spot, claiming the diversion of funds to the Contras was an Israeli operation from start to finish, with minimal involvement by him. Meese, sensing a cover-up and knowing the political disaster that it would cause, decided the matter needed to be publicly disclosed as soon as possible. Meese and his assistants weren't immediately sure whether the diversion was necessarily illegal, but the specter of impeachment was plain.

One very large question loomed: had Reagan known about this? The circumstantial evidence suggests he did not. Don Regan said that "the color drained from Reagan's face" when Meese told him of the diversion the next morning. In his diary Reagan wrote: "Our Col. North (NSC) gave the money [from the Iran arms sale] to the 'Contras.' This was a violation of the law against giving the Contras money without authorization from Congress. North didn't tell me about this." Reagan later told the media, in response to a question as to whether he could have forgotten he had been told: "Oh, no. You would have heard me without opening the door if I had been told that." North's "diversion memo," as it came to be known, included the standard check boxes at the end for Reagan to indicate his approval or disapproval. There was no check mark on the copy Meese's team had found and there is no other evidence that North's memo ever got to Reagan, which doesn't rule out the possibility that Reagan could have seen or checked off another of the five copies of the diversion memo that North is known to have prepared and destroyed.

Don Regan observed: "I doubt there was a single reporter who believed in his or her heart that Oliver North, a mere lieutenant colonel, had done what he had done without the approval of higher—much higher—authority."[16] Much later North would assert that Reagan knew of the diversion and approved "enthusiastically," though North never claimed to have received a signed copy of the diversion memo. But North was a decidedly less-than-trustworthy source. (In the weeks after the initial scandal broke—but before the diversion was discovered—North put out one story to sympathetic journalists that the Iranian arms transactions were part of an urgent initiative to prevent a Soviet invasion of Iran. To an NSC colleague, North put out a markedly different story—that he had ordered the kidnapping of senior Iranian officials, whom he was planning to swap for the American hostages.)[17] Reflecting on this claim, Peter Wallison wrote, "I have never understood why North—who can so easily call Ronald Reagan a liar—has been treated as a hero by the same people who profess to admire Reagan."[18] The final irony is that the enemies and critics of Reagan who hoped to take him down with his approval of a possibly illegal act were hoisted by their own petard: having claimed for six years that Reagan was "out of touch" and a "creature of his staff," they were now stuck with a narrative theme that made his denials wholly plausible to the public. "What did Reagan know," Jeff Greenfield asked, "and when did he forget it?"

The question of Reagan's direct knowledge, while important, was secondary because he was responsible and accountable as chief executive for the actions of his administration. As soon as Reagan disclosed the diversion in a tumultuous press conference the next day (along with the firings of Poindexter and North), it was inevitable that Washington would go into full-scale post-Watergate scandal mode, complete with televised congressional hearings, a special presidential commission, an independent counsel investigation that would last years, and above all a media feeding frenzy.

Over the next three months the *Washington Post* published 555 separate stories about the scandal; the *New York Times* printed 509. The glittering spectacle of a Watergate rerun was on the mind of every partisan Democrat in Washington. Despite all the sanctimonious pontificating of the pundits and "responsible" party leaders on the disastrous prospect of "another failed presidency," liberals and most Democrats were positively giddy—a fact that Michael Kinsley was at least honest enough to admit: "Am I really the only one here who is having a good time? Simple honesty requires any Washington type to admit that this is the kind of episode we all live for. The adrenaline is flowing like Perrier. . . . Dry those tears and repeat after me: Ha. Ha. Ha."[19] "Young reporters all over town have visions of Pulitzer Prizes dancing in their heads," Hugh Sidey admitted in *Time*. Liberal author Greg Grandin recalled the mood: "Democrats couldn't believe their luck. After years of banging their heads on Reagan's popularity and failing to derail his legislative agenda, they had not only taken back the Senate, but follow-up investigations soon uncovered a scandal of epic proportions, arguably the most consequential in American history, one that seemed sure to disgrace every single constituency that had fueled the upstart conservative movement. The Reagan Revolution, it appeared, had finally been thrown into reverse."[20]

In other words, it was showtime in Washington.

*   *   *

THE FIRST AND most immediate difficulty for Reagan and the White House staff was that they simply *didn't know all the facts*. Key documents had been destroyed. The central figures, especially Poindexter and North, had lawyered up and weren't talking, and couldn't be trusted even if they did talk. Rumors flew that Poindexter and North would implicate Reagan as having had full knowledge of the diversion. But North and Poindexter, called hastily before congressional hearings, pled the Fifth and refused to testify.

Reagan was determined not to repeat the blunders of Nixon that had protracted the Watergate agony, so he quickly (but unwisely) waived executive privilege with regard to White House documents, sought the appointment of an independent counsel to pursue possible criminal charges, and brought in a cabinet-level outside counselor, the well-regarded David Abshire, to troubleshoot the matter from inside the White House and coordinate with the special Tower Commission that Reagan appointed to look into the matter. These decisions, taken in understandable haste, meant yielding much of the principled ground upon which to defend his policy and his administration.

These concessions exacerbated the second problem: getting Reagan to acknowledge and admit publicly what really had happened—an ill-advised arms-for-hostages transaction with Iran. "As the crisis continued," Peter Wallison wrote, "the White House staff came unanimously to the conclusion that the President should tell the American people that he had made a mistake by not properly supervising his national security staff. To us, this was an easy call—reminiscent of Kennedy's successful mea culpa after the Bay of Pigs." Reagan stoutly resisted this advice. Wallison attributes his stubbornness to the implicit rebuke it would have meant for Reagan's delegation-heavy management style.[21] But Reagan was also misled by his potent imagination. As far back as the TWA 847 hijacking crisis, he had entertained the view that meeting terrorist demands without directly bargaining with terrorists—through the kind of indirect, two-steps-removed process that became central to the Iranian arms transactions—was compatible with his sense of morals and honor. To be told otherwise was a bitter pill. "I don't care if I am the only person in America that does not believe it," Reagan barked at David Abshire when Abshire tried to persuade him of the necessity to acknowledge arms-for-hostages; "I *don't* believe it was arms for hostages."[22] It was going to be an uphill battle to change his mind.

Several other well-known Reagan traits were in evidence in the early going of the controversy, such as his reluctance to fire people who deserved it. He expressed genuine regret at Poindexter's departure (technically a resignation, but in reality a firing), and he called Oliver North on the telephone to express sympathy and laud him as "an American hero." (It would be some weeks before Reagan, better informed about North's improvisations, became shocked and angry.) And he mishandled the dismissal of Chief of Staff Don Regan, at first resisting the mounting calls (including from Vice President Bush and the first lady) for his firing, and then failing to execute the deed in a dignified manner. In his encounters with the Tower Commission he was confused and contradictory, displaying lack of memory of key details (such as whether he had approved the first arms shipment to Iran before or after the fact) and ultimately drafting a disconcerting letter in which he pled that "I don't remember—period. I'm afraid that I let myself be influenced by others' recollections, not my own." Above all, by every account his reserves of optimism and cheerfulness were fully depleted; at times he was visibly downcast or subdued. His annual State of the Union speech to Congress, delivered on January 27, 1987, ten days before his seventy-sixth birthday, was widely panned as a lackluster performance for the Great Communicator. (The fact that Reagan unveiled the federal government's first trillion-dollar budget, not the kind of milestone to make a conservative cheerful, contributed to the downbeat mood.) His own advisers commiserated that the administration was "dead in the water," and after the last lingering contacts with Iran regarding further arms-for-hostage swaps were finally ended decisively in January, three more Americans were taken hostage in Beirut: Robert Polhill, Alann Steen, and Jesse Turner.

It took the Tower Commission report, released the last week of February, to begin to turn the tide. The report was harsh on Reagan for his lax management style, and also gave low scores to all of Reagan's top appointees, including Shultz and Weinberger, but especially his national security advisers, McFarlane and Poindexter. The normal deliberative and review processes of the National Security Council were not followed, and the NSC was improperly placed in charge of conducting covert operations directly. "The NSC system will not work unless the President makes it work," the Tower Commission concluded in its summary findings. The Tower Commission did not, however, find any conclusive evidence of illegality on either end of the Iran-Contra affair, though it admitted that its legal investigation was not exhaustive, and it exonerated Reagan of any attempted cover-up. As R. W. Apple of the *New York Times* summarized the meaning of the Tower Commission report, "This is not a portrait of venality. It is a portrait of ineptitude verging on incompetence."

The Tower Report was the last nail in Don Regan's political coffin: "More than almost any chief of staff of recent memory, he asserted personal control over the White House staff and sought to extend his control to the national security adviser. He, as much as anyone, should have insisted that an orderly process be observed." Regan was in the grip of the kind of pincer movement that Washington's media and political class had down to an art form, and he was out a week later. His replacement was the man who had posed the fatal question to Nixon ("What did the president know and when did he know it?"), former Tennessee senator Howard Baker. One dramatic sign of how demoralized the White House had become was the suggestion that Baker and the cabinet consider invoking the Twenty-fifth Amendment, which provides for the involuntary retirement of the president in the event that he is unable to discharge the office due to incapacity.

The Tower Commission broke down Reagan's last resistance to acknowledging that the Iran initiative, however it began and whatever he thought its best motives might be, had degenerated into a ransom scheme. A few days after gulping through the Tower Commission's briefing in the White House, Reagan faced the public in a televised address from the Oval Office.

"A few days ago, I told the American people that I did not trade arms for hostages. My heart and my best intentions tell me that was true, but the facts and the evidence tell me it is not."[23] He again denied knowing of the diversion of funds to the Contras, "but as president I cannot escape responsibility." There would be "no more freelancing by individuals when it comes to our national security."

The speech worked. The *New York Times* noted, as Reagan's staff had expected, that "not since John F. Kennedy took the blame for the catastrophic Bay of Pigs invasion in 1961 has any president so openly confessed error." Opinion polls showed an immediate uptick in public approval for Reagan; for the first time in three months, he was back over 50 percent (51 percent in the CBS News poll). It was Reagan's second recovery from a very low public approval rating (the first being in 1983 when the economy turned around), making him the first and only president ever to come back from two such steep swoons in public esteem. Reagan was ready to move on, but this was not the end of the story, nor even the end of his political peril. Congress still had to get in its licks. The completion of the Tower Commission's work was merely intermission; the climax was just beginning.

*　　*　　*

IN TYPICAL FASHION, the intricate and sordid details that fed the Washington theater surrounding Iran-Contra and the sustained outrage of what might be called the scandal industry subsumed the deeper constitutional and political issues at the heart of the matter. While it was wholly legitimate to investigate whether the CIA violated the Boland Amendment or whether McFarlane, North, and their compatriots violated the Arms Export Control Act and other statutes, there was something perverse about the fact that, in regard to the diversion of funds to the Contras, Congress and an independent counsel were looking to criminalize a policy that Congress now *approved*.

The constitutional controversy over Iran-Contra was the latest skirmish in the institutional struggle between the president and Congress to control foreign policy. The tensions between the president and Congress over foreign policy go back to the Founding, as the Constitution is deliberately ambiguous about the dividing line between the branches. The Constitution singles out the president as the commander in chief of the armed forces—giving him the power to make war—as well as denoting his clear authority to conduct foreign policy and diplomacy. Yet the Constitution reserved for Congress the power to declare war, as well as the power of the purse over the military and the "advice and consent" function on treaty making. In fact, a seldom-noted clause of Article I holds that no congressional appropriation for military purposes "be for a longer term than two years," a restrictive clause undoubtedly owing to the Republican suspicion of standing armies. But there is no express requirement of congressional consent for the president to make war, and in fact Congress has formally declared war only five times in American history, while the nation has engaged in more than a hundred armed conflicts, always at the instigation of the president.

Congress was within its rights to deny using taxpayer funds for the Contras, but whether it could restrain the president from supporting the Contras in other ways, such as soliciting private support or support from other nations, is doubtful. Private American support for the Abraham Lincoln Brigade in the Spanish Civil War was mentioned as a precedent (and indeed, several left-wing groups such as CISPES sent private funds to the Marxist guerillas in El Salvador in the 1980s), along with the powerful precedent of President Franklin Roosevelt transferring fifty U.S. destroyers to Britain in defiance of the Neutrality Act—a step that, legally speaking, was arguably just as impeachable as any of the Reagan administration's actions. The *Wall Street Journal*'s L. Gordon Crovitz put his finger on the crux of the issue: "The same Constitution can't give Presidents Wilson and Roosevelt the power to get the country into world wars, while at the same time deny today's executive branch the right to send TOW missiles to Iran and funding to the contras."[24] To which might be added that there was something obviously wrong with a legislative landscape in which it was permissible for the administration to provide support to anti-Communist resistance forces in faraway Afghanistan, Angola, and Cambodia but not in nearby Nicaragua.

By its very nature as a plural body, the legislative branch cannot be as responsible and accountable as the executive branch—a distinction that was much on the mind of the Framers in Philadelphia in 1787.[25] In fact, there is a strong case that it was the inconstant actions of Congress that led to the circumstance in which a marine lieutenant colonel was operating major foreign policy initiatives on behalf of the president—initiatives that would have been legitimate in the absence of pusillanimous congressional restrictions. It is highly debatable whether any version of the Boland Amendment legally applied to the president and his staff. But if the fundamental constitutional latitude of the president to conduct foreign policy limited the reach of the Boland Amendment, then its limits on executive branch agencies such as the CIA were perhaps equally dubious. Ironically, the person who best understood this was Oliver North, who sent a memo to Poindexter in June 1986 that read: "What we most need is to get the CIA re-engaged in this effort so that it can be better managed than it is now by one slightly confused lieutenant colonel."

Reagan would have vetoed most or all of the five successive Boland Amendments had they been presented to him as stand-alone laws rather than wrapped into omnibus budget bills that he could not veto without shutting down the government.[26] But neither did he ever challenge the constitutionality or legal reach of Boland, either directly through litigation or through signing a statement that would have put an executive branch interpretation on the record.

The constitutional questions involved are essentially unsolvable in any bright-line way because of the necessary ambiguity of executive power itself.[27] During the course of the Iran-Contra affair numerous scholars and intellectuals dusted off John Locke's *Second Treatise on Government*—the text that had been the primary inspiration for the Declaration of Independence. Locke's understanding of the nature of prerogative in the executive was equally important to the Founders as they designed the office of the presidency. Locke defined *prerogative* simply as *"nothing but the power of doing public good without a rule"* (emphasis in original). Why "without a rule"? Because, Locke explained, "[M]any things there are which the law can by no means provide for. . . . [M]any accidents may happen wherein a strict and rigid observation of the laws may do harm." Indeed, Locke went as far as to say that "it is fit that the laws themselves should in some cases give way to the executive power. . . . [The executive must have] the power to act according to discretion for the public good, without the prescription of the law, *and sometimes even against it"* (emphasis added).[28]

Locke's defense of prerogative is plainly a holdover of the historical latitude of European monarchs, whose frequent abuses prompted the rise of parliamentary democracy. Executive prerogative is a concept that cannot by its very nature be delimited through formal legal means, and as such it sits uneasily within the context of American formalistic constitutionalism. In the view of the Founders the abuse of executive prerogative is meant to be checked by the separation of powers, and congressional oversight and legislation are both necessary and proper. But even within congressional assertion of its own prerogative to check executive power, the residue of the Lockean understanding of the executive's latitude for action is evident. The National Security Act, for example, recognizes the general need for secrecy and discretion by providing that the president must notify Congress about covert operations "in a timely manner," but there are no legislative or judicial parameters of timeliness. Reagan never notified anyone in Congress of the Iran initiative during the year prior to its exposure in November 1986. But obviously if he had it would have been on the front page of the *Washington Post* the next day, just as deliberations of possible covert actions against Libya in 1986 were leaked to the *Post* and caused the idea to be abandoned.[29]

Examples of presidential use of prerogative power in American history include Jefferson's decision to consummate the Louisiana Purchase despite his own constitutional doubts, Lincoln's suspension of habeas corpus in 1861 (the Constitution expressly stipulates that suspension of habeas corpus "in times of rebellion" is a congressional, not executive, power), Theodore Roosevelt's sailing of the Great White Fleet in 1907 in the absence of congressional authorization, and Franklin Roosevelt's various transgressions of the Neutrality Act.[30] These and other examples fit Alexander Hamilton's conception in the *Federalist* of the presidency as the locus of the government's "extensive and arduous enterprises." Jefferson, channeling Locke, argued in 1810: "A strict observance of the laws is doubtless *one* of the high duties of a good citizen, but it is not *the highest*. The laws of necessity, of self-preservation, of saving our country when it is in danger, are of higher obligation. To lose our country by a scrupulous adherence of written law, would be to lose the law itself."[31] On the other hand, Nixon showed the limits of the concept when he infamously argued that "[i]f the president does it, it's not illegal"—an assertion the American public rejected.

Between Jefferson and Nixon, how is this delicate matter to be judged? While scholars and constitutional lawyers will argue for bright-line standards, the example of Nixon suggests the answer that Locke gives explicitly: the people shall judge. "The people," Locke wrote, "observing the whole tendency of their actions to be the public good, contested not what was done without law to that end, or, if any human frailty or mistake—for princes are but men, made as others—appeared in some small declinations from that end, yet it was visible the main of their conduct tended to nothing but the care of the public. The people, therefore, finding reason to be satisfied with these princes whenever they acted without or contrary to the letter of the law, acquiesced in what they did."[32]

The outcome of the constitutional struggle over the Iran-Contra matter would be decided in the same way—by public judgment of the political clash in Washington. Reagan and his political advisers, noting low poll numbers on his Nicaraguan policy, had shied away from a sustained public fight over the issue. On the other hand, moderate Democrats didn't want to be tagged with the responsibility for "losing Nicaragua" and halfheartedly supported Contra aid some of the time at least. The scandal put an end to this debilitating equilibrium and forced the partisan divisions into the open. The American people finally paid close attention to the most extensive debate to date on the issue of Central America, albeit confused by its combination with the ill-considered Iran initiative. What Democrats and the media didn't grasp was that the arms sales to Iran were much more objectionable to the public than was the covert support of the Contras. But it was the Contra diversion that played to the political left. Senator Daniel Inouye (D-Hawaii), the co-chair of the subsequent congressional investigation, made clear in his opening statement that it was the Contra diversion that was the chief target of the investigation. Democrats immediately seized upon the fund diversion angle to attempt to cut off the Contras once again. "They will not get another nickel," an aide to Senator Alan Cranston (D-Calif.) told a reporter. In March the House voted by a margin of 230–196, largely along party lines, to withhold the final $40 million of Contra aid that had passed the year before; a week later the Senate voted down the same measure by the close vote of 52–48. (Eight Republican senators voted with most Democrats for the cutoff.)

Like Watergate, Iran-Contra was portrayed as a legal controversy, and there were direct echoes of Watergate, such as the query "What did the president know, and when did he know it?" If Reagan could be shown to have known about the dubious diversion of funds to the Contras, he could be impeached and potentially convicted. Historian Louis Fisher, author of a leading study of presidential war powers, argued: "If President Reagan had authorized the theory propounded by Poindexter and North, he would have invited, and deserved, impeachment proceedings."[33] If the cherished goal of impeachment proved out of reach, at least the investigation could be used to put the nail in the coffin of Reagan's Central America policy. "No one wanted another Nixon," Theodore Draper wrote, while Democratic congressman Lee Hamilton, chairman of the House Intelligence Committee, said, "There's no one who wants to see a presidency crippled." Both statements were nonsense. No amount of legalese could disguise the partisan and ideological fault lines at the base of the scandal. Congressional Democrats licked their chops at the prospect of televised summer hearings, at which the ghosts of H. R. Haldeman, John Ehrlichman, Howard Hunt, John Dean, and Gordon Liddy would haunt the visages of McFarlane, Poindexter, and especially

Iran-Contra's Hunt and Liddy analogue, Oliver North. Just as North was the key figure in generating the scandal in the first instance, he would now be the pivot on which the scandal reached its denouement.

The Democrats, who now ran both houses of Congress, made three key decisions that altered the dynamic of the subsequent Iran-Contra hearings to their detriment. First, they decided to form a special joint House-Senate committee co-chaired by Senator Inouye and Representative Lee Hamilton (D-Ind.), instead of allowing each house to conduct its own separate hearings, which would be duplicative, cumbersome, and confusing. But this meant that the committee would include feisty House Republicans such as Henry Hyde, Jim Courter, William Broomfield, and especially House GOP whip Dick Cheney—Republicans used to brawling effectively against Democrats on the House floor. Among the Senate Republicans on the joint committee, only Utah senator Orrin Hatch matched the fighting spirit of the House Republicans. Second, because North invoked his Fifth Amendment right against self-incrimination, the committee struck a bargain with the reluctant independent counsel, Lawrence Walsh, to grant North immunity in exchange for his testimony. Democrats were convinced that North would be the star witness and the key to the success of the hearings. Third, North's aggressive defense counsel, Brendan Sullivan, won a crucial concession from the committee in addition to immunity: he got the committee to waive deposing North privately before his appearance at the public hearings. Unknown to most of the viewing public, most high-profile congressional hearings are largely scripted in advance by means of prior depositions. In this case, the committee didn't know what North's testimony would be.

Democrats weren't worried by this concession. The committee had been very tough on many of the witnesses preceding North. But it did not go according to the Watergate-revival script. Several of the early witnesses gave robust performances before the committee, especially retired air force major general Richard Secord, the point man in North's Contra supply operation, and former national security adviser Robert McFarlane. The public was reacting negatively to the televised hearings. Fred Barnes observed, "Both the members and the staff seemed mean, prosecutorial, petty, and unfair."

Committee Democrats thought North would turn things around. Much of the testimony was highly damaging to him, culminating with the testimony of Justice Department attorney Charles Cooper, a highly respected conservative, that North could not be trusted to tell the truth, even under oath. The White House had begun putting as much distance as possible between themselves and North, calling him a "rogue colonel." "The committee members and staffers expected a ritual sacrifice, with North the victim," Michael Ledeen recalls. North had reportedly been hospitalized for "emotional distress" in 1974 (though no medical records of this could be found), and "[h]ours were spent discussing what to do if, as many of them fully expected, North broke down in the witness chair."[34] Senate Democratic counsel Arthur Liman promised a "rigorous cross-examination" of North "in full view of the American people." Many of the Republicans on the joint committee were ready to cast North to the wolves.

On the morning of July 7, 1987, North showed up in the Senate Caucus Room on the third floor of the Russell Senate Office Building—the same room where Joe McCarthy had held forth in the 1950s and the Watergate hearings of 1973 had taken place—dressed in his crisp marine officer's uniform, festooned with six decks of service ribbons and a row of medals. North's formal military bearing and rugged handsomeness offered a stark visual contrast to the motley appearance of his chief inquisitors, Democratic legal counsels John Nields and Arthur Liman. Opposite North, both men appeared slightly seedy; one reporter called Nields "the most wonderful geek I've ever seen." Nields sported a mop of stringy, greasy hair, near shoulder length in back but receding in front. Liman's visage was even worse; with his wavy black hair and round face (not to mention caustic demeanor) he resembled H. L. Mencken out of the 1940s. Liman became, in the words of Brit Hume of ABC News, "the Howard Cosell of the hearings—the man the TV audience would love to hate."

Democrats were determined to get right to work on North, invoking a seldom-enforced rule denying North the opportunity to make an opening statement to the committee because he had failed to submit his statement forty-eight hours in advance. Directly Chairman Inouye turned the hearing over to House Democratic counsel Nields. North may have been imprudent and untruthful, but before the committee his was not the countenance of a guilty man. He understood that offense is the best defense and charged at the committee as if he were charging an enemy position on the battlefield, quickly turning the tables and never yielding the initiative for the duration of his seven days of testimony.

From the outset it was clear Nields was after evidence and testimony that would incriminate Reagan, and to set perjury traps with which to ensnare North. North promptly blunted Nields with a stout defense of the propriety of covert operations and a lecture on the constitutional principle of the separation of powers. Sometimes Nields led with his chin, giving North perfect openings to display his brio.

MR. NIELDS: [Covert] operations are designed to be secrets from the American people?

LT. COL. NORTH: Mr. Nields, I'm at a loss as to how we could announce it to the American people and not have the Soviets know about it. . . .

MR. NIELDS: In certain Communist countries, the government activities are kept secret from the people. But it's not the way we do things in America, is it?

LT. COL. NORTH: I would like to go back to what I said just a few moments ago. I think it is very important for the American people to understand that this nation is at risk in a dangerous world. And that they ought not to be led to believe, as a consequence of these hearings, that this nation cannot or should not conduct covert operations. By their very nature covert operations or special activities are a lie. There is great deceit, deception practiced in the conduct of covert operations. . . . The American people ought not to be led to believe by the way you are asking that question that we intentionally deceived the American people, or had that intent to begin with.

Nields had the wit to see he was losing this debate and changed tactics, but North had established his mastery.[35] North defiantly celebrated that he had shredded documents and lied to Congress, confounding the efforts of the committee to put him on the defensive. Nields's efforts at sarcasm fell flat.

MR. NIELDS: When you pushed the "delete" button on the PROF system, it didn't erase your memory, did it?

LT. COL. NORTH: No.

North, who had won a famous boxing match against James Webb (in 2006 elected a Democratic U.S. senator from Virginia) at the Naval Academy, got in many effective jabs at Nields.

MR. NIELDS: I think the first thing to do is refer you to Exhibit 18. That is a chronology that bears the date and time, November 17, 1986, two thousand—which I take is 8 p.m.

LT. COL. NORTH: Twenty hundred.

MR. NIELDS: I'm sorry, twenty hundred.

LT. COL. NORTH: Military time.

It was a small slip on Nields's part, but it reinforced the contrast between the duty-conscious military officer and the partisan civilian lawyer. Another exchange:

LT. COL. NORTH: I have Exhibit 88. Begins with a unit?
MR. NIELDS: Yes. And up at the top it says F. M. Goode [a code name].
LT. COL. NORTH: Yes.
MR. NIELDS: I take it you were Goode?
LT. COL. NORTH: I was very good.

But it was North's long soliloquies attacking Congress and defending the "freedom fighters" and "democratic resistance" in Nicaragua that proved most resounding.

LT. COL. NORTH: I don't know, to this day, what the President knew I, personally, was doing. I hope to God that people were keeping him apprised as to the effect of it. Because if we hadn't done it, there wouldn't have been a Nicaraguan resistance around when the Congress got around to putting up $100 million for it—sir. . . . The President ought to be aware of what a handful of people did to keep the Nicaraguan resistance alive at a time when nobody in this Congress seemed to care. And it's important that the President know that good men gave inordinate amounts of time, and some gave their lives, to support that activity. And some of them have been brutally treated by what has come about in these two parallel investigations—brutally treated.

North ended the first day on a high note.

MR. NIELDS: And [the President] certainly didn't tell you to stop?
LT. COL. NORTH: Why would he? We were conducting a covert operation to support the Nicaraguan resistance, to carry out the President of the United States' stated publicly, articulated foreign policy. Why should he tell me to stop? We weren't breaking any laws, we were simply trying to keep an operation covert.

He might as well have added: *You got a problem with that?*
Nields questioned North for a second full day, during which North readily admitted lying to Congress, falsifying and destroying key documents, and conducting covert operations without correct legal authorization, arguing that "we all had to weigh in the balance the difference between lives and

lies." He also said defiantly, "I still, to this day, counsel, don't see anything wrong with taking the Ayatollah's money and sending it to support the 'Nicaraguan freedom fighters." Most important, though, was his spirited defense of executive prerogative:

LT. COL. NORTH: [T]his great institution can pass laws that say no such [covert] activities can ever be conducted again. But that would be wrong, and you and I know that. The fact is, this country does need to be able to conduct those kind of activities. And the President ought not to be in a position, in my humble opinion, of having to go out and explain to the American people, on a biweekly basis or any other kind, that I, the President, am carrying out the following secret operations. It just can't be done. No nation in the world will ever help us again—and we desperately need that kind of help—if we are to survive, given our adversaries.

On the third day of his testimony North was finally allowed to give his opening statement, and he unloaded on Congress for its lack of responsibility and seriousness in the conduct of foreign policy:

I believe that it is a strange process that you are putting me and others through. Apparently, the President has chosen not to assert his prerogatives, and you have been permitted to make the rules. . . . One thing is I think for certain—you will not investigate yourselves in this matter. There is not much chance that you will conclude at the end of these hearings that the Boland Amendments and the frequent policy changes therefore were unwise or that your restrictions should not have been imposed on the Executive Branch. You are not likely to conclude that the Administration acted properly by trying to sustain the freedom fighters in Nicaragua when they were abandoned, and you are not likely to conclude by commending the President of the United States who tried valiantly to recover our citizens and achieve a vital opening that is strategically vital—Iran.

North was just warming up. He reached back and threw a roundhouse punch directly at Congress:

It is difficult to be caught in the middle of a constitutional struggle between the Executive and legislative branches over who will formulàte and direct the foreign policy of this nation. . . . [S]ome here have attempted to criminalize policy differences between co-equal branches of government and the Executive's conduct of foreign affairs. I believe it is inevitable that the Congress will in the end blame the Executive Branch, but I suggest to you that it is the Congress which must accept some of the blame in the Nicaraguan freedom fighters' matter. Plain and simple, Congress is to blame because of the fickle, vacillating, unpredictable, on-again off-again policy toward the Nicaraguan Democratic Resistance. . . . [By cutting off funds] the Congress of the United States left soldiers in the field unsupported and vulnerable to their Communist enemies. When the Executive Branch did everything possible within the law to prevent them from being wiped out by Moscow's surrogates in Havana and Managua, you then had this investigation to blame the problem on the executive branch. It does not make sense to me. In my opinion, these hearings have caused serious damage to our national interests. Our adversaries laugh at us, and our friends recoil in horror.

North punctuated these prepared remarks with extemporaneous panegyrics to a soldier's duty during Liman's ineffective cross-examination:

LT. COL. NORTH: Let me make one thing very clear, counsel. This Lieutenant Colonel is not going to challenge a decision of the Commander in Chief, for whom I still work. And I am proud to work for that Commander in Chief. And if the Commander in Chief tells this Lieutenant Colonel to go stand in the corner and sit on his head, I will do so. . . . I saluted smartly and charged up the hill. That's what lieutenant colonels are supposed to do.

North was dramatic, emotional, animated, and devastatingly effective. The nation, hitherto uninterested in or dubious of Reagan's Central America policy, was suddenly riveted by the spectacle of North humbling the committee. Not since the Army-McCarthy hearings of 1954 had anyone so humiliated a congressional committee investigation.[36] Senators William Cohen (R-Maine) and George Mitchell (D-Maine) wrote afterward that the contest of "one Marine against twenty-six lawyer-politicians wasn't even close. North held a Gatling gun while we sat like ducks in a shooting gallery. The American people loved it."[37] Newt Gingrich was ecstatic, telling a reporter, "The country, for the first time in my lifetime, saw the left wing of Congress face to face." The *Wall Street Journal*'s Suzanne Garment, who called Iran-Contra "the scandal Olympics," observed, "The post-Watergate operating rules had boomeranged on the legislators, who discovered that he who lives by the tube can die by the tube."[38]

North became an instant cultural phenomenon: Olliemania was born. A deli in Pennsylvania began offering the Ollie Sub—thinly sliced steak on a roll with "*shredded* lettuce" (emphasis in original menu), while a California café concocted an Ollie North shredded cheese omelet and Ollie's Gottem Buffaloed Burger made with bison meat. Before North was done testifying, more than $100,000 in unsolicited cash poured into his legal defense fund; within a month he had banked $1.4 million. In the ensuing months he became the hottest attraction for conservative groups and GOP candidates, who had yet to learn of North's more reckless and unreliable side. Capitol Hill offices were flooded with more than 150,000 pro-North letters and telegrams, the largest avalanche of mail since Nixon fired Archibald Cox at the height of Watergate in 1973. More than five thousand calls came into the White House, with only 222 expressing criticism—the rest were in enthusiastic support. *USA Today* set up a North hotline and received 66,973 calls by the end of his first week of testimony; 58,863 were pro-North, with many urging that he be given a medal. When North was spotted getting out of a car near his lawyer's Seventeenth Street office late in the week of his testimony, Washington pedestrians applauded and cheered. Marine Corps recruiting offices reported anecdotal accounts of an uptick in enlistment inquiries. Even TV network news coverage warmed to North. On CBS, correspondent Bernard Goldberg noted that "in a world where so many lack convictions, we're drawn to people who passionately believe in what they're doing and then do it." Liberal Hollywood producer Norman Lear told the *New York Times*, "I can't take my eyes off it. I've seen every second of it." OLLIE NORTH FOR PRESIDENT T-shirts quickly appeared at the tourist kiosks along the National Mall. North's hairstyle became a momentary fashion; barbers reported a surge in requests for the "Ollie cut." Book publishers lined up to sign him as an author.

Few of the Democrats on the committee deigned to argue with the geopolitical or constitutional views North offered. Recall the revealing comment of Contra aid opponent Representative Mike Barnes (D-Md.) the year before: "We just didn't have the votes if Reagan ever presented it that way." Well, North had now "presented it that way" with the whole nation watching and debating the issue attentively for the first time—and applauding the valiant marine. A *Newsweek* poll found that a 48 percent plurality thought the committee was harassing North; a *Los Angeles Times* poll found that only 6 percent thought the committee was being fair, and more people thought Congress was to blame for the scandal than the president, by a margin of 43 to 30 percent. Support for the Contra cause surged. A *Washington Post*/ABC News poll found that two-thirds of the public would have approved if Reagan *had* okayed the diversion to the Contras. As North's testimony continued, several Democrats on the committee began to make prominent mention of their prior support for the Contras.[39]

Over the weekend, Democrats took stock and recognized that they were being routed. When North resumed his testimony the following Monday, Senator George Mitchell, a former prosecutor and federal judge, argued eloquently that North didn't have a monopoly on patriotism, closing with a plea to North to "respect the patriotism and motives of those who disagree with you." Senator Inouye attempted a clumsy and morally obtuse comparison of North to the Nazi defendants at the Nuremberg trials ("just following orders"), drawing a sharp blast from North's attorney, Brendan Sullivan. Inouye had overruled all twenty-two objections Sullivan made during the course of North's testimony, contributing to Inouye's image as a hanging judge. Outside the hearing room Democrats fumed. Illinois senator Paul Simon, a declared candidate for president in 1988, said, "Oliver North is *not* a hero." Representative Richard Gephardt of Missouri, also gearing up for a presidential campaign in 1988, told an audience in New Hampshire, "When people walk over the law, they shouldn't be celebrated, they should be thrown in jail, and that's where he belongs, with all of his charisma." "North put the Constitution through the shredder," he added, "making Watergate look like a Sunday school picnic."[40] And Gephardt was a moderate among Democrats. A few moderate Republicans openly dissented from the conservatives. New Hampshire senator Warren Rudman offered a profile in leadership in lecturing North that "the American people have the constitutional right to be wrong. . . . if the American people say enough, that's why this Congress has been fickle and has vacillated."

But it was too late to turn around the North juggernaut. The last two days of North's testimony were mostly long speeches by committee members, with most Republicans, emboldened by North's performance, joining the attack on the committee. Seizing on a mistake of Liman's, Republicans managed to enable North to present his pro-Contra slide show that he had used to assist private fund-raising efforts. (Dick Cheney yielded his allotted time for this purpose.) Polling data showed that North's presentation to the committee boosted popular support for the Contras, closing a fifteen-point gap between opposition and support to Contra aid to a dead-even proposition. Whatever hope remained that the hearings might implicate Reagan were decisively ended when Poindexter, who appeared immediately after North, testified that he had not informed Reagan of the diversion of funds to the Contras. "The buck stops with me," he told the committee. "This was the bombshell I've been waiting for 7 months," Reagan wrote in his diary that night. "The day is brighter."

In the end, the attempted congressional coup against Reagan's foreign policy—which might have culminated in Reagan's impeachment—fell flat.[41] It was a remarkable turnabout. In January a *New York Times*/CBS poll found that the public trusted Congress more than the president to make the right decisions on foreign policy by a 61 to 27 percent margin. Congress had squandered that advantage. The disappointment in newsrooms was palpable. Haynes Johnson wrote in the *Washington Post* that "it seems almost certain now that there will be no impeachment." Foreign media got the point too; *Le Monde* wrote, "Congress could have won a lot from the process, but was unable to score even one point." Committee co-chairman Lee Hamilton effectively threw in the towel at the end of the hearings by saying, "The solution to the problems of decision-making revealed in these hearings lies less in new structures or new laws than in proper attitudes." Had the hearings gone better, congressional Democrats surely would not have settled for new attitudes but would have demanded new concrete prerogatives to share foreign policy making with the executive, modeled after the War Powers Resolution of 1973 that was enacted in the aftermath of Vietnam and Watergate. The committee produced a seven-hundred-page final report in November that, while harshly critical of the White House, drew back from finding criminal fault: "The Committees make no determination as to whether any particular individual involved in the Iran-Contra Affair acted with criminal intent or was guilty of any crime."[42] In the fullness of time North, Poindexter, and other targets of the independent counsel's investigation would never be charged with violating the Boland Amendment or the Arms Export Control Act and were at length charged mostly with secondary legal violations such as lying to Congress and, in North's case, accepting an illegal gratuity. Reagan breezily dismissed the committee report: "They labored, and brought forth a mouse."

Republicans filed a strongly argued minority report that was in equal parts critical of the Democratic majority in Congress and of President Reagan—for not defending executive prerogative vigorously enough. As the minority report noted, "A substantial number of the mistakes of the Iran-Contra affair resulted directly from an ongoing state of political guerrilla warfare over foreign policy between the legislative and executive branches. . . . The Administration decided to work within the letter of the law covertly, instead of forcing a public and principled confrontation that would have been healthier in the long run." As for Reagan, the minority report said: "The President's inherent constitutional powers are only as strong, however, as the President's willingness to defend them. . . . Thus, the President should have vetoed the strict Boland Amendment in mid-October 1984, even though the Amendment was only a few paragraphs in an approximately 1,200 page long continuing appropriations resolution, and a veto therefore would have brought the Government to a standstill within three weeks of a national election. . . . Matters of war and peace are too important to be held hostage to government decisions about funding Medicare or highways." Representative Henry Hyde was more direct in his separate opinion, appended to the report: "There are members of the House and Senate who do not believe that Communism in Central America is a grave threat to peace and freedom that requires a vigorous response from the United States. . . . We have had a disconcerting and distasteful whiff of moralism and institutional self-righteousness in these hearings. Too little have these committees acknowledged that the Executive may well have had a clearer vision of what was at stake on Central America."

The grand irony of the affair was that Oliver North, the man who almost single-handedly brought down the Reagan presidency, turned out to provide the most robust and effective defense of the Reagan Doctrine. Conservative columnist M. Stanton Evans observed, "Ollie North was able to do in six days of testimony what the rest of the Reagan Administration hadn't been able to accomplish in six years," and *National Review* lamented, "The Administration's Central American policy should not have had to wait two years for a lieutenant colonel of the Marines to present it forcefully." But even as they lauded his performance, a few conservative leaders discerned the difficulty with North. David Keene of the American Conservative Union remarked, "North has performed heroically before the committee, but even if you're a good man with good motives, it doesn't mean you can't mess things up." North's actions, Keene added, "have damaged our ability to aid the Contras and crippled the President."[43]

Despite these few conservative misgivings, the liberal onslaught over the Iran-Contra crisis had helped to alleviate Reagan's fraying relationship with many conservatives, who in 1987 were starting to become restive about Reagan's impending arms control agreements with the Soviets. Conservatives resented the way the media and liberals were attacking Reagan over Contra policy, and rallied to his cause. By this time Reagan wanted to put the matter behind him and move on. After the hearings concluded in early August, Reagan reprised his February speech:

> Secretary Shultz and Secretary Weinberger both predicted that the American people would immediately assume this whole plan was an arms-for-hostages deal and nothing more. Well, unfortunately, their predictions were right. As I said to you in March, I let my preoccupation with the hostages intrude into areas where it didn't belong. The image—the reality—of Americans in chains, deprived of their freedom and families so far from home, burdened my thoughts. And this was a mistake.
>
> My fellow Americans, I've thought long and often about how to explain to you what I intended to accomplish, but I respect you too much to make excuses. The fact of the matter is that there's nothing I can say that will make the situation right. I was stubborn in my pursuit of a policy that went astray.
>
> The other major issue of the hearings, of course, was the diversion of funds to the Nicaraguan contras. Colonel North and Admiral Poindexter believed they were doing what I would have wanted done—keeping the democratic resistance alive in Nicaragua. I believed then and I believe now in preventing the Soviets from establishing a beachhead in Central America. Since I have been so closely associated with the cause of the contras, the big question during the hearings was whether I knew of the diversion. I was aware the resistance was receiving funds directly from third countries and from private efforts, and I endorsed those endeavors wholeheartedly; but—let me put this in capital letters—I did not know about the diversion of funds.
>
> Yet the buck does not stop with Admiral Poindexter, as he stated in his testimony; it stops with me. I am the one who is ultimately accountable to the American people. The admiral testified that he wanted to protect me; yet no President should ever be protected from the truth. No operation is so secret that it must be kept from the Commander in Chief. I had the right, the obligation, to make my own decision.

Reagan announced changes to the management of future covert action procedures, and then changed the subject to economic matters.[44]

*   *   *

ALTHOUGH REAGAN HAD survived the firestorm and to a small extent saw his larger policy aims in Central America vindicated, the nine-month saga had left the Contras in limbo and frozen Reagan in place. In the middle of the hearings Reagan wrote in his diary, "I don't see how I can do anything until they close down this investigation." For the moment the Contras had the resources to carry on as an effective fighting force, and in 1987 they fielded as many as ten thousand men, often routing Sandinista forces in battle. Like the Afghan *mujahadeen,* the Contras supplied with better weapons were exacting a higher toll; as much as 60 percent of Nicaraguan territory was contested, and the Nicaraguan economy was near collapse.[45] The Contras shot down as many as ten Mi-24 helicopters in the first half of 1987. But there was little confidence Congress would approve new aid when U.S. funds ran out in a few months. Reagan included $180 million over the next two years in his current budget proposal but was rebuffed by Democratic congressional leaders. And there remained the fundamental ambiguity that had plagued the policy from the beginning: were the Contras out to overthrow the Sandinistas or get them to allow genuine democratic reforms? The commander of the U.S. Southern Command, General John Galvin, testified to Congress in the spring that the Contras could win a protracted military struggle, overturning the conventional wisdom up to that point. Some conservatives were outspoken in the view that if Congress wouldn't support the contras, Reagan should consider breaking off diplomatic relations, recognizing an exile government, and perhaps invading Nicaragua. *Human Events* editorialized: "[T]here is a growing school of thought in both diplomatic and military circles that only a Grenada-style invasion can eventually salvage Nicaragua from Marxist-Leninist control."[46]

Two new players soon entered the fray and altered the political landscape: Costa Rica's new president, Oscar Arias, and new U.S. House Speaker Jim Wright. Elected in 1986, Arias broke with previous Costa Rican policy. He declared that henceforth Costa Rica would be neutral in the Nicaraguan conflict, which meant the Contras were no longer welcome to make bases in and conduct sorties from Costa Rica. Arias also opposed further U.S. military aid to the Contras and called for an end to the Contras' military efforts. But he also spoke critically of the Sandinistas, refused to include Managua on his itinerary of regional state visits, and called for negotiations between the

Sandinista "dictators" and the Contras. These reversals and inconsistent gestures marked Arias as an opportunist and an unstable partner for diplomacy.

Encouraged by Senator Christopher Dodd, who was in regular contact with Nicaragua's Washington embassy during this period, Arias soon emerged with his own full-blown regional peace plan that aimed not only to resolve the Nicaraguan civil war but also to end the guerilla struggles of El Salvador and Guatemala. It was a plan plausible only to a high school civics class (or the UN General Assembly): cease-fires on all sides, amnesty for all guerilla fighters, "comprehensive dialogue" to achieve "national reconciliation," political pluralism, and scheduled elections. Although the Arias plan appeared to put unacceptable political conditions on the Sandinistas, its requirement that the Contras disband also made it unpalatable to Reagan, who pronounced it "lousy" in his diary. (Unlike the successive Contadora proposals of 1984–86, the Arias plan didn't require that Nicaragua reverse its arms buildup or reduce the number of Soviet and Cuban advisers.) Reagan noted in an entry about a White House visit by Arias in September 1987: "[Arias] admitted to being concerned that the Sandinistas would try to cheat & agreed the contras should be supported. Then he went up to Congress & reversed himself." Amidst the agony of the Iran-Contra scandal, however, the Arias plan caused Reagan fits. Robert Kagan observed, "The very inconsistency of Arias's proposals made them attractive to members of Congress who, in the aftermath of the Iran-Contra scandal, were looking for a way out of their own political impasse."[47] When the Senate passed a resolution endorsing the Arias plan by a vote of 97–1, Reagan reluctantly gave a lukewarm endorsement to Arias's efforts. Fortunately, Honduras and El Salvador were publicly unenthusiastic about the Arias plan. Arias stubbornly refused to discuss changing his scheme, and his initiative began its inevitable collapse.

House Speaker Jim Wright then entered the picture. With political sentiment on Capitol Hill rubbed raw by the Iran-Contra debacle, the White House hoped it could avoid another bitter battle for Contra aid by reaching a compromise with Speaker Wright, whose position on Contra aid was thought to be less fixed than Tip O'Neill's had been. The White House essentially offered to make Wright a full partner in making Central American policy: Wright and Reagan would put forward their own peace proposal, and if the Sandinistas refused, Wright would support another installment of military aid for the Contras. Many House Democrats feared it was a Reagan trap, but the crafty Wright thought he could turn the tables on Reagan and agreed to move forward with the idea. Wright wanted to kill Contra aid but was wary of Democrats being blamed as the party that lost Nicaragua in the event that things went badly. He sought to maneuver Reagan into conditions that would amount to a bipartisan bug-out.

The opening to Wright was a major blunder, as it surrendered the political advantages of the collapse of the Iran-Contra hearings. Wright began conducting his own diplomacy, contacting Nicaragua's ambassador to the United States to inquire about the Sandinistas' willingness to enter peace talks with the United States. At length Wright struck a deal with the White House that called for a cease-fire in place in Nicaragua, during which time the United States would suspend military aid but continue humanitarian aid. In return the White House agreed not to demand a Hill debate on new Contra funding for at least two months (this became known as the "gag rule"), while, Wright hoped, Olliemania would dissipate. Wright and the White House were immediately disabused of the hope that this gambit would dampen the partisan and ideological fervor over the issue. Democratic opponents were unhappy, and conservatives inside Congress and in the administration cried betrayal. There were fresh calls from the right for Reagan to fire Secretary of State Shultz, even though Shultz privately shared their dismay. Shultz wrote, "Getting close to Jim Wright was not a pleasant experience. . . . He could smile at you while he cut your throat."[48]

The Sandinistas muddled the picture once again by rejecting the Wright-Reagan proposal, calling it "a declaration of war against Nicaragua." The other Central American countries announced their rejection of Wright-Reagan soon after, greatly cheering the White House. But then Arias reentered the picture, brokering a deal between Nicaragua and El Salvador at a meeting in Guatemala that represented a sellout of the Contras more or less along the lines of the original Arias proposal. (For this effort Arias would receive the Nobel Peace Prize two months later, in a transparent attempt by the Nobel Committee to hobble Reagan's Contra support even further.) Wright immediately hailed the agreement, saying that there was no need for further military aid to the Contras. The White House was stunned but hoped to make the best of things by pressing hard against the ambiguities of the agreement and pushing back against Wright's position on ending Contra aid. Reagan countered with an announcement that Shultz was willing to meet directly with Ortega so long as the Contras and regional leaders were included in the talks.

The White House opening to Wright had failed to defuse the partisan

split over Nicaragua but had elevated Wright to the position of co-equal partner in making policy, mistakenly conferring legitimacy on congressional foreign policy meddling. Matters now depended on whether the Sandinistas
would follow their previous pattern of maladroit moves that undermined
Democratic opposition to the Contras back in Washington; as *National Review* worried, "the Sandinistas will not be stupid forever." The agreement,
which called on Nicaragua to cease its support for Marxist guerillas in El Salvador and lift its restrictions on political opposition at home, was controversial within the Sandinista directorate back in Managua. In a secret meeting in
mid-August, Daniel Ortega reassured his comrades that he had no intention
of ceasing support for revolution in Central America, and the Sandinistas
told the Salvadoran guerillas that they would step up arms shipments. Ortega
told the directorate, "As in the case of Vietnam, we will win this war in
Washington," adding that the Sandinistas must do nothing to undermine
Speaker Wright or "anything that will upset the majority vote in Congress."[49]
Identifying Wright as a "parallel power" to Reagan, the Sandinistas went so
far as to invite Wright to serve as the official mediator of regional peace talks.
Wright sensibly demurred from this formal role but later engaged in more of
his own freelance diplomacy by holding meetings with Sandinista and Contra
representatives in an attempt to broker a deal. The normally stolid Shultz
wrote that "Jim Wright was trying to blindside President Reagan and me,
subvert our policies, and become the de facto secretary of state in the process.
This was outrageous!" Wright backed down only when Reagan publicly (and
more forcefully in private) attacked Wright for his recklessness—a sentiment
that found editorial echo in the *Washington Post*.

Back in Nicaragua someone down the line didn't get the memo about
staying on good behavior, and when opposition groups attempted a peaceful
march in Managua on August 15, Sandinista police set upon them with riot
sticks, cattle prods, and attack dogs. The leaders of the march were arrested
and jailed for thirty days, and the lifting of restrictions on political opposition was postponed indefinitely. (The *New York Times* covered the story on
page 4, the *Washington Post* on page 15.) Democrats in Washington were
dismayed and told the Sandinistas in blunt terms not to make such a stupid
mistake again. The Sandinistas reluctantly backed off, lifting press censorship
for the first time in years and allowing opposition political forces to rally
publicly. *La Prensa* resumed publication and wasted no time before staking
out a position of strong opposition to the Sandinistas. The Sandinistas calculated that they could allow just enough liberalization to forestall additional

Contra aid from Congress, and they still resisted negotiating with the Contras, whose growing popularity inside Nicaragua drew the notice of the front page of the *New York Times* in the fall of 1987.[50]

A fresh revelation in December dealt the Sandinistas another blow in Washington. A high-ranking Nicaraguan defector, Roger Miranda, revealed that the Sandinistas had secret plans to expand their army to six hundred thousand men and that the Soviets would increase their military supplies to the regime. The White House initially suspected Miranda was a plant—the Sandinistas had run false-flag defectors before—but when the Sandinistas confirmed the accuracy of Miranda's information, congressional Democrats were once again embarrassed and angry. Wright complained that Nicaragua was "snatching defeat from the jaws of victory." Congress voted for a short-term extension of Contra military aid to the end of February 1988.

As the year drew to a close both the United States and Nicaragua had achieved part of their political aims. The prospects for further Contra military aid in Congress remained uncertain, but, as Kagan summarized, "[T]he Sandinistas found themselves in precisely the position they had hoped to avoid. They had permitted enough of an opening to allow an emboldened opposition to be heard by the world."[51] With a year to go in Reagan's presidency, the fear among the Contras and other Central American nations was that the Sandinistas would run out the clock, hoping a Democrat would succeed Reagan in 1989 and end Reagan's policy. Ortega candidly expressed his objective in the summer of 1988: "The revolution stays and Reagan leaves." Virtually all of the announced Democratic candidates for president in 1988 had stated that they would end Contra aid once and for all if elected.

The uncertainty in Washington led to political and military ambiguity in Nicaragua in the early months of 1988. In February the Senate approved, on a 51–49 vote, new military aid for the Contras, but the House voted it down twice. With the Contras once more running low on military supplies in the absence of a fresh U.S. commitment (and with the CIA once again prohibited from providing assistance), their offensive began to wither and the pendulum swung in favor of the Sandinistas. As the Contras withdrew to their bases in Honduras, the Sandinistas launched a major offensive designed to finish them off, an act that again dismayed centrist Democrats in Washington and revived the prospects for new military aid. When Sandinista troops crossed into Honduras in force in March, Reagan announced he was dispatching the 82nd Airborne to Honduras. It had the desired effect; fearing a direct

American attack, the Sandinistas halted their offensive and suddenly relented in their opposition to negotiating directly with the Contras.

What followed was an ambiguous interim agreement neither side wanted but both needed, calling for a cease-fire that, significantly, allowed the Contras to keep their weapons and remain in place in designated safe havens. This represented a major concession from the Sandinistas, but it gave the Sandinistas what they needed most—a respite from the specter of renewed U.S. military aid while they ran out the clock on Reagan's second term. It got Democrats in Washington off the hook—Wright and other Democrats pressured and advised the Sandinistas on the course they should take, and Ortega publicly thanked Wright for his help after the deal was struck. Congress passed a large package of humanitarian aid to keep the Contras intact, and the Contras and the Sandinistas entered months of negotiations over political reform and a permanent end to the civil war. The White House had little optimism for these negotiations and took the unusual step of sending copies of the 1973 Vietnam Peace Treaty to American embassies throughout Latin America as a reminder that Communist nations regard diplomacy as war by other means. Amidst endless waves of recrimination and mistrust between the Contras and their supporters back in the United States, the negotiations made little progress and eventually broke down. Déjà vu: the Sandinistas re-arrested opposition leaders, suspended publication of *La Prensa,* and shut down the Catholic Church's radio station.

Robert Kagan summarized the state of affairs as the 1988 election campaign was reaching full swing: "The intransigence on both sides was the product of a divided American Congress which could not choose between abandoning the contras and letting them fight the Sandinistas."[52] The problem of Nicaragua was going to be held over for Reagan's successor, whoever it might be. The eruption of the Iran-Contra scandal had neither ended nor compelled a final decision in favor of Reagan's policy. A stalemate was better than a rout of the Contras but less favorable than the downfall of the Sandinistas. The inter-branch struggle over foreign policy would continue.

*   *   *

THE OLLIE NORTH show wasn't the only incandescent scene on Capitol Hill in the second half of 1987. In late June, with almost no prior notice, Associate Supreme Court Justice Lewis Powell abruptly announced his retirement. Reagan swiftly announced his choice to replace Powell: Robert Bork, the name that everyone had expected since 1981. Conservatives were ecstatic. Richard Viguerie said, "This is the most exciting news for conservatives since President Reagan's re-election." Bork was to jurisprudence what North was to geopolitics; surely the Senate Judiciary Committee would be no match for this brilliant mind.

Thus began an unprecedented political firestorm that would funamentally reorder judicial politics for decades to come.

CHAPTER 12

CRASH

———————

*And so the free world yet again watches its leader, the U.S.A.,
afflicted by a political and economic nervous breakdown. . . . [T]he
Republican Administration has lost its nerve and seeks popularity
instead of respect. And the Democratic Congress is enjoying the
collapse of its political opponents and hopes to benefit by peddling
sweet-tasting poison packaged to resemble medicine.*
—SIR JAMES GOLDSMITH

NINETEEN EIGHTY-SEVEN was a tale of two crashes: that of Bork's
Supreme Court nomination, and that of Wall Street. By the end of the
year conservatives were worrying that the Reagan presidency had crashed
as well.

The White House assumed that Bork's nomination would be controversial but that he eventually would be confirmed after some heat inside the Senate. Bork had been confirmed unanimously for the D.C. Circuit Court of Appeals in 1982, at which time the American Bar Association had given him a "highly qualified" rating. Several days before Reagan announced his nomination, Howard Baker and Ed Meese met with Judiciary Committee chairman Joe Biden and Senate majority leader Robert Byrd to go through a list of possible nominees, and neither man indicated that Bork was unacceptable, with Byrd saying to a reporter: "I frankly think he would probably be confirmed," and cautioning fellow Democrats that Bork's nomination should not become "a litmus test of party affiliation and loyalty." Senator Dennis DeConcini (D-Ariz.) said, "I start with the assumption that the President has the right to appoint whom he wants," and freshman senator Al Gore said he would take a wait-and-see attitude toward a Bork nomination.

The White House and many in the media thought Senator Ted Kennedy had gone too far when he took to the Senate floor the day of Bork's nomination to blast what he called "Robert Bork's America":

Women would be forced into back alley abortions, blacks would sit at segregated lunch counters, rogue police could break down citizens' doors in midnight raids, school children could not be taught about evolution, writers and artists could be censored at the whim of government, and the doors of federal courts would be shut on the fingers of millions of citizens for whom the judiciary is—and is often the only—protector of the individual rights that are the heart of our democracy. President Reagan is still our president. But he should not be able to reach out from the muck of Irangate, reach into the muck of Watergate and impose his reactionary vision of the Constitution on the Supreme Court and the next generation of Americans. No justice would be better than this injustice.

The White House and others thought Kennedy's intemperate remarks would backfire. The new chairman of the Senate Judiciary Committee, Joe Biden, never at a loss for words—even if they were someone else's—had told a reporter in 1986: "Say the administration sends up Bork, and, after our investigation, he looks a lot like another Scalia. I'd have to vote for him, and if the groups tear me apart, that's the medicine I'll take. *I'm not Ted Kennedy*" (emphasis added).

But Kennedy knew exactly what he was doing. Bork's nomination, as *New York Times* reporter Linda Greenhouse put it, sent "a kind of metaphysical shudder . . . through the liberal community." George Will was not alone in calling Bork "the most intellectually distinguished nominee since Felix Frankfurter." That was exactly the problem for the Left.

The activist Left was gearing up for the political equivalent of Armageddon, and Kennedy, in close touch with the Left's leadership, whipped up the grassroots with his extreme rhetoric. And Biden was running for president in 1988, which meant that the opinion and demands of the activist Left had to be heeded. Biden announced a few days after Bork's nomination that he would oppose Bork, that he might lead a filibuster against him in the full Senate, and that the Judiciary Committee would delay Bork's confirmation hearings until mid-September.[1] The average interval between a Supreme Court nomination and the start of confirmation hearings in the twentieth century had been thirteen days, with the longest ever being forty-one days. The seventy-one-day delay in the beginning of confirmation hearings meant the Supreme Court might well begin its fall term in October with only eight justices. The purpose of the delay was transparent: Biden and Kennedy wanted time for the activist Left to organize and execute a campaign against Bork. Biden met with leaders of the nascent anti-Bork forces and essentially turned over his Senate staff to coordinate the outside effort that was taking shape. The *Washington Post* raised an editorial eyebrow at Biden's extraordinary stance, noting that it would be hard for Bork to get a fair hearing when the Judiciary Committee chairman "has already cast himself in the role of a prosecutor instead of a juror."

The subsequent public campaign of the activist Left was stunning in its breadth, depth, and dishonesty. It also made evident the startling politicization of civic organizations in America.[2] By the time the Bork battle was over, about three hundred organizations had joined the anti-Bork coalition, which raised and spent more than $10 million for advertisements and lobbying efforts. Leading the way was Norman Lear's People for the American Way, which sponsored among other efforts a television ad featuring Gregory Peck telling viewers: "Robert Bork could have the last word on your rights as citizens, but the Senate has the last word on him. Please urge your senators to vote against the Bork nomination, because if Robert Bork wins a seat on the Supreme Court, it will be for life—his life and yours." Planned Parenthood took out full-page newspaper ads: "Robert Bork is an extremist who believes you have no constitutional right to personal privacy." The *Washington Post* editorialized that "the campaign against him did not resemble an argument so much as a lynching" and said the attacks were marked by "intellectual vulgarity and personal savagery." Despite this clarity of perception, the *Post* ultimately came out against Bork anyway.

The barrage was not limited to public advertisements. Liberal activists played hardball with Democratic senators, threatening primary challenges to any who cast a vote for Bork, including Florida's Lawton Chiles, New York's Daniel Patrick Moynihan, and Louisiana's Bennett Johnston. At least two black witnesses who were to testify on behalf of Bork were threatened with personal and professional reprisals and cancelled their testimony. Many of the opposition groups were predictable, such as the ACLU, the NAACP, feminists, environmentalists, and labor unions. But also joining the list were the Association of Flight Attendants, the Jewish War Veterans, the National Council of Senior Citizens, the YWCA, the United Cerebral Palsy Association, and the Epilepsy Foundation of America. The American Bar Association, while ranking Bork "well qualified," also leaked the news that four members of its judicial appointments review committee—all associated with left-wing views— had voted "not qualified," dealing a superficial blow to the White House strategy of stressing Bork's unquestionable stature in the field. Arkansas governor Bill Clinton, who had been a student of Bork's at Yale Law School, planned to be among the lead witnesses against Bork during the confirmation hearings, but a schedule conflict prevented him from appearing. George Will commented: "The ease with which such groups have been swept together for the first time in such a campaign reflects, in part, the common political culture of the people who run the headquarters of the compassion industry."[3] The effect of this onslaught, Will added, "turned Bork's confirmation process into the first national plebiscite on a nominee."

The White House, weakened and preoccupied by the Iran-Contra scandal, was slow to recognize the gathering storm from the Left and how effective it would be in defining Bork's public image in a negative way. They were not alone. Right after the nomination was announced George Will dismissed the initial caterwauling with a prediction of "a confirmation process that is going to be easy." *National Review* wrote on the eve of confirmation hearings in September—after the anti-Bork ad blitz had reached a frenzy—that "[i]t seems clearer and clearer that the Senate will confirm Robert Bork for the Supreme Court," adding that "[c]onservatives would be wise not to overreact to the leftist zealots on the Bork matter." The *New Republic* wrote in their September 7 issue, "From the time he was nominated, Bork was oddson to win confirmation. He still is."

The sheer demagoguery and dishonesty of the assault were breathtaking, as was the hypocrisy of Democratic senators, including Kennedy, who had long argued that ideology should not play a role in confirming a president's Supreme Court nominees.[4] The assault wasn't limited to distorting Bork's political and judicial views. There were false rumors that he was a drunk and a tax cheat and that his wife, Mary Ellen, was a Holocaust denier. While attacking Bork's views on privacy, his opponents violated his by obtaining his movie rental records. (They were disappointed: Bork's viewing tastes ran to Fred Astaire, Cary Grant, and other old-fashioned fare.) The White House made a crucial strategic error at the outset in deciding to cast Bork as a moderate and to have him keep a low profile, rather than campaigning vigorously on Bork's conservative philosophy. The Justice Department wanted to fight on this ground but was overruled. White House congressional liaison

William Ball said, "The idea was to set forth Bork's record, not to engage in a political battle." The White House did not perceive that the rules had changed, that it was planning to show up for a political knife fight armed only with Occam's razor.

The strategy of presenting Bork as a mainstream moderate played into the hands of the activist Left, which hung its campaign on the theme that Bork was out of the mainstream and lacked a judicial temperament. The charge was preposterous. During his tenure on the D.C. Circuit he had written or joined 416 opinions, many of them on the same side as fellow D.C. Circuit judge Ruth Bader Ginsburg, who in 1993 would take a seat on the Supreme Court. Bork's three-judge panels were unanimous 90 percent of the time, and Bork was in the majority 95 percent of the time. The Supreme Court had reversed not a single majority opinion he wrote or joined, while in six cases adopting one of his dissenting opinions. Bork's critics said he was hostile to minorities and civil rights, yet he sided with minority plaintiffs in seven out of eight cases that came before him as a judge. As political scientist Aaron Wildavsky noted, "How could a superb legal craftsman be outside the mainstream when he was one of the leaders in determining what constituted excellence in legal reasoning [as a professor at Yale Law School and Solicitor General of the United States]? How could a judge who had written some 150 opinions, and had never been reversed by a higher court, be outside the mainstream?"

The out-of-the-mainstream charge attained a patina of substance from a number of legal scholars, especially Laurence Tribe, of Harvard Law School, and Ronald Dworkin, of Yale Law School. Tribe had written an entire book, *God Save This Honorable Court,* arguing that the Senate should explicitly take a nominee's ideology into account. He became "the intellectual architect of the opposition," conferring almost daily with Biden's staff, role-playing Bork in rehearsals with Biden, organizing fellow academics to speak out publicly against Bork, and testifying against Bork in the confirmation hearings.[5] Dworkin, in a long article in the *New York Review of Books*, said, "Bork's views do not lie within the scope of the longstanding debate between liberals and conservatives about the proper role of the Supreme Court. Bork is a constitutional radical." Dworkin and Tribe also introduced a theme that has taken its place as a prominent talking point for opposition to conservative judicial nominees: because Bork would be replacing a moderate justice, he would unbalance the composition of the Court, as though the Supreme Court or the judicial branch generally is supposed to have the ideological equivalent of proportional representation.

Transforming the judiciary was a key goal of the Reagan administration from day one, and they had approached the task with more seriousness and forethought than any administration since FDR. By the end of his second term, Reagan would fill 372 of 736 Article III federal judgeships—one for every eight days of his presidency. Liberals were understandably dismayed at losing their dominance of the judiciary, but they were not willing to argue the issue on the merits of jurisprudence. As Terry Eastland noted, "The views of Bork's opponents were never forced into public view," and Aaron Wildavsky concurred: "The passion of these attacks reflected the unwillingness of Bork's antagonists to permit their egalitarian dogma to be questioned." Bork on the Court, in alliance with Scalia and Rehnquist, would have formed a formidable intellectual bloc that might have dominated the Court's main lines of jurisprudence for generations to come. Hodding Carter, a press spokesman in the Jimmy Carter administration, was candid when he told ABC News that Bork's nomination "forces liberals like me to confront a reality we don't want to confront, which is that we are depending in large part on the least democratic institution, with a small 'd,' in government to defend what it is we no longer are able to win out there in the electorate." Liberal activist Ann Lewis confessed the same: "If this were carried out as an internal Senate battle, we would have deep and thoughtful discussions about the Constitution, and then we would lose." Hence, a smear job was the only possible strategy. Suzanne Garment observed:

> The irony here is large. For a long time now liberals in America have denounced conservatives for anti-intellectualism and represented themselves and the institutions they control, like universities and the courts, as preservers and defenders of intellect. In the Bork campaign they acted with a contempt for intellect at least as bad in its way as anything that came out of the fundamentalist Right of the 20s.[6]

Despite the ferocity of the attack and opinion polls showing public skepticism of Bork, there was still confidence that Bork's confirmation hearings would reverse the course of things. With the image of Oliver North's bravura performance fresh in mind, conservatives thought the brilliant Bork would surely humble the Senate Judiciary Committee. NBC News had described Bork as "a *combative ex-Marine* who has enjoyed doing battle against liberals in the courts and law schools for 25 years" (emphasis added). Richard Vigilante wrote in *National Review* shortly before the hearings opened, "If

Ollie was the first blow, Robert Bork may be the last straw. Like Ollie, when Bork comes up before his congressional tribunal he will set the agenda. . . . Bork is in the position of an intellectual Ollie North."[7] Dan Casey of the American Conservative Union told *New York Times* reporter Ethan Bronner: "It was inconceivable to us that he wouldn't be confirmed. We were euphoric and cocky. We had just seen what Ollie North had done, and we figured Bork is a lot smarter. He'll run circles around those guys."[8]

This was a fatal miscalculation. Here was an opportunity for liberal Democrats to get even for their humiliation at North's hands; if they could not get North, they could get Bork, who lacked North's flair for the dramatic. He resisted as undignified the idea that he should engage in the low arts of public relations and image craft, such as shaving off his scraggly beard. In prehearing rehearsal sessions, Bork resisted advice on how to "package" himself for the Judiciary Committee. He brushed aside such suggestions with the retort "I'm a lawyer, not a politician."

The hearings opened on September 15, two days before the bicentennial of the signing of the Constitution. If Bork thought his cool, erudite manner and authoritative baritone voice would win over the undeclared or undecided senators, he was mistaken. The *Wall Street Journal* and other media observers described his bearing as "cold and aloof" and his answers as "clinical and without compassion." His worst moment came when Senator Alan Simpson (R-Wyo.) tossed him a softball: why did he want to be on the Supreme Court? Bork gave an antiseptic answer wholly inadequate to his predicament that included his most infamous line: "I think it would be an intellectual feast just to be there and read the briefs and discuss things with colleagues." As Ethan Bronner put it, the "intellectual feast" remark seemed to confirm that "the bearded egghead from Yale just wanted to play with ideas." The man who had been said to lack a judicial temperament was now criticized for having too much of it. Aaron Wildavsky observed: "Even when senators on his side set him up with 'fat pitches,' he steadfastly refused to hit home runs. . . . Bork would neither repeat back the egalitarian code words—compassion, sensitivity, let alone 'touchy-feely' warmth—nor would he keep repeating the word [justice] on which he had spent his life and to which his record as a man and a lawyer and judge spoke."[9] *National Review* commented: "Like it or not, this is a television age, and on TV he flunked."

Beyond the theatrical aspect of Bork's testimony lay the unacknowledged split within conservative jurisprudence about originalism that hobbled Bork to an extent that is still underappreciated, especially by the Left and the media. Bork's version of original intent was narrowly textual—if an individual right or prohibition on government power does not appear in the black-and-white text of the Constitution, then judges have no basis for overruling an act of the legislative branch or discerning such a right or prohibition. As such, Bork believed more in judicial restraint than in originalism—they are not the same thing. He was highly critical of any appeals to natural law, notwithstanding the centrality of the natural law tradition to the American Founding and therefore to any faithful understanding of the Founders' originalism. For example, Bork pointed to Justice Samuel Chase's cautious and tentative appeal to natural law in the 1798 case of *Calder v. Bull* as the beginning of dangerous judicial activism or "judicial authoritarianism." Justice Chase had entertained the view that an act of a legislature might be unconstitutional even if it did not violate an express provision of the Constitution. "The Constitution was barely in place," Bork wrote, "when one Justice of the Supreme Court cast covetous glances at the apple that would eventually cause the fall."[10]

While many conservatives objected to the way judges had used the equal protection clause of the Fourteenth Amendment as a virtual hunting license to strike down laws and invent new individual rights, Bork went further, challenging the idea of a constitutional basis for a general right to privacy that was the hallmark of *Griswold v. Connecticut* in 1965, the key antecedent to *Roe v. Wade*. (Hence, in judicial confirmation discourse *privacy* is a code word for abortion.) Bork did not deny that there are specific aspects of privacy protected in the Bill of Rights, and he was on reasonable ground to object that a generalized right to privacy has no intelligible limiting principle. In response to sharp questioning from Senator Kennedy, Bork sensibly replied: "For example, if it really is a right of sexual freedom in private, as some people have suggested, then *Bowers v. Hardwick,* which upheld a statute against sodomy as applied to homosexuals, is wrongly decided. Privacy to do what, Senator? You know, privacy to use cocaine in private? Privacy for businessmen to fix prices in a hotel room? We just do not know what it is."[11]

But Bork was so wedded to textual literalism that he compared the nonspecific Ninth Amendment ("The enumeration in the Constitution, of certain rights, shall not be construed to deny or disparage others retained by the people") to an "inkblot"—as a clause without usable meaning, saying, "Nobody has ever to my knowledge understood precisely what the Ninth Amendment did mean and what it was intended to do." It was hard to escape the conclusion that much of Bork's dislike of the Ninth Amendment stemmed from its use by Justice Arthur Goldberg as the basis for discovering a right to privacy in *Griswold*. Bork's position would imply that a passage of the Constitution is practically meaningless, that there are rights judges are powerless to protect, and that the Founders were bad draftsmen.[12]

Bork could not have been unaware of Alexander Hamilton's argument in *Federalist 84* against including the Bill of Rights in the Constitution—namely, that a positive enumeration would have the effect of misinstructing the people as to the nature and extent of their rights, as well as laying a pretext, by omission, for the government to grab more power than the Constitution intended. Hamilton's argument was rejected, though his logic has certainly been vindicated with the passage of time. But Bork had no tolerance for natural law jurisprudence. His jurisprudence partook of the same legal positivism at the root of liberal jurisprudence, with the distinction that his position came close to the view that the only rights individuals possess are those enumerated specifically in the Constitution or enacted into positive law by the legislative branch, whereas liberals think it fine for courts to make them up. Many conservative legal thinkers parted company with Bork, as his view provided only minimal safeguards against majoritarianism, which in the minds of the Founders was the major hazard of popular government.[13] Douglas Kmiec, a Reagan Justice Department lawyer and law professor, wrote: "Bork's inkblot assertion cannot stand. If the Constitution is law, then no part of it can go unenforced." Even *National Review* looked askance at this aspect of Bork in an editorial entitled "Second Thoughts on Bork": "The trouble is that judicial restraint may run head-on into original intent. At times the Constitution may require the Court to be, if not 'activist,' at least very active. . . . A Court devoted to original understanding would make very sweeping rulings indeed."[14]

In other words, for all his formidable intellectual gifts, Bork was a poor defender of the Founders' constitutionalism. Of all people, Senator Biden was on to this weakness:

> I believe all Americans are born with certain inalienable rights. As a child of God, I believe my rights are not derived from the Constitution. My rights are not derived from any government. My rights are not derived from any majority. My rights are because I exist. They were given to me and each of my fellow citizens by our creator and they represent the essence of human dignity.

Ironically, when Clarence Thomas came before the Judiciary Committee for his Supreme Court confirmation hearings in 1991 espousing that very basis for his jurisprudence, it became the reason Biden opposed him. The continued confusion over this split on the Right today can be illustrated by reference to the frequent slogan of Republican candidates to appoint Supreme Court justices "like Scalia and Thomas." One is tempted to ask: which one? They are not the same. Scalia is closer to Bork; Thomas is closer to George Sutherland or John Marshall.

It became the fate of this intransigent man to see his name become a transitive verb: *borked*.[15] So massive was this borking that his chances were virtually doomed at the conclusion of his five days of testimony before the committee. Polls showed that public support for Bork declined as a result of the hearings. But the hearings had to go on—for another seven days and ninety-nine witnesses, chiefly because so many special-interest groups needed to justify their direct-mail boasts of their "key role" in the Bork battle by appearing before the committee, and the egos of virtually the entire elite law school professoriate required their appearance on the hustings.[16] The list of witnesses included a who's who of leading legal academics and political figures. Jimmy Carter wrote to the committee urging Bork's rejection. The complete hearing record was nearly four thousand pages; by contrast, Rehnquist's hearing record the year before was only 114 pages. It is hard to pick out the lowest point of the testimony. Perhaps the artist Robert Rauschenberg, claiming to testify on behalf of all artists against Bork, took the prize: "I am speaking [and] writing to express the unanimous fears that the art world has toward the nomination of Bork. Young, old, rich, and hopeful are united by repulsion that a neauveau [*sic*] changeling by his tongue and unproven change of ideology might entrap decades of innocences. . . . Law is not a fixed point of view. Even supremely. But just a love of people." Biden finally called an end to this circus on September 30, turning away demands from Ralph Nader and NOW's president, Molly Yard, that they be allowed to testify against Bork.

After the hearings ended, senators began to declare their intentions. The first blow came from Republican senator Bob Packwood of Oregon, who declared the day the hearings ended that he would vote against Bork. Packwood's no vote was expected, as he was a champion of abortion rights, but the public announcement the day Bork's testimony ended was a sign that the battle was lost. The following day Senator Arlen Specter (R-Penn.) announced that he would vote against Bork, along with three southern Democratic senators. Not for the first time Reagan expressed his anger toward Specter in his diary, writing on October 9: "Senator Specter has 2 candidates for Fed. Judgeships—after his performance I'll not reward him for his no vote on Bork."

The most squalid rejection of Bork came from Alabama senator Howell Heflin. Heflin, regarded as a conservative Democrat, disingenuously attacked Bork from the *right,* saying he "was troubled by Judge Bork's extremism—an admission that he had been a socialist, a libertarian, that he nearly became a Communist, and actually recruited people to attend Communist Party meetings, and had a strange life style. I was further disturbed by his refusal to discuss his belief in God—or the lack thereof." Heflin added that Bork had a "fondness for the strange," a comment that Republican senator John Warner of Virginia cited in announcing his own decision to vote against Bork.

The White House was asleep at the wheel throughout the entire saga. Reagan's call logs show that he did not make his first telephone call to senators to lobby for Bork until September 30, long after the tide had turned. Moreover, he did not call most southern Democrats, who were the key to Bork's dwindling chances. Reagan's one and only national speech on behalf of Bork was delivered in the middle of the afternoon on October 14, nearly a week after the Judiciary Committee had already voted against Bork by a vote of 9–5, and with only CNN choosing to broadcast it live. It was too little, too late. Bork refused to withdraw his nomination in the face of certain defeat, ensuring several days of bitter argument on the Senate floor before the foregone end arrived on Friday, October 22. Bork was rejected by a 58–42 vote.

Bork's was not the first nomination to fail for political reasons, but the demagogic nature of the public campaign against him made it a watershed moment in American politics, permanently deforming the nomination process for the judiciary, with ideological battles nowadays extending to the lower federal courts as well. The Bork episode demonstrated the continuing strength of the Left when aroused, and the bitter consequence of losing control of the Senate in the 1986 election. By far the most significant lasting consequence of the Bork inquisition is that it ensured that no future high court nominee would ever again candidly discuss his or her judicial philosophy before the Judiciary Committee, and before reaching that threshold many judges and legal figures self-censor their public comments, lest a speculation or argument be dredged up in a prospective confirmation hearing someday. It will likely deprive the judiciary of many colorful and imaginative judges from across the ideological spectrum; Hugo Black, Felix Frankfurter, and William O. Douglas might not have been able to be confirmed in an atmosphere like the one the Bork debacle created. In the 1990s a few liberals were heard to complain that President Clinton's two Supreme Court nominees, Stephen Breyer and Ruth Bader Ginsburg, were not as liberal as the judges they thought Clinton should have appointed. But Clinton made sure to avoid a Bork-like nomination fight.

Reagan was so outraged that he was tempted to appoint no one and leave the Court with only eight justices until the next president came to office in 1989. He was also urged (by Bob Dole, among others) to consider putting Bork on the Court through a recess appointment. But Court appointments are too precious to pass up or make on a short-term basis with long-term political costs (the Senate would have been in an uproar over a recess appointment after a negative vote), so Reagan soon proclaimed that he'd name someone "they'll object to just as much as the last one."

He came up with Douglas Ginsburg, then serving as a judge on the same court as Bork, the D.C. Circuit. Ginsburg, forty-one, had an unusual profile, having clerked for the liberal icon Justice Thurgood Marshall, and taught at Harvard Law School. But he was a stalwart Reaganite deregulator at the Justice Department and in the White House. There was some nervousness among conservative groups about the little-known nominee, especially when it was revealed that Ginsburg's wife, an obstetrician, had once performed abortions. His nomination collapsed ignominiously when it was revealed that he had smoked marijuana at a party a few years before while teaching at Harvard Law School. It was a trivial stumbling block, except in the context of Nancy Reagan's "Just say no" antidrug campaign.[17]

So the White House was left with a remarkably short list of prospective nominees. They settled on a name that had survived previous screenings: Judge Anthony Kennedy of the Ninth Circuit Court of Appeals. Kennedy's name came up immediately after Bork but was rejected in favor of Ginsburg. The judicial selection committee at the Justice Department was opposed to naming Kennedy. Former attorney general William French Smith told Reagan: "I know Anthony Kennedy, and he won't be there in the trenches." Ed Meese felt the same way, telling Reagan: "I can't look you in the eye and say he's the kind of justice you want on the Supreme Court."[18] But with Ginsburg gone, Kennedy was the last man standing, and time was running out. If the White House waited to develop a new list of prospective nominees, the matter might drag over into 1988 and Democrats might block any nominee in hopes that a Democrat would win the election.

The anti-Bork coalition worried that Kennedy was simply a more congenial Bork, and criticized Biden for scheduling prompt confirmation hearings, which went smoothly for Kennedy. After cooing suitably before the Senate Judiciary Committee that the Constitution was "a covenant with the future," Kennedy was confirmed unanimously (97–0) on February 3, 1988. The *People's Daily World* (an avowedly Communist newspaper) worried that "Kennedy would not provide a swing vote for the liberal members of the Court on issues like abortion and affirmative action, as Powell did." It turned out they needn't have worried. Reagan had lost his last chance to reshape the Supreme Court decisively.

As the Bork nomination reached its sorry denouement, a fresh cataclysm knocked Bork from the headlines. The stock market, perhaps the most popular barometer of Reagan-era prosperity, crashed. Seemingly in the blink of an eye, the morning-in-America economy became darkness at noon on Black Monday.

*   *   *

THE INTERPLAY OF the various causes of the crash of October 19, 1987, remains obscure and contested up to this day, and the full inventory of antecedents is complex and extensive, most often yielding to the overused simile of the perfect storm. Beyond the data and the theory, there was the social and cultural importance of Wall Street. The bull market of the mid-1980s was more than just an indicator of the nation's revived prosperity; it became a totem of yuppiedom and a talisman of consumption. The most junior securities analyst required at least a 3-series BMW, and the Wall Street–luxury nexus became the chief evidence for the "decade of greed" slogan popular on the left. Coincidentally, Oliver Stone was readying for release at the time of Black Monday a new film called *Wall Street,* whose central character, a humorless update of J. R. Ewing, argued that "greed is good." His name was Gordon Gekko, after the lizard, just to make sure no one missed the point.

While the real-world takeover financiers and corporate raiders inspired the hand-wringing scolds in Hollywood and dominated the public perception of Wall Street, the real action affecting macroeconomic trends lay in the much less glamorous world of interest rates and currency valuations. These two factors fueled the ongoing political battle over the federal budget deficit and the steadily growing trade deficit. At the beginning of Reagan's second term in 1985, real interest rates—interest rates above the rate of inflation—remained at historic highs, at least 2 percent higher than the long-term average. The persistence of high real interest rates was a reflection of the deep-seated residual inflationary expectations of the marketplace. The benchmark thirty-year Treasury bond was fetching 10.8 percent, while the three-month T-bill rate stood at 7.5 percent and the Federal Reserve's discount rate rested at just above 8 percent.[19] Corporations with triple-A credit ratings faced interest rates of more than 11 percent, while rates on so-called junk bonds were often over 14 percent. It was thought that such high rates would eventually strangle economic growth and contribute to the overvaluation of the dollar.

But interest rates had gradually fallen in 1985 and 1986. By the spring of 1986 the Fed funds rate had fallen to 6.6 percent and the thirty-year Treasury bond to 7.8 percent. Even the *New York Times* took note of the favorable direction of things in 1985: "Americans are enjoying the lowest interest rates they have seen in five years or more. Mortgage rates are down. Car loan rates are down. The cost of business borrowing has fallen. Even the Treasury Department's borrowing costs have plunged. . . . If the rate relief persists—and most economists expect stable or lower interest rates for the next few years—it will bolster such basic industries as housing and automobiles."

Behind the scenes of these falling interest rates was the ongoing controversy over monetary policy at the Federal Reserve. Supply-siders and many of Reagan's economic advisers continued to argue that Fed chairman Paul Volcker should loosen the reins on the money supply and that the prospect of renewed inflation was overestimated, but Volcker remained stubborn. Volcker feared that cutting interest rates would reignite inflation and spur a return to the stagflation of the late 1970s, and that further reductions in short-term Fed rates would eventually backfire in the bond market, driving up long-term rates out of concern that the Fed was relenting in its vigilance against inflation.

But Reagan slowly filled seats on the Fed's Board of Governors with appointees more to his liking, and by early 1986 had appointed a majority of the Board of Governors.[20] Reagan's four appointees wasted no time before putting their stamp on Fed policy, and in February 1986 they took the unusual step, in a heated meeting, of outvoting Volcker on a proposal to lower the Fed's discount rate from 7.5 percent to 7 percent. It was the first time in eight years that a Fed chairman had been outvoted, and Volcker stormed out of the Fed's conference room in a huff. When news of Volcker's humiliation leaked out a few weeks later rumors began to circulate that he would resign; this kind of internal dissent, the *Washington Post* editorialized, is "always a sign of serious trouble." *Business Week* called the vote "a palace coup . . . a power struggle more befitting a Hollywood set than the Fed's Washington headquarters."

Volcker needn't have fretted that interest rates would sink too far. The happy trend of falling interest rates halted and reversed starting in the early months of 1987. By the spring of 1987, the robust economic expansion that began in late 1982 had reached fifty-five months, nearly a record. The longevity of this expansion and the supposed natural course of the business cycle lent verisimilitude to the thought that a recession was overdue. "For months," the *American Banker* wrote in February 1987, "the consensus in the financial community has been that for all practical purposes, the economy would be mired in weakness in early 1987." On the other hand, some economic data early in the new year suggested that the economy, after slowing to about a 2.2 percent annual growth rate in 1985 and early 1986, might be accelerating again, rekindling the threat of inflation. Job growth in the last quarter of 1986 had been robust, and in January an eye-popping 450,000 new jobs were generated; first-quarter growth looked to be coming in at about a 5 percent annual rate.

In addition to ordinary worries about the business cycle there was an ongoing fretfulness over the twin deficits—the federal budget deficit and the trade deficit, which had soared in the middle 1980s to heretofore unimaginable levels. The budget deficit in 1986 had been $283 billion, or 5.3 percent of GDP.[21] Although it was not widely recognized at the time, the budget deficit was falling sharply in 1987 and would come in at $222 billion in the next fiscal year—a healthy drop to 3.4 percent of GDP. America's balance of trade, meanwhile, had gone from a surplus of $5 billion in 1981 to a deficit of $147 billion in 1986.

There is always a lag between gathering the data and seeing its significance, and the favorable developments on the budget couldn't overcome the anxiety about the trade deficit.[22] Classical economic theory suggested that a large and growing trade deficit would put significant downward pressure on the value of the dollar. To the contrary, between 1981 and 1985 the dollar had risen over 50 percent in value against the mighty West German mark, the sturdy British pound, and the fickle French franc. At one point in 1985 the dollar almost reached nominal parity with the British pound.

In September 1985, Treasury Secretary James Baker convened his counterparts from France, West Germany, Japan, the United States, and the United Kingdom at the Plaza Hotel in New York and brokered an agreement to lower the value of the dollar through coordinated intervention in the international currency markets. Essentially this meant central banks dumped dollars on the market to drive down their value. Over the next two years the dollar declined more than 50 percent against the Japanese yen, and began to have the predicted effect: by the end of 1987, U.S. exports had risen 38 percent over the year before.

But by early 1987 the dollar's value was thought to be falling too fast, and in February Baker and his counterparts convened again at the Louvre in Paris, this time to find a way to break the dollar's fall lest the economies of our trading partners falter and tip the United States into a recession. The central bankers reversed course, intervening to prop up the dollar and putting upward pressure on interest rates. Long-bond rates started first creeping and then galloping back up, reaching almost 10.2 percent for the ten-year Treasury bond by October 19. The stock market, which usually moves down in response to increases in interest rates, blithely ignored this reversal and continued soaring, eventually rising by 45 percent on the year at its peak of just over 2,722 on the Dow on August 25. Coincidentally, the market top occurred just as Volcker's term as Fed chairman ended. Reagan's new Fed chairman, Alan Greenspan, was sworn in on August 11.

There was considerable doubt in the markets about the durability of the dollar stabilization regime. While the United States was publicly committed to stabilizing the dollar, there was suspicion that unofficially the Reagan administration was happy to let the dollar's value slide further to alleviate the trade deficit with Japan. Then West Germany raised its interest rates, which put added upward pressure on U.S. interest rates, much to the annoyance of Treasury Secretary Baker, who had been leaning on West Germany to lower its rates.

In hindsight the harbingers of a stock market breakdown become easier to make out. The stock market could not maintain its level in the face of rising interest rates and extreme valuations; the Standard and Poor's 500 Index was trading at twenty-two times trailing earnings at the market top in August, far out of line from its historic range. A study in the *Harvard Business Review* would later conclude that the market was 17 percent overvalued at its peak. The market became increasingly volatile, with 40- and 50-point swings in the course of a trading day—the equivalent of 200 points nowadays. At the market peak in August, big institutional buyers—mutual and pension funds—were net buyers of about 2.8 million shares a day. But by mid-September, the funds had become net sellers, shedding 300,000 shares a day. By mid-October institutional funds were dumping shares, with daily net sales accelerating to 4.4 million shares.

Right after Labor Day, the New York Stock Exchange's president, Gerald Corrigan, said that "the storm clouds were visibly gathering."[23] A few prescient observers sounded the alarm in real time. Commodities trader Paul Tudor Jones had been saying since late 1986, "There will be some type of decline in the next 10, 20 months, and it will be earth-shaking; it will be saber-rattling." Robert Prechter, an advocate of the esoteric Elliott wave hypothesis of market behavior, said on October 5, "The overvaluation of stocks is more extreme than the 1929 high."[24] The legendary investor Philip Fisher—who had gone through the crash of 1929, after having famously predicted that stock prices would go still higher—told *Forbes* magazine that the stock market looked to him like 1927 or 1929. The advance cover date of the *Forbes* issue where his remarks appeared was October 19. A little-known stock adviser named Elaine Garzarelli advised her clients to sell everything a week before October 19; she would be little known no longer. But as the signs of a market meltdown accumulated, the market would stage robust rallies that lulled investors; on September 22, the Dow rallied for 75 points, a record rise at the time.

During the week of October 5, the Dow fell 150 points. Volatility increased the following week. On Monday, October 11, the Dow fell 11 points, but it rallied Tuesday by 37 points. Kidder, Peabody reassured its clients: "The long-term bull market remains intact. On an intermediate-term basis, early 1988 should still witness 2900 on the Dow Jones Industrial Average." On Wednesday, October 13, the trade deficit figure for the previous month was released; it was $1.5 billion higher than expected. Bond yields spiked above 10 percent for the first time in two years. The Dow fell 95 points, at that time the largest one-day drop ever. On Thursday, the market seemed steady until the last half hour, when a wave of heavy selling drove the Dow down another 57 points. It was the fourth-busiest day in market history. The Dow had declined in eight of the past nine trading days.

Reacting to the trade deficit numbers, Treasury Secretary James Baker said late in the day on Thursday that the United States could "accommodate further adjustments" in the value of the dollar, meaning that the United States was willing to let the dollar's value fall further. Baker's comments reinforced market suspicions that further weakening of the dollar was the unofficial policy of the Reagan administration; a falling dollar would put more upward pressure on interest rates. Friday was another debacle. After trading evenly for most of the morning, at lunchtime the bottom fell out. The Dow fell 108 points—another new mark—dropping the last 50 points in the final half hour of trading. In yet another record, 338 million shares had changed hands.

The market turmoil got the attention of the White House. Late in the day Reagan met with Greenspan, Baker, Treasury Undersecretary Beryl Sprinkel, and others to take stock. Reagan expressed his concern that the money supply was too tight. As he recorded in his diary, "Alan [Greenspan] doesn't agree & believes this is only an overdue correction." Over the weekend, Baker returned to his dollar-bashing theme, telling *Meet the Press,* "We will not sit back in this country and watch [trade] surplus countries jack up their interest rates and squeeze growth worldwide on the expectation that the United States somehow will follow by raising its interest rates." On Sunday the eighteenth the *New York Times* ran a story quoting a "senior administration official" (Baker adamantly denied being the source) saying the United States would allow the dollar to decline against the West German mark. Unrest in the Persian Gulf added further to Wall Street's jitters. Late in the week Iran had fired on an American oil tanker, and over the weekend the U.S. Navy destroyed two Iranian oil platforms in retaliation (the platforms had been used as staging areas for Iranian attacks on Gulf shipping).

Many individual investors who had flocked to the market during its bull phase panicked and jammed the phone lines at mutual fund companies. Fidelity received eighty thousand calls. Joseph Nocera wrote: "The people who ran the likes of Fidelity and Schwab and Vanguard knew—absolutely knew—what was going to happen next."

The turmoil and declines of the previous week left the markets deeply shaken at the open on Monday morning. The Dow fell 68 points in the first half hour of trading; eleven of the Dow's thirty stocks were unable to open because of severe imbalances between sell and buy orders. With no buyers, more than two hundred stocks—one-twelfth of the New York Stock Exchange's listings—could not open for trading. At 11:00 a.m. the market appeared to have stabilized, down 200 points. Then the new chairman of the Securities and Exchange Commission, David Ruder, blundered. At the completion of a speech in Washington, Ruder mused aloud to reporters about halting trading on the NYSE. His comments hit the trading floor shortly after 1:00 p.m. Ruder claimed later to have been misunderstood, and even though the SEC quickly issued a statement saying it was not going to close the markets, the psychological damage was done. (This was not a new idea for

Ruder; he had mentioned the idea of a trading halt to combat volatility in a speech on October 6.)²⁵ The afternoon was a one-way rout. The system for handling large orders seized up under the huge volume, and computer screens on the trading floor went blank. Many trades cleared at prices far from the price in effect when the orders were placed. Orders for sales of more than a hundred million shares were never completed at all, and the trading tape, which could handle nine hundred trades a minute, ran two and a half hours behind.

Some evidence suggests that selling by individual investors drove the magnitude of the crash; the volume of large trades (twenty-five thousand shares or more) by institutions was only 2 percent higher on October 19 than the average of the preceding fifty trading days. But a larger factor in driving the market over a cliff was an innovation that was supposed to protect investors against this very risk—portfolio insurance in the form of index futures options. Starting in 1982, the Chicago Mercantile Exchange had begun selling a new financial product—futures options on the price of various stock indexes. Index options allowed for pure speculation on the short-term movement of the market and were thought to be a perfect hedge against losses. Owners of large stock positions with big paper gains could hedge against the prospect of a large decline in price by selling a futures contract on the price level of one of the major stock indexes, such as the S&P 500, and thereby lock in gains. The complexity of portfolio insurance had two effects: it gave rise to automatic computerized trading on a wide scale, which in turn increased volatility in the stock market, especially on the Fridays that became known as "triple-witching days," when index options expired and had to be settled.

While in theory index options should have helped to smooth the market during ordinary conditions, their highly leveraged nature meant they increased the risk of a market meltdown in any episode of extraordinary volatility or market panic. On October 19 automatic computer trading programs flooded the market with billions of dollars in index option sell orders, but with no buyers the prices collapsed and pulled down the prices of underlying stocks. It was the financial equivalent of a runaway nuclear war by computer rather than human decision. Reflecting on the problem of computerized trading, Greenspan would later say: "The market plunge was an accident waiting to happen." One of the market reforms enacted after the October 19 crash was limits and halts on computer trading in conditions of extraordinary volatility.

When the dust settled at the end of the day, the Dow finished down 508 points on 604 million shares of volume, closing at 1,739, down from 2,516 just eleven days earlier. It was a 22 percent loss in one day, representing a half trillion dollars in market capitalization. Forty stocks declined for every one that rose; normally a three-to-one ratio is considered a rout. The one-day figure understated the damage: along with the previous Thursday and Friday, the Dow had lost 769 points—a third of its value—in three days. By contrast, the crash of 1929 had taken the market down 13 percent. And the crash was global. As the market closed in New York, the contagion spread to the markets opening in the Far East. In Hong Kong the main stock index dropped 45 percent, and the stock market closed for the rest of the week. Japan's stock market dropped 15 percent; Australia's market plunged 20 percent, and the London stock market fell 12 percent. Many investors fled to Treasury bonds, but gold jumped $10 an ounce to a five-year high.

Blue chips became black-and-blue chips: Westinghouse lost one-third of its value, Exxon one-quarter, IBM one-quarter. The value of Sam Walton's share of the company he founded, Wal-Mart, fell $1.1 billion. George Soros lost $800 million. Securities firms feared a classic run on the bank from panicky account holders and, fearing violence from customers, Donaldson, Lufkin & Jenrette posted uniformed security guards outside its New York office. Alan Greenspan was on a commercial airline flight to Dallas during trading hours; when he deplaned he was relieved to hear that the market had fallen "five-oh-eight," assuming it meant 5.08 on the Dow. "Some people are talking of panic," Reagan wrote in his diary that night. The president was slow to pay attention to the market's action, as it had been a busy day elsewhere: he had spent the late afternoon with Nancy at Bethesda Naval Hospital, where she was recovering from breast cancer surgery two days before.

The first order of business at the White House the next morning was another meeting between Reagan and his economic advisers. Greenspan was still in Dallas, where he issued a short statement first thing Tuesday morning to reassure the market of the Fed's "readiness to serve as a source of liquidity to support the economic and financial system." He then cancelled his morning speech and returned to Washington on the first available plane.

The panic Reagan worried about nearly came to pass on Wall Street the following day. History—and Reagan's diary for October 20—records that the markets settled down and the Dow rose 102 points, providing some measure of relief to Washington and a nervous public. Neither the White House nor the public learned until later that, in fact, October 20 was more unsettling than the nineteenth had been, as the stock market came within a hairbreadth of collapsing and shutting down. Financier Felix Rohatyn told the *Wall Street Journal* that "Tuesday was the most dangerous day we had in 50 years; I think we came within an hour" of the disintegration of the market.[26]

The immediate problem at the end of the day Monday and at the market open on Tuesday is that many securities firms and specialists (the firms on the trading floor who perform the all-important function of making a market for individual stocks by buying and selling from their own inventory) were facing margin calls on account of the fallen value of their now-swollen holdings and, according to market rules, needed to settle their accounts within five business days. Many firms lacked sufficient cash to do so. But banks that normally extended credit to brokers and specialists were reluctant to step into the breach. Specialists and brokers were stunned when their banks said Monday night and early Tuesday morning that they wouldn't make new loans. Some specialist firms faced immediate insolvency; a few were forced into shotgun mergers with larger firms. One small specialist firm that faced immediate insolvency, A. B. Tompane, merged overnight with Merrill Lynch; the deal was completed at three o'clock Tuesday morning.

Despite the Fed's promise of liquidity, the market opened slowly, with many leading blue chip stocks taking an hour or more to begin trading. Initially the Dow Jones average was up an encouraging 200 points, but this gain quickly evaporated as specialists and securities firms tried to unload the large unwanted positions built up the day before. As buy orders dried up, blue chip stocks ceased trading one by one. Merck stopped trading at 9:52 a.m., Sears at 11:12, Eastman Kodak at 11:28, Philip Morris at 11:30, Dow Chemical at 11:43. Some blue chips didn't open at all. Stocks that remained open were trading sporadically and in small volumes. With so many stocks closed, the American Stock Exchange and the Chicago Mercantile Exchange halted options trading. By noon the Dow was off 100 points and market watchers feared it was about to fall another 200 points.

During the lunch hour rumors swept trading floors nationwide that the New York Stock Exchange was going to close. In fact the NYSE's president and senior executives were meeting to decide whether to take such a dramatic step. Behind the scenes, several securities firms—Goldman Sachs and Salomon Brothers were said to be among them—were calling the SEC in Washington and urging it to close the exchange (the SEC does not have the power to do this but presumably could ask the president, who does). White House chief of staff Howard Baker encouraged the markets to stay open. The

NYSE's president, John Phelan, recoiled from the thought of closing the market: "If we close it, we would never open it."

At about 12:40 p.m. a sudden turnabout occurred that traders later described to the *Wall Street Journal* as "a miracle." At the Chicago Board of Trade, buy orders started flooding in for the Major Markets Index, the only major index option still trading. Within five minutes the price of the MMI swung from an implicit 60-point discount to the underlying value of the stocks in its index to a 12-point premium. The *Wall Street Journal* described it as "the equivalent of a lightning-like 360-point rise in the Dow." Where this flood of buy orders came from is not fully known, but circumstantial evidence pointed to a small number of sophisticated buyers acting deliberately to force the market back into positive territory. News of the surge in the MMI reached the trading floors in New York at the same time several major corporations announced major share buybacks.[27] Several banks reversed their earlier position and now agreed to extend credit to specialists and brokers. Shortly after 1:00 p.m., most blue chip stocks reopened for trading; the crisis was over. The Dow ended the day up 102.2 points—a record increase at the time, once more on record volume of 608 million shares. Gainers outnumbered decliners 1,398 to 537. Wednesday, October 21 was even better: the Dow rose 186 points, and 1,749 stocks posted gains.

*　　*　　*

ALTHOUGH THE MARKETS had stabilized, the parallel with 1929 was on everyone's mind, and the political marketplace began its own convulsions. The October 19 crash was, at the time, regarded as a harbinger of the end of Reaganomics, if not the beginning of another depression. Senator Al Gore said, "The voodoo chickens of Reaganomics have come home to roost." John Kenneth Galbraith commented that the crash "is the end product of Arthur Laffer's supply-side economics and Milton Friedman's experiment with monetarism." Galbraith added, "After the 1929 crash, the universal phrase was 'The economy is fundamentally sound.' Expect to hear that out of Washington over the next few days." Sure enough, Reagan remarked: "All the economic indicators are solid; everyone is a little puzzled. There is nothing wrong with the economy." On Thursday, by which time the market had recouped half its loss from Black Monday, Reagan said "the crisis would appear to be over." Reagan also used the old joke that the stock market had predicted nine out of the last six recessions. Nonetheless, consumer confidence surveys, no doubt reflecting media pessimism, showed a sharp drop in consumer sentiment, and Wall Street firms laid off sixteen thousand employees over the next three months. Year-end bonus envelopes on Wall Street were much thinner.

Reagan would turn out to be correct about the economy. Instead of a prolonged bear market, stocks resumed their slow upward march, and the economy continued to grow rather than stalling out. GDP grew by 3.4 percent for 1987 as a whole, and a robust 6.1 percent in the fourth quarter. The economy grew 4.1 percent in 1988, and corporate profits were up by more than one-quarter. Surveys showed a quick rebound in consumer confidence, and there was no apparent impact on consumer spending. Within a few months *USA Today* noted "a host of signs that recession worries are overblown," and *National Review* taunted the naysayers: "What if the press threw a recession and nobody showed up?" A year later, the *Financial Times* looked back: "The prophets of doom have been confounded. Far from being pitched into recession, the world economy is approaching the anniversary of the crash with the fastest growth since 1984."

Anyone who bought stocks the day after the crash made out handsomely. By the end of 1988, the Dow Jones Industrial Average was 25 percent higher than at the close of Black Monday. But as with any such startling event, there was an urgent need to understand causation to prevent its recurrence. Market mavens and bankers were quick to blame James Baker and his feud with the West German Bundesbank. The vice chairman of the Bundesbank pushed back: "The crash was the consequence of an attack on the Bundesbank by the very respected James Baker." Supply-siders were split on the role of monetary policy in causing the crash. Paul Craig Roberts sided with Reagan, arguing that tight money contributed to the crash.[28] Art Laffer thought money was too loose. This disagreement among Reaganite supply-siders indicates the difficulty of understanding economic forces at work throughout the 1980s; Laffer and Roberts couldn't even agree on the rate at which the money supply had been growing, though implicit in this disagreement was the recognition that monetary policy under Volcker had been highly erratic. James Cramer, not yet known as the screaming man of cable TV business news, wrote: "No esoteric explanation of the crash was necessary. The market had simply been too high." The Securities and Exchange Commission studied factors in the crash and gave the usual government-panel shrug: "We may never know what precise combination of investor psychology, economic developments and trading technologies caused the events of October." Some even counted the failing Bork nomination as a factor in shaking market confidence.

Needless to say, politicians jumped at the opportunity to capitalize on the events. "Crash Promises to Benefit Democrats," read a *Wall Street Journal* headline on October 21. Pundits and analysts rushed to declare that "the day of reckoning is at hand." "The Reagan era is over," announced the *New Republic*. Leading Democrats all said the crash was "an early warning" that the budget deficit needed to be closed, which was a euphemism for a tax increase. This was expected, but moderate Republicans were quick to agree. Bob Dole said the crash "creates an opportunity, an opportunity to do something about the deficit," and Republican congresswoman Marge Roukema of New Jersey said, "The supply-siders have been totally discredited." Dole agreed: "It's going to be tough to sell that stuff now."

Reagan appeared to relent on opposition to a tax increase when he agreed to a new round of budget negotiations with Congress and said that he'd "be willing to look at" congressional proposals for a tax hike, though budget director Jim Miller quickly contradicted the president and dismissed the idea. Two days after the crash, Reagan announced $23 billion in automatic spending cuts required by the Gramm-Rudman deficit reduction law.

But as nerves calmed down it became clear that the twin deficits had little to do with the crash; to the contrary, fears that Washington might roll back Reagan's economic policies contributed to the loss of confidence in the stock market. The *Wall Street Journal* editorialized, "The 1982–1987 bull market resulted from the Reagan policies, and the fall in the last two months resulted from renewed doubts about whether those policies would be sustained." *National Review* concurred: "The crash was 'a vote of no confidence' in the Congress, and in a White House increasingly unwilling to do battle over serious issues."

Two political factors in particular stood out. The first was the progress of the Omnibus Trade Bill in the House of Representatives, the brainchild of Democratic House majority leader Richard Gephardt of Missouri. Gephardt's bill would not impose direct tariffs on imports but would direct the president to "enter negotiations" with any country that had a trade imbalance with the United States; in the event that negotiations failed to open foreign markets, the bill required mandatory but unspecified measures to reduce trade surpluses by 10 percent. The Gephardt bill passed the House by four votes in the spring and was headed to a House-Senate conference committee near the time of the crash. Reagan had assailed previous congressional attempts to punish trade as "kamikaze protectionism," but there was fear that momentum for trade protectionism was growing. "Trade Vote Deals Blow to Bonds," read the *New York Times* headline the day after the Gephardt bill passed the

House. Late in the summer the *Times* speculated that Reagan's deteriorating political position might compel him to accept a restrictionist trade bill.

Then the Tuesday before the crash the House Ways and Means Committee announced plans to pass a bill to limit the deductibility of interest payments on debt used to finance corporate takeovers. It was an extraordinarily counterproductive idea, aimed at the so-called corporate raiders and leveraged-buyout specialists who took over and restructured major corporations chiefly with borrowed money. The practice was controversial chiefly because several raiders and their financiers (especially junk bond king Michael Milken) turned huge personal profits through the practice, which was obscure to the public and infuriating to wealth-hating liberal politicians. Robert Reich expressed the typical view of the intelligentsia, calling takeovers "greed, contributing nothing to economic performance." Reich predictably endorsed the Ways and Means proposal as "just what the economy needs to improve economic efficiency." But both corporate profits and productivity growth were sluggish in the 1970s, when corporate merger and takeover activity was at a standstill, and profits and productivity had soared in the mid-1980s. Numerous economists and market watchers made the compelling case that corporate takeover activity was an important spur to corporate management to achieve better results from assets.[29] Even though the bill faced long odds of passage, it was seen as the possible first step in a New Deal–style political attack on finance capital. The SEC report on the crash fingered this measure as a contributing factor in investor sentiment, and companies that had been takeover targets were especially hard hit on October 19. Takeover specialist Carl Icahn called the proposed bill "the match that ignited the dynamite."

*   *   *

THE TRIPLE WHAMMY of Iran-Contra and its unsatisfactory aftermath, the failed Bork nomination, and the stock market crash meant that the media headlines from 1983 about the stench of failure at the White House were dusted off and recycled. *Newsweek* reported in July: "Washington's judgment is already in: Reagan is politically crippled, personally faltering and lapsing toward irrelevance." "The sound being heard around here is the sound of the Reagan administration running out of steam," the *Wall Street Journal* reported the Friday before the stock market crash in October.[30] Reagan was said to have entered his lame duck period, more than a year ahead of the election to choose his successor. As far back as the spring, *Time* magazine ran a cover story on what the post-Reagan future would bring, because "the nation is beginning to look beyond Reagan now." *Time* presented a thoroughly gloomy backdrop for its look ahead: "Some of the new American imagery is very different. It suggests something closing down, a darkness crowding at the margins. One sees not the sunshine of Reagan's American morning but touches of Thomas Hobbes." The author was Lance Morrow, who only nine months before had authored a soaring paean to Reagan's greatness but here added without a touch of irony, "The gloom probably is just as exaggerated as the earlier optimism."[31] The *Economist* ran a cover drawing of a frowning Statue of Liberty with the headline "Whatever Happened to America's Smile?" Britain's sober premier news organ discerned "sulkiness, defensiveness, and pessimism" in America.[32]

The new pessimism of the chattering class coincided with the literary-intellectual sensation of the moment, Paul Kennedy's bestselling book *The Rise and Fall of the Great Powers*.[33] Ostensibly a sweeping history of the arc of great powers from sixteenth-century Spain through twentieth-century Britain, it made the Spenglerian argument that the United States was in a condition of "imperial overstretch" because of its global military commitments and precarious economic position. Suggesting that high defense spending hindered long-term economic growth was an elegant argument for Democrats who wanted to cut Pentagon spending. Reagan trumped Paul Kennedy with another Kennedy, pointing out that even with his increases the United States in the mid-1980s was still spending less of its GDP on defense than it had under President John F. Kennedy. Kennedy's "imperial overstretch" thesis did have one perfect fit that no one pointed out: the Soviet Union. (One person who did—later—was Soviet scholar Alexei Arbatov, who wrote in 2008: "Kennedy's description accurately fits what was happening in the Soviet Union at the beginning of the 1980s.")[34]

What was different as 1987 drew toward a close was that many conservatives joined the chorus of dismay and disillusionment. Fred Barnes wrote in August that Reagan "is weakened, aged, and sometimes disconsolate." *National Review*'s pseudonymous Washington correspondent "Cato" reported in early September, "Many big-name conservatives here think Ronald Reagan has lost his soul." A *Human Events* front-page headline blared, "Conservatives Depressed by Rudderless Administration." The lead of the story read: "The Reagan Administration appears to have lost its will to survive."[35] Sir James Goldsmith, a prominent British conservative with close ties to America, wrote a widely noted article for the *Wall Street Journal* entitled "America, You Falter."[36]

There were clear signs of Reagan's declining clout on Capitol Hill. His frequent meetings with Hill Republicans over budget and tax issues were contentious. Congress ostentatiously voted to override two Reagan vetoes of spending bills. In January Reagan vetoed a Clean Water Act reauthorization.[37] He had proposed $6 billion for new wastewater treatment facilities in his previous budget, and offered to compromise at $12 billion when Congress demanded more. The House wouldn't even hold hearings or a vote on the proposal, instead passing a bill that cost $18 billion. Reagan drew his veto pen, calling it "a program that is so loaded with waste and larded with pork I cannot in conscience sign it."[38] But local sewage treatment plants offer the right kind of popular pork smell, and both houses of Congress overrode Reagan's veto with lopsided votes: 401–26 in the House, 93–6 in the Senate. It was Reagan's sixtieth veto to that point in his presidency; only five had been overridden.

Reagan knew ahead of time that his veto of the water bill would lose, but his other high-profile veto was a more bitter and close-run affair. In March Reagan vetoed a five-year, $87 billion transportation bill on the grounds that it exceeded his budget target by $10 billion in unnecessary pork projects (and 152 earmarks—minor league compared to the three thousand earmarks in the 2006 transportation bill that many conservatives regarded as the nadir of fiscal responsibility in the George W. Bush years). Half of the Republicans in the House abandoned Reagan and passed the override by a vote of 350–73. After Reagan's veto was initially upheld by a single vote in the Senate, Democrats arm-twisted Senator Terry Sanford of North Carolina into switching his vote. Reagan was unable to sway any of the thirteen Republican senators who voted to override, despite a personal plea made in Bob Dole's Senate office. Among the thirteen were staunch conservatives including Steve Symms, Thad Cochran, and Mitch McConnell. Reagan wrote in his diary, "I knew when I left [Dole's office] I'd failed, but I have no respect left for that 13 . . . they were voting against a balanced budget." Stung by these overrides, the White House (especially former Senate majority leader Howard Baker) decided the better course was to avoid veto fights and seek compromise with Congress. In exasperation, *Human Events* ran another critical headline: "Bring Back Don Regan."[39]

Meanwhile, the domestic policy proposals coming out of the White House were drearily conventional, and were signs of slippage from Reagan's hardheaded attitude toward expansion of government. Reagan's second-term secretary of health and human services, former Indiana governor Otis Bowen, was pushing a scheme to add catastrophic health insurance coverage to Medicare. Reagan had invited Bowen to develop a catastrophic health coverage plan in his 1986 State of the Union speech, but Bowen was unable to come up with a private sector alternative to Medicare. For a premium of a mere $4.92 a month, the federal government would offer complete catastrophic health coverage for elderly Americans. Despite warnings from several cabinet members and his Council of Economic Advisers that expanding Medicare would have perverse consequences, Reagan signed off on Bowen's proposal in late 1986. He was partly swayed by pollster Richard Wirthlin's finding that the idea was popular with the public and could help Reagan rebound from the Iran-Contra mess. Ted Kennedy hailed the proposal, while the Heritage Foundation's health care expert, Stuart Butler, wrote in dismay, "It is ironic that Ronald Reagan's Health Secretary may make the liberals' dream come true." (Congress eventually adopted the Bowen plan with the usual additions and extra spending the critics had forecast, but repealed it in 1989 after furious seniors protested against the additional $800 per person annual premium. The lesson was clear: don't ask people to pay directly for program benefits.)

The White House was also working haltingly and unconvincingly on a welfare reform plan that mostly called for allowing the states greater latitude to experiment with reform ideas and work requirements. There was nothing wrong with that from a pure Reaganite point of view—it was not far removed from his view as governor of California that states could innovate better than Washington—but it represented a missed opportunity and a remarkable failure of intellectual imagination to go after an area of social policy where revisionist views were gaining strength. One of the great mysteries of the Reagan White House, especially in its second term, is why it never embraced Charles Murray's critique of social policy in his blockbuster 1984 book *Losing Ground*, which argued that the problem with welfare programs was not their expense but their debilitating moral and social effect on the underclass. Despite the efforts of some Reagan aides (particularly Michael Horowitz) to promote Murray's analysis within the administration, Murray's provocative thesis fell victim to a not-invented-here mentality. It would be left to Bill Clinton and the Republican Congress of the mid-1990s to push reform along Murray's lines. For the meantime, the White House was content to follow the lead of Senator Moynihan in crafting a reform measure.

Finally, the White House produced a 750-page "competitiveness" bill, which was intended to blunt congressional momentum for protectionist trade legislation. But the White House bill included $980 million for "worker adjustment" and $800 million for youth job training, exactly the kind of feel-good boondoggles that Reagan used to criticize and target for elimination in his first term. Fred Barnes observed of these three policy areas: "All three measures could have been proposed by Jimmy Carter, the ultimate slur on the guy who defeated him. The worst fear of conservatives has been realized."[40] Barnes was not alone in making the ultimate invidious comparison. Newt Gingrich told the *Wall Street Journal* that Reagan is "in some danger of becoming another Jimmy Carter." Gingrich decried "the self-imposed debilitation of the Reagan presidency. None of us on the Hill knows what to expect in any given week."[41]

The only recognizably Reaganite initiative of the moment was the Economic Bill of Rights (EBOR), a package of five constitutional reforms that included a federal spending limit, a line-item veto, a balanced budget amendment, a prohibition on wage and price controls, and a requirement for a two-thirds majority in Congress to pass tax increases. The idea to package these reforms in a single bill—a Reaganite antidote to the statist Economic Bill of Rights that FDR first articulated in 1944—grew straight from work Martin Anderson had done for Reagan before the 1980 campaign.[42] Reagan announced the idea with great flourish in a speech at the Jefferson Memorial on July 4, and he returned to EBOR repeatedly throughout the summer and fall. It might have been a great idea in 1981, but in 1987 it had no chance of passing Congress.

There were some achievements that drew little notice at the time but which have loomed much larger subsequently, most notably the Federal Communication Commission's repeal of the Fairness Doctrine. The Fairness Doctrine was a rule from the 1960s requiring TV and radio broadcasters to provide equal time for opposing points of view. The Supreme Court upheld this constraint on free speech on the rationale that the broadcast airwaves were public property since the government allocated the broadcast spectrum. Broadcasters hated it, and the rule contributed to the blandification of the airwaves, as broadcasters avoided controversial points of view to keep from tripping a regulatory snare. The FCC's Reaganite chairman, Mark Fowler, worked patiently to build a record to justify dumping the Fairness Doctrine, producing a report in 1985 that concluded the Fairness Doctrine no longer served the public interest because it had a "chilling effect" on free speech.[43] Democrats in Congress saw where Fowler's work was heading and attempted to codify the Fairness Doctrine. Reagan vetoed the bill, calling the Fairness

Doctrine unconstitutional, and Congress lacked the votes to override this veto. This set the stage for Fowler and the FCC to abolish the rule in August 1987, and Democratic attempts to restore the Fairness Doctrine in Congress in 1989 and 1990 were beaten back, helping to pave the way for the rise of conservative talk radio.

But these disappointments and victories were small beer. Much worse for conservatives was the news that Reagan was going to reach an arms control agreement with the Soviet Union, and sign it alongside Gorbachev at a summit in Washington.

*   *   *

DESPITE SHULTZ'S CONVICTION that the concessions on nuclear arms Gorbachev offered at Reykjavik would form the basis for rapid progress, in the three months after Reykjavik the official Soviet diplomatic channels reverted to their old snail's pace. Shultz and Shevardnadze had a futile follow-up meeting in Vienna a few weeks after Reykjavik. Tempers and mutual suspicion were still running too high. The Soviets sent word they did not wish to speak with America's two senior arms control specialists (Paul Nitze and Richard Perle), and began sending back-channel messages to the United States through the staff of Senator Ted Kennedy. At year's end Gorbachev refused to allow Reagan to broadcast greetings to the Soviet people on Soviet TV, as he had done at the end of 1985. In January the Soviets refused to issue a visa to Ron Reagan (the president's son), who wanted to visit Moscow for ABC's *Good Morning America*.

Inside the Kremlin, Gorbachev and his advisers were convinced that Reagan didn't want any arms control agreement, and thought that the best course was to call Reagan's bluff and play to the president's domestic opposition. A December 1986 memo to Gorbachev from Alexander Yakovlev argued, "[We are facing] the task of incessant and effective political pressure on the United States with the objective of countering Reagan's course and of providing support for those forces within the U.S. ruling class who stand against this course. . . . Under the current correlation of forces, the USSR is confronting the USA not only in the international arena, but also inside the U.S. itself. Of course, we cannot elect a 'good' President for ourselves, we cannot persuade him to make 'good' policy for us. However, we can protect ourselves from the worst. Today it would mean: to increase pressure on Reagan and the circles standing behind him."

Yakovlev's recommendation was that Gorbachev "untie the package" offered at Reykjavik—in other words, unbundle the grand deal and work for separate agreements on INF missiles in Europe and on strategic weapons (the START talks), strengthen the ABM Treaty, and make a new agreement on nuclear testing. Despite the technical differences that arose at Reykjavik, the basic outline of each component part was clear. "Will the U.S. go for such decisions?" Yakovlev asked. "It is already clear that *not under Reagan!*" (emphasis in original). But offering to reach quick deals, Yakovlev thought, might provide considerable political leverage: "[It would] uncover the true positions of the U.S., become a powerful and long-term instrument of pressure on the Americans, and their course; [it would] play a role of a stimulus to limit appropriations for the SDI in the American Congress."[44] Although killing SDI remained a key objective, Yakovlev thought it best not to link the separate arms agreements to restrictions on SDI. Congress would do the heavy lifting for them.

Yakovlev read domestic American politics accurately. In late 1986 and early 1987 Congress voted for measures to reduce funds for SDI development and to force Reagan to obey the SALT II limits. The most transparent case of political calculation was Senator Sam Nunn (D-Ga.). Nunn, chairman of the Senate Armed Services Committee, was known as a Democratic hawk but was contemplating a run for president in 1988, so he needed to play to the Democratic left. He did so by picking a public fight with Shultz and the State Department over the interpretation of the ABM Treaty. Nunn argued in favor of the most restrictive interpretation, the one the Soviets favored, and said that the administration's interpretation was "the most flagrant abuse of the Constitution's treaty power in 200 years of American history." Reagan complained about Congress in his diary: "They are actually sitting on the Soviet side of the negotiating table," and he referred to Nunn as "a highly overrated Senator" who is "kicking a tantrum."[45]

Politburo minutes suggest Gorbachev's view was not as cynical as Yakovlev's, but after the first of the year he moved quickly to exploit the moment. In February he invited Shultz to Moscow to push ahead with an INF treaty on the terms agreed in the Reykjavik package—the zero option for Europe, with each side allowed one hundred intermediate-range missiles in Asia (for the Soviet Union) and Alaska (for the United States). He also reiterated his call for an across-the-board 50 percent reduction in strategic nuclear weapons and indicated new flexibility on how the ABM Treaty could be understood to allow U.S. testing of SDI outside the laboratory. Gorbachev still wanted to scupper SDI above all, but he and his inner circle recognized that, having failed to shake Reagan at Geneva or Reykjavik, they needed a subtler negotiating strategy. Separately U.S. diplomats received word from various channels that the Soviets were serious about their desire to get out of Afghanistan, but wanted some U.S. concessions to do so.

American arms control experts pointed out that the simple-sounding 50 percent across-the-board reduction in strategic nuclear weapons was a bad deal for the United States because of the asymmetry of force structure. Even with a 50 percent cut in Soviet ICBMs, they still would have a large enough force to wipe out America's land-based missiles in a first strike and, most importantly, still have plenty of missiles with which to threaten Europe. It was the aim of American arms control strategy to reduce or eliminate this threat, and Gorbachev's proposal would leave the Soviets with a greater relative advantage than they had presently. Hence the American emphasis on the sublimits of different kinds of delivery systems and the Soviet resistance to such limits. There were additional problems of verification that defied solution, especially involving mobile Soviet missiles and American submarine-based cruise missiles. And whenever useful, the Soviet would throw SDI restrictions back into the pot. It would be slow going on this front.

When Shultz arrived in Moscow in April, Gorbachev immediately retreated on a sticking point of the INF agreement: the hundred missiles slated for Asia and Alaska. The United States worried about verification, since INF missiles were mobile and could be moved back to Europe on short notice. Fine, said Gorbachev, then get rid of them all: a global zero-zero. Though Shultz told Gorbachev he would have to consult with the NATO allies, he knew a deal was close at hand. Gorbachev renewed his argument about SDI and the ABM Treaty but then overplayed his hand, trying to corner Shultz into making concessions by saying that he didn't think an INF treaty alone would justify a summit with Reagan in Washington. It was a blunder: Shultz, the former labor negotiator, coolly responded that it shouldn't be hard to find another way to have the INF treaty signed. As Shultz told Reagan later, "I was low-key. . . . If we look too interested [in a summit], they will raise the price." Gorbachev changed the subject.

As Yakovlev had predicted, Gorbachev's renewed offer on INF missiles played to European anxieties and American divisions of opinion. Now that the zero option for European missiles was in sight, European leaders, especially Thatcher, Kohl, and Mitterrand (who called it "a nuclear Munich"), felt it would leave Europe *less* secure from Soviet attack, even though the deal would result in the Soviets destroying three times as many nuclear warheads as the United States. The removal of American intermediate-range missiles would leave the Soviets with their massive conventional force advantage and a potentially weakened U.S. commitment to European defense. There was no prospect the United States or European nations would spend the resources necessary to match the Soviets' conventional forces, and there was little reason to think the Soviets would bargain away their advantage. The Soviets had turned the tables: their goal of splitting the NATO alliance by placing INF missiles in Eastern Europe might now be achieved by removing them. "NATO Fears Erosion of U.S. Shield," ran a headline in the *International Herald Tribune* in the spring of 1987. Back home, Weinberger argued against the deal. Reagan noted this in his diary: "He is opposed to a zero zero deal for short range nuclear missiles. . . . He & I disagree on this one." Weinberger pushed for an early commitment to begin deploying SDI as soon as possible.

Weinberger's resistance was only the beginning of the storm. As the final treaty took shape in the fall and the Washington summit where it would be signed drew near, criticism came from across the entire political spectrum. But it was the dyspepsia of conservatives that turned heads. Richard Nixon, Henry Kissinger, Alexander Haig, and Brent Scowcroft came out against the treaty. Kissinger was certain the treaty was the first step in the dissolution of the NATO alliance. "If the president persists in his assault on nuclear weapons and establishes denuclearization as a pre-eminent American objective," Kissinger wrote in *Newsweek,* "a crisis with the European nuclear powers, Britain and France, is certain."[46] Former NATO commander General Bernard Rodgers came out forcefully against it.

"Some conservatives worry that Reagan has been beguiled by Gorbachev," Hedrick Smith reported in the *New York Times Magazine,* "to the detriment of American interests. . . . [T]he disenchantment of right-wingers is at a peak. They feel jilted by their prince and compelled to fight him to try to stem the tide of history." Republican senator James McClure of Idaho worried, "We've had leaders who got into a personal relationship and have gotten soft—I'm thinking of Roosevelt and Stalin."[47] Other conservatives were even less subtle. Conservative activist Howard Phillips said Reagan was "fronting as a useful idiot for Soviet propaganda." There was talk among some conservative activist groups of forming an Anti-Appeasement Alliance to oppose Reagan's diplomatic overtures to the Soviet Union. Advertisements compared Reagan to Neville Chamberlain and the INF treaty to the Munich accord. Representative Jack Kemp and other conservatives in the House called for Shultz to be fired. It was hard to escape the conclusion that Reagan was knuckling under to pressures for détente out of desperation to halt the political damage suffered from the Iran-Contra scandal. The departure of Cap Weinberger, by 1987 the second-longest-serving secretary of defense in the nation's history, for personal reasons (his wife was ill) and his replacement by Frank Carlucci added to conservative anxieties.

These doubts were not limited to the know-nothing ranks of right-wingers. George Will charged that Reagan was engaging in "the moral disarmament of the West by elevating wishful thinking to the status of political philosophy."[48] Patrick Glynn, recently departed from the Arms Control and Disarmament Agency, wrote in *Commentary*: "This avowedly most conservative of recent American Presidents has emerged as a champion of nuclear disarmament measures far more radical and sweeping than even many arms-control proponents deem advisable."[49] *National Review* came out in full opposition: "The impending INF deal requires observers to come to an unfortunate conclusion: that Ronald Reagan is no longer predictable on matters of nuclear strategy. . . . It is simply impossible any longer to count on the Reagan Administration one way or another." Before long *National Review* came to call the INF treaty "a suicide pact." Privately William F. Buckley exchanged several letters with Reagan expressing his dismay: "Damn I wish I could be on your side on that one," Buckley wrote. "Haven't had a significant difference with you since the Panama Canal."[50] Jeane Kirkpatrick publicly opposed the treaty, along with a number of other conservatives who had left the administration. *Human Events* joined the critical chorus, but did pause long enough to notice a significant anomaly to the story line: "Conservatives should also comprehend a central point: that the INF Treaty is *not*—repeat *not*—a product of the doves within the Reagan Administration, but a product of the hardliners. Indeed, this is the treaty built by former Assistant Secretary of Defense Richard Perle, and backed by hawking elements of the National Security Council staff."[51] Perle, who left the Defense Department in the spring of 1987, would become the most vocal conservative defender of the INF treaty over the following year.

Reagan was annoyed that so many among his conservative base were bashing him and the treaty. In early December Reagan hit back at his critics in an interview with the network anchors:

QUESTION: Mr. President, a point of information—did I understand you correctly to say that you have not changed your mind from the time you described the Soviet Union as the "evil empire"?
REAGAN: The Soviet Union has, back through the years, made it plain, and

certainly leader after leader has declared his pledge that they would observe the Marxian concept of expansionism: that the future lay in a one world, Communist state. All right, we now have a leader that is apparently willing to say—or has never made that claim, but is willing to say that he's prepared to live with other philosophies in other countries. But again, as I say, that doesn't mean that we take his word for that and sign a treaty *he alone may not be able to deliver on something of that kind*. . . . And I would like to call your attention to the fact that in 1981, when I proposed the zero option of these intermediate weapons, they indignantly walked out of the negotiations and said they wouldn't be back. Well, they came back. And as a matter of fact, they came back and announced a zero-zero as their own idea. Now, I think that some of the people who are objecting the most and just refusing even to accede to the idea of ever getting any understanding, whether they realize it or not, those people, basically, down in their deepest thoughts, have accepted that war is inevitable and that there must come to be a war between the two superpowers. (Emphasis added)

It should be noted that this is nearly identical to the formulation Reagan gave to a reporter late in 1981: "I've always recognized that ultimately there's got to be a settlement, a solution. The other way, if you don't believe that, then you're trapped in the back of your mind, the inevitability of a conflict some day . . . That kind of conflict is going to end the world."[52] Conservatives didn't buy it, though. William Safire took dead aim in the *New York Times:* "His overnight abandonment of realism—his notion that a change of line and style marks a basic change of purpose—suggests that Mr. Reagan has slipped his strategic moorings."

The treaty looked to be heading for heavy weather in the Senate. Senator Sam Nunn (D-Ga.) balked at endorsing the treaty, suggesting the Senate might wish to attach a number of amendments to the treaty, requiring its renegotiation and effectively killing it. Over in the House, the leading Democratic Party defense figure, Les Aspin, said Reagan was "irresponsible." But it was from conservative Republicans that Reagan took the most serious fire. In a meeting with Reagan in Bob Dole's office, Senator Malcolm Wallop asked the question on many minds: "The Soviets have broken most every treaty they have ever signed. How do we assure compliance with the new treaty? And if they don't comply, what do we do about it?" The administration had produced five detailed reports of Soviet cheating on existing arms treaties. Reagan's answer to Wallop—start building Pershing missiles again—was not reassuring. Dole said, "I don't trust Gorbachev," though in typical Dole fashion he would eventually endorse the treaty. Another vocal critic was first-term Indiana senator Dan Quayle, who said, "This is a watershed treaty, a very high-risk, high-stakes treaty. You will see the gradual neutralization of Europe through de-nuclearization."[53]

The central fear of conservatives was that Reagan had embarked upon a slippery slope that would lead to giving up SDI to get a START agreement. Washington was rife with rumors, and the occasional published news story, that Shultz or Carlucci or someone was working on the formula for a sellout. They needn't have worried. Reagan wrote in his diary in October: "We still believe [Gorbachev] wants a summit but is playing a game thinking I want a summit so bad I'll pay a price regarding SDI. He's wrong."

A number of conservatives fixed upon remarks from Reagan that the Soviet Union had given up its imperialist goal of spreading Marxism-Leninism to the four corners of the earth as a sign that he had given in to the conventional wisdom. "Possibly," Reagan told four conservative journalists, "the fundamental change is that in the past Soviet leaders have openly expressed their acceptance of the Marxist theory of the one-world Communist state; that their obligation was to expand in the whole world. They no longer feel that way." He went on to mention what he had observed privately to Gorbachev in Reykjavik, that Gorbachev "is the first and only leader that has never affirmed that, that has never stood up there before their great Soviet Congress and openly stated that goal as all the others have." The same person who had written in his diary two years before that he was "too cynical" to believe reports that Gorbachev was different was now inferring a new era from the absence of rhetorical continuity from the general secretary.

But for all the focus on the questionable subtlety of Reagan's assessment of change in the Soviet Union, he was not falling for a revival of flabby 1970s-style détente. Consider the Berlin Wall speech of June 1987. It is a commonplace error, then and now, to suppose that his famous "tear down this wall" challenge was a one-off event and a contrivance of his speechwriters. Not so. He repeated the phrase in a televised speech to the nation upon his return from Europe three days later, and then again the very next day at a luncheon with Republican senators. "If Mr. Gorbachev's actions match his words then—I said it there: Tear down the wall! Open the gate!" A month later at a Captive Nations conference Reagan upped the ante: "I challenged [Gorbachev] to tear down the Berlin Wall and to open the Brandenburg Gate. I renew that challenge today and expand it to include opening up those countries that are now under the domination of the Soviet Union or its Leninist protégés, from the Baltic States through Bulgaria, from Vietnam to Ethiopia." Reagan wrote in his diary: "The Soviets will be unhappy."

Over the next year and a half before Reagan left office, he repeated his call to tear down the wall another fourteen times: four times in his Saturday radio addresses,[54] three times in special radio broadcasts to Europe,[55] five times in speeches to U.S. audiences,[56] and twice during interviews with foreign journalists.[57] The Soviets did not take it well. In the laughable doublespeak of Soviet and East German propaganda, the wall was an "anti-fascist protective structure," and the Soviets criticized Reagan for "antisocialist rhetoric" (the only accurate part of their complaint) and of wanting to "instigate a new wall of mistrust."[58] The official Soviet news agency, TASS, accused Reagan of advocating terrorism.[59] Yet Reagan's public stand had immediate practical effects. While East Germany took steps in the months after Reagan's visit to reinforce the wall, U.S. intelligence started picking up cable traffic from Moscow to East Germany in which Moscow suggested the East Germans ease restrictions on passage through the wall.[60] The State Department took the cue, and within a short time senior State Department officials were treating Reagan's call as policy during diplomatic missions in Europe.[61]

Reagan's attack on the Berlin Wall, made for simple and sentimental reasons, had the effect of turning the tables on the Eastern bloc by reopening the issue of German reunification. A neutral, Finlandized Germany was the Western anxiety, but a neutral *free* Germany was the Soviet nightmare, and the removal of the Berlin Wall—the keystone of the Eastern bloc police states—could bring down the entire edifice of Communism. Reagan spoke directly to this question in Berlin: "President von Weizsäcker has said: 'The German question is open as long as the Brandenburg Gate is closed.' Today I say: *As long as this gate is closed, as long as this scar of a Wall is permitted to stand, it is not the German question alone that remains open, but the question of freedom for all mankind*" (emphasis added).

There were other signs throughout 1987 that, despite the prospective arms agreements, the Cold War was far from over. While Shultz was first vising Moscow and then meeting with Foreign Minister Shevardnadze in Washington, there was a new espionage scandal involving the U.S. embassy in Moscow, and bad news out of the CIA, which reported that *every single one* of its recruited agents in the Soviet Union had been rolled up and in most cases executed. The new U.S. embassy building under construction in Moscow was found to be riddled with bugs, and a story that two marine embassy guards had been compromised by the KGB caused a firestorm in Washington. The case of the marine guards would turn out to have been grossly exaggerated, and it would be more than a decade before the United States discovered that moles in the CIA (Aldrich Ames) and FBI (Robert Hanssen) were responsible for the blown agents.

There were also cultural signs of the endurance of the Cold War. In February ABC television, in an about-face from 1983's *The Day After,* broadcast a $40 million, seven-part, fourteen-hour miniseries depicting the United States under Soviet occupation, called *Amerika.* The same critics who had praised *The Day After* panned *Amerika.* The *Washington Post* called it "14 torturous hours on the rack" and ranked it as the worst TV show of the year. Protestors picketed outside ABC headquarters in New York, chanting, "World War Three brought to you by ABC," and hoisting signs reading "ABC, AmeriKKKan Broadcasting Company." Outside the United Nations, the Mobilization for Survival peace group released a statement that said, "We're very concerned about the negative impact it could have on U.S.-Soviet relations and public support for the United Nations." Left-wing groups agitated for a boycott and pressured advertisers; Chrysler knuckled under and cancelled its ad buy.

*   *   *

THE UNITED STATES did not perceive clearly at the time that Gorbachev's attempt at reform was encountering predictable resistance and leading to a political crisis. *Perestroika* was failing to make progress for the simplest of reasons: the bureaucrats and Party apparatchiks resisted and undermined reform at every turn. In Moscow, Yeltsin replaced two-thirds of the Party hierarchy but was baffled when nothing changed.

Perestroika was only succeeding at causing economic confusion. In fact, economic decline under Gorbachev was accelerating. *Perestroika* might well be considered the Soviet New Deal—a politically and rhetorically popular policy that was ineffective at achieving its goals. At the beginning of 1987, Gorbachev attempted to move his reform program into higher gear. Dimly he perceived that economic reform required political reform. Russian scholar Leon Aron summarized the state of play:

> Between April 1985 and January 1987 the new Soviet leadership sought to implement something very much like a Chinese option: effecting economic reform without touching the foundations of the

political order. January 1987 marked the forced abandonment of this attempt and the entry into the completely uncharted waters of "democratization."[62]

Gorbachev recognized that the only way *perestroika* would work was if there was real pressure on party cadres and managers to perform. More pressure from the top would not work; there needed to be pressure from the bottom—from the people. In a speech to the January Plenum of the Central Committee, Gorbachev called publicly for *glasnost* to begin in earnest. He called for "more light," for allowing more public criticism, and even for the possibility of contested, secret-ballot elections for party positions, though this was still a long way from questioning the continuation of one-party rule. Aron called it "Gorbachev's first revolutionary act . . . For the first time, the Party's leader, speaking at the Plenum of the Central Committee, appealed over the heads of its members for the people's support in exchange for a dramatic expansion of liberties."[63]

Even though Gorbachev's general program of liberalization stopped far short of contemplating genuine pluralism or multiparty democracy, the Party apparatchiks did not like what they heard. Elite resistance to Gorbachev increased, but Gorbachev had calculated correctly, if not with full prescience of its final effects, that the public response would set in motion a train of events that would box in the Party reactionaries. Over the next few months there occurred the first spontaneous mass protests since the 1920s, along with wildcat strikes at mines and industrial facilities. The USSR in 1987 was starting to look like Poland in 1980. Gorbachev was playing a dangerous game, and political opposition among Kremlin insiders was growing.

In the midst of backroom political struggles there occurred a bizarre incident that gave Gorbachev a temporary boost. In May 1987, Mathias Rust, a West German teenager, flew a single-engine Cessna airplane from Helsinki to Moscow, crossing 400 miles of Soviet airspace at low altitude, circling over the Kremlin several times, and finally landing in Red Square, where he declared that he had come on a peace mission. It took the bewildered Soviet police an hour to arrest him. Rust's flight had been so suspiciously easy that there was speculation it must have been an inside job. Gorbachev exploited the embarrassment of the flight to remove senior defense ministers and officers—more than 150 in all—replacing them with junior figures more to his liking and more supportive of his arms control agenda. The Rust caper was a source of great mirth in the West; who needed high-tech stealth technology, late-night comedians joked, when we could use low-tech prop planes to penetrate Soviet air defenses?

The CIA was skeptical, believing that Gorbachev was merely attempting a repeat of Lenin's New Economic Plan of the 1920s and Khrushchev's limited thaw of the 1950s to gain some breathing space by which to regroup and resume the Soviet Union's historical expansionism. The sporadic signals that the Soviets wanted to get out of Afghanistan were regarded with similar skepticism. The suspicion that Gorbachev's program was largely intended for Western political consumption received a boost when news of an affair involving Boris Yeltsin emerged late in the year.

At a meeting of the Central Committee Plenum in late October, a few days before the official observance of the seventieth anniversary of the October Revolution, Yeltsin launched a vociferous and imprudent attack on Gorbachev, arguing that Gorbachev was taking too much power into his hands and seeking to create his own cult of personality. Yeltsin announced his intention to resign his position as a candidate member of the Politburo, though he left open the possibility of staying on as Party boss of Moscow in what looked like an attempt to cause a split in the ranks and set himself up as a full-scale rival to Gorbachev. "Never in seventy years had the Central Committee heard anything like this," Leon Aron observed. With Gorbachev leading the counterattack, the Central Committee turned on Yeltsin with considerable bitterness and unanimously voted to oust him from his several posts, casting him into the political wilderness for the time being.

News of the Yeltsin affair was suppressed initially, so when Shultz arrived in Moscow a few days later to finalize the INF treaty and see whether the long-discussed Washington summit would proceed he was unaware of the recent turmoil. The Americans were by now used to Gorbachev's negotiating style, which always included at least one moment of heightened contentiousness over something; like a boastful street gang leader, he seemed to need to prove either his toughness or his ability to compel explicit signs of respect from the other superpower. Shultz always stood firm and rode out the tempests, but this time Gorbachev's petulance seemed more extreme and unhinged. His grievances went beyond his usual frustration with U.S. unwillingness to bend on SDI; he affected great offense at a routine State Department report on Soviet anti-American propaganda. It was a frivolous and marginal thing to fix upon, unworthy of a head of state. And why bother coming to Washington, Gorbachev kvetched, if they were just to talk in generalities again as they had in Reykjavik? Shultz thought something was wrong; borrowing a line from Carl Sandburg, Shultz said, "This boxer has been hit." While the last details of the INF treaty were close at hand, Shultz returned to Washington without a final agreement for a Washington summit.

Shultz had barely unpacked his bags back in Washington before word came from Moscow that Gorbachev wanted the summit to take place soon. Shevardnadze would be in Washington within two days to see to the final details of the INF treaty and the summit. "The Soviets blinked," Reagan wrote in his diary on October 28. Two days later the news about the Yeltsin affair began leaking out, and it added to Western confusion about what was really taking place in the Soviet Union. That Gorbachev was throwing out genuine liberal reformers such as Yeltsin suggested limits to *perestroika* and *glasnost*. At the same time, stories were emerging of growing resistance to Gorbachev's reformism within the Politburo itself, led by Yegor Ligachev; this cast Gorbachev as a moderate reformer precariously caught between extremes. Reagan had gotten wind of this prospect months before. In a February diary entry, he recounted a rumor Suzanne Massie passed along: "A top Soviet official told her Gorbachev might well be killed if he came here. There is so much opposition to what he's trying to do in Russia—they could murder him here & then pin the whole thing on us. I don't find the warning at all outlandish. The KGB is capable of doing just that."[64] Over the summer, Reagan took note, along with other heads of state, of a six-week period when Gorbachev disappeared entirely from public view, fueling rumors of a putsch. Early in 1988 Reagan recorded in his diary intelligence reports of the split between Gorbachev and Ligachev. Reagan may have judged Gorbachev to be different, but he also knew the "evil empire" was still in business.

Compared to the previous two summits and the internal drama within the Kremlin, the Washington summit in December 1987 was anticlimactic. In their six head-to-head sessions Reagan and Gorbachev went through a familiar list of issues such as human rights; Afghanistan, Central America, and other regional conflicts; and the slow pace of the START negotiations. Most of the arguments were the same as in Geneva and Reykjavik, though on the subject of human rights Gorbachev threw a curveball with the suggestion that a group of experts from each nation could debate the merits of the two nations' rival conception of human rights in a joint seminar, an indication that for all his professions of being a liberal reformer, he still had a residual attachment to the Marxist view of human rights. And in a typical Reagan negotiating move, when Gorbachev indicated Soviet flexibility on START sublimits, Reagan countered by pocketing the prospective concession while saying the United States might wish to deploy missile defenses sooner than ten years. Gorbachev didn't jump at the bait, instead turning the conversation to broader areas of potential future arms reductions, such as chemical and conventional weapons. Reagan offended Gorbachev with another recent anti-Soviet joke he had heard; Gorbachev asked Ambassador Matlock to stop collecting jokes for the president. "A good rousing meeting," Reagan wrote in his diary, though he noted that "things got a little heated."

While Gorbachev and Reagan publicly signed the Intermediate-Range Nuclear Forces Treaty, behind the scenes the working groups made some progress on the START issues. The treaty eliminated nuclear weapons that made up about 4 percent of the arsenals of both sides—a modest amount, but it was the first-ever arms agreement that reduced the number of nuclear weapons rather than merely regulating their further expansion. Gorbachev, significantly, didn't insist on completing a START agreement as a condition of a Moscow summit the following year, and a tentative date in the spring was agreed.

But it was Gorbachev's flair for American-style public relations that stole the spotlight at this summit. Driving down Connecticut Avenue with Vice President Bush in his limousine, Gorbachev ordered his driver to pull over to the curb, whereupon Gorbachev got out of the car and began pressing the flesh with startled downtown D.C. office workers on their lunch hour. The populist stunt caused pandemonium as he was mobbed by the crowd. "It looked like a scene out of the Keystone Kops," one observer told the *Washington Post*. Gorbymania took its place alongside Olliemania as the public's latest fascination. Education Secretary William Bennett coined the sarcastic term *Gorbasm* to describe the uncritical swooning over the man who stood at the apex of what was still, after all, a tyranny. The usual intellectuals and literary figures were smitten. Antinuclear siren/crusader Helen Caldicott said Gorbachev was "the only sane leader in the world. He is like Jesus. He just keeps giving out things like arms control proposals and getting hit with rejections." (In the same speech Caldicott called Richard Perle, author of the zero-option INF treaty, "a war criminal.") Novelist Joyce Carol Oates, a guest at a luncheon with Gorbachev, remarked, "The things he said were almost too good to be true. It's as if he came from another planet." *Washington Post* columnist Mary McGrory may have hit her all-time low: "He is a political leader to make Americans weep. None of the men who want to be president are in his intellectual league."

Gorbachev's only miscue of the summit week was his visible anger at being asked, on more than one occasion, questions about human rights and the plight of Soviet dissidents. He said he would not be "lectured to" by a nation that used machine guns to keep people out; to Reagan he insisted he would not appear as the accused before a prosecutor. But despite their tough bargaining, Reagan and Gorbachev ended their last session together swapping jokes about bureaucrats and stories of their respective origins far from the national capitals. These two men were becoming genuinely fond of each other. Reagan wrote in his diary, "I think the whole thing was the best summit we'd ever had with the Soviet Union." If the minutes of the Politburo meeting held after Gorbachev's return to Moscow are to be taken at face value, Gorbachev felt the same way. He did caution, however, that there would continue to be voices in the West that "keep searching for some kind of dirty trick from Gorbachev, some kind of change in the Kremlin, which, it turns out, planned *perestroika* in its entirety only to trick the West and lull them out of their vigilance."[65]

That would be mostly American conservatives, whose largest worry—that Reagan would yield on SDI to get a START agreement at the summit—did not come to pass. In fact, though it was not known publicly at the time, Gorbachev had begun the process of backing away from his opposition to SDI deployment in one of his sessions with Reagan; the final communiqué of the summit essentially said that the United States and Soviet Union had agreed to disagree about this point. But conservatives remained in a funk anyway. *National Review* editorialized: "The darkest days of the Carter Administration were always brightened by the prospect of a united conservative resistance. This summit has fractured the Right."[66] *Human Events* ran a banner headline: "Reagan's Summit Performance Stuns Conservatives." George Will wrote: "December 8 will be remembered as the day the Cold War was lost." Pat Buchanan, who had left his White House post in the spring to resume his newspaper column, wrote: "The Great Communicator who preached Peace Through Strength today preaches peace through parchment."

As the year ended with both parties looking intently forward to the election contest to succeed Reagan in 1988, conservatives were starting to echo the line liberals had taken since 1985: the post-Reagan era had arrived. While Democrats looked with optimism at recapturing the White House, among many conservatives it appeared that the most successful strategy would be to run to the *right* of Ronald Reagan.

CHAPTER 13

A MIGHTY WOMAN
WITH A TORCH

―――➤●◄―――

*By far the greatest influence on the 1988 presidential campaign,
largely unheard and unseen but all-powerful, was the presence of
Ronald Reagan. When people ask why the campaign said so little
about issues, the startling answer is that their president had
preempted virtually all the issue space there was.*
—AARON WILDAVSKY

*The interesting question is how much difference it would make if a
Democrat is elected in 1988—an eventuality that is still far short of a
foregone conclusion. Will such a President be able to reverse the
conservative trend that brought Ronald Reagan to office? Or will he
become a prisoner of that trend?*
—IRVING KRISTOL, JUNE 1987

A LL PRESIDENTIAL ELECTIONS are construed as referendums on something, and the question of the election of 1988 was whether it would be a referendum on Reagan's presidency—especially if Vice President George Bush was the GOP nominee—or a referendum on the liberalism that Reagan had challenged so effectively in the last two elections. The outcome would also answer the questions of whether there would be an Age of Reagan lasting beyond him and whether he had transformed the two parties. While the media ignored Reagan in favor of the horse-race drama of the two parties' primary battles and the fall general election campaign, he still cast a large shadow, contributing to the march of events leading to the unexpected outcome of the Cold War.

Between his lame duck status and the partisan assertiveness of the Democratic Congress, Reagan was forced to swallow a number of political concessions. His veto of a civil rights bill overturning a Supreme Court rebuke of racial quotas in higher education was overridden. He signed an extension of the independent counsel statute against his better judgment. His veto of a protectionist trade bill was upheld, but he signed a compromise version that stripped out the most objectionable features. Later in the year Congress sustained a veto of another trade protection bill, this time for textiles. The budget for the next fiscal year was the usual fiasco; a vague agreement between Reagan and congressional leaders reached in the weeks after the stock market crash to cut $30 billion and avoid the automatic Gramm-Rudman rescissions became a mischievous continuing resolution (CR) that Reagan reluctantly signed two days before Christmas in 1987. Congress had adjourned and left town; if Reagan vetoed the CR, the government would have shut down for the holidays. He was surely tempted. In his last conversation with Gorbachev at the end of the December summit, Reagan said he "often wondered what would happen if he and other leaders closed the doors of their offices and quietly slipped away. How long would it be before people missed them?"

In his State of the Union address in late January, Reagan began with his by-now familiar perorations, but then pivoted to some unusually hard criticism of Congress for its failure to obey its own budget laws. He brought with him to the well of the House the three most recent CRs, each more than a thousand pages long, as props:

> With each ensuing year, the spectacle before the American people is the same as it was this Christmas: budget deadlines delayed or missed completely, monstrous continuing resolutions that pack hundreds of billions of dollars worth of spending into one bill, and a Federal Government on the brink of default. [L]et's recall that in seven years, of 91 appropriations bills scheduled to arrive on my desk by a certain date, only 10 made it on time. Last year, of the 13 appropriations bills due by October 1st, none of them made it. Instead, we had four continuing resolutions lasting 41 days, then 36 days, and two days, and three days, respectively. And then, along came these behemoths.

Reagan then dropped each massive document with a thud on the table beside the podium. "Congress shouldn't send another one of these," he said.

"No, and if you do, I will not sign it." Here he can be criticized for not hav-ing taken more opportunities to assert himself in such a manner in his previ-ous seven years. Reagan had vetoed only two CRs—one in November 1981 and another in October 1986—and both led to brief government shutdowns.[1] The experience of President Bill Clinton a few years later suggests that the president has the advantage in budget confrontations with Congress. As a part of the annual budget wrangle, Reagan was forced to relent on his de-fense budget request. One consequence was that the goal of a six-hundred-ship navy had to be scaled back, which prompted his navy secretary, James Webb, to resign in protest. The National Republican Senatorial Committee tried to recruit Webb to run for the Senate in Virginia, but he declined.

As he approached his seventy-seventh birthday, Reagan's diary entries convey a portrait of a chief executive still actively engaged in the full range of problems and issues, including Manuel Noriega in Panama, Ferdinand Mar-cos's attempts in exile to midwife a coup in the Philippines, new Middle East peace initiatives, and congressional opposition to Contra aid. He took the trouble to read Gorbachev's bestseller, *Perestroika*. He also took note of the media refrain that he wasn't up to the job: "On ABC News Sam Donaldson had somehow gotten a sheet of my talking points for one of the meetings and used it to show (his interpretation) that I could no longer be trusted to attend meetings without having everything I was to say written out for me."[2] In the spring Don Regan's tell-all book, *For the Record*, was published, revealing the embarrassing fact of Nancy Reagan's fascination with astrology. On the whole the book was not as critical of Reagan as other memoirs (such as David Stockman's), but the media sensation surrounding the astrology story caused Reagan to call it a "vile attack." "The media are behaving like kids with a new toy," Reagan wrote in his diary, "never mind that there is no truth in it." (But the evidence suggests that Reagan allowed Nancy's astrologer friends to set the timing of some public events. Stranger things have happened in the White House. President Carter told *GQ* magazine that he once asked the CIA to consult a psychic to assist in finding a missing American airplane.)

On February 8 Gorbachev announced publicly that the Soviet Union would begin withdrawing from Afghanistan by May 15 and would be com-pletely out within ten months. The Soviets had hoped they could get the United States to stop arming the Afghan resistance and allow the Soviet-installed government in Kabul to remain, but Reagan had stood firm and the Soviets gave in. The United States yielded a little ground in the interest of se-curing a formal peace treaty through the United Nations, but the withdrawal still represented a tangible abandonment of the Brezhnev Doctrine and a clear victory for the Reagan Doctrine.

Shultz went to Moscow in late February to push along the START negotiations and prepare for Reagan's prospective springtime summit in the Soviet capital. As he always did, Shultz made human rights his first order of business, this time by paying a visit to Andrei Sakharov, whose internal exile Gorbachev had ended. It was a sore point for the Soviets. Shultz met with Shevardnadze the same day and, flanked by Assistant Secretary of State Roz Ridgway and Reagan's new national security adviser, Colin Powell, couldn't help being amused as Shevardnadze attacked human rights in the United States with the example that women and blacks were denied opportunity. (Only later in 1988 did the Politburo finally have its first woman member.)

The relentless American pressure on human rights, along with Reagan's constant jokes to Gorbachev about the dysfunctional Soviet socioeconomic system, aggravated the Soviets' latent inferiority complex. Gorbachev was additionally offended during the Washington summit when congressional Republicans blocked his desire to address a joint session of Congress. Though Reagan had not used the "evil empire" line since 1983, Politburo minutes and other Soviet documents from as late as 1988 contain repeated references to Reagan's infamous label; it had obviously stuck in their craw. Suzanne Massie, Reagan's informal adviser and back-channel messenger on Soviet matters for the previous five years, brought up this problem with Reagan in meeting in early March. Massie had just come from Moscow, where Dobrynin, acting on instructions from high up (meaning presumably Gorbachev), told Massie that

> the Soviet belief that the Administration's overall perception of Soviet international behavior has not changed—that the President still thinks of the USSR as an evil empire whose social and political positions have placed it on the ash heap of history. The Soviets request that, if this is not the President's perception, if the President believes there have been changes or could be changes in Soviet international policies, then it would be important for the President to state this prior to the Moscow summit. The Soviets ask what concrete steps they could take over the next few months to prompt such a statement by the President.[3]

Reagan responded by giving another anti-Communist speech in Springfield, Massachusetts, in April, the day before Shultz's next meeting with

Gorbachev in Moscow. Although he spoke positively, saying that "Soviet-American relations have taken a dramatic turn into a period of realistic engagement . . . negotiations are underway between our two governments on an unparalleled number of issues," the heart of the speech was a restatement of the moral dimension of the Cold War and Reagan's strategy:

> We spoke plainly and bluntly. We rejected what Jeane Kirkpatrick calls moral equivalency. We said freedom was better than totalitarianism. We said communism was bad. . . . Well, at first, the experts said this kind of candor was dangerous, that it would lead to a worsening of Soviet-American relations. But far to the contrary, this candor made clear to the Soviets the resilience and strength of the West; it made them understand the lack of illusions on our part about them or their system. By reasserting values and defining once again what we as a people and a nation stood for, we were of course making a moral and spiritual point. So, we were candid. We acknowledged the depth of our disagreements and their fundamental, moral import. In this way, we acknowledged that the differences that separated us and the Soviets were deeper and wider than just missile counts and number of warheads.

The American media barely covered the speech, but the Soviets paid close attention. When Shultz, who had not been in Reagan's meeting with Massie the month before, arrived at the Kremlin the next day, Gorbachev was livid. "He soon flew into a tantrum," Shultz wrote.

"I have to conclude that there is backward movement and an attempt to preach to us, to teach us," Gorbachev complained to Shultz. "So how am I to explain this? Is this summit going to be a catfight?" It was bad enough that Shultz constantly embarrassed the Soviets by his visits to dissidents such as Sakharov; what Gorbachev was trying to get across with his indignation was that he didn't want Reagan to embarrass him in Moscow. "The message was clear," Shultz wrote; "tell the president not to make a speech like that in Moscow."[4] Shultz gently changed the subject, but Gorbachev wouldn't let go, startling Shultz with what the secretary of state regarded "as a truly remarkable statement" for the boss of the Communist Party: "The Soviet Union does not pretend to have the final truth. We do not impose our way of life on other people." If he was serious, it meant the repudiation of Marxist dialectical materialism. The following week in Washington, the new Soviet ambassador, Yuri Dubinin, sounded out Colin Powell on the same subject: what were Reagan's aims for the summit? Powell knew what was on Dubinin's mind, and reassured him, "There is no intention on our part to have a confrontation in Moscow or do anything to embarrass the General Secretary. . . . You can be sure the President will be a gracious guest."[5]

On the surface it appeared that Reagan heeded these appeals when he arrived in Moscow for the summit a month later. For the American media the most memorable moment of the Moscow summit in late May was when Sam Donaldson asked Reagan, standing next to Gorbachev in Red Square, if he still thought the Soviet Union was an evil empire. After a short hesitation, Reagan answered tersely, "No." "Why not?" "I was talking about another time in another era." But Reagan did give a speech that was more subversive and problematic than a reprise of the "evil empire" theme. To the student body of Moscow State University, standing beneath a large statue of Lenin and wearing the same necktie he had worn for the Berlin Wall speech the year before, Reagan presented an ode to the technology and information revolution under way in the West. It was similar to the mini-lectures Shultz had given to Gorbachev repeatedly since 1985:

> Like a chrysalis, we're emerging from the economy of the Industrial Revolution—an economy confined to and limited by the Earth's physical resources—into, as one economist [Reagan was referencing Warren Brookes here] titled his book, *The Economy in Mind,* in which there are no bounds on human imagination and the freedom to create is the most precious natural resource. . . .
>
> But progress is not foreordained. The key is freedom—freedom of thought, freedom of information, freedom of communication. . . . And that's why it's so hard for government planners, no matter how sophisticated, to ever substitute for millions of individuals working night and day to make their dreams come true. . . .
>
> But freedom is more even than [elections]. Freedom is the right to question and change the established way of doing things. It is the continuing revolution of the marketplace.

He added that barriers between peoples, such as the Berlin Wall, should come down, but he couched his argument as a reinforcement of Gorbachev's *perestroika,* even as he subtly shamed it by hinting how much further it needed to go to be authentic.

After much back-and-forth, the Senate ratified the Intermediate-Range

Nuclear Forces Treaty without amendment by a 93–5 vote on the eve of Reagan's departure, allowing him to present Gorbachev with the ratified agreement. Most accounts of the Moscow summit characterize it as more ceremonial than substantive. This is true only insofar as the goal of having a second major arms agreement was not achieved. The two plenary sessions between the top staffs of both sides were businesslike and productive. But on the more important plane of dynamic political argument, this summit was a good barometer of the changing political weather of the late Cold War. In their first one-on-one meeting on May 29, Gorbachev's insecurities about his regime were made apparent when he asked Reagan if he would agree to a joint statement about the basis for Soviet-American relations that read in part: "Equality of all states, non-interference in internal affairs and freedom of socio-political choice must be recognized as the inalienable and mandatory standards of international relations." In other words, *Stop it with the "evil empire" talk.* Gorbachev wanted Reagan on record acknowledging the political legitimacy of the Soviet regime. Reagan said he liked the draft statement and would have his people look at it. Then he asked if he could digress for a moment, whereupon he produced a list of individual human rights cases in the Soviet Union that he wanted to bring to Gorbachev's personal attention. Gorbachev knew better than to lose his temper at this direct rebuff, as he had in past meetings with Reagan, so he responded ludicrously that he was eager to help the United States with its own human rights problems, such as racial discrimination and poverty.

"He did not want to teach lessons to the United States President on how to run America," the summary of their conversation reads. "He just wanted to note that the President had ideas about the Soviets, and the Soviets had ideas about the U.S. . . . he thought the President's successors would be more self-critical than he was." Rather than give in to this attempt at asserting moral and political equivalence, Reagan pressed ahead to an area where Gorbachev could not follow so easily—religious freedom. Reagan had planned this argument in advance, but Gorbachev's human rights gambit was a perfect setup. Reagan made clear he didn't want to embarrass Gorbachev publicly and would deny having discussed the subject if word got out, thereby implying he thought Gorbachev should be embarrassed privately by the Soviet lack of religious freedom. Gorbachev replied that atheists were criticized in the United States, and finally tried to change the subject: could they consider some joint missions in space? Delighted to, Reagan said, though he added "that space went toward heaven, but not as far as he had been talking about before." Poor Gorbachev. He had three more meetings with Reagan still to come.

In the second one-on-one meeting three days later, Gorbachev didn't even try to put up a fight, and the two mostly just swapped stories as though they were two pals at happy hour. In the course of the conversation, however, were several astonishing concessions. In making a general defense of socialism, Gorbachev allowed that it must be "capable of movement" and "far-reaching forms of reorganization." But he abandoned egalitarianism: "In their socialist society, they did not want to level things out like a table"—here Gorbachev slammed the flat of his hand on the coffee table. "The principle of the economy had to be that as you produce, so you earn." In other words, gone was the Marxist adage "From each according to his abilities, to each according to his needs."

Gorbachev saved his main argument for the last plenary session, where he brought up the proposed joint political statement he had showed Reagan in their first meeting. Reagan's people had indeed objected to the wording of the statement and proposed alternative language (which the Soviet working group accepted), the key phrase of which read: "[The two leaders] do not minimize the real differences of history, tradition, and ideology which will continue to characterize the U.S.-Soviet relationship." In other words, the United States was not going to stop arguing with the Soviets about the nature of their regime. In the final session Gorbachev was desperate to get agreement to his original statement. "What it said was that we all have to respect the rights of others," Gorbachev said. "What is wrong with that? Why can't we incorporate this basic idea into our statement? The President read it and said he liked it. I think his exact words were, 'I respond positively to this.' I think that the President's wishes should be respected." When Shultz and Frank Carlucci pointed out the American objections, Gorbachev changed the subject. But he made another run at it toward the end of the session, an indication of how strongly he wanted to win the point: "I would appreciate it if the President could look again at the political statement, which he was shown on Sunday." When Reagan demurred, Gorbachev petulantly attempted to drive a wedge between Reagan and his senior advisers: "Should we record that the Americans would not agree to the paragraph because of George Shultz or Frank Carlucci? Are they the intransigent parties? Is one of them a revisionist? If not, perhaps we need to look for a scapegoat elsewhere. Perhaps Ambassador Matlock or Assistant Secretary Ridgway . . . Tell me, Mr. President, that you will accept this text after all." Shultz and Reagan conferred briefly but came back with the same answer—no.

While Reagan was ready—indeed, eager—to head off the prospect of superpower war, he was not ready to call off or ignore the ideological roots of the Cold War. The conservatives back home who thought Reagan was going soft on the Soviet Union were overreacting. Despite Gorbachev's disappointment at not getting Reagan to acknowledge formally that the Soviet Union was a legitimate, civilized nation, he had developed a genuine fondness for the president, which Reagan reciprocated. "There is no question in my mind but that a certain chemistry does exist between us," Reagan wrote in his diary in the middle of the Moscow summit. It was at this summit that the two men began calling each other by their first names, and their follow-up letters from that point forward were addressed "To Mikhail, from Ron," and vice versa. Gorbachev expressed satisfaction with the summit at the next Politburo meeting a few days later, saying, "[T]he human factor, which we regard so highly in foreign policy for a good reason, has played its essential role." Chernyaev, who participated in the plenary sessions at the summit, wrote in his diary: "Reagan saw that we are not an 'empire of evil,' but normal people, with a rich history at that, and we are such a giant that you cannot intimidate or dazzle us."

One reason for Gorbachev's extreme sensitivity about whether Reagan would seek an embarrassing confrontation is that he was under growing attack from Kremlin hard-liners in the spring of 1988. In March, while both Gorbachev and his reformist adviser Yakovlev were out of the country, there appeared in the newspaper *Sovetskaya Rossiya* a stinging attack on Gorbachev's reform program entitled "I Cannot Forsake My Principles." It was, Chernyaev wrote in his diary, "an anti-*perestroika* manifesto" that defended Stalinist values. Its author was an unknown science professor from Leningrad, Nina Andreeva, and whether that name was a pseudonym or not was beside the point: articles such as this didn't happen by accident. The Nina Andreeva affair, as it became known, created a political sensation and was the talk of Moscow for weeks.

It is hard to pinpoint the moment when Gorbachev's reform program spun out of his control and set in motion the dissolution of the Soviet Union, but his response to the Nina Andreeva affair is a worthy candidate. Rather than pull in his horns, Gorbachev responded aggressively, using the controversy to marginalize his opponents in the Politburo and push the frontier of political reform. A series of Politburo meetings over the next few days became, in Chernyaev's description, "a two-day thrashing of Ligachev," who sat "red as a lobster" and "started lying" about his role in the genesis of the article. Gorbachev went around the table, requiring every Politburo member present to state his opinion of the article, dividing the house between supporters and foes, and he used the division to isolate Ligachev and prepare the way for his demotion. Gorbachev cleverly said the article was an excellent example of *glasnost* at work and that there should be more of it. (He then published a point-by-point rebuttal in *Pravda* a few days later, and began exerting greater control over the party's media apparatus.) From then on it was not long before *glasnost* came to resemble freedom of speech in the Western sense. Between the backlash against the Andreeva article's pro-Stalinism and the view that he really meant it about ending censorship and allowing free expression, intellectuals, writers, and editors wasted little time before starting to question and criticize not just Stalin but the founding fathers and founding myth of the Soviet Union itself. Starting in 1988, long-suppressed books by Solzhenitsyn and other dissidents were published openly in the Soviet Union. Leon Aron observed, "The water is swirling perilously close to Lenin's pedestal and is rising higher and higher every day. . . . The fall of the Founding Fathers may mark the final destination of the Soviet crusaders, beyond which lies a gaping void."

Moreover, he argued, the time had arrived to implement "deep transformations" in the political and legal structure of the country. At the Nineteenth Party Conference in late June, shortly after the Moscow summit with Reagan, Gorbachev rolled out a proposal for replacing the Supreme Soviet, a rubber-stamp legislative body, with a Congress of People's Deputies to be chosen in secret-ballot contested elections. The first elections under the new scheme would come in 1989. He called for diminished Communist Party control over the economy. In succeeding weeks he cut down the size of the Central Committee, abolishing eleven out of twenty existing departments and pensioning off apparatchiks who had resisted *perestroika*. Though he still invoked socialism and Lenin, it was becoming increasingly apparent that these were throwaway adjectives in his vocabulary. It didn't quite add up to democratic pluralism yet, but it sounded the death knell for Communist Party control of the country. All of these positive-sounding ideas actually represented Gorbachev doubling down on his reform gamble—*perestroika* was not working. The shelves in the stores were still mostly bare. Toward the end of the year it would become clear that the grain harvest would be down about 7 percent from 1987, the worst in years.

U.S. conservatives remained suspicious but began to allow that beneath the fog and contradictory language, Gorbachev might be up to something genuine. "Strange things appear to be happening in the Communist world,"

Jeffrey Hart wrote in *National Review*. "We remain skeptical about the ultimate outcome of what Gorbachev is doing, but he is certainly attempting something. . . . The odds against his effecting change are enormous, but it is not wise or realistic to interpret his every move and statement as a ruse to fool the United States."[6] Separately *National Review*'s Cold Warrior columnist Brian Crozier wrote that "the All-Union Conference of the Communist Party at the end of June was a gigantic funeral service: the burial of a doctrine and of the hopes and delusions built upon it."[7] Reagan noted in his diary about the new head of ideology in the Politburo, Vadim Medvedev: "One of Gorbachev's new appointees, Medvedev, is making speeches that sound like he's pushing for free enterprise."

*   *   *

BACK IN THE United States, the primary contests in both parties dominated political attention. Despite the Republican Party habit to nominate the person next in line from the last contest, it was not automatic that Vice President George Bush would succeed Reagan in the Republican Party, on account of his Eastern establishment background, which made conservatives suspicious. The famously grouchy *Manchester Union Leader* in New Hampshire called Bush "a spoon-fed rich kid wet-nursed to success." There was also what *Newsweek* magazine called "the wimp factor."[8] But Bush had the most formidable campaign organization.

Most observers handicapped the race as follows: Representative Jack Kemp and Senator Bob Dole were the most formidable challengers to Bush, with former Delaware governor Pete du Pont and former general and secretary of state Al Haig in the second tier, and the Reverend Pat Robertson in the wild card slot. Each could claim a corner of the conservative movement, but each had his weaknesses, which became apparent as the campaign unfolded. Kemp, the pioneer of supply-side economics, had difficulty branching out from that signal accomplishment, turning the answer to every question into a monologue about the gold standard and the need for more tax cuts. Despite early strength in polls, he fizzled quickly. Although du Pont received good buzz among the party elite, he never showed strength. The well-organized and well-funded Robertson demonstrated the growing importance of the religious right by running a strong second in the Iowa caucuses and winning the later caucus states of Washington and Nevada. But his candidacy was always implausible, and he faded as soon as the regular primary contests started. A significant feature of the Robertson campaign bears notice—his success in reregistering thousands of Democrats, especially in the South, as Republicans. After his campaign ended, he morphed his apparatus into the Christian Coalition.

Early on the race came down to Vice President Bush and the 1976 vice presidential nominee, Dole. Dole won the Iowa caucuses, but not before Bush pulled off the political coup of the primary season by humiliating Dan Rather on a live CBS News interview, dispatching the wimp factor in one stroke. Dole reacted badly when Bush won the New Hampshire primary, lashing out at Bush on TV for "lying about my record." The race was effectively over on Super Tuesday in March, when Bush won all sixteen primaries, racking up 578 of the 705 delegates up for grabs that day. He reassured conservatives at the Republican convention by declaring his fealty to Reaganism with the pledge "Read my lips: No new taxes." The man who once derided tax cuts as "voodoo economics" in 1980 now offered his own supply-side fillip: Bush proposed to cut the capital gains tax from 28 percent to 15 percent. (In the fullness of time George Bush lived up to these pledges—just not *this* George Bush.)

The Democratic nominating contest was more interesting, in part because of the spectrum of personalities in the field and in part because of the uncertainty over how the party would respond to the political environment Reagan had created. There was optimism that after eight years of Reagan, Democrats were well positioned to recapture the White House. In the spring of 1987 Richard Nixon wrote a memo to his close associates in which he predicted that "the Democrats could nominate a jackass and probably win." Despite Reagan's personal popularity, opinion surveys revealed anxiety over the economy in the wake of the stock market crash, not to mention the general media pessimism. An ABC News/*Washington Post* poll in January 1988 found that the public disapproved of Reagan's handling of the economy by a 52 to 46 percent margin; 45 percent thought the economy was getting worse, with only 18 percent believing it was getting better. On the generic ballot question of whether the public wanted a Democratic or Republican president in 1988, Democrats led by a plurality of 42 to 33 percent. Bush trailed every prospective Democratic candidate in hypothetical matchups; he even trailed Ted Kennedy, 48 to 47 percent, in the ABC/*Post* January poll. By a 55 to 41 percent margin, the public wanted "a new direction" for the country.

The Democratic candidates that emerged in 1987 were derisively called the "Seven Dwarfs"—not one of them was an obvious heavyweight. Senator Gary Hart was the early front-runner, reprising his content-free "new ideas" campaign from 1984. Early polls in New Hampshire found Hart running two to one over neighboring Massachusetts governor Michael Dukakis. But Hart self-destructed in the spring of 1987 in a sex scandal, throwing the race wide open. The successor to Hart at the top of the polls was Jesse Jackson, rising chiefly on account of his successes in the 1984 campaign. Jackson showed considerable strength in the Democratic primaries, carrying not just the black vote (as expected) but a decent segment of the white vote, enabling him to win several states in the Super Tuesday primary, which was supposed to be a boon to moderate Democrats in the South. Jackson handily won the union-dominated Michigan caucuses and finished a strong second in the New York primary. He would arrive at the Democratic convention in July with the second-largest number of votes, a large slate of delegates, and an inflated ego requiring massive care and feeding from party leaders.

Throughout the primary season no one in the Democratic establishment would say openly what everyone knew—that a Jackson nomination was unthinkable, a certain landslide loser. Jackson's problem wasn't his race or his liberalism—it was his radicalism, though he typically played the race card whenever someone pointed this out. He indignantly told columnist William Raspberry that "calling me a leftist is just another way of saying 'nigger.' "[9] Yet he made George McGovern look like a chamber of commerce Republican. At one point in the 1988 campaign, Jackson told David Frost his three favorite world leaders at the moment were Gorbachev, Zambian president Kenneth Kaunda, and Zimbabwe's Robert Mugabe—three Marxists. At the convention he pushed for a plank in the Democratic platform calling for a Palestinian state. There was a subterranean current of panic among Democrats; there had to be a stop-Jackson campaign without admitting it.

The rest of the 1988 field consisted of Illinois senator Paul Simon, whose plodding bow-tie liberalism excited no one; Representative Richard Gephardt, running as a pessimistic protectionist at a time when union membership was plummeting; former Arizona governor Bruce Babbitt, a moderate who squandered his opening by emulating Mondale and calling for tax increases; Governor Dukakis, who ran on his record of having generated the "Massachusetts miracle"; and forty-year-old Senator Al Gore, who ran as the southern conservative of the field. (Senator Joe Biden was an early candidate, but he self-destructed in a plagiarism scandal, while Arkansas governor Bill Clinton pondered a run but decided to wait for another cycle after he saw what befell Gary Hart.)

Dukakis emerged as a strong contender, based on an ample campaign war chest (raised in large part from the Greek American community), his high name recognition in New Hampshire, and his ability, as a governor, to distinguish himself from the other Democratic liberals by citing his executive experience. Dukakis, coming from a key Democratic state (part of Babbitt's problem was that he hailed from Republican-leaning Arizona and had little policy legacy to boast of), played this advantage masterfully, if not quite accurately. Most of the economic growth in Massachusetts that Dukakis touted had occurred between 1978 and 1983, when Dukakis was out of office. Dukakis had raised taxes sharply during his first term, from 1974 to 1978; by 1978 Massachusetts had the fifth-highest tax burden in the nation—one reason why the Bay State came to be called "Taxachusetts," and a factor that contributed to his loss in the Democratic primary that year to Edward King. In the fall of 1978 Massachusetts voters passed Proposition 2½, a property tax cut modeled after California's Proposition 13, and Governor King cut other taxes during his one term in the statehouse. By the time Dukakis returned to office in 1983, the tax burden had been reduced by a fifth. The Massachusetts economy also enjoyed the benefits of Reagan's higher defense spending and the proliferation of high-tech companies along Boston's Route 128 corridor— the Silicon Valley of the Northeast. Dukakis was claiming credit for the benefits of the tax revolt. Even Dukakis supporter Robert Reich admitted that "Dukakis had very little to do with it," and James Howell, chief economist of the Bank of Boston, said, "Baptists will have air-conditioned Hell before the business community sees [Dukakis] as pro-business."[10] His claims of being a frugal governor were laughable; taxes, spending, and the size of Massachusetts government soared again after he returned to office.

For obvious reasons these were not vulnerabilities other Democrats were able to exploit. After the usual up-and-down jostling—Gephardt and Gore showed some early strength before fading—Dukakis became the person to stop Jackson because, as the *Boston Globe*'s Mike Barnacle put it, he was "the last white guy standing." After choosing as his running mate Texas senator Lloyd Bentsen, a Democrat with some conservative credentials (he had backed tax cuts and aid to the Contras in the early 1980s), Dukakis unveiled his signature line that "this election isn't about ideology—it's about competence." Dukakis emerged from the Democratic convention in July with a seventeen-point lead over Bush. Surely only an incompetent could blow that big a lead over the drab Bush, and Dukakis had just declared competence to be the central issue of the campaign.

Herein lies the entrance to the central subtext of the 1988 campaign and the lesson of Reagan's impact on the decade. Throughout the campaign, the entire Democratic field, except for Jackson, attempted to avoid being identified as liberal. The field was responding to the new political situation, unfavorable to Democrats, that Reagan had established. Hart, Gephardt, Simon, Babbitt, and Gore tried to claim the mantle of neoliberalism or make other acknowledgments that the political landscape had fundamentally changed. Babbitt remarked in 1987: "The Democrats have got to understand that the New Deal is dead. The rules have changed and the Democratic Party is going to have to come to grips with that."

Dukakis tried to deny flatly that he was a liberal of any kind, declaring, "I don't think these labels mean a thing." Why is it, the *American Spectator*'s Tom Bethell pointed out, that only liberals seem to want to reject labels? "This becomes clear when you realize that someone running for President as a conservative cannot be harmed by being clearly labeled a conservative."[11] Bethell noted that a Nexis database search found that label rejecters were uniformly liberals (with one notable exception: Ronald Reagan, in his famous 1964 Goldwater speech, rejected the labels of "left" and "right").

As Harvey Mansfield put it, "The Democrats decided they could win by concealing who they were."[12] Democratic National Committee chairman Paul Kirk was forthright about this ducking and weaving: "We should avoid a long list of legislative proposals and a litany of social, cultural, and ideological buzzwords." After listening to Kirk's evasions, the *Washington Post*'s David Broder concluded that the theory seemed to be "the less the Democrats say as a party on the issues, the better chance Democrats have to win." In an attempt to reduce the size of the target for the GOP, the 1988 Democratic platform was only four thousand words—mostly an attack on Reagan—down from forty thousand words in 1984. The L-word, as it came to be called, was for all practical purposes banned at the convention podium. An aide to Senator Bentsen admitted as much, telling Fred Barnes that "Democrats have finally learned that you can be a liberal, but you can't say you're a liberal." The media noticed the absence of the L-word. The *New York Times*'s Abe Rosenthal wrote: "In Atlanta it's been hard to hear the word that once was the proudly accepted label of the majority of the Democratic Party—liberal." If pressed, liberals would call themselves "progressives."

Dukakis was a perfect exemplar of process liberalism, believing that partisan disputes over issues could be subsumed or avoided by managerial competence. He was, as Fred Barnes observed, the George Bush of the Democratic field, running on his résumé rather than the issues. Hubert Humphrey had complained of this trait way back in 1975: "There are two kinds of liberals. Dukakis is a process liberal, and I'm not. All he cares about is that the pipeline is neat and shiny and clean. He doesn't care if shit comes out the other end."[13] The *New Republic* observed, "He has a tendency (not rare among politicians) to act as if a problem has been solved once he's thought up a name for the committee that's going to look into it."[14] Mansfield observed that Dukakis liked to talk about making tough choices without saying much about what he would choose.

It didn't help that Dukakis was a stiff. "Zorba the Clerk" was one derisive label. Columnist Mark Shields said Dukakis was "Jimmy Carter without the humor." Martin Peretz wrote, "The fact is that to know Dukakis—to know him even from afar—is to dislike him." Molly Ivins said, "Dukakis is an unbelievable stick." On the campaign trail he remained buttoned up in blue business suits, and he could be awkward on the stump. When a factory owner in Tyler, Texas, presented Dukakis with a silver western-style belt buckle at a campaign stop, "Dukakis acted as if a cow pie had been deposited in his hand," in the words of Fred Barnes. He was unembarrassed to admit that he'd once read a book on Swedish land use planning on a beach vacation, and his absurd advice to Iowa farmers to grow Belgian endive came back to haunt him. This passionless quality came home dramatically in his second televised debate with Bush, where he matter-of-factly told CNN's Bernard Shaw that he would still oppose the death penalty even for the hypothetical rapist and murderer of his wife. At that late point most Democrats wondered if they could furlough their nominee, and he became, in William Schneider's lacerating phrase, "the first remaindered candidate in the history of American politics."

Running on a platform of managerial competence at a time when the character and status of liberalism were tenuous with the American people left Dukakis wide open to be defined by the opposition. Newt Gingrich figured this out early, remarking in the spring, "It is very hard to elect George Bush in an election that focuses primarily on George Bush. It is remarkably easy to elect George Bush in an election that focuses primarily on defining Mike Dukakis."[15] Gingrich's point was corroborated by an unlikely observer, the Left-leaning journalist Sidney Blumenthal, who wrote that Dukakis was "a man for all vacuums . . . the candidate for the age of safe sex—stable and steady, no peaks or valleys. The avoidance of intellectual risk became his strategic imperative."

Finding evidence of liberalism in Dukakis's record was easy. Al Gore started the process for Republicans in the New York primary in April, where he landed a roundhouse punch on Dukakis in a debate: "You've been the principal advocate and defender of a program in Massachusetts that has just been cancelled over your objections by the legislature, that provided for weekend passes for convicted criminals including those convicted of first degree murder or serving life sentences without parole. If you were elected president would you advocate a similar program for federal penitentiaries?" Although Gore did not mention a specific case, he had in mind a story first reported in the Lawrence, Massachusetts, *Eagle-Tribune* in 1987 (for which the paper won a Pulitzer Prize) about Willie Horton, a convicted murderer who kidnapped and raped a Maryland couple while on a three-day furlough from a Massachusetts state prison. A detail Gore mentioned bears repeating— Horton was serving a sentence of life *without parole,* a sentence ordinary citizens regard as the tough alternative to the death penalty (which Dukakis had vetoed restoring). Horton's was not the only such case, merely the most spectacular; seventy-one felons had escaped while on furlough. Dukakis offered a lame defense: more than forty states had furlough programs. He vetoed a bill to prohibit furloughs for first-degree murderers, and he later tried to stop the legislature from repealing the furlough program after the Horton episode had received wide publicity in Massachusetts. Republicans watching Gore eviscerate Dukakis on this issue in April perked up their ears and filed it away. GOP consultant Alex Castellanos called it "an agenda-changing battlefield nuclear weapon against Dukakis in the fall." Gingrich said in June that Bush should ask Dukakis: "Did you really think murderers would come back on Monday?" It didn't help when Willie Horton told *USA Today* in October, "Obviously I am for Dukakis."

This was only the beginning of Dukakis's exploitable record of evasive process liberalism. As governor he vetoed a bill to require public school teachers to lead students in reciting the Pledge of Allegiance each morning. Based on an old Supreme Court decision about a different circumstance, Dukakis said he felt the bill was unconstitutional, and he had an advisory opinion from the Massachusetts state supreme court to back him up. But he had tipped his hand ahead of time, telling the court that he felt the bill was unconstitutional. It didn't help his case that his hometown of Brookline had done away with reciting the pledge at town council meetings, and the state attorney general sided with him against the pledge bill "because [some teachers] believe the phrase, 'with liberty and justice for all,' which is part of the pledge, is untrue." When the Democratic-dominated state legislature voted to override Dukakis's veto, the legislators sang "God Bless America" in the capitol chamber. Dukakis never could bring himself to make a sentimental public embrace of the pledge. So Bush visited flag factories and hammered away: "What is it about the Pledge of Allegiance that upsets him so much?" Add to these issues Dukakis's support for gun control and his membership in the American Civil Liberties Union, and it added up to an easy target for Republican campaign strategists.

Dukakis's foreign and defense policy orientation was equally vulnerable. He opposed every new weapons system "since the slingshot," according to Bush, who was exaggerating only slightly. He opposed every strategic weapons modernization program in the 1980s, opposed SDI (as did all the Democratic candidates, for that matter), and supported the nuclear freeze. He said the United States needed to rely more on the United Nations and the Organization of American States on regional problems. He opposed aid to anti-Communist resistance forces not just in Nicaragua but also in Africa, and he criticized Reagan's invasion of Grenada and the 1986 reprisal raid against Libya. David Broder wrote that Dukakis "sometimes sounds as if the ghost of Eleanor Roosevelt controls his whole body." Bush had an endless supply of Reaganesque one-liners: "I wouldn't be surprised if Dukakis thinks a naval exercise is something you find in Jane Fonda's workout book." The Democrat's running mate, Senator Bentsen, drew boos when he defended Dukakis at an appearance before the Veterans of Foreign Wars. Dukakis's vulnerability led to the biggest gaffe of the campaign: visiting a General Dynamics weapons plant, Dukakis donned a tank helmet and gear and allowed the media to film him driving the tank around a proving yard. It became the campaign's "killer rabbit" moment; the media fell over themselves thinking up analogies for its goofiness, including "Pee-Wee's armored adventure" and Dukakis as "Rocky the Flying Squirrel." The Bush campaign turned the tank footage into a negative TV spot.

Dukakis's early lead in the polls vanished as Bush succeeded in transforming the election into a referendum on Dukakis's unconfessed liberalism. Polling by CBS and the *New York Times* found that the proportion of voters who perceived Dukakis as a liberal rose from 27 percent in July to 43 percent in October. The labeling of Dukakis as a liberal was the source of liberal fury about the 1988 election campaign, because for most liberals these cultural or values issues weren't genuine issues the way, for example, health care was. Herein one can discern another trait of modern cosmopolitan liberalism—the idea that elections should be purely wonky affairs, decided along the lines of a Socratic seminar. That campaigns and elections are equally broad expressions of our sentiments is an idea that has become anathema to the media-academic complex. Reagan is credited, even by most of his critics, with restoring Americans' confidence and optimism through his leadership; exactly what concrete policy issue is confidence or optimism? Symbolic issues such as the Pledge of Allegiance are shorthand means of discerning if a candidate has leadership qualities that command a voter's confidence and trust. And it is a bit precious that the same people who savaged Robert Bork the year before would now complain that a presidential candidate was being treated roughly.

Starting first with the Dukakis campaign and spreading out in concentric circles through the media was a denial that Bush's attacks were meaningful or important. Dukakis's campaign manager, attorney Susan Estrich, dismissed the pledge attack: "If Bush thinks he's going to get anywhere with the pledge stuff, he's crazy. We've got this Supreme Court decision." She and others in the campaign also dismissed the Willie Horton issue. Novelist Philip Roth had a new complaint: "Why is [Bush] turning the Pledge of Allegiance into a loyalty oath?" A few liberals understood the error of this cloistered thinking. Lefty economist Robert Kuttner wrote, "Dukakis and his people never quite grasped the potency of issues like crime and the Pledge of Allegiance; they took these for cheap manipulation of symbols and dirty, negative campaigning, rather than the assertion of *a set of values closer to those of the average voter*" (emphasis added).[16] Another liberal who understood this was Bill Clinton. Journalist Peter Brown recalls Governor Clinton trying to alert Dukakis to the resonance of the pledge issue:

> "How are you going to answer this Pledge of Allegiance thing?" Clinton asked Dukakis during a prep session in a plush suite in the Lexington Hotel. "The general consensus around the table," Clinton recalled, "was, 'Do we need to spend a lot of time on this in this debate?' And Mike, bless his heart, and this wasn't being liberal, this was his government mindset, said, "What does that have to do with being president?" Dukakis said, "It's hard for me to believe it is going to be a big deal." "I told him it is a big deal," Clinton replied. "Where I come from, people will not vote for a president who doesn't like to pledge allegiance to the flag. . . . But words matter, values, symbolism matters. We had this long talk, and finally I sat down and wrote out a proposed 56-second statement about this

Pledge issue and how you could argue it in terms of values. But Dukakis never used it. To him, his values as a citizen were not relevant to his campaign for president, because the president was the person who did government. That is a huge problem for Democrats," Clinton lamented.[17]

Dukakis was still denying his liberalism two weeks before the election in November, telling Ted Koppel on *Nightline,* "Ted, I'm not a liberal." Then all of a sudden, a week before the election, he admitted he *was* a liberal after all, but not a McGovernite liberal. "I am a liberal in the tradition of Franklin Roosevelt and Harry Truman and John Kennedy," he said on October 30. A couple of days later he added Lyndon Johnson to the list, even though Dukakis had been active in Eugene McCarthy's dump-Johnson movement in 1968. The tacit message was that he wasn't a McGovern-Mondale liberal, prompting McGovern himself to throw a penalty flag: "To repudiate the McGovern Democrats in 1988 is to repudiate what is now the mainstream of the Democratic Party."

On Election Day a week later Bush swamped Dukakis by a popular vote margin of 54 to 46 percent, but the electoral college result was more lopsided, with Bush winning forty states and 426 electoral votes to just ten states (plus the District of Columbia) and 111 electoral votes for Dukakis. A few Democrats looked at the bright side: Dukakis did better than Mondale and Carter. But most were more realistic. Democratic pollster Harrison Hickman was despondent: "If we couldn't beat Bush, I don't know who we *can* beat." Hendrik Hertzberg wrote in the *New Republic:* "If Dukakis is too liberal then any Democrat is probably too liberal." However, the daily tracking polls showed that Dukakis gained on Bush the last week of the campaign, after he professed to being an old-style liberal. His small late surge may reflect the natural tightening that often happens in the closing days of presidential campaigns. But it is also possible that semicandid expressions of his ideology did him some good with swing voters who had mixed attitudes about modern liberalism. Some exit poll data support this speculation. Ted Kennedy certainly thought so, commenting after the election that "I believe if he had started campaigning that way a few weeks earlier this fall, Mike Dukakis and not George Bush would be taking the oath of office next January."[18]

Harvey Mansfield drew attention to the heart of the matter. "Bush's three attacks on Dukakis exposed not only a liberal but also a liberalism that is politically exhausted and bored with itself." Some liberals understood that self-examination of the nature of modern liberalism was necessary. The *Washington Post*'s Meg Greenfield dissented from the liberal chorus that the Willie Horton attack was unalloyed racism: "Many Democrats seem unwilling or unable to think about violent crime as a matter of public policy." The *New Republic* ran what it called its "quadrennial recriminations issue," with no shortage of intelligent self-criticism of modern liberalism. Robert Kuttner noted correctly that "our overall public philosophy was so garbled that the standard bearer didn't seem to stand for anything." There was lots of sensible reflection that presaged Bill Clinton's successful campaign four years later; Clinton himself reflected some months after the 1988 election that Democrats like Dukakis felt "the only legitimate action that a politician takes is not what he says, or what he feels, but what he does in terms of a program or a bureaucracy."[19] Writing in the *Nation,* Jefferson Morley argued that Democrats "must turn to national leaders who can perform comfortably in the culture of poor and middle-income Southern whites, like Bill Clinton of Arkansas."

But there was no getting around the central fact William Schneider presented: "Why has liberalism become such a scare word? The reason is that Reagan has changed the shape of American politics."[20] While the dwindling band of conservative Democrats chorused an I-told-you-so, the dominant reaction on the left was denial. Rather than examine whether contemporary liberalism was unpopular with a majority of voters, the media-academic complex took up the rallying cry that Bush had won unfairly and unscrupulously, an approach that has become the template for liberal interpretation of national elections ever since. But as Aaron Wildavsky observed, "A negative campaign is one in which the wrong candidate loses."

Newsweek said that Bush's campaign "was nationalist and nativist, a thinly-coded way of suggesting that Dukakis was less than 100-percent American." *Time* magazine said, "Little can justify Bush's cynical exploitation of the pseudo-issues of crime and patriotism." NBC's Bryant Gumbel said Bush "tapped a rather rich vein of American racism." While very tough on Dukakis, the *New Republic* joined other liberals in taking offense at Bush's "pledgehammer" attack: "Making an issue of the other side's love of flag and country is simply repulsive." Kathleen Hall Jamieson of the Annenberg Public Policy Center lamented that "many of us were naive in thinking that the nation as a whole was adequately protected from this kind of campaigning." Marvin Kalb, formerly of CBS and NBC News, said that Dukakis was "too principled" to win, and Ellen Goodman attributed Dukakis's loss to "the candidate's irrational belief in reason." The Horton furlough episode has had an especially long half-life. In 1990, Sam Donaldson interviewed Horton on ABC's *Primetime Live* and concluded his interview with this question: "If [Bush campaign manager] Lee Atwater should walk through that door tomorrow and say, 'Mr. Horton, I think I did you wrong,' would you forgive him?" This kind of thinking, George Will noted, "encourage[s] in the Democrats the soothing belief that their party's problems are in the nuts and bolts of the machinery and not in the party's mind."

The secondary theme of this analysis was that, like Reagan in 1984, Bush had no mandate to do anything. To be sure, Bush had no coattails in the election: Democrats picked up two Senate seats and five House seats.[21] Representative Pat Schroeder quipped that "Bush got elected in a bikini," and the *New York Times* reassured its readers that "Mr. Bush's victory . . . cannot fairly be called a mandate."

And yet Bush became the first vice president to succeed a sitting president in 150 years, and his victory has been interpreted justly as a third term for Ronald Reagan. His lack of Reagan's rhetorical gifts and hard-edged ideological conservatism diminished the clarity of Bush's politics. Beyond pledging to continue Reaganomics—a pledge he did not keep—and the main outlines of Reagan's foreign policy, Bush had gone to some trouble to distinguish himself from Reagan stylistically, most pointedly with his convention-speech language of seeking to bring about "a kinder, gentler nation." *Kinder and gentler than whom?* Nancy Reagan is reported to have asked. George W. Bush tried to reassure conservative movement leaders about his father, telling them, "You'll be astounded at how conservatively he will govern. George Bush to the conservatives will be like Richard Nixon in China."[22]

But the first order of business for the Bush transition was turning out all of the Reaganites as quickly as possible. It was said of Bush appointees that, unlike Reaganites, they had mortgages rather than ideologies. Paul Weyrich said that he had always feared that the election of Bush meant the arrival of "country club Republicans who couldn't wait for the end of the Reagan administration." George Shultz's top aide at the State Department, Charles Hill, recalled, "It was suddenly clear that this would be an adversarial transition. The new people were not friendly. The signals were: get out of here as fast as you can."[23] Newt Gingrich cautioned, "We are not Bush's movement."

*   *   *

ONE AREA WHERE Bush was more traditionally conservative than Reagan was his view of the Soviet Union. Bush was skeptical and wary of Gorbachev, and not in a hurry to meet him. He would bring in as his national security adviser Brent Scowcroft, an opponent of the INF treaty and a critic of Reagan's Soviet diplomacy, and James Baker as secretary of state. Shultz worried that "George Bush and Jim Baker seemed concerned and wary that Ronald Reagan and I had become too impressed with Soviet personalities—Gorbachev, Shevardnadze—too ready to believe that genuine change was occurring in the Soviet Union." For their part, Gorbachev and Shevadnadze said several times in the Moscow summit in May that they wished Reagan and Shultz could stay on.

As the summer wore on, it became clear that the United States and the Soviet Union would not be able to complete the START agreement on strategic nuclear weapons before Reagan's term ended. So Gorbachev prepared a bold stroke on another front. In late October, as he looked ahead to a speech at the United Nations in early December, Gorbachev told his senior aides that he wanted the address to be an answer to Churchill's "Iron Curtain" speech in Fulton, Missouri, in 1946, which could be said to have announced the Cold War. The speech should be "an anti-Fulton—Fulton in reverse." He also sent word to Washington that he'd like to meet Reagan one last time while he was in New York.

Gorbachev kept the content of his speech closely guarded (he did not circulate it to the Politburo before departing Moscow). It was dramatic and specific: within the next two years, he said, the Soviet Union would reduce the size of its armed forces by half a million men, "*unilaterally*, without relation to the talks on the mandate of the Vienna meeting."[24] They would remove not just troops but also most of their offensive equipment and supplies, such as bridging equipment, combat aircraft, and tanks, from Eastern Europe. This was real news, and lent credibility to the earlier parts of his speech that amounted to his calling off the Cold War. By embracing "freedom of choice," the "de-ideologization of interstate relations," and similar concepts, he implicitly disavowed the Marxist ideology of international class struggle and the Brezhnev Doctrine. He was most emphatic that the use of force was not a legitimate instrument of foreign policy.[25]

After his speech Gorbachev took the ferry across New York Harbor to Governor's Island to have lunch with Reagan and President-elect Bush. The White House had made it clear to the Soviets that because the Reagan-Bush transition was just beginning this was to be purely a social lunch and not a serious negotiating session; no Reykjavik-style surprises, please. After lunch Reagan posed outside with Gorbachev and Bush for a photo with the Statue of Liberty in the background.

Though Reagan spoke often of the "shining city on a hill," it was the Statue of Liberty that was his greatest symbol. He had formally launched his fall campaign for president on Labor Day in 1980 across from the Statue of Liberty, and marked the midpoint of his restorative presidency at the unveiling of the refurbished Lady Liberty in 1985. I wonder whether Reagan noted to himself that the tableau of that day marked the bookend to his story—that Emma Lazarus's unforgettable sonnet celebrating "the new colossus" also points the way to his shining city:

> *Here at our sea-washed, sunset gates shall stand*
> *A mighty woman with a torch, whose flame*
> *Is the imprisoned lightning, and her name*
> *Mother of Exiles.*

EPILOGUE

THE REAGAN REVOLUTION
AND ITS DISCONTENTS

————⟶✦⟵————

*The Reagan years will be for conservatives what the Kennedy
years remain for liberals: the reference point, the breakthrough
experience—a conservative Camelot. At the same time, no lesson
is plainer than that the damage of decades cannot be repaired
in any one administration.*
—FORMER REAGAN HOUSE STAFF MEMBER AND
INDIANA GOVERNOR MITCH DANIELS

THE SPECTER THAT haunted America's containment policy during the
Cold War was the domino theory. In 1989 the theory came true in re-
verse—nearly the entire Communist world fell almost in the blink of an eye.
In 1983 Leszek Kolakowski had written, "Certainly in Poland or Czechoslo-
vakia (or in Hungary) Communism would fall apart within days without the
Soviet threat." The Captive Nations of Eastern Europe decided to test Gor-
bachev's UN declaration that the Brezhnev Doctrine was well and truly over.
The Communist regimes didn't have a chance.

The final collapse began in 1988 in Poland, where the revival of Solidarity led the demoralized Communist government to miscalculate. A series of
effective general strikes and other agitation prompted the ruling Communists
to enter formal negotiations—the roundtable talks—with Solidarity. Solidarity wanted one thing above all: real elections. While the Soviet Union talked
of having contested elections within the Communist Party structure, in
Poland the strength of Solidarity meant that elections had to permit the participation of the opposition. Grudgingly General Jaruzelski agreed to a deal

calling for opposition candidates to fill 35 percent of the seats in the crucial lower house of a bicameral legislature (the Sejm) but allowing all one hundred seats of a new Senate to be freely contested. The Communists thought they would win quick elections against an unorganized opposition. They underestimated both their unpopularity and the spontaneous organizing ability of Solidarity, which swept ninety-nine of the one hundred Senate seats and captured virtually all of the 35 percent of the opposition seats in the Sejm. A wrinkle in the Polish election law dealt an additional devastating blow to the ruling Communists. Voters were allowed to cross off names from the single-candidate lists, and any candidate receiving less than 50 percent of votes cast was ineligible for office. In massive numbers Polish voters crossed out the names of thirty-three of thirty-five major Communist officials on the ballot, including the prime minister. Solidarity ended up forming the new government; while Jaruzelski remained president for the time being, the first non-Communist prime minister of Poland took office in August.

The Polish election took place on June 4, and as the landslide results were coming in that evening, news arrived from Beijing of a bloody crackdown on prodemocracy demonstrators in Tiananmen Square. Here was a reminder—and a puzzle—of dictatorial systems. Since the late 1970s China had enjoyed a reputation as a liberalizing Communist nation, but now it was reverting to the same kind of violent repression the Soviets had used in 1953, 1956, and 1968. There was little prospect of such a course succeeding again in Europe in 1989, however. Historian Mark Kramer commented on this extraordinary spectacle: "History offers no previous instances in which revolutionary political and social change of this magnitude transpired with almost no violence."[1] What explains the different courses of the Soviet bloc and China?

For all of the sophisticated structural and materialist analyses of the Communist world, it comes down to the simple fact that most of the Communist rulers lost the will to shoot their own people in large numbers. This might seem an inevitable consequence of the loss of belief in the Marxist ideology of class struggle, but the will to power of rulers has never been dependent on ideology, and it might have turned out differently. As Princeton historian Stephen Kotkin puts it in his concise book *Armageddon Averted*, the Soviet Union "was lethargically stable, and could have continued muddling on for quite some time." Moreover, Kotkin argues,

> although it had been destabilized by romantic idealism, the Soviet
> system still commanded a larger and more powerful military and re-

pressive apparatus than any state in history. It had more than enough nuclear weapons to destroy or blackmail the world, and a vast storehouse of chemical and biological weapons, with all requisite delivery systems. . . . [W]ith the horrid example of much smaller Yugoslavia's catastrophic break-up right next door, one shudders to think of the manipulative wars, indeed the nuclear, chemical, or biological Armageddon, that *could have* accompanied the Soviet collapse.[2]

Kotkin concludes: "The greatest surprise of the Soviet collapse was not that it happened—though that was shocking enough—but the absence of an all-consuming conflagration."

From Poland the next domino to fall was Hungary. A combination of a disheartened Communist Party leadership and a confident opposition movement that prompted growing public protests against the regime culminated in an agreement in September for full and free parliamentary elections. As in Poland, the Communists hoped to hang on through the same divide-and-rule strategy, and after some backing and filling a new constitution was proclaimed in October. A crystallizing moment occurred when, during the public announcement of the new constitution, a Communist Party leader told the crowd assembled outside the parliament building: "We continue to regard the undisturbed and balanced development of our relationship with our great neighbor, the Soviet Union, as being in our national interest." The crowd erupted in boos and whistles. It was over.

Hungary embarked on a strategy that started other dominoes falling in quick succession. Hungary's reformers knew that they faced great hazards during the transitional phase, and they feared that another 1956-style military crackdown might be in store, perhaps from East Germany, whose aging Stalinist tyrant, Erich Honecker, had never sympathized with Gorbachev's program. The Hungarians decided on a bold stroke: they opened their border with Austria and stopped detaining East Germans who transited through Hungary en route to Austria. A back door around the Berlin Wall had opened up, and thousands poured through. The Hungarians did not inform the Soviet Union or East Germany in advance. "We were pretty sure," Hungarian reformer Imre Pozsgay said later, "that if hundreds of thousands of East Germans went to the West, the East German regime would fall, and in that case Czechoslovakia was also out."

They were right. Throughout the fall protests in East German cities were growing, reaching a climax on November 4, when a million people took to the streets of East Berlin. Honecker stepped down in October after

Gorbachev showed him the back of his hand, but it was too late for the regime to save itself. In the face of the mounting exodus of its citizens and unprecedented public protests in East German cities (fifty thousand turned out in Leipzig on October 9, and half a million flooded the streets of East Berlin on November 4), on November 9 the Politburo quietly decided to lift all travel restrictions. At the end of a routine daily press briefing at 7:00 p.m., a Politburo spokesman made a low-key announcement that "private trips abroad can be applied for, and permits will be granted promptly . . . Permanent emigration is henceforth allowed across all border crossing points between East Germany and West Germany and West Berlin."

Within hours thousands of Germans from both sides of the Berlin divide descended on the wall, where bewildered guards didn't know what to do. Soon people with picks and hammers climbed atop the wall and started its destruction. "We did not suspect," the East German foreign minister wrote, "that the opening of the Wall was the beginning of the end of the Republic."

In Bulgaria the Communist rulers went quietly the day after the wall came down. In the face of rising popular opposition, Prime Minister Todor Zhivkov, an unreconstructed Stalinist who had been in office since 1954, resigned in November. The Party Central Committee forced him out (having apparently consulted with Moscow), announced plans for competitive elections, and in effect abolished the Communist Party.

In less than a week Czechoslovakia started a quick journey down the same road. A series of general strikes and huge public protests following the killing of a student protestor (later revealed to have been a secret-police infiltrator) on November 17 led the ruling Communists to capitulate by the end of the month without further bloodshed, announcing that a coalition government would be formed and an election held the following year. Non-Communists dominated the new cabinet that was formed in December, and the national assembly elevated Vaclav Havel, who at the beginning of 1989 was in jail for his human rights activism, as the new president. Romania's Nicolae Ceauşescu lasted another month. Ceauşescu attempted to hold on to power the old-fashioned dictator's way, having openly admired the Chinese solution to the Tiananmen Square problem. He and his wife ended up with bullets in their heads on Christmas Day.

The formal breakup of the Soviet Union was more protracted. Gorbachev used force to put down a drive to independence by the Baltic nations of Latvia, Estonia, and Lithuania, and a coup attempt against Gorbachev in 1991 led to some nervous moments all around. Eventually his rival Boris

Yeltsin swept him away in a free election. Yeltsin finished what Gorbachev had haltingly begun. One of Yeltsin's first acts as president was to slash defense spending by 80 percent. Yeltsin cashiered more than five hundred generals, and the number of men under arms in Russia was cut from 2.7 million to 1.2 million. The Soviet Union had spent roughly a quarter of its GDP on defense in the 1980s; by 1999, Russian spending for defense was down to 2.3 percent of GDP. In accordance with the START Treaty finally reached with the United States in 1990, the number of nuclear warheads in the Russian arsenal declined from more than 10,000 in 1990 to under 4,500 today. In 1991 the famous Doomsday Clock of the *Bulletin of Atomic Scientists* was reset at seventeen minutes to midnight, down from three in 1984—the farthest it had been since its invention early in the nuclear age. (It is today, in the aftermath of 9/11, back to five minutes to midnight.)

Even Nicaragua succumbed. The Sandinistas, faced with renewed American and regional pressure and the withdrawal of Soviet subsidies, agreed to free elections in 1990. Between their bully apparatus and the disorganization of the opposition, they expected to win; the CIA expected them to win too. They were crushed in a landslide. Before long the scholarly journal *Problems of Communism* had to change its name to *Problems of Post-Communism*. In 2007 Gorbachev turned up in expensive full-color ads in the Sunday *New York Times* touting Louis Vuitton luggage from the comfort of his limousine driving past a fragment of the Berlin Wall. A Las Vegas casino reportedly offered Gorbachev millions to be a greeter. While he declined that offer, he did appear in a Pizza Hut ad. With the passage of time Russians do not regard these changes as an unalloyed good. In 2008, an opinion survey found that three-quarters of Russians regret the demise of the Soviet Union, and the survey also found residual admiration for Stalin.

*   *   *

THE ABRUPT FALL of the Berlin Wall caught the West by surprise. At the White House, President Bush, wary of inflaming a potentially unstable situation, issued a statement so low-key it made people wonder if he was on Valium. "You don't seem elated," Lesley Stahl said to Bush. "I'm not an emotional kind of guy," Bush replied. With the time difference between Europe and the United States, the American news media scrambled to catch up to the story. Naturally, the TV news shows began looping Reagan's call to "tear down this wall." ABC News reached Ronald Reagan at home in Los Angeles, and he agreed to go on ABC's *Primetime Live,* where he appeared to be as astonished as everyone else. Sam Donaldson asked Reagan, "Did you think it would come this soon?" Reagan, subdued throughout the interview, replied, "I didn't know when it would come, but I'm an eternal optimist, and I believed with all my heart that it was in the future." Like Bush, Reagan didn't wish to embarrass or humiliate Gorbachev, so Reagan denied to Donaldson that he'd ever directly spoken to Gorbachev about the wall, though subsequent transcripts show that he had.

Mostly Reagan repeated some of the better-known public themes from his Cold War diplomacy ("Trust but verify"), but he did take a mild shot at his critics: "Contrary to what some critics have said, I never believed that we should just assume that everything was going to be all right." Asked to revisit his "evil empire" comment, Reagan said, "I have to tell you—I said that on purpose. . . . I believe the Soviet Union needed to see and hear what we felt about them. They needed to be aware that we were realists"—a final confirmation of his conviction that the anti-Communist "ideologues" were the true realists all along. Prompted to revisit his 1982 prediction that Communism was headed to the "ash heap of history," Reagan ended the interview with the short observation: "People have had time in some 70-odd years since the Communist revolution to see that Communism has had its chance, and it doesn't work."

But it was the end of more than a twentieth-century story. Some of the East German protestors in the streets of Leipzig in early November carried banners that read 1789–1989. If the storming of the Bastille in 1789 could be said to have marked the beginning of utopian revolutionary politics, then the storming of the Berlin Wall in 1989 marked its end. As Timothy Garton Ash observed, "Nineteen eighty-nine also caused, throughout the world, a profound crisis of identity on what had been known since the French revolution of 1789 as 'the left.' "[3] The deep unpopularity of the Communist regimes revealed by the peoples of Eastern Europe in 1989 was an embarrassment to moderate liberals and value-free social scientists who had regarded these nations as stable and legitimate forms of governance, and it was a faith-shaking crisis for the far Left, which openly sympathized with these regimes. On an intellectual level the death of revolutionary socialism has found a successor in postmodern philosophy, which preserves some aspects of decayed Marxism. But its obscurity limits its power to convince, and it is unlikely to advance beyond the barricades of academic English departments.

The issue of who won the Cold War aggravated partisan sentiment as well as the liberal neo-Kantian analytical framework that disapproved of

Reagan's simple philosophy of peace through strength and renewed ideological warfare with the Soviet bloc. The initial impulse in the early 1990s was to deny Reagan credit and lionize Gorbachev. In 1990 *Time* magazine selected Gorbachev—not Reagan—as its "man of the decade." Strobe Talbott's five-thousand-word valentine to Gorbachev mentioned Reagan only once, and then only to dismiss as "smug" the central features of his Soviet strategy. Gorbachev was awarded the Nobel Peace Prize; there was no mention of Reagan.

Gorbachev and his circle of courageous reformers (Yakovlev, Chernyaev, et alia) deserve their share of credit, but the dissolution of the Soviet empire formed no part of his purpose. *Time* essayist Lance Morrow wrote that "Gorbachev is the Copernicus, Darwin, and Freud of communism all wrapped in one." Gorbachev himself had a better grasp, however; when a reporter asked him shortly after his Nobel Prize whether he was moving to the right, he quipped, "Actually, I'm going round in circles."[4]

The churlish treatment of Reagan proved unsustainable, even by his ideological opponents. The release of documents and the new testimony of witnesses eroded their condescension. Numerous high former Soviet officials testified that Reagan's SDI hastened their demise. And Gorbachev himself was more charitable toward Reagan than Reagan's American detractors were, telling the History Channel in 2002, "I am not sure what happened would have happened had he [Reagan] not been there."[5] More significant perhaps than Gorbachev's words was the most remarkable scene at the observances of Reagan's passing in June 2004, when Gorbachev, his onetime enemy, paid his respects at Reagan's casket as it lay in state at the Capitol, and then sat next to Margaret Thatcher at the memorial service the next day.

Princeton's Sean Wilentz, no friend of conservatives or Republicans, wrote recently: "His success in helping finally to end the cold war is one of the greatest achievements by any president of the United States—and arguably the greatest single presidential achievement since 1945."[6] Jonathan Schell, author of the overwrought *Fate of the Earth* in 1982, wrote at Reagan's death in 2004: "Reagan had been prescient early in his term in foreseeing the dimensions of the Soviet crisis . . . to his great credit, Reagan began to understand that the rise of Gorbachev to the leadership of the Soviet Union heralded fundamental change."[7]

There has been much speculation among counterfactual historians about how the course of events might have gone without Reagan and Gorbachev. George Breslauer and Richard Ned Lebow conjectured that, "[l]ed by cautious and conservative General Secretary Viktor Grishin [instead of Gorbachev], the Soviet Union might have shunned serious reform at home and continued to regard the West as its principal foreign foe." Breslauer and Lebow, no enthusiasts for Reagan generally, concluded after a lengthy academic exercise that Reagan and Gorbachev were "indispensable" to the ending of the Cold War in the late 1980s and early 1990s. Separately, Richard Hermann and Lebow suggested, "It is worth considering the proposition that it was Reagan's maximalism and resolve, coupled with his willingness to strike deals and abandon hostile rhetoric when his maximalist demands were met, and the personal rapport and vision he shared with Gorbachev, that ended the Cold War when and how it did."[8]

The marginalization of Reagan's role in ending the Cold War was merely of a piece with the larger denigration of Reagan by the American chattering classes. When Bill Clinton challenged a weakened George H. W. Bush in 1992, he made a point of attacking the entire Reagan-Bush legacy of "the past 12 years." "The Reagan-Bush years," Clinton said, "have exalted private gain over public obligation, special interests over the common good, wealth and fame over work and family. The 1980s ushered in a Gilded Age of greed and selfishness, of irresponsibility and excess, and of neglect."

And yet for all of Clinton's political gifts and his success in raising income tax rates slightly, he had to give way to the Age of Reagan, most obviously when the 1994 election (which some observers called "Reagan's third landslide") delivered the House to GOP control for the first time in forty years. It was an election result that some academics—and pessimistic conservatives—had thought was no longer possible. Newt Gingrich said the campaign's main innovation, the Contract for America, "stood on Reagan's shoulders. It was the culmination of 30 years of Reaganism, dating back to 'The Speech.' " The election of 1994 was a sign that the Reagan realignment was genuine and enduring; nearly all Republicans today profess to being Reagan Republicans, and many of them mean it. Michael Barone points out that the high-water mark for the number of Democrats imbued with New Deal ideology came with the election of 1958, thirteen years after FDR's passing.

This enduring realignment within the Republican Party also represents the triumph of a practical principle the Reaganites understood clearly but were unable to implement with complete success: personnel is policy. *National Review* publisher William Rusher wrote in 1984: "[Reagan] has put conservatives into lower echelons of government. This means that in the next conservative administration, conservatives can go to the higher echelons." Rusher added: "Reagan has been criticized for drawing his top people from outside the conservative ranks. But previously, there was not a soul in the conservative movement who had been postmaster of Dogpatch, Kentucky. How can you have a reasonable agenda for redesigning the Environmental Protection Agency when no conservative has ever served there? Reagan has been like Columbus. He has led us ashore on a continent many of us have never seen or been on." One of the notable aspects of the George W. Bush years was the many junior Reaganites who emerged in key senior positions, such as Paul Wolfowitz, John Bolton, Paula Dobriansky, and most especially John Roberts and Samuel Alito.

One of Clinton's significant concessions to Reaganism was welfare reform. Reagan signed a welfare reform bill with weak work requirements in his closing weeks in office in 1988, and it changed nothing. The 1996 reform bill, which President Clinton reluctantly signed after vetoing two previous versions, incorporated the principles of reform that Reagan had advocated in the early 1970s: it ended welfare as an entitlement, set time limits for eligibility, and imposed serious work requirements. Welfare rolls have fallen by more than 50 percent since its enactment.

Watching the squandering of the Clinton years led some liberals to an honest reappraisal of Reagan, with surprising results. Perhaps the most dramatic was the elegant liberal scribe Richard Reeves. In 1979 Reeves wrote a long feature in *Esquire* with the self-evident title "Why Reagan Won't Make It." "Reagan seems to be a nostalgia figure whose time has passed," Reeves concluded; "he looks like the past, he talks about the past. It is hard to imagine America turning to a candidate whose standard pitch is 'I told you so!' " When Reagan left office in 1989, Reeves's judgment was immediate. "Reagan gave it his best shot, but he failed." Throughout the George H. W. Bush years Reeves filed column after column embellishing the liberal campfire ghost stories that Reagan favored the rich, reduced the middle class, and saddled our children with endless debt.

With the coming of Bill Clinton, Reeves thought he had found vindication. "It is a pleasure to watch this president work," Reeves wrote in early 1994. "Whatever else he has done in his first year, Clinton has shown he has both ideas and testosterone—and maybe he thinks that will be enough to move the nation off the Reagan detour and back into more caring directions." Shortly before the 1994 election this author suggested to Reeves in a debate in California that if the imminent election went as the polls suggested it would, he might need to reissue his 1985 book *The Reagan Detour* under a new title, *The Reagan Main Road*.

At first Reeves shared in the liberal denial, writing that the 1994 election was a populist revolt by white men who wanted to be back in control again. But then something seemed to snap; perhaps it was the recognition that Bill Clinton had more testosterone than ideas. Starting in 1996, Reeves began to upgrade Reagan's status: "I was no fan of Ronald Reagan, but I think I know a leader when I see one, even if I do not want to follow where he is leading. . . . He was a man of conservative principle and he damned near destroyed American liberalism. Reagan was larger than he seemed, indeed larger than life, even if our historians do not quite get it yet." A year later Reeves wrote of Clinton: "Wittingly or not, the Democrat who ran as the agent of change gave up after a couple of years and joined the Reagan revolution." By 1999 Reeves's capitulation was complete: "Reagan, in fact, is still running the country. President Clinton is governing in his shadow, trying, not without some real success, to create a liberal garden under the conservative oak. In the next wave of history, when Americans have forgotten some of his failings, Reagan will probably be classed as a 'near-great' president." In 2005 Reeves published a full-length book entitled *President Reagan: The Triumph of Imagination,* in which he adumbrated this view further. Twenty-five years ago bookmakers would have given very long odds against ever seeing a liberal grandee such as Richard Reeves using the words *Reagan* and *triumph* in the same sentence, let alone in the title of a book.

In 2007 John Patrick Diggins, a neighbor, friend, and ideological soul mate of Arthur Schlesinger Jr., published *Ronald Reagan: Fate, Freedom and the Making of History,* in which he made the case that Reagan deserves to be considered among the greatest American presidents, alongside Washington, Lincoln, and Franklin Roosevelt. Diggins calls Reagan our "Emersonian President," and certainly Reagan lived up to Emerson's aphorism that a foolish consistency is the hobgoblin of little minds. However, Diggins wants to make Reagan into a crypto-liberal: "Far from being a conservative, Reagan wa the great liberating spirit of modern American history, a political romantic impatient with the status quo. . . . Reagan's relation to liberalism may illuminate modern America more than his relation to conservatism. . . . What Reagan sought to do for America has been the goal of liberalism since the 18th century Enlightenment: to get rid of authority, the meddlesome intrusions of controlling institutions, whether of church or state."

Atlantic Monthly writer Joshua Green noted in the *Washington Monthly* in January 2003 that "many of [Reagan's] actions as president wound up facilitating liberal objectives. What this clamor of adulation is seeking to deny is that beyond his conservative legacy, Ronald Reagan has bequeathed a liberal one."[9] He raised taxes. He—gasp!—talked to the Soviets and reached arms agreements. Green's article was provocatively adorned with a cartoon rendering of Reagan assuming the mantle of FDR, complete with upturned cigarette holder. Reagan was fond of saying that he didn't leave the Democratic Party—the party left him. Now, in the years after his death, Democrats seem to be returning to him. Indeed, Barack Obama's successful presidential campaign of 2008 emulated a number of Reaganesque notes, and not merely in his impressive stagecraft.

It is one thing for academics and intellectuals to appreciate Reagan, but political animals drew the line when Barack Obama said, "I think Ronald Reagan changed the trajectory of America in a way that, you know, Richard Nixon did not and in a way that Bill Clinton did not. He put us on a fundamentally different path because the country was ready for it. . . . I think it's fair to say that the Republicans were the party of ideas for a pretty long chunk of time there over the last 10, 15 years, in the sense that they were challenging conventional wisdom." That this was said as a way of denigrating Hillary Clinton is secondary to the fact that it was possible for a liberal candidate even to think, let alone speak, such heresy.

*   *   *

THE IRONY IS that the counterpoint to the growing liberal appreciation of Reagan can be found among conservatives. Reagan may have ended liberalism's near-monopoly in American politics, but he did not supplant it with a dominant conservative monopoly. A few conservatives, such as David Frum in *Dead Right,* noted not long after Reagan left office that Reagan fell far short of his first inaugural speech promise "to curb the size and influence of the federal establishment." Although Reagan added no new agencies or major regulatory programs in his two terms, his announced intention to abolish the Departments of Education and Energy got nowhere. The budget deficit should be regarded as an embarrassment by any self-respecting fiscal conservative. Reagan himself said that the inability to control spending was his biggest disappointment.

The late Thomas B. Silver wrote: "Judged by the highest goal he set for himself, Reagan was not successful. That goal was nothing less than a realignment of the American political order, in which the primacy of the New Deal was to be challenged and overthrown. It cannot be said that Reagan in any fundamental way dismantled or even scaled back the administrative state created by FDR."[10]

More recently William Voegeli surveyed the scene in the *Claremont Review of Books* in terms that Ronald Reagan would use if he were alive today:

> In 1981, the federal government spent $678 billion; in 2006, it spent $2,655 billion. Adjust that 292% increase for inflation, and the federal government is still spending 84% more than it did when Reagan became president—in a country whose population has grown by only 30%. To put the point another way, if per capita spending after 1980 had grown at the rate of inflation, federal outlays would have been $1,883 billion in 2006 instead of $2,655 billion. The 41% increase from 1981 to 2006 *is* considerably lower than the 94% increase in real, per capita spending in the previous 25 years from 1956 to 1981. In the last two decades, the federal establishment grew steadily, rather than dramatically. Nonetheless, Reagan's pledge to curb the government's size and influence has hardly been fulfilled. Inflation-adjusted federal spending increased in every year but two over the past 26 years.[11]

While there is some truth to this, it is worth noting that Reagan almost surely lowered the growth rate of government spending substantially below what it would have been in a second term of Jimmy Carter or even under some other less ideological Republican president such as Howard Baker or George H. W. Bush. And the spending record under George W. Bush made Reagan look frugal. Under Reagan, nondefense discretionary spending grew at an annual rate of 2.6 percent, about the rate of inflation. Under George W. Bush, it grew at an annual rate of 6.2 percent.

One area where George W. Bush kept faith with Reaganomics was tax cuts. Bush rolled back some of the income tax hikes that his father and President Clinton had put through, and although he did not bring top marginal rates back down to the 28 percent level of Reagan's 1986 tax reform, his cuts on dividends and long-term capital gains (to 15 percent) were superior to the levels of the Reagan years. Reagan's supply-side economics remains the most controversial aspect of his legacy on two grounds—its supposed favoritism for the rich, and its role in the large federal budget deficits of the late 1980s and again today. This is an argument without end, in part because of the lack of an agreed-upon methodology for the quantitative aspect of the issue, and in part because it represents a clash of fundamental principles (egalitarianism versus opportunity) that resists empirical analysis.[12] Even if tax cuts could be definitively proved to maximize economic growth and tax revenue, many liberals would still oppose lower rates. When Barack Obama was confronted during the 2008 campaign with the evidence that lower capital gains tax rates increased revenue to the Treasury, he said he still favored higher rates out of "fairness."

Today, nearly half of American wage earners pay little or no federal income tax, which may be a problem from a conservative point of view—all who enjoy the benefits of government ought to share in paying for it. Upper-income earners now pay a much *larger* share of total income taxes than they did before Reagan, just as supply-siders predicted, but the sight of individual wealthy earners paying less on the margin than they did before Reagan distracts liberals from this larger fact.[13] Finally, it cannot escape a fair-minded review of the data that the huge deficits of the 1980s stemmed more from rapid spending growth than from tax cuts, though this point will never be conceded. Lawrence Lindsey's thorough review of the data in 1990 concluded that only 21 percent of the cumulative deficits of the period from 1981 to 1987 could be attributed to the Reagan income tax rate cuts. Lindsey further predicted in 1990 that the federal budget would be in surplus by 1999 if tax rates were kept low or lowered further—more or less exactly as it happened.

The basic logic of tax rate reductions, and its premise that taxes matter, seems secure (which is one reason why Obama felt compelled to present himself as a tax cutter for the middle class), though it will always grate against liberal egalitarian sensibilities. Reagan's tax cuts are still assailed, but no one—not even Ted Kennedy on a bender—proposes going back to the 50 to 70 percent marginal rates of the pre-Reagan years.

Voegeli offers more counterarguments in the realm of broad fiscal policy:

> One yardstick may help conservatives feel a little better about themselves. In 1981 federal spending was 22.2% of GDP; last year it was 20.3%. This measure hovered in a very narrow band for the whole era, never exceeding 23.5% or falling below 18.4%. Adding expenditures by states and localities confirms the picture of a rugby match between liberals and conservatives that is one interminable scrum in the middle of the field. Spending by all levels of government in America amounted to 31.6% of GDP in 1981, and 31.8% in 2006.

The record in regulation is susceptible to a similar criticism. Unable to achieve wide-scale regulatory reform, the Reagan administration settled for regulatory relief, which, while effective, proved transient. Some retreats didn't wait for successor administrations. When at length (and under order from the courts) the administration retreated on repealing mandates for air bags in new cars in 1984, Walter Olson at *Regulation* magazine let out an anguished complaint: "Something like this makes me think, for this we elected Ronald Reagan? This is an issue that sticks out like a sore thumb, because there's an element of people being protected against a hazard they knew they were facing. It's a pure form of paternalism." Reagan surely didn't disagree. Regulatory expert Kip Viscusi commented after Regan left office: "Short-term efforts to alter regulatory policies by slowing the pace of regulation or altering the enforcement effort will not yield long-run changes in the regulatory approach. Ultimately, the agency's enabling legislation will determine the shape of these policies. A major failure of the Reagan regulatory reform effort is not just that such reforms were never achieved but that they were never even attempted."[14]

Reagan was more successful in rolling back the Soviet empire than he was in rolling back the domestic government empire *chiefly because the latter is a harder problem.* While the partisan Democratic House that Reagan faced through his entire eight years was an important factor, it does not entirely explain Reagan's failures. Rolling back big government was a harder problem for constitutional reasons, but also because of public opinion. The experience of the 1990s, after the Gingrich revolution delivered both houses of Congress to Republicans, suggests the public doesn't support shrinking the government to the same extent as the conservative movement does. Conservatives resist facing this problem directly and openly, preferring to deploy expanded versions of the sound critiques from public choice theory to explain why the public really doesn't like big government but can't break the "iron triangle" that preserves big government piecemeal. This is a cop-out.

The Reagan experience should also be a meditation on the limitations of politics. William F. Buckley Jr. reminded the Philadelphia Society during Reagan's presidency that the most powerful man in the world is not powerful enough to do everything that needs to be done. Reagan's second solicitor general, Charles Fried, wrote: "The Reagan administration tried to make a revolution. It proposed dismantling large parts of the welfare-bureaucratic state which had grown up over the previous half-century. Revolutionary as it was, it required (in Danton's phrase) boldness, more boldness, ever more boldness. This boldness was not always in evidence, and often when it was it met ignominious defeat at the hands of Congress, the news media, and timorous Republicans."

Reagan successfully curbed the excesses of liberalism; he did not curb liberalism itself. The inexorable logic of modern American government is to expand by degrees—the intended legacy of the Progressive and New Deal revolutions, which were constitutional in purpose and effect. The shortcomings of the Reagan Revolution stemmed from its failure to be a full-fledged constitutional movement of its own. This was not for lack of perception. As mentioned several times in the main narrative, Reagan advocated constitutional changes, such as his Economic Bill of Rights and Attorney General Meese's public fight about constitutional originalism, that were worthy endeavors. If the Reagan Revolution is finally to be consummated, the movement that cherishes his name will need to return to this mode of constitutional thinking and press to achieve the reforms Reagan could only dream of. Reagan's would-be successors would do well to recall Machiavelli's counsel: "There is nothing more difficult to take in hand, more perilous to conduct, or more uncertain in its success, than to take the lead in the introduction of a new order of things." One of the great shortcomings of conservative political leadership since Reagan is the near-total absence of any serious, broad-gauge constitutional argument such as Reagan and his team made from time to time. And there was little or no effort under the George W. Bush administration to reform or roll back regulation in a significant way. It is possible, though, to change the course of a nation in profound ways that fall short of a full-blown revolution. In the Prologue, Midge Decter delivered her judgment that "there was no Reagan Revolution." But she added this valuable coda: "But what he did leave behind was something in the long run probably more important—a series of noisy open debates about nothing less than the meaning of decency, the limits of government, the salience of race, the nature of criminal behavior." And Gary McDowell, one of Ed Meese's Justice Department aides, offers a suitable companion summary: "Domestically Ronald Reagan did far less than he had hoped, he did far less than he had promised, less than people wanted—and a hell of a lot more than people thought he would."

NOTES

—————◆—————

PROLOGUE: THE LION AT THE GATE

1. Peter Robinson, "Tearing Down That Wall," *Weekly Standard*, June 23, 1997, p. 8. Robinson was the principal author of the speech.

2. Gerald M. Boyd, "Raze Berlin Wall, Reagan Urges Soviet," *New York Times*, June 13, 1987, p. 3.

3. Peter Robinson, *It's My Party: A Republican's Messy Love Affair with the GOP* (New York: Grand Central Publishing, 2000), p. 17.

4. David Binder, "Revival of the Berlin Wall Debate: If We Had Knocked It Down . . . ," *New York Times*, August 14, 1986, p. A-16.

5. See especially Lou Cannon's application of Howard Gardner's theories of multiple types of intelligence in *President Reagan: The Role of a Lifetime* (New York: Simon & Schuster, 1991), pp. 137–39.

6. Bernard J. F. Lonergan, *Insight: A Study of Human Understanding* (London: Longmans, Green, 1958), p. 4.

7. I have written of the striking parallels between Churchill and Reagan in *Greatness: Reagan, Churchill, and the Making of Extraordinary Leaders*—a book that grew unexpectedly out of an earlier draft of this chapter.

8. See especially Robert Rhodes James, *Churchill: A Study in Failure* (London: Weidenfeld and Nicolson, 1970).

9. *National Review*, "For the Record," July 22, 1983, p. 852.

10. Ibid., December 18, 1987, p. 11.

11. Harry V. Jaffa succinctly describes the dynamic of realignment as follows: "Once a party has demonstrated a winning formula in American politics, then the opposition, to survive, must recast itself—at least to considerable extent—in the image of its victorious rival. This remains the case until radically different conditions and different issues arise—conditions and issues which portend a drastic realignment of the entire bipolar arrangement. Sometime during this process of realignment, and then only, is there apt to be an election in which the parties stand for radically different things" (Harry V. Jaffa, *Equality and Liberty: Theory and Practice in American Politics* [New York: Oxford University

Press, 1965], pp. 8–9). For a contrary view of the realignment thesis, see David R. Mayhew, *Electoral Realignments: A Critique of an American Genre* (New Haven: Yale University Press, 2002).

12. Cited in James MacGregor Burns, *Roosevelt: The Lion and the Fox, 1882–1940* (New York: Harcourt, 1956), p. 375.

13. Midge Decter, "Ronald Reagan and the Culture War," *Commentary*, March 1991, p. 46; William Niskanen, *Reaganomics* (New York: Oxford University Press, 1988), p. 332.

14. *National Review*, November 20, 1987, p. 49.

15. Harvey C. Mansfield, *America's Constitutional Soul* (Baltimore: Johns Hopkins University Press, 1991), p. 44.

16. Other Republican senators often cool to Reagan or throwing roadblocks in his path included John Warner, Slade Gorton, Mark Andrews, James Abnor, Lowell Weicker, Robert Stafford, William Cohen, Warren Rudman, and John Chaffee.

17. In a 1983 interview with *USA Today* Reagan dilated the point: "I understand that in the past, Cabinets, for example—each person had his own turf and no one else in the Cabinet would talk about a decision affecting the turf of that one Cabinet member. I don't do business that way. Ours is more like a board of directors. I want all the input, because there are very few issues that don't lap over into other areas. . . . The only thing different from a board of directors is that I don't take a vote. I know that I have to make the decision."

18. Newt Gingrich, "What Conservatives Think of Ronald Reagan," *Policy Review*, Winter 1984, p. 16.

19. Haynes Johnson, *Sleepwalking Through History: America in the Reagan Years* (New York: Norton, 1991), p. 41.

20. Lou Cannon, *President Reagan: The Role of a Lifetime* (New York: Simon & Schuster, 1991), p. 36.

21. Reagan was not entirely unique in this regard among his peers at the summit of politics. John F. Kennedy's aide Theodore Sorenson wrote that one of Kennedy's favorite lines was from a character in John Buchan's *Pilgrim's Way:* "He disliked emotion not because he felt lightly but because he felt deeply."

22. At a conference preceding the 1992 election, former *New York Times* political reporter Susan Rasky said that she was offended that Ross Perot could presume to be president, as he had no government experience of any kind. This prompted the author, a fellow panelist, to ask whether she had ever heard of Wendell Willkie.

23. Evans and Novak, *The Reagan Revolution* (New York: Dutton, 1981), p. 22.

24. See Steven F. Hayward, *Greatness: Reagan, Churchill and the Making of Extraordinary Leaders* (New York: Crown Forum, 2005), especially ch. 4, "The Education of Statesmen."

25. Andrew E. Busch, *Ronald Reagan and the Politics of Freedom* (Lanham, MD: Rowman & Littlefield, 2001), pp. 4–6.

26. George F. Will, " 'Fresh Start'?" *Washington Post*, October 31, 1985.

27. *U.S. News & World Report,* June 30, 1980, p. 51.

28. "One More 'Disposable President,' " *U.S. News and World Report,* November 17, 1980, p. 64.

29. *Newsweek,* January 26, 1981.

30. Fred Greenstein and Robert Wright, "Reagan . . . Another Ike?" *Public Opinion,* December 1980/January 1981, p. 51.

31. Godfrey Hodgson, *All Things to All Men* (New York: Simon & Schuster, 1980), p. 253.

32. Theodore Lowi, "Ronald Reagan—Revolutionary?" in Lester Salamon and Michael S. Lund, eds., *The Reagan Presidency and the Governing of America* (Washington, DC: Urban Institute, 1984), p. 47.

33. Burns cited in *New Republic,* June 9, 1982, p. 39.

34. Everett Carll Ladd Jr., "The Candidates and the State of the Presidency," *Fortune,* December 3, 1979, pp. 38–44.

35. Lloyd N. Cutler, "To Form a Government," *Foreign Affairs,* Fall 1980, pp. 126–43.

36. *Newsweek,* January 26, 1981.

37. Dom Bonafede, "Presidential Scholars Expect History to Treat the Reagan Presidency Kindly," *National Journal,* April 6, 1985, pp. 743–47.

38. Quoted in Paul Duke, ed., *Beyond Reagan: The Politics of Upheaval* (New York: Warner Books, 1986), p. 132.

39. Quoted in ibid., pp. 122–23.

40. Reagan's successor, George H. W. Bush, applied this label during his eulogy during Reagan's funeral at the National Cathedral in June 2004. More recently, the liberal author John Patrick Diggins, in his surprising book about Reagan, calls Reagan "one of the three great liberators" in American history, along with Abraham Lincoln and Franklin D. Roosevelt. John Patrick Diggins, *Ronald Reagan: Fate, Freedom and the Making of History* (New York: W. W. Norton, 2007), p. xx.

CHAPTER 1: "THE TOWN TREMBLED"

1. There was giddy talk of a possible GOP deal with conservative southern Democrats to oust House Speaker Tip O'Neill. Not even close.

2. *Washington Post,* November 6, 1980, p. A18. The *National Journal* concurred, writing that the election result "brings into question not only the news media's political perspicacity, but also their ability to gauge or even detect the voting public's deep-seated concerns and sensitivities" (*National Journal,* November 29, 1980, p. 2032).

3. John P. Roche, "The Passing of the Class of 1941," *National Review,* October 19, 1984, p. 26.

4. Cited in Rowland Evans and Robert Novak, *The Reagan Revolution* (New York: Dutton, 1981), p. 11.

5. Wallace Turner, "Anti-Reagan Protests Continue for 3rd Day on California Campus," *New York Times,* November 7, 1980, p. A-16.

6. Herbert H. Denton, "Black Leaders Read Election Results with Foreboding and Alarm," *Washington Post,* November 6, 1980.

7. Stein later became a conservative, writing a book entitled *How I Accidentally Joined the Vast Right-Wing Conspiracy (and Found Inner Peace)* (New York: Delacorte Press, 2000).

8. Alan Wolfe, "The New Right's Road to Power," *New Left Review,* July–August 1981, p. 3.

9. *Nation,* January 31, 1981, p. 109.

10. Richard Pipes, *Vixi: Memoirs of a Non-Believer* (New Haven: Yale University Press, 2003), p. 190.

11. Mansfield, *America's Constitutional Soul,* p. 23.

12. Quoted in Duke, ed., *Beyond Reagan,* p. 45.

13. Dom Bonafede, "The Press Does Some Soul Searching in Reviewing Its Campaign Coverage," *National Journal,* November 29, 1980, p. 2032.

14. *New Republic,* October 25, 1980, p. 9.

15. *National Journal,* November 29, 1980, p. 2034.

16. Spencer quoted in Deborah Hart Strober and Gerald S. Strober, eds., *Reagan, the Man and His Presidency: The Oral History of an Era* (Boston: Houghton Mifflin, 1998), p. 38.

17. *National Journal,* November 29, 1980, p. 2036.

18. Reagan also took a congratulatory phone call from Senator Ted Kennedy.

19. Jerry Adler, "Reagan: Easy Rider," *Newsweek,* November 17, 1980, p. 30.

20. See Ben Stein, *The View from Sunset Boulevard* (New York: Basic Books, 1979).

21. Quoted in *Grand Strategy: Countercurrents,* September 1, 1981, p. 1.

22. The Freedom House 1981 tally classified fifty-one nations as "free," fifty-three as "partly free," and fifty-seven as "not free."

23. Jean-François Revel, *How Democracies Perish* (New York: Doubleday, 1984), p. 3.

24. This was literally the case with onetime Yippie leader Jerry Rubin, who had helped organize the Chicago protests of 1968. In 1980 Rubin turned up as an investment banker in New York with the slogan, "Here I come! Let's make millions together!"

25. Quoted in James Traub, "Party Like It's 1994," *New York Times Magazine,* March 12, 2006, p. 44.

26. This formula was originally used by Jacques Barzun to describe Walter Bagehot.

27. Paul Duke, ed., *Beyond Reagan: The Politics of Upheaval* (New York: Warner Books, 1986), p. 13.

28. Robert J. Samuelson, "The Republican Dilemma," *National Journal,* December 6, 1980, p. 2086.

29. Howell Raines, "He Has a Way with Words," *New York Times,* November 6, 1980, p. A-1. Raines's article, ostensibly a news story, was a thinly disguised editorial, presaging his later ruinous reign as the *Times*'s executive editor. "Mr.

Reagan's message was rooted in the romanticized America of Western movies and in the idealized nation of Mr. Reagan's own nostalgia-wrapped Illinois boyhood," Raines wrote. "The world that Mr. Reagan remembers as formative—a world of horse-drawn carriages on an uncle's farm, of tinny voices over a crystal radio, of swimming in unpolluted rivers—has disappeared. But Mr. Reagan retains his reverence for small-town values, his trust of business and, despite the experience of his luckless father and the Depression, his contempt for Government activism."

30. Richard Eder, "Hopefulness and Anxiety Characterize the Reaction Abroad to Reagan's Victory," *New York Times,* November 6, 1980, p. A-10.

31. Steve Lohr, "Business Counts on Reagan," *New York Times,* November 6, 1980, p. D-1.

32. Though Reagan would begin to change perceptions on Inauguration Day, his relative weakness would carry over into the early months of his administration. Pollster Samuel Kernell observed that Reagan had "the lowest approve-to-disapprove ratio the Gallup Poll had ever recorded for a president in his second month in office." Quoted in John W. Sloan, *The Reagan Effect* (Lawrence, KS: University Press of Kansas, 1999), p. 126.

33. John A. Farrell, *Tip O'Neill and the Democratic Century* (Boston: Little, Brown, 2001), p. 543.

34. Democratic Senate candidates received 29,011,889 votes to the Republicans' 25,696,546 votes. On the other hand, GOP House candidates outpolled Democrats by 230,000 votes nationwide (the first time since 1952 that Republicans had won more votes) but received only 44 percent of House seats.

35. O'Neill address to House Democratic Caucus, May 5, 1981, cited in Hedrick Smith, *The Power Game: How Washington Works* (New York: Random House, 1988), p. 517.

36. O'Neill, being an Irish Catholic, had once opposed abortion, calling it "morally indefensible," and supported the Human Life Amendment and the Hyde Amendment that barred Medicaid funding for abortion. By the 1980s he had abandoned this position.

37. Cited in Farrell, *Tip O'Neill,* p. 576.

38. Elisabeth Bumiller, "The Reagans' Hello Party," *Washington Post,* November 19, 1980, p. E-1. Carter had been scorned for refusing to serve hard liquor at the White House, prompting one guest to relish Reagan's full-service bar: "Oh, make it Scotch and water! The Carters are gone."

39. "Reagan Courts Legislators in Visit to Hill," *National Journal,* November 22, 1980, p. 3394.

40. The most thorough account and analysis of this episode is found in Lou Cannon, *President Reagan: Role of a Lifetime,* pp. 105–6. Also unknown to Carter at the time, Reagan promptly but quietly honored one of the outgoing president's requests in that meeting. Carter was concerned that South Korean leader

Chun Doo Hwan might carry out a death sentence against human rights activist Kim Dae Jung. Reagan wrote to Hwan to echo Carter's request that Jung's sentence be commuted. Jung was later elected president of South Korea.

41. The Reagan administration had only slightly more than half of its appointments made by May 1981. This problem has only gotten worse in subsequent administrations.

42. Evans had a corollary from the Nixon years: "Why is it that whenever one of us gets into a position of power, they are no longer one of us?"

43. Martin Anderson offers an extensive description of what lessons Reagan's team learned from Nixon's botched transition in *Revolution: The Reagan Legacy,* rev. ed. (Stanford, CA: Hoover Institution Press, 1990), pp. 191–95.

44. Haynes Johnson, *Sleepwalking Through History: America in the Reagan Years* (New York: Norton, 1991), p. 75.

45. One reason for Meese's reputation for being unorganized is the visible evidence of his office, in which it was typical for every square foot to be buried in stacks of papers and documents. The best place to make a document disappear in Washington, a frequent joke went, was in Meese's briefcase. However, Meese has a highly organized mind; he was the architect of much of the effective transition structure, and much else besides. David Stockman described Meese's design for cabinet councils as "an organizational chart that looked like a plan for the invasion of Normandy."

46. Martin Anderson offers this account in Strober and Strober, eds., *Reagan,* 63.

47. Baker pointedly declined to take cabinet rank as a concession to Meese, but revealingly told an interviewer after leaving office, "In the White House cabinet rank doesn't mean a thing because you have the power whether you have the rank or not" (Strober and Strober, eds., *Reagan,* p. 63).

48. Richard Darman, *Who's in Control? Polar Politics and the Sensible Center* (New York: Simon & Schuster, 1996), pp. 19, 35, 63.

49. "Far more than we condescending Easterners had assumed, or that he let the general public know, he was intelligent, disciplined, and hardworking. . . . He had a clearheaded capacity for writing and editing, a compulsive insistence on completing whatever work was given him—and, when he applied himself, a natural analytic facility." On the other hand, Darman also says that Reagan "had none of the upper-class mannerisms of the Northeastern elite." It is not clear whether this was meant as criticism or praise. Darman, *Who's in Control?,* pp. 39–40, 81.

50. Elizabeth Wehr, "Centrists, 'Old Hands' Get Key Posts on Transition Team," *Congressional Quarterly,* November 15, 1980, p. 3368.

51. "Mixed Reviews for Reagan Transition Team," *Human Events,* November 22, 1980, p. 1.

52. Nicholas Lemann, "New Right: Unsettled by Its Man," *Washington Post,* November 19, 1980, p. A-1. See also Steven R. Weisman, "Campaign Aides for Reagan Fear They're Left Out," *New York Times,* January 12, 1981, p. A-16.

53. "George Shultz for Secretary of State?" *Human Events,* November 22, 1980, p. 3.

54. "Caspar Weinberger: Reagan's Budget Watcher," *Human Events*, November 22, 1980, p. 4.

55. Lou Cannon, *Reagan* (New York: Putnam, 1985), p. 309.

56. The incoming Reagan administration was the first subject to the public financial disclosure requirements of the 1978 Ethics in Government Act. The completeness of public financial disclosure and the cumbersome disclosure process itself (most cabinet appointees had to hire lawyers to shepherd them through the process) proved to be a deterrent to several potential cabinet appointees, including Reagan's first choices for Treasury (William Simon and Walter Wriston) and the Energy Department (Michael Halbouty).

57. Donald Regan, *For the Record: From Wall Street to Washington* (New York: Harcourt Brace, 1988), p. 176.

58. Donald Rumsfeld had been briefly considered for the Pentagon, but he wanted to stay in private industry.

59. There was also vocal opposition to Shultz from some conservatives. *Human Events* reported that the prospect of Shultz "sent shivers down the spine of some hard-liners in the Reagan foreign policy camp."

60. Nixon made several other personnel recommendations, many of which were followed, such as Casey to the CIA.

61. Strober and Strober, eds., *Reagan,* p. 69.

62. Lou Cannon, *President Reagan: The Role of a Lifetime* (New York: Simon & Schuster, 1991), pp. 78–79.

63. Ibid., pp. 86, 111. For a scholarly assessment of the Reagan transition, see James P. Pfiffner, "The Carter-Reagan Transition: Hitting the Ground Running," *Presidential Studies Quarterly* 13, 4 (1983): p. 623–45.

64. Wallace Earl Walker and Michael R. Reopel, "Strategies for Governance: Transition and Domestic Policy Making in the Reagan Administration," *Presidential Studies Quarterly,* Fall 1986, p. 1.

65. *Final Report of the Initial Actions Project,* January 29, 1981, p. 7.

66. The Initial Actions Project was equally shrewd in its assessment of Carter's style of handling foreign policy issues, especially the Iranian hostage crisis: "Crises should be managed with minimum public drama, and maximum private resolve and commitment. . . . Jimmy Carter allowed himself to become the president of the hostages, rather than president of the people. . . . The country was not well served by this situation."

67. Anderson, *Revolution,* p. 227.

68. "President Reagan's America," *Washington Post,* January 21, 1981, p. A-18.

69. Cannon, *President Reagan: The Role of a Lifetime,* pp. 98–100. Reagan had learned of the Treptow story in a letter from one of his California supporters, Preston Hotchkiss.

70. Oddly enough, Cannon did grasp this point in his contemporaneous reporting.

In his *Washington Post* news article on Reagan's inauguration the day after, Cannon noted, "Usually, the heroes he cites are American patriots, or soldiers, or prisoners of war. Today he expanded the theme to include the everyday Americans who expect the Reagan administration to reduce the burdens of government. These everyday Americans were depicted as having the qualities of Treptow even though, said Reagan, they will not even be called upon to make the same kind of sacrifice." This correct analysis did not, however, find its way into the pages of *President Reagan: The Role of a Lifetime.*

71. Richard Cohen, "Heroism and Futility: Difficult Distinction," *Washington Post,* January 22, 1981, p. C-1.

72. Tom Wicker, "America the Greatest," *New York Times,* January 23, 1981, p. A-23.

73. In his classic 1959 book *Suicide of the West,* James Burnham, an author Reagan read regularly in *National Review,* noted: "Liberals, unless they are professional politicians seeking votes in the hinterland, are not subject to strong feelings of national patriotism and are likely to feel uneasy at patriotic ceremonies. These, like the organizations in whose conduct they are still manifest, are dismissed by liberals rather scornfully as 'flag-waving' and '100 percent Americanism.' The national anthem is not customarily sung or the flag shown, unless prescribed by law, at meetings of liberal associations. When a liberal journalist uses the phrase 'patriotic organization,' the adjective is equivalent in meaning to 'stupid, reactionary and rather ludicrous.' The rise of liberalism to predominance in the controlling sectors of American opinion is in almost exact correlation with the decline in the ceremonial celebration of the Fourth of July, traditionally regarded as the nation's major holiday. To the liberal mind, the patriotic oratory is not only banal but subversive of rational ideals; and judged by liberalism's humanitarian morality, the enthusiasm and pleasures that simple souls might have got from the fireworks could not compensate the occasional damage to the eye or finger of an unwary youngster. The purer liberals of the Norman Cousins strain, in the tradition of Eleanor Roosevelt, are more likely to celebrate UN day than the Fourth of July" (pp. 84–85).

74. Newcomb Stillwell, "A Chat with Wilbur Mills," *Forbes,* April 13, 1981, p. 56.

75. Henry Fairlie, "The First 100 Days," *Washington Post,* April 19, 1981, p. C-1.

CHAPTER 2: DUNKIRK

1. A then little-known congressman named Newt Gingrich described Kemp as "the most important Republican since Theodore Roosevelt, the first Republican in modern times to show that it is possible to be both hopeful and conservative at once" (*Washington Post,* August 11, 1981).

2. *US News and World Report,* January 19, 1981, p. 23.

3. "Reagan's Bleak Inheritance," *Newsweek,* December 8, 1980, p. 28.

4. See especially Anderson's Policy Memorandum No. 1 on economic policy, dated August 1979, reprinted in his memoir *Revolution.*

5. "The specific danger is this: If President Reagan does not lead a creatively orchestrated high-profile policy offensive based on revision of the fundamentals—supply-side tax cuts and regulatory relief, stern outlay control and Federal fiscal retrenchment, and monetary reform and dollar stabilization—the thin Senate Republican majority and the de facto conservative majority in the House will fragment."

6. Telling this often confusing story with tolerable accuracy and completeness requires extended discussion of both economic theory and data, yet a blizzard of budget numbers and percentages and the arcana of revenue streams choke the life out of narrative. This account attempts to keep the amount of eye-glazing numbers to a minimum in the interest of readability. Those specialists and readers with an appetite for more technical depth should see any of the several fine books dedicated solely to economic policy in the Reagan years. Among these are Paul Craig Roberts, *The Supply-Side Revolution* (Cambridge, MA: Harvard University Press, 1984); Niskanen, *Reaganomics;* Robert Bartley, *The Seven Fat Years* (New York: Free Press, 1992); Lawrence Lindsey, *The Growth Experiment* (New York: Basic Books, 1990); Martin Feldstein, ed., *American Economic Policy in the 1980s* (Chicago: University of Chicago Press, 1994); John W. Sloan, *The Reagan Effect: Economics and Presidential Leadership* (Lawrence: University Press of Kansas, 1999); Anderson, *Revolution;* Michael J. Boskin, *Reagan and the Economy: The Successes, Failures, and Unfinished Agenda* (San Francisco: Institute for Contemporary Studies, 1987); Richard B. McKenzie, *What Went Right in the 1980s* (San Francisco: Pacific Research Institute, 1994).

7. Boskin, *Reagan and the Economy,* p. 27.

8. Arthur Laffer, for whom the curve is named, wrote: "Supply-side economics is little more than a new label for standard neoclassical economics."

9. William Niskanen's formulation (*Reaganomics,* p. 18), is: "Supply-side economics is most accurately described as the application of microeconomic theory to the effects of fiscal policy on the incentives to work, save, and invest and on the allocation of resources in the economy." Economist Norman Ture, one of the leading supply-side proponents, wrote: " 'Supply-side' economics is merely the application of price theory—widely and tastelessly labeled 'microeconomics'—in analysis of problems concerning economic aggregates—widely and tastelessly labeled as 'macroeconomics' " (from Bartley, *The Seven Fat Years,* p. 56).

10. Lindsey, *The Growth Experiment,* p. 5.

11. Stein, in William Fellner, ed., *Essays in Contemporary Economic Problems,* 1981–82 ed. (Washington, DC: American Enterprise Institute, 1981), p. 57.

12. Robert Lekachman, "The Postponed Argument," *The New Leader,* November 23, 1964.

13. Cited in Feldstein, ed., *American Economic Policy,* p. 25.

14. Bartley, *Seven Fat Years,* p. 74.

15. *Wall Street Journal,* February 21, 1981 (cited in Sloan, *The Reagan Effect,* p. 118).

16. Lynde McCormick, "Laffer: The Man Behind the Curve," *Christian Science Monitor,* April 9, 1981, p. B-16.

17. Anderson, *Revolution,* p. 147. Nobel laureate Paul Samuelson went as far as to give a lecture at the University of Chicago in 1971 (years before the Laffer curve was conceived) entitled "Why They Are Laughing at Laffer."

18. *New Republic,* September 20, 1980, p. 3.

19. Edward Cowan, "President Reagan's Recession," *New York Times,* December 14, 1980, Sec. 3, p. 1.

20. John Berry, "Supply-Side Men Worry," *Washington Post,* November 16, 1980, p. F-1.

21. *Newsweek,* December 1, 1980, p. 64.

22. *Newsweek,* December 8, 1980, p. 28.

23. Niskanen, *Reaganomics,* p. 19.

24. Roberts, *The Supply-Side Revolution,* p. 4.

25. Ibid., p. 5.

26. William Niskanen, William Poole, and Murray Weidenbaum, "Economic Reports of the President," in James Tobin and Murray Weidenbaum, eds., *Two Revolutions in Economic Policy: The First Economic Reports of Presidents Kennedy and Reagan* (Cambridge, MA: MIT Press, 1988), p. 279.

27. Reagan was oblivious to or uninterested in the divisions of opinion among his advisers. In 1983 Reagan wrote to R. Emmett Tyrrell of the *American Spectator:* "You know Bob I'm not sure I really understood simon-pure 'supply-side' or that I agreed with every facet. It's always just seemed to me that when the government goes beyond a certain percentage of what it takes as its share of the people's earnings we have trouble" (Reagan to Tyrrell, private correspondence), in *Reagan: A Life in Letters,* eds. Martin Anderson, Annelise Anderson, and Kiron Skinner (New York: Free Press, 2003), p. 318.

28. Evans and Novak, *The Reagan Revolution,* p. 69.

29. He explained it this way in his autobiography: "I think my own experience with our tax laws in Hollywood probably taught me more about practical economic theory than I ever learned in a classroom or from an economist, and my views on tax reform did not spring from what people called supply-side economics. At the peak of my career at Warner Bros., I was in the ninety-four percent tax bracket; that meant that after a certain point, I received only six cents of each dollar I earned and that the government got the rest. The IRS took such a big chunk of my earnings that after a while I began asking myself whether it was worth it to keep on taking work" (Reagan, *An American Life* [New York: Simon & Schuster, 1991], p. 231).

30. Stein in Fellner, ed., *Essays,* p. 58.

31. Press conference, February 19, 1981.

32. Quotations complied by Werner Meyer, "Snake Oil Salesmen," *Policy Review,* Summer 1986, pp. 76–77.

33. Bartley, *The Seven Fat Years,* p. 169.

34. Anderson, *Revolution,* pp. 151–52.

35. Silver, *Coolidge and the Historians* (Durham, NC: Carolina Academic Press, 1983), p. 7.

36. *Newsweek,* January 26, 1981, p. 50. In a 1976 radio commentary on Coolidge, Reagan said: "Who cares if he was a 'do nothing' president. Do you suppose doing nothing had something to do with balancing the budget, reducing the debt, and cutting taxes four times?" From Anderson, Anderson, and Skinner, eds., *Reagan's Path to Victory* (New York: Free Press, 2004), p. 65. See also Reagan, *A Life in Letters,* p. 287.

37. Mark Shields, "With All Due Respect to Cal Coolidge," *Washington Post,* July 24, 1981, p. A-13.

38. *Newsweek,* January 26, 1981, p. 49.

39. Haynes Johnson, "Resurrection of Coolidge," *Washington Post,* June 7, 1981, p. A-3.

40. Lindsey, *The Growth Experiment,* p. 24.

41. Walter Heller protested: "The tax cuts succeeded, not by miraculously evoking new supplies of work effort and savings, but by stimulating demand for goods and services in a slack economy and thereby putting idle workers and excess factory capacity back to work" (*New York Times,* December 17, 1980, p. D-2).

42. Lewis Beman, "The Lessons for Reagan of Kennedy's Big Tax Cut," *Business Week,* February 23, 1981, p. 128. Lawrence Lindsey adds: "Upper income groups . . . reported substantially more income than could be accounted for if economic growth had been spread evenly across the population."

43. Lindsey, *The Growth Experiment,* p. 40.

44. To add to the confusion, *Time* magazine dredged up a supply-side endorsement from Keynes himself: "I believe you have first of all to do something to restore profits and then rely on a private enterprise to carry the thing along" (*Time,* January 19, 1981).

45. *Time* magazine (March 2, 1981): "[Reagan's] plan challenges all the assumptions that have powered Government economic and social policy for nearly half a century. The key assumption—which prevailed in practice, if not in rhetoric, through Republican as well as Democratic administrations—was that the people had to look to Government to ensure material prosperity and a reasonably fair distribution of wealth for all citizens."

46. Peter Grier, "Galbraith on Reaganomics: 'For the Forgotten Rich,' " *Christian Science Monitor,* May 5, 1981, p. 11.

47. "Kennedy Attacks Reagan Economic Policies," Associated Press, April 4, 1981.

48. Mansfield, *America's Constitutional Soul,* pp. 47–59. Mansfield offers this summary of the heart of the matter: "In the narrow sense *entitlement* is a budget

item that cannot be touched because the law awards it without reference to the number of people who claim it or to the cost. But the term has escaped into political philosophy and settled into American political practice. There it challenges the distinction, essential to liberal constitutionalism, between the rights the government exists to protect and the exercise of those rights by private individuals, or between state and society. For an entitlement is a right whose exercise is guaranteed to a certain degree by the government—a right that is therefore exercised to that degree by the government. An equal right to seek a job, for example, becomes an entitlement to a job or rather to the proceeds of a job, which the government performs as it were instead of the worker. In this way the government spreads into society, looking for more private activities to equalize and, with decreasing reluctance, to exercise itself of, yet on behalf of, those it wishes to benefit. Thus it grows unchecked by the liberal understanding that constitutional government must be limited in scope and in methods, because the defenders of liberalism, the followers of Locke and Mill, have surrendered to the criticisms made by Marx and Nietzsche of the essential liberal distinction. The main obstacle to the growth of entitlements has been popular suspicion and opposition, applauded by a few conservatives, which have been more faithful to liberalism than have liberal intellectuals."

49. Owen Ullmann, *Stockman: The Man, the Myth, the Future* (New York: Donald I. Fine, 1986), p. 72.

50. Stockman, *The Triumph of Politics, Why the Reagan Revolution Failed* (New York: Harper & Row, 1986), p. 54.

51. Ibid., p. 89.

52. Anderson, *Revolution*, p. 263.

53. Daniel Patrick Moynihan, *Came the Revolution: Argument in the Reagan Era* (San Diego: Harcourt, Brace, Jovanovich, 1988), p. 6.

54. Bartley, *Seven Fat Years*, pp. 120, 121.

55. Anderson, *Revolution*, p. 236.

56. *Time*, March 2, 1981.

57. *Time* magazine noted (March 23, 1981): "The Administration has never given a satisfactory explanation for exempting these programs, even though eliminating indexing could save $22 billion in 1982. It argues that Social Security pensions and veterans' benefits form part of a 'social safety net' protecting the 'truly needy'—though many of the beneficiaries hardly meet any reasonable definition of that term."

58. Lou Cannon considers the early months of 1981 to be the greatest lost opportunity for controlling Social Security spending growth, as Reagan rejected plans by Republican senator Pete Domenici and Democratic congressman J. Pickle to develop a bipartisan plan on Social Security. (See *President Reagan: The Role of a Lifetime,* pp. 245–49.) However, it is equally possible that Democrats might have found springing a mousetrap on Reagan to be irresistible, as indeed a few

months later Tip O'Neill made it emphatically clear to the House Democratic Caucus that they would politicize Social Security to the maximum extent possible. According to David Stockman's account, Reagan anticipated exactly this outcome, telling Republican senators in a March 10 meeting, "Fellas, I promised I wouldn't touch Social Security. We just can't get suckered into it. The other side's waiting to pounce" (Stockman, *Triumph of Politics,* p. 176). Pounce they did three months later.

59. Stockman, *Triumph of Politics,* p. 89.
60. Jimmy Carter never used the term *malaise* in his famous 1979 speech, and Nixon never said he had a secret plan to end the Vietnam War; in both cases, faulty media reports became ineradicable false memories of what really occurred. See *Age of Reagan: The Fall of the Old Liberal Order, 1964–1980* (Roseville, CA: Forum Prima, 2001), pp. 578, 294.
61. Niskanen, *Reaganomics,* p. 8.
62. *The Supply-Side Revolution,* p. 112.
63. George Gilder, *Wealth and Poverty* (New York: Basic Books, 1981).
64. Washington journalist Tom Bethell wrote in *National Review* in April, 1981: "If [supply-side economics] succeeds, who becomes the heir apparent to the Republican Party? George Bush or Jack Kemp? You can believe that there are some people in the White House who have thought this one through carefully."
65. Roberts, *The Supply-Side Revolution,* p. 103.
66. More from *Time* on this theme: "Crammed as it was with fiscal details, the speech could not display Reagan at his rhetorical best. For once, the master of the TV homily and the after-dinner pep talk appeared not only ill at ease but even a bit defensive."

CHAPTER 3: "LIE, CHEAT, STEAL . . ."

1. Reagan conferred the Presidential Medal of Freedom on Burnham in 1983. Reagan also referred to Burnham in early 1982 with the remark that "the columnist and journalist Burnham once said that when even the most skillful surgeon operates on a Democratic politician, he cannot separate demagogic from solid tissue without causing the death of the patient."
2. Reagan's liberal critics, and later Mikhail Gorbachev, argued that Reagan used spurious quotations from Lenin and Marx. Russian scholar Leon Aron, however, identifies the following quotation from Lenin, which is very close to Reagan's account: "Our morality is completely subordinate to the interests of the class struggle of the proletariat. . . . In the foundation of Communist morality lies the struggle for the strengthening and completion of Communism."
3. Cited in John Lewis Gaddis, *The United States and the Origins of the Cold War, 1941–1947* (New York: Columbia University Press, 1972), p. 204.
4. Reagan proved completely unembarrassed by his statement. He proudly recalled and repeated it two years later in his most famous anti-Soviet speech—the

March 8, 1983 "evil empire" speech to the National Association of Evangelicals in Orlando, Florida. "During my first press conference as president," Reagan recalled, "I pointed out that, as good Marxist-Leninists, the Soviet leaders have openly and publicly declared that the only morality they recognize is that which will further their cause, which is world revolution. I think I should point out that I was only quoting Lenin, their guiding spirit, who said in 1920 that they repudiate all morality that proceeds from supernatural ideas—that's their name for religion—or ideas that are outside class conceptions. Morality is entirely subordinate to the interests of class war. And everything is moral that is necessary for the annihilation of the old, exploiting social order and for uniting the proletariat."

5. *Newsweek,* May 4, 1981.

6. Walter Laqueur, "Reagan and the Russians," *Commentary,* January 1982, p. 26.

7. *National Review,* November 27, 1981, p. 1391.

8. Private correspondence with John Koehler, in *Reagan: A Life in Letters,* p. 375. In public Reagan turned the foreign policy vacuum to his advantage with a typical quip. In a speech on June 12, 1981, Reagan joked: "There's been some criticism that we don't have a foreign policy . . . and that's just not true at all. Just the other day, before he left for China, Al Haig sent a message to Brezhnev that said, 'Roses are red, violets are blue, stay out of El Salvador, and Poland, too.' "

9. See Hayward, *The Age of Reagan,* pp. 678–80.

10. *National Review,* September 18, 1981, p. 1064. *National Review* changed its mind after the memorial was built, editorializing in 1982, "Experienced directly, however, rather than in theory, the memorial possesses considerable power and even eloquence. . . . Miss Lin has created something unusual and beautiful" (November 26, 1982, p. 1461).

11. I owe this shorthand definition of détente to Martin Malia, *The Soviet Tragedy* (New York Free Press, 1995), p. 381.

12. Pipes, *Vixi,* p. 166. Foreign policy wasn't Schmidt's only complaint; he was also a vocal critic of Reagan's economic policy.

13. Anatoly Dobrynin, *In Confidence: Moscow's Ambassador to America's Six Cold War Presidents* (New York: Times Books, 1995), p. 486.

14. As Martin Malia put it, "three or four years of détente were a kind of diplomatic NEP [New Economic Plan] designed to build Soviet strength for a new offensive."

15. Angelo Codevilla, *Informing Statecraft: Intelligence for a New Century* (New York: Free Press, 1992), p. 430.

16. Margaret Thatcher, *The Downing Street Years* (New York: HarperCollins, 1993), p. 157.

17. Robert Gates, *From the Shadows* (New York: Simon & Schuster, 1996), p. 171.

18. Kenneth Adelman, "Beyond MADness," *Policy Review,* Summer 1981, p. 84.

19. The *Sovetskaya Voennaya Entsiklopedya* (Soviet Military Encyclopedia), whose

eighth volume was published in 1980, contained such gems as "The transition of all countries and peoples to Communism is inevitable," and "Under conditions of nuclear war, superiority over the enemy may be obtained along several avenues." From "The New Soviet Military Encyclopedia," *Grand Strategy: Countercurrents,* April 1, 1982, pp. 11–12. This was a long-running theme. The 1972 edition of *Marxism-Leninism on War and Army* said: "Today's weapons make it possible to achieve strategic objectives very quickly. The very first nuclear attack on the enemy may inflict such immense casualties and produce such vast destruction that his economic, moral-political and military capabilities will collapse."

20. Typical of Reagan's many comments on the Soviet Union's offensive configurations was this from August 1981: "The Soviet Union has been engaged in the greatest military buildup in the history of man, and it cannot be described as necessary for their defense. It is plainly a buildup that is offensive in nature."

21. The July 1981 Soviet-Syrian amphibious exercises on Syria's Mediterranean coast included fifty-three Soviet warships as well as sixteen heavy bombers and thirty-eight antisubmarine aircraft.

22. "The Middle East: Soviet Maneuvers," *Grand Strategy: Countercurrents,* August 1, 1981, p. 5.

23. Connie De Boer, "The Polls: Our Commitment to World War III," *Public Opinion Quarterly* 45 (1981): pp. 126–34.

24. *SPD Parteitag Berlin 1979* (uncorrected transcripts), *Protokoll,* no. 7, p. 75, cited by Hans Ruhle, "The Theater Nuclear Issue in German Politics," *Strategic Review,* Spring 1981, p. 55.

25. Codevilla, *Informing Statecraft,* p. 227.

26. David Pryce-Jones, *The War That Never Was: The Fall of the Soviet Empire, 1985–1991* (London: Weidenfeld & Nicolson, 1995), p. 99.

27. Two Soviet economists, Grigory Khanin and V. Selyunin, argued in 1987 that the Soviet economy peaked and began its decline in the early 1960s. The real long-term growth rate of the Soviet Union from the 1920s to the 1980s had been no better than 3.3 percent a year; the official statistics claimed a 7.9 percent growth rate.

28. There is evidence that a few Soviet economists recognized as early as the mid-1960s that their system was fatally flawed and destined to decline. According to Moshe Lewin, author of *The Soviet Century* (London: Verso, 2005), economist V. Nemchinov wrote a report that concluded the Soviet system "is paralyzed from top to bottom," and in 1967 a team of Soviet economists concluded that the Soviet Union was falling behind the United States economically in every area except coal and steel.

29. Nicholas Eberstadt, "The Health Crisis in the USSR," *New York Review of Books,* February 19, 1981, p. 29.

30. Robert Skidelsky, *The Road from Serfdom: The Economic and Political Consequences of the End of Communism* (London: Penguin, 1997), p. 100.

31. Kotkin, *Armageddon Averted,* p. 67.

32. According to one account, Reagan told the following joke to Gorbachev: Two men are walking down a street in Moscow. One asks the other, "Is this full communism? Have we really passed through socialism and reached full communism?" The other answers "Hell, no. It's gonna get a lot worse first."

33. Cited in Benjamin B. Fischer, "Cold War Conundrum," unclassified CIA report, 1997.

34. There are plenty of reasons to doubt the accuracy and veracity of Soviet life expectancy statistics from the 1950s, as the last formal population census, conducted in the 1930s in the aftermath of the Ukrainian famine and the purges, had been doctored to please Stalin. A complete census was not conducted again until 1959, six years after Stalin's death.

35. Eberstadt, "Health Crisis," p. 23.

36. Dmitry F. Mikeyev, "The Soviet Union: Might It Collapse?" *National Review,* May 1, 1981, p. 480.

37. Reagan wanted to use this anecdote in his 1982 speech at Westminster, London (see ch. 6), but his speechwriters were not able to verify the story.

38. Harry Rositzky, cited in Codevilla, *Informing Statecraft,* p. 217.

39. See Nicholas Eberstadt, *Tyranny of Numbers: Mismeasurement and Misrule* (Washington: AEI Press, 1995), p. 130.

40. The dissident Soviet writer Andrew Amalrik put the matter in stark terms in his 1970 book, *Will the Soviet Union Survive Until 1984?:* "It should be noted, however, that there is another powerful factor which works against the chance of any kind of peaceful reconstruction and which is equally negative for all levels of society: this is the extreme isolation in which the regime has placed both society and itself. This isolation has not only separated the regime from society, and all sectors of society from each other, but also put the country in extreme isolation from the rest of the world. This isolation has created for all—from the bureaucratic elite to the lowest social levels—an almost surrealistic picture of the world and of their place in it. Yet the longer this state of affairs helps to perpetuate the status quo, the more rapid and decisive will be its collapse when confrontation with reality becomes inevitable."

41. Leon Aron, *Yeltsin: A Revolutionary Life* (New York: St. Martin's Press, 2000), p. 71.

42. Derek Leebaert, *The Fifty-Year Wound: The True Price of America's Cold War Victory* (Boston: Little, Brown, 2002), p. 491. The minutes of Politburo meetings that have become available since the collapse of the Soviet Union read like a parody of decrepit Marxist ideology, with Western imperialism portrayed in cartoonish fashion. Many Politburo transcripts and other translated materials can be found at the Cold War International History Project housed at the Woodrow Wilson Center, http://www.wilsoncenter.org/index.cfm?fuseaction=topics.home &topic_id=1409.

43. *Newsweek*, November 19, 1979, pp. 144, 147.

44. Churchill, *The World Crisis: The Aftermath* (London: Thornton-Butterworth, 1929).

45. Nicholas Eberstadt, *Prosperous Paupers and Other Population Problems* (New Brunswick: Transaction, 2000) p. 102.

46. The Notre Dame speech was something of a lost opportunity for Reagan, as it was given at the same venue as Carter's "inordinate fear of Communism" speech in 1977. Instead of using the occasion to make a major foreign policy address and implicitly correct Carter's view, it was a general speech in which Reagan couldn't resist spending nearly a third of its length recounting his portrayal of George Gipp in the movie *Knute Rockne: All American*.

47. Gates, *From the Shadows,* p. 197.

48. Codevilla, *Informing Statecraft,* p. 221.

49. Daniel L. Bond and Herbert S. Levine, "An Overview," in Abram Bergson and Herbert S. Levine, eds., *The Soviet Economy: Toward the Year 2000* (London: George Allen and Unwin, 1983), p. 21.

50. Joseph Berliner, "Planning and Management," in Bergson and Levine, eds., *The Soviet Economy,* p. 360.

51. Reagan to John O. Koehler, private correspondence, in *Reagan: A Life in Letters,* p. 375.

52. Richard N. Ostling, "Cross Meets Kremlin," *Time,* December 4, 1989, p. 74.

53. Vasil Bilak, a member of the Czech Politburo, said openly, "The choice of Krakow bishop Wojtyla for Pope was not an accident. . . . It was part of a plan worked out by the United States with the aim of attacking another socialist country" (cited in Oldrich Tuma, "The Czechoslovak Communist Regime and the Polish Crisis, 1981–1981," Cold War International History Project, *Bulletin 11*, p. 61).

54. John Lukacs, "Open Your Eyes, for God's Sake," *National Review,* March 5, 1982, p. 224.

55. *Time,* January 4, 1982.

56. Stalin is also reported to have said that imposing Communism on Poland was like putting a saddle on a cow.

57. *Time,* January 4, 1982.

58. George Weigel, *Witness to Hope: The Biography of Pope John Paul II* (New York: HarperCollins, 1999), p. 281.

59. Weigel, Ibid., p. 301.

60. Timothy Garton Ash, *The Polish Revolution: Solidarity,* 3rd ed. (New Haven: Yale University Press, 2002), p. 32.

61. *National Review,* March 5, 1982, p. 224.

62. Tad Szulc, "Papal Secrets," *Newsweek,* April 10, 1995.

63. Ash, *Polish Revolution,* p. 293. Ash adds: "It is hard to think of any previous revolution in which ethical categories and moral goals have played such a large part."

64. Cited in ibid., p. 294.

65. Alexander Haig, *Caveat* (New York: Macmillan, 1984), p. 88.

66. Strober and Strober, eds., *Reagan*, p. 112.

67. Gregg, Hill, and Anderson comments, ibid., pp. 86, 116.

68. Quoted in Cannon, *President Reagan: The Role of a Lifetime*, p. 196.

69. Pipes, *Vixi*, p. 144.

70. Strober and Strober, eds., *Reagan*, p. 91.

71. Ibid., p. 42.

72. Deaver-Hannaford Papers, Hoover Institution, Box 3.

73. Ford, in Strober and Strober, eds., *Reagan*, p. 72.

74. Gates, *From the Shadows*, p. 225.

75. Michael Ledeen, "Intelligence, Anyone?" *American Spectator*, January 1995.

76. Jeffrey Anteval, Reuters wire report, March 18, 1981.

CHAPTER 4: THE SHOT HEARD ROUND THE WORLD

1. Cited in John A. Farrell, *Tip O'Neill and the Democratic Century* (Boston: Little, Brown, 2001), p. 552.

2. At the annual White House Correspondents Dinner on April 25, at which Reagan spoke briefly by telephone while recuperating at Camp David, Bob Pierpont joked to Reagan: "Among these people are many of your Cabinet Secretaries. There's only really one that I think is very noticeable by his absence. I haven't seen Secretary Haig. I wondered if you've been watching television tonight. We are a little worried who's in the Situation Room and who's in control." On the *Tonight* show, Johnny Carson joked: "There is good news and bad news today. The good news is that President Reagan is coming home from the hospital. The bad news is that Alexander Haig has barricaded himself inside the Oval Office with a four year supply of Spam."

3. Quoted in Farrell, *Tip O'Neill*, p. 553.

4. Strober and Strober, eds., *Reagan*, p. 121.

5. *The Nation*, April 11, 1981, p. 420.

6. Sure enough, in his first post-shooting media interview, Reagan reiterated his opposition to new gun control proposals.

7. Reagan: "I now seem to have her faith that there is a divine plan, and while we may not be able to see the reason for something at the time, things do happen for a reason and for the best. One day what has seemed to be an unbearable blow is revealed as having marked a turning point or a start leading to something worthwhile."

8. Reagan to Mrs. Van Voohis, in *Reagan: A Life in Letters*, pp. 277–78. In 1984 Reagan wrote to Sister Mary Ignatius: "Abe Lincoln once said that he would be the most stupid human on this footstool called Earth if he thought for one minute he could fulfill the obligations of the office he held without help from one

who was wiser and stronger than all others. I understand what he meant completely." In *Reagan: A Life in Letters,* p. 280.

9. Reagan made this passage public in a speech on November 18, 1981.

10. Reagan to Vice Admiral Marmaduke Bayne, September 13, 1983, in *Reagan: A Life in Letters,* p. 410.

11. Friedersdorf memo to Baker, Meese and Deaver, March 19, 1981 (David Gergen Papers, Reagan Library).

12. This was a widespread theme. Bill Clinton, at that moment out of office, said: "Reagan's budget mathematics don't work."

13. Speech to the Sacramento Host Breakfast, September 4, 1970. Reagan included such jabs at the left as "Do not be surprised if the New Left turns out to be the Old Left, in sandals and jeans."

14. Stockman, *Triumph of Politics,* p. 246.

15. Close observers recognized this at the time. In a 1982 study, political scientist Samuel H. Beer observed: "[The Reagan budget cuts] do not, however, constitute a deep penetration into the 1982 base of federal spending for domestic purposes. This conclusion is somewhat at variance with the popular view. We think this is because there is a strong tendency for public officials to overstate the size of the cuts. This tendency is not hard to explain. Conservatives tend to exaggerate the budget cuts because they supported them and want to take credit for them. Liberals also tend to exaggerate the size of the cuts, but for different reasons. They want to create public concern about their impact and build up political support for resisting further cuts." Samuel H. Beer, "The Reagan Budget," in John William Ellwood, ed., *Reductions in U.S. Domestic Spending* (New Brunswick, NJ: Transaction Books, 1982).

16. In the case of the school lunch program, eligibility was lowered to 185 percent of the poverty line; even after the change, the program served more than twenty-three million children a day. The Medicaid caseload actually grew in 1982 by 500,000 people.

17. See Fred Barnes, "TV News: The Shock Horror Welfare Cut Show," *Policy Review,* Spring 1983, pp. 57–73.

18. See Michael J. Boskin, *Reagan and the Economy: The Successes, Failures and Unfinished Agenda* (San Francisco: ICS Press, 1989), p. 56: "The social safety net actually grew as a percentage of the budget and in real terms. The social safety net is defined to include basic Social Security benefits (retirement, disability, and Medicare); unemployment benefits; cash benefits for dependent families, the elderly, and the disabled; and income support and medical benefits for veterans. In addition, Headstart, summer youth employment, and subsidized nutritional programs to low income families were left untouched. These programs were projected to grow at 9 percent per year in *current* dollars through 1984."

19. Gerald Ford had attacked Reagan's 1976 comment that perhaps Social Security trust funds could be invested in the stock market as "back-door socialism," as

such a step would increase government control of the economy. Conservatives returned to this criticism when President Clinton briefly flirted with a form of this idea in 1997.

20. The closest liberalism comes to making this case is John Rawls's highly abstract book *A Theory of Justice*.

21. Lindsey, *Growth Experiment*, p. 89.

22. The long-running debate over media bias took a fresh turn in 1981 with the publication of Stanley Rothman and Robert Lichter's study on media attitudes. Done under the auspices of the Research Institute on International Change at Columbia University, the Rothman-Lichter study surveyed 240 journalists and editors at the most influential major media outlets (*New York Times, Washington Post,* weekly newsmagazines, and broadcast networks). The study reported that these media leaders voted Democratic by a margin of four to one and by the same margin believed that government should redistribute wealth.

23. Johnson, *Sleepwalking*, p. 111.

24. Herbert H. Denton, "Broad-Based Coalition Forms to Fight Reagan on Cuts," *Washington Post,* February 28, 1981, p. A-1.

25. *New York Times*, May 5, 1981, p. A-7.

26. *Newsweek*, February 16, 1981.

27. Some of the headlines include "Is Britain a Warning?" (Flora Lewis, *New York Times*); "Are the Streets of Britain a Warning to the U.S.?" (William Raspberry, *Washington Post*); "The Grim Warning of Britain's Riots" (Henry Fairlie, *Washington Post*).

28. Cited in Farrell, *Tip O'Neill*, p. 575.

29. One of columnist Robert Novak's favorite axioms is that "God put Republicans on the earth for one purpose—to cut taxes." Other than that, he usually adds, Republicans aren't good for much.

30. Indexing did not begin, however, until 1985, ensuring the government a few more years of inflation-induced income tax revenue gains.

31. See Richard J. Powell and Dan Schloyer, "Public Presidential Appeals and Congressional Floor Votes," *Congress and the Presidency,* Autumn 2003.

32. Others include Australia, which cut its top tax rate from 62 percent to 49 percent; New Zealand, from 60 percent to 33 percent; Israel, from 66 percent to 48 percent; Canada, from 58 percent to 45 percent; Austria, from 62 percent to 40 percent; Japan, from 75 percent to 50 percent; Singapore, from 55 to 33 percent; South Korea, from 89 to 48 percent.

33. See Lindsey, *The Growth Experiment*, pp. 129–35.

34. See Steven R. Weisman, "White House Rebuts Charges That Nominee Has Voted for Abortions," *New York Times,* July 9, 1981, p. A-17.

35. Terry Eastland, "The O'Connor Nomination," *American Spectator,* September 1981, pp. 24–26.

36. George F. Will, "The Gender of Justice," *Newsweek,* July 20, 1981, p. 76.

37. Reagan to Harold O. J. Brown, in *Reagan: A Life in Letters*, p. 552.
38. *Time*, August 10, 1981, p. 12.
39. James W. Ceaser, "The Theory of Governance of the Reagan Administration," in Lester M. Salamon and Michael S. Lund, eds., *The Reagan Presidency and the Governing of America* (Washington, DC: Urban Institute Press, 1984), p. 57.
40. Throughout the 1930s Roosevelt was relentless not only in his attack on "economic royalists" but also in associating "economic royalists" with the Republican Party. As Charles Kesler explains, "The key to FDR's strategy was to read the Republican Party as previously constituted right out of American politics, to cast it beyond the pale of the Declaration of Independence, to pronounce it excommunicate and heretic and to anathematize its doctrines." Examples include FDR's Commonwealth Club speech of 1932, his nomination acceptance speech in 1936, and also his nomination acceptance speech of 1932, wherein he compared Republicans to the British Tories overthrown in 1776: "There are two ways of viewing the government's duty in matters affecting economic and social life. The first sees to it that a favored few are helped and hopes that some of their prosperity will leak through, sift through, to labor, to the farmer, to the small businessman. That theory belongs to the party of Toryism, and I had hoped that most of the Tories had left this country in 1776."
41. Anderson also memorably described Reagan as "a warmly ruthless man."
42. The Teamsters endorsed Nixon in 1972.
43. The average controller's earnings at the time were $33,000—one-third above median household income at the time—but with overtime, night work, and seniority, many controllers were averaging more than $40,000.
44. Federal employees, including air traffic controllers, take the following oath: "I am not participating in any strike against the Government of the United States or any agency thereof, and I will not so participate while an employee of the Government of the United States or any agency thereof."
45. William Niskanen, a member of Reagan's Council of Economic Advisers, points out that in 1983 the Reagan administration was "scrupulously neutral" toward a systemwide strike against AT&T, which was the largest strike in thirty-seven years.
46. This, despite a series of anti-Reagan TV commercials that the public employees union (AFSCME) began running in thirteen major markets.
47. Feldstein, ed., *American Economic Policy in the 1980s*, p. 162.
48. Quoted in David Blundy and Andrew Lycett, *Qadhafi and the Libyan Revolution* (Boston: Little, Brown, 1987), p. 26.
49. *Newsweek*, August 24, 1981, p. 13.
50. "Off Tripoli's Shores," *New Republic*, September 9, 1981, p. 7.
51. Reagan's personal assistant Jim Kuhn relates the story of Reagan traveling to Louisiana in 1986 to help the Senate campaign of Henson Moore, who crassly introduced Reagan with the attempted joke that "you wouldn't sleep through

anything with Libya this time, like you did in 1981." Kuhn writes that "I thought he was going to take his neck off, he was that angry." Reagan looked at Moore and said "in a precise and firm tone," "My staff now has orders to wake me up the minute something like that happens again. We made a big mistake, but *it won't happen again.*" Moore lost his election bid. (From Jim Kuhn, *Ronald Reagan in Private: A Memoir of My Years at the White House,* New York: Sentinel, 2004, p. 181.)

52. In the tit-for-tat world of the Cold War, one response came on August 27, when North Korea fired a Soviet-made antiaircraft missile at an American SR-71 spy plane flying outside of North Korean airspace.

53. Reagan observed in his diary (October 6): "[Kaddafi] goes on radio (clandestine) and began broadcasting propaganda, calling for holy war, etc. before Sadat's death was confirmed. This material had to have been already prepared. In other words, he knew it was going to happen."

54. When Reagan addressed the UN's General Assembly in September, the secret service contrived to have agents seated across the table from the Libyan UN representatives, since UN delegates could not be made to pass through metal detectors.

55. *Time,* December 21, 1981, p. 18.

56. See Shai Feldman, "The Bombing of Osiraq Revisited," *International Security,* 7, 2 (Autumn 1982): pp. 114–42.

57. Angelo Codevilla, *Informing Statecraft: Intelligence for a New Century* (New York: Free Press, 1992), p. 96.

58. In his diary (September 14, 1981), Reagan wrote: "Was annoyed to learn that PM Begin had gone to the hill & had lobbied against the sale after leading me to believe he wouldn't."

CHAPTER 5: STAY THE COURSE

1. Darman wrote: "Entering stage left, stage right, and stage everywhere were puff after puff and gust after gust of thick white fog. It was relentless. The ranch in the sky had become the ranch in the clouds. One could see neither hills, nor valleys, nor even the backdrop. . . . The inescapable fact of the matter was that the President of the United States was enacting his would-be revolutionary economic program in a cloud of fog." According to Paul Craig Roberts, one of the architects of supply-side policy in the Treasury Department, the White House political staff wanted Reagan to sign the tax cut at his ranch rather than the White House so as to avoid having to share the credit and the spotlight with Jack Kemp and the other supply-side pioneers.

2. This formulation is Richard Darman's recollection. Stockman recalls Reagan saying, "Maybe Tip O'Neill was right all along." Darman's version sounds more authentic and consistent with Reagan's general attitudes.

3. See James Fairhill, "The Case for the $435 Hammer," *Washington Monthly,* January 1987, pp. 47–52.

4. In fact military spending in real terms grew 12.4 percent in 1981, and 14.6 percent in 1982; military spending would rise from $178 billion in 1981 to $367 billion in 1986.

5. The *New York Times*'s Steven Weisman, for example, quoted an anonymous White House aide—probably Darman—that "a full-scale battle" was under way "for the soul of the Reagan Administration and the mind of Ronald Reagan" (*New York Times,* December 12, 1981).

6. Darman, *Who's in Control,* p. 95.

7. See Joshua Muravchik and John E. Haynes, "CBS Versus Defense," *Commentary,* September 1981, pp. 44–56.

8. *Time* magazine's Board of Economists, meeting in mid-September, predicted 4 percent growth by the second half of 1982. Morgan Stanley predicted that "in the spring [of 1982] we may see the beginning of the first sustained expansion in U.S. economic activity since the beginning of 1979." The Congressional Budget Office, thought to be hostile to Reaganomics, issued an upbeat forecast for the coming year and projected declining budget deficits. CBO director Alice Rivlin told the media, "We are quite optimistic about the outlook for the economy." By then, however, the economy was already in a recession. The National Bureau of Economic Research, the organization that enjoys the privilege of designating the beginning and ending of economic cycles, would later determine that the recession began in July 1981, the same month the tax cut passed.

9. A. F. Ehrbar, "What the Markets Are Telling Reagan," *Fortune,* October 19, 1981, pp. 62–63.

10. A reporter asked Reagan in a press conference: "Mr. President, the style of your administration is being called 'millionaires on parade.' Do you feel that you are being sensitive enough to the symbolism of Republican mink coats, limousines, thousand-dollar-a-plate china at the White House, *when ghetto kids are being told they can eat ketchup as a vegetable?*" (emphasis added).

11. Hayward, *The Age of Reagan,* pp. 126–27.

12. *National Review* had presciently anticipated Stockman's defection in an editorial five months before the *Atlantic* article appeared. The emphasis on budget cutting, *National Review* wrote on June 26, 1981, "made it inevitable that OMB Director David Stockman's job would be constrained in a way that would pull him out of the supply-side camp. Stockman, who rode Jack Kemp's coattails to power, is finding that his perceived success as OMB director depends less on how much taxes and spending are cut and more on whether he produces that balanced budget in 1984 or sooner. This has made him less of a tax-cutter, as he sees on paper, the revenues flowing away from his balanced-budget success-indicator."

13. CBS's Lesley Stahl said: "The *Atlantic* said that Mr. Reagan's policymakers knew their plans were wrong, or at least inadequate in some respects, but the President went ahead and conveyed the opposite impression to the American people."

14. This is the case Paul Craig Roberts makes forcefully in his book *The Supply-Side Revolution.*

15. Paul Craig Roberts (*The Supply-Side Revolution,* p. 175) summarized Niskanen's evidence as follows: "Niskanen found that the rate of inflation was determined by the rate of money growth and the rate of money growth was not related to the deficit: 'Over the whole period (1948–1976), about 15–20 percent of the federal deficit appears to have been monetized. This effect, however, nearly disappears when one controls for the substantial shift in monetary policy in the last decade. In any given year, the federal deficit does not appear to have any significant effect on the rate of change of the money supply.' " Niskanen concluded that "federal deficits do not have any significant effects on the inflation rate operating either through or independent of the rate of money growth."

16. "The deficits are a product of Mr. Reagan's tax cuts and military spending increases," Steven Weisman wrote authoritatively in a "news story" in the *New York Times.*

17. Some among Reagan's economic team believed this too. Treasury Secretary Don Regan commented in December 1981: "I honestly believe that the recession might never have happened if we had gotten our full 10 percent tax cut last July as scheduled."

18. Lindsey, *Growth Experiment,* p. 52.

19. In a personal letter dated February 22, 1981—days after Reagan's first economic policy speech—Reagan wrote, "The goal is to have a steady and reasonable growth in money supply instead of the roller-coaster we've had over the last several years with wild surges and then equally wild cutbacks." Reagan to Paul Trousdale, in *Reagan: A Life in Letters,* p. 295.

20. Quoted in Robert Samuelson, "Unsung Triumph," *Washington Post,* June 9, 2004, p. A21.

21. William Greider, *Secrets of the Temple: How the Federal Reserve Runs the Country* (New York: Simon & Schuster, 1989), pp. 355, 356.

22. Roberts, *Supply-Side Revolution,* pp. 116, 197; Niskanen, *Reaganomics,* p. 155; Bartley, *Seven Fat Years,* pp. 125, 167; Lindsey, *Growth Experiment,* pp. 107, 110.

23. *Newsweek,* December 8, 1981: "But some economists suggest another outcome: political pressure from the recession's victims—the unemployed and troubled businessmen—and huge government deficits could force the Federal Reserve Board to relax its monetary grip and allow the inflation rate to return to double digits by 1984."

24. Niskanen, *Reaganomics,* pp. 168–69.

25. Public Papers of the President, October 16, 1981.

26. Friedman quoted by Peter Robinson, *How Ronald Reagan Changed My Life* (New York: Harper, 2003), p. 65.

27. Michael Mussa, "Monetary Policy," in Martin Feldstein, ed., *American Eco-*

nomic Policy in the 1980s (Chicago: University of Chicago Press, 1994), p. 136. Mussa added: "[O]ne can imagine what Lyndon Johnson or Richard Nixon would have done had their personal political popularity dropped substantially and their party faced significant midterm electoral losses because of excessively tight monetary policy directly by a group of appointed officials at the Federal Reserve."

28. Paul Volcker and Toyoo Gyohten, *Changing Fortunes: The World's Money and the Threat to American Leadership* (New York: Random House, 1992), p. 175.

29. Robinson, *How Ronald Reagan Changed My Life,* p. 53.

30. Michael J. Boskin, *Reagan and the Economy: The Successes, Failures, and Unfinished Agenda* (San Francisco: ICS Press, 1989), pp. 89–90.

31. Paul Craig Roberts and Norman Ture left the Treasury Department for more agreeable climes in late 1981 and early 1982, respectively.

32. Brooks Jackson, *Honest Graft: Big Money and the American Political Process* (New York: Knopf, 1988), p. 3.

33. Ibid., p. 79.

34. Ibid., p. 93.

35. See Hayward, *The Age of Reagan,* pp. 160–62.

36. A few—but only a few—observers noted this at the time. Steven Weisman of the *New York Times* reported (March 7, 1982): "To many of the President's aides, his insistence on not compromising is reminiscent of the way he dealt with the California Legislature when he was Governor of that state. 'I've seen this pattern so many times before,' a longtime Reagan aide said. 'He's out there saying, "My feet are in concrete on this," but at the same time he's looking to see what the other side comes up with.' "

37. Dole cited in *National Review,* April 16, 1982, p. 395.

38. There were some exceptions. *Time* magazine noted the "unintended policy consequences" of sensational personalized coverage, asking in 1983: "Which story more truly reveals the state of the economy and the performance of Reaganomics: the drop in inflation from 12.4% in 1980 . . . to about 5% in 1982, a change that is often conveyed flatly and numerically? Or the simultaneous rise in unemployment from 7.4% to 10.8%, a development that lends itself to anecdotes and dramatic interviews with the jobless?" (Cited in Cannon, *President Reagan: Role of a Lifetime,* p. 265.)

39. See Gregg Easterbrook, "Examining a Media Myth," *Atlantic Monthly,* October 1983, pp. 10–24.

40. Remarks to the New York City Partnership, January 14, 1982.

41. Hedrick Smith, *The Power Game: How Washington Works* (New York: Random House, 1989), pp. 523–24.

42. *New Republic,* August 2, 1982, p. 5.

43. Duberstein memo to the president, July 2, 1982, David Gergen Papers, Ronald Reagan Presidential Library.

44. *Reagan: A Life in Letters,* p. 554.

45. Ibid., p. 555.

46. Ibid., p. 595.

47. Cited in Donald T. Critchlow, "Mobilizing Women: The 'Social' Issues," in W. Elliott Brownlee and Hugh Dans Graham, eds., *The Reagan Presidency* (Lawrence, KS: University Press of Kansas, 2003), p. 312.

48. Winston Churchill, *Thoughts and Adventures* (London: Thornton-Butterworth, 1932), p. 39.

49. Richard Rahn, "What Conservatives Think of Ronald Reagan," *Policy Review,* Winter 1984, p. 17.

50. Boskin, *Reagan and the Economy,* pp. 106–7.

51. Bruce Yandle, "The Evolution of Regulatory Activities in the 1970s and 1980s," in Philip Cagan, ed., *Essays in Contemporary Economic Problems, 1986* (Washington, DC: AEI, 1986), p. 111.

52. George C. Eads and Michael Fix, "Regulatory Policy," in John L. Palmer and Isabel V. Sawhill, eds., *The Reagan Experiment* (Washington, DC: Urban Institute, 1982), p. 137.

53. John L. Peterman, "The Brown Shoe Case," *Journal of Law and Economics,* April 1975, p. 143.

54. The major intellectual figures and some of their pathbreaking books included Robert Bork (*The Antitrust Paradox*); Yale Brozen and Domenick Armentano (*Antitrust and Monopoly: Anatomy of a Policy Failure*); George Stigler (*The Organization of Industry*); Timothy Muris, Fred McChesney, and William Shughart (*The Causes and Consequences of Antitrust: The Public-Choice Perspective*).

55. Cited in Jonathan R. Hughes, *The Governmental Habit Redux: Economic Controls from Colonial Times to the Present* (Princeton: Princeton University Press, 1991), p. 14.

56. Cited in George Stigler, *Memoirs of an Unregulated Economist* (New York: Basic Books, 1988), p. 97.

57. Niskanen, *Reaganomics,* p. 134.

58. Baxter didn't win all the antitrust fights he picked. When the Justice Department and the FCC proposed to open up the television syndication market, Hollywood studios opposed to the idea lobbied Reagan personally through Charlton Heston. Baxter squared off against Heston in the Oval Office. Reagan sided with Heston. "I have lost many arguments that I should have won," Baxter reflected, "but never one to so vacuous an opponent." In 1984 Baxter returned to Stanford Law School. (Cited in Feldstein, *American Economic Policy in the 1980s,* p. 614.)

59. Cited in Stephen D. Cohen, "The Route to Japan's Voluntary Export Restraints on Automobiles: An Analysis of the U.S. Government's Decision-Making Process in 1981," Working Paper No. 20, School of International Service, American University, 1998, http://www.gwu.edu/~nsarchiv/japan/scohentp.htm.

60. Herman Belz, *Equality Transformed: A Quarter-Century of Affirmative Action* (New Brunswick: Transaction, 1991), pp. 186, 202.

61. Address to National Black Republican Council, September 15, 1982.

62. "Statements of Commissioners Blandina Cardinas Ramirez and Mary Frances Berry," *Toward an Understanding of Stotts* (U.S. Commission on Civil Rights: Clearinghouse Publications 85, January 1985), p. 63.

63. The key cases in the development of "disparate impact" affirmative action policy were *Griggs v. Duke Power* (1971), *United Steelworkers v. Weber* (1979), and *Fullilove v. Klutznick* (1980).

64. Lewis and Glasser cited in Robert Detlefsen, *Civil Rights Under Reagan* (San Francisco: ICS Press, 1991), pp. 176–78.

65. Charles Fried, *Order and Law: Arguing the Reagan Revolution* (New York: Simon & Schuster, 1991), pp. 41–42.

66. Bennett had written one of the first serious books criticizing affirmative action in the 1970s, and in his NEH announcement said, "To believe in human equality and equal liberty can mean nothing less than to treat white and black, male and female, Jew and Gentile as morally equal. We strongly believe that different or special treatment by this agency on the basis of these characteristics offends our best principles as a nation." Bennett told a *Washington Post* reporter that his actions were justified "by the rights of man, the moral teaching of generations, the ancient founding faith of this country, constitutional principle and the determination of the Justice Department. Not bad support, not bad company, that."

67. Thomas, interview with *U.S. News and World Report,* March 14, 1983, p. 67.

68. Belz, *Equality Transformed,* p. 198. Belz quoted an unnamed General Motors executive: "I hate to think where this corporation would be today without these [affirmative action] programs. G.M. should be a reflection of the larger community and society around us."

69. Cannon, *President Reagan: Role of a Lifetime,* pp. 180, 364.

70. Reagan was not alone in bringing the matter up with Justice. Mississippi congressman Trent Lott also sent a series of letters to the Justice and Treasury departments in 1981 complaining of the tax treatment of Bob Jones University and Goldsboro Academy, the other party in litigation against the IRS.

71. "Private Schools, Tax Exemption, and the IRS," *Regulation,* January/February 1982, p. 7.

72. Peter Wallison, oral history, Miller Center for Public Affairs, University of Virginia, http://millercenter.org/scripps/digitalarchive/oralhistories/detail/3236.

73. House Committee on Ways and Means hearing, February 4, 1982.

74. Chester E. Finn Jr., "Affirmative Action Under Reagan," *Commentary,* April 1982, p. 26.

75. *Memphis Firefighters v. Stotts* (1984), and *Wygant v. Jackson Board of Education* (1986) both chipped away at the legal basis for quotas and set-asides, while

other decisions upheld the practice. Several decisions after Reagan left office further eroded quotas and set-asides, especially *Adarand v. Pena* (1995).

76. *New Republic,* November 1, 1982, p. 5.

77. Beth A. J. Ingold and Theodore Otto Windt Jr., "Trying to 'Stay the Course': President Reagan's Rhetoric During the 1982 Election," *Presidential Studies Quarterly* 14 (1984): p. 90.

78. Reagan taped nearly a hundred television spots for individual GOP candidates, an indication that he was a liability only in selected areas.

79. See, e.g., Hadley Arkes, "A Lover's Lament for the Reagan Administration," *National Review,* May 28, 1982, pp. 615–19. Sample: "And yet there can be no gainsaying that the emphasis on the management of the economy in the first year has involved more than a focusing of the public attention. It has also diminished the energy that may be invested in other concerns, and it has distracted the Administration from some of its other commitments."

80. Alan I. Abramowitz, "National Issues, Strategic Politicians, and Voting Behavior in the 1980 and 1982 Elections," *American Journal of Political Science* 28, 4 (November 1984): p. 710.

81. Robert C. Rowland and Rodger A. Payne, "The Context-Embeddedness of Political Discourse: A Re-Evaluation of Reagan's Rhetoric in the 1982 Midterm Election Campaign," *Presidential Studies Quarterly,* 14 (1984): pp. 500–11.

82. J. Michael Hogan and Ted J. Smith III, "Public Opinion and the Nuclear Freeze," *Public Opinion Quarterly* 55 (1991): p. 534.

83. Ladd cited in Donald R. Baucom, *The Origins of SDI, 1944–1983* (Lawrence: University Press of Kansas, 1992), p. 241.

84. The freeze wasn't the only skirmish line in the cultural debate over American defense and foreign policy. Concurrent with the freeze movement was a similar push in Congress to establish a United States Academy of Peace to be on par with the national military academies for the army, navy, and air force. Like the freeze, there was an organized National Peace Academy Campaign, whose membership had risen tenfold since Reagan took office.

CHAPTER 6: THE GATHERING STORM

1. Niskanen, *Reaganomics,* p. 30. There were many reasons to second-guess Reagan's military buildup. Niskanen reviews the numbers, concluding that "the focus of the defense buildup was on weapons modernization rather than an increase in the size or readiness of the military forces."

2. Bernard Gwertzman, "Allied Contingency Planning Envisions a Warning Atom Blast, Haig Says," *New York Times,* November 5, 1981, p. A-1.

3. *Washington Post,* April 11, 1982, p. B1.

4. Robert Scheer, "U.S. Could Survive in Administration's View," *Los Angeles Times,* January 16, 1982. See also Scheer's book, *With Enough Shovels: Reagan, Bush and Nuclear War* (New York: Random House, 1982).

5. Gates, *From the Shadows,* p. 261.

6. Reagan: "I do have to point out that everything that has been said and everything in their manuals indicates that, unlike us, the Soviet Union believes that a nuclear war is possible. And they believe it's winnable, which means that they believe that you could achieve enough superiority, then your opponent wouldn't have retaliatory strike capacity. Now, there is a danger to all of us in the world as long as they think that. And this, again, is one of the things that we just want to disabuse them of. . . . I also feel that one of the things that's been lacking in the last several 'years in any negotiations was they sat on their side of the table and had nothing to lose. And we had nothing to threaten them with. Now, I think that we can sit down and maybe have some more realistic negotiations because of what we can threaten them with." Reagan also averred his desire to develop missile defense and his oft-stated belief that the Soviet Union's economy could not keep up with the United States in a real arms race. Reagan's exact words were: "So, we've got the chip this time, that if we show them the will and determination to go forward with a military buildup in our own defense and the defense of our allies, they then have to weigh, do they want to meet us realistically on a program of disarmament or do they want to face a legitimate arms race in which we're racing."

7. The infighting over the zero option is often personalized as the clash between the two Richards, Richard Perle at the Pentagon and Richard Burt in the State Department. For a detailed account of this rivalry, see Jay Winik, *On the Brink: The Dramatic, Behind-the-Scenes Saga of the Reagan Era and the Men and Women Who Won the Cold War* (New York: Simon & Schuster, 1996).

8. Reagan also made a direct argument to the peace movement: "[T]oday, a new generation is emerging on both sides of the Atlantic. Its members were not present at the creation of the North Atlantic Alliance. Many of them don't fully understand its roots in defending freedom and rebuilding a war-torn continent. Some young people question why we need weapons, particularly nuclear weapons, to deter war and to assure peaceful development. They fear that the accumulation of weapons itself may lead to conflagration. Some even propose unilateral disarmament. I understand their concerns. Their questions deserve to be answered. But we have an obligation to answer their questions on the basis of judgment and reason and experience. Our policies have resulted in the longest European peace in this century. Wouldn't a rash departure from these policies, as some now suggest, endanger that peace?"

9. Bradley Graham, "Schmidt Takes Credit for U.S. Stance," *Washington Post,* November 18, 1981, p. A-27.

10. The Soviet news agency TASS said the U.S. proposal "is a mere propaganda ploy designed to stalemate the Geneva talks and to present the American course of escalating the arms race and ensuring military superiority as a peace initiative."

11. *Washington Post* foreign affairs reporter Walter Pincus wrote: "The so-called 'zero option' negotiating posture . . . is seen by the Europeans who have pressed it on

Reagan as a public opinion gesture, not a true negotiating posture." "Arms Decision Stirred Storm Around NATO," *Washington Post,* November 17, 1981, p. A-1.

12. The Associated Press, for example, reported on November 17: "The *New York Times,* quoting 'high-ranking administration officials,' said in its editions today that if the Soviets do not agree to this so-called 'zero option,' the United States will propose a more limited agreement under which the Soviets would accept scheduled deployment of new American nuclear warheads on Pershing 2 and ground-based cruise missiles in exchange for Soviet reduction of the number of warheads on the SS-20 and other missiles to the same level."

13. Pat Moynihan liked to remark that anyone who won the Order of Lenin deserved it.

14. Ash, *The Polish Revolution,* p. 172.

15. Ash makes this argument (ibid., p. 308): "Solidarity missed its chance of overthrowing the Party . . . They should have gone for the general strike, in March, and if not in March, then in the summer."

16. Aleksandr Solzhenitsyn nominated Lech Walesa for the Nobel Peace Prize, which Walesa duly received the following October. He was also *Time*'s "Man of the Year" for 1981.

17. Pipes, *Vixi,* p. 169.

18. See, e.g., Richard T. Davies, "The CIA and the Polish Crisis of 1981," *Journal of Cold War Studies* 6, 4 (Summer 2004): pp. 120–23.

19. The U.S. Ambassador to Poland at the time, Francis J. Meehan, makes this case in "Reflections on the Polish Crisis," Woodrow Wilson Center, Cold War International History Project, available at http://www.wilsoncenter.org/index.cfm ?topic_id=1409&fuseaction=library.document&id=370.

20. Douglas J. MacEachin, *U.S. Intelligence and the Confrontation with Poland, 1980–81* (University Park: Pennsylvania State University Press, 2002), p. 230.

21. Jaruzelski later portrayed himself as a desperate and reluctant Polish patriot who developed an "internal solution" to prevent an "inevitable" Soviet invasion. But evidence shows that he desperately wanted Soviet intervention and pleaded for the Soviets to commit troops. The Politburo rebuffed all of Jaruzelski's demands; Poland would have to solve its problems on its own, the Politburo told him. Historian Mark Kramer observed, "[B]y all indications he was devastated when his requests were turned down. . . . Far from having 'saved' Poland from a Soviet invasion, Jaruzelski was desperately promoting the very thing he now claims to have prevented." See Mark Kramer, "Jaruzelski, the Soviet Union, and the Imposition of Martial Law in Poland: New Light on the Mystery of December 1981," Woodrow Wilson Center, Cold War International History Project, available at http://www.wilsoncenter.org/index.cfm?topic_id= 1409&fuseaction=library.document&id=62.

22. Ash speculates about these curious indicators (*The Polish Revolution,* p. 363): "Thus the new evidence actually reinforces the argument . . . that there was a

chance, albeit a slim one, of a different outcome. Even within the severe, objective constraints of the autumn of 1981, Jaruzelski might have acted otherwise. Andropov's remark [that the Soviet Union might have to let Poland go] suggests that his acting otherwise might just possibly have meant that some of what happened all over Central Europe in 1989 could have happened in Poland already in 1981."

23. Ibid., p. 328. Ash adds, "There were therefore a few Reagan advisers who actually said, in so many words, that it would be better for America—and therefore for the 'free world'—if the Soviet Union would be forced to invade Poland. West European peace movements would be confounded." Ash does not, however, offer any specific examples of any administration advisers who argued this "in so many words" or any other words.

24. Honecker had repeatedly urged Brezhnev to crush Solidarity, writing at one point in 1980: "Any delay in acting against the counterrevolutionaries would mean the death of socialist Poland."

25. Reagan repeated this in his diary: "We can't let this revolution against Communism fail without offering our hand. We may never have an opportunity like this in our lifetime."

26. Minutes of NSC meeting, December 22, 1981.

27. Allen had accepted a $1,000 cash payment from a Japanese journalist—a typical Japanese journalistic courtesy—in return for helping arrange an interview with Nancy Reagan on Inauguration Day, and put the money in a White House safe and forgot about it. Its discovery months later led to an ethics investigation.

28. Ash, *The Polish Revolution*, p. 337.

29. According to Richard Pipes, Jaruzelski later claimed the sanctions cost Poland $12 billion (*Vixi*, p. 173). This figure sounds implausible.

30. "After I wrote that article," Podhoretz later recalled, "Reagan called me and spent half an hour on the phone reassuring me he was serious about the Soviets. What he basically said was: Trust me, they're in more economic trouble than people realize, and I'm going to put the squeeze on them."

31. "Is Reagan Foreign Policy Different from Carter's?" *Human Events,* December 26, 1981, p. 1.

32. Thatcher, *The Downing Street Years*, pp. 254–55.

33. The U.S. Chamber of Commerce, and most of the American business community, also opposed tough pipeline sanctions.

34. Cited in Peter Schweizer, *Reagan's War* (New York: Doubleday, 2002), p. 171.

35. The French government was guaranteeing loans to the Soviet Union at an interest rate of 7½ percent when the going bank rate was over 12 percent. The Reagan administration wanted the French to charge the going rate.

36. See Cannon, *President Reagan: Role of a Lifetime*, pp. 199–204.

37. Shultz notes in his memoirs: "I was struck whenever I was involved in negotiations that the most important bargaining took place *within* one's own negotiating team and that those internal negotiations were the most difficult of all"

(*Turmoil and Triumph: Diplomacy, Power, and the Victory of the American Ideal* [New York: Simon & Schuster, 1993], p. 21).

38. Michael Ledeen, *Perilous Statecraft* (New York: Scribner's, 1988), p. 67.

39. Pipes's complete account of this interlude appears in his memoir *Vixi*, pp. 194–202.

40. The five are: his Westminster address (discussed here) of June 1982; the "evil empire" and Strategic Defense Initiative speeches of March 1983; the January 1984 speech calling for an improvement in relations with the Soviets; and the "tear down this wall" speech of June 1987.

41. From Lady Thatcher's memoirs: "I remember the speech for another reason as well. I was full of admiration that he seemed to have delivered it without a single note. 'I congratulate you on your actor's memory,' I said. He replied, 'I read the whole speech from those two Perspex screens'—referring to what we had taken to be some security device. 'Don't you know it? It's a British invention.' And so it was that I made my acquaintance with Autocue."

42. Reagan's more conventional alliance rhetoric did not mitigate German media reaction. *Der Spiegel* wrote: "Reagan is synonymous for dangerous atomic helmsmanship, as a cowboy who shoots from the hip, who plays with rockets and bombs, who has the mania to grab the red steer by the horns and drag it to the ground."

43. Pipes, *Vixi*, p. 200.

44. Weigel has in mind here the sensational reporting of Watergate veteran Carl Bernstein and Marco Politi in *His Holiness*. John O'Sullivan concurs with Weigel in *The President, the Pope and the Prime Minister* (Washington, DC: Regnery, 2006), and two U.S. ambassadors to the Vatican under Reagan privately disputed Bernstein's specific claims to this author. See Weigel, *Witness to Hope*, pp. 441–42, and especially footnotes 9–13.

45. NSC paper, "Response to NSSD 11-82, U.S. Relations with the USSR," December 6, 1982, p. 12.

46. *New York Times*, January 2, 1982, p. D-19.

47. Susan Sontag, "Some Thoughts on the Right Way (for Us) to Love the Cuban Revolution," *Ramparts*, April 1969, p. 16. Sontag would eventually repent of her tergiversation over Poland in the aftermath of September 11, 2001, when she suggested that the United States had brought the attack upon itself.

48. Richard Sobel, "A Report: Public Opinion About U.S. Intervention in El Salvador and Nicaragua," *Public Opinion Quarterly*, 53, 1 (Spring 1989): p. 115.

49. Asner cited in Gerald Kaufman, "A Makeshift Toast to Nicaraguan Libre," *New Statesmen*, September 11, 1987, p. 16.

50. Peter N. Rodman, *More Precious Than Peace: The Cold War and the Struggle for the Third World* (New York: Scribner's, 1994), p. 244.

51. John Brentlinger, *The Best of What We Are: Reflections on the Nicaraguan Revolution* (Amherst: University of Massachusetts Press, 1995), p. 2.

52. Cited in Ronald Radosh, "Darkening Nicaragua," *New Republic,* October 23, 1983, p. 7.

53. For an exhaustive catalogue of such sentiments as applied to Nicaragua and elsewhere and a general analysis see Paul Hollander's *Political Pilgrims: Western Intellectuals in Search of the Good Society,* 4th ed. (New Brunswick: Transaction Books, 1998; originally published by Harper Colophon, 1981). See also Hollander's *Anti-Americanism: Irrational and Rational* (New Brunswick: Transaction Books, 1995; originally published by Oxford University Press, 1992), esp. ch. 5, "The Pilgrimage to Nicaragua."

54. Codevilla, *Informing Statecraft,* p. 137.

55. Rodman, *More Precious Than Peace,* p. 242.

56. Cited in Hollander, *Anti-Americanism,* p. 294.

57. American members of the Brandt Commission included Katharine Graham, owner of the *Washington Post,* and Pete Peterson, head of Lehman Brothers.

58. The Soviet news agency TASS accurately described the premise of the New International Economic Order: "The industrialized western countries would share with developing countries a part of their wealth, *plundered as a result of exploiting them both in the colonial times and the present period"* (emphasis added). TASS Comments on Reagan's Philadelphia Speech, October 15, 1981.

59. Speech delivered on October 15, 1981. See also Peter Bauer, *Equality, the Third World, and Economic Delusion* (Cambridge, MA: Harvard University Press, 1981).

60. In light of the Vietnam analogy applied to Central America, it was notably insulting that one Sandinista arms shipment consisted of 1,500 American M-16 rifles and a million rounds of ammunition that had been captured in Vietnam at the end of the war in 1975.

61. Robert Kagan, *A Twilight Struggle: American Power and Nicaragua, 1977–1990* (New York: Free Press, 1996), pp. 197–98.

62. American policy was further complicated by the political support Nicaragua received from several European nations (especially France) and also Mexico, whose tilt toward the Sandinistas was a combination of anti-Americanism and appeasement.

63. Diary entry, October 16, 1981.

64. Cited in Rodman, *More Precious Than Peace,* p. 238.

65. Kagan, *A Twilight Struggle,* p. 204.

66. For a compact account of the political and legal history of covert operations in American history, see Louis Fisher, *Presidential War Power* (Lawrence, KS: University Press of Kansas, 1995), pp. 162–84.

67. See Joshua Muravchik, "Misreporting Lebanon," *Policy Review,* Winter 1983, pp. 11–66.

68. Reagan, like Carter, did not care for Begin personally: "Boy, that guy makes it hard for you to be his friend."

69. Cannon, *President Reagan: Role of a Lifetime,* p. 390.

70. See "Arafat: Major Israeli Move Likely," *Journal of Palestine Studies* 10, 3 (Spring 1981): pp. 146–148.

71. See Clifford Wright, "The Israeli War Machine in Lebanon," *Journal of Palestine Studies,* 12, 2 (Winter 1983): pp. 38–53.

72. A joke making the rounds in Moscow and Damascus after the battle had Soviet defense minister Ustinov asking the Syrians, "What happened to the missiles we sent you?" To which the Syrians replied: "They were ground-to-air missiles. This time we want ground-to-plane missiles."

73. Leslie H. Gelb, "Who Won the Cold War?" *New York Times,* August 20, 1992, p. 27.

74. Galia Golan, "The Soviet Union and the Israeli Action in Lebanon," *International Affairs,* 59, 1 (Winter 1982–83): p. 8.

75. Cited in *Grand Strategy: Countercurrents,* February 1, 1982, p. 10.

76. Diary entry, November 13, 1982.

77. In fact the United States was not certain of Andropov's age. According to some accounts, he was seventy-one; other records had his age at sixty-eight.

78. There was some evidence at the time that Andropov had reformist inclinations and had long thought the Soviet system was dysfunctional; subsequent findings since the collapse of the Soviet Union tend to confirm this. See especially Moshe Lewin, *The Soviet Century* (London: Verso, 2005), pp. 253–67.

79. Only *U.S. News and World Report* seemed immune from the euphoria, running a short item under the headline "A 'Closet Liberal'? Don't Bet on It."

80. Russian scholar Robert Conquest noted the absurd incongruity of all this: "There are those in the West who would simply have us ignore the historical and psychological background of men like Andropov. They would pay no attention to the fact that he and those like him are products of a history quite alien to our own and are exemplars of a political psychology of a type hardly seen in the West outside of small sects of millenarian psychopaths." (Quoted in *Policy Review,* Fall 1983, pp. 99–100.)

81. *Time* magazine acknowledged a year later, on the eve of Andropov's death (January 2, 1984), that the Western press had got it badly wrong: "Not only was he a somewhat unknown figure to those outside the Kremlin even before illness removed him from public view, but some of what the West thought it knew about him was wrong. The picture of Andropov as a Westernized intellectual, fond of American music and books, that circulated widely in the months before he assumed power following the death of Leonid Brezhnev in November 1982, was mostly the product of wishful thinking, possibly aided by deliberate Kremlin disinformation."

CHAPTER 7: THE YEAR OF LIVING DANGEROUSLY

1. "I had hoped there would not be a second term," Clark said later in an oral history. "I told the president that I hoped he would consider the fact that we had accomplished what we had set out to do, both on the domestic front and internationally, and that I hoped he would consider handing the reins instead to the vice president. . . . I'd rather not go into his reaction." (Clark, in Strober and Strober, eds., *Reagan*, p. 301.)

2. George Church, "Playing Hide and Seek," *Time*, May 2, 1983, p. 15. One of Reagan's comments to reporters demonstrates his acute political sense: "I think to do it [declare candidacy] too early leaves you open to the charge that everything you do is based on politics. And if you say the other way too soon, why, you're a lame duck prematurely."

3. Erich Heinemann, "Washington's New Mood Stirs Hopes of Growth," *New York Times*, January 1, 1983, p. 19.

4. Steven R. Weisman, "Tax Increase Options Unlikely, Reagan Aides Say," *New York Times*, January 1, 1983; Steven R. Weisman, "Aides Say Reagan Has Shelved Plan to Cut $26 Billion," *New York Times*, January 2, 1983.

5. An across-the-board freeze, Gingrich said, was the "only step which is politically possible, which is simple and clear enough that the nation could rally to it." In his diary Reagan wrote that "it's a tempting idea except that it would cripple our defense program. And if we make an exception on that every special interest group will be asking for the same."

6. Paul Weaver, "The Networks vs. the Recovery," *Commentary*, July 1984, p. 39.

7. William A. Henry III, *Visions of America: How We Saw the 1984 Election* (New York: Atlantic Monthly Press, 1985), p. 35.

8. Greider, *Secrets of the Temple*, p. 562.

9. Several observers had predicted this at the outset of Reagan's presidency. George Will wrote, "Folks laughed in 1980 when Reagan invoked FDR's name, but in 1981 he began doing for the welfare state what FDR did for capitalism: saving it by tempering its excesses." Lou Cannon wrote that "Reagan may turn out to be the salvation of the New Deal as much as his idol Franklin Roosevelt proved the savior of capitalism."

10. Typical is this *Time* magazine report of May 9, 1983: "Yet the Reagan Administration has worked only half-heartedly in Congress for laws that would permit organized school prayer, stop busing and ban abortion, and none of that social agenda has been passed."

11. This is William Clark's recollection, as recorded in *National Review*, June 28, 2004, p. 20.

12. Reagan's Justice Department filed an ambivalent brief in the *Akron* case that stopped short of calling for *Roe* to be overturned. When Justice Harry Blackman asked directly during oral argument whether the Reagan administration wished *Roe* overturned, solicitor general Rex Lee answered, "Not at this time, your honor."

13. This involved the controversial charge that Dr. Robert Gallo had stolen the work of French researchers and claimed it as his own.

14. Larry Kramer, "Adolf Reagan," *Advocate,* July 6, 2004.

15. For a complete account of this remarkable man, see Nitze's memoirs, *From Hiroshima to Glasnost: At the Center of Decision* (New York: Grove Weidenfeld, 1989).

16. Cited in Jay Winik, *On the Brink,* p. 202.

17. Various accounts of this sequence exist. The most copious is Jay Winik's *On the Brink* (pp. 196–204), but see also Nitze, *From Hiroshima to Glasnost* (pp. 366–98), Jack F. Matlock, *Reagan and Gorbachev: How the Cold War Ended* (New York: Random House, 2004), pp. 41–45.

18. Nitze wrote in his memoir *From Hiroshima to Glasnost* (p. 389): "The Moscow group had decided that INF could best be used as a political device to sow dissension within NATO and to drive wedges between the United States and its European partners." Jack Matlock, *Reagan and Gorbachev* (p. 43), was emphatic that the Soviets had committed a major mistake: "[T]he Soviets could have gained powerful leverage over NATO's ability to deploy if they had agreed to negotiate on that basis. If they had, the Reagan administration would probably have been forced, despite the reservations many of its officials held, to adopt the positions Nitze had outlined. Otherwise, opposition to the U.S. deployments, already dangerously high, would have grown in Europe. . . . Verification, however, would have proven a most difficult issue, and the negotiations could easily have stalled. In that case, NATO would probably have found it politically impossible to proceed with the deployments planned for the fall of 1983."

19. Ken Adelman, *The Great Universal Embrace* (New York: Simon & Schuster, 1989), p. 163.

20. James Fallows, "The Ordeal of Kenneth Adelman," *Atlantic,* July 1984, pp. 33–34.

21. Cited in Frances FitzGerald, *Way Out There in the Blue: Reagan, Star Wars, and the End of the Cold War* (New York: Simon & Schuster, 2001), p. 191.

22. Dobrynin, *In Confidence,* p. 523.

23. The bishops' statement contained some theologically odd language, such as "Today the destructive potential of the nuclear powers threatens the sovereignty of God over the world he has brought into being." Did the bishops really mean to say that God had lost His omnipotence?

24. A reviewer noted, "Schell does not actually say 'better red than dead,' but he surely could not disavow such a position." Peter deLeon, "Freeze: The Literature of the Nuclear Weapons Debate," *Journal of Conflict Resolution* 27, 1 (March 1983): p. 187.

25. Unnoticed by most of the press, in February Reagan issued an official proclamation designating 1983 as "the Year of the Bible in the United States."

26. Shultz, *Turmoil and Triumph,* p. 267.

27. Caspar Weinberger Transcript, Ronald Reagan Oral History Project, Miller Center for Public Affairs, University of Virginia, p. 11.

28. Paul Kengor offers a copious roundup of these admissions in ch. 16 of his book *God and Ronald Reagan: A Spiritual Life* (New York: Regan Books, 2004).

29. Talbott, *The Russians and Reagan* (New York: Vintage, 1984), p. 33. Talbott continued: "After all, the Soviets do lie, cheat, and reserve the right to commit any crime; they do preside over the last great empire on earth; and many aspects of their behavior, both toward their own people and toward those of other lands, are so offensive and threatening to the democratic and human values that evil is not an outrageous characterization of them."

30. The full story of Reagan's dramatic unveiling of a missile defense initiative has been amply told by writers across the political spectrum. The best and most detailed of these accounts are Paul Lettow's *Ronald Reagan and His Quest to Abolish Nuclear Weapons* (New York: Random House, 2005), Frances FitzGerald's *Way Out There in the Blue: Reagan, Star Wars, and the End of the Cold War* (New York: Simon & Schuster, 2001), and Paul Kengor's *The Crusader: Ronald Reagan and the Fall of Communism* (New York: Regan Books, 2006).

31. Lieutenant "Brass" Bancroft was a recurring role for Reagan. He made three Bancroft movies previous to *Murder in the Air,* all in 1939: *Secret Service of the Air; Code of the Secret Service;* and *Smashing the Money Ring.* For an extended discussion of Reagan's films from that era and their possible political effect, see Stephen Vaughn, "Spies, National Security, and the 'Inertia Projector': The Secret Service Films of Ronald Reagan," *American Quarterly* 39, 3 (Autumn 1987): pp. 355–80.

32. FitzGerald, *Way Out There,* p. 206.

33. Ibid., p. 205.

34. Shultz, *Turmoil and Triumph,* p. 250.

35. Thatcher, *Downing Street Years,* p. 463. Reagan's speech was careful to include language reassuring our NATO allies that we were not abandoning either Europe or the doctrine of deterrence through retaliation: "As we pursue our goal of defensive technologies, we recognize that our allies rely upon our strategic offensive power to deter attacks against them. Their vital interests and ours are inextricably linked. . . . I clearly recognize that defensive systems have limitations and raise certain problems and ambiguities. If paired with offensive systems, they can be viewed as fostering an aggressive policy, and no one wants that."

36. Gates, *From the Shadows,* p. 266.

37. Bessmertnykh quoted in William C. Wohlforth, ed., *Witnesses to the End of the Cold War* (Baltimore: Johns Hopkins University Press, 1996), pp. 14, 33.

38. Typical was New York Democratic representative Ted Weiss, who said: "Never in my wildest dreams could I ever imagine our president taking to the national airwaves to promote a strategy of futuristic 'Star Wars' schemes as Mr. Reagan did last night."

39. BBC interviewer: "Are you saying then, Mr. President, that the United States, if it were well down the road towards a proper SDI program, would be prepared to share its technology with Soviet Russia, provided, of course, there were arms reductions and so on on both sides?" Reagan: "That's right. There would have to be the reductions of offensive weapons. In other words, we would switch to defense instead of offense."

40. FitzGerald, *Way Out There*, p. 206.

41. See especially Robert Jastrow, "The War Against 'Star Wars,' " *Commentary*, December 1984; Angelo M. Codevilla, "How SDI Is Being Undone from Within," *Commentary*, May 1986; Angelo M. Codevilla, *While Others Build: A Commonsense Approach to the Strategic Defense Initiative* (New York: Free Press, 1988).

42. The usual constellation of left-leaning groups seized upon the heightened technical thresholds to bolster their ideological opposition to the idea. The Union of Concerned Scientists produced a series of reports attacking the feasibility of missile defense, and attempted to organize academic scientists into making public pledges not to work on missile defense research. Eventually the UCS would garner the signatures of 6,500 scientists who pledged not to work on the "ill-conceived and dangerous" project. *Nature* magazine editorialized, "The scientific community knows that it will not work." The Office of Technology Assessment issued a report concluding that the prospects for effective missile defense were "so remote that it should not serve as the basis for public expectations or national policy."

43. Abshire quoted in Strober and Strober, eds., *Reagan*, p. 240.

44. Powell quoted in Strober and Strober, eds., *Reagan*, p. 244.

45. Oleg Grinevky, "The Crisis that Didn't Erupt: The Soviet-American Relationship, 1980–1983," in Kiron K. Skinner, ed., *Turning Points in the Cold War* (Palo Alto: Hoover Institution Press, 2008), p. 71.

46. "Blood for No Oil," *Atlantic Monthly*, May 2006, p. 135.

47. The previous year Reagan commented in an interview: "The most upsetting letters I receive are from schoolchildren who write me as class assignments. It's evident they've discussed the most nightmarish aspects of a nuclear holocaust in their classrooms. Their letters are often full of terror. Well, this should not be so."

48. One of the few news accounts that got the matter right was Nicholas Daniloff, the Moscow correspondent for *U.S. News and World Report*. "Samantha Smith: Pawn in Propaganda War" was the headline for his story of July 18, 1983. Three years later the Soviets would arrest Daniloff on charges of spying.

49. BBC Summary of World Broadcasts, July 14, 1983.

50. Cannon, *President Reagan: Role of a Lifetime*, p. 358.

51. Weigel, *Witness to Hope*, pp. 455–56.

52. The mischievous cables were the handiwork of Tom Enders, the assistant secretary of state for Latin America, who had been doing his own freelancing in the

region, often unbeknownst to Shultz. "He went off doing deals on his own, and his trail was hard to follow," Shultz laconically recorded in his memoirs. This and other mistakes led shortly to Enders's ouster at State.

53. Strobe Talbott, "Playing Nuclear Poker," *Time,* January 31, 1983.
54. Jeffrey Herf, *War by Other Means: Soviet Power, West German Resistance, and the Battle of the Euromissiles* (New York: Free Press, 1991), p. 165.
55. See especially ibid., ch. 10, "History, Language, and Strategy," pp. 164–95.
56. Ibid., p. 174.
57. Quoted in Shultz, *Turmoil and Triumph,* p. 358.
58. Most significant from the point of view of international diplomacy was Japan's joining the endorsement of missile deployment. The Soviet Union had been toying with the idea of trying to split off Japan with some territorial and trade concessions.
59. See Hayward, *The Age of Reagan,* pp. 702–4.
60. Letter to Paul Trousdale, May 23, 1983, in *Reagan: A Life in Letters,* p. 409.
61. One worthwhile review of the many books and studies on the episode is Murray Sayle, "KE007: A Conspiracy of Circumstance," *New York Review of Books,* April 25, 1985.
62. The Soviets most likely believed this because their own civilian airliner, Aeroflot, routinely flew "off course" over American military installations in an apparent espionage mode.
63. *Human Events,* September 17, 1983, p. 21.
64. Shultz, *Turmoil and Triumph,* p. 370.
65. Ibid., p. 372.
66. Cannon, *President Reagan: The Role of a Lifetime,* p. 411.
67. Letter to WFB, January 5, 1984, in *Reagan: A Life in Letters,* p. 448.
68. Letter to Paul Trousdale, February 20, 1984, in *Reagan: A Life in Letters,* p. 449.
69. The best account of the strange political history of Grenada during this period is Gregory Sandford and Richard Vigilante, *Grenada: The Untold Story* (Lanham, MD: Madison Books, 1984). Grenada was the only Latin American nation, for example, that voted against the UN resolution in January 1980 condemning the Soviet invasion of Afghanistan. Even Nicaragua had the good sense to abstain.
70. See especially Constantine C. Menges, *Inside the National Security Council* (New York: Simon & Schuster, 1988), p. 63.
71. Shultz, *Turmoil and Triumph,* p. 329.
72. Strober and Strober, eds., *Reagan,* p. 291.
73. Mona Charen provides a comprehensive inventory of liberal reaction to Grenada in *Useful Idiots: How Liberals Got It Wrong in the Cold War and Still Blame America First* (Washington, DC: Regnery, 2003), pp. 187–93.
74. Moynihan's great friend George Will responded: "It is bad enough we pay for the United Nations; surely we do not have to listen to it." Moynihan replied: "That is not a satisfactory retort."

75. Dinesh D'Souza, "Paddy, We Hardly Knew Ye," *Policy Review,* Spring 1984, p. 42.

76. Theodore A. Blanton, "Neo-Moynihan?" *Claremont Review of Books,* December 1983, p. 8.

77. Cited in Godfrey Hodgson, *The Gentleman from New York: Daniel Patrick Moynihan, a Biography* (New York: Houghton Mifflin, 2000), p. 311.

78. Paul Seabury and Walter A. McDougal, *The Grenada Papers* (San Francisco: ICS Press, 1984).

79. Strober and Strober, eds., *Reagan,* p. 290.

80. Stephen Haseler, "The Euromissile Crisis," *Commentary,* May 1983, p. 32.

81. The most complete account of this episode is the original reporting of Hedrick Smith, *The Power Game: How Washington Works* (New York: Random House, 1988), pp. 320–24. See also Lou Cannon, *President Reagan: The Role of a Lifetime,* pp. 431–35.

82. Reagan, *An American Life,* p. 448.

83. David Hoffman, " 'I Had a Funny Feeling in My Gut': Soviet Officer Faced Nuclear Armageddon," *Washington Post,* February 10, 1999, p. A-19.

84. A few days after Able Archer concluded, Ustinov wrote in *Pravda:* "The dangerous nature of the military exercises conducted by the U.S. and NATO in recent years commands attention. These exercises are characterized by an enormous scope, and they are becoming increasingly difficult to distinguish from a real deployment of armed forces for aggression" (cited in Beth Fischer, p. 131).

85. Politburo Minutes, May 31, 1983, published by the Cold War International History Project, Woodrow Wilson Center.

86. Dobrynin, *In Confidence,* p. 523.

87. Cited in Christopher Andrew and Oleg Gordievsky, *Comrade Kryuchkov's Instructions: Top Secret Files on KGB Foreign Operations, 1975–1985* (London: Hodder & Stoughton, 1991), p. 85.

88. However, the Pentagon was alarmed that the Soviets were somehow tracking American submarines and surface ship movements anyway. In 1985 the Walker spy ring was uncovered; the Walker ring had provided navy code books to the Soviets, in what is regarded as perhaps the most serious security breach in the Cold War, and one that could have been decisive in the event of hostilities.

89. Much of this information derives from NSC member Gus Weiss's unpublished "Farewell Dossier," on file with author.

90. Fischer, "Cold War Conundrum."

91. John Prados, "The War Scare of 1983," in Robert Cowley, ed., *The Cold War: A Military History* (New York: Random House, 2005), p. 448.

92. One forceful and credible demurral comes from Anatoly Chernyaev, deputy chief of the International Department of the CPSU at the time, who said in 1993 when asked directly about the matter: "So far as I remember that situation, in the highest echelon of Soviet government there really was no serious fear that this situation might really provoke a nuclear conflict or a large-scale

international conflict. Perhaps in individual military districts certain steps were taken, but so far as the political level, I think we can rule out that there was real fear of a nuclear attack." See William C. Wohlforth, ed., *Witnesses to the End of the Cold War* (Baltimore: Johns Hopkins University Press, 1996), pp. 72–73. Another senior Soviet foreign ministry official, Sergei Tarasenko, portrayed the Soviet anxiety as a deliberate propaganda effort to make the West nervous.

93. Prados, "The War Scare of 1983," p. 440.

94. Massie in Strober and Strober, eds., *Reagan,* p. 224. Reagan liked Massie because, as he put it in his diary, "she has no truck with the govt. types."

95. Akhromeyev quoted in Dobrynin, *In Confidence,* p. 525.

96. Beth A. Fischer, *The Reagan Reversal: Foreign Policy and the End of the Cold War* (Columbia: University of Missouri Press, 1997), p. 123.

97. Accounts differ as to when Reagan finally submitted to a full SIOP briefing. According to Derek Leebaert (*The Fifty-Year Wound*), who worked from NSC sources, Reagan didn't receive a full SIOP briefing until the middle of 1982, as did Thomas Reed, Reagan's secretary of the Air Force. But Fischer (*The Reagan Reversal*) wrote that Reagan didn't get a full SIOP briefing until the fall of 1983.

98. Fischer, *The Reagan Reversal,* p. 121.

99. Some of the limited information available on SIOP can be found in the National Security Archive at George Washington University: http://www.gwu.edu/~nsarchiv/NSAEBB/NSAEBB173/index.htm.

100. For more on this startling aspect of Reagan, see especially Lettow, *Ronald Reagan and His Quest to Abolish Nuclear Weapons;* see also Fischer, *The Reagan Reversal,* and Matlock, *Reagan and Gorbachev: How the Cold War Ended.*

101. It is worth recalling that in the early 1970s the single bestselling paperback book was Hal Lindsey's *The Late Great Planet Earth,* which made the case for the contemporary fulfillment of biblical prophecies of the Book of Revelation. There is no evidence, however, that Reagan was familiar with Lindsey's book. Reagan was not alone in his belief in biblical Armageddon. Defense Secretary Weinberger told a Harvard audience in 1982: "I have read the Book of Revelation and, yes, I believe the world is going to end—by an act of God, I hope—but every day I think that time is running out."

102. Reagan to Peter and Irene Hannaford, February 10, 1983, in *Reagan: A Life in Letters,* p. 278.

103. See especially Fischer's discussion of this point in *The Reagan Reversal,* pp. 148–49.

104. The CIA revisited the entire episode again in 1990 and reached the same conclusion that the Soviet alarm had been real.

105. Cited in Prados, "The War Scare of 1983," p. 450.

106. Quoted in Don Oberdorfer, *The Turn from the Cold War to a New Era: The United States and the Soviet Union, 1983–1990,* revised edition (Baltimore: Johns Hopkins University Press, 1998) p. 67.

107. Herbert E. Meyer, "Why Is The World So Dangerous?" Memorandum to William Casey, November 30, 1983, available at http://www.foia.cia.gov.

108. The most famous is *Dr. Strangelove* (1964), but other notable nuclear war movies prior to *The Day After* include *On the Beach* (1959), *Fail Safe* (1964), and *World War III* (1982).

109. The *New Republic*'s reviewer, Paul Attanasio, savaged the movie: "*The Day After* recalls one of the worst tendencies of the 1960s, the tendency to reduce everything—politics, drugs, rock 'n' roll, divorce—to equivalent occasions for phatic community, starter cultures for a glutinous mass of good feelings. . . . *The Day After* stands as another example of TV's ability to corrupt pretty much everything."

110. Marshall Ogarkov later confirmed that senior Soviet officials also screened the film.

111. ABC naturally made a civic virtue of this problem, with Brandon Stoddard of ABC boasting that "commercial success has never been ABC's prime consideration with the project." ABC's director of programming, Tom Mackin, told the *New Republic*'s Paul Attanasio that "we would have put it on the air with no ads."

112. See Stanley Feldman and Lee Sigelman, "The Political Impact of Prime-Time Television: 'The Day After,'" *Journal of Politics* 47 (1985): pp. 556–78.

113. *New Republic,* February 20, 1984, p. 7.

114. Cited in Charen, *Useful Idiots*, p. 162.

CHAPTER 8: REALIGNMENT MANQUÉ

1. Two notable exceptions are several essayists contributing chapters to Dennis J. Mahoney and Peter W. Schramm, eds., *The 1984 Election and the Future of American Politics* (Durham: Carolina Academic Press, 1987), and Marc Landy and Sidney M. Milkis, *Presidential Greatness* (Lawrence: University Press of Kansas, 2000), pp. 220–25.

2. Reagan set up the effort in 1982, and it carried out its work entirely with resources provided by the private sector.

3. For an intelligent dissent on the Grace Commission's findings, see Steven Kelman, "The Grace Commission: How Much Waste in Government?" *Public Interest,* Winter 1985, pp. 62–82. Kelman's conclusion: "The horror stories one hears are almost always gross exaggerations."

4. Moynihan, *Came the Revolution: Argument in the Reagan Era* (San Diego: Harcourt Brace Jovanovich, 1988), p. 163.

5. Charles W. Ostrom Jr. and Dennis M. Simon, "The Man in the Teflon Suit? The Environmental Connections, Political Drama, and Popular Support in the Reagan Presidency," *Public Opinion Quarterly* 53, 3 (Autumn 1989): p. 356.

6. In the essay "You and the Atomic Bomb," published on October 19, 1945, Orwell wrote: "[L]ooking at the world as a whole, the drift for many decades has

been not towards anarchy but towards the reimposition of slavery. We may be heading not for general breakdown but for an epoch as horribly stable as the slave empires of antiquity. James Burnham's theory has been much discussed, but few people have yet considered its ideological implications—that is, the kind of world-view, the kind of beliefs, and the social structure that would probably prevail in a state which was at once *unconquerable* and in a permanent state of 'cold war' with its neighbors."

7. Johanno Strasser, "1984: Decade of the Experts?" in Irving Howe, ed., *1984 Revisited: Totalitarianism in Our Century* (New York: Harper & Row, 1983), pp. 151, 153.

8. Norman Podhoretz, "If Orwell Were Alive Today," reprinted in *The Bloody Crossroads: Where Literature and Politics Meet* (New York: Simon & Schuster, 1986), p. 65.

9. The complete ad copy, which had to be shortened to fit the sixty-second time limit, was even more explicitly Orwellian. It began: "My friends, each of you is a single cell in the great body of the State. And today, that great body has purged itself of parasites. We have triumphed over the unprincipled dissemination of facts. The thugs and wreckers have been cast out. And the poisonous weeds of disinformation have been consigned to the dustbin of history. Let each and every cell rejoice!"

10. *New Republic,* February 6, 1984, p. 7.

11. *The Nation,* February 4, 1984, p. 114.

12. Jack Matlock, U.S. ambassador to the Soviet Union during Reagan's second term and a principal author of the January 16 speech draft, wrote: "Subsequently, we learned that the delay had not been based on policy considerations, but on the advice of Mrs. Reagan's astrologer friend [Joan Quigley] in California."

13. Shultz, *Turmoil and Triumph,* pp. 468–70.

14. Quoted in Matlock, *Reagan and Gorbachev,* p. 87.

15. The complete postscript read: "In thinking through this letter, I have reflected at some length on the tragedy and scale of Soviet losses in warfare through the ages. Surely those losses, which are beyond description, must affect your thinking today. I want you to know that neither I nor the American people hold any offensive intentions toward you or the Soviet people. The truth of that statement is underwritten by the history of our restraint at a time when our virtual monopoly on strategic power provided the means for expansion had we so chosen. We did not then nor shall we now. Our common and urgent purpose must be the translation of this reality into a lasting redirection of tensions between us. I pledge to you my profound commitment to that goal." Reagan to Chernenko, April 16, 1984, in *Reagan: A Life in Letters,* p. 743.

16. Jackson's typically self-promoting role prompted Navy Secretary John Lehman to remark that survival packets for American pilots should henceforth include a

roll of quarters and Jackson's phone number (cited in Robert Timberg, *The Nightingale's Song* [New York: Free Press/Touchstone, 1996], p. 341).

17. Cannon, *President Reagan: The Role of a Lifetime,* p. 453.

18. "Who Lost Lebanon?" *New Republic,* February 27, 1984, p. 8; *National Review,* meanwhile, said, "It is time for the Marines to withdraw offshore. . . . The most difficult step a great power can take is to cut its losses and retreat from a conflict not worth wasting lives on."

19. The bipartisan report concluded, "Present levels of U.S. military assistance [to El Salvador] are inadequate," promoting this comment from the *New Republic:* "There is indeed a war taking place in El Salvador, and it may be one of the political achievements of the commission to have provoked from some of the leaders of the Democratic Party this assent to a fact of Salvadoran life which many Democrats prefer to ignore."

20. Cited in Kagan, *A Twilight Struggle,* pp. 303–4.

21. This led directly to an embarrassment for Reagan in his second debate with Walter Mondale on October 17. Georgie Anne Geyer asked Reagan whether the manual amounted to "our own state-supported terrorism." Reagan replied, "We have a gentleman down in Nicaragua who is on contract to the CIA, advising—supposedly on military tactics—the Contras. And he drew up this manual. It was turned over to the agency head of the CIA in Nicaragua to be printed." The grim bits were supposed to have been excised, Reagan said, but due to a slip-up mistakenly got through. Geyer's eyes widened; had Reagan just given up a classified operation, or acknowledged the CIA's presence in Nicaragua against the express law of Congress? Reagan immediately realized his error and beat a hasty retreat: "I'm afraid I misspoke when I said a CIA head in Nicaragua. There's not someone there directing all of this activity. There are, as you know, CIA men stationed in other countries in the world and, certainly, in Central America. And so it was a man down there in that area that this was delivered to, and he recognized that what was in that manual was in direct contravention of my own Executive order, in December of 1981, that we would have nothing to do with regard to political assassinations." The unexpurgated manual was indeed highly compromising. It included language such as: "If possible, professional criminals will be hired to carry out selective jobs," and "It is possible to neutralize carefully selected and planned targets, such as court judges, police and State Security officials, CDS chiefs, etc."

22. Draper, *A Very Thin Line* (New York: Simon & Schuster, 1991), p. 72.

23. *National Review,* January 21, 1983, p. 11.

24. Bartley, *Seven Fat Years,* p. 150.

25. *National Review,* "For the Record," March 23, 1984, p. 9.

26. A good account of the neoliberal moment is provided by William Voegeli, "Crisis of the Old Liberal Order," *Claremont Review of Books,* Summer 2007, pp. 20–23.

27. Robert Kuttner, "The Left's Recovery," *New Republic*, February 14, 1984, p. 26.

28. Melville J. Ulmer, "The War of the Liberal Economists," *Commentary*, October 1983, p. 53.

29. Cited ibid., p. 56.

30. Cited in Jack Germond and Jules Witcover, *Wake Us When It's Over* (New York: Macmillan, 1985), p. 178.

31. Cited in Henry, *Visions of America*, p. 39.

32. Almost unnoticed in the Hart surprise in New Hampshire was that Reagan received more write-in votes from Democrats than three of the official Democratic candidates on the ballot.

33. Quoted in Peter Beinart, "Good Old Boy," *New Republic*, June 19, 2006, p. 6.

34. Jackson's 1984 campaign is reported to have been the first ever to have an official "gay desk" in his campaign headquarters.

35. Ronald Radosh, *Divided They Fell: The Demise of the Democratic Party, 1964– 1996* (New York: Free Press, 1996), p. 197.

36. Henry added: "It was the classic New Deal argument, movingly spoken. But Cuomo took it too far. He began to envision the unemployed, the dispossessed, the homeless sleeping on city streets. As he talked, he evoked a nation reminiscent of fifty years before, at the height of the Depression, an America remembered from his childhood. The scenes he described were distant from the lives of ordinary suburban Americans of 1984. The deprivation he so piteously depicted seemed all but impossible in a modern, prosperous welfare state" (*Visions of America*, pp. 185–86).

37. Ibid., p. 183.

38. Joshua Muravchik, "Why the Democrats Lost," *Commentary*, January 1985, p. 15.

39. Jeffrey H. Birnbaum, and Alan S. Murray, *Showdown at Gucci Gulch: Lawmakers, Lobbyists, and the Unlikely Triumph of Tax Reform* (New York: Random House, 1987), p. 35.

40. Germond and Witcover, *Wake Us When It's Over*, pp. 413, 409, 415.

41. This was not a new note for Mondale. In 1981 he commented that he "can't understand why the Soviets in the last few years have behaved as they have. Why did they have to build up all those arms? Why did they have to go into Afghanistan? Why can't they relax just a little bit about Eastern Europe? Why do they try every door to see if it is locked? Maybe we have made some mistakes with them."

42. Reagan's moving homage to the "boys of Pointe du Hoc" who charged the cliffs on D-Day was one of the rhetorical and emotional high points of his presidency. Mondale campaign aide William Galston recalls: "As President Reagan spoke, the camera showed grainy black and white military footage of the young, superbly conditioned soldiers as they made their way up the face of the cliff. As the

film ended, the television camera panned around to the hobbled, white-haired survivors of that day, seated in rows of chairs in front of the president. He gestured toward them and said, 'These are the boys of Pointe du Hoc.' As he uttered that sentence, tears welled up in my eyes. I was standing in a crowd in the Mondale campaign's press office. I looked around me and saw that everyone was crying. I realized then that we could not win the election because we were up against a man with an unerring ability to find and tap the emotional core of his country." Galston, unpublished conference paper, "The Meaning of American Citizenship: What We Can Learn from Disputes Over Naturalization," October 2008, on file with author.

43. Niskanen, *Reaganomics*, p. 284.
44. Cited in Jane Mayer and Doyle McManus, *Landslide: The Unmaking of a President, 1984–1988* (Boston: Houghton Mifflin, 1988), p. 4.
45. One dissenter from this approach on the campaign team was Ken Khachigian, who told Mayer and McManus: "I thought we needed to at least convey something of the sense that this election was an epic ideological contest. . . . But instead of engaging [Mondale], we were just waltzing through the campaign. It was like we were heading for a dignified coronation" (ibid., p. 15).
46. Cannon, *President Reagan: The Role of a Lifetime*, p. 535.
47. Burns, *The Lion and the Fox*, p. 314.
48. Reagan wrote in his diary: "Well the debate took place & I have to say I lost. I guess I'd crammed so hard on facts & figures in view of the absolutely dishonest things he's been saying in the campaign, I guess I just flattened out." Other witnesses recall Reagan being privately angry with himself for having "left his game in the locker room." "God I was awful," Reagan said.
49. See Cannon, *President Reagan: Role of a Lifetime*, p. 538.
50. Landy and Milkis, *Presidential Greatness*, p. 223.
51. Mahoney and Schramm, eds., *The 1984 Election*, pp. 270–71.
52. The six senators were: Lowell Weicker (Conn.), Robert Stafford (Vt.), Charles Mathias (Md.), Mark Hatfield (Ore.), Mark Andrews (N.D.), and John Chaffee (R.I.).
53. This account of the platform fight owes to the on-scene reporting of Douglas A. Jeffrey and Dennis A. Teti, in Mahoney and Schramm, eds., *The 1984 Election*, pp. 59–64.
54. It was around this time that Newt Gingrich is said to have first labeled Dole as "the tax collector for the welfare state."
55. The executive director of the platform committee in 1984 was a young Washington lawyer named John Bolton.
56. Michael J. Robinson, "The Media in Campaign '84," *Public Opinion*, February/March 1985, p. 45.
57. James Reston, "Reagan Beats the Press," *New York Times*, November 4, 1984.
58. Oberdorfer, *The Turn*, p. 90.

59. Cited in Henry, *Visions of America,* p. 259.

60. A few pollsters and analysts noted this aspect of the results. Lou Cannon quotes Jerry Alderman of ABC News remarking that Mondale "had bigger problems with male voters than Reagan had with females."

61. Mahoney and Schramm, eds., *The 1984 Election,* p. 270.

62. Quoted in the *Washington Monthly,* November 1986.

63. Smith in Duke, ed., *Beyond Reagan,* pp. 154–55.

64. Cited in Muravchik, "Why the Democrats Lost," p. 25.

65. Richard Reeves, *The Reagan Detour* (New York: Simon & Schuster, 1985), pp. 13, 14.

66. Cited in Peter Brown, *Minority Party: Why Democrats Face Defeat in 1992 and Beyond* (Washington, DC: Regnery, 1991), p. 64.

67. Cited in Radosh, *Divided They Fell,* p. 214.

68. Brown, *Minority Party,* p. 247.

INTERMISSION: REAGAN AT THE RANCH

1. *Daily Telegraph* (London), December 29, 1929.

2. Edwin Harper interview, August 13, 2002, Ronald Reagan Oral History Project, Miller Center for Public Affairs, University of Virginia, p. 61, http://www.miller center.virginia.edu.

3. Because of government ethics rules, Reagan could not accept several horses given by foreign leaders during his presidency. El Alamein was received before he took office in 1981.

4. John Barletta, author interview, October 23, 2001.

5. Peter Hannaford, ed., *Recollections of Reagan* (New York: Morrow, 1997), p. 43.

6. *Time,* August 24, 1981, p. 12.

7. Diary entry, February 12, 1984.

CHAPTER 9: THE FULCRUM: THREE DAYS IN GENEVA

1. Arkansas governor Bill Clinton delivered the Democratic response to Reagan's 1985 State of the Union speech and road-tested some themes that would play well for him seven years later: "Our critics have said we [Democrats] want too much government, while they want government off our backs. Well, we want the government off our backs, too; but we need it by our side."

2. Diary entry, February 5, 1985.

3. Quoted in Detlefsen, *Civil Rights Under Reagan,* p. 11.

4. Nowadays nearly every administration appointee engages outside counsel to help fill out disclosure forms.

5. Ledeen, "Meese Mess," *New Republic,* August 27, 1984, p. 16.

6. *New Republic,* November 19, 1984, p. 4.

7. Adam Wolfson, "The New McCarthyism: William Bradford Reynolds and the Politics of Character Assassination," *Policy Review,* Winter 1986, pp. 60–62.

8. Nor did the liberal wrath at Reagan's political momentum end with Reynolds and Meese. The Senate Government Affairs Committee, again with Mathias and Specter joining the Democrats, rejected Donald Devine's reappointment as director of the Office of Personnel Management. By one estimate, Devine's personnel reforms during Reagan's first term had reduced costs by $18 billion. Although Democrats seized upon management controversies, the real reasons were political. One Devine move that had angered liberals was cutting Planned Parenthood as a recipient of OPM's qualified employee charity drives.

9. Sample: "The past several decades of American life have been influenced by an aggressively secular liberalism often driven by an expansive egalitarian impulse. The result has been nothing less than an abandonment of many of the traditional political and social values the great majority of Americans still embrace. . . . Foremost among those values—indeed the common constitutional denominator of most of the social policies of this administration—is the principle of federalism."

10. Meese dilated this argument more fully in a 1986 speech at Tulane University: "The Supreme Court, then, is not the only interpreter of the Constitution. Each of the three coordinate branches of government created and empowered by the Constitution—the executive and legislative no less than the judicial—has a duty to interpret the Constitution in the performance of its official functions. In fact, every official takes an oath precisely to that effect."

11. *Wall Street Journal,* May 6, 1980.

12. Frank Goodnow, *Social Reform and the Constitution* (New York: Macmillan, 1991), p. 6.

13. Theodore Roosevelt, Special Message to Congress, December 8, 1908, *Messages and Papers of the Presidents,* U.S. Government Printing Office, p. 7594.

14. The best explanation and critique of Wilson's constitutionalism is R. J. Pestritto, *Woodrow Wilson and the Roots of Modern Liberalism* (Lanham, MD: Rowman & Littlefield, 2005). See also Paul Eidelberg, *A Discourse on Statesmanship: The Design and Transformation of the American Polity* (Urbana: University of Illinois Press, 1974), pp. 279–362. "The government of the United States was constructed upon the Whig theory of political dynamics," Wilson wrote in his most notorious formulation of the Constitution's defects, "which was a sort of unconscious copy of the Newtonian theory of the universe. In our own day, whenever we discuss the structure or development of anything, whether in nature or in society, we consciously or unconsciously follow Mr. Darwin. . . . The trouble with the [Newtonian] theory is that government is not a machine, but a living thing. . . . Living political constitutions must be Darwinian in structure and in practice. . . . All that Progressives ask or desire is to interpret the Constitution according to the Darwinian principle." About the separation of powers, Wilson

extended the evolutionary metaphor: "No living thing can have its organs offset against each other, as checks, and live."

15. See especially FDR's Commonwealth Club address of September 23, 1932.

16. Jonathan O'Neill, *Originalism in American Law and Politics: A Constitutional History* (Baltimore: Johns Hopkins University Press, 2005), p. 157.

17. Stephen G. Calabresi, ed., *Originalism: A Quarter-Century of Debate* (Washington, DC: Regnery, 2007), p. 7.

18. Meese aide Terry Eastland described the process for Supreme Court appointments as follows: "[Brad] Reynolds assembled a team of Justice Department officials (about twenty in all) who examined about twenty prospects, most of them sitting federal judges, many appointed by Reagan. The group reviewed everything known about the candidates. And it focused especially on judicial philosophy. Each candidate's published writings, including judicial opinions, and speeches were collected and placed in notebooks, and then read and assessed by three-person units assigned by Reynolds. . . . As the final leg of the process, Reynolds convened sessions during which the group debated the relative merits of the candidates." Terry Eastland, *Energy in the Executive,* p. 239.

19. Tribe later reversed his judgment of Siegan in correspondence with Siegan's widow. Mrs. Siegan wrote to Tribe in 2006 after discovering a cordial correspondence between Bernard and Tribe and asked: "In the 19 years since you penned your letter to Joe Biden, I wonder if you have reconsidered your comment regarding Bernie's competence as a constitutional lawyer and a serious scholar?" Tribe replied to Mrs. Siegan on September 21, 2006. "Please permit me to apologize to you here for the unnecessarily ad hominem character of what I wrote to Senator Biden in May of 1987. To help correct the record, if only posthumously, I am sending a copy of this letter to Senator Biden. Despite the differences in our perspectives, I came to think of Bernie, just as you write that he thought of me, as a colleague in the profession we both truly love and consider to be one of the noblest." http://www.govtrack.us/congress/record.xpd ?id=110-h20070712-46.

20. Leszek Kolakowski, "A General Theory of Sovietism," *Encounter,* May 1983, p. 21.

21. Good accounts include Oberdorfer, *The Turn;* Kengor, *The Crusader;* Schweizer, *Reagan's War;* Leebaert, *The Fifty-Year Wound,* esp. chs. 10 and 11; Matlock, *Reagan and Gorbachev;* Melvyn P. Leffler, *For the Soul of Mankind: The United States, the Soviet Union, and the Cold War* (New York: Hill and Wang, 2007).

22. Letter to Alan Brown, January 22, 1985, in *Reagan: A Life in Letters,* p. 413.

23. The entry in Anatoly Chernyaev's diary typifies the restiveness of the rising generation of party apparatchiks: "Chernenko died last night. Everyone saw it coming, sneered and sniggered at it, told anecdotes about how our leadership and propaganda, by demonstrating the complete vitality of the General Secretary on the screen, at elections and numerous statements, talks and interviews, made us

the 'land of fools.'" Chernyaev's translated diary for 1985 is available at: http://www.gwu.edu/~nsarchiv/NSAEBB/NSAEBB192/index.htm.

24. Chernyaev recorded in his diary (p. 41): "The Plenum took place at five o'clock. Everyone stood up to honor [Chernenko]; Gorbachev said (without excess) the appropriate words. But there was not a drop of sadness or distress in the air, as if to say, you suffered, poor bloke, for accidentally landing in a position inappropriate for you . . . and made a pause in the acceleration that Andropov had almost given the country. A suppressed 'satisfaction,' if not joy, then reigned in the atmosphere—as if to say, the uncertainty has come to an end, and the time has come for Russia to have a real leader."

25. David Pryce-Jones, *The War That Never Was: The Fall of the Soviet Empire, 1985–1991* (London: Weidenfeld & Nicolson, 1995), p. 101.

26. Matlock, *Reagan and Gorbachev*, p. 110.

27. Quoted in Archie Brown, *Seven Years That Changed the World: Perestroika in Perspective* (Oxford: Oxford University Press, 2007), pp. 60–61.

28. Cited in Moshe Lewin, *The Gorbachev Phenomenon: A Historical Interpretation* (Berkeley: University of California Press, 1988), p. 120.

29. Chernyaev's translated diary. See also Chernyaev's *My Six Years with Gorbachev*, trans. and ed. Robert English and Elizabeth Tucker (University Park: Pennsylvania State University Press, 2000).

30. As Chernyaev explained in his diary: "[Gorbachev] did this not because they were not ready to serve the new 'first,' the more so not because of some ideological reasons; but by reason of their worthlessness, incompetence, ignorance, their 'accidental' assignment to high posts (the products of Brezhnev's, Chernenko's favoritism); or because they discredited themselves glaringly at their posts, giving rise to well deserved contempt in their circles and in society."

31. Pipes, "Gorbachev's Russia: Breakdown or Crackdown?" *Commentary*, March 1990, p. 18.

32. Shultz, *Turmoil and Triumph*, pp. 587–91. Shultz reprised this argument at greater length to Foreign Minister Shevardnadze in April 1987 (ibid., pp. 888–89). Shevardnadze listened without comment but told Shultz in 1989 that he had gone over Shultz's argument with Gorbachev and that "[w]hat you said had a profound impact." On still a third such occasion, Gorbachev told Shultz, "We should have more meetings like this."

33. Brown, *Seven Years That Changed the World*, pp. 242, 263.

34. Most accounts suggest Gromyko wanted to be elevated to the largely ceremonial post of president as a sort of emeritus reward for a long career. Though Gromyko remained involved in Soviet-American diplomacy for several more months, Shultz's impression was that Gorbachev had reduced Gromyko to being "an errand boy."

35. Cited in Richard Pipes, *Vixi*, p. 161. The *Washington Post*'s deputy editorial page editor, Stephen Rosenfeld, echoed this sentiment in the Spring 1986 issue of

Foreign Affairs: "Now the possibility exists that Washington, in a heady mood, could push too hard for Soviet tolerance in the 1980s. A new leader in the Kremlin, one may speculate, could have more to prove on this front."

36. Kagan, *A Twilight Struggle*, p. 361.

37. See ibid., pp. 318–36.

38. Before the House Foreign Affairs Committee on February 19, Shultz said: "I believe very strongly that we in the democracies simply cannot put up with a 'Brezhnev doctrine.' As you know, the Brezhnev doctrine, in effect, states that once a country has been taken into the socialist camp, it never can leave. Or, to put it more colloquially, under the Brezhnev doctrine, what's mine is mine, and what's yours is up for grabs. I don't see any reason why we should put up with that."

39. Kagan, *A Twilight Struggle*, p. 383.

40. In conversation with this author Deaver selected Bitburg as the single biggest mistake of his entire service to Reagan.

41. "I'm worried about Nancy," Reagan wrote in his diary on April 28, a week before the trip. "She's uptight about the situation and nothing I say can wind her down."

42. Diary entries, April 5 and April 22.

43. Reagan's only support came from Nixon and Kissinger, both of whom called Reagan to urge that he not back down.

44. George Shultz records in his memoir (*Turmoil and Triumph*, p. 663) that "the NSC staff produced a 'time line' of steps . . . leading eventually to 'declaring war on terrorism' "—something Shultz had been advocating since 1982.

45. The CIA "burn notice" said that Ghorbanifar "should be regarded as an intelligence fabricator and a nuisance." A redacted version of the CIA's burn notice can be found at http://www.gwu.edu/~nsarchiv/NSAEBB/NSAEBB210/12-Ghorbanifar%20Fabricator%207-25-84%20(IC%2000505).pdf.

46. The best account of Ghorbanifar is found in Ledeen, *Perilous Statecraft*, pp. 104–27.

47. Theodore Draper's critical account of the whole affair, *A Very Thin Line*, comments about this period: "The record keeping of this affair was often so deficient or nonexistent that even at key moments we have only the memories of participants to fall back on. These memories can differ so much that one can almost believe that they were present at different meetings" (p. 168).

48. Bob Woodward, *Veil: The Secret Wars of the CIA, 1981–1987* (New York: Simon & Schuster, 1987), p. 416.

49. Ledeen, *Perilous Statecraft*, p. 127.

50. The possible manifestation of Reagan's Alzheimer's disease during his presidency will always be a matter of debate. Reagan was poor at remembering names as far back as his governorship. There is one curious entry in his diary from August 26, 1986, that is worth noting: "Coming down the coast in the

helicopter I watched for landmarks I remembered and was a little upset when I could locate them & then couldn't remember their names—Topanga Canyon for example."

51. *Nicomachean Ethics,* 1115b.

52. There is good reason to suppose that this description of the extra-legal "Enterprise" was another exaggeration or fabrication of North's and that in fact CIA director William Casey had in mind an unorthodox but strictly legal operation unencumbered by the CIA's bureaucracy. See Draper, *A Very Thin Line,* pp. 530–34.

53. The congressional investigation concluded that only about 20 percent of the privately raised funds reached the contras.

54. Richard Sobel, "Contra Aid Fundamentals: Exploring the Intricacies and the Issues," *Political Science Quarterly* 110, 2 (1995): p. 290.

55. Joel Brinkley, "Nicaragua Rebels Getting Advice from White House on Operations," *New York Times,* August 8, 1985, p. A1.

56. Joanne Omang, "McFarlane Aide Facilitates Policy: Marine Officer Nurtures Connections with Contras, Conservatives," *Washington Post,* August 11, 1985, p. A1.

57. Abbas made his way eventually to Iraq, where he was captured by U.S. forces in 2003. He died in captivity a year later.

58. The CIA subsequently prepared a retroactive finding covering only its own activities.

59. At the time of Stalin's death in 1953, Churchill, who is thought to have originated the use of the term *summit,* was eager for President Eisenhower to seek a summit with Stalin's successors, who Churchill thought might be uncertain and willing to approach East-West problems afresh. Eisenhower, for his own reasons, was not interested and brushed off Churchill. Historian John Lukacs has written recently that "perhaps a great chance may have been missed fifty years ago, when Churchill, as so often during his life, was willing to act on his own vision and go against the tide, and when he was right and his opponents were wrong." See John Lukacs, "Blood, Sweat, and Fears," *New Republic,* January 13, 2003, p. 37.

60. A CIA/NSC memo to Reagan conveyed the same advice: "His concern to demonstrate equality may prompt him at times to take an aggressive tack so as not to appear on the defensive over such issues as human rights and the Soviet role in regional disputes."

61. Reagan's memo is discussed at length in Matlock, *Reagan and Gorbachev,* pp. 150–54.

62. Yakovlev's memo, "About Reagan," March 12, 1985, can be found at http://www.gwu.edu/~nsarchiv/NSAEBB/NSAEBB168/yakovlev01.pdf.

63. Ken Adelman, Oral History, Miller Center, University of Virginia (http://millercenter.virginia.edu/programs/poh/reagan/index.html), p. 52.

64. Reagan had written in his diary before the summit: "Gorbachev is adamant that we must cave in on SDI. Well, this will be a case of an irresistible force meeting an immovable object."

65. *National Review,* December 31, 1985, p. 16.

66. Matlock, *Reagan and Gorbachev,* p. 168. Matlock mused: "Gorbachev could have molded Reagan's position without making commitments himself just by asking a few questions. When Reagan spoke of sharing, he could have asked what specific guarantees Reagan was willing to undertake and how he would have made them enforceable. He could have asked for more details on 'open laboratories' and whether the idea should be applied to offensive weapons research and development as well. He might have asked whether Reagan would accept a joint SDI program. My guess is that, in many of these areas, Reagan would have been willing to make some far-reaching commitments in order to gain Gorbachev's acquiescence to SDI research."

67. Letter to Mrs. William Loeb, November 25, 1985, in *Reagan: A Life in Letters,* p. 414.

68. Letter to Alan Brown, November 25, 1985, and letter to Elsa Sandstrom, in *Reagan: A Life in Letters,* pp. 414–15.

69. Letter to Suzanne Massie, February 10, 1986, in *Reagan: A Life in Letters,* p. 417.

CHAPTER 10: I LIFT UP MY LAMP: THE ROAD TO REYKJAVIK

1. Lance Morrow, "Yankee Doodle Magic," *Time,* July 7, 1986.

2. "Life After OPEC," *BusinessWeek,* December 23, 1985, p. 24.

3. Thane Gustafson, cited in Stephen Kotkin, *Armageddon Averted: The Soviet Collapse, 1970–2000* (Oxford University Press, 2001), p. 17.

4. Between 1955 and 1980 real short-term interest rates averaged about 1.5 percent; between 1980 and 1988, real short-term interest rates ranged from 5.6 percent (1981) to 2.8 percent (1987). (Source: Margaret M. Blair, ed., *The Deal Decade: What Takeovers and Leveraged Buyouts Mean for Corporate Governance* [Washington, DC: Brookings Institution, 1993], Table 5–6, p. 170.)

5. Robert M. Collins, *Transforming America: Politics and Culture During the Reagan Years* (New York: Columbia University Press, 2007), p. 110.

6. William F. Long and David J. Ravenscraft, "Decade of Debt: Lessons from the LBOs in the 1980s," in Blair, ed., *The Deal Decade,* p. 222.

7. John Greenwald, "Let's Make a Deal," *Time,* December 23, 1985, p. 42.

8. Hedrick Smith, *The Power Game: How Washington Works* (New York: Random House, 1988), p. 495.

9. John Ehrman, *The Eighties: America in the Age of Reagan* (New Haven: Yale University Press, 2005), p. 131.

10. Rostenkowski would later go to prison for fifteen months on charges of mail fraud after personal corruption on a wide scale came to light.

11. Roberts, "The Seduction of the Supply-Siders," *National Review,* June 6, 1986, pp. 41–42.

12. Birnbaum and Murray say House Republicans simply made a mistake, but one wonders whether this is plausible.

13. Niskanen, *Reaganomics,* p. 99.

14. Quoted in *National Review,* July 18, 1986, p. 12.

15. See especially Paul Lettow's account of staff resistance to Reagan's nuclear abolitionism in *Ronald Reagan and His Quest to Abolish Nuclear Weapons,* pp. 190–96.

16. Kenneth L. Adelman, *The Great Universal Embrace: A Skeptic's Guide to the Politics of Disarmament* (New York: Simon & Schuster, 1989), p. 114.

17. A typical diary entry on this problem is from June 3, 1986: "A brief NSC meeting—in which we talked about yesterday's N.S.P.G. [National Security Planning Group] meeting on leaks & how our account of the entire meeting was on the front page of today's Wash. Post."

18. The ACDA report identified nine specific Soviet violations of SALT II.

19. "Half Right and All Wrong on SALT," *New York Times,* June 1, 1986, Sec. 4, p. 24.

20. "The Reagan Arms Strategy," *Chicago Tribune,* June 23, 1986, p. 12.

21. The Soviets ultimately admitted that the Krasnoyarsk radar violated the ABM Treaty.

22. Senator Sam Nunn (D-Ga.), chairman of the Senate Armed Services Committee, held hearings and issued a report disputing the Reagan administration's broad interpretation of the ABM Treaty. A number of Republican senators endorsed Nunn's position, largely out of solicitude for the prerogative of the Senate, as the treaty-ratifying body, to have a say in the interpretation of treaties.

23. Wolf quoted in *New York Times,* November 12, 2006, Sec. 4, p. 3.

24. A few contemporary observers discerned that Gorbachev was up to something, and noted also Yeltsin's strong stands. Archie Brown wrote in *Foreign Affairs* shortly after: "The evidence available on Gorbachev's position suggests not only that he takes seriously the deficiencies of the Soviet economy, but also that he does not believe that tinkering with the economic mechanism will be enough." A month after the Party Congress, Gorbachev told the workers of the Volga Car Works: "Can you manage an economy which runs into trillions of rubles from Moscow? It is absurd, comrades. Incidentally, it is in this—in the fact that we have attempted to manage everything from Moscow up until very recently—that our common and main mistake lies." ("Change in the Soviet Union," *Foreign Affairs,* Summer 1986, pp. 1055–56.)

25. Also giving a reformist speech at the Twenty-seventh Party Congress was the newest candidate for full Politburo membership, Boris Yeltsin. Yeltsin provoked the insiders with an attack on special privileges. Yeltsin asked the pregnant question: "Why, Congress after Congress, do we deal with the same problems over and over again?"

26. Cited in Odom, *The Collapse of the Soviet Military*, p. 96; Robert D. English, "The Road(s) Not Taken: Causality and Contingency in Analysis of the Cold War's End," in William C. Wohlforth, ed., *Cold War Endgame* (University Park: Pennsylvania State University Press, 2003), p. 260.

27. English, "The Road(s) Not Taken," p. 258.

28. Chernyaev diary entry, February 2, 1986.

29. Gates, *In the Shadows*, p. 380.

30. The split generally fell out between political appointees, who favored supplying Stingers, versus career bureaucrats, who opposed the idea. See Marin Strmecki, "The Stinger Finds a Home," *American Spectator*, November 1987, pp. 19–21.

31. The news statement in its entirety read: "An accident has occurred at the Chernobyl Nuclear Power Plant as one of the reactors was damaged. Measures are being taken to eliminate the consequences of the accident. Aid is being given to those affected. A government commission has been set up."

32. See Nicholas Daniloff's account, *Of Spies and Spokesmen: My Life as a Cold War Correspondent* (Columbia: University of Missouri Press, 2008), p. 344.

33. Felicity Barringer, "Kiev Journal: In Chernobyl's Zone, Streets Are Still Vacuumed," *New York Times*, December 15, 1986.

34. "Chernobyl: Poverty and Stress Pose 'Bigger Threat' than Radiation," *Nature*, September 5, 2005. The UN report concluded that about four thousand people remained at risk from the long-term effects of radiation exposure; this is far less than the tens of thousands of deaths predicted at the time.

35. http://www.project-syndicate.org/commentary/ gorbachev3/English.

36. Christian Neef, "Diary of a Collapsing Superpower," *Der Spiegel*, November 22, 2006.

37. Peter Rutland, "Sovietology: Notes for a Post-Mortem," *National Interest*, Spring 1993.

38. The matter of Kaddafi was not far removed from U.S.-Soviet relations. Reagan took up the issue in his February letter to Gorbachev: "And I must say that some recent actions by your government are most discouraging. What are we to make of your sharply increased military support of a local dictator who has declared a war of terrorism against much of the rest of the world, and against the United States in particular? . . . And more importantly, are we to conclude that the Soviet Union is so reckless in seeking to extend its influence in the world that it will place its prestige (and even the lives of some of its citizens) at the mercy of a mentally unbalanced local despot?"

39. Evidence found in East German secret police (Stasi) files following German reunification in 1991 revealed full East German knowledge of the bombing plot and enabled the successful prosecution in 1997 of five people for their roles in the bombing.

40. Weinberger oral history, p. 27.

41. The raid had to be conducted at night because the U.S. desire to minimize civil-

ian casualties meant that warplanes had to come in very low, exposing them to antiaircraft fire. For a detailed account of the planning and execution of the raid, see Joseph T. Stanik, *El Dorado Canyon: Reagan's Undeclared War with Qaddafi* (Annapolis, MD: Naval Institute Press, 2003).

42. Anthony Lewis, "A Real Evil," *New York Times*, April 17, 1986, p. A31. Within days Lewis began to have second thoughts and became more critical of the raid.

43. Stanik, *El Dorado Canyon*, p. 212.

44. Quotations from Anatoly Chernyaev's notes of Politburo and Reykjavik advisory group preparation meetings, September 22, October 4, and October 8, 1986, available from the National Security Archive, http://www.gwu.edu/~nsarchiv/NSAEBB/NSAEBB203/index.htm.

45. *Human Events* (September 20, 1986): "What particularly concerns conservative foreign policy analysts about the way the Administration is handling the Daniloff affair is that the President now looks as if he's overly eager to go to another summit with Mikhail Gorbachev, a poor posture to be in when dealing with the Kremlin."

46. Nofziger in Strober and Strober, eds., *Reagan*, p. 347.

47. After it was all over, a State Department evaluation confessed, "Reykjavik demonstrated once again how poor we are at guessing what the Soviets will do."

48. The Soviet transcript of the Reykjavik summit, declassified and released in 1993, is more complete than the American transcript, and is available at http://www.gwu.edu/~nsarchiv/NSAEBB/NSAEBB203/index.htm. There are numerous first- and secondhand accounts and analyses of the Reykjavik summit worth consulting, including Shultz, *Turmoil and Triumph*, pp. 751–80; Matlock, *Reagan and Gorbachev*, pp. 215–50; Oberdorfer, *The Turn*, pp. 174–209; Talbott, *Master of the Game* (New York: Knopf, 1988), pp. 314–26; Winik, *On the Brink*, pp. 500–20; Adelman, *The Great Universal Embrace*, pp. 19–88; FitzGerald, *Way Out There in the Blue*, pp. 314–69; Lettow, *Ronald Reagan and His Quest to Abolish Nuclear Weapons*, pp. 217–29.

49. Cited in English, "The Road(s) Not Taken," p. 262.

50. Paul Kengor discusses the nature and evidence of this episode in *Crusader*, pp. 210–11.

51. In this regard see especially Angelo Codevilla, "How SDI Is Being Undone from Within," *Commentary*, May 1986, pp. 21–29.

52. When the Soviets later claimed in Geneva not to have agreed to follow-up talks on sublimits, Nitze called the Soviet lead negotiator "a damn liar." "There are times when diplomatic language is simply not adequate," Nitze wrote. "This was one of those times."

53. These quotations come from the more detailed Soviet transcript but in this case are likely a mistranslation, as Reagan was surely referring to his leaving office in 1988 as a result of the regular election cycle.

54. Matlock, *Reagan and Gorbachev*, pp. 237–38.

55. Thatcher, *Downing Street Years,* p. 472.

56. Geoffrey Smith offers a complete account of Thatcher's November 1986 mission to Washington in *Reagan and Thatcher* (New York: W. W. Norton, 1991), pp. 214–26.

57. Chernyaev's diary, December 15, 1986.

58. James Schlesinger, "Reykjavik and Revelations: A Turn of the Tide?" *Foreign Affairs,* 1986 year-end special edition, "America and the World."

59. Aaron Wildavsky, *The Beleaguered Presidency* (New Brunswick, NJ: Transaction, 1991), p. 229.

60. Talbott, *Master of the Game,* p. 205.

61. Strober and Strober, *Reagan,* p. 356.

62. Chernyaev, *My Six Years with Gorbachev,* p. 85.

63. Cited in English, "The Road(s) Not Taken," p. 262.

64. See Raymond Garthoff, *The Great Transition* (Washington, DC: Brookings Institution Press, 1994), p. 289, n. 103; William C. Wohlforth, ed., *Witnesses to the End of the Cold War,* p. 311 n. 2.

65. Richard Rhodes, *Arsenals of Folly: The Making of the Nuclear Arms Race* (New York: Knopf, 2007), p. 272.

66. The Soviets would reiterate their "flexibility" on SDI testing "outside the laboratory" in the spring of 1987 in a back-channel communication through Senator Ted Kennedy. See Shultz, *Turmoil and Triumph,* pp. 884–85.

67. Wildavsky, *The Beleaguered Presidency,* p. 233.

CHAPTER 11: "TEMPEST-TOST": THE IRAN-CONTRA CLIMAX

1. Telling this complicated story in its fullness fills several large single volumes, to which curious readers are advised to refer. See, e.g., Theodore Draper, *A Very Thin Line* (New York: Simon & Schuster, 1991); Michael Ledeen, *Perilous Statecraft: An Insider's Account of the Iran-Contra Scandal* (New York: Scribner's, 1988); Peter J. Wallison, *Ronald Reagan: The Power of Conviction and the Success of His Presidency* (Boulder, CO: Westview, 2003), chs. 7–9; George Shultz, *Turmoil and Triumph,* chs. 37–39, 42; David M. Abshire, *Saving the Reagan Presidency* (College Station: Texas A&M University Press, 2005); *Report of the Congressional Committees Investigating the Iran-Contra Affair* (Washington, DC: U.S. Government Printing Office, 1987); and the Tower Commission Report.

2. Kagan, *A Twilight Struggle,* p. 391.

3. Ibid., p. 412.

4. Doyle McManus, "Some Democrats Back Reagan; Liberals Split on Whether to Support Aid for Contras," *Los Angeles Times,* December 22, 1985.

5. Robert Leiken, "Nicaragua's Untold Stories," *New Republic,* October 8, 1984.

6. Paul Berman, "Nicaragua 1986: Notes on the Sandinista Revolution," *Mother Jones,* December 1986, pp. 23, 27.

7. McManus, "Some Democrats Back Reagan."

8. Leiken, "Nicaragua's Untold Stories."

9. Farrell, *Tip O'Neill*, p. 671.

10. Quoted in Kagan, *A Twilight Struggle*, p. 461.

11. *New Republic*, April 11, 1986, p. 12.

12. "The Case for the Contras," *New Republic*, March 24, 1986.

13. For example, see Reagan's January 10, 1986, diary entry: "The answer is 'yes' we must come to their aid. This does not mean however use of Am[erican] troops."

14. The diversion memo of April 4, 1986 can be found at http://www.gwu.edu/~nsarchiv/NSAEBB/NSAEBB210/16-Diversion%20Memo%204-4-86%20(IC%2002614).pdf.

15. Terry Eastland, then a top aide to Attorney General Meese, later reflected critically on the decision not to invoke executive privilege: "Reagan also failed to defend the presidential office when he complied with the congressional request, unprecedented in its reach, for NSC and even presidential records of matters not involving allegations of executive malfeasance. Reagan refused to assert executive privilege—the power of a President to withhold certain information from Congress—thus setting an unfortunate precedent for the future" (*Energy in the Executive*, [New York: Free Press, 1992], p. 227). Perhaps, but as then–White House counsel Peter Wallison perceived, "[It] is appropriate to waive the privilege—as many presidents have done—when invoking it would do more harm to the presidency, or the president then in office, than waiving it. . . . I foresaw a long series of investigations looming before us, and believed that the President would be hurt far more by an appearance that he was covering up wrongdoing than by disclosure of any of the lapses that may have occurred" (Wallison, *Ronald Reagan*, p. 181).

16. Regan, *For the Record*, p. 50.

17. See Neil Livingstone, "What Ollie North Told Me Before He Took the Fifth," *National Review*, January 30, 1987. "Far from constituting ransom to achieve the freedom of the American hostages," Livingstone wrote of what North told him on November 14, "the military goods provided Iran were part of a rapprochement process designed to deliver Iran from the clutches of the Soviet Union and to block the Soviet drive to the Persian Gulf." William F. Buckley, a long-ago veteran of the spy trade, may have smelled a rat. In an editorial note, Buckley said that *National Review* could not verify the details of the story and admitted the possibility that "North was having his breakfast guest on: that Ollie North was romancing, dealing in surrealisms, testing hypotheses." For the kidnapping angle, see Eric Alterman, "Inside Ollie's Mind," *New Republic*, February 16, 1987, p. 14.

18. Peter J. Wallison, *Ronald Reagan: The Power of Conviction and the Success of His Presidency* (Boulder, CO: Westview Press, 2003), p. 200.

19. Michael Kinsley, "The Case for Glee," *New Republic*, December 22, 1986.

20. Greg Grandlin, "Still Dancing to Ollie's Tune," http://www.tomdispatch.com (October 17, 2006).

21. Wallison, *Ronald Reagan*, p. 169. As Wallison observes: "It violated a management principle and a style of governing that he considered central to his success. It took me a while to recognize this, and I doubt that many others have yet understood it. For many people, and most politicians, it may not be credible to say that they willingly absorbed punishment because of their adherence to something so inconsequential as a management principle, but Ronald Reagan was not like most people or virtually any other politician."

22. Abshire, *Saving the Reagan Presidency*, p. 89.

23. Privately Reagan still resisted this view, telling journalist Fred Barnes in an interview a few months later, "It was not trading arms for hostages." Barnes's account continued: "He was merely trying to influence the government that would succeed the man he called 'the Khomeini.' I glanced at Fitzwater and Griscom as Reagan spoke. They had that look of terror I'd seen on the face of Reagan aides at press conferences" ("Covering the Gipper," *Weekly Standard*, February 5, 2001).

24. "Presidents Have a History of Unilateral Moves," *Wall Street Journal*, January 15, 1987.

25. See, e.g., *Federalist* 70, where Alexander Hamilton reviewed the arguments against a plural executive (such as a council) and sharing power with the legislative branch.

26. Another irony to note in passing: the omnibus spending bills to which the Boland Amendments were attached were themselves irresponsible acts on the part of Congress, as they violated the terms of the Budget Act of 1974 that required thirteen separate appropriation bills.

27. The most extensive treatment of this issue is Harvey C. Mansfield Jr., *Taming the Prince: The Ambivalence of Modern Executive Power* (New York: Free Press, 1989).

28. John Locke, *Second Treatise of Government*, Chapter XIV ("Of Prerogative"), paras. 159, 160.

29. Iran-Contra was not the only such controversy over Reagan's use of presidential foreign policy power going on at the time. In response to increasing Iranian harassment of oil shipping in the Persian Gulf, in May 1987 the United States embarked upon a scheme in which Kuwaiti oil tankers sailed under the U.S. flag and were thus extended the protection of the U.S. Navy. The navy conducted minesweeping operations and engaged Iranian gunboats in a number of minor skirmishes, usually to the detriment of the Iranians. The operation was not without significant battlefield risk, however. In May an Iraqi warplane mistakenly fired a missile at the USS *Stark,* a navy frigate, killing thirty-seven American sailors. (Iraq promptly apologized, claiming it had intended to strike an Iranian

target, though the *Stark* had twice identified itself to the Iraqis as a U.S. warship. Iraq later paid $27 million in restitution.) As had been the case with the Grenada invasion, the 1982–84 peacekeeping excursion to Lebanon, and the Libya bombing raid of 1986, Congress wanted Reagan to invoke the notification and consultation requirements of the War Powers Resolution as well as starting the War Powers Resolution's sixty-day clock, which mandated either an affirmative congressional vote or the withdrawal of U.S. forces. Reagan resisted until September, at which time he invoked not the War Powers Resolution but Article 51 (the self-defense clause) of the United Nations Charter (as he had done in the Libya air raid), pursuant to "my constitutional authority with respect to the conduct of foreign affairs and as Commander-in-Chief." Congress backed down and did not pursue the matter further. Presidents of both parties have insisted the War Powers Act is unconstitutional, but so far no chief executive has sought a formal legal challenge to the statute. (See Fisher, *Presidential War Power,* pp. 144–45.)

30. There are numerous other examples of significant constitutional controversy over the propriety of executive acts, starting with Andrew Jackson and including Woodrow Wilson, Harry Truman, Dwight Eisenhower, and of course Richard Nixon and George W. Bush.

31. Jefferson letter to J. B. Colvin, September 20, 1810 (http://www.Teaching AmericanHistory.org/library/index.asp?document-1916). Lincoln offered a restatement of Jefferson's comment with his justification for the suspension of habeas corpus in 1861: "Are all the laws but one to go unexecuted, and the government go to pieces? Even in such a case, would not the official oath be broken if the government should be overthrown, when it was believed that disregarding a single law would tend to preserve it?" (http://www.TeachingAmerican History.org/library/index.asp?document-1063).

32. Locke, *Second Treatise of Government,* para. 165.

33. Fisher, *Presidential War Power,* p. 182.

34. Ledeen, *Perilous Statecraft,* p. 281.

35. Arthur Liman didn't do much better than Nields. His first question to North when he got his turn to ask questions on the third day of North's testimony was: "Colonel, is it fair to say that November 25, 1986 [the day Reagan fired North from the NSC], was one of the worst days of your life?" North: "I will tell you honestly, counsel, that I have had many worse days than that. Most of those days were when young Marines died."

36. There were some striking echoes of that famous long-ago hearing, including a misleading composite photo of Reagan's signature next to the text of the 1984 Boland Amendment. In fact Boland had been a short passage buried in an eight-hundred-page continuing resolution. Republicans pounced on this legerdemain and embarrassed Democratic counsel Liman.

37. William S. Cohen and George J. Mitchell, *Men of Zeal: A Candid Inside Story of the Iran-Contra Hearings* (New York: Viking, 1988), p. 165.

38. Suzanne Garment, *Scandal: The Culture of Mistrust in American Politics* (New York: Random House, 1991), p. 209.

39. Of the twenty-six members of the joint committee, seventeen had voted in favor of the 1986 Contra aid package.

40. Gephardt cited in *Human Events*, August 1, 1987, p. 639.

41. I am indebted for this interpretation to Dennis Teti's excellent account, "The Coup That Failed: An Insider's Account of the Iran/Contra Hearings," *Policy Review*, Fall 1987, pp. 24–31.

42. The investigating committees also looked but did not find any corroborating evidence of the widely alleged U.S.-condoned drug trafficking by the Contras.

43. Martin Anderson openly doubted North's account and speculated that North might have skimmed money from the process. See Anderson's *Revolution: The Reagan Legacy*, ch. 31, "The Mystery of the Missing Money (1990)."

44. Richard Nixon wrote to Reagan the day after the speech: *"The speech last night was one of your best,"* Nixon wrote with emphasis. "You sounded and looked strong. You gave the lie to the crap about your being over-the-hill, discouraged, etc. If I could be permitted one word of advice: Don't *ever* comment on the Iran-Contra matter again."

45. Robert Kagan offers an excellent summary of Contra strategy and battlefield successes in 1987 in *A Twilight Struggle*, pp. 523–26.

46. "Will the U.S. Need to Invade Nicaragua?" *Human Events*, November 15, 1986.

47. Kagan, *A Twilight Struggle*, p. 503.

48. Shultz, *Turmoil and Triumph*, p. 957.

49. Quoted in Kagan, *A Twilight Struggle*, p. 549.

50. Lindsey Gruson, "For Contras in One Area, Growing Civilian Support," *New York Times*, November 5, 1987, p. A1.

51. Kagan, *A Twilight Struggle*, p. 551.

52. Ibid., p. 611.

CHAPTER 12: CRASH

1. Biden's early commitment drew criticism from a surprising source—Mario Cuomo: "It's the worst kind of irony to condemn Bork on the grounds that he's not open-minded about the law when you yourself haven't waited for the hearings to take place."

2. The seemingly inexorable politicization of so many civic organizations contributed to the origin of O'Sullivan's First Law, coined by *National Review* editor John O'Sullivan in the early 1990s: "Any institution or organization that is not explicitly right-wing will become explicitly left-wing over time."

3. "The Compassion Industry Against Bork," *Washington Post*, October 1, 1987.

4. When President Carter nominated Abner Mikva to an appeals court in 1979, Biden rebuffed conservative complaints about Mikva's activist liberal philosophy: "I think that the advice and consent responsibility of the Senate does not

permit us to deprive the President of the United States from being able to appoint that person or persons who have a particular point of view unless it can be shown that their temperament does not fit the job." Ted Kennedy said on the Senate floor: "If strong political views were a disqualifying factor from serving on the federal bench, then all of us here today—and every man and woman who has ever served in either house of Congress, or held political office—would be disqualified." Kennedy had made a similar argument in 1967 in defense of Thurgood Marshall's appointment to the Supreme Court.

5. The irony of Tribe's outspoken opposition was surely not lost on him. He became the "Bork of the Left," and as such would be as unconfirmable as Bork were he ever to be nominated to the Supreme Court.

6. Suzanne Garment, "The War Against Robert H. Bork," *Commentary,* January 1988, p. 26.

7. Richard Vigilante, "Who's Afraid of Robert Bork?" *National Review,* August 28, 1987, p. 25.

8. Cited in Ethan Bronner, *Battle for Justice: How the Bork Nomination Shook America* (New York: Union Square Press, 2007 [originally published 1989]), p. 174.

9. Wildavsky, *The Rise of Radical Egalitarianism,* p. 209.

10. Robert H. Bork, *The Tempting of America: The Political Seduction of the Law* (New York: Free Press, 1989), p. 19.

11. What Bork said of *Bowers v. Hardwick* is precisely what the Supreme Court subsequently decided, on the very logic Bork noted, in *Lawrence v. Texas* (2003).

12. The Ninth Amendment is not the only clause that requires republican imagination to interpret; for example, there is Article IV, Section 4: "The United States shall guarantee to every State in this Union a Republican Form of Government."

13. See Harry V. Jaffa, *Storm Over the Constitution* (Lanham, MD: Lexington Books, 1999); Hadley Arkes, *Beyond the Constitution* (Princeton: Princeton University Press, 1992).

14. *National Review,* September 25, 1987, pp. 18–19.

15. *Bork* entered dictionaries with the definition "to deny Senate confirmation of a nominee, especially for a U.S. Supreme Court or federal judgeship, by use of sustained public disparagement" (*Encarta World English Dictionary*).

16. One direct-mail consultant told the *Wall Street Journal* that he had five anti-Bork client organizations. More than thirty organizations submitted requests to testify against Bork.

17. Reagan initially shrugged off Ginsburg's pot smoking, writing in his diary, "I don't see any reason why I should withdraw his name." But as support for Ginsburg collapsed on Capitol Hill, Reagan relented.

18. Jan Crawford Greenburg, *Supreme Conflict: The Inside Story of the Struggle for Control of the United States Supreme Court* (New York: Penguin Press, 2007), pp. 52–53.

19. Though it bears noting these rates were down from their historic highs of over 16 percent (short) and 13.4 percent (long) in 1981.

20. Reagan's four appointees were Preston Martin, Martha Seger, Wayne Angell, and Manuel Johnson.

21. This was a new record in nominal dollars, but represented a slight decline in its proportion to GDP, which had been 6.3 percent in 1983 and 5.4 percent in 1985.

22. *American Banker* magazine, however, noted in February 1987: "A major improvement in the U.S. foreign trade deficit now appears to be well under way."

23. Cited in Matt Rees, "The Hunt for Black October," *The American,* September/October 2007, p. 48.

24. Quoted in Landon Thomas, "The Man Who Won as Others Lost," *New York Times,* October 13, 2007, p. B1.

25. Thomas E. Ricks, "Ruder Says Trading Halt Is a Way to Ease Volatility Caused by Program Trading," *Wall Street Journal,* October 7, 1987.

26. James B. Stewart and Daniel Hertzberg, "Terrible Tuesday: How the Stock Market Almost Disintegrated," *Wall Street Journal,* November 20, 1987, p. A1.

27. Among the companies publicly announcing buybacks on the twentieth were Shearson Lehman Brothers, Merrill Lynch, Citicorp, Honeywell, ITT, four of the regional Bell telephone companies, and U.S. Steel.

28. Paul Craig Roberts, "Monetary Policy Caused the Crash—Too Tight Already," *Wall Street Journal,* October 22, 1987.

29. Warren Brookes, "Takeover Boom Spurs Competitiveness," *Detroit News,* December 14, 1987.

30. Gerald Seib and Ellen Hume, "Administration Seems Paralyzed in Wake of Bork Fight," *Wall Street Journal,* October 16, 1987, p. 1.

31. Lance Morrow, "America's Agenda After Reagan," *Time,* March 30, 1987, p. 28.

32. *Economist,* September 12, 1987, p. 11.

33. Paul Kennedy, *The Rise and Fall of the Great Powers: Economic Change and Military Conflict from 1500 to 2000* (New York: Random House, 1987).

34. Alexei Arbatov, "What Lesson's Learned?" in Kiron K. Skinner, ed., *Turning Points in Ending the Cold War* (Palo Alto, CA: Hoover Institution Press, 1988), p. 47.

35. *Human Events,* November 28, 1987.

36. James Goldsmith, "America, You Falter," *Wall Street Journal,* November 12, 1987.

37. It was actually his second veto; he had vetoed the identical bill in November 1986, but as the lame duck Congress didn't have time to cast an override vote, the new Congress passed the identical bill as its first order of business in January 1987.

38. There was also a regulatory component to the act for nonpoint-source water

pollution that Reagan found objectionable. "This new program threatens to become the ultimate whip hand for Federal regulators," Reagan said in his veto message.

39. *Human Events*, September 5, 1987. Quote: "If the President continues to embrace Baker's advice, he may yet end his eight years in office as the man who not only permitted the Soviets to establish a major beachhead on the American continent, but who also presided over the greatest increase in the welfare state since Lyndon Johnson gave us the Great Society."

40. "White House Watch," *New Republic*, March 16, 1987, p. 14.

41. There were several other minor skirmishes that dismayed the right. HHS Secretary Bowen fired an HHS deputy, Jo Ann Gasper, in 1987 after she moved to cut off federal funding for Planned Parenthood. Don Devine, director of the Office of Personnel Management in Reagan's first term, had done something similar, and it played a role in the Senate's refusal to confirm him to a second term at OPM.

42. See Anderson, *Revolution: The Reagan Legacy*, pp. 120–21, 180–81, 186–87. FDR's Economic Bill of Rights, first outlined in his 1944 State of the Union message, called for guaranteed rights to employment, housing, health care, education, and "protection from economic fears of old age, sickness, accident, and unemployment." This was also the speech in which FDR equated Republicans with the fascists against whom the nation was fighting in World War II: "One of the great American industrialists of our day—a man who has rendered yeoman service to his country in this crisis—recently emphasized the grave dangers of 'rightist reaction' in this Nation. All clear-thinking businessmen share his concern. Indeed, if such reaction should develop—if history were to repeat itself and we were to return to the so-called 'normalcy' of the 1920's—then it is certain that even though we shall have conquered our enemies on the battlefields abroad, we shall have yielded to the spirit of Fascism here at home."

43. "In sum," the FCC's report said, "[T]he fairness doctrine in operation disserves both the public's right to diverse sources of information and the broadcaster's interest in free expression. Its chilling effect thwarts its intended purpose, and it results in excessive and unnecessary government intervention into the editorial processes of broadcast journalists."

44. Yakovlev's memo is available from the National Security Archive: http://www.gwu.edu/~nsarchiv/NSAEBB/NSAEBB168/yakovlev03.pdf.

45. Diary entry, October 29, 1987.

46. Henry Kissinger, "A New Era for NATO," *Newsweek*, October 12, 1987.

47. Hedrick Smith, "The Right Against Reagan," *New York Times Magazine*, January 17, 1988, p. 38.

48. Will, *Ronald Reagan: How an Ordinary Man Became an Extraordinary Leader* (New York: Free Press, 1997).

49. Patrick Glynn, "Reagan's Rush to Disarm," *Commentary*, March 1988, p. 26.

50. Buckley to Reagan, January 24, 1988, reprinted in William F. Buckley Jr., *The Reagan I Knew* (New York: Basic Books, 2008), p. 207.

51. "Richard Perle's INF Treaty," *Human Events*, December 19, 1987, p. 3.

52. Oval Office interview with print reporters, December 23, 1981.

53. Quoted in Smith, "The Right Against Reagan," p. 38.

54. August 8, 1987; August 29, 1987; March 5, 1988; December 3, 1988.

55. November 9, 1987; February 23, 1988; May 23, 1988.

56. September 16, 1987; February 29, 1988; April 10, 1988; May 27, 1988; July 13, 1988.

57. September 28, 1987; March 10, 1988.

58. BBC Moscow World Service in English, August 15, 1987.

59. Ibid., August 10, 1987.

60. Peter Robinson, e-mail communication with author, December 5, 2002.

61. See "U.S. Aide Urges E. Germany to Tear Down Berlin Wall," *Chicago Tribune*, October 13, 1988, p. 4.

62. Leon Aron, *Yeltsin: A Revolutionary Life* (New York: St. Martin's Press, 2000), p. 177.

63. Ibid., p. 187.

64. Diary entry, February 25, 1987.

65. Politburo session, December 17, 1987, available at the National Security Archive: http://www.gwu.edu/~nsarchiv/NSAEBB/NSAEBB238/russian/Final1987-12 -17Politburo%20Session.pdf.

66. *National Review*, December 31, 1987.

CHAPTER 13: A MIGHTY WOMAN WITH A TORCH

1. Reagan's veto of the 1986 CR was prompted in part by a provision allowing the rehiring of the fired air traffic controllers. Following this example, Reagan might have vetoed the CRs with the troublesome Boland Amendments.

2. Diary entry, February 25, 1988.

3. National Security Council memorandum of conversation, March 11, 1988, available at http://www.gwu.edu/~nsarchiv/NSAEBB/NSAEBB251/4.pdf. On the issue of the Soviets' self-esteem, Massie told Reagan that she "perceived a feeling of malaise among the Soviets she talked to, mostly educated persons and intellectuals. Rising expectations born of Gorbachev's reforms were tempered by the realization of the basic inertia of the working force—nothing seemed to be happening. 'Soviet society is undergoing an agonizing reappraisal,' she said, likening the Soviet people to someone breaking out of concrete."

4. Shultz, *Turmoil and Triumph*, pp. 1096–97.

5. National Security Council memorandum of conversation, April 29, 1988, available at http://www.gwu.edu/~nsarchiv/NSAEBB/NSAEBB251/9.pdf.

6. Jeffrey Hart, "Thinking the Unthinkable," *National Review*, June 24, 1988.

7. Brian Crozier, "The Collapse of Communism," *National Review*, August 5, 1988.

8. Reagan of course held a position of strict neutrality during the primary season, but privately favored Bush, in part as a reward for his dutiful vice presidential loyalty.

9. William Raspberry, "There Is No Black Agenda," *Washington Post,* November 18, 1988.

10. *National Review,* February 5, 1988, p. 18.

11. Tom Bethell, "Ducks and Bees," *American Spectator,* February 1985.

12. Mansfield, *America's Constitutional Soul,* p. 60.

13. Cited by Fred Barnes, "Odds on Mike," *New Republic,* April 18, 1988.

14. "Dukakis's Deceptions," *New Republic,* October 10, 1988.

15. Quoted in Fred Barnes, "Sticky Wicket," *New Republic,* June 13, 1988.

16. Robert Kuttner, "Incompetent Ideology," *New Republic,* December 5, 1988.

17. Peter Brown, *Minority Party: Why Democrats Face Defeat in 1992 and Beyond* (Washington, DC: Regnery-Gateway, 1991), p. 124.

18. This quotation and several others from this section are compiled in Joshua Muravchik, "Why the Democrats Lost Again," *Commentary,* February 1989, pp. 13–22.

19. Clinton quoted in Brown, *Minority Party,* p. 125. In the *New Republic* Martin Peretz posed this question: "Who among the liberals even will be willing to say that school districts may insist that their students wear white blouses or shirts as a modest way of bringing some visual order and esprit de corps to the chaos of urban education?" President Bill Clinton did, in 1996.

20. William Schneider, "Tough Liberals Win, Weak Liberals Lose," *New Republic,* December 5, 1988.

21. One of the Democratic winners in 1988 was Joe Lieberman in Connecticut, who knocked off incumbent liberal Republican Lowell Weicker. Reagan so disliked Weicker that he wanted to donate to Lieberman's campaign; chief of staff Ken Dubertsein had to talk him out of it.

22. Cited in Fred Barnes, "Sore Winners," *New Republic,* December 5, 1988.

23. Molly Worthen, *The Man on Whom Nothing Was Lost: The Grand Strategy of Charles Hill* (Boston: Houghton Mifflin, 2006), p. 260.

24. The reference to Vienna is to the Mutual Balanced Force Reduction (MBFR) negotiations about conventional forces in Europe. These long-running talks had been stalled for years.

25. A few weeks before arriving in New York, Gorbachev announced that the Soviet Union would stop jamming transmissions of Radio Free Europe and Radio Liberty, release more than a hundred political prisoners, and allow greater freedom of religious practice.

EPILOGUE: THE REAGAN REVOLUTION AND ITS DISCONTENTS

1. Mark Kramer, "The Collapse of the Soviet Union," *Journal of Cold War Studies* 5, 1 (Winter 2003): p. 3.

2. Kotkin, *Armageddon Averted,* pp. 2–4.

3. Timothy Garton Ash, *The Magic Lantern* (New York: Vintage, 1999 [originally published by Random House, 1990]), p. 158.

4. Cited in Kotkin, *Armageddon Averted,* p. 92.

5. Gorbachev wrote in the *New York Times* the week of Reagan's funeral: "I don't know whether we would have been able to agree and to insist on the implementation of our agreements with a different person at the helm of American government. . . . [Reagan] was not dogmatic; he was looking for negotiations and cooperation" (*New York Times,* June 7, 2004).

6. Sean Wilentz, *The Age of Reagan: A History, 1974–2008* (New York: Harper, 2008), p. 281.

7. *Nation,* June 28, 2004.

8. George W. Breslauer and Richard Ned Lebow, "Leadership and the End of the Cold War: A Counterfactual Thought Experiment," in Richard K. Hermann and Richard Ned Lebow, eds., *Ending the Cold War: Interpretations, Causation, and the Study of International Relations* (New York: Palgrave Macmillan, 2004), p. 184.

9. Joshua Green, "Reagan's Liberal Legacy," *Washington Monthly,* January/February 2003.

10. Thomas B. Silver, "Reagan's Failure," unpublished paper, on file with author.

11. William Voegeli, "The Trouble with Limited Government," *Claremont Review of Books,* Fall 2007, http://www.claremont.org/publications/crb/id.1495/article _detail.asp.

12. Lawrence Lindsey's copious book on the subject, *The Growth Experiment,* laments the lack of a solid empirical basis for evaluating the effect of tax cuts on federal revenues: "One yearns for down-to-earth numbers. There are none to be had" (p. 77).

13. Lindsey again: "The great American middle class, people earning between $20,000 and $60,000 in the early 1980s, saw their tax share fall from 67 percent to 60 percent between 1981 and 1986. It was they who received the bulk of the Reagan tax cuts" (p. 83).

14. Viscusi, "The Misspecified Agenda," in Feldstein, ed., *American Economic Policy in the 1980s,* p. 457.

SELECTED BIBLIOGRAPHY

Books

Abshire, David M. *Saving the Reagan Presidency.* College Station: Texas A & M University Press, 2005.

Adelman, Ken. *The Great Universal Embrace.* New York: Simon & Schuster, 1989.

Anderson, Martin. *Revolution: The Reagan Legacy.* New York: Harcourt, Brace, 1988.

Anderson, Martin, Annelise Anderson, and Kiron Skinner, eds. *Reagan: A Life in Letters.* New York: Free Press, 2003.

———. *Reagan's Path to Victory.* New York: Free Press, 2004.

Andrew, Christopher, and Oleg Gordievsky. *Comrade Kryuchkov's Instructions: Top Secret Files on KGB Foreign Operations, 1975–1985.* London: Hodder & Stoughton, 1991.

Aristotle. *Nicomachean Ethics.*

Arkes, Hadley. *Beyond the Constitution.* Princeton: Princeton University Press, 1992.

Aron, Leon. *Yeltsin: A Revolutionary Life.* New York: St. Martin's Press, 2000.

Ash, Timothy Garton. *The Magic Lantern.* New York: Vintage, 1999.

———. *The Polish Revolution: Solidarity* (3rd edition). New Haven: Yale University Press, 2002.

Bartley, Robert. *The Seven Fat Years.* New York: Free Press, 1992.

Baucom, Donald R. *The Origins of SDI, 1944–1983.* Lawrence: University Press of Kansas, 1992.

Bauer, Peter. *Equality, the Third World, and Economic Delusion.* Cambridge, MA: Harvard University Press, 1981.

Belz, Herman. *Equality Transformed: A Quarter-Century of Affirmative Action.* New Brunswick, NJ: Transaction, 1991.

Bergson, Abram, and Herbert S. Levine, eds. *The Soviet Economy: Toward the Year 2000.* London: George Allen & Unwin, 1983.

Birnbaum, Jeffrey H., and Alan S. Murray. *Showdown at Gucci Gulch: Lawmakers, Lobbyists, and the Unlikely Triumph of Tax Reform.* New York: Random House, 1987.

Blair, Margaret M., and Martha A. Schary, eds. *The Deal Decade: What Takeovers and Leveraged Buyouts Mean for Corporate Governance.* Washington, DC: Brookings Institution, 1993.

Blundy, David, and Andrew Lycett. *Qadhafi and the Libyan Revolution.* Boston: Little, Brown, 1987.

Bork, Robert H. *The Tempting of America: The Political Seduction of the Law.* New York: Free Press, 1989.

Boskin, Michael J. *Reagan and the Economy: The Successes, Failures, and Unfinished Agenda.* San Francisco: Institute for Contemporary Studies, 1987.

Breitlinger, John. *The Best of What We Are: Reflections on the Nicaraguan Revolution.* Amherst: University of Massachusetts Press, 1995.

Bronner, Ethan. *Battle for Justice: How the Bork Nomination Shook America.* New York: Union Square Press, 2007.

Brookes, Warren T. *Unconventional Wisdoms: The Best of Warren Brookes.* Ed. Thomas J. Bray. San Francisco: Pacific Research Institute, 1997.

Brown, Archie. *Seven Years That Changed the World: Perestroika in Perspective.* Oxford: Oxford University Press, 2007.

Brown, Peter. *Minority Party: Why Democrats Face Defeat in 1992 and Beyond.* Washington, DC: Regnery-Gateway, 1991.

Brownlee, W. Elliott, and Hugh Davis Graham, eds. *The Reagan Presidency: Pragmatic Conservatism and Its Legacies.* Lawrence: University Press of Kansas, 2003.

Burnham, James. *Suicide of the West: An Essay on the Meaning and Destiny of Liberalism.* Washington, DC: Regnery, 1985. [Originally published by John Day, 1964.]

Burns, James MacGregor. *Roosevelt: The Lion and the Fox, 1882–1940.* New York: Harcourt, 1956.

Busch, Andrew E. *Ronald Reagan and the Politics of Freedom.* Lanham, MD: Rowman & Littlefield, 2001.

Cagan, Philip, ed. *Essays in Contemporary Economic Problems, 1986.* Washington, DC: AEI, 1986.

Calabresi, Stephen G., ed. *Originalism: A Quarter-Century of Debate.* Washington, DC: Regnery, 2007.

Cannon, Lou. *President Reagan: The Role of a Lifetime.* New York: Simon & Schuster, 1991.

———. *Reagan.* New York: Putnam, 1985.

Charen, Mona. *Useful Idiots: How Liberals Got It Wrong in the Cold War and Still Blame America First.* Washington, DC: Regnery, 2003.

Chernyaev, Anatoly. *My Six Years with Gorbachev.* Trans. and ed. Robert English and Elizabeth Tucker. University Park: Pennsylvania State University Press, 2000.

Churchill, Winston S. *The World Crisis: The Aftermath.* London: Thornton Butterworth, 1929.

Codevilla, Angelo M. *Informing Statecraft: Intelligence for a New Century.* New York: Free Press, 1992.

———. *While Others Build: A Commonsense Approach to the Strategic Defense Initiative.* New York: Free Press, 1988.

Cohen, William S., and George J. Mitchell. *Men of Zeal: A Candid Inside Story of the Iran-Contra Hearings.* New York: Viking, 1988.

Collins, Robert M. *Transforming America: Politics and Culture During the Reagan Years.* New York: Columbia University Press, 2007.

Daniloff, Nicholas. *Of Spies and Spokesmen: My Life as a Cold War Correspondent.* Columbia: University of Missouri Press, 2008.

Darman, Richard. *Who's in Control? Polar Politics and the Sensible Center.* New York: Simon & Schuster, 1996.

Detlefsen, Robert. *Civil Rights Under Reagan.* San Francisco: ICS Press, 1991.

Diggins, John Patrick. *Ronald Reagan: Fate, Freedom and the Making of History.* New York: W. W. Norton, 2007.

Dobrynin, Anatoly. *In Confidence: Moscow's Ambassador to America's Six Cold War Presidents.* New York: Times Books, 1995.

Draper, Theodore. *A Very Thin Line.* New York: Simon & Schuster, 1991.

Duke, Paul, ed. *Beyond Reagan: The Politics of Upheaval.* New York: Warner Books, 1986.

Eastland, Terry. *Energy in the Executive: The Case for the Strong Presidency.* New York: Free Press, 1992.

Eberstadt, Nicholas. *Prosperous Paupers and Other Population Problems.* New Brunswick, NJ: Transaction, 2000.

———. *Tyranny of Numbers: Mismeasurement and Misrule.* Washington, DC: AEI Press, 1995.

Ehrman, John. *The Eighties: America in the Age of Reagan.* New Haven: Yale University Press, 2005.

Ellwood, John William, ed. *Reductions in U.S. Domestic Spending.* New Brunswick, NJ: Transaction Books, 1982.

Evans, Rowland, and Robert Novak. *The Reagan Revolution.* New York: Dutton, 1981.

Farrell, John A. *Tip O'Neill and the Democratic Century.* Boston: Little, Brown, 2001.

Feldstein, Martin, ed. *American Economic Policy in the 1980s.* Chicago: University of Chicago Press, 1994.

Fellner, William, ed. *Essays in Contemporary Economic Problems, 1981–1982.* Washington, DC: American Enterprise Institute, 1981.

Fischer, Beth A. *The Reagan Reversal: Foreign Policy and the End of the Cold War.* Columbia: University of Missouri Press, 1997.

Fisher, Louis. *Presidential War Power.* Lawrence: University Press of Kansas, 1995.

FitzGerald, Frances. *Way Out There in the Blue: Reagan, Star Wars and the End of the Cold War.* New York: Simon & Schuster, 2001.

Fried, Charles. *Order and Law: Arguing the Reagan Revolution.* New York: Simon & Schuster, 1991.

Frum, David. *Dead Right.* New York: Basic Books, 1994.

Gaddis, John Lewis. *The United States and the Origins of the Cold War, 1941–1947.* New York: Columbia University Press, 1972.

Garment, Suzanne. *Scandal: The Culture of Mistrust in American Politics.* New York: Random House, 1991.

Garthoff, Raymond L. *The Great Transition: American-Soviet Relations and the End of the Cold War.* Washington, DC: Brookings Institution, 1994.

Gates, Robert. *From the Shadows.* New York: Simon & Schuster, 1996.

Gedman, Jeffrey. *Hidden Hand: Gorbachev and the Collapse of East Germany.* Washington, DC: American Enterprise Institute, 1992.

Germond, Jack, and Jules Witcover. *Wake Us When It's Over.* New York: Macmillan, 1985.

Gilder, George. *Wealth and Poverty.* New York: Basic Books, 1981.

Greenburg, Jan Crawford. *Supreme Conflict: The Inside Story of the Struggle for Control of the United States Supreme Court.* New York: Penguin, 2007.

Greider, William. *Secrets of the Temple: How the Federal Reserve Runs the Country.* New York: Simon & Schuster, 1989.

Haig, Alexander. *Caveat.* New York: Macmillan, 1984.

Hannaford, Peter, ed. *Recollections of Reagan.* New York: Morrow, 1997.

Hayward, Steven F. *The Age of Reagan: The Fall of the Old Liberal Order, 1964–1980.* Roseville, CA: Prima, 2001.

———. *Greatness: Reagan, Churchill and the Making of Extraordinary Leaders.* New York: Crown Forum, 2005.

Henry, William A., III. *Visions of America: How We Saw the 1984 Election.* New York: Atlantic Monthly Press, 1985.

Herf, Jeffrey. *War by Other Means: Soviet Power, West German Resistance, and the Battle of the Euromissiles.* New York: Free Press, 1991.

Hermann, Richard K., and Richard Ned Lebow, eds. *Ending the Cold War: Interpretations, Causation, and the Study of International Relations.* New York: Palgrave Macmillan, 2004.

Hodgson, Godfrey. *All Things to All Men.* New York: Simon & Schuster, 1980.

———. *The Gentleman from New York: Daniel Patrick Moynihan, A Biography.* New York: Houghton Mifflin, 2000.

Hofstadter, Richard. *The American Political Tradition.* New York: Alfred A. Knopf, 1948.

Hollander, Paul. *Anti-Americanism: Irrational and Rational.* New Brunswick, NJ: Transaction Books, 1995.

———. *Political Pilgrims: Western Intellectuals in Search of the Good Society,* 4th ed. New Brunswick, NJ: Transaction Books, 1998.

Howe, Irving, ed. *1984 Revisited: Totalitarianism in Our Century.* New York: Harper & Row, 1983.

Jackson, Brooks. *Honest Graft: Big Money and the American Political Process.* New York: Knopf, 1988.

Jaffa, Harry V. *Equality and Liberty: Theory and Practice in American Politics.* New York: Oxford University Press, 1965.

———. *Original Intent and the Framers of the Constitution: A Disputed Question.* Washington, DC: Regnery, 1994.

———. *Storm over the Constitution.* Lanham, MD: Lexington Books, 1999.

James, Robert Rhodes. *Churchill: A Study in Failure.* London: Weidenfeld & Nicolson, 1970.

Johnson, Haynes. *Sleepwalking Through History: America in the Reagan Years.* New York: Norton, 1991.

Jones, Gordon S., and John A. Marini, eds. *The Imperial Congress: Crisis in the Separation of Powers.* New York: Pharos Books, 1988.

Kagan, Robert. *A Twilight Struggle: American Power and Nicaragua, 1977–1990.* New York: Free Press, 1996.

Kengor, Paul. *The Crusader: Ronald Reagan and the Fall of Communism.* New York: Regan Books, 2007.

———. *God and Ronald Reagan: A Spiritual Life.* New York: Regan Books, 2004.

Kotkin, Stephen. *Armageddon Averted: The Soviet Collapse, 1970–2000.* Oxford: Oxford University Press, 2001.

Kuhn, Jim. *Ronald Reagan in Private: A Memoir of My Years at the White House.* New York: Sentinel, 2004.

Landy, Marc, and Sidney M. Milkis. *Presidential Greatness.* Lawrence: University Press of Kansas, 2000.

Ledeen, Michael. *Perilous Statecraft.* New York: Scribner's, 1988.

Leebaert, Derek. *The Fifty-Year Wound: The True Price of America's Cold War Victory.* Boston: Little, Brown, 2002.

Leffler, Melvyn P. *For the Soul of Mankind: The United States, the Soviet Union, and the Cold War.* New York: Hill & Wang, 2007.

Lettow, Paul. *Ronald Reagan and His Quest to Abolish Nuclear Weapons.* New York: Random House, 2005.

Lewin, Moshe. *The Gorbachev Phenomenon: A Historical Interpretation.* Berkeley: University of California Press, 1988.

———. *The Soviet Century.* London: Verso, 2005.

Lindsey, Lawrence. *The Growth Experiment.* New York: Basic Books, 1990.

Lonergan, Bernard J. F. *Insight: A Study of Human Understanding.* London: Longmans, Green, 1958.

MacEachin, Douglas J. *U.S. Intelligence and the Confrontation with Poland, 1980–81.* University Park: Pennsylvania State University Press, 2002.

Mahoney, Dennis J., and Peter W. Schramm, eds. *The 1984 Election and the Future of American Politics.* Durham, NC: Carolina Academic Press, 1987.

Malia, Martin. *The Soviet Tragedy: A History of Socialism in Russia.* New York: Free Press, 1994.

Mansfield, Harvey C., Jr. *America's Constitutional Soul.* Baltimore: Johns Hopkins University Press, 1991.

———. *Taming the Prince: The Ambivalence of Modern Executive Power.* New York: Free Press, 1989.

Matlock, Jack. *Reagan and Gorbachev: How the Cold War Ended.* New York: Random House, 2004.

Mayhew, David R. *Electoral Realignments: A Critique of an American Genre.* New Haven: Yale University Press, 2002.

McKenzie, Richard B. *What Went Right in the 1980s.* San Francisco: Pacific Research Institute, 1994.

Meiners, Roger E., and Bruce Yandle, eds. *Regulation and the Reagan Era: Politics, Bureaucracy, and the Public Interest.* New York: Holmes & Meier, 1989.

Menges, Constantine C. *Inside the National Security Council.* New York: Simon & Schuster, 1988.

Moynihan, Daniel Patrick. *Came the Revolution: Argument in the Reagan Era.* San Diego: Harcourt, Brace, Jovanovich, 1988.

———. *Loyalties.* Orlando: Harcourt, Brace, Jovanovich, 1984.

Niskanen, William A. *Reaganomics.* New York: Oxford University Press, 1988.

Nitze, Paul. *From Hiroshima to Glasnost: At the Center of Decision.* New York: Grove Weidenfeld, 1989.

Oberdorfer, Don. *The Turn: From the Cold War to a New Era.* New York: Simon & Schuster, 1991.

Odom, William E. *The Collapse of the Soviet Military.* New Haven: Yale University Press, 1998.

O'Neill, Jonathan. *Originalism in American Law and Politics: A Constitutional History.* Baltimore: Johns Hopkins University Press, 2005.

O'Sullivan, John. *The President, the Pope and the Prime Minister.* Washington, DC: Regnery, 2006.

Palmer, John L., and Isabel V. Sawhill, eds. *The Reagan Experiment.* Washington, DC: Urban Institute, 1982.

Pestritto, R. J. *Woodrow Wilson and the Roots of Modern Liberalism.* Lanham, MD: Rowman & Littlefield, 2005.

Pipes, Richard. *Vixi: Memoirs of a Non-Believer.* New Haven: Yale University Press, 2003.

Podhoretz, Norman. *The Bloody Crossroads: Where Literature and Politics Meet.* New York: Simon & Schuster, 1986.

Pryce-Jones, David. *The War That Never Was: The Fall of the Soviet Empire, 1985–1991.* London: Weidenfeld & Nicolson, 1995.

Radosh, Ronald. *Divided They Fell: The Demise of the Democratic Party, 1964–1996.* New York: Free Press, 1996.

Reagan, Ronald. *An American Life.* New York: Simon & Schuster, 1990.

———. *The Reagan Diaries.* Ed. Douglas Brinkley. New York: HarperCollins, 2007.

Reeves, Richard. *President Reagan: The Triumph of Imagination.* New York: Simon & Schuster, 2005.

———. *The Reagan Detour.* New York: Simon & Schuster, 1985.

Regan, Donald. *For the Record: From Wall Street to Washington.* New York: Harcourt Brace, 1988.

Report of the Congressional Committees Investigating the Iran-Contra Affair. Washington, DC: U.S. Government Printing Office, 1987.

Revel, Jean-François. *How Democracies Perish.* New York: Doubleday, 1984.

Rhodes, Richard. *Arsenals of Folly: The Making of the Nuclear Arms Race.* New York: Knopf, 2007.

Roberts, Paul Craig. *The Supply-Side Revolution.* Cambridge, MA: Harvard University Press, 1984.

Robinson, Peter. *How Ronald Reagan Changed My Life.* New York: Harper, 2003.

———. *It's My Party: A Republican's Messy Love Affair with the GOP.* New York: Grand Central Publishing, 2000.

Rodman, Peter. *More Precious than Peace: The Cold War and the Struggle for the Third World.* New York: Scribner's, 1994.

Salamon, Lester, and Michael S. Lund, eds. *The Reagan Presidency and the Governing of America.* Washington, DC: The Urban Institute, 1984.

Sandford, Gregory, and Richard Vigilante. *Grenada: The Untold Story.* Lanham, MD: Madison Books, 1984.

Scheer, Robert. *With Enough Shovels: Reagan, Bush and Nuclear War.* New York: Random House, 1982.

Schweizer, Peter. *Reagan's War: The Epic Story of His Forty-Year Struggle and Final Triumph over Communism.* New York: Doubleday, 2002.

Seabury, Paul, and Walter A. McDougal, eds. *The Grenada Papers.* San Francisco: ICS Press, 1984.

Shultz, George P. *Turmoil and Triumph: Diplomacy, Power, and the Victory of the American Idea.* New York: Simon & Schuster, 1993.

Silver, Thomas B. *Coolidge and the Historians.* Durham, NC: Carolina Academic Press, 1982.

Skidelsky, Robert. *The Road from Serfdom: The Economic and Political Consequences of the End of Communism.* London: Penguin, 1997.

Skinner, Kiron K., ed. *Turning Points in the Cold War.* Palo Alto, CA: Hoover Institution Press, 2008.

Sloan, John W. *The Reagan Effect: Economics and Presidential Leadership.* Lawrence: University Press of Kansas, 1999.

Smith, Geoffrey. *Reagan and Thatcher.* New York: Norton, 1991.

Smith, Hedrick. *The Power Game: How Washington Works.* New York: Random House, 1988.

Stanik, Joseph T. *El Dorado Canyon: Reagan's Undeclared War with Qaddafi.* Annapolis, MD: Naval Institute Press, 2003.

Stein, Ben. *The View from Sunset Boulevard.* New York: Basic Books, 1979.

Stockman, David. *The Triumph of Politics: Why the Reagan Revolution Failed.* New York: Harper & Row, 1986.

Strober, Deborah Hart, and Gerald S. Strober, eds. *Reagan, the Man and His Presidency: The Oral History of an Era.* Boston: Houghton Mifflin, 1998.

Talbott, Strobe. *Master of the Game: Paul Nitze and the Nuclear Peace.* New York: Alfred A. Knopf, 1988.

————. *The Russians and Reagan.* New York: Council on Foreign Relations, 1984.

Thatcher, Margaret. *The Downing Street Years.* New York: HarperCollins, 1993.

Timberg, Robert. *The Nightingale's Song.* New York: Free Press/Touchstone, 1996.

Tobin, James, and Murray Weidenbaum, eds. *Two Revolutions in Economic Policy: The First Economic Reports of Presidents Kennedy and Reagan.* Cambridge, MA: MIT Press, 1988.

Ullmann, Owen. *Stockman: The Man, the Myth, the Future.* New York: Donald I. Fine, 1986.

Volcker, Paul, and Toyoo Gyohten. *Changing Fortunes: The World's Money and the Threat to American Leadership.* New York: Random House, 1992.

Wallison, Peter J. *Ronald Reagan: The Power of Conviction and the Success of His Presidency.* Boulder, CO: Westview, 2003.

Weigel, George. *Witness to Hope: The Biography of Pope John Paul II.* New York: HarperCollins, 1999.

Wildavsky, Aaron. *The Beleaguered Presidency.* New Brunswick, NJ: Transaction, 1991.

————. *The Rise of Radical Egalitarianism.* Washington, DC: American University Press, 1991.

Wilentz, Sean. *The Age of Reagan: A History, 1974–2008.* New York: Harper, 2008.

Winik, Jay. *On the Brink: The Dramatic, Behind-the-Scenes Saga of the Reagan Era and the Men and Women Who Won the Cold War.* New York: Simon & Schuster, 1996.

Wohlforth, William C., ed. *Witnesses to the End of the Cold War.* Baltimore: Johns Hopkins University Press, 1996.

Woodward, Bob. *Veil: The Secret Wars of the CIA, 1981–1987.* New York: Simon & Schuster, 1987.

Worthen, Molly. *The Man on Whom Nothing Was Lost: The Grand Strategy of Charles Hill.* Boston: Houghton Mifflin, 2006.

Archives and Special Collections

Cold War International History Project, Woodrow Wilson Center; http://
www.wilsoncenter.org/index.cfm?topic_id=1409&fuseaction=topics.home.

The "Farewell Dossier" of Gus Weiss (unpublished).

Hoover Institution, Stanford University.

National Security Archive, George Washington University; http://www.gwu
.edu/~nsarchiv/index.html.

Ronald Reagan Oral History Project, Miller Center for Public Affairs, University of Virginia; http://millercenter.org/academic/oralhistory/projects/
presidential/reagan.

Ronald Reagan Presidential Library, Simi Valley, California.

ACKNOWLEDGMENTS

―――❦―――

A long list of people deserve thanks for their invaluable help and insight into this project, including Martin Anderson, Leon Aron, Karlyn Bowman, Mark Burson, Michael Deaver, Stephen Entin, Newt Gingrich, Clark Judge, Jeane Kirkpatrick, Michael Ledeen, Derek Leebaert, Edwin Meese III, Daniel Oliver, Senator Robert Packwood, Al Regnery, Peter Robinson, Peter Schramm, R. Emmett Tyrrell Jr., Michael Ullmann, Jeff Van Schaick, Peter Wallison, Gus Weiss, and Martin Morse Wooster.

Special thanks are owed to Ron Robinson, Floyd Brown, Andrew Coffin, and the good people at the Young America's Foundation and the Reagan Ranch Center in Santa Barbara. My three research assistants at AEI, Ryan Stowers, Kathryn Boateng, and Abigail Haddad, provided crucial research help and fact checking; AEI librarian Gene Hosey always came through with my requests for obscure materials. A succession of interns eagerly chased down sources and factoids: Daniel Fichter, Erin Hertog, Lauren Jones, Sean McGregor, and Tom Rickeman.

I could not have carried out this ambitious project without the unfailing support and encouragement of AEI's immediate past president, Christopher DeMuth, and the intrepid leader of the Pacific Research Institute, Sally Pipes. Special thanks are also owed for financial support from the Earhart Foundation and the Searle Freedom Trust.

My editorial team at Crown Forum, Jed Donahue, Julian Pavia, and Nathan Roberson, labored mightily and contributed numerous refinements that greatly improved the final manuscript. This installment includes more footnotes than the first volume, chiefly to satisfy Professor Elizabeth Spalding, who has a well-known footnote fetish. General readers can safely skip them.

INDEX